Achieving Software Quality through Teamwork

For a listing of recent titles in the *Artech House Computing Library,*
turn to the back of this book.

Achieving Software Quality through Teamwork

Isabel Evans

Artech House
Boston • London
www.artechhouse.com

Library of Congress Cataloging-in-Publication Data
A catalog record for this book is available from the U.S. Library of Congress.

British Library Cataloguing in Publication Data
Evans, Isabel
  Achieving software quality through teamwork.—(Artech House computing library)
  1. Computer software—Quality control 2. Computer software—Development—Management
  3. Teams in the workplace
  I. Title
  005.1'0684

ISBN 1-58053-662-X
Cover design by Yekaterina Ratner

© 2004 ARTECH HOUSE, INC.
685 Canton Street
Norwood, MA 02062

The following are registered in the U.S. Patent and Trademark Office by Carnegie Mellon University: Capability Maturity Model®, CMM®, and CMMI®. CMM Integration^{SM}, CMMI^{SM}, Personal Software Process^{SM}, PSP^{SM}, Team Software Process^{SM}, and TSP^{SM} are service marks of Carnegie Mellon University; Capability Maturity Model® and CMM® are registered in the U.S. Patent and Trademark Office.

Special permission to reproduce "Quotations from the SEI website (www.sei.cmu.edu)," "©2003, "Pathways to Process Maturity: The Personal Software Process and Team Software Process" © 2000 and "A Framework for Software Product Line Practice Version 4.1" ©2003 by Carnegie Mellon University, is granted by the Software Engineering Institute. No warranty. This Carnegie Mellon University and Software Engineering Institue material is furnished on an "as is" basis. Carnegie Mellon University makes no warranties of any kind, either expressed or implied as to any matter including, but not limited to, warranty of fitness for purpose or merchantability, exclusivity or results obtained from use of the material. Carenegie Mellon University does not make any warranty of any kind with respect to freedom from patent, trademark, or copyright infringement.

All material related to the EFQM model is Copyright © 1999–2003 by the European Foundation for Quality Management and is reproduced here by permission of EFQM. Information about use of the EFQM Model is on the EFQM Web site http://www.efqm.org.

Crown copyright material is reproduced with the permission of the Controller of HMSO and the Queen's Printer for Scotland. Extracts from the "McCartney report" are under licence C02W0003641.

Extracts from DISC PD 0005: 1998 have been reproduced with the permission of BSI under license number 2003DH0297. British Standards can be obtained from BSI Customer Services, 389 Chiswick High Road, London, W4 4AL. Tel +44 (0)20 8996 9001. E-mail: cservices@bsi-global.com.

MBTI® and Myers-Briggs Type Indicator® are registered trademarks of Consulting Psychologists Press Inc. Oxford Pyschologists Press Ltd. has exclusive rights to the trademark in the UK. Extracts describing the MBTI are reproduced from the Team Technology Web site by permission of Team Technology.

TPI® is a registered trademark of Sogeti Netherland B.V.

Appendix A, Table A.1: Belbin® is a registered trademark of Belbin Associates. Belbin Team Roles, from the work of Dr. Meredith Belbin, are reproduced by permission of Belbin Associates and are © e-interplace, Belbin Associates, UK 2001. Reproduced by permission of Belbin Associates.

All rights reserved. Printed and bound in the United States of America. No part of this book may be reproduced or utilized in any form or by any means, electronic or mechanical, including photocopying, recording, or by any information storage and retrieval system, without permission in writing from the publisher.

All terms mentioned in this book that are known to be trademarks or service marks have been appropriately capitalized. Artech House cannot attest to the accuracy of this information. Use of a term in this book should not be regarded as affecting the validity of any trademark or service mark.

International Standard Book Number: 1-58053-662-X

10 9 8 7 6 5 4 3 2 1

*For my brother, James, statistician, rock climber, mountaineer, 1958–2003.
You encouraged me to write this book.*

Contents

Forward	*xv*
Preface	*xvii*
Acknowledgments	*xxiii*

1 Software Quality Matters — 1

1.1	Defining software quality	1
1.2	Fundamental concepts of excellence	5
1.3	EFQM Excellence Model	7
	1.3.1 Enablers	7
	1.3.2 Results	9
	1.3.3 Excellence, the EFQM Excellence Model, the Malcolm Baldrige model, and other related models	10
1.4	ISO 9000:1994 and ISO 9000:2000	10
1.5	IT maturity models—CMM® and relations	11
1.6	Team Software Process and Personal Software Process	12
1.7	Bringing the models together	13
	References	15
	Selected bibliography	16

2 Defining the Software Team — 17

2.1	Teams in disunity	17
2.2	Defining the team	19
	2.2.1 People who are customers and users of software	20
	2.2.2 People who manage software projects	20
	2.2.3 People who build software	21
	2.2.4 People who measure software quality	21
	2.2.5 People who provide the support and infrastructure for the project and the deployment of software	22

vii

	2.3	Interaction between the groups and within each group	22
	2.3.1	Differences in quality viewpoints	22
	2.3.2	Intergroup relationships in CMM® and Personal and Team Software Processes	24
	2.3.3	Intergroup relationships and excellence frameworks—the EFQM Excellence Model	25
	References	28
	Selected bibliography	28

3   Roles and Quality: Customers 31

3.1		Introducing the customers	31
3.2		Who could be in this group?	32
	3.2.1	In-house customer	33
	3.2.2	Third-party custom-made system customer	35
	3.2.3	Third-party package or commercial off-the-shelf (COTS) customer	36
	3.2.4	The IT specialist as customer	38
3.3		Quality viewpoint	38
3.4		Quality framework using the EFQM Excellence Model	39
	3.4.1	The EFQM Excellence Model and the customer organization	39
	3.4.2	EFQM Excellence Model enablers for customers	40
	3.4.3	EFQM Excellence Model results for the customers	43
3.5		Communication between the customers and other groups	45
3.6		Summary of the group	47
	References	49
	Selected bibliography	49

4   Roles and Quality: Managers. 51

4.1		Introducing the managers	51
4.2		Who could be in this group?	52
4.3		Quality viewpoint	53
4.4		Quality framework using the EFQM Excellence Model	54
	4.4.1	The EFQM Excellence Model and the manager	54
	4.4.2	EFQM Excellence Model enablers for the managers	57
	4.4.3	EFQM Excellence Model results for the managers	65
4.5		Communication between the managers and other groups	68
	4.5.1	Managers and communication cycles	68
	4.5.2	The reporting process	70
4.6		Summary of the group	73
	References	74
	Selected bibliography	75

Contents ix

5 Roles and Quality: Builders 77

5.1	Introducing the builders	77
5.2	Who could be in this group?	79
5.3	Quality viewpoint	80
5.4	Quality framework using the EFQM Excellence Model	86
	5.4.1 *The EFQM Excellence Model and the builders*	86
	5.4.2 *EFQM Excellence Model enablers for builders*	87
	5.4.3 *EFQM Excellence Model results for the builders*	92
5.5	Communication between the builders and other groups	95
5.6	Summary of the group	96
	References	97
	Selected bibliography	98

6 Roles and Quality: Measurers 101

6.1	Introducing the measurers	101
	6.1.1 *Why do we need QA and QC?*	101
	6.1.2 *Just measurers or also improvers of quality?*	102
	6.1.3 *Defect prevention*	103
	6.1.4 *The Hawthorne effect*	105
6.2	Who could be in this group?	106
6.3	Quality viewpoint	106
6.4	Quality framework using the EFQM Excellence Model	113
	6.4.1 *The EFQM Excellence Model and the measurers*	113
	6.4.2 *EFQM Excellence Model enablers for the measurers*	114
	6.4.3 *EFQM Excellence Model results for the measurers*	123
6.5	Communication between the measurers and other groups	125
6.6	Summary of the group	128
	References	129
	Selected bibliography	129

7 Roles and Quality: Supporters 131

7.1	Introducing the supporters	131
7.2	Who could be in this group?	133
7.3	Quality viewpoint	134
7.4	Quality framework using the EFQM Excellence Model	136
	7.4.1 *The EFQM Excellence Model and the supporter*	136
	7.4.2 *Enablers for the supporters*	138
	7.4.3 *Results for the supporters*	143
7.5	Communication between supporters and other groups	146
7.6	Summary of the group	147

7.7	Summary of all the groups	148
References		150
Selected bibliography		151

8 The Life Span of a Software System 153

8.1	Life span or life cycle?	153
	8.1.1 Start-up	155
	8.1.2 Development	155
	8.1.3 Delivery	156
	8.1.4 Postdelivery	156
8.2	Entry and exit criteria between stages	157
8.3	Changes in quality viewpoints across the life span of a system	158
References		159

9 Start-Up for a Software-Development Project . . 161

9.1	Start-up—description	161
9.2	Start-up viewpoints	163
9.3	Entry criteria for start-up	164
9.4	Start-up—typical activities	165
	9.4.1 Understanding the problem/idea	165
	9.4.2 Decide whether the problem/idea is worth solving	168
	9.4.3 Set general constraints and parameters for the solution	170
	9.4.4 Agree on next stage	170
	9.4.5 Contract for work	171
9.5	Exit from start-up stage	178
References		179
Selected bibliography		180

10 Software-Development Life Cycle 181

10.1	Software-development life cycle—description	181
	10.1.1 Types of software acquisition project	182
	10.1.2 Identifying the software products	183
	10.1.3 SDLC task summary	183
10.2	SDLC viewpoints	184
10.3	Entry criteria for SDLC	186
	10.3.1 Entry criteria following a detailed start-up	186
	10.3.2 When no entry criteria have been defined	187
	10.3.3 When entry criteria have not been met	187
	10.3.4 Tailoring entry criteria	189
	10.3.5 When no start-up stage took place	190

10.4	SDLC—typical activities	190
	10.4.1 Planning and monitoring	190
	10.4.2 Managing change	191
	10.4.3 Requirements	192
	10.4.4 Design	193
	10.4.5 Build	193
	10.4.6 Testing	194
10.5	Entry and exit points within the SDLC	195
10.6	SDLC models	195
	10.6.1 Waterfall model (big bang or phased)	196
	10.6.2 Spiral, incremental, and iterative models	199
	10.6.3 Evolutionary model	203
	10.6.4 V-model	203
	10.6.5 Advantages and disadvantages of the models	204
10.7	Quality views and the models—why we might wish to combine models	204
10.8	Exit from the SDLC	208
	10.8.1 Exit criteria following a detailed acceptance test	208
	10.8.2 When no exit criteria have been defined	209
	10.8.3 When exit criteria have not been met	210
	10.8.4 Tailoring exit criteria	210
	10.8.5 When no acceptance criteria have been set	210
10.9	Conclusion	211
	References	212
	Selected bibliography	213

11 Delivery and Support When Going Live 215

11.1	Delivery—description	215
	11.1.1 Delivery considerations	215
	11.1.2 Identifying the delivery	217
11.2	Delivery viewpoints	218
11.3	Entry criteria for delivery	221
11.4	Delivery—typical activities	221
	11.4.1 Person buys PC and software for self-installation	223
	11.4.2 Single-site delivery of software	224
	11.4.3 Multisite rollout of new software to existing infrastructure	224
	11.4.4 Data migration project software and hardware changes	225
11.5	Exit from delivery	226
11.6	Conclusion	226
	References	227
	Selected bibliography	227

12 The Life of a System Postdelivery 229

12.1	Postdelivery—description	229
	12.1.1 Postdelivery for different types of software acquisitions	230
12.2	Delivery viewpoints	231
12.3	Entry criteria for postdelivery	233
12.4	Postdelivery—typical activities	233
	12.4.1 Use of the system	233
	12.4.2 IT infrastructure and service management activities	234
	12.4.3 Making changes to an existing system	236
	12.4.4 Monitoring and evaluation	241
12.5	Exit from postdelivery	244
12.6	Conclusion	244
	References	246
	Selected bibliography	247

A Techniques and Methods 249

A.1	Communication, team dynamics, and meeting behavior	249
	A.1.1 Belbin Team Roles	250
	A.1.2 De Bono's Six Thinking Hats	251
A.2	Communication styles	253
	A.2.1 Myers-Briggs Type Indicators	253
	A.2.2 Honey and Mumford Learning Styles	254
	A.2.3 Kirton adaptors and innovators	255
	A.2.4 Motivation studies	256
	A.2.5 Transactional analysis	257
A.3	Techniques to identify and classify problems and assess ideas for solutions	259
	A.3.1 Cause–effect, root cause, and solution analysis	259
	A.3.2 Prototyping and ideas modeling	261
	A.3.3 Assessing whether an idea is worth pursuing	262
A.4	Understanding aims and objectives	265
A.5	Review techniques	266
A.6	Improving graphics in reporting	267
A.7	Useful sources and groups	269
	References	270
	Selected bibliography	272

B Quality Planning Documents and Templates . . 273

B.1	The document family	273
B.2	Why we use document templates	275

B.3	Using the document standards to provide your own templates	278
B.4	Auditing considerations	278
B.5	The team's information needs	278
B.6	Adapting templates	279
B.7	Keep it brief—do not repeat or copy information	279
B.8	Do you need a document at all?	279
B.9	Simple project audit plan and report templates	280
References		282

About the Author 283

Index 285

Foreword

If you are in IT, you probably think of yourself as a technical person. Often the emphasis is very much on the "technical" rather than the "person." Yet, as Isabel points out, the majority of problems in IT are due to people problems, not technical ones. Yes, producing quality software is a technical activity, but software is produced by people, complete with talents and abilities, but also personalities, idiosyncracies, foibles, and emotions, and these people produce IT systems in teams, where the roles and perspectives of each team can differ significantly, especially about what constitutes quality.

If every person has a different view of what quality is, and the people involved don't communicate well, is it any wonder that major problems arise? What is the solution? Is it better processes? That has been tried. Is it a maturity model? That has been tried. Yet problems still abound, and people are still surprised by the fact that there are still problems with people!

Isabel sprinkles this book with numerous "overheard conversations" within IT organizations. Why do customers find developers arrogant? Why do developers lack appreciation of business issues? Why do support staff feel left out? Why do managers not appreciate the value of testing? I frequently find myself in conversation with IT people, particularly testers and test managers, and I hear them saying many of the things that Isabel describes. This book not only explains what is going on, but also shows how things can be improved, bringing the ideas to life through Isabel's rich source of anecdotes. Reading this book will help you understand the viewpoint of the very people you often complain about!

The use of the EFQM Excellence Model as a framework to structure the book gives a solid foundation for comparing different models of quality and shows where the different roles of the people involved fit together in a software development project and the life of that system. From a technical perspective, the book gives useful guidance on achieving quality; Appendix B includes a summary of quality documents.

The project advice contained in the start-up section in Chapter 9 alone could be worth the price of this book; it could save you a lot of time, money, and mistakes and is an aspect frequently overlooked and underemphasized. Appendix A is also a useful handbook on its own—a concise summary of people- and teamwork-related techniques and methods and where to go for further information.

This book will increase your understanding of the people with whom you work. It may cause a wry smile or two as you recognize the behavior described "to a T" of a colleague. Then you may find yourself thinking, "So that's what they're thinking, that's why they do that; I never realized." Perhaps you will even recognize yourself and realize why other people don't seem to understand your view of quality.

This book is a rare breed. It explains why people issues are important, yet it does so in a way that will appeal to technical people.

Dorothy Graham
Senior Consultant
Grove Consultants
Macclesfield, United Kingdom
May 2004

Preface

The cost of failed IT projects in the United States was recently estimated at $84 billion in just 1 year [1], so software quality matters more now than it ever has, and it matters to you and me because we use that software. For all of us, our reliance on software is increasing year by year whether we realize it or not. More of us are using software for more tasks than ever before, in information technology (IT), information systems (IS) for businesses, embedded systems in consumer goods such as phones, and, of course, across the Internet [2]. The risks associated with software failure have increased with the use of software; these include greater exposure for organizations when software fails or is unsatisfactory, and greater disappointment or loss for individuals when they are let down by software.

Meanwhile, pressures on modern organizations, including businesses, have increased in recent years. Pressures on organizations—the importance of time to market, cost reduction, value for money, increased expectation and knowledge of customers, global communications, constant change, and the need to find new markets—become pressures on software teams to produce more software, more quickly, with increased expectations of what that software can deliver as benefits.

Why is IT so often disappointing? Why isn't software built correctly? One reason is quite simple: IT systems are built by people, and people make mistakes. This is true for any human activity, but in IT we have a number of exacerbating circumstances:

- IT systems are often built by teams of people other than those who will use them. In these circumstances, any poor communication between people and teams increases the chances of mistakes.
- IT is relatively new, and we are working on a continuous learning curve. Both the suppliers and users of software rarely have time to consolidate knowledge before they face yet more change.
- IT departments are notorious for their failure to align the software they produce with the culture, processes, or objectives of the business for which the software is intended.

- IT systems are complex, and are becoming increasingly so in themselves and in their intercommunications with other systems.

Only one of these (the last) is a technical problem, yet most of the emphasis for IT groups seeking improvement is on technical processes. All the other points in the list have to do with people, their ability to communicate well and understand each other, and their ability to learn from each other and from experience.

We need a framework for IT projects that addresses the issues of software quality through an emphasis on teamwork and communication set in a framework aligned with the customers, their organizations, and their goals. To help achieve this goal, *Achieving Software Quality through Teamwork* answers the following questions:

- Who should be involved in the development and deployment of software? People are going to work in teams to provide the software, so we need the right teams.
- What are the differences and similarities between these people, especially in their assumptions about quality? To achieve quality, the team needs to agree on what quality is.
- What are the ways of understanding communication preferences and how conflict can arise from differences between these preferences? Teamwork requires mutual understanding and tolerance in communication.
- How can that understanding be improved? By providing opportunities for communication within and around the IT and organizational processes, teamwork and communication are encouraged so that quality is achieved.
- How can IT suppliers understand the goals of their client organizations, whether nonprofit or commercial businesses, and how they measure success? IT suppliers must have an understanding of the quality framework used by their customers in order to produce quality software. IT teamwork means including the customers.

This book was written in response to a number of people with whom I have worked over the years. It is for you if you, like they, have ever said things like:

- We've improved the processes, so why are the customers still unhappy?
- I just can't talk to the people in the business units (or IT, or management, and so forth). How can we understand each other?
- Why do they keep sending e-mails to me when I'd rather talk face-to-face?
- How can I provide quality if the managers just talk about costs?

- How can I align my goals with what the customer really needs?
- Why do the IT people always deliver the wrong thing?
- What do the managers really do?
- I have just started as a team leader. What do I need to think about?
- Who needs to be involved at this stage?
- Why don't the people in my team get along?
- Why do we always end up having an argument?
- We could get on with this if people stopped arguing!
- We've done some process improvements, and we've still got problems.
- I can't stand all this touchy-feely people stuff. Can't you just give me a process?
- Why do the IT people always cringe when I want to do a team-building exercise?

I hope you enjoy yourself!

As I wrote, I imagined you reading this book. One colleague who reviewed some chapters said to me, "I want to imagine that we are sitting by the fire with a glass of wine, sharing ideas and experiences," and that is what I wanted the atmosphere of the book to be like. I have used experience-based anecdotes rather than scientifically gathered evidence. The stories I tell include lessons I have learned (and am still learning!) from my own mistakes, situations I have observed, and anecdotes from colleagues and clients, and I hope that when you read them you will respond with "Oh, yes! That reminds me of when...."

So enjoy this book; feel free to browse and dip into it as well as read it through. A key message from it is that there is more than one way of thinking, and we are sensible to acknowledge them all, however strange they seem to us. So bring your own ideas to the book and read interactively!

This is a huge subject

This book is for you if you need an overview of a huge subject in one book, and the chance to find out more about the details that particularly interest you. I have covered the whole life of a software system, together with describing all the people involved, so this is a sketchbook of what you need to consider, with extensive references to further information.

As you are busy, when you want further information you will need to get to it quickly and easily. To help you, wherever possible I have given several references whenever possible to newer publications, including Web sites, short books or papers, or books that I have been able to locate in a library rather than have to order, so that you can get the next level of detail quickly and easily. I have also provided original book or paper citations, either in the references or in the selected bibliography in each chapter, so that if you just need a little more information you can get it easily, but you can also find more depth when you need it.

In Appendix A, I have given some suggested Internet search words for each technique that I describe, as some of the references, especially for Web sites, may change. I have also provided a list of useful organizations from which you will be able to find more information.

Remember, this book is an overview and as a result there are many references, techniques, standards, methods, and frameworks that I have not covered, but that should not inhibit you from considering them for your own situation. If you prefer a different method at a particular point, simply incorporate it into your recipe for success.

Finding your way around this book

Three of the chapters in the book provide overviews of ideas presented in the chapters that follow them:

- Chapter 1 provides an overview of quality concepts used throughout the book.
- Chapter 2 provides an overview of the groups discussed in Chapters 3 to 7.
- Chapter 8 provides an overview of the software life span described in Chapters 9 to 12.

Chapter 1 sets out some ideas and definitions that are used throughout the book. Read this chapter first, as the ideas introduced are used throughout the book. I describe five definitions of quality and a number of quality or excellence frameworks that provide the basis for the discussion in the rest of the book. Each definition of quality provides a different viewpoint about quality—what it is and how we might measure it. Some of the frameworks are organizational—the business will use them to set and check its direction. Others are IT-specific. I show how the organizational and IT standards can fit together.

Chapter 2 provides an overview of the groups of people who are involved in software, whether as producers or users. I have divided people into five groups: customers, managers, builders, measurers, and supporters. I am not suggesting that an individual is assigned a role within a group, or always stays within one group. Instead, I show how the five groups fit with particular quality viewpoints, and that many people move between groups.

Chapters 3 to 7 each describe one of the groups in detail. Most readers will find that they fit most closely into one of the groups, but spend some time in the other groups. Read these chapters to get an overview of what each group does and what its viewpoints are, so that you understand each other better. Each of these chapters provides an overview of that group, based on the organizational framework and the quality viewpoints described in Chapter 1:

- Chapter 3 describes the customers and users of software systems.
- Chapter 4 describes the people who manage software projects and services.
- Chapter 5 describes people who build products, not just the developers but also technical authors, training providers, business analysts, and designers.
- Chapter 6 describes people who measure the quality of products and processes: the testers, inspectors, document reviewers, and auditors.
- Chapter 7 describes the people who support the software during its development and deployment, by providing infrastructure for the software and tools used to build and test it, as well as supporting the people who build, test, deliver, service, and use the system.

Chapter 8 gives an overview of the life of a piece of software or a system from the moment it is conceived as an idea, through the software development life cycle, as it is installed or delivered, throughout its deployment as a live or production system, its maintenance and updating, and, finally, its decommissioning. It introduces Chapters 9 to 12, in which I discuss how communication needs to be considered and improved by all the groups throughout the life of a software system. I have only described the techniques applied by particular groups when they have an effect on communication and teamwork; the chapters are not intended to explain everything about software projects but to highlight some aids to mutual understanding. For example, quality gates, or entry and exit criteria, between stages in a project are important for process definition, and reviews are important for identifying defects in products but they are both also important communication points between the groups described in Chapters 2 to 7.

- Chapter 9 discusses what happens before we start to build software—we realize we have a problem to solve or an opportunity to grab, and we must decide whether we need software or something else to solve our problem. It covers problem and solution analysis, risk analysis, and setting the contract for the software development life cycle, describing how to improve communication and understanding in order to launch the right project.
- Chapter 10 describes the software development life cycle and provides an overview of some models for software development, comparing and contrasting the models' effect on effective communication and teamwork between groups.
- Chapter 11 describes the point of implementation of the software, types of delivery, and what information is needed by different groups at this point.

- Chapter 12 describes the life of software once it is in use, and discusses the importance of continued communication for evaluation of the previous stages and for maintenance and optimization of the software.

Throughout these chapters I refer to a number of techniques for understanding other people's communication styles. In Appendix A, I provide a summary of these techniques and sources for more detailed information. In Appendix B, I provide more information about tailoring standards and documents for a project based on published national and international standards.

References

[1] Smith, K., "The Software Industry's Bug Problem," *Quality Digest*, reproduced on http://www.qualitydigest.com, April 2003.

[2] Sol, E. -J., "The Embedded Internet—Towards 100 Billion Devices," *EuroSTAR Conference*, Stockholm, Sweden, 2001.

Acknowledgments

Naturally, a book like this is only built on other people's work and efforts, and you will see from the references that many practitioners and authors have supported me by being earlier writers in the same areas of thought. This book weaves together threads that others have spun. I thank them all for their inspiration over the years.

Many people helped me while I was writing this book, by their encouragement, discussing ideas, providing support, and reviewing material. Colleagues and clients have contributed with enormous generosity, discussing and challenging ideas, commenting and reviewing material and drafts, suggesting additional references, and providing valuable insights into the subject. They encouraged me to continue; their comments, stories, and ideas have improved the book immeasurably. I wish to thank, among others, Rick Craig, Dorothy Graham, Frank Johnstone, Mike Bowdon, Stuart Reid , Paul Gerrard, Richard Warden, Tom Gilb, Julian Harty, David Hayman, Mike Holcombe, Brenda Hubbard, John Smith, Norman Hughes, Kai Gilb, Jane Jeffs, Simon Mitchley, Fiona Powell, Lloyd Roden, Mike Smith, Jayne Weaver, Graham Thomas, Geoff Thompson, Neil Thompson, Erik van Veenendaal, John Watkins, Steve Allott, Jayne Weaver, Clive Bates, Mark Fewster, Pat Myles, and Ian Bennett. I could not have completed this without the help of Barbara Eastman, who encouraged me, proofread drafts, and pursued permissions. Richard Delingpole's graphic design expertise turned my rough ideas into elegant figures. Tiina Ruonamaa, Tim Pitts, and the team of editors at Artech House supported me throughout the project and kept me on track.

It is an honor for me that Dorothy Graham has written the foreword to this book. Thank you, Dorothy, for your help, encouragement, and friendship.

My family has supported my writing during a bad year for us all—thank you. Finally, my partner, Dave, has been an unfailing support throughout—thank you, Dave, for everything you have done.

My thanks to all of you for your help; the book would not have been possible without you. As I am human, there will be mistakes in the book; the mistakes, of course, are my own.

CHAPTER 1

Contents

1.1 Defining software quality

1.2 Fundamental concepts of excellence

1.3 EFQM Excellence Model

1.4 ISO 9000:1994 and ISO 9000:2000

1.5 IT maturity models—CMM® and relations

1.6 Team Software Process and Personal Software Process

1.7 Bringing the models together

Software Quality Matters

In this chapter I shall:

- Demonstrate that there is no universal definition of quality: it varies with people and situation;
- Offer several definitions of quality;
- Show why it is necessary for all stakeholders in the software to agree on what they mean by "quality";
- Introduce some models for managing quality;
- Show how you can integrate these models.

The developers are always so enthusiastic about the wonderful new software when they hand it over for me to develop the training. Then the "buts" start … they tell me that when I demonstrate the software I need to keep away from this transaction because of the outstanding defects, and to watch out for the finance director who's still sore about the budget overrun. They tell me the interface the users wanted wasn't feasible and preparation of user manuals has been de-scoped to a postlaunch activity. Once, on the morning of the first course, the company announced that the new software would "enable moving 40% of jobs overseas." "Negative trainees" would be an understatement!

—Trainer pointing out some forgotten aspects of quality

1.1 Defining software quality

Let us start looking at quality by examining the story above. What do the trainer's frustrations reveal about our views of quality?

1. The delivered software includes *other products and services* as well as code; the people buying and using software do not just need the code, they also need services and products such as training, user guides, and support.

2. *Quality cannot be defined by technical excellence alone*—it also includes human factors such as communication and motivation, as well as value for money. The customer must be able to afford the products and services, and enjoy the experience of dealing with the supplier as well as using the products.

3. Different people will hold various views on whether quality is delivered *to the customer*. The developers produced a fine product, with lots of wonderful new features, so they were rightly enthusiastic, but the product had flaws, cost too much, did not meet the customer's needs, and made the lives of their colleagues in training much harder. Also, the people losing their jobs would take a decidedly different view about whether a quality solution had been delivered.

We will find throughout this book that different people give different definitions if we ask them what they mean by quality. When I ask people working with software as users or on software development projects what quality means, all sorts of ideas emerge. Some might mention cost, time, scope, specification, value, or standardization, whereas others talk about perfection, expectations, relationships, feelings, and emotions. Some of this can be accomplished by delivering code, but much is achieved from other software products and services such as documentation and training. Some can only be realized through less tangible things such as relationships and expectations.

Why is this important? Because it causes difficulties when people involved in a project have different views of quality. If people do not have shared goals and aspirations, their view of quality is affected. It means that, if they do not communicate their differences and negotiate a common goal, they may work against each other, while thinking they are all pulling together. There will be confusion about whether a delivered software product provides quality. So many systems are delivered that are not used, or not liked, or cannot be supported by training, documentation, and help provisioning. Yet the IT project teams are either unaware of, or surprised by, the reaction to what they have perceived as a successful project. We all believe we have done a good job and are mortified if our work is not well received! We commonly find a different view of whether a project has delivered a "quality product" if we talk to the customers and to the project team. Furthermore, we frequently find differences of opinion if we talk to the project manager, the developers, the testers, the trainers, and other groups within the project team. Each person may seem to hold a different view of the quality of the product and service, and, indeed, a different underlying assumption of how to measure quality. So I will start by defining quality from a variety of viewpoints.

Five distinct definitions for quality can be recognized.[1] The definitions I will use are from [1]. They are the *product*-based, *manufacturing*-based, *user*-based, *value*-based, and *transcendent* definitions.

---

1. The definitions of quality in this chapter and throughout the book are based on Chapter 1 of [1], reused by permission of UTN Publishing. These definitions are based on work by [2] and were adapted by [3].

1.1 Defining software quality

Two definitions of quality favored by IT people are the product-based and the manufacturing-based definitions. In projects, we favor definitions that allow us to measure progress and success in delivery. We want to fix quality to something that is deliverable and measurable.

- In the product-based definition, quality is based on a well-defined set of software quality attributes that must be measured in an objective and quantitative way. We can derive acceptance criteria to objectively assess the quality of the delivered product. *Example: Standards such as ISO 9126 [4] define attributes such as reliability, usability, security, and functionality, together with measures for them. "The software is 98% reliable when running continuously over a 7-day period. Recovery time is less than 1 minute at each failure."*

- The manufacturing-based definition focuses on the manufacture of software products, that is, their specification, design, and construction. Quality depends on the extent to which requirements have been implemented in conformance with the original requirements. We measure faults and failures in products. Success is measured as our ability to follow a process and deliver products against agreed specifications. We *will* verify (is the system correct to specification?) but if we do not take account of the *user-based* definition of quality (see below), we *may forget* to validate (is this the right specification?). *Example: Repeatable, auditable process with delivery that conforms to specification. "The software was built to specification, and there are a low number of defects."*

There are two other definitions of quality that reflect the views of the software user and purchaser. These perspectives are about supporting the needs of the organization and its stakeholders, within the organization's constraints. Because the pressures on an organization change over time, what constitutes "quality" may change over time to match. Sometimes the changes will be tactical—*"We must cut costs this quarter!"*—and sometimes they may be strategic—*"We want to be market leaders!"*—and these may conflict.

- The user-based definition says that quality is fitness for use. Software quality should be determined by the user(s) of a product in a specific business situation. Different business characteristics require different types of software products; not only to do different things, but also to cater to how different people want to carry out their tasks. This can be subjective and cannot be determined only on the basis of quantitative metrics. It is the user-based definition that encourages us to validate *as well as* to verify the system. *Example: Fit for purpose. "I can do my work efficiently and effectively when I use this software."*

- The value-based definition is focused on things that impact on the running of the business as a whole. Software quality should always be determined by means of a decision process on trade-offs between time, effort, and cost aspects. This is done by communicating with all parties involved, for example, sponsors, customers, developers, and producers. *Example: Return on Investment (ROI).* "*If we release the software now, we will spend $250,000 extra on support in the first month. If we are a month late, it will cost the organization $1 million in fines and lost business. Should we release or do more testing?*"

Finally, we must acknowledge that we all know quality when we see it; our knowledge is based on our experiences, taste, affections, loyalties, and emotions. Unfortunately, this means different people will have different reactions to a product: The transcendent definition states that quality can be recognized easily depending on the perceptions and the affective feelings of an individual toward a type of software product. This means that we consider someone's emotional response to a product or service. *Did they enjoy it? Did they like the people they met? Are they happy?* This is not easily measurable, but understanding this aspect of quality can be a first step toward the explicit definition and measurement of quality. *Example: Brand loyalty based on affection.* "*I like using this software—it appeals to me.*"

In a single project, we may have several definitions of quality in use, perhaps inadvertently and unacknowledged by all the people in the project. It is important to realize that there is no "right" definition of quality. How we define "quality" for a particular product, service, or project is situational. We say, "*It depends on....*" Contrast the following:

- *Air traffic control system:* We are considering using the product/manufacturing definitions because we need to ensure technical excellence above all else.
- *Package to improve usability of Web pages for the visually impaired:* We are considering using the user-based definition because we need to ensure it is fit for the purposes of this group.
- *Software to launch an innovative new product and achieve "first mover" advantage:* We are considering using a value-based definition because if we spend more to get a better product we may miss the market.

For most commercial or custom-made software, the customer is best served by balancing the definitions. In our particular project, we should ask ourselves: What is the greatest number or level of attributes (product-based) that we can deliver to support the users' tasks (user-based) while giving the best cost–benefit ratio (value-based) while following repeatable/quality-assured processes within a managed project (manufacturing-based)?

As a colleague remarked to me, "Compromise and a balance between the quality definitions is essential" (Frank Johnstone, personal communication, April 18, 2003). We *need* to define quality and to understand which definitions people buying, using, developing, testing, and supporting software use. This prevents the conflicts between stakeholders and enables us to understand *why* we are developing the software. In Chapters 2 to 7, we will explore the different groups and which quality definitions they favor, and then, in Chapters 8 to 12, we will look at how the different groups contribute throughout the life of software and systems, and the benefits that each quality view brings.

Whichever definition(s) of quality we use—that of software users or suppliers—we all want to try to avoid mistakes. One way to try and do this is to adopt strong processes within a quality management framework. In *quality management*, our concern is to decide which processes to use and to adapt those processes appropriately for a project. During the project, we will carry out *quality assurance* activities to check that the chosen process has been followed and is suitable. *Quality control* processes will check the products for defects. The processes sit within an organizational culture and framework of management systems. Some quality management models are entirely *process driven*; our task as people operating within the processes is to follow the processes as defined. If we are lucky, we might be asked to suggest improvements to the processes. Other models, specifically those described as excellence models to differentiate them from process-driven quality models, are more focused on *people and their capabilities and needs*; here the activities of the project are focused on the ability of people to deliver services and products that satisfy the customers. Some models have a greater emphasis on improvement cycles than others; the *Deming cycle,* for example, proposed by W. Edwards Deming [5], has four stages, sometimes called the "Plan, Do, Check, and Act" cycle, and sometimes the "Plan, Do, Review, Improve" cycle. Here, we plan what to do and we do it. Then we review what we did. Was it successful? Did it go as planned? What should we improve? We then put improvements in place, and plan the next cycle of activities. We will see through this book that this Deming improvement cycle works on a large scale, for example, when looking at the excellence framework for an organization or for a project, but is particularly effective for making incremental improvements as we do work, whether as a team or individually.

We need to look at these models and understand the advantages and disadvantages of each one.

1.2 Fundamental concepts of excellence

To compare models, I shall use the Fundamental Concepts of Excellence set out by the European Foundation for Quality Management (EFQM) [6]. These concepts are used in a number of models, including the EFQM Excellence Model, which is used by more than 20 member countries in the European Union. Similar organizational models based on these concepts have been developed in other countries. For example, Puay et al. [7] compare nine schemes, including the Malcolm Baldrige model [8] and the EFQM Excellence Model [6], in different countries (three European, two North American, three Asian-Pacific, and one South American) against nine criteria: leadership, impact on society, resource management, strategy and policy, human resource management, process quality, results, customer management and satisfaction, and supplier/partner management and performance. It is these criteria that are reflected in the Fundamental Concepts of Excellence.

Other organizational quality and excellence initiatives, such as Six Sigma and the Balanced Scorecard, also provide a way of discussing the goals of an organization, deciding how to achieve those goals, and measuring whether they have been achieved.

In this book, I focus on the EFQM Excellence Model, but whichever model your organization uses, whether Baldrige or one of the others, you should be able to map your model onto the ideas in this book. This is because, although the different models use slightly different words and place a different emphasis on the different criteria, the fundamentals of running a successful organization apply, worldwide. For example, I will link the EFQM Excellence Model to a number of other standards, specifically for use in IT. In the same way, in [9] the authors have linked Six Sigma to IT frameworks.

The Fundamental Concepts of Excellence of the EFQM Excellence Model [6] are:

- *Results orientation*: "Excellence is dependent upon balancing and satisfying the needs of all relevant stakeholders (this includes the people employed, customers, suppliers, and society in general, as well as those with financial interests in the organization)."
- *Customer focus:* "The customer is the final arbiter of product and service quality, and customer loyalty, retention, and market share gain are best optimized through a clear focus on the needs of current and potential customers."
- *Leadership and constancy of purpose:* "The behavior of an organization's leaders creates a clarity and unity of purpose within the organization and an environment in which the organization and its people can excel."
- *Management by processes and facts:* "Organizations perform more effectively when all inter-related activities are understood and systematically managed, and decisions concerning current operations are planned. Improvements are made using reliable information that includes stakeholder perceptions."
- *People development and involvement:* "The full potential of an organization's people is best released through shared values and a culture of trust and empowerment, which encourages the involvement of everyone."
- *Continuous learning, innovation, and improvement:* "Organizational performance is maximized when it is based on the management and sharing of knowledge within a culture of continuous learning, innovation, and improvement."
- *Partnership development.* "An organization works more effectively when it has mutually beneficial relationships, built on trust, sharing of knowledge, and integration, with its Partners."
- *Public responsibility.* "The long-term interest of the organization and its people are best served by adopting an ethical approach and exceeding the expectations and regulations of the community at large."

How can we encourage the Fundamental Concepts of Excellence and get the best from our software teams? If you look at the Fundamental Concepts of Excellence, you will see that process, which emphasizes manufacturing and product-based viewpoints, is only one part we need to consider. When we look at the concepts, we see they involve considering and working with different groups of people, and thinking about balancing the views of different stakeholders. To help us do this, I will use the concepts throughout the book, to encourage a teamwork approach and allow all five quality definitions. Some quality models define quality processes for an individual to use, some are for teams, and some for organizations. The coverage of the quality definitions and the emphasis on teamwork varies across the models. In this book, I will use a selection of the models. They are:

- A framework for organizational excellence, known as the EFQM Excellence Model [6] in Europe, which is similar to others, such as the Malcolm Baldrige model [8], used in the United States;
- Two process standards—ISO 9000:1994 and ISO 9000:2000 [10];
- A group of IT maturity models based around CMM® (Capability Maturity Model®) [11, 12] and two models for implementing CMM®: the Team Software Process (TSP) [13] and the Personal Software Process (PSP) [14].

1.3 EFQM Excellence Model

The European Foundation for Quality Management (EFQM) Excellence Model [6] is an organizational excellence model using a nonprescriptive framework. It is not specifically an IT framework. It may be used with organizations of any size and type and is intended for corporations, companies, or nonprofit organizations. Here I am using it to help discuss a "mini-organization": the software project. The EFQM Excellence Model provides a framework for excellence under nine criteria; five of these are "Enablers" for excellence and four are measures of the "Results." These are interlinked with a continuous improvement feedback loop known as RADAR (Results, Approach, Deployment, Assessment, and Review) (Figure 1.1).

1.3.1 Enablers

The Enablers are *Leadership, Policy and Strategy, People, Partnerships and Resources,* and *Processes*. The results are *Customer, People, Society,* and *Key Performance Results*. In the following descriptions, I will first give the description for an entire organization and then for a project as a "mini-organization."

1.3.1.1 Leadership

Excellence is led from the top. Leaders facilitate the achievement of the mission and vision, and develop values for success. Leaders are personally

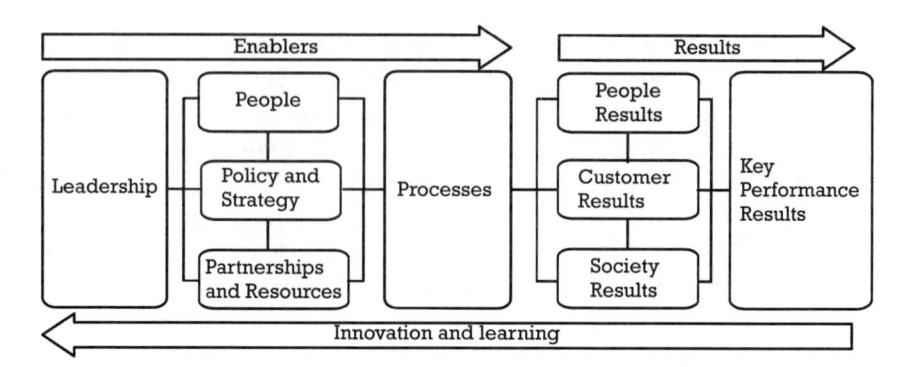

Figure 1.1 EFQM Excellence Model. (*From:* [6]. © 1999–2003 EFQM. Redrawn by permission of EFQM.)

involved in ensuring that the management system is developed and implemented.

Project managers provide leadership for their projects under the leadership of the project board and sponsor. In the mini-organization the project manager is the leader.

1.3.1.2 Policy and Strategy

The vision of leaders is implemented via policies and strategies. Leaders focus policy and strategy around the needs of the stakeholders and ensure they are reflected in policies, plans, objectives, targets, and processes.

The specific strategy for the project (including any quality strategy) is derived from the organization's overall policy and strategy. Additionally, it will show where changes have been made to reflect the needs of a particular project. The mini-organization requires its own strategies.

1.3.1.3 People

The organization manages, develops, and releases the knowledge and full potential of its people at individual, team-based, and organization-wide levels. The organization must consider how people are treated and valued.

In a project, for example, we need to consider not only who is working on the project and the skills they bring, but also how their skills and experience are enhanced during the project. During and after the project, people must feel that they and their contributions were valued.

1.3.1.4 Partnerships and Resources

The organization plans and manages its external partnerships and internal resources in order to support its policy and strategy and the effective operation of its processes. The organization considers partnerships with other organizations and how resources such as technology and information are managed. This divides into two distinct categories. The first includes the people outside our organization with whom we interact.

In the context of the mini-organization, I mean those external to our project. This might include how we liaise with suppliers and other projects. The second includes the (nonhuman) resources we require in order to complete our tasks, for example, management of the organization's information, IT infrastructure, and negotiation for scarce facilities such as development/test environments.

1.3.1.5 Processes

The organization designs, manages, and improves its processes in order to support its policy and strategy and fully satisfy, and generate increasing value for, its customers and other stakeholders. In a project, we need to consider which processes are appropriate. If we have experienced people and low-risk problems to solve, we might consider a lightweight, agile method for our IT project. If we have a high-risk project or inexperienced people, we may find that heavy-duty processes with an audit trail may give us more confidence. We select processes appropriate to our problem and our team.

1.3.2 Results

There are four sets of results measurements. The first three have a perception and a performance measure, whereas the fourth, key performance results, focuses on outcomes in relation to planned performance. As in the Enablers, I will show how the mini-organization of a project relates to the larger organization.

1.3.2.1 Customer Results

These measure whether the organization is meeting the needs of its external customers. Customer perception can be assessed through satisfaction surveys. Performance could be monitored by tracking the number of complaints and volume of repeat business. For a project team, or an IT team undertaking a series of projects, we might measure the perception of that team or project by its customers, the users of the software, and the managers of the purchasing organization.

1.3.2.2 People Results

Here, we measure what the organization is achieving for its people. The organization may survey employee perception and set performance targets for staff turnover and absence. Similarly, we could measure the motivation of the project team, people's attitude to working on the project, and factors such as illness and turnover.

1.3.2.3 Society Results

Society results measure what the organization is achieving in relation to local, national, and international society where appropriate. We can measure how our organization is perceived in society, for example, through favorable press. A performance measure could be the attainment of awards, perhaps for corporate social responsibility.

Within a project, we might measure how the project measures against corporate targets for waste and energy management. We might also plan for, and measure use of, time for project members to carry out activities in the local community.

1.3.2.4 Key Performance Results

These results measure what the organization is achieving in relation to its planned performance, including financial measures such as return on investment, profit, and turnover, and nonfinancial outcomes such as market share and sales success rates. For the project, indicators of its success might include contribution to achieving increased business and decreasing costs, but we might also want to measure how well the project delivers against its planned budget.

1.3.3 Excellence, the EFQM Excellence Model, the Malcolm Baldrige model, and other related models

As we might expect, the EFQM Excellence Model meets the Fundamental Concepts of Excellence well. It is a European model, but is closely related to other models such as the U.S. model, the Malcolm Baldrige model [8]. The Baldrige model has the same aims and a very similar framework. In both, organizations score points against the enablers and the results to accumulate a total excellence score out of 1,000. Organizations compete against themselves—they seek to improve their score year by year. If organizations wish, they can compete against other organizations in an award scheme. The point of both models is to encourage the continuous improvement of organizations, rather than to achieve a specific level.

1.4 ISO 9000:1994 and ISO 9000:2000

ISO 9000:1994 [10] is a quality assurance standard for design and manufacturing processes. It is rigid in its definition and interpretation of quality. A large number of processes are defined and must be adhered to by means of audit trails and evidence, regardless of whether these processes give the best outcome for the customer or for the project team on a particular project. In ISO 9000:2000 [10], there are a smaller number of defined and documented processes and a greater emphasis both on people understanding the tasks that they have to perform and on customer satisfaction. ISO 9000:2000 includes continuous improvement and moves toward the EFQM framework. Although the ISO 9000 standards meet some of the Fundamental Concepts of Excellence, there are significant gaps, especially in ISO 9000:1994. However, the standards are useful in IT projects as a guide for auditability.

1.5 IT maturity models—CMM® and relations

The concept of organizational maturity and capability for an IT organization was developed at the Software Engineering Institute (SEI) [11] to define a better way of producing software. It regards software as an engineering discipline and groups organizations into five levels within the Capability Maturity Model® (CMM®):

- *Level 1—Initial:* Projects are ad hoc and chaotic. "Everyone has their own process."
- *Level 2—Repeatable:* Requirements are managed and projects are performed according to documented plans. "Every team has its own process; teams can repeat work."
- *Level 3—Defined:* Software engineering and management processes are stable and do not break down under stress. "Every team in the organization uses the same process; we can start to deal with change."
- *Level 4—Managed:* The organization manages its processes quantitatively and measures performance and quality across all projects. "The whole organization is measuring so we KNOW how we are doing."
- *Level 5—Optimizing:* Continual improvement and proactive defect resolution. "We can build on our knowledge to improve."

Progress through these levels is measured by key process indicators (KPIs). All the indicators at one level must be met before an organization can be considered to be at that level. The levels and KPIs are focused on the software development process and measurement of that process:

> The CMM® provides a staged approach to IT process improvement. The underlying premise is good common sense: the IT organization needs to walk before it runs. Sophisticated engineering and measurement processes cannot be sustained unless they are built upon a framework of strong basic management practices. Organizations that omit embedding Level 2 processes normally return to "ad hoc and chaotic" in periods of stress. (Frank Johnstone, personal communication, April 18, 2003)

CMM® covers software development, and considers testing as a part of this, with explicit requirements for testing included at Level 3 and above. To enhance this, number of testers started to develop related models specifically for testing. These include TMM® [15] and TPI® [16], among others [17]. These are all process models. They differ from the Fundamental Concepts of Excellence in that they generally focus on process and measurement of process to the exclusion of other issues, although, as the models develop, increasing heed is taken of the wider aspects of excellence. Difficulty with the implementation and use of CMM® gave rise to two further process models: the Team Software Process (TSP) and the Personal Software Process (PSP), which are described below. CMM® and its relations continue to develop. Recently the Software Engineering Institute has introduced the

CMMI® (CMM® Integration) and PCMM® (People CMM®) models, which attempt to widen the applicability of the CMM® concept to any engineering discipline and to cover management of people. For the latest news on CMM® and its relations, please visit the Software Engineering Institute Web site [11]. A paper comparing some test assessment and improvement processes was given by Stuart Reid at EuroSTAR 2003 [17].

1.6 Team Software Process and Personal Software Process

The Team Software Process (TSP) was developed at the Software Engineering Institute "to help integrated engineering teams more effectively develop software-intensive products. This process method addresses many of the current problems of developing software-intensive products and shows teams and their management explicitly how to address them" [11]. The TSP identifies that software projects fail because of teamwork problems and not because of technical issues. In [13] Watts Humphrey identifies ineffective leadership as a key problem for teams. The TSP requires the establishment of goals, the definition of team roles, the assessment of risks, and the production of a team plan. TSP permits whatever process structure makes the most business and technical sense. Teams are self-directed; in other words, they plan and track their own work. Managers operate by coaching and motivating the teams. In using the TSP, compliance to CMM® Level 5 is expected. We can see some common ground with the Fundamental Concepts of Excellence, particularly in the areas of leadership, people, process, improvement, and measurement. There are gaps in focus on the needs of the customer. In addition, the assumption of CMM® Level 5 means that the TSP is not so useful for organizations with less mature processes.

The Personal Software Process (PSP), developed by the Software Engineering Institute and based on CMM®, is a process definition for software engineers enabling them to plan and track work. PSP provides a framework of processes for the software engineer. It emphasizes the need for individual software engineers to receive intensive training before they use the processes. Good process is needed, but that will only work if people understand and are motivated to use the process. "Seventy percent of the cost of developing software is attributable to personnel costs; the skills, experience, and work habits of engineers largely determine the results of the software development process" [11]. This fits well with some aspects of the Fundamental Concepts of Excellence; it considers process and people's skills. However, the needs of the customer are not a focus for these models:

> The Personal Software Process helps individual engineers to improve their performance by bringing discipline to the way they develop software. ... It is not a matter of creativity versus discipline, but of bringing discipline to the work so that creativity can happen. ... The PSP shows engineers how to manage the quality of their products and how to make commitments they can meet. It also provides them with the data to justify their plans. [11]

1.7 Bringing the models together

Having briefly outlined these models, we can see how they complement each other. CMM® uses a staged approach to IT process improvement, which prescribes processes that the organization is ready to receive. PSP and TSP acknowledge the importance of people and teamwork in implementing and using processes. ISO 9000 shows us how to develop auditable processes. It is possible to fit all our organizational standards into a framework like the EFQM Excellence Model, and the ethos of the awards scheme is to encourage organizations at a low level of maturity to take the first steps toward excellence by assessment and improvement. It is possible to self assess and work for initial improvements, but continuous improvement is encouraged by assessment and comparison with other organizations at a regional, national, and European level. However, it does not have an IT focus, so in Figure 1.2 I have overlaid onto the EFQM Excellence Model the methods, processes, and standards that have been mentioned so far. In Chapters 3–7, I will discuss how the EFQM Excellence Model can be used as a framework to help leadership, strategy, and policy aid individuals or teams in understanding their own objectives and how they fit with their organization.

Each model has gaps and most do not encourage all the five definitions of quality (see Table 1.1). Only the EFQM Excellence Model, with its measurements of perception as well as performance, acknowledges the *transcendent* view of quality. At present, only the EFQM Excellence Model, with its measures of key performance results, including financial results, acknowledges the *value-based* view of quality. PCMM® performance measurement is set against the organization's business objectives, but not yet, as far as I can ascertain, as a value-based quality. However, together the models have strength; from the ISO 9000 family we can use the idea of evidence and audit trails, from the CMM® family we can use the idea of developing maturity of process, and from the EFQM we can use the quality concepts of

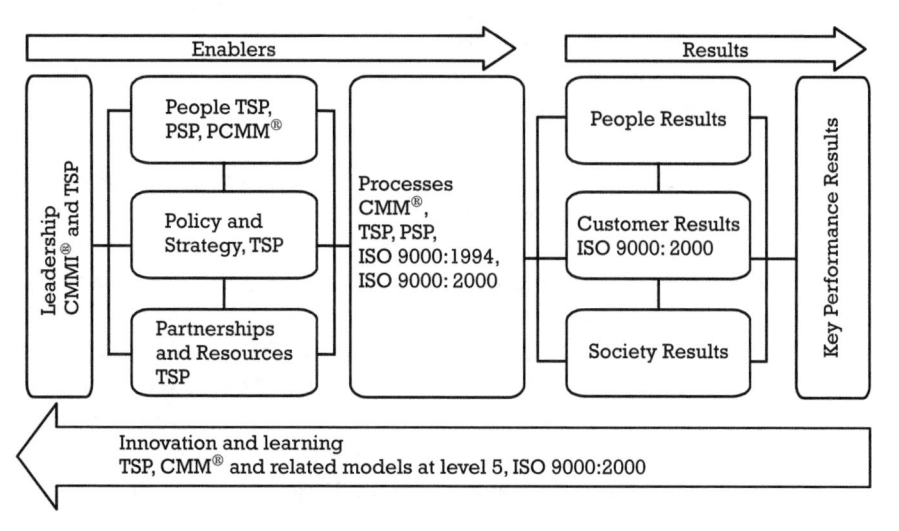

Figure 1.2 How the models fit in the EFQM Excellence Model. (*After:* [6].)

Table 1.1 Views of Quality Across the Models

Quality View	Model EFQM/Baldrige	CMM® and Relations	ISO 9000:1994	ISO 9000:2004
ISO 9000:2000	✓			
Transcendent	✓			
User	✓			✓
Value	✓	(✓)		
Product	✓	✓		
Manufacturing	✓	✓	✓	✓

✓ is a primary quality view.
(✓) is a quality view that may be taken by some people in this group.

value and transcendent excellence. Organizations can benefit from any or all of these models. Meeting all the requirements of a model is rarely necessary or an end in itself. Organizations can select aspects of the models and choose from the techniques suggested, to meet their specific needs. This is an approach that I encourage throughout this book.

There are other standards that apply to software development, delivery, and support. It is important to realize that these standards will always sit within an organizational and cultural framework. Our choice of particular standards will reflect how we define quality, our industry/sector, our process maturity, and what is appropriate for our particular project. These other standards I will cover as needed in the rest of the book. I will note here three references that also place software standards in a framework. We have already mentioned a paper that sets software standards within Six Sigma [9]. In addition, the Software and Systems Quality Framework (SSQF), [18] mentions the EFQM Excellence Model and Baldrige model, Six Sigma, CMM®, and ISO 9000 as possible frameworks within which software standards might be adopted, but concentrates on ISO 9000 as the example framework. A useful paper concentrating on testing-related standards can be found on the Testing Standards Web site [19], although it does not mention the EFQM Excellence Model and Baldrige model.

Finally, the move toward integrating standards together is becoming increasingly important; organizations are moving toward *integrated management systems* that integrate quality, environmental, security, and financial management systems into one framework, and also include information management within and beyond the IT systems. Standards for IT work cannot stand alone; they must be part of the organization's integrated management system in order to align with the organization's aims. These will align with excellence frameworks, whether these are the EFQM Excellence Model, Baldrige model, or another framework. Frameworks for IT service management already align with the EFQM Excellence Model and the Baldrige model [20]. Whether providing new technology or exploiting existing technology, what is needed is for IT development and for project management to share that alignment. As organizations develop new excellence and management frameworks to face their changing world, IT development and support standards will need to follow.

References

[1] Evans, I., "Testing Fundamentals," in *The Testing Practitioner*, E. van Veenendaal, (ed.), Den Bosch, the Netherlands: Uitgeverij Tutein Nolthenius, 2002, pp. 13–30.

[2] Garvin, D., "What Does Product Quality Really Mean?" *Sloan Management Review*, Vol. 26, No. 1, 1984.

[3] Trienekens, J., and E. van Veenendaal, *Software Quality from a Business Perspective*, Deventer, the Netherlands: Kluwer, 1997.

[4] International Standards Organization/International Electrotechnical Commission (ISO/IEC), DTR 9126 Software Engineering—Software Product Quality (Parts 1–4, 2000/2001).

[5] The W. Edwards Deming Institute, "Deming's Teachings," http://www.deming.org/theman/ articles/articles_gbnf04.html, November 2003.

[6] European Foundation for Quality Management, "EFQM Excellence Model" and "Fundamental Concepts of Excellence," http://www.efqm.org, August 2003.

[7] Puay, S. H., et al., "A Comparative Study of the National Quality Awards," *TQM Magazine*, Vol. 10, No. 1, pp. 30–39.

[8] Malcolm Baldrige model, http://www.quality.nist.gov/index.html, August 2003.

[9] Gack, G. A., and K. Robison, "Integrating Improvement Initiatives: Connecting Six Sigma for Software, CMMI®, Personal Software Process, and Team Software Process," *Software Quality Professional*, September 2003, pp. 5–13.

[10] International Standards Organization, ISO 9000:1994 and ISO 9000:2000 Quality Systems.

[11] Software Engineering Institute, "Capability Maturity Model®," http://www.sei.cmu.\edu, July 2003.

[12] Caputo, K., *CMM® Implementation Guide: Choreographing Software Process Improvement*, Reading, MA: Addison-Wesley, 1998.

[13] Humphrey, W., *Introduction to the Team Software Process*, Reading, MA: SEI, 2000.

[14] Humphrey, W., *Introduction to the Personal Software Process*, Reading, MA: SEI, 1997.

[15] van Veenendaal, E., and R. Swinkels, "Testing Maturity Model," in *The Testing Practitioner*, E. van Veenendaal, (ed.), Den Bosch, the Netherlands: Uitgeverij Tutein Nolthenius, 2002, pp. 289–300.

[16] Koomen, T., and M. Pol, *Test Process Improvement*, Reading, MA: Addison-Wesley, 1999.

[17] Reid, S. C., "Test Process Improvement—An Empirical Study," *EuroSTAR Conference paper*, Amsterdam, the Netherlands 2003.

[18] British Standards Institute, PD0026:2003, *Software and Systems Quality Framework—A Guide to the Use of ISO/IEC and Other Standards for Understanding*

Quality in Software and Systems, London, England: British Standards Institute, May 2003.

[19] Reid, S. C., "Software Testing Standards—Do They Know What They Are Talking About?" http://www.testingstandards.co.uk/publications.htm, August 2003.

[20] IT Infrastructure Library, *Best Practice for Service Delivery*, Norwich, England: Office of Government Commerce, 2002.

Selected bibliography

British Quality Foundation, *How to Use the Model*, London, England: British Quality Foundation, 2002.

British Quality Foundation, *The Model in Practice 2*, 2nd ed., London, England: British Quality Foundation, 2002.

Burnstein, I., T. Suwannasart, and C. R. Carlson, "Developing a Testing Maturity Model," *CrossTalk*, August/September 1996.

European Foundation for Quality Management and British Quality Foundation, *EFQM Excellence Model*, London, England: British Quality Foundation; Brussels, Belgium: European Foundation for Quality Management, 2002.

Handy, C., *Understanding Organizations*, New York: Penguin, 1993.

Hayes, L., "Hello Up There! Will the Sarbanes–Oxley Act Finally Catapult QA to the Boardroom?" Sticky Minds Web site, http://www.stickyminds.com/sitewide.asp?Function=FEATUREDCOLUMN&ObjectId=6544&ObjectType=ARTCOL&btntopic=artcol&tt=LIMITCAT_6544_**WHERE**&tth=H, August 2003.

Kaplan, R. S., and D. P. Norton, *The Balanced Scorecard*, Boston, MA: Harvard Business School Press, 1996.

Larson A., *Demystifying Six Sigma*, New York: AMACOM, 2003.

Mullins, L. J., *Management and Organisational Behaviour*, 5th ed., New York: Financial Times/Pitman, 1999.

Seddon, J., and Vanguard Consulting, "Lean Service: Systems Thinking for Service Organisations—The Business Excellence Model—Will It Deliver?" http://www.lean-service.com/6-3.asp, November 2003.

Sticky Minds Web site Round Table, facilitator Craig, R., "What Is Software Quality and How Do You Measure Its Value?" http://www.stickyminds.com/s.asp?F=S6540_ROUND_46, August 2003.

Woodruff, W. D., "Introduction of Test Process Improvement and the Impact on the Organisation," *Software Quality Professional*, September 2003, pp. 24–32.

CHAPTER 2

Defining the Software Team

Contents

2.1 Teams in disunity

2.2 Defining the team

2.3 Interaction between the groups and within each group

In this chapter I shall:

- Describe the stakeholder groups that make up the software team;
- Discuss the mutual distrust between the team members and how it might be overcome;
- Identify which definitions of quality from Chapter 1 best fit to each group;
- Identify which of the quality models from Chapter 1 best fit the groups;
- List techniques to help improve communication between the groups.

It makes me wonder why senior managers don't knock a few heads together. After all, we are all fighting on the same side, or should be.

—*Comment from a test consultant, noting the disagreements between members of the software teams*

2.1 Teams in disunity

Some years ago, I was working with a software team to help them improve the quality of their delivered software. I met a succession of people—first the testers, then the developers, then the business analysts, and, finally, a group of project managers. What was astounding was that each group was convinced that they were the least respected group and that they were the group that cared most about quality. They all described themselves as being "on the bottom of the heap," and commented on the lack of support and the grief they received from the other three groups. They all pointed to the software user and to senior management as "awkward customers." What was going on?

Each person held strong views about their own contribution and that of other people to the project and to quality. Studies of the motivation of IT personnel and users of IT systems have shown that people believe that their own group enhances the project and other groups detract from it. Warden and Nicholson, in their 1996 survey of motivation in IT staff [1], remarked:

> IT is not a close-knit community of like-minded professionals. Many negative attributions are made about other groups lacking the motivation for quality. Senior managers are accused of paying lip-service to quality, while starving it of resources in pursuit of profit. Software developers are accused of focusing on technical excellence, completely disregarding customers' need for a quality product. Customers are accused of demanding levels of quality which they are not prepared to pay for. These are among the most common criticisms but there are many others. Each group within the profession makes negative attributions about other groups.

Table 2.1 shows that each group has a positive self-perception, but often feels negatively about other groups. Many of you will recognize these interactions and misunderstandings.

I have illustrated all the chapters in this book with anecdotes from my own experience, and I hope that you will add stories of your own. Here are

Table 2.1 Group Attitude Results

View	*How* Developers	IT Infrastructure Staff	Software Maintainers	IT Managers	Quality Practitioners	Testers	Users
Developers	We're OK.	Don't listen. Poor quality.	Will not document.	No business awareness or interpersonal skills.	Resist change. A law unto themselves.	Resent criticism.	Computers are difficult to use and unreliable.
IT infrastructure staff	Always complaining.	We're OK.	Should filter requests.	Better customer orientation.	Understand.	Understand.	
Software maintainers	Unpleasant job, low status.	Long delays	We're OK.	Long delays.	Resist change.	Resent criticism.	
IT managers	Want delivery too soon to get quality.	Should force developers to attend to users.	Want delivery too soon to get quality.	We're OK.	No interest, no support. Don't understand.	Don't know the cost of letting bugs through.	
Quality practitioners	Waste time. Unrealistic. Don't understand.	Understand	Waste time. Unrealistic. Don't understand.	A luxury. Only if customers demand it.	We're OK.	Understand.	
Testers	Unnecessary —we do that!	Understand	Unnecessary —we do that!	Little skill needed.	Understand.	We're OK.	
Users	Don't know what they want.	Complain to us about software.	Ask for trivial changes.	Will not pay for quality but expect it.	Will not pay for quality but expect it.	Understand.	We don't want to know about technology.

Source: [1].

a few to start us off. Some are from colleagues and some are from my own experiences.

- On one project I worked on, testers and developers were not allowed to talk to each other because it would waste time!
- The testers didn't check whether the reports they sent to the developers were duplicates. They did not talk to other testers about what they were reporting. It really wasted the developers' time.
- When I said I had not used a PC before, he treated me like an idiot ... they are always so rude in the IT department.
- When I was asked to build the new software, I wanted to find out what I should be building—there was no specification—so I went to talk to the system users to see what they wanted. No one had told them the system was being changed, and they were furious. They spoke to my manager to ask what was happening. Main result: I was reprimanded for talking to people outside the IT department.

Why don't we get along? Maybe it's because we should be talking to each other and listening to each other more.

2.2 Defining the team

To help us understand how to overcome this problem of mutual distrust, let us examine who is in the software team. I will include in "the team" all the stakeholders for quality. This is not only people who commission, design, build, deliver, and support the software, but also people who use or are affected by the software. These definitions are based on my own experience of software projects and customers.

I have divided the team into five groups of stakeholders, based upon their main interests in the software project and, therefore, the definition of quality that they favor. These groups do not map to skill sets or organizational functions, and the people in each group will have various job titles. A person may be in more than one group for a particular project, or may move between groups in different projects. We will see how each group contributes to the success of the software project in a particular way. The groups are:

- People who are customers and users of software: *customers*;
- People who manage software projects: *managers*;
- People who build software: *builders*;
- People who measure software quality: *measurers*;
- People who provide the support and infrastructure for the project and the deployment of software: *supporters*.

In Chapter 1, we saw that there are five definitions of quality:

- Product-based quality is based on a well-defined set of software quality attributes that must be measured in an objective and quantitative way.
- Manufacturing-based quality focuses on the manufacture of software products, that is, their specification, design, and construction.
- User-based quality is fitness for use.
- Value-based quality is focused on things that impact on the running of the business as a whole.
- Transcendent quality can be recognized easily depending on the perceptions and the affective feelings of an individual toward a type of software product.

We will see that each group favors particular views of quality, and this is one of the causes of disunity between the groups.

2.2.1 People who are customers and users of software

Customers include all the people who buy, use, and are affected by software. They include the people who will pay for the software: the project sponsor, budget holder, or purchaser. The people who will use the software belong in this group (see "Users" in Table 2.1). I also include here the customers of the end users—they do not use the software but are affected by it when they interact with the end users.

When I refer to customers later in the book, I mean anyone in this group. They are all stakeholders for the quality of software because they commission, buy, use and, are affected by the software.

This group will hold a transcendent view of quality; as we saw in Chapter 1, this includes one's emotional reaction to a product or service. Their primary quality viewpoint is the user view of quality, so they will want the software to be fit for their purposes. The purchasers will also hold the value-based view of quality, wherein quality is concerned with a product or service being affordable and good value for money. This group is discussed in more detail in Chapter 3.

2.2.2 People who manage software projects

Managers include all the people who control the planning and management of the software project (see IT Managers in Table 2.1). For a particular project there may be a hierarchy of control starting from a project/program board. Reporting to the project board might be a program manager, one or more project managers, and, working under them, project leaders and team leaders. These people are stakeholders for quality because they are responsible for the time and budget control of the project, and for meeting planned delivery requirements. These are important aspects of quality: the customer needs a product they can afford.

2.2 Defining the team

This group will hold a transcendent view of quality. They will share with the purchasers the value-based view of quality. They may also support a manufacturing view of quality—an interest in process and identifying defects—especially if they come from an IT development background.

This group is discussed in more detail in Chapter 4.

2.2.3 People who build software

Builders are the people who specify, design, and build the software and other products. This includes the development team (see Developers in Table 2.1). The people in this group include business and system analysts, software architects, designers, software engineers, programmers, developers, technical writers, and trainers. They are stakeholders for quality because they build quality into the product, which includes not just the deliverables (for example, code, user guides, and training material) but also the interim products (for example, requirement definitions, designs, and specifications).

This group will hold a transcendent view of quality. Their primary quality viewpoints are the manufacturing and product-based view of quality. The product-based viewpoint measures quality against the attributes of the product or service; its performance and reliability characteristics, for example. This group is discussed in more detail in Chapter 5.

2.2.4 People who measure software quality

Measurers include people who check the conformance to and suitability of processes, as well as those who check the quality of the products, including software (see Quality Practitioners and Testers in Table 2.1). This group might include the quality assurance (QA) teams (e.g., audit and compliance) and quality control (QC) teams (e.g., test and inspection). By QA I mean processes and activities that check the suitability of and adherence to processes. QC, in contrast, includes processes and activities that check products for completeness, correctness, suitability, and adherence to specification. The QA activities might include process review and quality or process audit. The QC activities include software testing, software inspection, and product review. The membership of this group may be drawn from the other groups or they may be specialists. Beware of believing that this group improves the quality of products; in fact, what they do in this group is measure quality and provide information to the other groups. The measurers support decision making and quality improvement. You may be surprised by this idea, but consider this: the builders build quality into the products, the measurers measure the quality of the product. I will enlarge on this discussion in Chapter 6. This group will hold a transcendent view of quality. They will also favor the manufacturing and product-based views of quality. Some people in this group work mainly in user acceptance testing and will support the user view of quality. The group is discussed in more detail in Chapter 6.

2.2.5 People who provide the support and infrastructure for the project and the deployment of software

Supporters have an important part to play in achieving software quality. They are involved in two areas. First, this group maintains the software when it is delivered and accepted by the customers. They provide support and infrastructure and are therefore stakeholders for quality in that they will have requirements for the software. These relate particularly to its quality attributes: security, performance, portability, and maintainability will all be factors for this group. Second, this group will provide the support and infrastructure for the other groups. They will supply the environments for the building and testing of the software and will support the tool sets used by all the groups in their work. The group includes the IT infrastructure team, comprising IT operations, support, and maintenance; IT security; the help desk; service management; networking; and database administration (see IT Infrastructure Staff and Software Maintainers in Table 2.1).

This group will hold a transcendent view of quality. Their primary focus for quality is the product-based view of quality, and they will also hold a user-based view of quality, especially as related to service levels. The group is discussed in more detail in Chapter 7.

2.3 Interaction between the groups and within each group

2.3.1 Differences in quality viewpoints

Because of the difference in quality viewpoints across the groups, and because different groups bring different expertise, there should be interaction between these five groups before, during, and after a software project. Each person will identify with one of the groups, and, for a particular project, may take roles drawn from one or more of the groups. If we look again at Table 2.1, we see the evidence for mistrust between the groups. I suggest from my own observations two possible reasons for this unfortunate state of affairs.

First, among other differences, the groups hold different viewpoints of quality (see Table 2.2) and so will contribute effort toward achieving their

Table 2.2 Views of Quality across the Groups

| | Group | | | | |
Quality View	Customer	Manager	Builder	Measurer	Supporter
Transcendent view	✓	✓	✓	✓	✓
User view	✓			(✓)	✓
Value view	✓	✓			(✓)
Product view			✓	✓	✓
Manufacturing view		✓	✓	✓	

✓ is a primary quality view.
(✓) is a quality view which may be taken by some people in this group.

2.3 Interaction between the groups and within each group

own view of quality and not value the other groups contributions and opinions.

Second, if all the groups are not explicitly involved in the project from inception to postdelivery, although they are all stakeholders for quality, they do not interact and communicate effectively throughout the project. How does this lead to unproductive conflict? We have already acknowledged that each group wants to do a good job, but as each group pursues its own definition of what a good job entails in isolation, conflict between the groups becomes inevitable. Conflict increases as feedback between groups becomes negative or ceases altogether:

> The main cause of mistrust between groups comes from poor motivational dynamics. People's jobs are not designed to create constructive feedback between groups or members of groups. Individuals usually hear only when things go wrong and rarely get feedback to understand and learn from their successes. The outcomes are groups that may be in conflict, or a group is marginalized in terms of project involvement. Both are highly demotivating and can lead to serious under-performance. (Richard Warden, personal communication, April 24, 2003)

It is possible to address and resolve both these problems. Essentially, it is a matter of communication. To overcome them, we need to provide the means to improve communication between groups, so that each hears and understands the others' point of view. Each group will interact with all the other groups (Figure 2.1), either by direct or indirect communication, or because of views held from previous encounters. Some of these may be positive viewpoints and some may be negative.

Warden and Nicholson [1] particularly noted that groups attribute problems to people outside their own team. These biased attributions of faults are summarized in Table 2.3, based on the MIP Report, and show that "No matter how badly my group behaves or how well the other group behaves, I will see minor faults outside my own group before I see major faults within it. The other side is doing the same thing" [1]. The table summarizes how people react to others; in general we tolerate quite bad behavior from "our

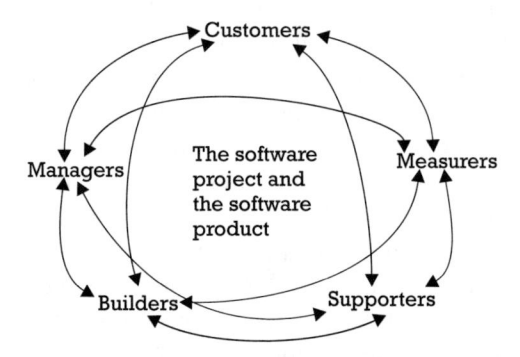

Figure 2.1 Interactions between groups during a software project.

Table 2.3 Attribution of Faults and Problems Inside and Outside "My Group"

If someone in my group behaves well,	I make a positive attribution. I attribute their good behavior to personal goodness.
If someone outside my group behaves well,	I look for a negative attribution. I attribute their good behavior to ulterior motives.
If someone in my group behaves badly,	I struggle to make a positive attribution. I make excuses for their bad behavior.
If someone outside my group behaves badly,	I make a negative attribution. I attribute their bad behavior to personal badness.

gang," but are quicker to take offense at the behavior of other groups. This is human nature and we must struggle to overcome it.

Each of the groups claims that they are motivated to improve performance. However, as each group has its own set of priorities and definition of quality, each often hears the others' views as if they were in direct opposition to their own. For example, Warden and Nicholson [1] found that infrastructure staff measure quality as reliability and service level. They consider the pursuit of the latest technical excellence as an attack on quality, perhaps because use of "leading edge" technology will be more difficult to support. At the same time, developers may see this as a demand for more primitive, hence, less excellent, technology because they measure by product attributes, and perhaps by a transcendent view of excellence. Both sides assume that the others' aspirations are equivalent to their own fears.

Do the quality, process, and excellence models that we looked at in Chapter 1 help us with this problem?

2.3.2 Intergroup relationships in CMM® and Personal and Team Software Processes

In the Personal Software Process [2], the emphasis of the process described is on the individual software engineer (the builder). Individuals are asked to plan and track their tasks and time in order that they can make and meet commitments made to others. This individual self-discipline is an essential ingredient in the success of the software project as a whole. In the Team Software Process [3], the team is made up of software engineers, each of whom is following the PSP, and is therefore using CMM® Level 5 processes; it has been used with "pure software teams and with mixed teams of hardware, software, systems, and test professionals" [4]. The PSP and TSP do not include the customer (see Table 2.4).

The software engineers must interact with their customers in order to understand the requirements, budget, and timescale, but the customer is not seen as part of the team. It is often true as well that the support group (IT infrastructure, operations and so on) are only involved in a minimal way.

This isolation of the software engineers from other groups is very common in software project teams, but is it counterproductive? I would suggest that it is. I have noticed that IT groups and software engineers are not well

Table 2.4 PSP, TSP, and the Groups

PSP	TSP	Matches to:
Software engineer	Software engineer	Builder, Measurer, Manager
Does not include	Does not include	Customer
Does not include	Infrastructure	Supporter

regarded by many of their customers. Why is this? Partly it is the number and effect of defects in delivered software; this is the problem that software engineering processes such as CMM®, the PSP, and the TSP are designed to overcome.

However, there are significant problems in communication between the groups. On occasion, I have asked software customers their view of IT group. Typical responses are "arrogant," "do not listen," and "in a world of their own." If you ask IT people about their customers, typical responses are "ignorant about IT," "do not listen," and "in a world of their own." Do we see a pattern here?

In my experience, the more the customers and supporters are involved in the project, the greater the mutual understanding of the groups, the better the project, and the more well received the software product. What is important is the interaction between people. At the European Software Testing and Review (EuroSTAR) Conference in 2002, one speaker remarked that although we talk about the HCI (human–computer interface), all the interfaces are human to human—the people who designed and built the software and the people who use it [5].

2.3.3 Intergroup relationships and excellence frameworks—the EFQM Excellence Model

The EFQM Excellence Model (see Chapter 1 and [6]) has four criteria that are relevant. These are people (i.e., employees, the team doing the work), customers, partners (i.e., second or third parties, suppliers), and society. These are matched to the groups I suggest in Table 2.5. A similar grouping is found in other models, for example, the Malcolm Baldrige model [7], which is the equivalent model in the United States.

Table 2.5 EFQM Excellence Model and the Groups

EFQM Criteria	Matches to:
People—Enabler	Builders, managers, measurers, and supporters
People—Results	
Partners—Enabler	Supporters (e.g., infrastructure)
	Builders (e.g., third-party software house)
	Measurers (e.g., third-party test services company)
Customers—Results	Customers
Society—Results	Customers—people affected by the software

The EFQM Excellence Model does not tell you how to organize these groups or how to improve communication between them, but it does expect improvement in the perceptions each has of the organization, and of the performance measures of the organization in relation to that group.

It is important for the software team (including all five groups) to consider responsibilities and ownership for tasks and problems. For example, Obeng [8] points out that poorly focused communication between project leaders and project sponsors can lead to a vicious circle of ineffective risk management and increased time spent on getting projects back on track. He suggests actions for the project owners to improve their communication and control. Similar charts of miscommunication and improved communication could be built for other role pairs in the project.

I am not suggesting that everyone has to agree the whole time! For example, the groups' different expertise and viewpoint for quality should be welcomed, as it provides a balance. Some conflict between groups is good!

> In an environment of honest dialogue, the groups constructively challenge each other. In most software situations, the interests of the customers are best served by balancing several definitions of quality. Unchecked, a dominant group will follow their own definition to an extreme. In effective software teams, the supporters ensure that the technologies the builders favor can be maintained. The managers guard the customer's budget by preventing the developers' overengineering and the measurers being inappropriately cautious. In a healthy project, the builders challenge the customers' requirements, pointing out attributes that they haven't considered. (Frank Johnstone, personal communication, April 18, 2003)

What we need are ways to improve our interrelationships and communication. There are a number of techniques and tools that can help with improving communication and fostering understanding between people. Some of these are summarized in Table 2.6, and there is more information in Appendix A.

These methods of improving empathy and communication between people are vital because each of the five groups contributes to and benefits from the software. Each group will require information from the other groups in order to progress and make decisions, but if you are trying to introduce these ideas, you may find resistance. Remember we can only change our own behavior, but how we behave to others will influence how others treat us. In the next five chapters, I will explore each of the groups in turn, suggesting what they can contribute to the project and what they require from other groups during the project. Then, in Chapters 8 to 12, I will look at each stage in the software project life cycle and how each group contributes at each stage. In these chapters, I will refer to techniques for improving and understanding communication, such as those in Table 2.6. I will provide more explanation as particular techniques are demonstrated, either in later chapters or in Appendix A, together with sources for further information.

2.3 Interaction between the groups and within each group

Table 2.6 Summary of Techniques for Improving Communication Between People

Subject Area	Technique Examples	Brief Description (see Appendix A for more)
Motivation measurement and job design	MIP [1]	MIP is based on the Job Characteristics Model of Motivation [9]. The job diagnostic survey provides a comprehensive set of motivational measures. As a process model, it can diagnose problems with motivational dynamics caused by poor job design. Psychometric measurement techniques do not provide this capability.
Team relationships and natural roles/ team skills	Belbin team scores [10]	Teams need to understand their strengths and weaknesses as a team. A balance of roles/skills is required in the personalities in the team. Example roles: plants have new ideas, completer–finishers want to finish to fine detail. Too many plants and you will never finish anything.
Improve communication— Empathy with others	MBTI [11]	Different people have different personalities and communication styles. People who wave their arms around and talk a lot can annoy people who like to be quiet and think, and vice versa. Myers-Briggs Type Indicator (MBTI) identifies four contrasting type pairs (e.g., Introvert/Extrovert) leading to 16 "types" (e.g., INTJ is Introvert-iNtuitive-Thinking-Judging).
	Honey & Mumford Learning Styles [12]	Honey & Mumford Learning Styles Questionnaire identifies preferred learning styles (e.g., Pragmatists and Theorists require different experiences to learn).
	Kirton Adaptors and Innovators [13]	Kirton identifies preferred problem-solving methods (Adaptors versus Innovators)—do we break the rules or work within them?
Motivation	Maslow Hierarchy of Needs [14]	Until someone's basic needs (e.g., food, shelter) are met, this is likely to be all they are interested in. Once they have enough at one level, then other motivators become more important. The cutoff point for moving from one point in the hierarchy to another is different for different people.
Improve meetings	De Bono's Six Thinking Hats [15]	Improve meetings by setting rules for behavior. Six "hats" are used. Everyone wears the same color hat at the same time. Example roles: Black Hat— pessimistic, Yellow Hat—optimistic, Red Hat— feelings, White Hat—facts. Allows meeting members to move outside their stereotypes and allows time for different, sometimes difficult, types of communication.
Helping groups agree on goals, aims, objectives, targets, and indicators	Weaver Triangle [16]	On a one-page diagram, the group identifies and agrees on the aim of the project (why it is being done) and associated indicators of success, then the objectives of the project (what is to be done) and associated targets. This helps identify where stakeholders have different aims for the project.
Identify problems and root causes, find solutions	Ishikawa fishbones [17, 18]	Use to identify problems, root causes of problems, and solutions. On a fishbone diagram, brainstorm problems, their possible causes, their root causes, and, therefore, solutions to the root cause.
Walkthrough reviews	Reviews [19]	A type of review with the purpose of increasing understanding of a document. The author introduces the audience to the document and takes them through it, explaining the content.

References

[1] Warden, R., and I. Nicholson, *The MIP Report—Volume 2—1996 Motivational Survey of IT Staff,* 2nd ed., Bredon, England: Software Futures Ltd., 1996.

[2] Humphrey, W., *Introduction to the Personal Software Process,* Reading, MA: SEI, 1997.

[3] Humphrey, W., *Introduction to the Team Software Process,* Reading, MA: SEI, 2000.

[4] Software Engineering Institute Web site http://www.sei.cmu.edu, accessed April 2003.

[5] Hatton, L., "Quantifying Test Value: Some Examples and a Case Study," *EuroSTAR Conference,* Edinburgh, Scotland, 2002.

[6] European Foundation for Quality Management Web site, http://www.efqm.org, accessed August 2003.

[7] Malcolm Baldrige model, http://www.quality.nist.gov/index.html, accessed August 2003.

[8] Obeng, E., "It's Nobody's Baby," *Project Manager Today,* Vol. XV, No. 3, March 2003.

[9] Hackman, J. R., and G. R. Oldham, *The Job Diagnostic Survey: An Instrument for the Diagnosis of Jobs and the Evaluation of Job Redesign Projects,* Technical Report No. 4, New Haven, CT: Yale University, Department of Administrative Sciences, 1974.

[10] Belbin Associates, "Belbin Team Roles," http://www.belbin.com/belbin-team-roles.htm, accessed October 2003; also for assessment information.

[11] Team Technology, "Articles," http://www.teamtechnology.co.uk/articles.html, November 2003.

[12] Honey, P., "What Are 'Learning Styles'?" http://www.peterhoney.com/product/learningstyles, accessed November 2003. PeterHoney.com, 10 Linden Avenue, Maidenhead, Berks, SL6 6HB. Tel.: 01628633946. Fax: 01628633262. E-mail: info@peterhoney.com.

[13] McHale, J., "Innovators Rule OK—Or Do They?" *Training & Development,* October 1986, http://www.kaicentre.com/.

[14] Gywnne, R., "Maslow's Hierarchy of Needs," http://web.utk.edu/~gwynne/maslow.HTM, November 2003.

[15] de Bono, E., *Six Thinking Hats*®, New York: Penguin, 1999.

[16] Evans, I., "The Troubled Project—Best Practice from Theory to Reality," *EuroSTAR Conference,* Stockholm, Sweden, 2001.

[17] Robson, M., *Problem Solving in Groups,* Hampshire, England: Gower, 1995.

[18] TQMI, *Problem Solving—Tools and Techniques,* Cheshire, England: TQMI, 2001.

[19] IEEE 1028™ Standard for Software Reviews, 1997.

Selected bibliography

Honey, P., and A. Mumford, *The Learning Styles Helper's Guide,* Maidenhead, England: Peter Honey Publications, 2002. PeterHoney.com, 10 Linden Avenue, Maidenhead,

Berks, SL6 6HB. Tel.: 01628633946. Fax: 01628633262. E-mail: info@peterhoney.com.

Kroeger, O., J. M. Thuesen, and H. Rutledge, *Type Talk at Work: How the 16 Personality Types Determine Your Success on the Job*, New York: Bantam Doubleday Dell, 2002.

Maslow, A., *Motivation and Personality*, New York: Harper and Row, 1970.

Mullins, L. J., *Management and Organisational Behaviour*, 5th ed., New York: Financial Times/Pitman Publishing, 1999.

Rothman, J., "Team Building at Work," *STQE*, July/August 2003, p. 64.

CHAPTER 3

Roles and Quality: Customers

Contents

3.1 Introducing the customers

3.2 Who could be in this group?

3.3 Quality viewpoint

3.4 Quality framework using the EFQM Excellence Model

3.5 Communication between the customers and other groups

3.6 Summary of the group

In this chapter I shall:

- Introduce the members of the customers group and their roles and activities;
- Introduce their quality viewpoint;
- Provide a framework for customers' activities within the EFQM Excellence Model;
- Identify information flows between customers and the other groups.

"Why do so many IT people think the world was started with a requirements catalog? Don't they understand there's more to my business than that.... I want them to understand what makes my business tick...." "And why are they so arrogant and rude? Personally I'd take on the guy who has fewer technical skills if I thought he understood my world, and he treated me like a human being."

—*Two customers for IT services compare notes on just why they hate their IT departments*

3.1 Introducing the customers

If it were not for customers, we would not build IT systems. Software is only there to solve people's problems and help them carry out tasks more easily. The context for the tasks might be in home computer use, for example, to play a game or shop on-line. It might be a work context, for example, to reorder stock or produce a report. The use of the computer may be essential to the task, for example, to carry out complex calculations or to control a remote robotic arm in a dangerous environment. It may be intended to make the task easier, for example, intraoffice communication.

The customers for IT systems do not love their IT suppliers or the software. Software is only a tool, and if it is technically excellent but not seen as useful, it will be rejected. In one organization I visited, a staff satisfaction survey showed that almost all the problems associated with staff dissatisfaction were perceived to be caused by poor IT provision. We saw in the quote above that customers have various reasons for dissatisfaction; the IT work itself may be poor, and the IT people may not be liked, either. IT people are seen as self-satisfied and arrogant; customers may feel sneered at if they do not understand the technical jargon. The second customer in the quote above told me that the IT support person they chose eventually for their team was the least well qualified technically, but was the politest and the one who was able to work as part of the team. In order that the customers receive the software they need, they have to communicate with those who supply the software, either directly or by representation; communication is vital to success.

Not only do the customers observe that IT "solutions" fail to solve their problems, they often believe that software in fact *adds* to them, for example, by adding steps or by hiding information. Additionally, if IT people are focused on providing functionality against a requirements list, they may lose sight of *why* the customer wanted the software.

When I visit large IT organizations, it is easy to see who in the IT department is well regarded by the customers; look for the queues by particular desks and you will know that those are people who have troubled themselves not only to understand IT technicalities but also to understand their customers.

In this chapter, I will examine who the customers of IT systems are, what they want, and how the communication gap between IT people and their customers can be bridged.

3.2 Who could be in this group?

For customers, the software is a tool, a means for them to perform tasks efficiently and effectively. This group includes:

- People who will pay for the software, for example, the project sponsor, budget holder, or purchaser.
- People who will use the software delivered (see "users" in Chapter 2, Table 2.1), for example, the customer service agents working at the call center of a financial services organization also request a change to the software they are using to match a new business process.
- *The customers of the end users:* They do not use the software but are affected by it when they interact with the end users; for example, someone who contacts the call center to make a change to an investment may comment on the services provided, and this may lead the customer service agents to request a business process change, which leads to a software change.

- *Society and government as customers:* There may be a legislative change that requires change in business processes, supporting systems, or both.
- *Organizational customers:* Other people in the organization who need particular outcomes; for example, the finance group may want to reduce costs and so request streamlining changes.
- In IT organizations without a direct customer, for example, those companies building and selling packages for commercial or home use, the marketing or product design groups may commission software and are customers in that sense, but they will not use the software.
- The IT organization itself may request changes; for example, the operational support group may wish to improve the maintainability, performance, or reliability of IT systems without changing the functionality and usability for the customer service agents.

These people are all stakeholders for the quality of software because they commission, buy, use, and are affected by the software.[1]

Let us examine some different types of customers and their relationship with software and with other groups.

3.2.1 In-house customer

In this situation, the IT department works for the same company as the people who will use the software and those who will pay for it. The managers, builders, measurers, and supporters may have a captive audience of customers who must use their services, or they may need to bid for projects if the customers choose to put work out to tender. I have seen this happen, with the IT department bidding against external third parties, and with teams within the IT department bidding against each other for projects.

When the customer is in-house, the relationship between the groups can become very close. The managers, builders, measurers, and supporters have the chance to understand the customer and the organization in enormous detail. At best, this has the advantage that the IT people can provide a real depth of service to the customers, who, in turn, can become involved easily throughout the process of commissioning, building, delivering, and using the software. Careful choice of processes and methods, as described in Chapters 9 to 12, can allow the customers' constantly changing business needs to be met because all the groups are in the same organization and should, therefore, have the same overall strategic goal. One IT customer remarked to me:

> If staff turnover in customer departments is much higher than in IT, the builders and supporters may have *more* business knowledge, which enables them to help the customers identify how software can create profitable

---

1. The IT Infrastructure Library (ITIL) [1] differentiates customers who pay for the software, and users who actually use the software. In this book, I have included both those groups together as customers.

opportunities. This can, however, become detrimental to the relationship if it reaches the point where the IT people are dismissive of the customers and feel it is their role to *tell them* what they want.

So we see that it can be disadvantageous if the IT people become complacent about their customers, leading to the types of comments we saw at the start of the chapter. The costs of work can be hidden; the IT work may be seen as "free" because no invoices change hands. Alternatively, if work is charged by a system of internal billing, with customers having a budget to use for IT work and the IT group having charging rates to bill against the budget, then both the customer and the other groups can monitor the cost of the software, including the cost of changes. Communication difficulties can arise because of the personality and cultural differences between the groups. I am struck by how often customers complain that the others, especially IT specialists, whether managers, builders, measurers, or supporters, are uncommunicative, arrogant and rude. Meanwhile, IT specialists complain that customers do not know what they want, and also misunderstand the communication style of their customers. In one organization, I remember the business users remarking on the difficulty of getting what they needed from the network support specialists; the technical team would not respond to questions, and often did not even reply if spoken to directly. One day, I asked a member of the technical team if he thought there were communication difficulties across the teams. "No," he said, "the network has been up 100% this week." So, I changed my question to "Do you talk with the business people very often? Do they come and ask you when they have a technical problem, for example?" He said that they did come and ask if they had problems and that he would deal with the problems, but that the business users tended to chat, fuss, and waste his time. What I observed taking place were dialogues like the one in Table 3.1.

In truth, the people on the technical team didn't see the need to provide feedback at the level their customers required it. How do we deal with this problem? The Myers-Briggs Type Indicator (MBTI) [2] seems to show that different personality types require and give different types and amounts of feedback during communication. This means that we need to try and

Table 3.1 Typical Dialogue Between a Technical Team and Its Customers in One Organization

Tom Customer says:	"Hi—how are you? I'm trying to do my e-mail and I can't get access to the network—it just doesn't seem to be working and . . . "
Ted Technical thinks:	*I'd better look into that.*
Tom Customer thinks:	*Did he hear me?*
Ted Technical	Solves problem but does not tell anyone
Tom Customer, some time later:	"Is the network available yet?"
Ted Technical replies (irritated):	"Yes, of course it is."
Ted Technical thinks:	*Why does this person ask me stupid questions?*
Tom Customer thinks:	*Why is this person so rude and unhelpful?*

understand other people's communication styles. As customers, we need to consider whether we have communicated in a way that puts our message across, and that results in the feedback we require. The dialogue could be managed differently (see Table 3.2). This improved dialogue allows Tom Customer to know what is going on, while acknowledging Ted Technical's desire to minimize "unnecessary" conversation.

3.2.2 Third-party custom-made system customer

Here the customer asks another company to provide a software system, and the supplying company is going to design and build the software to meet the customer's specific requirements. Like a custom-made suit, it will be made to fit the particular customer rather than being bought ready-made. This allows the customer to ask for tenders from a number of suppliers, and to make a choice based on reputation, confidence, ease of relationship, understanding of the customer's organization and needs, expertise in a particular application or software type, standards followed, price, or whatever the key factor is for the customer organization. This allows the customer to pick the most suitable supplier to meet their needs and to pay them on a partnership or contract-by-contract basis.

The third party will be keen to get repeat business and this should focus them on making every effort to meet the customer's changing needs; they will not be complacent about their position as a supplier. However, if the customer and supplier are working to a fixed-price contract, the supplier will resist change if this means that the service or product will be delivered at a loss. We will see in Chapter 9 how much work is required to reach the point where we can agree on a contract for a software development life cycle (SDLC), and the importance of involving all parties in understanding what is required. For a third-party supplier, the risks associated with agreeing to a fixed-price contract when there are uncertainties are enormous, so customers need to be consider what type of contract is best not only for them but also for their suppliers. As one customer manager remarked to me:

> A fixed-price contract that is not competitive to the supplier does not necessarily make good business sense for the customer. Third parties have quit punitive fixed price contracts, forcing the customer to reissue for tender. On occasion, the delay caused has prevented the customer from realizing the benefits predicted from the software.

Table 3.2 Improved Dialogue Between a Technical Team Member and a Customer

Tom Customer says:	"I can't get access to the network. Will you look at it please?"
Ted Technical says:	"Sure, give me five minutes to finish this reboot."
Tom Customer says:	"No problem. Give me a shout when the network is running, please."
Ted Technical says:	"Yup!"
Ted Technical	Solves problem and shouts across, "OK now!"
Tom Customer says:	"Thank you!"

Options for a single project might include a time and materials contract; time and materials to a budget ceiling; a series of short investigative projects to reach a decision about the content of and type of contract; or agreement to use an evolutionary, iterative, or incremental approach (see Chapter 10 for an explanation) in which the budget and scope could be renegotiated on a stage-by-stage basis.

Some customers prefer to build a partnership relationship with their third-party suppliers, rather than working on a project-by-project basis. This can be more satisfying for the customer and for the supplier, as relationships build up over time; the supplier's staff feel like real stakeholders in the customer's success, and they can see the outcome of their work, which increases their satisfaction and motivation. In turn, this means that they are happy to work with the customer, and, therefore, provide a better service to the customer, who in turn reports increased satisfaction with the supplier.

A closely embedded relationship with a third-party supplier can lead to similar advantages and disadvantages as the relationship with in-house IT groups that we discussed in Section 3.2.1, but, additionally, if the customer's circumstances change very significantly it can be difficult to disentangle the two organizations. Communication difficulties can arise because of cultural differences between the organizations, as well as because of personality differences between the groups and individuals. Often, a supplier organization will put its most "customer-friendly" people in the jobs that require customer contact. This improves the customer–supplier interactions, but may have the effect of moving the dialogues in Tables 3.1 and 3.2 from the customer organization to the supplier organization.

With third parties, one great advantage is the "fresh look"; sometimes, an outsider can see our strengths and weaknesses and how to improve more clearly than we can ourselves.

3.2.3 Third-party package or commercial off-the-shelf (COTS) customer

Sometimes, instead of ordering a custom-made solution tailored to our specific problem, we may choose a "ready-made" or "off-the-shelf" product. This is referred to as commercial off-the-shelf (COTS) software. The customer should be able to buy, install, and run this software without any tailoring or changes built especially for them, although there may be options they can set within the package. In this case, the relationship between the customer and supplier may be quite limited or consultancy and support may be offered as part of the purchase. It is likely that the builders and measurers never meet the customer directly. Instead, the customer relationship is managed via the sales, marketing, support-line, or client-management functions within the supplier. For the customer, the contact is minimal, perhaps limited only to the support line when problems arise. However, customers can influence what is built into future versions of the package, for example, by taking part in user groups, lobbying suppliers for change, and reporting problems or improvement suggestions.

Many different types of customers will become involved with COTS software, such as the following:

- *Large organizations:* Such customers are likely to have their own IT departments or commission custom-made software; however, they will probably choose COTS to automate those generic business processes that do not give them a competitive advantage and so do not need to be different from their competitors' processes. We see this in the success of some payroll and accounting packages, which are used across many industries. In such COTS acquisitions, the large organizations normally change their business processes to fit those required by the package, this being seen as a more economical solution than commissioning custom-made software.

- *Small businesses:* Many small businesses do not have IT departments and cannot afford to engage third parties to build custom-made software; they are likely to buy COTS. Companies can get competitive advantage from COTS by using it differently to their competitors. For example, one colleague reported to me that several years ago that one small importer became the first participant in the (then) niche active sports goods market to use a stock control system that was standard in more mature sectors. For a while, this gave the company an edge over its rivals.

- *Home and hobby users:* These customers use software for entertainment, socializing, pursuing a hobby, or doing chores. Sometimes they buy COTS to change the way they do an existing activity, for example, using e-mail to write to friends or using a spreadsheet to manage their personal finances. Most computer games are, of course, creating a *new* need.

- *The niche user:* There are very specialized COTS systems [3], for example, those used in military applications. You may see these referred to as NOTS (niche off-the-shelf) or MOTS (military off-the-shelf).[2]

With COTS suppliers, one of the supplier's problems is that sometimes there is no clear customer group; sales, marketing, client management, and the support line or help desk act as a proxy customer for the other groups. The customers' goals and requirements are found by market research, or by looking at complaints and improvement suggestions. Market researchers interview groups of likely or existing customers to help focus the supplier's understanding of the customer's viewpoints. However, the customers will see these immediate contacts—the sales, marketing, client-management, or help-desk teams—as the face of the supplier, and direct any frustration with the quality of the software at them. As a result, these contacts may become builders by proxy!

---

2. Definition copyrighted and used with permission of whatis.com (http://www.whatis.com) and TechTarget, Inc.

We mentioned earlier that games programs are examples of an entirely new product; before a computer game is invented, people do not know they need it. What happens when a product is entirely new? We may not, as customers, know that we need it; we have not specified requirements, and we have not noticed a need, we do not know we have a problem. I have seen cases in which one of the builders, a developer, or software engineer has invented a piece of software and then asked, "What could we use this for?" or has identified a way to solve a particular problem. Development of the ideas will then be led by sales and marketing based on their knowledge of the end customers' likely buying habits, and by market research.

3.2.4 The IT specialist as customer

Interestingly, people from all the groups become customers at some point, because all the groups use software tools to aid them in their work. For example:

- Managers use planning and reporting tools.
- Builders use compilers and software engineering and support tools.
- Measurers use test and review tools.
- Supporters use operational support tools and networking monitoring tools.

It is always instructive to see members of the IT group in receipt of a software tool, complaining about the lack of help messages, user guide, usability, functionality, and so on, and then to look at the customer reports on their last release. The IT specialists may also request changes to existing software in order to make it easier to support, for example, changes to make it more reliable or have better throughput. User and business customers must be involved in these projects from the start-up discussions, even if they are not the originators of the request for change. This is because any change may have an impact on them; for example, I remember a performance upgrade for a system that theoretically did not change the functionality but, in practice, resulted in a complete retest of functionality because the code had been entirely rewritten. This was decided on by the builders of the system, but the user and support-line groups had not realized the amount of testing that would be required from them, as they had not been involved in the discussions at the start. As a result, the project was late in completing because the system and acceptance tests took longer than expected and resulted in more problems than expected.

3.3 Quality viewpoint

The customer perspective is about supporting the needs of the individual customer, but also those of the organization and its stakeholders. These needs must be met within the individual or organization's constraints, whether of time, money, or expertise.

The user-based definition says that quality is fitness for use. Software quality should be determined by the user(s) of a product in a specific situation, either in a home or a business. Different customer characteristics require different "qualities" of a software product. This can be subjective and cannot be determined on the basis of quantitative metrics alone. It is the user-based definition that encourages us to validate *as well as* verify the system. For example, fit for purpose might mean that I can do my work efficiently and effectively when I use this software.

This group may hold a transcendent view of quality. As we saw in Chapter 1, transcendent quality is based on an emotional response to the product. For the supplier, especially of COTS software, the transcendent qualities will be very important. What is it that makes one software package more appealing than another? Different customers will hold views based on fashion, culture, prejudice, and previous experience. Customers need the answers to these types of questions:

- When will I get it?
- Will it do what I want?
- Can I afford it?
- Can I rely on it?
- Will I enjoy using it?
- Will it make my life easier?
- Will it support our improvement strategy?

3.4 Quality framework using the EFQM Excellence Model

3.4.1 The EFQM Excellence Model and the customer organization

For a business customer, software is used to help in tasks that allow the organization's goals to be met. In the EFQM Excellence Model (see the description in [4], for example) information systems come under the heading of "partnerships and resources," that is, information and information systems are resources that enable the organization to achieve its strategic goals.

Similarly, if we look at an organizational measurement system, such as the Balanced Scorecard, information systems are seen as critically important tools that enable employees to work effectively, so that they can contribute to the goals of the organization. We will look at how managers use the Balanced Scorecard in Chapter 4.

This means that the customer's quality framework should influence the quality framework used by the other groups. For example, in one software company that provides third-party, custom-made software to its customers, the software company's quality manual says that a project's standards should always at least equal the customer's. If the customer has processes or practices that exceed the software company's standards, those will be adopted for a project, but if the customer's processes are less rigorous than those of the software company, then the software company's processes will be used.

The other groups need to be aware of the customer's strategy and quality framework, including any measurements and targets, in order that they can deliver services and products that help the customer meet the organization's quality targets. The emphasis will change, and this will change what constitutes quality for the organization. The organization may be driven by a need to meet a particular external standard, to keep within legislative or regulatory bounds, to increase market share, to reduce time to market, or to be a world leader for excellence of service. The supplier's ability to recognize and adapt to the customer's quality framework is a critical success factor in the effectiveness of their relationship. The framework for the customer translates into departmental goals and, finally, into the personal objectives and targets for an individual system user, but it also translates into a complementary subset of the supplier's goals and, hence, into personal objectives and targets for managers, builders, measurers, and supporters. This quality framework will drive what the customer needs from the software.

In Chapter 1, we looked at the EFQM Excellence Model and how it is divided into nine parts: five enabling criteria and four criteria for measuring results. In Section 3.4.2, we will look at how the EFQM Excellence Model enablers could be interpreted for the customers of an IT project, and in Section 3.4.3, we will look at customer results. Remember that the EFQM Excellence Model is based on the fundamental concepts of excellence we discussed in Chapter 1, and that equivalent models such as the Baldrige model are available.

3.4.2 EFQM Excellence Model enablers for customers

3.4.2.1 Leadership

Leadership for customers is the leadership of their organization. If the vision and goals of the organization have not been communicated to the specific customers who are commissioning software, then they will not commission software that meets the quality goals of the organization. The pressures on organizations will change the goals for the customers. Lately, for example, issues like information security and IT governance are playing an increasingly important role in organizations. Now, leadership in IT governance is expected from the board of directors and the executive management, so it is integral to enterprise governance. Leadership from the top is required to ensure that the organization's information systems sustain and extend the organization's strategies and objectives. Leadership from the top is also required to ensure that information and systems are secure [5].

3.4.2.2 Policy and Strategy

The policies and strategies for the organization reflect the vision of the leaders. Customers of IT software and systems need to consider the policy and strategy for acquiring software that supports their information, improvement and organizational goals. As customers, we implement IT strategies to reflect organizational strategies; for example, different customers might need IT strategies to:

- Support the work in a particular industry sector, for example, different strategies for supplying the avionics industry, education sector, or home computing.
- Support a marketing need, for example, different strategies to support quick time to market with new products, high market demand, increased market share, or emphasis on a small number of high-value customers.
- Support the administration of the rest of the business, for example, accounts and payroll.

Policies are brief statements that are the basic rules for how an organization conducts itself. As customers for IT, we want policies for obtaining IT systems that enable us to fulfill our strategies. For example, different customers might have policies about:

- Acquisition types—"We will only buy COTS."
- Supplier choice—"All suppliers must have achieved at least CMM® [6] Level 3."
- Supplier quality processes—"All acquired software must be designed and built complying to standards within the BSI Software and Systems Quality Framework (SSQF) [7]."
- Relating to the supplier and involvement—"We want the supplier to use evolutionary delivery methods and to be involved at every stage."

3.4.2.3 People

The people we are considering here are the customers themselves, because of their part in the software team. As we will see in Chapters 8 to 12, it is useful if customers are involved throughout the life of software, not just as the users of software, but also during the definition, build, and testing of the software. One of the advantages of the evolutionary delivery method, for example, is that the feedback cycle between the customer and the other groups is very fast. The customer is sent frequent improvements to their software, and is also able to feed back to the supplier improvement ideas needed to cope with changing requirements. According to Tom Gilb (at a seminar on Evolutionary Delivery, London, September 20, 2003), this feedback loop enhances the customer's satisfaction with the software delivery.

Customers can improve their contribution to the software quality and their understanding of the software project by learning how to take part in certain key activities. Some years ago, I worked at a software company where I helped to introduce a number of quality processes. We had put together an in-house document review process, based on experiences with walkthrough and inspection methods that several of us had used in different organizations. This process allowed us to make decisions about the type of review based on the risks associated with the document, for example, the value of the contract, the difficulty of the technical work, and so on. The reviews had the general structure of:

- Up to 2 hours preparation before the review to identify problems and suggestions for improvement;
- Up to 2 hours meeting to document those problems and identify new ones, with no more than six people attending, and optionally the second hour being used as a "solutions" meeting.

Time spent by each participant and the number of problems found were logged, so we could check that people were using their time effectively and efficiently. You will see that as a process, this does not match the rigor or structure of, for example, the Gilb and Graham inspection [8], but it was a vast improvement over the previous situation, which was quite unstructured. It was a good enough process. As part of an improvement program, we then decided to invite some of the customer organizations to take part in document review training courses. The benefit to us as supplier and to them as customers was that when we asked customers to review contracts or requirements, we all knew how to do it, how it was going to be organized, how much it would cost, and the purpose of the meeting. The customers enjoyed taking part and gained considerable satisfaction from contributing constructive criticism and seeing it acted on. The software development life cycle and the deliveries went far more smoothly; one of the directors commented to me that he spent far less time firefighting than ever before.

This principle of training customers to contribute more effectively can be applied to a number of activities:

- Training in document reviews. For basic understanding of a review process, but also for review of particular artifacts. For example, "If you are reviewing a use case, expect to see...."
- Training in user-acceptance testing, including an understanding of why user-acceptance testing is different from other types of testing, and what techniques might be applied. For example, "If you are testing a Web site you will need to consider usability and security as well as functionality."
- Training in process audits and reviews, including understanding why, during acceptance, the customer might want evidence of quality activities and how this might be found. For example, "If you are reviewing a supplier's work, ask to have some tests run and review the output from tests."

3.4.2.4 Partnerships and Resources

The customer's partners and resources for the software include all the groups: those who are supplying the software and those who will support it during use. The customers require a certain level of service from the software systems, and this will form the basis for the service level agreements (SLAs) with the supporters group. The criteria that the customers will use to decide whether to accept the software must reflect these SLAs because, in order that the supporters group can fulfill the SLA, the software must be capable of delivering according to the SLA. Therefore, the customers must work with the supporters to set acceptance criteria. We will see in Chapter 9 how to do this.

As well as partnerships with the supporters, customers will have partnerships with non-IT suppliers and their own customers. The software systems may need to share information, or they may need to be protected. One of the customer's acceptance criteria for system attributes may consider how well the delivered software supports control of interfaces with systems outside the customer's organization.

3.4.2.5 Processes

The customer's business processes must be supported by the software and systems. If the systems do not support and improve the organization, there is no point having them. The business processes may be industry-specific or general administration processes. They may also need to meet requirements in particular quality standards, for example, ISO 9000 [9]. The business processes should be designed to enable the customer to meet the organization's strategy and goals efficiently and effectively. Any software systems are there to make the work more effective and more efficient. The other groups need to understand the customer's processes and standards in order to support them.

3.4.3 EFQM Excellence Model results for the customers

3.4.3.1 Customer Results

The customers of the IT systems and software have their own customers. How does the software affect these customers? The customers need to find out how the services they offer to their customers could be improved, and this may include improvements to the IT systems and software. Results of satisfaction surveys, complaints, letters of praise, and comments all indicate where processes and, hence, systems could be improved.

3.4.3.2 People Results

Are the people in the customer group who work with the IT groups happy to do so? Do the others in the customer group see them as representative? It is important that the customer organization understands whether the IT suppliers are good to work with. Look again at the quotation at the start of this chapter. These customers are not unhappy with the technical excellence of the work done by their IT teams, nor are they questioning the number of coding defects. The two problems identified are lack of understanding of the business in its essence and poor interpersonal skills. In one organization that I visited, the staff satisfaction survey revealed that over 90% of the staff's complaints had to do with poor IT provision. This type of information allows the customers to show the other groups what changes are needed. Many authors, for example, Gilb [10] and Watkins [11], have observed that it is the nonfunctional rather than the functional attributes that cause complaints or cause people to reject a product. This fits in with my practical experiences. Functionality is taken for granted, and is usually delivered, but the real problems come in understanding what level of attributes such as reliability, security, and performance are required or deliverable. For this reason, in Chapter 9 we will focus on nonfunctional acceptance criteria.

3.4.3.3 Society Results

We have already noted in Section 3.4.2.1 that as part of the governance of the organization, the governance of IT systems and their security is increasingly important, for governments and for society as a whole. Customers need to consider what effect their organization has on society, and the view that society has of the organization. Consider how IT systems affect the impact of an organization on society, both the perception that society has of the organization and measures of how the IT systems help the organization to perform.

There will be legislative and regulatory controls set by government that must be obeyed. These include disability discrimination and data protection legislation. When looking at IT systems and projects, customers should consider how these support the organization in making products and services accessible, while protecting privacy. For example, is it reasonable to use a copy of live databases to test a new version of the software? Leaving aside all the technical reasons why this might be a bad idea, from a data protection and security viewpoint is it right to allow detailed access to the data to people who would not normally see it?

It is also useful to consider the effect on society when reviewing risks. In a financial services project, I looked at assessing the impact of problems with a group. We scored impact from 1 to 5, with 5 as highest impact. We set a "typical story" for each score to help us score the risks we were assessing, rather as in Table 3.3.

3.4.3.4 Key Performance Results

Key performance results measure financial results such as profit, return on investment, and turnover, but also measure nonfinancial results such as market share. The customer will want to know the efficiency and effectiveness of the IT systems in their contribution to the overall key performance

Table 3.3 Assessing Impact of Risks—Effect on Society Scores High

Impact Score	Description	Story
5	External publicity—external customers affected	Chief operating officer appears on a consumer affairs program to explain why the systems have gone wrong.
4	External awareness—external customers affected	Letters and calls of complaint, dealt with individually.
3	Internal publicity—internal customers affected	There are system failures; the call-center staff can work around these, but they are disruptive.
2	Internal awareness—internal customers affected	There are some minor system failures which the call-center staff can work round easily
1	No publicity—no customers affected	IT department affected by failures but can prevent the call-center staff from being affected.

measures. The bottom line question is "Was it worth investing in the software—did we get a return on investment?" We will look in Chapter 4 at how the manager can use measures in the project that tie into the customer's key performance measures; the customer needs to ensure that the manager knows what these are.

3.5 Communication between the customers and other groups

We will see in Chapters 8 to 12 that customers are involved in the whole life span of a piece of software, from its conception, through the software development life cycle (SDLC), during delivery, and postdelivery until decommissioning. We will see that some of the SDLC models encourage customer involvement and other models do not. The advantage of having little involvement to us as customers is that we order the software, and while it is being built and delivered we get on with other things. Superficially, it looks as though we are being efficient with our time. The disadvantage is that during the period of the SDLC, things will change; our problems as customers will change and the solutions we require will change. This means that by the time we get the software, it is out of date. The disadvantage of SDLCs with high customer involvement is that it is time-consuming for the customer, who also has "business as usual" to deal with as well as the SDLC. The advantage is that it is far more likely that a useful software solution will be delivered.

So we will see in the later chapters that communication between the customers and the other groups is needed throughout the whole life span and that each of the groups must communicate with all the other groups. The customer needs to exchange information with all the other groups (Figure 3.1).

In order to decide whether it is worth acquiring new software, for example, the customer needs to listen to the manager's view on cost effectiveness, the builder's knowledge of technical constraints, the measurer's

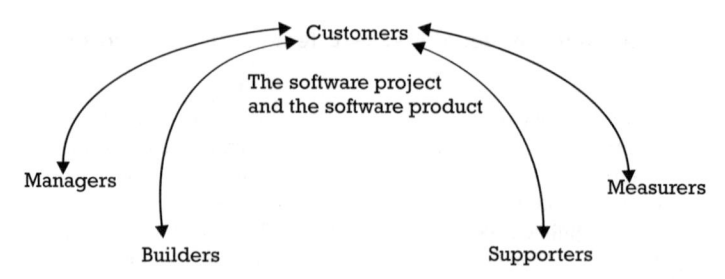

Figure 3.1 Communication between the groups.

experiences of likelihood of problems, and the supporter's view of impact on the existing systems. A risk assessment would be done at this point, and, in particular, customers need to assess the impact on the organization or business if the change is not made, if it goes wrong, or if it is late or over budget. In parallel with the risk assessment, therefore, the customers start to set constraints for cost and time. While doing this, they should be listening to the builders, supporters, and measurers' views about the technical risks and the technical constraints on what is being proposed. An SDLC may be appropriate, but it may not be the best solution. Whatever is decided on, a contract for the work needs to be agreed on. We will see in Chapter 9 how to reach agreement on aims, objectives, targets, and indicators, as well as measurable acceptance criteria. There may be constraints on the accuracy and precision of estimates, and customers should discuss this with the other groups, and expect that estimates may have a broad range. At this stage, particularly in the planning for an SDLC, there will be many things that are unknown, so we would expect to see accurate ranges in the estimates, rather than precision:

- "I can complete this in the next 5 to 50 days" is likely to be an accurate estimate, but it is not a precise one.
- "I can complete this on October 23 at 2:57 p.m." is a very precise estimate, but it may not be accurate.

It is also possible that the estimate makes us realize that it is not possible to build and test what the customer wants within time and budget constraints; something simpler must be agreed on. The customer must encourage honest estimation. Too often, I have seen the IT team attempting to produce an estimate that is acceptable rather than one that is realistic. If experience of the customer's reactions in the past has taught them that they will get praised for a low estimate and criticized for a high one, it is human nature to produce an "acceptable" estimate now, and try to avoid the consequences later. Customers should particularly watch for the situation in which the people making the estimate are not going to be involved in the work; their job is to get the contract, and they may not be focused on the effect of their estimate on the project team. Also beware of fixing the overall estimate too early; once changes are made to the requirements, whether these arise from change in the real world, correction of budget, or correction of mistakes, this may mean changes to the estimates. Customers will need to negotiate to deal with changes to requirements, whether these have been "set" and therefore require a contract renegotiation, or have been planned for. We know there will be change; we just cannot always anticipate what that change will be. Table 3.4 lists the information that customers have that the other groups need.

Customers need information from other groups in order to understand the constraints on delivering their wish list. Table 3.5 lists the information that customers need from the other groups.

3.6 Summary of the group

Without customers, there would be no software; their involvement and views are critical to the other groups' success. Customers have a vital contribution to make throughout the life of a software system. Their quality viewpoint, of the system being fit for its purpose, and their world, with its changing risks and demands, must influence how the other groups work. managers, builders, measurers, and supporters only exist to enable the customers to achieve the organization's goals.

Table 3.4   Information That Customers Have That Others Need

Before the SDLC starts and updated throughout the SDLC	Which problems/ideas are important to the customer/organization and why
	Changes in priority, new ideas, and problems
	Whether any of the proposed solutions/prototypes are suitable
	Reasons why they are/are not suitable
	What the customer's own customers need from them
	Business constraints (time, cost, process, legal) and why these are constraints risks (impacts) to the organization if we fail or do not deliver the solution
	Whether there are existing workarounds for this problem
	Why this is important; the difference it will make
	How we will measure success postdelivery
	How we will accept the software (acceptance criteria)
	What "fit for purpose" means in this case
During the SDLC	An initial set of detailed requirements
	User-acceptance testing—knowledge, business, budget, and time constraints
	Changes, corrections, and refinements to requirements and acceptance criteria
	Improvement suggestions for software, training, and documentation
	Design of any new business processes
	Delivery plan constraints and postdelivery SLA constraints
	Revisions to the plans
	Agreement on readiness to deliver
	Authorization that the acceptance test has passed or failed
At delivery	Confirmation that delivery is complete and accepted
	Ready to start "real work" signal
Postdelivery	Evaluation of the software in use; is it fit for its purpose?
	Evaluation of the processes used; how could they be improved?

Table 3.5 Information That Customers Need from Others

Managers	Possible solutions to problems/ideas
	Cost and resource constraints and why these are constraints
	Value quality viewpoint
	Whether proposed aims/indicators are understood
	Proposed objectives/targets for the solution
	Whether proposed acceptance criteria are SMART (specific, measurable, achievable, realistic, and time-bound)
	Nontechnical risks (likelihood of this going wrong) and nontechnical constraints such as resources, time, budget, and availability of people
	Precision and accuracy of estimates, when refined estimates will be possible
Builders	Possible solutions to problems/ideas
	Technical constraints and why these are constraints
	Why this problem/idea (for example, for a technical problem) is important and its impact on the customers
	Manufacturing/product quality viewpoint
	Whether proposed aims/indicators are understood
	Proposed objectives/targets for the solution
	Whether proposed acceptance criteria are SMART (specific, measurable, achievable, realistic, and time-bound)
	Technical risks (likelihood of this going wrong) and technical constraints
	Precision and accuracy of estimates, when refined estimates will be possible
Supporters	Possible solutions to problems/ideas
	Technical constraints and why these are constraints
	Why this problem/idea (for example, for a technical problem) is important and the impact on the customers
	Manufacturing/product quality viewpoint
	Shared user quality viewpoint
	Whether proposed aims/indicators are understood
	Proposed objectives/targets for the solution
	Whether proposed acceptance criteria are SMART (specific, measurable, achievable, realistic, and time-bound)
	Technical risks (likelihood of this going wrong) and technical constraints
	Precision and accuracy of estimates, when refined estimates will be possible
	Constraints on SLAs postdelivery
	Scope of supporters' operational acceptance testing
Measurers	Possible solutions to problems/ideas
	Technical constraints and why these are constraints
	Why this problem/idea (for example, for a technical problem) is important and the impact on the customers
	Manufacturing/product quality viewpoint
	Whether proposed aims/indicators are understood
	Proposed objectives/targets for the solution
	Whether proposed acceptance criteria are SMART (specific, measurable, achievable, realistic, and time-bound)
	Technical risks (likelihood of this going wrong) and technical constraints
	Precision and accuracy of estimates, when refined estimates will be possible
	Advice on acceptance testing
	Advice on review processes
	Assurance that QA and QC activities have taken place
	Results of those activities

References

[1] IT Infrastructure Library, *Best Practice for Service Support,* Norwich, England: Office of Government Commerce, 2002, p. 7.

[2] Team Technology, "Working Out Your Myers Briggs Type," http://www.teamtechnology.co.uk/tt/t-articl/mb-simpl.htm, October 2003.

[3] searchCRM.com (via http://www.whatis.com), "COTS, MOTS, GOTS, and NOTS," http://searchcrm.techtarget.com/sDefinition/0,,sid11_gci789218,00.html, September 2003.

[4] British Quality Foundation, *The Model in Practice 2,* 2nd ed., London, England: British Quality Foundation, 2002, p. 86.

[5] Smith, M., "Govern IT," *British Quality Foundation IT & T Group Meeting*, London, England, January 29, 2003.

[6] Software Engineering Institute, "Capability Maturity Model®," http://www.sei.cmu.edu, July 2003.

[7] British Standards Institute, PD0026:2003, *Software and Systems Quality Framework—A Guide to the Use of ISO/IEC and Other Standards for Understanding Quality in Software and Systems,* London, England: British Standards Institute, May 2003.

[8] Gilb, T., and D. Graham, *Software Inspection,* Reading, MA: Addison-Wesley, 1993.

[9] International Standards Organization, ISO 9000:1994 and ISO 9000:2000 Quality Systems 9000.

[10] Gilb, T., "Competitive Engineering," http://www.result-planning.com/, September 2003 (Web site now replaced by http://www.gilb.com).

[11] Watkins, J., "How to Set Up and Operate a Usability Laboratory," *EuroSTAR Conference,* Edinburgh, Scotland, 2002.

Selected bibliography

Buttrick, B., "Effective Project Sponsorship—Turning the Vision into the Reality of Success," *Project Manager Today,* September–October 2003, pp. 12–13.

Information Systems Audit and Control Association, http://www.isaca.org.

IT Governance Institute, http://www.itgi.org/ITGI.

Kaplan, R. S., and D. P. Norton, *The Balanced Scorecard,* Boston, MA: Harvard Business School Press, 1996.

The National Strategy to Secure Cyberspace, http://www.whitehouse.gov/pcipb/.

Obeng, E., "Helping Stakeholders to Understand Requirements," *Project Manager Today,* July 2003, pp. 14–17.

CHAPTER 4

Roles and Quality: Managers

Contents

4.1 Introducing the managers

4.2 Who could be in this group?

4.3 Quality viewpoint

4.4 Quality framework using the EFQM Excellence Model

4.5 Communication between the managers and other groups

4.6 Summary of the group

In this chapter I shall:

- Introduce the members of the managers' group, their roles, and activities;
- Introduce their quality viewpoint;
- Provide a framework for the managers' activities within the EFQM Excellence Model;
- Identify information flows between the managers and the other groups.

The tester challenges the project manager: "If we go live at the planned date, I predict there will be problems! I want to test the software more!" The project manager replies to the tester: "No! We go live when we planned to!"

4.1 Introducing the managers

In Chapter 3, we learned that customers want to acquire software to help them carry out their tasks. They may have a limited budget, among other constraints. They will want the software delivered as soon as possible so that they can start using it. They will need to be supported during the acquisition and use of the software.

The people who will provide the software and the support for its use are technical experts: builders, measurers, and supporters. They will focus on the details of the technical solution.

In contrast, the manager's focus is on nontechnical aspects of the work, such as budget control, planning, and reporting. Too often, the other groups see managers as the villains of the software development life cycle (SDLC). For example, our tester above will be angry that the project manager will not delay the project to allow more testing. She may say, "Surely, the manager can see there will be problems. And, anyway, what has the project manager contributed apart from calling meetings that no one wants to go to?" But the tester may be wrong if the overall organizational imperatives are to deliver early. In this chapter, I will examine what managers do, and their value-based view of quality and why it is useful.

Managers, if they are doing their jobs well, exist to enable other people to do what is required for the organization and the customer. They are needed because IT projects and IT support are often complex, not just technically but organizationally, involving large numbers of people, a restricted budget, and a tight timescale. The technical groups (builders, measurers, and supporters) are very focused on their own activities and, naturally, value them over other people's work. They lose sight of the big picture, as well as the budget and time constraints. There will be conflicts between groups and individuals, and competition for scarce resources. Risks will be perceived differently by different groups, and, as we are finding in Chapters 2 to 7, each group holds a radically different view of quality.

So what do managers contribute? They keep everyone aligned to the goals for the customer while keeping within the time and budget constraints. They will negotiate between parties to arrange sharing of scarce resources, make decisions about how to proceed in the face of risks, listen to complaints from all directions, and soothe, calm, coach, and motivate the team. Yes, managers make a contribution. A good manager will hold the team together, through thick and thin, to achieve the goal.

4.2 Who could be in this group?

Managers include all the people who control the planning and management of software delivery and support. This will include specialist project managers and team leaders, as well people who manage departments or teams that provide ongoing services and support (see IT Managers in Chapter 2, Table 2.1). For a particular project, there may be a hierarchy of control, starting from a project/program board. Reporting to the project board might be a program manager, one or more project managers and, working under them, project leaders and team leaders. There may also be a project office providing project management support. These people are stakeholders for quality because they are responsible for the time and budget control of the project, and for meeting planned delivery requirements. These are important aspects of quality: the customer needs a product they can afford.

Of course, we all need to manage our own work. We need to plan what we do, and manage it so, in that respect, we are all managers—it is the size of what we manage that changes. For many of us, making the move from managing our own time to managing our team's time is a very difficult transition and we will look at that in this chapter.

4.3 Quality viewpoint

Managers tend to focus on two key measures: time and money. These two constraints on any work are very important. If the customer spends beyond their budget or if the software arrives too late to be of use, however technically excellent it is, we have not delivered a quality solution to the customer's problem. Therefore, this group favors the value-based definition of quality.

As we saw in Chapter 1, the value-based definition is focused on things that impact on the running of the business as a whole. Software quality is determined by a trade-off between time, effort, and cost aspects. Managers will measure the cost–benefit ratio and return on investment (ROI). They will also plan and manage within a budget for time, effort, and cost. Because of their need to contain the work within a set budget, they may also support one aspect of the manufacturing-based views of quality, that is, delivery to an agreed specification. They will see any change to the agreed specification as "scope slip" and will want to avoid that. This is very important, particularly for teams delivering products or services within a fixed-price contract or to an immovable deadline. If a change in scope means additional work, the supplying organization may take a loss. In the long term, this could mean the collapse of the organization. Managers will support processes and activities that provide an immediate and a long-term ROI: a win now for the team and the customer, and long-term customer satisfaction leading to repeat business.

Although this group may hold a view of quality which focuses on value for money, they also hold transcendent quality views. We saw in Chapter 1 that we all "know quality when we see it"; our knowledge is based on our experiences, taste, affections, loyalties, and emotions. For managers, this may mean they have a strongly held view about excellence based on their previous experience; this will vary depending on whether their premanagement experience was as a customer, a builder, a measurer, or a supporter. The "taken for granted" assumptions of managers may align particularly with that one group. Managers find themselves wrestling with the quality views of all the groups in conflict during negotiations. Unfortunately, as different people will have different assumptions, a manager, when negotiating, needs to be particularly careful not to assume that one group is correct and the others are wrong.

A common cliché about managers is that they will deliver anything provided they meet the budget and timescale, and they are not interested in quality, just in meeting the plan. When we examine behavior patterns, we can see that the managers' drive to meet the plan is essential. In a particular training course that I present, groups carry out a series of six risk assessment tasks within a set time. What I have noticed is that when a group of project managers carry out these tasks, they divide their time evenly between the six tasks. However, a group of testers or developers given the same tasks and timescale may only complete the first one or two tasks, although they will have discussed and documented the risks in much more detail. The testers and developers did not see "missing the deadline" as a risk in itself, and, in fact, asked for more time; they "overengineered" their tasks. The project managers factored in "not meeting tight deadline" as one of the risks they needed to manage and produced a much sketchier, but adequate, solution to the tasks. This is an object lesson in why we need managers. As we will see in Chapters 5 and 6, when left to themselves, builders and measurers may pursue excellence at the expense of all other considerations. When managers negotiate with the other groups, they need to express what they require in a way that focuses on the other groups' quality views. We can see in Table 4.1 how a project manager could use the other groups' quality viewpoints to start putting across ideas about cost–benefit ratio and value.

Managers of IT projects are often recruited from the builders' group, but may also come from the customers, measurers, or supporters' groups. The group managers come from will tend to bias their quality viewpoint, but one of the jobs of the manager is to negotiate a balance between the viewpoints that is suitable for a particular situation.

4.4 Quality framework using the EFQM Excellence Model

4.4.1 The EFQM Excellence Model and the manager

There are qualifications, standards and methodologies for project management and for management processes in general, but I am not going to describe those here. I am not going to recommend a particular project management methodology. What I want to do is pick out a few important aspects of quality that are affected by management choices, and discuss these in the context of the EFQM Excellence Model we looked at in Chapter 1. We will

Table 4.1 A Project Manager Considering Other Viewpoints for Quality Impacts

Group and Quality View	Possible Routes In	Example Questions
Customer User quality view	Customer's performance measures and indicators of success	What are the financial and nonfinancial goals for you on this project? What strategic benefits do you need to realize from this project?
Supporter User and product quality view	Supporters' service-level measures	What SLAs do you have with the business? What support budget do you have for supporting the products from this project?
Builder Product and manufacturing quality view	Builder's knowledge of technical solutions	The customer needs to increase time to market for new products without compromising the excellence of service offered; what technical trade-offs do we need to make to support this? Do you know a technique or tool that would help with this?
Measurer Product and manufacturing quality view	Measurer's knowledge of quality processes	The customer needs to decrease time to market for new products without compromising the excellence of service offered; what quality processes do we need to apply to check the proposed solution? Given the limited budget, what are your recommendations for focusing testing and inspection processes?

see that we each need to tailor our methods in response to aspects of quality, culture, standards, risks, and expectations that affect our circumstances.

Whichever framework managers choose to follow, it should include some quality-management activities. The quality-management system for an organization provides a framework of policies, standards, processes, and procedures. Depending on the organization, these may be prescriptive and mandatory, perhaps because of external requirements, or they might be a framework of possible standards from which a manager chooses a suitable process for a particular project. This latter approach allows a manager to tailor the approach for a project to meet particular risks and customer expectations. I have seen it used successfully in a number of organizations. We will see an example in Chapter 6, where I will look at auditing. This selection of an appropriate process and controls is a quality-planning activity and should take place as part of project planning. The plan should include not just the schedule for the project, but also an assessment of risks and constraints, a statement of the aims and objectives for the project, and a series of planning documents describing the quality activities for the project (Figure 4.1).

This planning process will start during start-up (Chapter 9) and be refined at the start of the SDLC. However, it will continue during the SDLC and delivery (Chapters 10 and 11). Circumstances, risks, and what is important to the customer will change continuously and the management framework must reflect the need for managing constant change. Of course, managers working to fixed-price contracts will have a difficult time with this; they will either need to confine change to what can be achieved within the fixed price, agree with the customer that the fixed price is for a small, stable delivery, or renegotiate the contract. Some SDLC models, as we will see in Chapter 10, provide for managing change better than others do.

Quality planning sets the processes for this specific project for quality assurance and quality-control assessment and measurement activities, as well as setting the methods to be used for building the products. Quality assurance (QA) activities check that the processes are suitable and are being followed. Quality control (QC) checks the products for defects

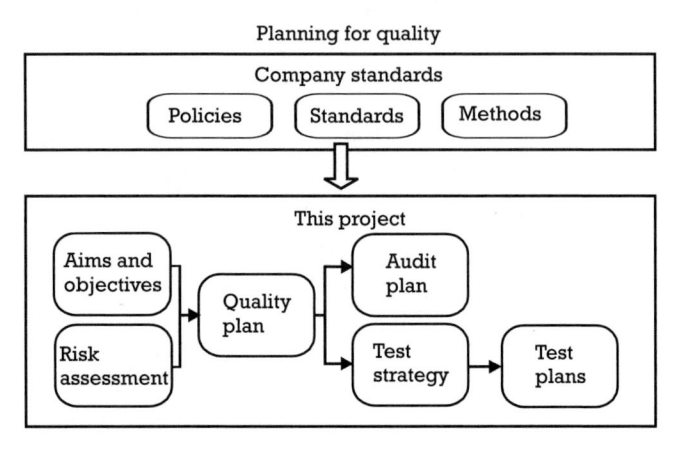

Figure 4.1 Planning for quality.

and improvements. These activities may provide feedback suggestions for improving processes and products. Figure 4.2 is an adaptation for planning that I have made of Deming's Plan–Do–Review–Improve cycle [1]. We will examine that again in Chapter 12.

If this evaluation is left until after delivery, it will be too late to learn and improve the product we are delivering, so it makes sense to build evaluation into the process steps. One of the key points about an evolutionary delivery, for example, is that it is accomplished in many small increments with a feedback loop in each increment, allowing continuous improvement and learning (see Chapter 10) [2].

In the EFQM Excellence Model [3], information systems come under the heading "partnerships and resources"—information and information systems are resources that enable the organization to achieve its strategic goals. If we look at an organizational measurement system, such as the Balanced Scorecard, information systems are seen as a critically important tool to enable employees to work effectively, so that they may contribute to the goals for the organization. We will look at how managers use the Balanced Scorecard later in this chapter.

Managers need to be aware of the customer's strategy and quality framework, including any measurements and targets, in order to deliver services and products that help the customers meet their organizations' quality targets. The emphasis will change, and this will change what constitutes quality for the organization. The organization may be driven by a need to meet a particular external standard, to keep within legislative or regulatory bounds, to increase market share, to reduce time to market, or to be a world leader for excellence of service. The manager's ability to recognize and adapt to the customer's quality framework is a critical success factor in the effectiveness of their relationship. The manager should refer to the customer's goals when setting team and project goals, translating these into personal objectives and targets for themselves, and the builders, measurers, and supporters. This quality framework will drive what the customer needs from the software.

In Chapter 1, we looked at the EFQM Excellence Model and how it is divided into nine parts; five enabling criteria and four criteria for measuring results. In Section 4.4.2 we will look at how the EFQM Excellence Model

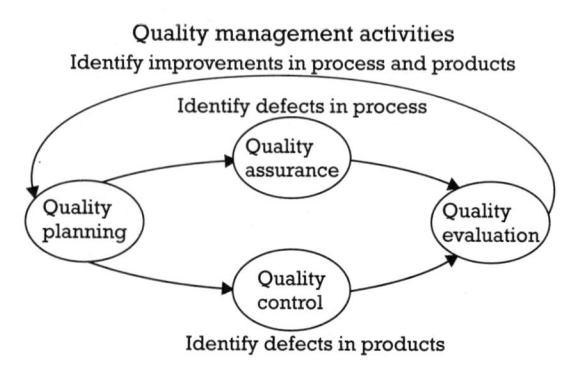

Figure 4.2 A quality-management planning cycle.

enablers could be interpreted for managers, and in Section 4.4.3 we will look at manager results. Remember that this model is based on the Fundamental Concepts of Excellence we discussed in Chapter 1, and that equivalent models such as the Baldrige model are available.

4.4.2 EFQM Excellence Model enablers for the managers

4.4.2.1 Leadership

Managers provide leadership for their teams. In order to provide leadership, they need leadership from their own managers and the board. The manager will follow the lead given by the organization in matters of quality viewpoint and, hence, on whether value, fitness for purpose, manufacturing defects, or product attributes will be the leading quality viewpoint. Managers may also be torn between conflicting leads from the customer organization and more senior management in their own organization.

The manager is often the main conduit between the customer and the rest of the team, relaying the customer's aims and objectives. Through leadership, the effective manager communicates these to the team in a way that creates a common vision and unity of purpose. The CMMI® framework that we discussed in Chapter 1 includes a specific management practice to "Establish a Shared Vision" [4] for the team. A colleague commented to me:

> This vital "big picture" increases commitment and enables all members of the team to think beyond their own specialism and use alignment to the customer's objectives to validate their activities. Asking a selection of team members to describe the objectives of one project resulted in a variety of incorrect answers. The reason was that the managers believed in communicating the minimum information that they thought the practitioners needed to carry out their tasks. Unsurprisingly, commitment in the team was low but it was also evident that a lot of activity in the team did not align with the project's objectives, and would have been challenged if the team were aware of the project's purpose.

The ability of a manager to inspire and motivate the team through leadership cannot be underestimated. The behavior of someone the team accepts as a leader is characterized by honesty, trustworthiness, the ability to keep a confidence, respect for others, and enthusiasm for achieving the aims and objectives. If the leader does not believe in the cause, no one else will. I remember visiting one project with some colleagues to provide consultancy. The project had been running for over a year and the team was tackling some extremely difficult but interesting problems. When we said, "It's difficult but we can do it—and it'll be fun!" a team member said to me that none of the management team leading the project to that point had indicated that achieving the project's aims was anything but difficult and unpleasant. If the managers were not positive, how could the team be? When the new management took a more robust attitude to the team's ability to solve problems, the project started to succeed. Of course, if managers lie about the difficulty, they will quickly lose their team's motivation, but part of a leader's role is to understand what is necessary and what is possible.

4.4.2.2 Policy and Strategy

Managers set policy and strategy for their own areas based on their organization's policy and strategy. This will include policy and strategy for QA and QC, but we also need to define how the build and support activities are done. In Chapters 5, 6, and 7, we will see some aspects of policy and strategy for builders, measurers, and supporters; what managers need to consider is how the customer policy and strategy are reflected in the strategy for the project and, hence, for the all the work done.

Policies are brief statements that are the rules for how an organization conducts itself. Managers also need policies for management activities; these may be documented or unwritten ("We always do it this way."). The decision about whether or not to document policy depends on the size of the organization. (In this case, for example, does a particular project require its own policy document, or does everyone in the project "know the rules"? Is the policy statement at the organization level sufficient?) Policy statements for management might include topics such as:

- Authorization, for example, "documents may not be released to customers without an authorization sign off by a team leader."
- Escalation, for example, "the project manager will always be informed of risks, issues and defects identified with an impact level of 4 or above."
- Reporting, for example, "test team leaders will report progress against plans to the test manager daily at 8:30 a.m."

Strategies for managing show how the policies will be applied and what approach will be taken in a particular case. One mistake I have seen inexperienced managers make is to believe that the project plan is just a schedule. In fact, the schedule is just part of what is needed to plan and control a project. Appendix B shows some of the documents we might need, including a quality plan, a configuration management plan, and a risk management plan.

On a small piece of work, these might be used as a checklist of things to think about, or a single document might be written that combines them all. In that case, keep it small—the size of the plan is not an indicator of its quality. One very good aspect of tailoring is to allow the manager to combine and abbreviate documents where this is appropriate.

On a major project, we might need a whole set of documents, each of which describes some aspect of the overall strategy for the work. Each document may have a different author, and part of the manager's job, with the team, is to make sure that the documents do make up a document family, do complement rather than contradict each other, there are no gaps, and the overlaps are minimized. Part of the reason for defining a document family is to allow child documents to just document differences and additional information. A common error in large projects is to become overwhelmed with paperwork and electronic documents. Keep repetition across documents to a minimum, as it saves reading and update time.

If you are following a published project management method, you will find that there will be a set of documents defined for your use. It is worth looking at the rules in the method to see whether it is allowable to tailor, combine, and minimize documents.

4.4.2.3 People

Managers spend much of their time dealing with people. They are often the hub of communication between the customer and the other groups, and they also deal with communications up and down any hierarchies. Managers need to be good communicators, and this means that they need to:

- Be good at receiving information and showing they have received it. They must read and listen well, and provide feedback.
- Be good at giving information and making sure people have received it. They must speak and write clearly and elicit feedback.
- Understand other people and treat them fairly. They must persuade, negotiate, empathize, and know when to compromise and when to be firm, treating everyone fairly and taking into account their different communication needs and quality viewpoints.

We have seen in Chapter 3 that one of reasons customers and builders sometimes do not get on is because of a difference in communication styles, and this is true for people in general. In Chapters 8 to 12, as we look at the stages of work that need to be managed, I will mention some techniques that help us improve communication.

Managers have a difficult mix of skills to acquire, and not all managers have all these skills (which of us has?). One trick I find useful is to use a "personal improvement cycle." As we saw in Section 4.4.1 and will see in Chapter 12 when we look at evaluating software development processes, we use a plan–do–review–improve cycle. On a personal level it simply means reflecting on how we manage ourselves during communication with others and what we could do to improve the communication, not just for ourselves, but also for the other people. Particular points to consider are cultural differences, personality differences, and communication styles, particularly when giving and receiving criticism [5–7].

I have noticed that one key factor in the success of a manager is consistency of behavior; if people know they can trust you, they work with you. I remember one project manager who was very hard on everyone, but this was less of a problem for us "down the hierarchy" when we realized that he gave the same grief "up the hierarchy" to the project board and executives.

Another key factor is not being remote. Another very good project manager helped during a crisis weekend when technical staff were working extra hours on some of the menial and housekeeping tasks to free time for the team. This effort was much appreciated; he was seen to be in and working when the team was doing overtime, and the work he was doing at that point contributed directly to removing some of their burden.

4.4.2.4 Partnerships and Resources

I have worked in situations where the customer chose to bring in specialists from a variety of organizations. For example, on one project, managers came from the customer organization and were also brought in from a specialist project-management consultancy; the builders and measurers came from third-party organizations as well as from the in-house IT group; and the supporters were a separate group from the IT group, reporting through a different management structure, although they were in-house. The project manager spent much time negotiating between these parties. All were partners in the project, and were controlling different resources that were required if the project was to be successful.

An IT manager has pointed out to me that one key skill that a good manager has is political astuteness:

> Managers often lead a virtual team that is united only by a shared task. Whereas team leaders manage a group of practitioners in their own discipline (such as builders or measurers), senior managers lead a matrix of specialists drawn from various functional areas (or companies), whose work they do not understand in depth. These managers cannot depend on traditional sources of power such as the line hierarchy or resource ownership; instead, they deploy a range of influencing tactics. They operate in two worlds simultaneously: the rational world of budgets and schedules and the shadowy world of organizational politics, which the specialists normally don't see.

Some new managers do all the things that I have recommended elsewhere in this chapter and still find unexpected opponents blocking or disrupting their projects. The same IT manager continued:

> The experienced manager who spends all day in meetings and every evening having dinner with key project stakeholders may be a joke in the team but always gets the best people and delivers the right product.

These organizational partnerships through influence are critical to success, and the ability to nourish them makes the difference between those of us who pursue technical careers and those of us who follow organizational careers. The ability to influence is not a sign of dishonesty, despite the suspicion of some IT technical staff; it is a way of communicating with people who are stakeholders and have different communication styles (see Appendix A for communication styles).

4.4.2.5 Processes

The processes used by managers include skills such as planning, estimating and reporting, for which there are various project management methods and tools available. What I will do is to pick out some aspects of the manager's processes that particularly affect teamwork and quality.

Learning to be a manager. One aspect of IT management that I have observed over the years is that people are given their first management responsibilities without having the role explained to them or their existing work removed; it is as though we believe that management activities are intuitive and take no time. In one typical instance, one of the development team, let us call him Jeff Teamleader, was asked to team lead part way through a major project. A few weeks later when I visited the project, Jeff came to me in a state of some distress; he was unable to carry out any of his work and was falling further and further behind. He could not understand what had happened.

When we talked it through, it turned out that until Jeff had been given the team leader role, he had a technically complex but organizationally simple role; he had never needed a to-do list or a plan of action. Now, as team leader, he had to plan and coordinate what the team as a whole was doing, produce some management deliverables such as estimates and reports, go to meetings with the project manager, and negotiate and deal with conflict inside the team and with other teams. Also, he still had his own technical work to do. He had simply become overwhelmed and unable to do anything as a consequence.

What was required? He needed a simple personal plan and a simple team plan, that would enable him with his team to make the big delivery in a few weeks time, by breaking it down into chunks. Every day, he needed to know what he and the team had to do that day, in order to deliver what was needed in the current week, so that the longer plan would work.

First, we sorted out his personal plan. We made a list of everything that he had been asked to do or thought he had to do, including all the nontechnical and nonproject tasks and building a plan for the team. We scored each item on the to-do list with an urgency, importance and size score. We quickly identified some things that he did not have to do. Then we divided up the to-do list as in Table 4.2, by deadline, importance, and urgency, putting together a day-by-day plan for the coming week, including a 5-minute progress review at the end of each day and a 10-minute session to plan the following week at the end of Friday.

Once Jeff had this simple plan for next few days, he could start to plan the team's work in the same way, and sort which parts of his own technical role to keep and which to delegate. It was much clearer to him and to them what really needed doing day to day. He calmed down; he could get a grip on the situation. Why hadn't his manager, Liz, explained this to him as he took over? I found two reasons when I talked to her:

Table 4.2 Simple Personal or Team Plan Layout

This week	Morning	Afternoon	
Monday			
Tuesday			
Wednesday			
Thursday			
Friday			
Next week start:			
Next week complete:			
This month complete:			
Goal: by (date) have completed (deliverable)			
To-do list			
Item	Importance	Urgency/deadline	Size

- Liz was dealing with larger and more complex problems, using project management tools and methods that would not be appropriate. Her attitude was that "Jeff Teamleader doesn't need that yet."
- Liz now took simple planning for granted and had forgotten that she too had struggled with her first team leader role. She said, "Well, I'm disappointed if he didn't realize that he needed to plan his time; I'd have thought it was obvious that he needed to...."

The problem that Jeff Teamleader then had was that his plan was disrupted by other people interrupting him and the team with questions and other meetings. A plan will always change; we plan partly to have an idea of what we need to do when, but also so that when things change we can deal with the change more easily. Ideas I have found useful are:

- Knowing your highest priorities: the things that you cannot compromise if the team is to meet its goal. That means you know which tasks you can delay or even cancel.
- Setting aside time that cannot be interrupted for particular individuals and for the team. This is time when people concentrate on the most important and most difficult tasks. You can achieve this by making appointments with yourself.
- Not making the plan too perfect; it just needs to be good enough to allow you to understand progress and changes.

4.4 Quality framework using the EFQM Excellence Model

Planning and estimating for quality activities. As part of planning, we need estimates of how long things will take to do. Estimates are really just guesses with more or less certainty behind them. As we saw in Chapter 3, the customers need to understand how precise and accurate our estimates are, so it is important to provide them as a range of times, costs, and resource usage, becoming more precise as we gain certainty and understanding. The teamwork aspects of estimating are:

- Listening to your team—they know how long different tasks will take and what resources are needed
- Listening to your customer and manager—what constraints are there that affect the estimate? For example, if the overall budget cannot exceed a certain amount, then your estimation task is to show what can be delivered for that price.
- Explaining to the customer the basis for the estimates—the assumptions made, the gaps, and the precision and accuracy of the estimates

There is a tendency to underestimate how long QA and QC tasks take, and to forget to estimate for changes and rework following the QA or QC. Table 4.3 suggests some tasks that you may need to include in your estimates, and to get the details, as a manager you would need to consult your

Table 4.3 QA and QC Tasks to Include in Plans and Estimates

Drivers for percentage of QA/QC activities to cost of project	Aims and objectives for the project/business, risks to be contained, constraints, how important are QA and QC activities for this project?
	All the deliverables for the project, their importance and risk associated with faults, what QA/QC does each need?
	Acceptance criteria for the project as a whole, Acceptance criteria for each deliverable, which QA/QC activities can measure against the acceptance criteria, and completion criteria for those activities
QA activities—audit and process review	Allow time, cost, resource usage for internal and external audit for:
	Planning
	Preparation (times number of auditors)
	Audit activities, for example, meetings (times number of auditors and interviewees)
	Follow-up and rework (time spent by auditor and auditee)
	Evaluation and process improvement (may be at audit end, increment/phase end, project end)
QC activities— document review	Allow time, cost, resource usage for:
	Planning, including selection of what is to be reviewed and the method to be used
	Preparation (times number of reviewers)
	Meeting (times number of reviewers)
	Follow-up and rework
QC activities—testing	Allow time, cost, resource usage for:
	Planning, including deciding on the level and types of testing, setup of management and control processes
	Acquisition—include test design, data, environment, tools
	Measurement—include execution, reporting
	Follow-up—include rework and rerun of tests

QA and QC experts to understand which techniques would be useful for your project. You also need to estimate what knowledge and resources you will require, and when you will need them. Tools, environments, and special skills may not be available to your team all the time, and there may be conflict with other teams for use of these resources, or they may not be available in your organization. In that case, you may need to estimate for outsourcing or purchasing resources.

Monitoring, control, and measurement of progress. Once we have our plan and our estimates, we need to track progress and make changes to the plan as necessary. If, like Jeff Teamleader, our team's work is contributing to a part of the overall plan, we need to be careful how we manage changes, as slippage in our work may have an effect on other people's work; there are dependencies between the tasks. In a large project, the overall project schedule may be controlled on a schedule of activities and tasks which shows these dependencies on a PERT (program evaluation review technique) chart. A PERT chart shows the length of time each task takes and the dependencies between tasks; it is a useful planning technique. A simple example is shown in Figure 4.3.

You can see from the figure that some tasks have to complete before others can start, but some can take place in parallel. You will see on each task the task name, the duration of the task, the earliest and latest days the task could start and finish, and the *slack* on the task. The slack is the amount of time you can let a task slip before it makes the subsequent, dependent tasks slip. The path through the tasks with zero slack is the *critical path*, shown in bold in the figure. If anything on this path is late, the whole project will be late. If finishing on time is important, planning using a PERT chart to

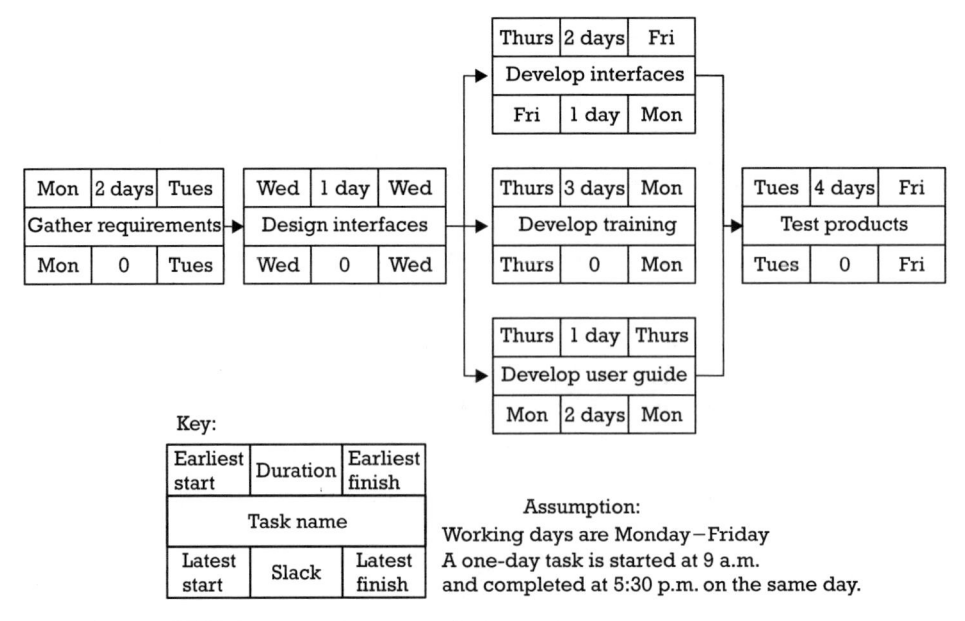

Figure 4.3 Simple PERT chart.

understand dependencies and slack can be very useful. When monitoring, small amounts of slippage within slack may not be important to us, but if the slippage means that later tasks on the critical path will not complete on time, it means we will not meet the deadline for the project. We might report using on a red–amber–green traffic lights system:

- Green tasks are completing within schedule.
- Amber tasks are finishing within slack.
- Red tasks have used up slack.

We can then identify where we have time problems: "If it weren't for task X, we'd be a green project." Different levels of management may require different levels of detail in reporting. I have seen some organizations concentrate on reporting on red and amber tasks only, whereas others only report to the project board if the slip exceeds a certain amount. This can cause problems with accumulated small slips. For example, if managers only track slippage by monitoring individual slips above a certain number of days, but there have been many small slips, they may not realize that the real hidden slippage in the project may be much larger than documented.

There are other things to track apart from time used and time to complete against estimated time. For example:

- Overall budget to date against spending to date.
- Number of deliverables completed against how many you expected to complete by now.
- Cost to produce deliverables to date compared with what we expected to spend on those deliverables.
- Quality of the deliverables against their acceptance criteria.
- Morale of the team (all groups—how happy are they now?).
- Delivery against targets.
- The organization's objectives and the customers/supporters' requirements and how these are changing; how the project is changing to meet the changing requirements.

We will talk in Chapter 10 about changing requirements during the software development life cycle, but here I want to discuss the use of a tracking and reporting mechanism that is used at the organizational level and could be adapted for an IT project: the Balanced Scorecard and its variants, sometimes referred to as the project dashboard, which we will look at below. Another mechanism, Earned Value, is discussed in Appendix A.

4.4.3 EFQM Excellence Model results for the managers

4.4.3.1 Customer Results

The customer results for the manager to track are:

- Customer perception of the other groups. Managers should meet their customers regularly, and as part of such meetings need to check how the customer feels about things. I remember a salesman once saying to me, "What do you think you deliver?" I came up with a number of answers—completed audits and tests, reports, tested software, and so on. He said, "No—what you are delivering is happiness. Is the customer happy to see you? Are they pleased you are there?" We can measure this right now, throughout our work, and we can adapt to deal with any problems
- Customer performance results are also important; for example, do we get repeat business or extended projects from the customer? Have we a good reputation as a team and individually as managers? These measures may not be apparent until too late if we have not worked on customer perceptions during the project.

4.4.3.2 People Results

Here, we consider the measures we might apply to managers themselves. Table 4.4 suggests some measures. The first of these are perceptions—how the managers feel about themselves in relation to the other groups and their work. The second group are the "harder" performance measures, staff turnover, for example.

4.4.3.3 Society Results

Managers have a role in ensuring that society as a whole is considered, in line with corporate objectives. Table 4.5 shows some example results for measurement. Quality here is not just the quality of the product itself, but the quality of its effect on the organization and on society as a whole. Managers will have a responsibility for ensuring that their own team's work does not breach standards in areas such as environmental management and impact, organizational security, and corporate governance.

Table 4.4 People Results—Managers

	Example of Possible Measures
Perceptions—surveys, interviews, compliments, and complaints	Has a motivational study provided positive feedback?
	Are managers satisfied with their career paths, rewards?
	Are the teams satisfied with their managers? Is the level of management and control right for the individuals in the team?
Performance indicators—internal to managers group	Does the managers group match up with the required qualifications and competencies? For example, do they have appropriate BCS qualifications [8]?
	Are there particular signals of stress among the managers: excessive hours, absenteeism, and sickness levels compared with other groups?
	What is the level of staff turnover compared with other groups and do people want to be recruited into this group? For example, if we advertise a team leader role internally, do people apply?

4.4 Quality framework using the EFQM Excellence Model

Table 4.5 Society Results—How the Managers Relate to Society

	Example of Possible Measures
Perceptions—external to the group: surveys, interviews, compliments, and complaints	Are the managers seen by the organization and wider society as acting ethically?
	Do the managers ensure that the processes and systems act properly with regard to health risks, safety, hazards, and the environment?
Performance indicators—internal to managers group	Has the manager encouraged the team to work toward accolades, for example, for paper- and energy-saving initiatives, in line with corporate initiatives?
	Have the managers supported the measurement group in checking compliance with external authorities' certification?
	Has the manager ensured that the team's work complies to standards such as the ISO 14000 family (Environmental Management) and the ISO 17799 family (Security Management)?

4.4.3.4 Key Performance Results

It is important that the manager choose an appropriate set of measures for monitoring and controlling the project. This may seem obvious, but often we choose measures that are not appropriate—we make the mistake of measuring what we have always measured, or what is easy to measure, rather than what we need to know.

Within the organization as a whole, there will be a strategy with associated measures, and both commercial and nonprofit organizations are starting to use Kaplan and Norton's Balanced Scorecard [9–12]. This is a method to balance different types of measure against each other. Examples might be:

- Long term versus short term;
- Financial versus nonfinancial;
- Leading and lagging indicators;
- Internal and external perspectives;
- Objective and subjective perspectives.

A simple example might be a balanced scorecard for a journey: We want to get there as fast as possible, which will be expensive, but we also want to travel as cheaply as possible, which may mean a slower journey to conserve fuel. There is a trade-off or balance between speed and cost.

Kaplan and Norton's scorecard typically looks something like Figure 4.4. Financial, customer, internal, and learning measures are balanced against each other, with balanced objectives and targets.

There are as many variations in scorecards as there are organizations using them; [9–12] present several examples from real companies. What I suggest is that if we know the goal and strategy for the organization, we can build a balanced scorecard for measuring quality in an IT project by balancing the quality views against each other. Figure 4.5 shows an example.

The measures in this scorecard can:

Balanced scorecard: simple organization example

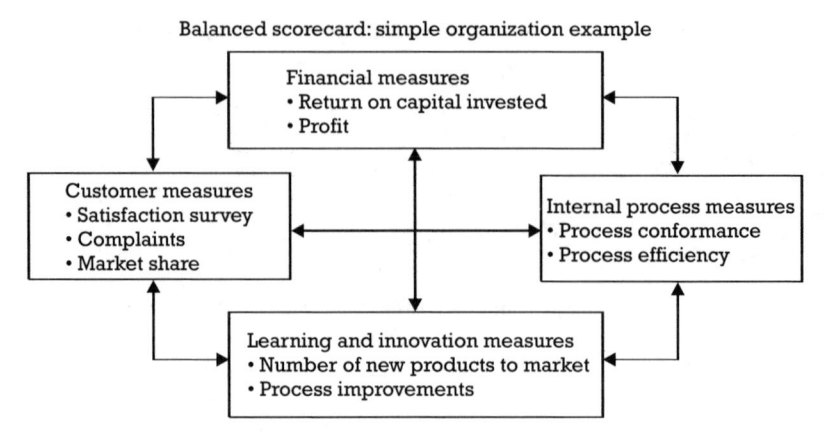

```
                    Financial measures
                    • Return on capital invested
                    • Profit

Customer measures                    Internal process measures
• Satisfaction survey                • Process conformance
• Complaints                         • Process efficiency
• Market share

                    Learning and innovation measures
                    • Number of new products to market
                    • Process improvements
```

Figure 4.4 Simplified typical balanced scorecard. (*After*: [9], p. 9.)

- Reflect the organization's strategic measures and ensure that those on the team all understand those measures;
- Balance the conflict between the value, user, product, and manufacturing views of quality;
- Be used continuously to report progress, not just against time and deliverables, but against quality targets;
- Be kept on one page or screen so it is easy to take in and agree upon;
- Be backed up by other measures and detailed explanation *if required* but does speak for itself.

4.5 Communication between the managers and other groups

4.5.1 Managers and communication cycles

We will see in Chapters 8 to 12 that managers are involved in the whole life span of a piece of software, from its conception, through the software development life cycle (SDLC), during delivery, and postdelivery until decommissioning.

Managers need to negotiate with others and also to control project progress. This can mean that the communication between managers and others can be difficult. Suppose that Liz Manager is waiting for a progress report from Jeff Teamleader. The report was due yesterday and she has heard nothing. How should she approach Jeff? Maybe Liz is not good at confronting people. She might be tempted to wait and see what happens. But as manager, she needs to know why the report is late; there may be a problem that she needs to resolve that Jeff is reluctant to tell her about. One manager I worked for was quite unable to ask people for late reports. He would put a notice on the project notice board: "Will all team leaders please ensure that their reports are delivered on time; the following have not yet delivered this week's report...." The end result of his being unable to speak to his team

4.5 Communication between the managers and other groups

Balanced scorecard for quality

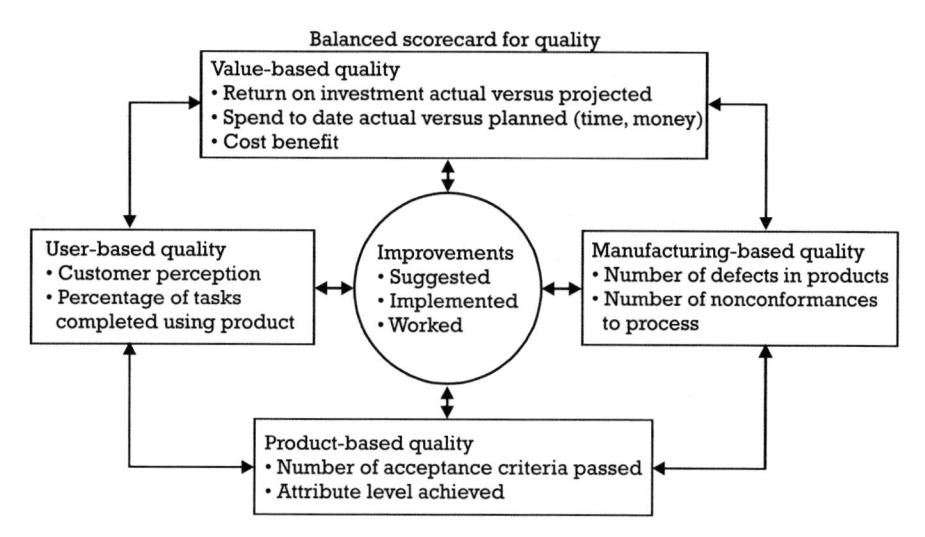

- **Value-based quality**
  - Return on investment actual versus projected
  - Spend to date actual versus planned (time, money)
  - Cost benefit

- **User-based quality**
  - Customer perception
  - Percentage of tasks completed using product

- **Improvements**
  - Suggested
  - Implemented
  - Worked

- **Manufacturing-based quality**
  - Number of defects in products
  - Number of nonconformances to process

- **Product-based quality**
  - Number of acceptance criteria passed
  - Attribute level achieved

Figure 4.5 Quality balanced scorecard. (*After*: [9], p. 9.)

leaders directly to ask for their reports was that the team leaders, who did not like the manager, did not understand the use of the reports, and who by and large were more experienced, started to put more energy into their "being late with the report" game. One particular old-timer said to me, "I always write the report on time, but I'm not going to give it to him unless he asks me himself; its an insult the way he puts those notices on the board without speaking to me, when I sit right next to it." I was too junior to ask the manager for his thoughts, but my reading of his behavior was he was frightened of the team leaders and so could not give or receive criticism successfully. All he needed to do was go to the team leaders and ask for the reports. I suspect that if he had done this once, they would have stopped the game. During complicated interactions, we can only alter our own behavior, and hope that if we behave well, others will be encouraged to behave well [5–7, 13]. So, Liz Manager needs to ask Jeff Teamleader for his report, and she needs to do that in a direct way. What affects Jeff's response to the request for the report is the manner in which it is made. Writers like Wagner [7] who use transactional analysis to describe behavior say we are several people at once—we have an internal dialogue that informs the dialogue we have with the external world. We can choose to behave like adults and treat others as adults, or we can behave like children or like parents. The ego states are:

- Adult—deals in facts: "The report was due yesterday."
- Nurturing parent—wants to help: "I see you are having problems with the report."
- Critical parent—tells people off: "Why are you always late with the report?"
- Natural child—likes to play and have fun: "Let's have lunch and think about it afterwards!"

- Rebellious child—does the opposite of what others want: "I'm not doing the report!"
- Compliant child—assumes the blame: "Oh, I'm hopeless. I'm late again."

Adult-to-adult transactions result in facts being communicated, but if you come and speak to me as though you are my parent, and are critical ("Why are you always late with the report?"), I may respond as a rebellious child ("I'm not doing the stupid report. It's a waste of time. You do it.") This is called a crossed communication; the unhelpful ego states feed off each other and we build up to an argument. We could have had a more constructive, uncrossed dialogue:

Adult: "Is the report ready?"
Adult: "No, but I will finish it this afternoon."

The question is couched neutrally as a request for facts and so is responded to with a neutral fact. Remember also that tone of voice and body language will also speak volumes; if the questioner uses "adult" wording but a "critical parent" tone of voice, she/he is still a "critical parent."

Figure 4.6 shows how we can build up an expectation of poor communication with those around us; our anticipation of problems causes us to communicate in a way that encourages a problematic response and it turns into a vicious circle. We give out the wrong signals and we get the wrong signals back.

4.5.2 The reporting process

One key process for all managers is the reporting process. Measurers gather information about processes and products and the managers, including test managers and quality managers, need to pass this on to other people in a way that will be acceptable and understandable. Good information design is

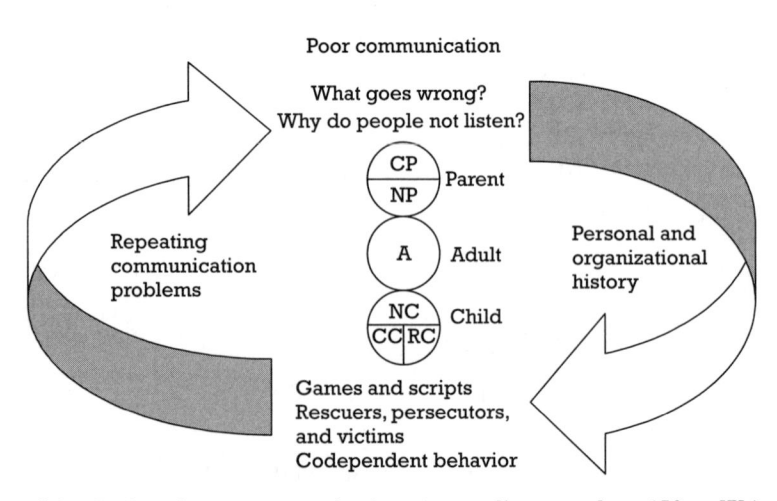

Figure 4.6 Cycles of poor communication—our audience and us. (*After:* [7].)

4.5 Communication between the managers and other groups

vital; it is easy to hide your message in your report so that it is ignored or misinterpreted. However well you have designed your audit or test process, however well you execute the process, if your reports are ignored, you may as well have not bothered doing it. Reports are the managers' deliverable to all the other groups:

- They help us understand progress and priorities.
- They help in decision making and risk assessment (they should show the bad news and good news!).
- They inform management, our colleagues, and our teams.

When deciding what to report, we need to examine the facts. First, do we have any facts? Managers need to report measurable facts, interpretation of those facts, and people's perceptions, but should distinguish between them. The measurers will provide the managers with data, which need to be interpreted and reported, for example:

- "The audit found 23 critical deviations from the configuration-management standard" is a fact.
- "The nature of the deviations increases the risk of failure in this project" is an interpretation of the fact.
- "The project team are worried that the lack of a configuration management process means that they cannot know whether they have completed the build" is a report of staff perception that comments on both the fact and the interpretation.

All three provide important information which should be reported.

When deciding what to report, do not collect information for the sake of it. One mistake many people make is reporting either on what has always been reported without questioning why, or only reporting on information that is easy to collect. Also, be prepared to report bad news as well as good news. In my experience, people want to hear the bad news; what they do not want is to get it when it is too late and without any ideas for improving the situation. Table 4.6 gives some ideas for consideration when deciding on measurement reporting.

Table 4.6 Planning Reporting—Questions

Who are our audience?	Customers, managers, builders, supporters, other measurers
Who is interested?	Internal and external bodies
	Who else?
What do they need to know?	Time, money, quality (and include the different quality viewpoints), progress toward a goal
What are they interested in?	
	What else?
When do they need it?	Daily, weekly, monthly, yearly
	When an emergency happens? As risks increase? When issues arise?
	What other cycles for your audience?
Why are they interested?	Making decisions, assessing risks, looking for improvements
	What else?

We often use graphics to report because they reveal data, especially for displaying complex ideas clearly, precisely, and efficiently but it is important to remember that graphics can be abused, either by using graphics that are not necessary or by distorting the data with the graphic [14–16]. Our eyes interpret the representation of two- and three-dimensional images as having area or volume, and if these are used to show one-dimensional data, we will see it as larger than it is, as we see in Figure 4.7.

One colleague remarked to me, "But I want to exaggerate the test results—I want the customers to be really, really worried...." I think he was joking, but the real point is, do you know that the graphs you produce are accurate and will be accurately interpreted? There are some notes and other examples in Appendix A about the measures Tufte [15] suggests for checking your graphics: the *lie factor*, the *data–ink ratio*, and the *data density* of the graphic.

Make sure you understand why you are using the graphic; is it for description, exploration, tabulation, or just decoration? Make sure you know what message you are trying to put across. We tend to overdecorate our graphics [14–16] and thus hide what we are trying to say. Edward Tufte [15] suggests that we use "the greatest number of ideas in the shortest time with the least ink in the smallest space" if we want to show the data. Many numbers in a small space encourages the eye to compare data. I strongly recommend that you look at his work to understand good and bad approaches to information design and reporting.

Managers need information from other groups in order to understand the constraints on delivering their wish list. Table 4.7 lists the information that managers need from the other groups.

Managers are conduits for information flow; they will gather information from all the groups and communicate it back to all the groups as reports, tactics, and decisions (Table 4.8 and Figure 4.8). They will do this at every stage in the life of the software.

The Lie Factor
Distorted data representation

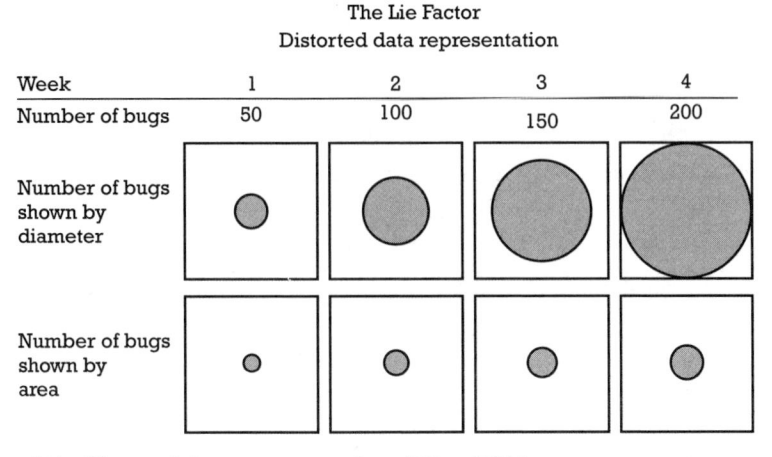

Week	1	2	3	4
Number of bugs	50	100	150	200

Figure 4.7 Distorted data representation. (*After:* [15].)

4.6 Summary of the group

Table 4.7 Information That Managers Need from Others

Customers	Goals, targets, strategy for the customer
	Business constraints
	Changes to circumstances
	Acceptance criteria, set, reported on as pass or fail
Other managers	Progress
	Changes to circumstances
Builders	Progress
	Problems
	Decisions required
Supporters	Technical constraints
	Timing constraints for delivery
	Changes to circumstances
	Acceptance criteria, set, reported on as pass or fail
Measurers	Quality measures—number of nonconformances, defects, number of acceptance criteria passed and failed
	Progress
	Problems
	Decisions required

Table 4.8 Information That Managers Have That Others Need

At all stages	Information gathered from each group
	Experiences from previous projects
	Constraints and policies
	Effect of changes
	Tactics and decisions based on policy, strategy, and circumstances

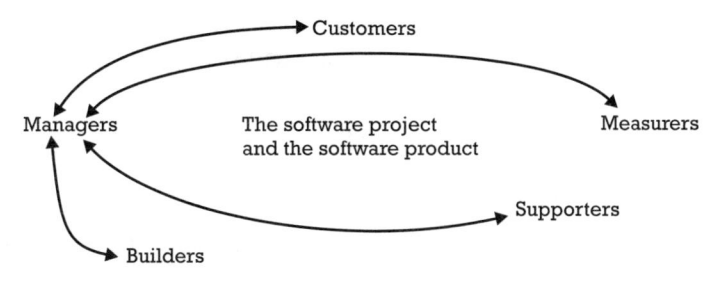

Figure 4.8 Communication between groups.

4.6 Summary of the group

Managers must communicate well with the other groups if they are to be effective. They are responsible for planning, estimating, and controlling work, as well as for making and enacting decisions. These are not intuitive skills, and new managers need help as they take on the role.

Managers are the conduit for information flow through and between the groups. Managers need to negotiate between the groups and ensure that the optimum course is taken at each point. Use of a Balanced Scorecard will help in this negotiation. Use of clear reports is vital; managers need to ensure that their reports tell the story they are intended to tell.

Managers are sometimes put in the position of being their team's "parent" and need to consider carefully how they give and receive criticism.

References

[1] The W. Edwards Deming Institute, "Deming's Teachings," http://www.deming.org/theman/articles/articles_gbnf04.html, November 2003.

[2] Gilb, T., see papers on Evolutionary Delivery on http://www.gilb.com, including "Competitive Engineering: A Handbook for Systems and Software Engineering," September 2003.

[3] European Foundation for Quality Management, "EFQM Excellence Model," http://www.efqm.org, August 2003.

[4] Software Engineering Institute, "Capability Maturity Model® Integrations (CMMI®), Version 1.1," http://www.sei.cmu.edu/pub/documents/02.reports/pdf/02tr004.pdf, October 2003.

[5] Tannen, D., "The Power of Talk," *Harvard Business Review*, September 1995, pp. 138–148.

[6] Hathaway, P., *Giving and Receiving Criticism*, Los Altos, CA: Crisp Publications, 1990.

[7] Wagner, A., *The Transactional Manager—How to Solve People Problems with Transactional Analysis*, Denver, CO: T.A. Communications, 1981.

[8] British Computer Society (BCS), "BCS Qualifications," http://www1.bcs.org.uk/link.asp?sectionID=574, September 2003.

[9] Kaplan, R. S., and D. P. Norton, *The Balanced Scorecard*, Boston, MA: Harvard Business School Press, 1996.

[10] Bourne, M., and P. Bourne, *Balanced Scorecard in a Week*, London, England: Hodder and Stoughton, 2000.

[11] Olve, N. G., and A. Sjöstrand, *The Balanced Scorecard*, Oxford, England: Capstone, 2002.

[12] British Quality Foundation and TQMI, "Using the Model and the Scorecard," *Seminar*, Kettering, United Kingdom, September 2003.

[13] Copeland, L., "Testing as Co-Dependent Behaviour," *SIGiST Conference, the BCS Specialist Interest Group in Software Testing*, London 1999.

[14] Evans, I., "Get Your Message Across!" *EuroSTAR Conference*, Edinburgh, Scotland, 2002.

[15] Tufte, E., *Visual Display of Quantitative Information*, Cheshire, CT: Graphics Press, 1983.

[16] Huff, D., *How to Lie with Statistics*, New York: Penguin, 1974.

Selected bibliography

Adair, J., *Effective Teambuilding*, London, England: Pan, 1986.

Adair, J., *Effective Time Management*, London, England: Pan, 1988.

Berne, E., *Games People Play*, New York: Penguin, 1970.

Boddy, D., and D. Buchanan, *Take the Lead: Interpersonal Skills for Project Managers*, London, England: Financial Times Press, 1992.

Brooks, F. P., *The Mythical Man Month*, Reading, MA: Addison-Wesley Longman, 1995.

Burnett, K., *The Project Management Paradigm*, London, England: Springer, Practitioner Series, 1998.

Chartered Management Institute (on-line checklists about management and quality topics), http://www.managers.org.uk.

Clarkson, M., *Developing IT Staff*, London, England: Springer, Practitioner Series, 2001.

Crosby, P., *Quality Is Free*, New York: Mentor, 1980.

de Bono, E., *Six Thinking Hats®*, New York: Penguin, 2000.

Evans, I., and I. Macfarlane, *A Dictionary of IT Service Management*, ITSMF, 2001.

Grove Consultants, "What Test Managers Say … and Why Project Managers Don't Listen," play presented at EuroSTAR Conference, Stockholm, Sweden, 2001.

Hadley, T., "More Than a Thank You," *UK Excellence*, August/September 2003.

Handy, C., *Understanding Organizations*, New York: Penguin, 1993.

Macfarlane, I., and C. Rudd, *IT Service Management*, Reading, England: IT Service Management Forum, 2001.

Mullins, L. J., *Management and Organisational Behaviour*, 5th ed., New York: Financial Times/Pitman, 1999.

Pas, J., "Emotional Intelligence," *EuroSTAR Workshop*, Stockholm, Sweden, 2001.

Project Management Today (monthly journal), http://www.pmtoday.co.uk.

Schein, E., *Organizational Culture and Leadership*, San Francisco, CA: Jossey-Bass, 1997.

Smith, J., *How to Be a Better Time Manager*, London, England: Kogan Page, 1997.

CHAPTER 5

Contents

5.1 Introducing the builders

5.2 Who could be in this group?

5.3 Quality viewpoint

5.4 Quality framework using the EFQM Excellence Model

5.5 Communication between the builders and other groups

5.6 Summary of the group

Roles and Quality: Builders

In this chapter I shall:

- Introduce the members of the builders group, their roles, and activities;
- Introduce their quality viewpoint;
- Provide a framework for the builders within the EFQM Excellence Model;
- Identify information flows between the builders and the other groups.

So I spent 2 months designing and building the new interface and its underlying software. It's got everything we discussed with the users, and I added some extras that looked useful, after I'd talked to the customer last week. You know I was here all night last Thursday getting it finished for delivery into test on Friday. And then at 10 o'clock on Friday morning, the tester comes up to me and starts moaning about the interface being too complex. How long could she have spent looking at it? I ask you! I just blew my top. I said, "It's my system; I designed it and I built it and I don't care what you think of it! It's not your business to criticize what it does! You weren't there when we discussed the spec." We do all the work and they do nothing but moan!

—Software engineer having a dramatic moment when the tester complained (rather rudely) about the complexity of the software interface

5.1 Introducing the builders

Of course, this group is vital to software quality—not only do they build the products, but they build in quality. The people in this group are wrestling with difficult problems as they create new products. Why is our software engineer so angry about the software being criticized by the tester? There are a number of reasons:

- Software engineers pride themselves in doing a good job; they want to build excellent products with few defects. In this case, the engineer had done groundbreaking work over a long period of concentrated effort.
- Once they build the product, it can be difficult to change it. In this case, a fundamental alteration to the design of the interface was being suggested.
- None of us likes having our work criticized, especially when we have put in a huge effort and been creative. The builders group is vulnerable to criticism by the other groups as they are responsible for the products.
- When we offer criticism of other's work, we need to consider the three points above. In this case, the tester phrased the criticism very tactlessly. How do I know? Reader, I was that young tester and I look back with embarrassment!

We have seen in Chapter 3 that customers need software to carry out their tasks, and that they want to do this as effectively and efficiently as possible. We saw in Chapter 4 that managers contribute by planning and controlling resources, budget, and time scales; by acting as an information conduit for decisions, to ensure that the proper communication takes place between people in the different groups; and by negotiating between the groups. The builders will realize the customer's requirements in products and services; this means that they need direct communication with the customers, so the managers should encourage that if it is not happening. A large group of people with a variety of roles and skills contribute to the build. Many people think first of the teams and individuals who design and write the code for the software. One IT manager said to me: "Why are you talking about 'builders'? 'Software engineer' is a perfectly good term!" However, many other products need to built along with the code itself, and these can be forgotten or neglected; remember our trainer in Chapter 1? Another trainer's comment is that the request for training material to be designed and built is often made very late in the project:

> I am so tired of being asked to write a training manual in two weeks, with supporting training database, and exercises from scratch, when the software has taken months to write, as though training development is easy to do and takes no time. The software is wonderful; don't they want the training to do it justice?

So, in this book, I emphasize that it is not just the code that is being built, and not just the software engineers who are involved. You might ask, "Will the software engineers write the training material, help guides, and operation support manuals? Those need building too!" Of course, the software engineers could build all the products, but we need to ask ourselves if they will have time and whether it is reasonable to assume that they have the skills required. For this reason I am using the term "builders" and include in that category all the people who build products, whether these are delivered to customers (software systems, training, user documentation), supporters (operations and support guides, system specifications, regression test packs), or only intended for use during the project itself.

5.2 Who could be in this group?

Builders are the people who specify, design, and build the software and other products. The group includes a number of specialists:

- Those who work on the design and build of software systems; sometimes referred to as the development team (see developers in Chapter 2, Table 2.1). In these roles, we find people who describe themselves as business and system analysts, software architects, designers, software engineers, analyst–programmers, programmers, and developers.
- Those who work on the development of textual and graphical supporting information for the code and software system, whether this is on-line, on paper, or delivered face to face. In these roles we find people who work as technical writers, authors, training developers, trainers, and graphic designers.

They are stakeholders for quality because they build quality into the product. The products include not just the delivered products (for example, code, user guides, training material) but also the interim products (for example, requirement definitions, designs, and specifications).

As well as the main products—software, training material, and so on—built by the specialists, other people will build products required to aid in the build and support of the products; these are sometimes called infrastructure, support, interim, or secondary products. Almost everyone involved will build something, including plans and reports. In this sense, we are all builders. Examples include:

- Supporters build supporting material, such as infrastructure and environments.
- Measurers build measurement material, such as review checklists, tests, and audit checklists.
- Managers build management material, such as plans and reports.
- Customers build inputs to the project, such as requirements and acceptance criteria.

This means that at some point we will all be builders, and we are all responsible for building quality into our own products. What do we mean by building quality in? To find out, let us next look at the quality viewpoint and framework of the builders.

5.3 Quality viewpoint

Although builders can be seen as date-driven, the pressure to deliver often comes from their managers and customers. Most builders tend to focus on building products as well as possible. In order to support this, they favor the manufacturing and product-based views of quality.

In Chapter 1, we saw that the manufacturing-based definition focuses on the specification, design, and construction of software products. Quality depends on the extent to which requirements have been implemented in conformance with the original requirements, and our success is measured on our ability to follow a process and deliver products against agreed specifications. Builders will adopt methods, processes, and tools that enable them to provide technically excellent solutions and to meet agreed specifications.

A problem with the manufacturing view is that if we focus on verifying that the system is correct to specification, we may forget to validate that we have the right specification. For the builders, the progression through the software development life cycle (SDLC) may move from product to product, with each product building on a foundation of the previous product in the stream. Once the customer's requirements are understood, the software design is based on those requirements. The builders use the design to develop the code and other material such as training courses and user manuals. If the requirements are wrong, the final products are wrong, even though the designs were followed faithfully. Measurers also favor the manufacturing-based quality viewpoint, as we will see in Chapter 6, so builders and measurers can work together to ensure that verification and validation are applied to products and defects are prevented and removed. We will see in Chapters 9 and 10 that there are ways to overcome this problem, by preparing for the SDLC properly: by choosing our SDLC model carefully, and by anticipating that change will happen throughout the SDLC.

In addition to the manufacturing-based view, builders also favor a product-based definition of quality. As we saw in Chapter 1, this is about working to a well-defined set of software quality attributes that can be measured in an objective and quantitative way. Builders can find customers vague about what they want, particularly in defining the nonfunctional attributes of a software system. This is partly because software attributes are difficult to describe and partly because it can be difficult to know what is possible, particularly with new technology. The supporters share the product-based view of quality; they will be interested in product attributes, especially nonfunctional attributes such as throughput, security, reliability, and maintainability, which affect the operability of the delivered software [1]. They will also be interested in the customer's user-based or fit-for-purpose viewpoint, because the supporters operate the help desk. We will look at the supporters in more detail in Chapter 7. It is, therefore, worthwhile for the builders and the supporters to engage in dialogue early on and throughout the SDLC. Their product-based view pins down vague "wants" to specific attributes. We will see in Chapter 9 how to derive acceptance criteria that allow objective assessment of the quality of the delivered product, using standards such as ISO 9126. These product-based qualities or attributes are also important to builders because the priority given to particular attributes will affect the design and build choices. For example, if maintainability is important, the code may be structured in a particular way to allow changes to be made easily, but if a different attribute, for example, security or performance, is more important, the code may be structured differently and perhaps be harder to maintain.

Builders also hold a transcendent view of quality, as everyone does, based on their "taken for granted" assumptions; in this case, based on their perceptions and their feelings toward a type of software product. For many builders, their transcendent view focuses on technical excellence or use of particular methods; for example, use of a particular SDLC model (see Chapter 10) or use of a particular technique or tool. A clichéd observation of builders (including my observation of my own work in training development, authoring user guides, and, in the past, writing code) is of a group of people who apply their expertise while obsessively pursuing technical excellence at the expense of a return on investment. They enjoy their own technical innovations and yet can be reluctant to change their processes.

We have seen that the builders favor the manufacturing and product-based views of quality. These viewpoints are shared by many measurers, and this leads them to provide technical solutions of the highest possible excellence; their dedication to quality cannot be overstated. However, their enthusiasm for what they do can blind them to the real quality aspirations of the customers, managers, and supporters. I discuss these groups in Chapters 3, 4, and 7, and show how they hold two other quality viewpoints that are quite different:

- The user-based definition says that quality is fitness for use. It is the user-based definition that encourages us to validate *as well as* to verify the system. The builders need to find out "Does the specification reflect what attributes are needed to enable people do their work efficiently and effectively?" This viewpoint is important to the customers and to the supporters, the two groups most affected by the software postdelivery (see Chapter 12).

- The value-based definition is focused on things that impact on the running of the business as a whole. Software quality should always be determined by means of a decision process based on trade-offs between time, effort, and cost aspects. The builders need to find out "What are the budget constraints for this build and how does that affect what we are able to deliver?" Value for money is important for managers and anyone responsible for budgets. The ROI for the software needs to be predicted before delivery, and scope against the budget managed carefully during the SDLC. It is worth noting here that employers of software engineering graduates complain that the graduates do not have sufficient business and enterprise skills [2].

Along with acknowledging the user-based and value-based views of quality, the builders need to understand others' transcendent view of quality. The builders must take into account the fact that other people's taken for granted viewpoints may well be different from their own. One important point here is to examine the slant that builders may put on the manufacturing- and product-based quality viewpoints. Let us look at some examples. Here are some real remarks from builders, including a developer, an author, and an analyst:

- "I met the specification so there can't be a problem," said Alice Developer.
- "If you introduce a set process, I'll just have to lower my standards to meet it," said Joe Author.
- "The specification defects arise because the testers won't review our specifications," said Jenny Analyst.

These are three comments that contain a nugget of truth but which are also flawed arguments. Let us look at them more closely.

Alice Developer is correct when she says, "I met the specification so there can't be a problem." The code met the specification. Unfortunately, specifications can be out of date, or just wrong. They are written by people, so they will have mistakes and gaps in them. In the translation through the different activities in the SDLC, the specification may have been worked on by several people as it was refined and detail was added. There may have been an initial misunderstanding that was compounded over the SDLC. Additionally, the customer's requirements may have changed during the SDLC. This happens so frequently that we might almost take it as a given—the requirements will change before delivery.

Corrections and changes will be needed, so builders, including Alice Developer, need to expect that. This makes some people wary of documenting any requirements specification at all: "Why write it down if it is going to change? We don't have time to keep updating a specification!" But it is useful to write down the original specification and changes made to it. Then we have a record of what has changed and why. Additionally, written specifications can be checked for consistency, completeness, and correctness. To encourage keeping specifications up to date, I like them to be as brief as they possibly can, to encapsulate the facts and satisfy any standards or contractual requirements. There is no virtue in writing long documents for their own sake. Some agile methods [3] suggest using media that restrict the length of the documents, for example, A5 cards. Keeping a record is worthwhile. I have been in the situation with technical documentation, for example, where the structure and material have changed back and forth over time. In order to explain to the managers and customers why I was behind time against the plan and over budget, it was useful to have a record of why changes had been requested as well as how long they had taken. Before I started keeping a written record of what changes were requested, it was easy to get into arguments about why changes had been made and the amount of time it had taken to get from A to B to C and back to A again.

So change is to be expected, but do we want the builders to just make those changes? Alice Developer was working within a contract and a budget, and had done exactly what was asked within those constraints. If she had made the changes requested, she may have exceeded the budget and time constraints, just as I was doing with the technical writing. We both needed to make some improvements in our process:

- We needed to assess the technical impact of the change requested; How big was it? How risky was it? How necessary was it?
- We needed to involve other groups in our assessment: the customers, managers, supporters, and measurers all would be able to contribute to the discussion about whether the change was necessary and what its impact would be (risks, changes to budgets and estimates, effect on other work, what would not get done if this took priority).
- We needed to get agreement on the change.

It is worth remembering that the impact of a change may be much larger than the immediate obvious change. One colleague was changing a training course recently. It looked like a simple change to combine two exercises into one. In fact, combining the two exercises into one document was quite simple, but far more time needed to be spent on changing the references in the slides, contents lists, tutor's notes, printing and binding instructions, and so on. In the same way, a one- or two-line code change can lead to changes in training material, help messages, support and user documentation, installation guides, code comments, and other code modules.

"If you introduce a set process, I'll just have to lower my standards to meet it," said Joe Author, an excellent practitioner with very high standards of work. Why was the suggestion of introducing what measurers and managers saw as a quality improvement (the use of defined, documented processes) seen as a threat to quality? Many builders see the introduction of standards as either a descent to the lowest common denominator, or as the introduction of bureaucracy that will prevent them from carrying out their work. If processes are poorly designed or badly introduced, this may be the case. What can the builders do to get the processes they need? The best way is to get involved in the work of the designing and implementing processes, so that they own them. The experts who believe that introduction of standards and processes will cause them to adopt poorer methods are the very people who design improved processes and to train others in using them.

Builders need sound processes at all stages to support them in the management of change and the development of low-defect and appropriate products, and this includes use of QC processes on specifications to make them as correct and complete as possible. The cost of changes to fix defects that could have been found earlier, saving rework, is a useful fact for builders to offer to customers and managers when asking for improvement in the specification of systems. Measurers can help them with this fact gathering. We will see in Chapter 10 that there are SDLC models that provide more opportunities both for checking that specifications are correct and complete, and for adapting to change during the SDLC, and in Chapter 12 we will discuss the difference between fixing defects and making enhancements.

In saying "The specification defects arise because the testers won't review our specifications," Jenny Analyst, the builder, has misunderstood where defects arise in products, and the tester has misunderstood that part of their role is to help the builder. In fact, this was just one comment in a catalogue of woe; the builders and measurers had a complete breakdown of relationship and simply did not cooperate at all. We will return to this story in Chapter 6.

Although measurers and builders can appear to exist on different planets, one reason that they come to loggerheads is that they are so similar. They share a manufacturing-based view of quality, with its emphasis on defect removal. It can happen that the testers' glee in finding defects is matched by the developers' irritation at being caught. One way to improve this is for the testers to couch their defect reports more politely. However, as this is the builder's chapter, let us think about what the builders can do to help. I have seen a number of things that have helped build the relationship between the groups:

- Workshops and training for the builders and the measurers together, where they can discuss what reviews and testing are needed and how these should be done.

- Clear roles and goals for reviews, as we discuss in Chapters 8–12, so that everyone understands what needs to be reviewed and why. The measurers and builders share responsibility for setting the goals and making the plans for the reviews.

- Review of the measurers' plans, test designs, and reports by the builders, thus allowing a reciprocal arrangement.

- Builders welcoming defect reports on their products (sometimes this might be through gritted teeth, as we all know when our own work is reviewed). Each identified defect is a chance to improve something—this product by correcting, future products and processes by introducing defect prevention methods, and the defect reporting process itself.

Communication is key, as always. In a recent software testing course, the group was an equal mix of developers and testers who worked together. I asked the developers and the testers two questions each:

- What information did the developers need when the testers sent them a defect report?

- What information did the testers send with a defect report?

5.3 Quality viewpoint

- What information did the developers return with a completed defect report?
- What information did the testers need when a completed defect report was returned?

When we put the results up on the flip chart, there was almost no relationship between the information supplied and that actually required. As soon as the two groups had a chance to reflect on what was happening, they were able to see how to improve the defect resolution cycle. The important information that each group needed was *not* obvious or intuitive to the other group. The developers needed to explain to the testers what information they required in the defect reports. The testers needed to explain to the developers what information they needed when a defect report was returned to them for retest.

In Table 5.1, we see how an example builder, a business analyst, might consider other quality viewpoints. We will look at communication between groups in Section 5.5; here, we are considering what questions about

Table 5.1 Analyst Considering Other Viewpoints for Quality Impacts

Group and Quality View	Possible Routes in	Example Questions
Customer User-based quality view	Find out the importance of *fit for purpose* on particular features, functions and attributes	What are the goals for the product; what do you want to achieve? What will be the impact on your work if this goes wrong? If it is not available, can you work without it? How much extra time would that take?
		Are there alternative ways you could achieve the same results?
Supporter User- and product-based quality view	Find out the importance for operability and *fit for purpose* of important attributes	What will be the impact on your work if this goes wrong?
		If this attribute is not available, can you work without it? How much extra time would that take?
		What is the minimum level of (reliability/security/and so forth) that is acceptable?
		If we delivered X, would that make your life easier or more difficult? What information do you need to be able to support the products? What service-level agreements do we need to consider/support?
Other builders Product and manufacturing quality view	Find out which attributes are technically possible	What information do you need in the specification in order to build the (code/training/support documentation/user guide/installation guide)
		How quickly do you need that?
		Can you build to an early draft expecting changes?
		Which attributes/technical areas will pose particular problems?
Measurers Manufacturing quality view	Find out what will make the product measurable and, hence, testable	What information do you need from me in order to review the document/test the software/audit the process?
		Which functional/nonfunctional areas have given rise to most problems for testing and where have you identified defect hot spots?
Manager Value-based quality view	Identify the *cost* of building and changing the specifications and the *cost* of repair/rework	The cost to the customer and supporter of *not* making the change is X, and the cost of making the change is Y. The cost impact if we make the change and it goes wrong is Z. Can we afford to make the change? Can we afford to not make the change?

quality we might consider in order to understand other people's assumptions about quality as a means of improving understanding.

Particular people in the builder group may have other quality views. In my experience, trainers and technical authors may be closer to the customers in their view of quality than the developers and business analysts. More experienced developers can often be very close in quality view to both the supporters and measurers in their organization.

5.4 Quality framework using the EFQM Excellence Model

5.4.1 The EFQM Excellence Model and the builders

There are a number of well-accepted process frameworks that specifically address the work of many of the roles within the builder group and how those roles interact. Within a particular organization or team, requirements gathering, business analysis, systems analysis, design, and coding work may be carried out by different people, with the work being passed from one person to another; or one person may undertake several or all of the roles. We will look at several generic SDLC models and a tailored model with roles in Chapter 10. In this chapter, I want to set the builders in a framework based on the EFQM Excellence Model [4].

As we saw in Chapter 1, there are a number of frameworks for software work, including the SEI's CMM® family [5], and means of implementing its requirements, such as TSP [6] and PSP [7]. Additionally standards bodies such as IEEE [8] and BSI [9] provide software engineering frameworks and standards. The IT Infrastructure Library (ITIL) has a framework for application management [1], which includes not just application development but also management and optimization of the application in use. This sets application management within an EFQM framework, and also discusses the similar Baldrige framework used in the United States. Other builders also have standards and process frameworks; for example, there are style guides for authors, such as *The Chicago Manual of Style* by the University of Chicago Press [10].

Each organization needs to draw from these models and frameworks to develop processes and standards in a framework appropriate for the type of work, the risks, the experience levels, and the customer expectations of process. For some customers, particular standards, methods or techniques are required, as discussed by Reid in [11]. Some customers, perhaps requiring an engineering approach to control risk, may demand achievement of a particular CMM® level with particular associated processes. Other customers may face risks in achieving time to market; there may be pressure for a fast-track process, which might lead to a different set of processes. The builder's quality framework must match to the customer's quality framework so that the delivered products are not underengineered and unfit for purpose, nor overengineered and too expensive.

The builders are suppliers, and any supplier's ability to recognize and adapt to their customer's quality framework is a critical success factor in the effectiveness of their relationship. The framework for the customer translates into departmental goals and, finally, into the personal objectives and targets for an individual system user, but it also translates into a complementary subset of the supplier's goals, and, hence, into personal objectives and targets for all the builders. This quality framework will drive what the customer needs from the software.

In Chapter 1, we looked at the EFQM Excellence Model and how it is divided into nine parts: five enabling criteria and four criteria for measuring results. In Section 5.4.2, we will look at how the EFQM Excellence Model enablers could be interpreted for builders, and in Section 5.4.3 we will look at builder results. Remember that this model is based on the fundamental concepts of excellence we discussed in Chapter 1 and that equivalent models such as the Baldrige model are available.

5.4.2 EFQM Excellence Model enablers for builders

5.4.2.1 Leadership

We saw in Chapter 2 that the Motivation Survey carried out by Warden and Nicholson [12] showed dissatisfaction between groups. One interesting finding is that although technical experts, for example developers, want to organize their own work, they often feel isolated because they lack feedback from their managers; they lack leadership. In the absence of leadership from their managers, people will either become demotivated, or they will look within their peer group for a leader. I have observed situations in development teams and in authoring teams where the actual line manager is not the natural leader of the team and may even be bypassed. I remember one excellent developer, Dave Tech-Expert, who disliked his manager for being weak both as a person and technically "He doesn't understand my work and he asks stupid questions, but he never listens and he never supports me in meetings," said Dave. Over the years, Dave built a strong relationship with a specific customer team, based on mutual respect and understanding of the technical difficulties in that customer area. The result was that, regardless of agreed-upon project plans, both Dave and the customer bypassed the manager to organize the work that actually happened in that area. The manager continued to report against the project plan, not realizing it was irrelevant; Dave had simply agreed to anything that would make his manager be quiet and go away. A vicious circle was in place, with each action by the manager, the customer, and Dave compounding the mutual suspicion (Figure 5.1).

Warden and Nicholson [12] found that the builders group needed leadership, but that their leaders had to have some technical expertise and understanding, so that the builders knew that they could trust the leader to make intelligent decisions. If they do not trust their managers, they will adopt unofficial leaders, sometimes known as *influence leaders*.

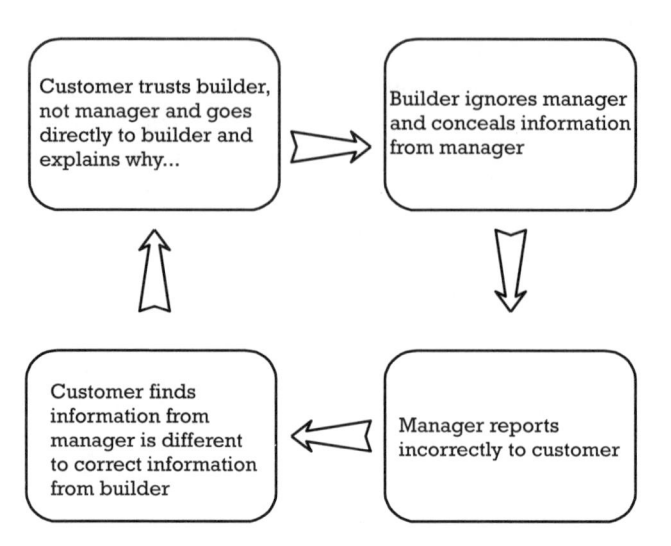

Figure 5.1 Vicious circle of poor and undermined leadership. (*After:* [12].)

5.4.2.2 Policy and Strategy

Builders need clearly defined policies and strategies, which set down what is expected of them and provide direction. We saw in Chapter 4 that managers set policy and strategy based on the higher-level policy and strategy for the organization. The builders need policies and strategies that not only state *what* must be done but also *why* the policy and strategy has been set. We saw in Section 5.4.2.1 that builders will work autonomously and may bypass anything they see as unnecessary or obstructive; generally, we have here a group of intelligent, well-educated, independently minded folk. It is best to set the policy and strategy after consulting with these experts.

Policies will be needed to cover the basic rules for approaching build activities, including rules for tailoring processes. Builders are often asked for fast responses (remember our trainer in Section 5.1?), whether to deal with an emergency, a change in circumstances, or do something that we forgot in our earlier planning. This means that if we have a policy and strategy that describes a normal set of build activities, we should also put together a policy and strategy for deciding when and how to provide a fast-track service, and how to decide how the risks of choosing the fast track weigh against the risks of using the normal approach. Of course, this might be a policy that says "we never tailor the processes," but that is unlikely to be successful. We will see in Chapter 10 an example of tailoring the SDLC. In this case, the policy might state: "A tailored SDLC with reduced steps may be used if the risk of failure has an impact of less than X," and the strategy would show how to tailor the life cycle based on experience, knowledge, clarity of problem definition, speed of response, and risk of failure.

Specialist builders should put together their own framework, with the agreement of the other groups and based on the appropriate practices and published standards, such as those described in the BSI SSQF framework [9] and in CMM® [5].

5.4.2.3 People

We have already noted in Sections 5.4.2.1 and 5.4.2.2 some of the characteristics of builders. This group faces the major challenge of using their creativity and skills to realize the products and services, and their work is measured and judged by the other groups.

The Motivation Survey [12] found that many IT staff want work that has a high motivating potential score, that is, it scores highly for things like the variety of skills required, autonomy of work, significance of the task to the organization, and the chance to complete a task from beginning to end and see the outcome. The survey also found that the range of work went from roles that were excessively understimulating to work that was more complex than it was possible to carry out. The latter was exacerbated by the tendency of IT people to automate parts of their tasks that are repetitive and boring, thus leaving them with only the complex parts. They are actually making their jobs harder.

Builders need a mix of skills, and these would generally be provided within a team rather than by a single individual. Their education, training, and work experiences will of course include all the technical skills and understanding of the methods, techniques, and tools for their tasks. It is worth considering the communication and team analysis techniques, for example, Belbin team roles and the MBTI analysis, discussed in Sections A.1 and A.2, as well as technical skills, when putting together a team. Builders' education, training, and work experiences should also include an understanding of:

- The measurement techniques they will need to apply to their own work and to other people's work. Not only do builders carry out QC activities such as reviews and testing, in which they will need training, but, in my experience, they also make excellent QA reviewers and auditors if trained in the techniques. I noted before that builders respect technical excellence, so having the technical experts carry out process and product reviews across projects spreads knowledge and increases the probability that the QA and QC processes will be accepted as useful.

- The management skills they require for control of their own time and work within a team. This is the focus of the TSP [6] and PSP [7], which emphasize the planning, control, and reporting required by individual software engineers and by teams.

- The interpersonal skills (sometimes called soft skills) to improve their communication with all the groups, including the builders themselves. Kent Beck [3] describes five values without which XP (eXtreme Programming) will not work. I think they are values without which any human endeavor will not work: good communication between people; simplicity in choice of action; concrete feedback to aid communication and simplicity; courage to confront and fix problems, if necessary by discarding work and starting again; and, finally, what Beck describes as the *deeper value* of respect for others.

- Their customer's goals and strategy in order that they focus their technical, measurement, management, and interpersonal skills toward solving the organization's real problems. This is increasingly important. For example misalignment of IT to the organizations' goals is cited in the McCartney report [13] as a reason for frequent IT project failures. I recently asked a number of IT customers in different organizations what they wanted from IT people. Although some of the responses asked for greater engineering or technical skills, others wanted greater business awareness. One customer said, "Perhaps one danger I perceive in the competency-aligned improvement model (which is generally strong) is that the focus may be 'professional' rather than 'entrepreneurial.' By that I mean more mature business/systems analysis is seen as an end in itself, rather than a means to doing things faster, smarter, and cheaper and making more money for us all."

5.4.2.4 Partnerships and Resources

As we saw in Chapter 1, partnerships cover people outside our team, our project, or our organization with whom we need to exchange information or cooperate with in some way. Resources are the things like IT environments, information, and equipment that we need to carry out our work.

Builders have partnerships with all the other groups and within the builder group, both to exchange information and because some work may be done by others and passed between individuals. They may also have partnerships with builders in other organizations. Some examples of typical partnerships might include:

- Between groups: with the customers and supporters to define the problem to be resolved and share information about possible solutions, risks, and the fit-for-purpose, user-based quality view;
- Between groups: with the measurers to define quality measures for products, carry out QA and QC processes to improve products and processes, and to resolve defects;
- Between groups: with the managers to understand constraints on time, budget, and resources, and the impact these may have on technical risk;
- Within the builders group: developers with designers and analysts to share information and review products concerned with building code;
- Within the builders group: software engineers with training designers and authors to share information and review products concerned with building supporting material such as training courses and user guides;

- Outside the SDLC, with builders and supporters for other projects to negotiate sharing of scarce resources such as environments and tools;
- Outside the organization, with third-party suppliers that the organization has selected to outsource some of the IT work.

5.4.2.5 Processes

As we saw in Section 5.4.1, there are a number of published frameworks for builders' work, and these tend to be biased toward process definition rather than to the other enablers that we looked at in Sections 5.4.2.1 to 5.4.2.4 above. The difficulty that software engineers in particular have is not finding a process definition, but in finding the right process definition for their circumstances. I am not going to describe the candidate processes here; each organization needs to select from those available and will undoubtedly want to adapt the chosen model to their own circumstances. I just want to note that we need to consider a number of factors in choosing a process. These include:

- *Builders' buy-in:* Do the builders understand the proposed process? Do they need training, support, and mentoring? Will the process bring them benefits and do they understand those benefits? If there are parts of the process that make life more difficult for the builders, is there a rational reason for them in terms of benefits to the organization as a whole?
- *Other groups' buy-in:* Do the other groups understand the process? How much are they involved in the process? Do they need training, support, and mentoring? Will the process bring them benefits and do they understand those benefits? If there are parts of the process that make life more difficult for them is there a rational reason for them in terms of benefits to the organization as a whole?
- *Flexibility and appropriateness of the processes:* If the organization has many types and sizes of project, is it clear and easy to tailor the processes? Has paperwork and bureaucracy been minimized? Is there enough documentation and not too much? Is there sufficient control to minimize technical risk and human error, balanced against the process not being excessively expensive to run? Is it easy to change and update the process? Does it meet any external process requirements? Is it easy to identify entry and exit criteria at each step? Are communication points where information is shared identified? Are responsibilities and authorities identified? Does the process allow for changes in the customer and supporter requirements, and for changes caused by rectifying mistakes?

The choice of process needs to balance the needs of different groups—part of the reason for having an agreed-on process is to give assurance to all the stakeholders that they can trust that the right things are being done. The different quality views of groups means that their expectations of what *should* be laid down in a process will vary. For example, when the builders design their processes, they will need buy-in from all the groups, by showing how the process will support them:

- Customers need the process to help them get what they need to solve their continuously changing problems and aspirations, and to know how the process will meet the demands of the organization, its customers, and society as a whole—all part of "fit-for-purpose," user-based quality.
- Managers need the process to support them in controlling budgets for cost, time, and resources within and across projects, to see how it will help them deal with change and offset technical against financial risks, and for it to support improvements to future planning, estimation, and control—all part of financial/corporate, value-based quality.
- Supporters need the process to include their involvement both in setting requirements and acceptance criteria for product attributes. They need assurance that the process will result in software that can be supported within the IT infrastructure and the IT service and application management standards—all part of "fit-for-purpose," user- and product-based quality.
- Measurers need the process to acknowledge their focus on defect identification, removal and prevention. They need to agree on how measurement processes (QA audits, QC reviews, and testing) are included in the process—for example, that they take place early enough for them to be effective and efficient—and mutual agreement on what information needs to be communicated and when, including information about change.
- Builders need to know that their tasks are included in the process, with links to their own processes early enough for them to complete their products, and with mutual agreement on what information needs to be communicated and when, including information about change.

5.4.3 EFQM Excellence Model results for the builders

5.4.3.1 Customer Results

Customer results are the measure of the effect we have on our customers. Who are the builders' customers? In fact, as well as the customers for the software itself, all the groups are customers of the builders. If we look at what the EFQM Excellence Model [4] refers to as customer perception results and customer performance indicators, we see that perception results are measured externally; we ask people outside our group for their views of us. Customer performance indicators measure what actually happens to our group; whether we get repeat business from a customer, for example. Both measures are needed so that we see the difference between a customer's reported perception: "We think you are doing a great job," and whether the customer actually *invites the builder back* for future projects. Examples of the type of results that could be measured are in Table 5.2.

5.4.3.2 People Results

In this case, the People Results measure what the builders think about themselves. As with the Customer Results, we measure perception and performance.

We have already seen that this group has quite specific motivational needs [12]. They need a stimulating environment and yet need support and leadership so that they are not alienated.

We will discuss SDLC models in Chapter 10, but I want to note here that some of the models encourage projects with team members involved throughout the SDLC and with frequent feedback loops, whereas others take a more production-line approach. I remember that in one organization, the business analysts would be involved in the first two to six weeks of a project to gather requirements, and after that would move on to their next project. They never saw the outcome of the projects. One person remarked to me, "I don't even know if any code is built as a result of my work, let alone whether it is delivered and worked. I don't know if I solve people's problems." This is the essence of the alienating production line—"People frustrated by work that goes nowhere and an increasingly intrusive system of management that means they have less and less control over what they do" [14]. SDLC models that encourage involvement throughout the SDLC, allow interaction and feedback between the groups, and allow the teams to make decisions and to control their own work, will provide a better working environment for builders. According to Tom Gilb (at a seminar on Evolutionary Delivery in London in September 2003), the frequent-feedback loop is particularly important in improving individual and group motivation. It seems reasonable to suppose that there may be improvements in individual's motivation using models such as XP, which encourage such feedback

Table 5.2 Customer Results—What the Other Groups Think of Builders

	Example of Possible Measures
Perceptions (external to the group), surveys, interviews, compliments, and complaints	Have the builders got a good image?
	Do other groups report that they find the builders easy to deal with (for example, helpful, flexible, honest, and proactive)?
	Are the builders seen as reliable, providing good value, providing a good service?
Performance indicators—measurement of outcomes	Do we get asked back for additional projects?
	Are people proactive in coming to us for help?
	Are our products usually accepted and used over a reasonable life span?
	Do other groups complain about our work?

loops, compared with the waterfall model, which has a production-line approach.

We mentioned in Section 5.4.2.3 that IT staff require stimulating work. One colleague described to me what happened when his teammates got bored; they had a competition to see who could use the most programming constructs in their programs, not because they were needed, but just to try them out. The result was programs that functionally did what they were supposed to do, but did it in a very convoluted way. I am glad I am not maintaining those programs! A measurable result of the boredom of those people was the number of lines of unnecessary code added for fun. Examples of the type of results that could be measured are shown in Table 5.3.

5.4.3.3 Society Results

For the EFQM Excellence Model, society means society at large, and although we might want to measure this, we could interpret "society" for a team as only including their organization. Again, we consider perception and performance indicators. Examples of the type of results that could be measured are shown in Table 5.4.

Table 5.3 People Results—What the Builders Think of Themselves

	Example of Possible Measures
Perceptions—"external" measurement of the group viewpoints by the organization asking for opinion through surveys, interviews, compliments, and complaints	Has a motivational study provided positive feedback? Are builders satisfied with their career paths, rewards?
Performance indicators—"internal" to builders group. Measurement of people's viewpoints by their actual behavior/attributes	Does the builders group match up to the required qualifications and competencies? For example, do they have appropriate BCS qualifications [15]
	What are absenteeism and sickness levels compared with other groups? Are trainers showing a different absence pattern to developers?
	What is the level of staff turnover compared with other groups and do people want to be recruited into this group? For example, if we advertise a business analysis course internally, is it over- or undersubscribed?

Table 5.4 Society Results—How the Builders Relate to Society

	Example of Possible Measures
Perceptions—external to the group—surveys, interviews, compliments, and complaints	Are the builders seen by the organization and wider society as acting ethically?
	Do the auditors and testers check that the systems act properly with regard to health risks, safety, hazards, and the environment?
Performance indicators—internal to builders group	Has the group won any accolades, for example, for paper- and energy-saving initiatives, in line with corporate initiatives?
	Has the group been recognized for its efforts to reduce security risks internally and externally, including customer data confidentiality, prevention of spam and virus attacks, and IT governance provisions?

5.4.3.4 Key Performance Results

The EFQM Excellence Model divides key performance measures into two areas: financial and nonfinancial measures. Some examples are shown in Table 5.5. It is important to reflect on *why* the organization needs an IT group; unless software is itself the revenue-earning product of the organization, the only reason for the software is to service the needs of the organization, allowing its customers and users to carry out their work more easily. For a business, this will mean that the key performance results for IT and, hence, the builders, must reflect the commercial drivers for the organization. For a nonprofit organization, again, the builders must support the organization's goals, increasing the efficiency and effectiveness of the services and products provided.

5.5 Communication between the builders and other groups

We will see in Chapters 8 to 12 that builders are involved in the whole life span of a piece of software, from its conception, through the software development life cycle (SDLC), during delivery, and postdelivery until decommissioning.

Builders have a large responsibility in communication to and from the other groups. They need to understand what is required, and they need to communicate back what is possible and what has been achieved. A problem with this is that IT people may have quite different personality types and communication styles than their customers [16–18]. It appears that a larger proportion of IT people tend to be introverts, working by intuition, thinking, and judgment skills. If across the general population and, therefore, among the builder's customers there is a bias toward extroverted behavior and working more by perception or emotional ways of thinking, we can see that there will be a clash of communication styles. I have seen this particularly where sales, marketing, or customer service staff need to work with IT. If Phil Marketing-Mann is emoting and waving his arms around, Dave Tech-Expert may just ignore him and, as he has brought his laptop into the meeting, just get on with some other work. One comment in [18] is that whereas many IT people prefer written communication, their customers may prefer

Table 5.5 Key Performance Results—Financial and Corporate

	Example of Possible Measures
Financial	What is the return on investment (ROI) for the software we have delivered this year (cost of software/money saved/number of new customers/market share gained)?
Nonfinancial	Number of projects/customers who request our team to carry out IT-related work, and the size of these projects
	Cycle times for responding to customer requests
	Innovation by the builders (e.g., new technology to support time to market with new products)

face-to-face communication. This alone can give rise to misunderstanding and resentment. This is an important factor in the success of the builders:

> ... [P]otential weaknesses for the organization lie in the lack of feeling and perception. These can become key issues if you need more flexibility and a greater focus on the customer for future success. A culture biased toward thinking and judgment is in danger of neglecting how the customer feels about the service he or she is getting, which can be an important factor in the decision to buy. [18]

Of course, in some builder–customer relationships the preferences may be reversed. What is important is that the communication preferences in a particular situation are understood. There is more about personality types and communication in Chapters 8 to 12 and Appendix A. In Figure 5.2, I have shown the communications between builders and the other groups. Builders have information that others need (Table 5.6) and they also need information from other people in order to understand the constraints on delivering their wish list. Table 5.7 lists the information that builders need from the other groups.

Remember, it is not just the content but also the manner of the communication that is important. All the groups need to understand that they will favor different communication styles, and that individuals within the groups may or may not fall into the usual pattern for the group; we must beware of pigeonholing people. The lesson is that each builder needs to understand their own favored communication style and to consider the favored communication styles of other people within their own and other groups. If you are interested in discovering your own preferred style, you may wish to look at the Myers-Briggs Type Indicator (MBTI) and take an MBTI quick test (see [17]).

5.6 Summary of the group

Builders are essential to the quality and success of software and systems, and their technical skills are needed throughout the life of software. However, builders must communicate well with each other and the other groups if they are to be effective. This means considering how they demonstrate

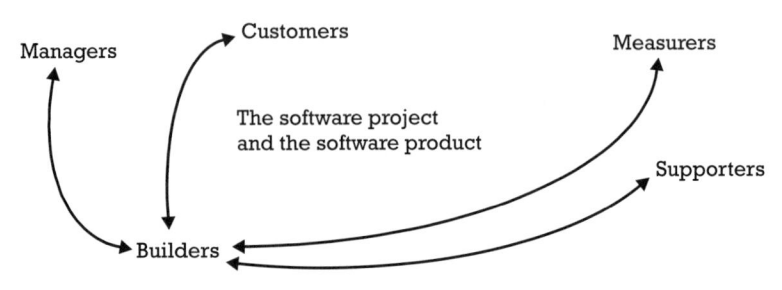

Figure 5.2 Communication between groups.

5.6 Summary of the group

Table 5.6 Information That Builders Have That Others Need

Before the SDLC starts and updated throughout the SDLC	Technical constraints
	Technical innovations
	Technical risks
During the SDLC	Results of QC done by the builders themselves
	Technical risks and areas on which to focus QA and QC work
	List of known problems when products are delivered to QC or go live
	Progress, problems, changes to risks, changes to constraints
At delivery	List of known problems
	List of incomplete products
	Delivery and installation requirements
Postdelivery	Evaluation comments
	Improvement ideas

Table 5.7 Information That Builders Need from Others

Customers	Business constraints
	Business risks
	Business requirements
	Evaluation of quality of system when it is in use
Managers	Financial, time, and resource constraints
	Progress toward goal
	Changes to goals and constraints
Other builders	Progress with products (different builders will be responsible for different products: specifications, designs, code, training material, and so on)
	Changes to products
Supporters	Technical constraints for live system
	Acceptance criteria
	Evaluation of quality of system when it is in use
Measurers	Acceptance criteria passed
	Defects and nonconformances identified

that they provide results and assurance for other groups, understanding other's quality views and communication styles, and explaining their own quality view and preferred communication style in a way that is understandable to the rest of the team. People with other communication styles and preferences, within and outside the builders group, should also have consideration for the builders' preferences as individuals. This will help to ensure that that the good communication that is essential for the builders' success is maintained.

References

[1] IT Infrastructure Library, *Best Practice for Application Management*, London, England: Office of Government Commerce, 2002.

[2] Holcombe, M., and M. Gheorgha, "Enterprise Skills in the Curriculum," *Ingenia*, Vol. 15, February/March 2003, pp. 56–61.

[3] Beck, K., *Extreme Programming Explained*, Reading, MA: Addison-Wesley, 2001.

[4] European Foundation for Quality Management, "EFQM Excellence Model," http://www.efqm.org, August 2003.

[5] Software Engineering Institute, "Capability Maturity Model®," http://www.sei.cmu.edu, July 2003.

[6] Humphrey, W., *Introduction to the Team Software Process*, Reading, MA: SEI, 2000.

[7] Humphrey, W., *Introduction to the Personal Software Process*, Reading, MA: SEI, 1997.

[8] IEEE standards; see Web site http://standards.ieee.org/.

[9] British Standards Institute, *PD0026:2003, Software and Systems Quality Framework—A Guide to the Use of ISO/IEC and Other Standards for Understanding Quality in Software and Systems*, London, England: British Standards Institute, May 2003.

[10] The University of Chicago Press, *The Chicago Manual of Style*, 15th ed., Chicago, IL: The University of Chicago Press, 2003.

[11] Reid, S. C, "Software Testing Standards—Do They Know What They Are Talking About?" http://www.testingstandards.co.uk/publications.htm, August 2003.

[12] Warden, R., and I. Nicholson, *The MIP Report, Volume 2: 1996 Motivational Survey of IT Staff*, 2nd ed., Bredon, England: Software Futures Ltd., 1996.

[13] Cabinet Office, *Successful IT: Modernising Government in Action*, London, England: HMSO, 2000.

[14] Smith, P., "Alien Resurrection," http://www.chartist.org.uk/articles/econsoc/jul03smith.htm, October 2003.

[15] British Computer Society Qualifications, http://www1.bcs.org.uk/link.asp?sectionID=574, September 2003.

[16] Kroeger, O., J. M. Thuesen, and H. Rutledge, *Type Talk at Work: How the 16 Personality Types Determine Your Success on the Job*, New York: Bantam Doubleday Dell, 2002.

[17] Team Technology Web site, "Working Out Your Myers Briggs Type," http://www.teamtechnology.co.uk/tt/t-articl/mb-simpl.htm, October 2003.

[18] Team Technology Web site, "The Mother of Strategic Systems Issues: Personality," http://www.teamtechnology.co.uk/tt/t-articl/news1.htm, October 2003.

Selected bibliography

Adair, J., *Effective Teambuilding*, London, England: Pan Books, 2003.

Adair, J., *Effective Time Management*, London, England: Pan Books, 2003.

Brooks, F. P., *The Mythical Man Month*, Reading, MA: Addison-Wesley, 1995.

Caputo, K., *CMM® Implementation Guide: Choreographing Software Process Improvement*, Reading, MA: Addison-Wesley, 1998.

5.6 Summary of the group

Clarkson, M., *Developing IT Staff*, London, England: Springer Practitioner Series, 2001.

Crosby, P. B., *Quality Is Free*, New York: McGraw-Hill, 1979.

Detiénne, F., *Software Design—Cognitive Aspects*, New York: Springer-Verlag, 2001.

Fowler, M., and K. Scott, *UML Distilled*, Reading, MA: Addison-Wesley, 1997.

Gershuny, J., *After Industrial Society*, New York: Macmillan Press, 1978.

Kruchten, P., *The Rational Unified Process*, Reading, MA: Addison-Wesley, 1999.

Nance, R. E., and J. D. Arthur, *Managing Software Quality*, New York: Springer-Verlag, 2002.

Parker, S. R., et al., *The Sociology of Industry*, London, England: George, Allen and Unwin, 1978.

Schein, E., *Organizational Culture and Leadership*, San Francisco, CA: Jossey-Bass, 1997.

Smith, J., *How to Be a Better Time Manager*, London, England: Kogan Page, 1997.

CHAPTER 6

Contents

6.1 Introducing the measurers

6.2 Who could be in this group?

6.3 Quality viewpoint

6.4 Quality framework using the EFQM Excellence Model

6.5 Communication between the measurers and other groups

6.6 Summary of the group

Roles and Quality: Measurers

In this chapter I shall:

- Introduce the members of the measurers group, their roles, and activities;
- Introduce their quality viewpoint;
- Provide a framework for the measurers' activities within the EFQM Excellence Model;
- Identify information flows between the measurers and the other groups.

I'm going to buy a magic wand, and then when the development manager says to me, "We've finished the build, now can you do the quality stuff," I can just wave the wand and make it happen.

—Quality assurance manager complaining about the way quality activities are regarded in projects

6.1 Introducing the measurers

6.1.1 Why do we need QA and QC?

Software projects generally include some activities such as testing, to check the software before it is released for live use, and auditing, to check that appropriate processes are followed during the project. We need to do this because humans make mistakes. This includes making poor decisions and building things with faults in them. Once we have made a mistake, it is often difficult for us to find it, so we ask someone else to check what we have done. A software project is generally quite complex, with many decisions to be made and many products leading to the final delivered software. This means that there are lots of opportunities for people to get things wrong. They may misunderstand each other, or make wrong assumptions, or simply slip up in what they are doing.

During the software-development life cycle (SDLC), testing and other quality activities are used to identify and prevent mistakes. So why was our quality assurance manager frustrated? The problem was that the development manager believed that the QA and QC activities introduced quality into the products and, therefore, that the QA manager was responsible for the quality. As we saw in Chapter 1, quality assurance activities (QA) are used for checking processes, and quality control (QC) for checking products. The output from QA and QC activities is a set of measures of quality. In fact, QA and QC activities do *not* change the quality of anything; all they do is to provide information about the quality of the processes and of deliverables from those processes, in order that the processes and products can be changed.

6.1.2 Just measurers or also improvers of quality?

Someone recently commented to me that "The test group does improve the quality by finding faults (early) in the requirements and later in the design and code. I do not think we spend up to half of the development budget just to measure quality," so let us consider that point.

I would say that the test group has *contributed* to the quality of the delivered product by identifying faults, and the earlier they find the faults, the greater the value of their contribution, because of the money and time saved. But the testers have not *changed* the quality of the deliverable; the deliverable does not change when the tests are run or the results analyzed.

The tests have provided information about the quality, that is, the identification of a number of faults and the areas of the product that meet their acceptance criteria. If the products are changed or if a suitable workaround to the defect can be provided, the tests have contributed to reducing failures during use.

This is true also for other forms of QC, for example, document review. The process of the review itself gathers information about the quality of the product under review, but does not in itself change it. However, the document reviewers contribute to the quality of the document by suggesting improvements and by identifying defects.

As a result of the testers' or reviewers' measurements, the team as a whole (customers, managers, builders, supporters and measurers) can make a decision about how to deal with the faults; they may be removed, or worked around, or ignored. That decision will be driven by the user-based quality view (is it fit for purpose?), the value-based quality view (will the cost of fixing it be less than the cost of leaving it?), and the transcendent quality view (do we like it?), as well as the manufacturing-based quality view (are there defects in the product?), and product-based quality view (does the product have the agreed attributes?).

We spend a large part of the budget on testing and other QC activities to understand all these quality views; we need information about the number of defects in the product to give us a view of its manufacturing- and

6.1 Introducing the measurers

product-based quality, so that we can form what will be a decision based on all the quality views.

Similarly, those measurers involved in looking at processes, for example, auditors, carry out QA tasks that provide information about processes, and a decision is then made about whether to enforce or change those processes. QA activities measure both the appropriateness of the chosen process and how well the process is adhered to. An audit or process review does not, in itself, change the processes; it simply comments on them. Auditors will also measure how closely a process adheres to standards and to legislative or regulatory demands. We hope that by choosing processes wisely and adhering to them, we will prevent people from making mistakes, and, hence, prevent them from breaking mandatory requirements or building defects into products.

Preventing defects in the products reduces the places where failure can occur when a product is used, and the process improvement aspect of QA is an important one. However, the people in this group, *while in this group*, can only observe, measure and recommend improvements in the process. It is the people who actually carry out the work who implement the process improvements, thus preventing defects.

This is why, instead of calling this group the testers, or the QA group, or the QC group, I have chosen to describe them as the measurers. This is to emphasize that their contribution is to provide information for all the groups by measuring the quality of the software, other products, the processes. The measurers support decision making and quality improvement.

These measures may be negative; for example, the number of defects in a product, or the number of times a process was not followed correctly. Additionally, we might want positive measures; for example, the number of requirements successfully delivered or the number of acceptance criteria passed. In Sections 6.1.3 and 6.1.4, I will enlarge on two aspects of QA and QC that do seem to directly affect improvement.

6.1.3 Defect prevention

QC activities need to be carefully timed. We will see in Chapters 9 to 12 how QA and QC activities are used appropriately at each stage in the life of a software system. Before we even start the software-development life cycle (SDLC) we need to decide whether we need an SDLC at all. Our biggest mistake can be to do the wrong project or to build something we just did not need.

We will see in Chapter 9 all the activities we need to do before we start an SDLC and that measurers, whether QA or QC specialists, are vital to this part of the process. Carrying out QA and QC on the processes and deliverables at this stage, for example, on the contract for the project, helps us start the right SDLC, which prevents us from making mistakes later on. The earlier QA and QC are carried out, the earlier defects are removed. These early defects tend to propagate through later deliverables; in other words, a mistake in the outline of the project aims and objectives, or an omission in the delivery list on the outline plan could lead to many mistakes in the project itself (Figure 6.1). In this figure, I illustrate two paths to problems; in path one, we simply do the wrong project; this one massive mistake leads to all the project activities and products being defective—a costly misunderstanding. In path two, although we are working on the right project, we make some mistakes in defining the requirements, which escalate through the SDLC.

For example, we need a periodic report from the system—(the period may vary)—but it is documented as monthly because that is given as an example during a meeting. This affects a number of design choices. The report is designed to deliver the previous month's data at the month end. The system archive and clear-down is designed to match the reporting cycle,

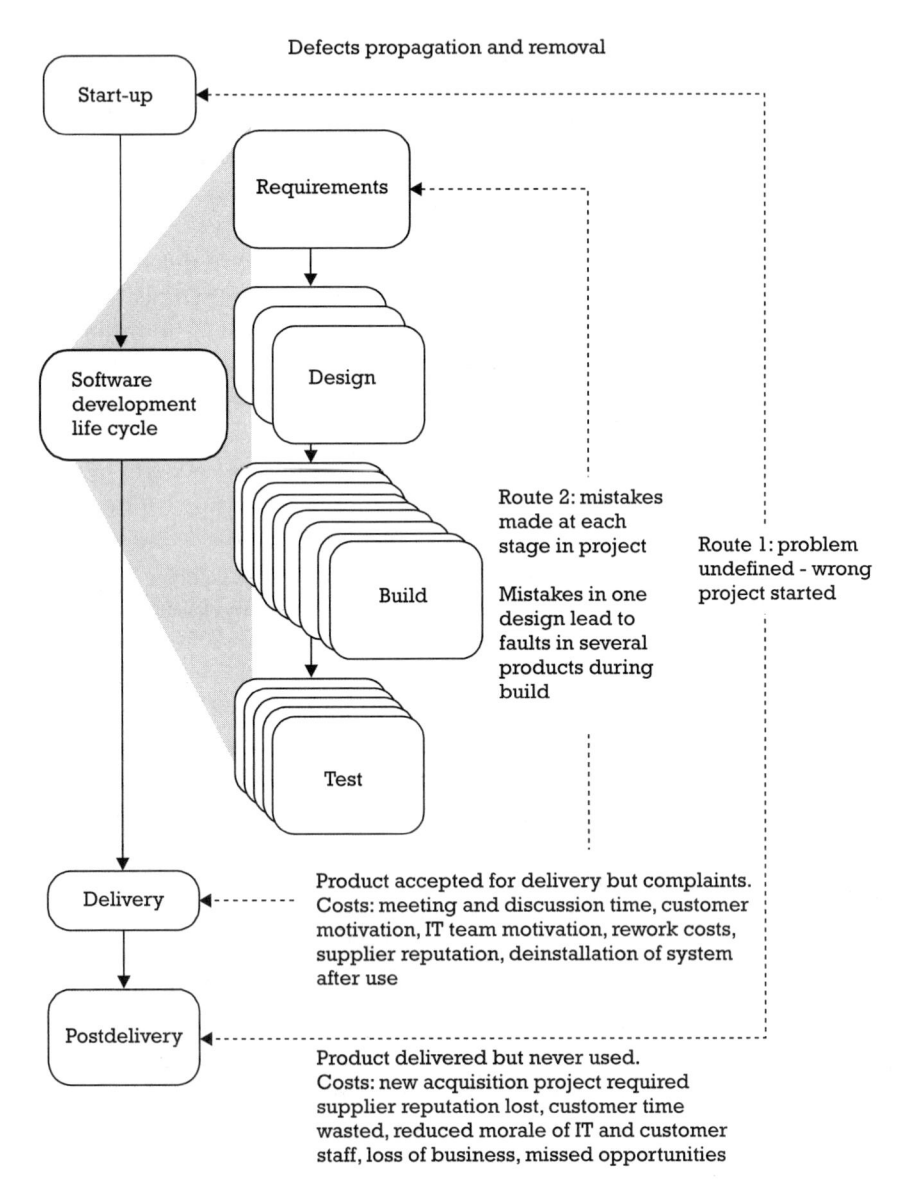

Figure 6.1 Defects propagation and removal.

so that the previous month's data is archived following the report; only 31 table lines are allowed on the current-month data collection fields. The designs affect nine programs, so each of them is wrong. Early tests are based on the requirements and design specifications, so they report no problems, but the user-acceptance test raises defects in all the programs. The IT team do not agree that they are defects, because the software meets specification. The software is accepted for delivery after much argument, but there are complaints after the first month that the reports can only be done at month end, and that data is autoarchived following the report so it cannot be used again. This is fixed, but when one user tries to report after three months, which is their preferred cycle, the data table cannot hold all the data because it is only 31 lines long. The resulting costs include meeting and discussion time, customer motivation, IT team motivation, rework costs, supplier reputation, maintenance to the system, and a recurrence of problems once the "fix" is in place.

Errors made in defining the requirements for the software solution can be found early on in the SDLC, by checking the requirements for defects and omissions immediately after the requirements have been gathered. Removing defects in the requirements prevents them from being propagated into later activities and deliverables such as design and build. We will see in Chapter 10 how different SDLC models encourage QA and QC to be carried out at different times, with a greater or lesser emphasis on defect prevention and defect removal.

6.1.4 The Hawthorne effect

One problem with understanding whether our quality measurements cause improvement or not is the Hawthorne effect. Named after the Hawthorne works of the Western Electric Company in Chicago, where the phenomenon was first observed, it indicates that people change behavior if they know they are being observed, or if they know that a process change is supposed to improve something. One definition of the Hawthorne effect is:

> An experimental effect in the direction expected but not for the reason expected; that is, a significant positive effect that turns out to have no causal basis in the theoretical motivation for the intervention, but is apparently due to the effect on the participants of knowing themselves to be studied in connection with the outcomes measured. [1]

This means that the very act of carrying out QA or QC may change the quality of the product or adherence to the process because people know they are being observed. This change can be positive or negative, in my experience, depending on the maturity of the organization and individuals. Some people will take a view that "someone else is going to check this…" and let their standards slip, whereas others' pride in their work means that they give it extra checks themselves before submitting it to QC or QA.

6.2 Who could be in this group?

Measurers include specialists who spend all their time in this group, and members of the other groups who take on a measurement role for a particular project, or carry out measurement tasks from time to time. Specialists in the measurers group include:

- People who audit or check the conformance to and suitability of processes; their measures are made against process standards—quality assurance specialists (see quality practitioners in Chapter 2, Table 2.1).

- People who measure the quality of the products, including software, using processes and activities to check for completeness, correctness, suitability, and adherence to specification—quality control specialists (see testers in Chapter 2, Table 2.1).

Although many organizations have specialists or teams focused on QA and QC activities, for example, audit and compliance teams, it is unusual for the measurement of quality to be left entirely to specialists. One common reason for this is that there are not enough specialists in the organization to carry out the work. We will also see in this chapter, and in Chapters 8 to 12, which describe the life span of software, that different types of checks are needed at different times. This means that, as required, the customers, managers, builders and supporters may all carry out measurement activities. These might include part-time or temporary membership in the quality assurance (QA) teams and quality control (QC) teams:

- The QA teams carry out activities that check that teams have selected suitable processes and are adhering to them. QA activities might include process review and quality or process audit.

- The QC activities include software testing, software inspection, and product review, and there may be, for example, test teams and inspection teams.

We all check our own work, and so we all measure quality; but specialist measurers hold a particular viewpoint of quality. Let us examine that next.

6.3 Quality viewpoint

Both QA and QC tend to focus on discovering defects against specifications or standards. This means that specialists for these activities favor the manufacturing view of quality. As we discussed in Chapter 1, manufacturing-based quality focuses on the manufacture of software products, that is, their specification, design, and construction. For specialist QA and QC people, therefore, quality depends on the extent to which requirements have been implemented in conformance with the original requirements.

When measurement focuses on faults and failures in products, success is measured by our ability to follow a process and deliver products against

6.3 Quality viewpoint

agreed-on specifications, so the report that "the software was built to specification and there are a low number of defects" might lead to a recommendation to release the system for live use, even if it does not do what the customer needs.

We can see this reflected in QA standards such as ISO 9000:1994 [2], and in QC standards, for example, BS 7925-1 [3] and BS 7925-2 [4]:

- An audit against ISO 9000:1994 will look for a documented process and evidence that the documented process is followed. It is concerned that a contract has been agreed on and met, but not whether that contract describes a suitable product for the customer.

- In BS 7925-1, testing is defined as the "process of exercising software to verify that it satisfies specified requirements and to detect errors." Using this definition, we *will* verify ("is the system correct to specification?"), but if we do not take account of the *user-based* definition of quality (see Chapter 3, Customers), we *may forget* to validate ("is this the right specification?").

As well as a manufacturing view, many measurers hold a product-based view of quality. Here, quality is based on a well-defined set of software quality attributes that must be measured in an objective and quantitative way. This quality viewpoint is particularly appealing to measurers because it provides a way of changing concepts which are often ill-defined and amorphous into neat, measurable acceptance criteria. We can use acceptance criteria to objectively assess the quality of the delivered product. Rather than reporting in vague, unquantified terms that "the software appears to be reliable," we can measure and report clearly, "The software is 98% reliable when running continuously over a 7-day period. Recovery time is less than 1 minute at each failure." We can use standards such as ISO 9126 [5] to help us define attributes measurably. These include reliability, usability, security, and functionality attributes. We will see how to do this in Chapter 9.

Most people, and that includes measurers, hold a transcendent view of quality. As we saw in Chapter 1, this means that we "know quality when we see it"; our knowledge is based on our experiences, taste, affections, loyalties, and emotions. Unfortunately, this means different people will have different reactions to a product, so it is hard to agree on what is "right." The transcendent definition for a particular person will be based on that individual's "taken-for-granted" assumptions. For many specialist measurers, their transcendent quality viewpoint is strongly attached to a taken for granted assumption that quality is related only to specification, number of defects, and product attributes. For these people, unless products and services can be measured against an agreed-on standard and meet or exceed that standard, they are inherently lacking in quality. For other specialist measurers, their taken-for-granted assumption is that a pursuit of defects (identification, removal, or prevention) and of product attributes (number and level of implementations) almost regardless of cost or time, must be a good thing.

A clichéd observation of specialist measurers (and I am one myself) is that common characteristics of people in the group are pedantry, obsessive attention to detail, a strongly developed ability to complain, and a delight in other people's mistakes. As a group, we can be difficult for others to deal with and perceived as unhelpful and focused on our own concerns (see Chapter 2).

So the measurers favor manufacturing and product views of quality and within those tend to focus on defects and non conformance. At its most extreme, the quality specialists' manufacturing-based quality view can be rigid and not focused on the overall needs of the customers and the organization. To improve their relationship with the other groups, they must consider the groups' quality viewpoints. As we saw in Chapters 1 and 2, two other definitions of quality reflect the views of the people using the software and those who pay for it. These perspectives are about supporting the needs of the organization and its stakeholders, within the organization's constraints; therefore, what constitutes "quality" may change over time.

- The user-based definition says that quality is fitness for use. It is the user-based definition that encourages us to validate *as well as* to verify the system. The measurers need to find out, "Can people do their work efficiently and effectively using this software?" This viewpoint is important to the customers and to the supporters, the two groups most affected by the software postdelivery (see Chapter 12).

- The value-based definition is focused on things that impact on the running of the business as a whole. Software quality should always be determined by means of a decision process based on trade-offs between time, effort, and cost aspects. The measurers need to find out, "If we release the software now, how much extra will we spend on support in the first month? If we are a month late, what will it cost the organization in fines and lost business? Should we release or do more testing?" Value for money is important for managers and anyone responsible for budgets. The ROI for the software needs to be predicted before delivery and measured postdelivery (see Chapter 12) in order that the organization as a whole can evaluate whether the project was worthwhile.

Along with acknowledging the user-based and value-based views of quality, the measurers must acknowledge that the transcendent view of quality depends on the individual. The measurers must take into account the fact that other people's taken-for-granted viewpoints may well be different from their own view. One important point here is to examine the different slant that builders and measurers may put on the manufacturing- and product-based quality viewpoints. As we saw in Chapter 5, builders, particularly those working in software development rather than other areas of product build, focus on technical excellence as a means for enhancing their work. They tend to be interested in the process aspects of manufacturing and in the enhancement of product attributes. They are also on the

6.3 Quality viewpoint

receiving end of criticism from the measurers about their processes and their products, which can cause communication problems (Chapter 2).

Let us look at some examples, looking at one subgroup within the measurers, specialist system testers. These people test software systems, often as part of an independent group within the project but separate from the builders. Here are three real remarks I have heard system testers make:

- Sam Tester: "We will not test without a written specification."
- Jo Senior-Tester: "If we're not aiming for zero defects how many do we want?"
- Jim Test-Expert: "We cannot sacrifice quality to cost."

These views are all correct, yet simultaneously wrong. Let us examine them one at a time.

"We will not test without a written specification." Sam Tester needs the specification in order to draw up tests and expected results for those tests. Without a written specification, it is difficult not just for the testers to proceed, but also for all the groups to remember what has been agreed on. However, simply to refuse to continue until a written specification is provided is unhelpful to the other groups if they had not expected to provide a written specification. The pragmatic approach *for this occasion* might be for the tester to agree to research the expected results by interviewing the customers. The tester then, as part of the measurement process, measures the cost of late development of the specification, in terms of additional work done and the number of defects in the build that could have been prevented had there been a written specification. This can be used to persuade all the groups to agree on improvements in process for the next project. For improvements to be accepted, the tester must provide the information showing how the other groups' quality viewpoints are met. This means that measurements must be changed into information that addresses those viewpoints, to make it easy for others to buy into the suggestion for change. For example, does the software do what the customers and supporters require, or does it stray from a "fit-for-purpose" model? Is it missing things that are needed? From the managers' viewpoint, what was the cost of exceeding "fit for purpose" by adding unnecessary things, and what was the cost and impact of defects found late that could have been identified in a written specification? When talking to the builders, focus on their transcendent view of quality as technical excellence (see Chapter 5), and the aspects of the manufacturing and product-based viewpoints that would be enhanced by a written specification. Would a clearer definition of what is required allow them to concentrate on building technically excellent solutions that will be more easily accepted, thus reducing boring rework? In Chapter 9, we will look at what we can do before we start to build software, to provide a clearer definition of what is required. In Chapter 12 we will look at evaluation of delivered systems.

"If we're not aiming for zero defects how many do we want?" Jo Senior-Tester is concerned that if the testing has not uncovered all the defects in the products, and that these defects have been corrected, the delivery will be of an unacceptable quality. Also, testers *know in their hearts* (transcendent quality) that they want to deliver a product that is *perfect*. Their argument is, "If we are not looking for perfection, how flawed is OK? With products and services outside software, we don't expect defects, do we?" In fact, customers and supporters are not bothered by defects as such. What they want to avoid is *failures*. By this I mean that the product not behaving as they expect it should. They will also differentiate between high and low impact failures. They need the products to be fit for purpose rather than perfect, and the software defects may not lead to high impact failures. The tester needs to work with the customer and supporter to define acceptance criteria that encapsulate a "fit-for-purpose" view. We will see how to do this in Chapter 9.

"We cannot sacrifice quality to cost," explained Jim Test-Expert. This comment is a continuation from the last one. The tester is concerned that the other groups are *only* interested in the cost, at present, but that later there will be a backlash, possibly directed at the tester, if the delivered products are disappointing. From a manager's viewpoint, cost and quality are inextricably linked in the value-based view of quality. For the customers and supporters, too, the budget they are prepared to spend must be balanced against their wish list. Builders, conversely, can be fixated on delivering additional attributes and see that as adding value and quality. Testing these additional attributes may be a problem for the tester if it adds unplanned scope and cost. If cost is the limiting factor in this project, the tester needs to explain what testing is possible within the budget, what testing cannot be done, and the risks associated with not doing that testing. In some projects, the goal is to deliver the minimum that will allow the customers to proceed—quality in that case is closely tied to fit for purpose and value for money. In other projects, the goal may be reducing risk in a safety-critical situation—quality in that case may be tied to product attributes such as reliability and to manufacturing goals such as defect prevention and removal. If, as testers, we believe quality will be impacted, we need to examine "what aspect of quality is now adversely affected and could be improved by increased spending?" In doing this, we need to not just focus on process, defects, and attributes (manufacturing and product views) but also to provide value, user, and transcendent examples of quality loss (see Table 6.1). The precise questions to use depend on the relationships between the groups, so these are just examples. Using questions allows each group to arrive at its own conclusion, based on its own quality view. As above, defining "fit-for-purpose" acceptance criteria will help prevent this problem, and in Chapter 9 we will also see how to arrive at a common understanding of risks and constraints across the groups.

When considering the quality costs and the impact of QA and QC activities on the project, it is important to remember that quality activities *can in themselves damage quality*. This idea surprises and offends some quality practitioners but it must be faced. Traditional quality economics supports the testers I described above because it assumes that all quality activities are inherently a "good thing." Yes, there is a trade-off between the cost of the quality activities and the cost of the failures that they may prevent;

6.3 Quality viewpoint

Table 6.1 Tester Considering Other Viewpoints for Quality Impacts

Group and Quality View	Possible Routes into a Discussion with This Group	Example Questions
Customer User-based quality view	Find out the impact on *fit for purpose* if things go wrong	What is the impact on your work if this goes wrong? If this feature is not available, can you work without it? How much extra time would that take? Where would you like testing to concentrate? From what you have said, it looks like if we find problems they will have X impact. Do you agree?
Supporter User and product-based quality view	Find out the impact on *fit for purpose* and important *attributes* if things go wrong.	What is the impact on your work if this goes wrong? If this attribute is not available, can you work without it? How much extra time would that take? Where would you like testing to concentrate? What is the minimum level of (reliability/security/...) that is acceptable? What is the postdelivery support budget? From what you have said, it looks like if we find problems they will have Y impact. Do you agree?
Builder Product- and manufacturing-based quality view	Find out the *likelihood* of different areas going wrong	Which attributes and areas would you like testing to concentrate on? Which areas were hardest/easiest to build? From what you have said, it looks like I might find it useful to look at areas A, B, and C. Do you agree? The software has just done this. Is that what you would expect? How difficult would it be to make changes in this area?
Manager Value-based quality view	Identify the *cost* of things going wrong and the *cost* of repair/support.	What budget do we have for support after going live? The impact of not testing these areas is X additional time (hence cost) for the customers and Y additional time (hence cost) for the supporters. The likelihood of them going wrong is Z, so the risk of them going wrong (likelihood times impact) is [Z * (proportion of X + proportion of Y)].

however, the possibility that quality activities can detract from a project is not considered. This view is now being challenged [6] and the distinction is sometimes made between quality costs (activities that contribute to the fitness for purpose) and quality losses (activities that cost money but make no contribution to the fitness for purpose of the product). Adopting this mindset goes some way to wedding the value-based quality definition to those quality viewpoints normally held by measurers. In one organization, a team of measurers were introduced to the concept of "quality loss," and on examining their activities found several examples of value-destroying quality activity. All of the following are failures in efficiency and effectiveness that colleagues and I have seen in more than one organization:

- Inspections and other document reviews for which participants have not prepared. These take time but have a low defect-detection rate. Just "having the inspection" in order to get the sign-off against the quality policy does not improve the quality of the product.

- Project audits carried out by staff who are not politically empowered. These require significant time investments from project teams as well as the auditors, and consistently fail to escalate significant nonconformances from standards. They may even make the situation worse because the political status of the auditors may be used as a reason to prevent measurements being taken.

- User-acceptance testing directly replicating the tests carried out in system testing (at cost), while not identifying additional defects, instead of carrying outtests at different levels, each having their own purpose and focus.

- Practitioners may be trained in quality methods that they consider to be only theoretically valid, and thus they may not implement them on their projects. In one organization, I found that the senior management had sent teams on a test techniques training course as a "treat." The view was that if they had some (any) training, this would keep them quiet for a while and improve their motivation, but there was no intention to allow any changes in working practice as a result of the training. As a result, the teams were more demotivated following their return to their desks because they were not allowed to apply the techniques they had learned. Additionally, a large proportion of the year's training budget had been used.

Carrying out this type of exercise helps eliminate costly but ineffective activities and it helps the measurers evaluate their own activities through the value-based quality definition.

It is important to note that, because this group is so widely supplemented by recruits from all the other groups, many individuals hold wider quality views. The important thing for each individual is to consider which quality view they are favoring, and then consider the other views:

- Some people in this group work mainly in *user-acceptance testing* and will support the user-based view of quality. They may be closer to the customer view and need to take extra time to consider value-, product-, and manufacturing-based views.

- An increasing number of measurers are *test automation specialists*; they can be closer to builders in outlook. They need to make sure that they do not forget the user- and value-based views.

- *Quality managers and test managers* may take on aspects of the manager's group, and be more focused on ROI and value for money, so they should make an additional effort to remember the user-, manufacturing-, and product-based views.

- The work of *audit and compliance groups* might take on aspects of the customers and/or managers groups and consider fit for purpose and ROI as well as compliance to standards and regulations, broadening their view from manufacturing defects to user and value views.

- If the *testers* look after the customer help desk as well as testing products, which does happen in some package suppliers, they become more focused on supporter activities during installation and postdelivery, and will be trying to consider user- and product-based quality as well as manufacturing-based quality.

6.4 Quality framework using the EFQM Excellence Model

6.4.1 The EFQM Excellence Model and the measurers

The measurers are, almost by definition, very interested in frameworks that include defined processes, standards, and specifications for work, including their own. Their measurements take place against that framework of processes, standards, and specifications. Quality assurance standards, including the ISO 9000 series, can be used to define the QA and QC processes as well as the organization's overall processes. There are also specific professional bodies, standards, frameworks, and best-practice guides for all aspects of QA and QC work. Some sources for these are listed in Appendix A, but you should remember that there are others, specifically country-based and industry-sector-based ones. I have chosen these examples for useful onward links as well as useful information. I would particularly recommend Stuart Reid's paper comparing test standards [7] and a BSI paper putting a number of software standards into a Software and System Quality Framework (SSQF) [8]. The BSI paper sets the software and systems standards within an organizational model taken from the ISO 9000:2000 [9] family of standards that we looked at in Chapter 1, but it compares this to the EFQM Excellence Model [10] and other quality frameworks, some of which are industry specific. It shows how a framework of standards can be used for the development and delivery of software, and places these within both a technical framework and an enterprise framework. It also sets out a measurement framework, including the QA and QC activities. For QA specialists, whether carrying out process reviews, auditing or making process improvement suggestions, this paper is a useful starting point. Reid's paper concentrates on standards that particularly relate to QC and, within that, software testing. This paper is good reading both for QC practitioners, whether testers or reviewers, and for QA specialists who are auditing or reviewing the test process.

When designing the quality framework for a particular set of measurers, it is essential to consider the quality framework for the customer (Chapter 3). The customer's goals inform their quality framework, and, in turn, this should inform the measurers' quality framework, and also the teams' and individuals' personal objectives and targets.

In Chapter 1, we looked at the EFQM Excellence Model [10] and how it is divided into nine parts: five enabling criteria and four criteria for measuring results. In Section 6.4.2 we will look at how the EFQM Excellence

Model enablers could be interpreted for measurers, and in Section 6.4.3 we will look at measurers' results. Remember that this model is based on the fundamental concepts of excellence we discussed in Chapter 1, and that equivalent models such as the Baldrige model are available.

6.4.2 EFQM Excellence Model enablers for the measurers

6.4.2.1 Leadership

In order that the measurers are supported in their role, the organization will require leadership. As we saw in Chapter 1, project managers provide leadership to their projects, drawing on the lead they are given by the organization's board and management. Measurers particularly require leadership support for their activities, for two related reasons:

- Because the measurers do not build products, their activities may not be seen as "adding" anything.
- Because the measurers are often messengers bringing bad news, their contribution is seen as negative.

This leads to comments like the one I heard from a programmer once: "I don't like testers; all they do is break things!"; and from a senior manager talking about a colleague he hoped would leave (!), "He doesn't contribute anything useful—let's put him in the quality group until he retires." Leaders in the organization and in the project must support the measurers' activities:

- By making the measurers' process and product measures clear to all parties;
- By helping all the groups to agree on a shared quality viewpoint.

6.4.2.2 Policy and Strategy

Policy and Strategy in an organization set down what is expected. For the measurers, an organization would need to have policies that lay down the basic rules for approaching these activities:

- A QA policy, including audit and process review;
- A QC policy, including test, inspection, and product review.

Strategies and high-level plans would be needed for the organization and, perhaps in more detail for particular programs of work or projects, for both QA and QC activities. The strategies and overall plans might include:

- An audit plan for the organization, including the approach, responsibilities, and a schedule of dates for audits;
- A strategy for testing for the organization or for a program, describing the risks to be addressed by testing, the approach, the test stages required in each project, and the completion criteria for the testing;

- A review plan for a particular project, listing the products to be reviewed, the type of reviews required for each product, the goal of each review, and the entry and exit criteria for the reviews.

I have not attempted to give the full list of strategies and plans, nor have I suggested complete contents lists. The specialist measurers should have their framework in place, including tailored standards based on ISO and IEEE standards (see Appendixes A and B for sources). Members of other groups should expect to support the use of those standards.

6.4.2.3 People

Specialist and nonspecialist measurers—skill and aptitude mix. The people who carry out measurement activities need to be selected for interest and aptitude in the area, but will require training in the QA and QC activities. When we examine the measurers group, as well as the specialists, we see people entering and leaving the group, carrying out QA and QC measurement activities. This means members of all groups will need training and support in these areas (Table 6.2).

Aptitude and interest are very important, but if we list what we might expect from people in this group, we see that it is most unlikely that a single individual will have all the aptitudes and skills we require:

- IT skills, for example, analysis and design skills, data modeling, coding;
- Knowledge of software engineering processes;
- Knowledge of QA processes, for example, audit, review, problem root-cause analysis;
- Business/industry sector knowledge;
- Specific software package knowledge;
- Knowledge of QC processes, for example, test design, inspection, review;

Table 6.2 QA and QC Training Requirements Across the Group

Group	QA/QC Activities That Require Support and Training
Measurers	Audit process, QA review process, document reviews (e.g., inspection, peer review, walkthrough, test design techniques)
Builders	Document reviews (e.g., inspection, peer review, walkthrough)
	Tests [e.g., component-test design and execution ("programmer testing" or unit testing), integration test design and execution]
Customers	Document reviews (e.g., inspection, peer review, walkthrough)
	Tests (e.g., acceptance-test design and execution
Supporters	Document reviews (e.g., inspection, peer review, walkthrough)
	Tests (e.g., acceptance-test design and execution)
Managers	Document reviews (e.g., inspection, peer review, walkthrough)
	Management reviews (e.g., plan reviews, progress reviews, examination of test-management reports and metrics)

- Test tool experience;
- Project management, planning, scheduling;
- Enthusiasm;
- Attention to detail;
- Tact;
- Firmness;
- Ability to negotiate;
- Ability to generate ideas;
- Ability to work under stress.

And you can no doubt think of others!

For this reason, it is best to build up teams of people with complementary skills. For example, Lloyd Roden, in his 1999 EuroSTAR presentation [11], identified four types of testers, with different styles of work (Table 6.3). These styles are all needed in a successful tester, but one individual is very unlikely to exhibit all these characteristics. So the QA and QC teams, including the test teams, need to have a mix of people.

Using the skill mix effectively. There are good reasons to organize the QA and the QC teams to use different personality traits effectively. This is both to allow individuals to shine in roles that allow them to use their skills and preferences, but also to match the team members' communication styles to their audience. In one organization I visited, the IT quality assurance group decided to have two groups of people in its QA review and audit team. The first group consisted of people chosen because they were known to be knowledgeable and experienced, and who were well liked and had a natural tendency to be helpful. This group carried out process reviews and audits with the project managers, agreed on lists of project risks, and reported a set of recommended improvements to processes. They were characterized as the "village bobbies" (old-fashioned local policemen, whose role was to patrol, advise, and gently admonish). Their objective was to "support projects and implement standards," and the consultants' unthreatening approach meant that projects invited them in. The second group were much fiercer, and their role was to work on projects that had refused the first group's help and were now failing or at risk. They were charged with

Table 6.3 Roden's Tester Type Matrix (Partial)

Pragmatist	*Pioneer*
Efficiency	Change
Results	Risks
Tasks	Involving others
Analyst	*Facilitator*
Accuracy	Networking
Proof	Consensus
Standards	Status quo

Source: [11].

6.4 Quality framework using the EFQM Excellence Model

enforcing processes and escalating problems on projects at risk of failure. The IT quality manager commented:

> One of the key features of our quality approach is recognition that (a) projects are very heterogeneous, thus standards are only a template; (b) we need to empower practitioners to optimize standards. The result is the recognition that an effective IT quality system is dynamic; this means that we recognize both adherence and adaptive quality controls. In one audit, the majority [of deviations from process] were deliberate, based upon considered assessment of the projects' circumstances. Was the project wrong? Absolutely not. When taking on QM, my second-highest issue was that *projects are not tailoring development standards to meet their needs; rather these are interpreted as an inflexible rulebook. This means that projects are not realizing the risk mitigation predicted from adopting a methodology.* Most of [the team's] time is spent selling the benefits of standards, then coaching the practitioners on them (point of need, desk-based) ... helping the teams to tailor the standards to their circumstances.

Team organization. One question I am often asked is, "How should the QA and QC teams be organized?" Unfortunately, this is one of those questions that does not have a single correct answer. Some possibilities are shown in Table 6.4. Generally speaking, the greater the risks associated with things

Table 6.4 QA and QC Team Independence

Review Team	Comment
Specialists—external (e.g., third-party testers, third-party inspection team, external auditors)	Effective at finding defects against defined process or specification, objective, independent, focused on their customer (may not be project team's customer). Customers and managers will listen to external bodies.
	May cause fear. May not know enough about the organization. May be seen as an obstacle. Problems may be disguised or hidden.
Independent specialists—internal (e.g., test team or audit reporting to quality director rather than development director)	Effective at finding defects against defined process or specification, objective, independent, focused on their customer (may not be project team's customer), understand the organization's quality drivers, voice on the board.
	May cause fear. May not know enough about the project. May not understand the project's quality drivers. May be seen as an obstacle. Problems may be disguised or hidden. Quality may be seen as owned by the QA/QC team.
Specialists—advise peer group teams *how to* carry out QA and QC. Carry out spot checks on the QA/QC.	Only a small group of specialists needed. Quality owned by the build teams. Knowledge transfer.
	May be not so effective or efficient as specialists have to learn new techniques. Builders may take a less objective stance in their QA/QC activities.
Peer group (e.g., walkthrough or test team reporting to the development manager). One project audits another project.	Effective at finding defects against defined process, also at making process improvement suggestions. Understand the problems, "in same boat," allies, will review each other.
	Less objective. Less independent. Can be difficult to report defects in peer's work. Needs strong leadership and support from managers, and from an independent QA/QC specialist group.
Buddy checks author's work; team leader checks team following processes.	Cheaper than a team, and quicker, but less likely to find defects. Not as effective or objective. Cheap. Team leaders should be "doing this anyway."
Author checks own work	Cheap for low-risk products but often not effective if there are any risks to contain.

going wrong or mistakes being made, the more likely we are to use an independent QA or QC team.

Typically, we find that different levels of independence are required depending on circumstances:

- The higher the risk, the more independent and specialist QA and QC teams will be appropriate.
- At different stages in the project, different levels of independence may be useful. For example, using specialist testers to help the developers design component tests should increase effectiveness. If the developers run the tests this keeps an efficient test run/debug cycle at this stage, which could be followed by independent specialists running integration and system tests.

Motivation and appreciation. When Warden and Nicholson carried out their motivational study [12] (see Chapter 2), one of their key findings was how very demotivated software quality practitioners were. It seemed to be, on examining their roles and their specific job design (the task mix and the opportunities for personal growth), that many of the interviewees had jobs that swung between being excessively stressful and very boring. Key points raised by Warden and Nicholson from the survey results include:

- Testers reported that they used a low variety of skills and could be confined to test execution rather than being able to spend time on test design and problem analysis.
- QA staff reported that they performed too many control tasks and not enough that create improvements.
- QA staff reported they did not get enough direction from management.
- Both QA staff and testers reported they did not get feedback from their jobs; it was difficult to tell if their efforts had made a difference.
- Both QA staff and testers reported that they did not get positive feedback from their colleagues, whether this was people from the customer, builder, manager, or supporter groups, and this was considered to be because they were the bringers of bad news.
- QA and QC staff had lower pay levels and less job security than other IT practitioners.

This finding is borne out by the BCS Industry Structure Model [13], which describes a career progression for various IT roles. The developer roles have a career progression to a higher level than testing roles, yet I cannot think of any real reason why a test specialist, *provided qualifications, aptitude, and experience levels are equivalent to a development specialist,* should not also aspire to an IT director role. Notice, however that QA/audit roles are shown to have a higher progression toward management than QC/testing roles, perhaps because a QA/audit view looks at process rather than specific products, and is focused toward improvement rather than toward defect identification. I am increasingly hearing testers talk about defect prevention, indicating, perhaps, that there is a move toward QA and away from QC by some individuals. Despite the career progression issues, most quality practitioners I meet, whether QA or QC specialists, are passionate about their work; they may feel unappreciated but they are filled with a belief about the importance of what they do and what they want to achieve.

6.4.2.4 Partnerships and Resources

As we saw in Chapter 1, partnerships cover people outside our team, our project, or our organization with whom we need to exchange information or cooperate in some way. Resources are the things like IT environments, information, and equipment that we need to carry out our work.

For measurers, there are partnerships with other measurement teams, both inside and outside the organization. For example, if I am working as a test manager, I find it useful to meet the audit and compliance teams to see if they have particular areas of interest in the testing. Similarly, I would want to find out what other test managers are doing. This might include discussions with testers working for other organizations on the same project to see where they are concentrating their testing and whether we are competing for resources. I might also look at the output from inspections/reviews and liaise with those teams in the same way. In each case, we are sharing information to ensure that our work complements the other groups' work rather than repeating it.

Resources for measurers include IT resources such as tools and test environments. These are often scarce. I remember arriving on one project at the point at which we had intended to use a particular test environment. Having been assured by the organization's IT and business management that ours was the most critical project and that nothing would stand in our way, we were surprised to find several other projects vying for the environment, all of whom had also been told their project was the most important. I would recommend liaison across the organization as well as within the project to make sure that there is no conflict.

6.4.2.5 Processes

Measurement framework. These are the processes specific to the measurers, not the processes and products they measure. These are the tasks, tools, and techniques that improve software quality by improving the way quality measures are collected and analyzed, and may be divided into two groups:

- QA audit processes, used to check adherence to processes;
- QC review and test processes, used to check products such as documents and code for defects

In the BSI SSQF [8], a group of standards are noted under the measurement framework, including standards for the software measurement process, audit, software product evaluation, software product metrics, problem resolution, process assessment, and process improvement. You will find standards bodies listed in Appendix A. Standards are important—not only because they should encapsulate best practice, but also because adherence to standards should give our customers some degree of assurance about how we have carried out work. However, they can be quite dry reading, and so you may prefer to refer to a textbook at first. There are a number of good books about QA and QC processes available; you will find a few of them listed in the selected bibliography at the end of this chapter. I am not going to explain the steps through the processes in this book, instead, I am going to concentrate on *how* to carry out the processes in a way that enhances teamwork and quality.

Measurement and improvement. One key point about these measurement processes is that they encapsulate the idea of improvement; not just of the processes and products being measured but also of the measurement processes themselves (Figure 6.2). Measurers must lead by acknowledging their own mistakes and improving their own processes if their suggestions for improvement to other people's products and processes are to be well received.

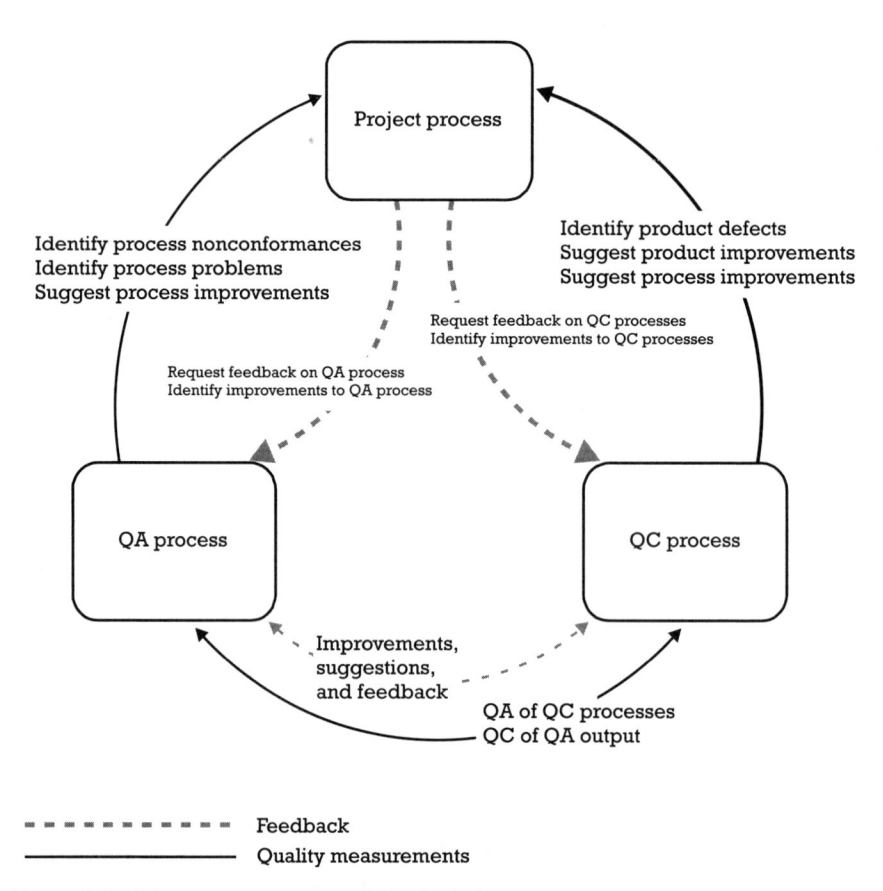

Figure 6.2 Measurement processes include improvement.

6.4 Quality framework using the EFQM Excellence Model

Table 6.5 Rules of Thumb for QA and QC Activities

It is the product or the process we are assessing and measuring, not the people	Try not to make it personal; check whether you have any personal baggage you are taking into the activity—you are not supposed to have favorites or be out for vengeance! If you have strong personal feelings that you cannot overcome (such as love or hate), maybe some else should do it instead of you.
Before the activity starts, it should be explained to anyone who is "on the receiving end" and not familiar with the activity	Why, how, who, where, what?—"Hi, I just wanted to introduce myself. Your manager may have said that I'm auditing this project to look at configuration management processes. What I'll need to do is visit you sometime this week to discuss what you do and to look at some examples."
The goals, rules, and plan for the activity should be clearly communicated to all the parties	Why, how, who, where, what?—"As we agreed at the start of the project, I'm going to be auditing your area in the next few days, in order to check adherence to configuration management standards. This is nothing to worry about; what we check is whether the process you use is suitable for your project. We will want to pick up your good ideas to share them with other teams, and we may be able to suggest some improvement ideas to help you. I'll need to interview some people and I'll need to look at the directory contents."
During the activity, collect and classify information, openly	During the activity, the measurers collect information, and this should carefully and clearly documented, differentiating between fact, interpretation, and perception (see Chapter 4). Typically, I make handwritten notes, or you could use a handheld tape recorder, and enter them into the logging tool or type them up immediately on concluding a session or each evening, if it is a several-day activity.
Use the interviewee's jargon, not our own	An example when auditing test processes is that if you ask a nontester, "Do you use the V-model?" they will probably say no, but if you ask them, "Do you review requirements before you start design?" they may well say yes. As people may not know the names of standards and processes, ask them questions about what they do, not what they call it. (If you want to know about the V-model, see Chapter 10.)
Find some positive and some negative things to say	There will always be at least one positive point you can make but, at the same time, everyone appreciates some constructive criticism.
After the activity, give feedback quickly	After the activity, immediate feedback should be given to all the authors and participants on the findings and they should have a chance to comment and add facts, interpretations, and perceptions.
Get feedback from others	Feedback is requested from the authors and participants on the activity—how could it be improved and what would make it more useful to the authors and participants? Facts, interpretations, and perceptions are logged about the activity.
Make sure people know the findings	This might be a detailed catalogue report, an overview management report, or simply access to a logging tool such as is used for test findings, but if the points logged so far are a "good enough" report, I might not write anything extra; I will make sure everyone who needs to know about the finding does know.
Monitor the outcomes—what happened as a result of the activity?	Monitor what actions were taken and why. This generally means follow-up conversations with all the interested parties.
Always ask other people to QA/QC our QA and QC work	"If it's sauce for the goose, then it's sauce for gander," as my grandmother used to say. Showing that we also need help will encourage others to receive help.

Whether we are planning to carry out QA processes such as audit or QC processes such as document review and testing, we should remember some simple general rules of thumb. Table 6.5 shows my rules of thumb. I do not always keep to them (it depends on circumstance), but they are my mental start point and checklist. The specific QA or QC process might be, for example, a document review, executing some testing, or carrying out an audit, so in the table I have called it the *activity* for brevity and to distinguish it from the product or process being assessed.

There are times when these rules of thumb do not apply or apply differently. As we saw above, we may need to follow up some gentle advisory reviews with a harsher audit if risks are escalating and teams are not responding to suggestions. We would also see a difference in emphasis in different types of QA and QC activities:

- In an external audit for compliance to a certification, the timing, rules, and goals for the audit would be set by the external body, and the conduct of the audit is very strict, with minimal feedback.

- In an internal audit or a QA process review, we might want to loosen the rules and allow discussion and information exchange. I have found this especially useful with peer reviews of processes—getting a couple of project managers or business analysts from different areas to talk to each other can be a great experience for both and a fine way to share good practice. I remember that in one organization, the consensus during the audit training was that just doing an ISO 9000-style audit [2] was not helpful; what the teams wanted was to share ideas for improvement, not just to look for compliance to an external standard.

The reporting process. One key process for all measurers is the reporting process. Measurers gather information about processes and products and need to pass this to other people in a way that will be acceptable and understandable. Good information design is vital; it is easy to hide your message so that it is ignored or misinterpreted. However well you have designed your audit or test process, however well you execute the process, if your results are ignored you may as well have not bothered doing it. Reports are the managers' deliverable to all the other groups, and the information that the measurers provide is vital for making these reports an accurate reflection of the quality of services and deliverables. In Chapter 4, I look at some aspects of report design that managers and measurers should consider when setting up reporting for QA and QC. When deciding what to report, do not collect information for the sake of it. One mistake many people make is reporting either on what has always been reported without questioning why, or only reporting on information that is easy to collect. As measurers, we need to reflect other quality views in our reports as we saw in Table 6.1. Also, be prepared to report bad news as well as good news. In my experience, people want to hear the bad news; what they *don't* want is to get it when it is *too late* and without any ideas for improving the situation.

6.4.3 EFQM Excellence Model results for the measurers

6.4.3.1 Customer Results

Customer Results are the measure of the effect we have on our customers. Who are the measurers' customers? In fact, as well as the customers for the software itself, all the groups are customers of the measurers: the managers, the builders, and the supporters. Measurers should look at what the EFQM Excellence Model [10] refers to as customer perception results and customer performance indicators. Perception results are measured externally; we ask the other groups for their views. Performance indicators are measured internally; what actually did other groups do? Both measures are needed so that we see the difference between "we think you are doing a great job" and actually *being invited back* for new projects. In one organization, the head of a new QA group said to me, "I'll know we've succeeded when the managers come to me to ask for audits." Examples of the type of results that could be measured are shown in Table 6.6.

6.4.3.2 People Results

In this case, the People Results measure what the measurers think about themselves. We saw in Section 6.4.2.3 that Warden and Nicholson found two groups within the measurers to be demotivated. The use of a sophisticated and proven measurement technique such as the motivational survey process used by Warden and Nicholson allows a much greater depth of understanding of people's motivation and of how to improve this. As with the customer results, EFQM Excellence Model people results are divided into two groups: the perceptions and the performance indicators. Examples of the type of results that could be measured are shown in Table 6.7.

6.4.3.3 Society Results

For the EFQM Excellence Model, society means society at large, and although we might want to measure this for the organization, we could also interpret it for a particular project as the wider organizational culture within which the measurers work. Again, we consider perception and performance

Table 6.6 Customer Results—What the Other Groups Think of Measurers

	Example of Possible Measures
Perceptions—external to the group—surveys, interviews, compliments, and complaints	Have the measurers got a good image?
	Do other groups report that they find the measurers easy to deal with (for example, are they helpful, flexible, honest, and proactive)?
	Are the measurers seen as reliable, providing good value, providing a good service?
Performance indicators—measurement of outcomes	Do we get asked back in for new projects?
	Are people proactive in coming to us for help?
	Are our reports usually accepted?
	Do other groups complain about our work?

Table 6.7 People Results—What the Measurers Think of Themselves

	Example of Possible Measures
Perceptions—external to the group—surveys, interviews, compliments, and complaints	Has a motivational study provided positive feedback?
	Are measurers satisfied with their career path, rewards?
Performance indicators—internal to measurers group	Does the measurers group match up to the required qualifications and competencies? For example, do they have appropriate BCS qualifications [14]?
	What are absenteeism and sickness levels compared with other groups? Are audit staff showing a different absence pattern to other staff?
	What is the level of staff turnover compared with other groups and do people want to be recruited into this group? For example, if we advertise a document inspection course internally, is it over- or undersubscribed?

indicators. Examples of the type of results that could be measured are shown in Table 6.8.

6.4.3.4 Key Performance Results

The EFQM Excellence Model divides key performance measures into two areas: financial and nonfinancial measures. There was a big debate among delegates at the EuroSTAR Conference in 2002 about how to measure return on investment in testing, and it quickly became apparent that nonfinancial as well as financial costs and benefits needed to be measured. Examples of the type of financial and nonfinancial results that could be measured are shown in Table 6.9. I recently asked a manager in a large IT organization in what ways his testers could improve their services to the organization. His response was that he wanted not just improved technical skills—"more bugs found"—but also an improved understanding of the financial drivers for the organization—"*will this make us money?*"

Table 6.8 Society Results—How the Measurers Relate to Society

	Example of Possible Measures
Perceptions—external to the group—surveys, interviews, compliments, and complaints	Are the measurers seen by the organization and wider society as acting ethically?
	Do the auditors and testers check that the systems act properly with regard to health risks, safety, hazards, and the environment?
Performance indicators—internal to measurers group	Has the test group won any accolades, for example, for paper- and energy-saving initiatives, in line with corporate initiatives?
	Has the audit group checked that certification and clearances with external authorities have been authorized and cleared properly?

Table 6.9 Key Performance Results—Financial and Corporate

	Example of Possible Measures
Financial	What is the return on investment (ROI) for the audits we have carried out this year (cost of audits, number of noncompliances detected, predicted failure costs of noncompliances)?
	What is the cost–benefit ratio of the system-testing activities, for example, cost of running the system test team, against predicted cost of failures if testing had not been done? (The benefit is the *money saved by doing testing*.) Compare with the cost–benefit ratio if testing and other QC activities had been carried out earlier. Consider quality losses.
Nonfinancial	Number of projects that request process reviews, and the size of these projects.
	Cycle times for testing and for document review; how quickly do the builders get feedback on their products and how accurate is that feedback?
	Innovation by the measurers (e.g., new techniques to enable faster implementation of systems to support time to market with new products).

6.5 Communication between the measurers and other groups

We will see in Chapters 8 to 12 that measurers are involved in the whole life span of a piece of software, from its conception, through the software-development life cycle (SDLC), during delivery, and postdelivery until decommissioning. We will see that some of the SDLC models encourage measurer involvement and other models do not.

First, let us think about what it is like to have your work tested, reviewed, or audited. If we think about people's feelings, we can see that communication before, during, and after a QA or QC process is very important. People are often apprehensive if their work is to be examined by other people and, therefore, can become defensive.

Here is a story from a colleague about interrelationships between some measurers and a group of builders.

> One of the main risks that I raised was that mutual distrust between groups—particularly business analysts and the test team—was inhibiting productivity, and until addressed would militate against improvement. The

Table 6.10 Some Measurers and Builders Indulge in Bad-Mouthing Each Other

Person	*Their Comment*
Test manager	"The problems in the project are caused by the poor quality specifications."
Business analyst 1	"The specification defects arise because the testers won't review our specifications."
Tester 1	"I would never speak to a business analyst!"
	(When asked why she did not highlight defects in the specification.)
Tester 2	"It's so frustrating—the analysts think we're a waste of space. It's the way that others carry on.... It reflects badly on me.... They don't see what I do."
Business analyst 2	"The testers are the problem—we have no idea what they do. They are over-resourced and don't have the right skills."
Tester 3	"The business analysts don't do anything—they're lazy."
Business analyst 3	"What does the (lead tester) do? ... plan his holiday, I think."

comments I got from interview sessions were revelatory [see Table 6.10]. Neither group had any awareness of what the other group was *actually* doing; all were frustrated with the situation.

Is the test manager right? Are the problems in the project caused by poor quality specifications? I do not think so; the poor quality of the specifications is a symptom and not a cause. The problems here are caused by distrust and poor communication. Once test execution had started, my colleague's pessimism about the outcome proved to be well founded: "During test execution, 50% of UAT conditions generated an error and 50% of these were specification defects."

My colleague also observed that the dissonant relationships were a big impediment to delivery:

> The most amazing manifestation of this was in how defects were resolved. The business analysts and testers sat together in an integrated team but didn't interact. Testers entered questions for the analysts in a spreadsheet, for example: *Is this word in the output meant to be capitalized?* Once a week, the business analysts would enter replies into the spreadsheet. As there had been a dispute about the format of the spreadsheet (the testers "won"), several business analysts refused to participate in the process. Directly observed result: simple queries about the specifications took *weeks* to resolve, causing the testing process to slip massively. The fascinating thing was that they had been provided with the environment to work closely (colocated, integrated team), but the relationships were totally broken.

What strikes me most here is how very badly both groups are behaving. Instead of partnership, we have conflict. As we each can only alter our own behavior and as this is a chapter about the measurers, I shall concentrate on their behavior—what could these testers do to improve the business analysts' view of them? Here are some ideas:

- Change the communication system; start talking to the business analysts instead of sending them spreadsheets.
- Ensure that the queries are not trivial; focus on what is important rather than what is easy.
- Be polite to the analysts—they are as busy you are.
- Be seen to work hard and concentrate; stop the "holiday planning."
- Ask the analysts what they need from you; treat them as a customer and provide a service.

Measurers need to share information with all the groups (Figure 6.3). In order to decide where to focus QA and QC activities, measurers need to understand the quality views of all the groups, particularly the customer's goal; the risks—both the impact and the likelihood of problems; and the budget for the project. For example, audit teams will concentrate on high-risk projects, where failure would have a high impact.

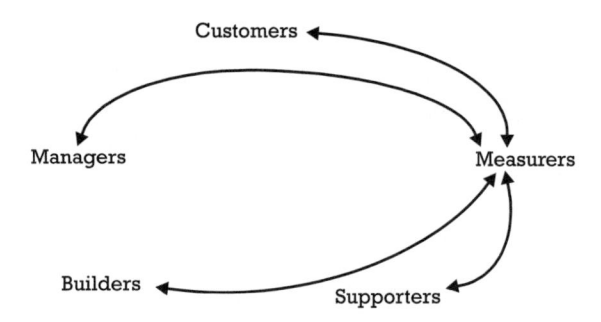

6.5 Communication between the measurers and other groups

Figure 6.3 Communication between groups.

In Table 6.11, I have identified information that the measurers gather that is needed by other parties. Some of these are measures directly made, for example, numbers of defects; some of them are extrapolations from

Table 6.11 Information That Measurers Have That Others Need

Before the SDLC starts and updated throughout the SDLC	Identification of similar problems/solutions
	Identification and assessment of technical and business risks
	What QA and QC is necessary to address the risks
	What QA and QC is possible within budget constraints
	Advice on methods, processes, and standards, generic and tailored
During the SDLC	Fast and early feedback on the success of the SDLC tailoring, by audit
	Reassessment of risks and consequent retailoring advice
	Improvement suggestions to make activities more effective and efficient
	Defect identification by review of requirements, design, specifications, code, training material, and documentation
	Defect identification by designing, executing, and following up tests of software and processes
	Advice on next steps if stage entry and exit criteria are not met
	Quality measures, including number of defects, risk assessments, cost projections, acceptance criteria passed, projected impact of leaving/repairing defects, including cost, time, and exposure
	Refinements to requirements, acceptance criteria, priorities, risks, constraints
	Advice to nonspecialists and members of other groups
At delivery	Known defects list
	Advice on next steps if stage entry and exit criteria are not met
	Quality measures, including number of defects, risk assessments, cost projections, acceptance criteria passed, projected impact of leaving/repairing defects, including cost, time, and exposure
Postdelivery	Evaluation of risk assessment. Were all the risks identified correctly? Did we have any surprises that we should have anticipated? If any risks were identified and did not become problems, is this because we misjudged the likelihood or whether it just did not happen this time?
	Evaluation of QA and QC processes, efficiency, and effectiveness of quality processes
	Evaluation of management, build, and support processes, improvement suggestions for all processes
	Advice on impact of change
	Aid in using tools and techniques (e.g., regression test packs)
	Aid in using known problem lists and workarounds

those measures, for example, projected costs of repairing the defects and the cost of leaving them; and some are information based on experience.

Measurers need information from other groups, in order to understand the constraints on delivering their wish list. Table 6.12 lists the information measurers need from the other groups.

6.6 Summary of the group

Measurers must communicate well with the other groups if they are to be effective. Indeed, many measurers will be in other groups. The contribution of QA and QC to the success of a project can be enormous, but if the

Table 6.12 Information That Measurers Need from Others

Customers	Who the customers are and their real needs;
	Constraints and risks for the customer;
	Understanding of the customer's user-based quality viewpoints;
	Aims and objectives and acceptance criteria for the project;
	Mandatory requirements;
	Business view of risks (likelihood and impact);
	Quality targets within the constraints;
	Changes to requirements, acceptance criteria, aims, risks, and constraints;
	Number and impact of defects reported during live use;
	Customer satisfaction with the delivered products;
	Improvement suggestions for quality processes;
	Test priorities for the next release;
	Evaluation of QA/QC effectiveness.
Managers	Constraints and risks for managers;
	Better understanding of the manager's value-based quality viewpoints;
	Understand and agree to an outline plan, including constraints such as dates and costs;
	Changes to requirements, acceptance criteria, aims, risks, and constraints;
	Evaluation of QA/QC efficiency from the managers.
Builders	Constraints and risks for builders;
	Better understanding of the builder's manufacturing and product quality viewpoints;
	Understand the technical view of risks (likelihood of errors being made in the build);
	Requests for changes to requirements, acceptance criteria, aims, risks, constraints, and changes to design, code and other products;
	Evaluation of QA/QC effectiveness.
Supporters	Constraints and risks for supporters;
	Better understanding of the supporters' user and product quality viewpoints;
	Understand the technical and business view of risks (likelihood and impact) on existing system;
	Supporters' requirements and acceptance criteria;
	Changes to requirements, acceptance criteria, aims, risks, and constraints;
	Number and impact of defects reported during live use;
	Customer satisfaction with the delivered products as expressed to help desk;
	Supporter satisfaction with the delivered products;
	Evaluation of QA/QC effectiveness.

behavior of measurement specialists alienates the other groups, then no benefits will be realized.

We will see in Chapters 8 to 12 how measurement, whether through QA or QC activities is necessary throughout the life of a software system.

References

[1] Draper, S. W., "The Hawthorne Effect: A Note," http://www.psy.gla.ac.uk/~steve/hawth.html (March 12, 2003), September 2003.

[2] International Standards Organization, ISO 9000: 1994 Quality Systems.

[3] British Standards Institute, BS7925-1:1998, "Software Testing, Part 1: Vocabulary."

[4] British Standards Institute, BS7925-2:1998, "Software Testing, Part 2: Software Component Testing."

[5] International Standards Organization/International Electrotechnical Commission (ISO/IEC), DTR 9126, Software Engineering—Software Product Quality (Parts 1–4, 2000/2001).

[6] Giakatis, G., T. Enkawa, and K. Washitani, "Hidden Quality Costs and the Distinction Between Quality Cost and Quality Loss," *Total Quality Management*, Vol. 12, 2001, pp. 179–190.

[7] Reid, S. C., "Software Testing Standards—Do They Know What They are Talking About?" http://www.testingstandards.co.uk/publications.htm, August 2003.

[8] British Standards Institute, PD0026:2003, *Software and Systems Quality Framework—A Guide to the Use of ISO/IEC and Other Standards for Understanding Quality in Software and Systems*, London, England: British Standards Institute, May 2003.

[9] International Standards Organization, ISO 9000:2000, Quality Systems.

[10] European Foundation for Quality Management, "EFQM Excellence Model," http://www.efqm.org, August 2003.

[11] Roden, L., "Choosing and Managing the Ideal Test Team," *EuroSTAR Conference*, 1999.

[12] Warden, R., and I. Nicholson, *The MIP Report—Volume 2—1996 Motivational Survey of IT Staff*, 2nd ed., Bredon, England: Software Futures Ltd., 1996.

[13] British Computer Society, "Industry Structure Model," http://www1.bcs.org.uk/link.asp? sectionID=574, September 2003.

[14] British Computer Society, "BCS Qualifications," http://www1.bcs.org.uk/link.asp?sectionID=574, September 2003.

Selected bibliography

The American Society for Quality Web site has articles and information about quality issues on http://www.asq.org, including a quality glossary at http://www.aq.org/info/glossary/index.html.

Craig, R. D., and S. P. Jaskiel, *Systematic Software Testing*, Norwood, MA: Artech House, 2002.

Crosby, P, *Quality Is Free*, New York: Mentor, 1980.

The W. Edwards Deming Institute Web site has articles on Deming's work at http://www.deming.org/theman/articles/articles_gbnf04.html.

Dustin, E., *Effective Software Testing*, Reading, MA: Addison-Wesley, 2003.

Galin, D., "Software Quality Metrics—From Theory to Implementation," *Software Quality Professional*, June 2003, pp. 24–31.

Gerrard, P., and N. Thompson, *Risk Based E-Business Testing*, Norwood, MA: Artech House, 2002.

Gilb, T., and D. Graham, *Software Inspection*, Reading, MA: Addison-Wesley, 1993.

Kaner, C., J. Bach, and B. Pettichord, *Lessons Learned in Software Testing*, New York: Wiley, 2002.

Pol, M., and E. van Veenendaal, *Structured Testing of Information Systems*, Deventer, the Netherlands: Kluwer, 1998.

Spaine, S., and S. P. Jaskiel, *The Web Testing Handbook,* Orange Park, FL: STQE, 2001.

The Sticky Minds Web site has roundtable sessions has a continuously changing range of articles and discussions on testing and software quality issues on http://www.stickyminds.com .

All issues of the *STQE Journal* (about to become *Better Software*).

Watkins, J., *Testing IT: An Off the Shelf Software Testing Process*, Cambridge, England: Cambridge University Press, 2001.

Wilborn, W., "Dynamic Auditing of Quality Assurance: Concept and Method," *International Journal of Quality and Reliability Management*, Vol. 7, No. 3, 1989, pp. 35–42.

CHAPTER 7

Contents

7.1 Introducing the supporters

7.2 Who could be in this group?

7.3 Quality viewpoint

7.4 Quality framework using the EFQM Excellence Model

7.5 Communication between supporters and other groups

7.6 Summary of the group

7.7 Summary of all the groups

Roles and Quality: Supporters

In this chapter I shall:

- Introduce the members of the supporters group, their roles, and activities;
- Introduce their quality viewpoint;
- Provide a framework for the supporters activities within the EFQM Excellence Model;
- Identify information flows between the supporters and the other groups.

So the first we hear about the new system is when we are asked to give it an operational acceptance test, just before the project team plan to put it live, so there's no time to do anything much. We get delivery of the software and run a quick test of the overnight batch; it now takes too long. Turns out the development guys and the testers never asked Operations about what constraints are on the time slots. That meant a last-minute fix! I didn't realize you didn't know about it.... I'd have told you if I'd realized. Yeah, we knew it was coming, but we didn't realize the mess they'd made of the user interface. The help desk is inundated with calls, and the extra network traffic is way over the capacity we'd planned for it. They should've come to talk to us; we'd have put them right. Now we've got to pick up the pieces.

—*Some supporters moan about the newly implemented software*

7.1 Introducing the supporters

Once the software has been and built and delivered, the customers will use it. This postdelivery period in the life of software, described in Chapter 12, is the longest period in the life of software, and its most important time; after all, if the software does not have a postdelivery life, what use is it?

Postdelivery, a group of IT specialists look after the software and the customers, providing a number of support and IT infrastructure services. These people provide the management, support, and infrastructure for the deployment, update, optimization, and use of the software. Additionally, this group plays an important role during the software-development life cycle (SDLC), providing the infrastructure and support within which the products are built as well as support for specialist tools used by all the other groups. They also keep "business as usual" going on the IT systems during the SDLC and the delivery.

Because of their role in supporting the software, this group has a breadth and depth of knowledge unrivaled by any of the other groups. They see the software in use and in context with the rest of the system. They work with the software from its delivery to its decommissioning, supporting it and its users. They are the first to hear about its faults from the user community, and they will be the people who fix those faults. I have chosen to call this group the *supporters* because they support all the IT-related activities of the other groups and, hence, the organization as a whole. They are critical to the success of the software and of the organization as a whole. Why, in our story at the start of the chapter, are the supporters so fed up? Well, you cannot provide a good supporting service unless the software is supportable, and the delivered software is unsupportable. They have information that would have helped the builders and measurers deliver better software. They have service needs that have not been met. They are on the receiving end of complaints about the software from the customers, but they were not involved in its design or build. They may even be subject to penalties against service-level agreements that have been compromised by the poor performance of the software.

Too often, in my experience, the supporters are involved too little and too late in the SDLC. So, why have I left them until last in this group of chapters? It is to emphasize their importance. Builders (Chapter 5) are central to this group of chapters and to the delivery of products, including software. They are aided in their work by managers (Chapter 4), who are conduits for information, and by measurers (Chapter 6), who provide information about the products and processes. All this work is done for the customers (Chapter 3); without them we would not need or build the products to support them in their work. Without the supporters, the customers might not be able to use the software. This is because customers may not have the technical knowledge, interest, or time to support the software themselves, for example, when:

- Software has to be deployed on a complex infrastructure of hardware, communications, and systems software.
- Software has to be protected against infiltration, losses, and other security risks, as does the information stored with it.
- Communications and on-line and batch-processing systems have to be monitored, and sometimes nursed, day and night.

- Software and its infrastructure require updates and changes, which need to be deployed without adversely affecting business as usual (BAU).
- Complex software is not learned quickly; the customers need the support of a help desk as they use more of the software's features.
- The software is optimized during its life and use [1].

The supporters have knowledge, experience, and information that none of the other groups have. Just like the customers, they have requirements and acceptance criteria for the software, which will enable it not simply to be functionally correct and provide the features the customers need, but also to provide quality in use [2], by having appropriate attributes of performance, security, reliability, and so on. So, the customer and supporter chapters "bookend" the chapters about the people they need to inform. Just like the customers, the supporters need to be involved right from the start of planning the software, through the SDLC, as well as during use and deployment. Many of the points about customer contact throughout the book also apply to supporters.

In this chapter, we will see that of all the groups, the supporters is the one that is most mature in its understanding of the importance of IT to the organization, and has standards that acknowledge and depend on wider organizational excellence frameworks. We will see in Chapters 8 to 12 that the involvement of the supporters is vital throughout the entire process of planning and executing the SDLC, not just at the point of delivery and after, because of this understanding of the attributes and the activities necessary to provide the IT services required by the organization and the customers.

7.2 Who could be in this group?

Supporters carry out all the IT service management activities required to support the organization. Generally, these jobs will be done by specialists. It is likely that the team that looked after the IT infrastructure, communications, and networks would be different from the team that manned the help desk. The specialists we might encounter include:

- Service-support specialists, including people who deal with the service desk, incident management, problem management, configuration management, change management, and release management;
- Service-delivery specialists, including those who work in capacity management, financial management for IT systems, availability management, service-level management, and IT service-continuity management;
- Information and communications technology (ICT) specialists, who are specialists dealing with network-service management, operations

management, management of local processors, computer installation, and acceptance and systems management;
- IT security specialists, who will deal with internal and external security of the IT systems and the information held within them;
- Software-maintenance specialists, including those who deal with systems and data conversion, as well as those who correct and enhance software.

Specialist supporters are important stakeholders for quality. There are two parts to their involvement:

- First, this group maintains the software when it is delivered and accepted by the customers; they provide support and infrastructure and are therefore stakeholders for quality in that they will have requirements for the software, particularly in its quality attributes. Security, performance, portability, and maintainability will all be factors for this group.
- Second, this group affects the quality of processes and products because they provide the support and infrastructure for the other groups during the SDLC. They will supply the environments for the building and testing of the software and will support the tool sets used by all the groups in their work. The group includes the IT infrastructure team, comprising IT operations, support, and maintenance; IT security; the help desk; service management; networking; and database administration (see IT infrastructure staff and software maintainers in Chapter 2, Table 2.1).

Many of us get involved in these activities in some way. Anyone who writes documents has to deal with change management and version control for those documents, for example. In smaller organizations, people may move between groups, sometimes building and supporting the software systems. Indeed, it could be argued that most software engineers work in software maintenance rather than software development. Most projects are about altering existing software rather than building entirely new systems. Similarly, in some organizations there may be an overlap between the measurers and supporters. In several organizations, I have seen the system testers also manning the help desk. This can be useful, as the testers develop their understanding of the customers' real use problems, but I have seen the situation were the team is overwhelmed by the volume of testing and help-desk calls for which they are responsible.

7.3 Quality viewpoint

Supporters need the software to be supportable; it needs to be fit for purpose and to have attributes that make it supportable. It needs to fit within infrastructure constraints and operational profiles. Remember our supporters at the start of the chapter—if the batch cannot run in its assigned slot, later processes are affected, and this may result in the on-line system not being available on time for the customers. Supporters tend to be more aware of organizational requirements that affect the wider organization than other IT staff, because they come up against problems more directly. I remember seeing a payroll system in which the overnight batch run for the weekly paid staff took somewhat longer than previously. It would not fit into the overnight schedule on Wednesday night, so someone in the development group suggested it could run in the freer Thursday night schedule. Weekly workers were either paid into their bank accounts, or by cash. Running the batch Thursday still left time for the head office weekly paid staff to get their cash envelopes by lunchtime as usual. What the head-office-based, monthly salaried development staff did not consider was that the manual workers for the organization worked remotely from head office, some as many as 50 miles away. This was why the payroll ran Wednesday; it left time to put cash into envelopes and take it to the remote sites, to enable the manual workers to be paid at lunchtime on Friday. If the payroll was run on Thursday, these workers would not receive their money until Monday, unless the courier could leave by 10 a.m., meaning that the cash clerks would need to start work at 7 a.m. instead of 9 a.m. every Friday. What implications does this have for the organization? It is an unplanned change in working practices. We would need to consider the reaction of the workforce and unions, the effect on management and the human resources department, adverse publicity in the press, possible strike action, and so on. Yet the IT development manager said to me, "Why does the time the courier leaves the pay office affect us? That's not an IT issue!" Yes, I am afraid it is, because the working of the IT system is affecting the organization and its staff. It was the *supporters* who understood and pointed out the problem, because they knew the special provisions that would be required if the Wednesday payroll failed in the existing system and it had to be run as one-off process on a Thursday night.

Supporters favor the product-based definition of quality, based on a well-defined set of software quality attributes that must be measured in an objective and quantitative way. We can derive acceptance criteria to objectively assess the quality of the delivered product. The supporters need this objective measurement of attributes to help them ensure that they will meet the service levels expected by their customers, the IT users, and the organization. For example, standards such as ISO 9126 [2] define quality—in-use attributes that directly affect the supporters' work. Typical attributes are reliability, usability, security and maintainability.

Supporters also favor the user-based definition that says that quality is fitness for use. This is because they will be using the software, as operations teams, for example, but also because they are in the first line for dealing with user inquiries and customer complaints. In the user-based view, software quality is determined by the user(s) of a product in a specific business situation. Different business characteristics require different "qualities" of a software product. For example, the usability of the interfaces for operations such as daily updating of security measures against virus and spam attack, running the daily batch systems, back-up and recovery, installing and deinstalling software, will all be of interest to the supporters, because they are the users of those programs.

The supporters' managers will focus particularly on service levels. This may include a provision for the cost of supporting the systems. In Chapter 12, we will meet a disenchanted support manager caught by service costs rising with a new software release. Failing to meet the service levels may incur a penalty clause. This means supporters and their managers have an interest in the value-based view of quality, specifically whether the money saved or spent during the SDLC is justified by savings in use of the system. We will look in Chapter 12 at evaluating postdelivery.

This group's transcendent view of quality—their taken-for-granted assumptions about the systems—include notions of stability, reliability of service levels, and long-term benefits. These assumptions about quality reflect the supporters' need to carry out their own work efficiently and effectively, as well as supporting the customers' use of the software to meet the organization's ends.

We can see in Table 7.1 how supporters, in this example a help-desk team, could consider the other groups' quality viewpoints to help them understand the supporters' quality requirements.

7.4 Quality framework using the EFQM Excellence Model

7.4.1 The EFQM Excellence Model and the supporter

As I mentioned earlier, the supporters have a mature standards framework. This is supported by a global organization, the IT Service Management Forum (itSMF) [3] which supports an associated library of process descriptions and guides, including the IT Infrastructure Library (ITIL). This library has been developed since 1989 [4], has recently been updated, and is being released as a series of seven guides. The ITIL books set service management within an EFQM Excellence Model [5] framework, and also discusses the similar Baldrige [6] framework used in the United States. The subjects in ITIL are:

- Service Support—covering service desk, incident management, problem management, configuration management, change management, and release management [7];
- Service Delivery—covering capacity management, financial management for IT systems, availability management, service-level management, and IT continuity management [8];
- Security Management—covering fundamentals of information security, relationship of security management to other aspects of service management, and security management measures [9];

7.4 Quality framework using the EFQM Excellence Model

Table 7.1 Help-Desk Team Considering Other Viewpoints for Quality Impacts

Group and Quality View	Possible Routes into a Discussion with This Group	Example Questions and Areas for Discussion
Customer User-based quality view	Shared viewpoint—discuss the impact on *fit for purpose* if things go wrong	Impact on business as usual (BAU) of failure, for example, cost of system outage to the business, work throughput efficiency for customer.
Builder Product- and manufacturing-based quality view	Shared product view; product attributes. Show empathy for manufacturing view; technical excellence and defect likelihood.	Which nonfunctional areas has the customer discussed with you? These are the nonfunctional attributes that experience shows us are important for BAU—the attributes most often commented on by customers calling the help desk. Volunteer to review specifications/requirements for possible attribute problems (functional and nonfunctional). Provide list of common help-desk issues and discuss technical innovations that could help improve these areas.
Measurer Product- and manufacturing-based quality view	Shared product view; product attributes. Show empathy for manufacturing view; defect likelihood and impact.	Priority of tests and document reviews. These are the nonfunctional attributes that experience shows us are important for BAU—the attributes most often commented on by customers calling the help desk. Volunteer to review and comment on test designs and test results; these are our acceptance criteria for product attributes. Discuss how to assign priority for defects, based on impact and likelihood for BAU. Provide support for setting up like-live environments for tests; provide example tests.
Manager Value-based quality view	Identify the *cost* of things going wrong and the *cost* of repair/support.	Service-level agreements and their penalty clauses, shared risk on penalty clauses. Cost of support, ROI on maintenance changes. This is the cost of system outage. This is the cost in customer and supporter time/efficiency loss in help-desk calls.

- The Business Perspective (was scheduled to be due in 2004)—covering business relationship management, partnerships and outsourcing, continuous improvement, and exploitation of ICT for business advantage [10];
- ICT Infrastructure Management (not yet available)—covering network services, operations, local processors, computer installation and acceptance, and systems management [10];
- Application Management—covering SDLC support, testing of IT services, and business change [1];
- Planning to Implement Service Management—a "how to start" guide [11].

Along with and aligned to ITIL, standards and qualifications are being or have been developed [12, 13] to cover service management.

Supporters may provide services to the customer as in-house suppliers or as third-party suppliers (see Chapter 3). The supporters' ability to recognize and adapt to the customer's quality framework is a critical success factor in the effectiveness of their relationship, whether they are internal or third- party suppliers. The framework for the customer translates into departmental goals and, finally, into the personal objectives and targets for an individual system user, but it also translates into a complementary subset of the service management supplier's goals and, hence, into service-level agreements (SLAs). These will lead to personal objectives and targets for all the supporters. This quality framework will drive what the customer needs from the software and from the SLAs.

In Chapter 1, we looked at the EFQM Excellence Model and how it is divided into nine parts: five enabling criteria and four criteria for measuring results. In Section 7.4.2, we will look at how the EFQM Excellence Model enablers could be interpreted for supporters, and in Section 7.4.3 we will look at supporter results. Remember that this model is based on the fundamental concepts of excellence we discussed in Chapter 1 and that equivalent models such as the Baldrige model are available.

7.4.2 Enablers for the supporters

7.4.2.1 Leadership

The supporters' activities are vital to the success of the organization, not just during BAU, but also during periods of change to the organization and IT provisions, and in enabling the organization to deal with threats to business continuity.

It is easy for the organization to take the supporters for granted; sometimes the only feedback they get is when things go wrong. For this reason, it is particularly important that the organization's leaders take account of service management in recognition schemes as well as in reward schemes [8]. For example, if the operations staff keep the overnight batches running on time through day-to-day problems, no one outside the group may notice, unless their leaders can alert senior management and, hence, the organization's leaders that a bonus (reward) and a thank you (recognition) is needed [14]. Supporters may also have to "pick up the pieces" after an unsuccessful software delivery, specifically in dealing with customer complaints and in fixing operational problems. We will meet in Chapter 12 a supporter reeling under the strain of looking after software delivered by a different team.

Similarly, it is easy for business managers to neglect areas that do not resolve immediate problems. Ensuring proper IT service continuity management plans [8] requires strong leadership and a strategy agreed to at the top level and implemented and communicated through the whole organization.

An interesting point raised by Warden and Nicholson in their motivational survey [15] is that the introduction of improved processes, for example, the adoption of the ITIL processes, while providing a process improvement, in some cases lowered staff motivation when jobs were changed radically without good communication from leaders. This is an important point for leaders. My observation is that professional staff in all groups will want and expect the adoption of appropriate recognized standards, but they do not respond to imposition of standards, especially without suitable training.

7.4.2.2 Policy and Strategy

The organization will need policies and strategies for all aspects of service management; these briefly set out the overall rules for the supporter team's work; for example, an organization might have a release policy [7] that defines release definition (for example "major releases are numbered v1.x, v2.x and must include significant changes to critical attributes of the system"), required deliverables, preferred timing for implementations, or times to avoid (for example "implementations always take place at least two weeks before month/year ends").

These policies must be agreed on and clearly communicated, whether they are documented (preferable in a large organization to ensure they are not miscommunicated) or passed on by oral tradition: "We always do it this way."

The policy rules will be translated into strategies for the supporter's activities. These will show the approach that the supporters will take to meet the goals of the organization. The different teams within the supporters group—IT Infrastructure, help desk, the software maintenance teams, and so on—will have strategies and detailed plans for their own work. Of course, it would be easy for these strategies to become misaligned with each other and with the strategies of the other groups, such as the builders. The ITIL books [e.g., 7] use a nice analogy—that of tectonic plates. The areas of interest and control overlap and demarcation lines are not clear. It is at these overlaps that friction occurs. We have seen in Chapters 3 to 6 that the other groups each have policies and strategies. Now, even if all the groups work for the same organization, some considerable effort in communication is needed to make sure each group understands the others. Policies and strategies need to be discussed, agreed on, and mutually understood, the overlaps of demarcation particularly being a focus for communication. The supporters' policy and strategy must support the customers' policy and strategy, but they also must support the managers, builders and measurers. If some or all of the supporters are from third-party organizations, the communication during agreement on the contract and SLAs as well as throughout the relationship will need to be nurtured across all the groups and across organizations, as we saw in Chapter 3.

7.4.2.3 People

The supporters group includes a variety of specialists, who may be working in different teams and through separate management structures. They may also work in a separate management structure from the builders and measurers. This isolation of teams can lead to one of the problems our supporters at the start of the chapter experienced: poor or nonexistent communication leads to ineffective, inefficient service delivery to the customers.

Increasing specialization also means that individual supporters may only see part of each problem or solution—work is divided up and passed along from one team to another. If little or no feedback is received by the supporters on the effectiveness of their work, this can be alienating and demotivating, just as we saw it was for the builders in Chapter 5. One finding of Warden and Nicholson [15] was that the feedback received by supporters was mainly negative, but was about the quality of the software—something they typically had no control over—rather than about their own service levels. Typically, an SDLC team of builders and measurers deliver the software and other products. The customer uses them, and when things go wrong complains to a supporter (e.g, one on the help desk). Thus, the supporter does not get feedback on the level of service *they* provided but on the poor product provided by another team. The customers do not ring up to say that the product is good, and when there have been problems they will not be in a mood to comment on the good aspects of the supporters' work. The efficient and effective running of the IT infrastructure, communications links, background processes, and so on is something we tend, as computer users, to take for granted. We only notice them when they go wrong, so the supporters receive poor feedback and, as a result, can become demotivated.

In addition to the problem of feedback, there can be a problem of status. The other groups may undervalue the supporters. I remember some years ago interviewing a software engineering graduate who explained that he did not expect to do any software support or maintenance because that was "boring, low-skill" work. For him, software engineering meant developing brand new systems from nothing, and then—in my view quite, bizarrely—never needing to change them or to support the customer. Instead, "in the unlikely event that anything was wrong with the software" or if the customer "changed their minds about what they wanted," a new system would be built. We had quite a painful conversation about the reality of life with software; the frequent problems and misunderstandings during the SDLC, and the need for constant change to reflect the customers' constantly changing world. In my own view, the work of supporters should be seen as high status; it is not only critical but also extremely difficult, requiring both technical and personal skills. For example, one of the central points of application management as described by ITIL [1] is that software in use will be optimized throughout its life. Changing software, as we will see in Chapter 12, is very difficult; the supporters' role in maintaining and optimizing the systems in order to meet the customers' changing needs and to improve service to them should not be undervalued. Some SDLC models—for example, XP [16] and Evolutionary Delivery [17]—acknowledge, indeed expect, change. We might even see these as software-maintenance life cycles (SMLCs) rather than SDLCs, and the people delivering via these life cycles as supporters rather than builders, software engineers as maintenance staff rather than development staff. Could it just be the poor perceived image of software maintenance that prevents this?

7.4 Quality framework using the EFQM Excellence Model

A breadth and depth of technical skills are also required to understand and be able to deal with the range of technology used by the customers, and to assess the technical and business implications of changes in technology. A recent example of change is the increased IT and commercial security risks posed by organizations requiring desktop machines to have Internet access as well as access to internal systems.

Supporters need a mix of skills. Their education, training and work experiences will, of course, include all the technical skills and understanding of the methods, techniques, and tools for their tasks. Just as for the builders, it should also include an understanding of:

- The *measurement techniques* they will need to apply to their own work and to other people's work. For example, supporters carry out QC activities such as reviews and testing, specifically the Operational Acceptance Test (OAT) in which they will need training. Supporters also employ measures that will be needed for the ongoing management of SLAs, and toolsets for providing these. An example might be the network traffic our supporters are discussing at the start of the chapter. They will have an optimum traffic volume calculated and be measuring against that. Too little traffic and we have a network that is not cost-effective: too much and the traffic takes too long. Supporters like the maintainers and the help desk will be interested in measures of products on delivery. For example, we can measure code complexity and use it to understand the difficulty of future maintenance, while measures of the usability, reliability, and stability of the software will give the help-desk team a view of how busy they may be after delivery.

- The *management skills* they require for control of their own time and work within a team. Supporters need the skills, experience, and support to assess risk, negotiate between parties, and manage against SLAs. The focus of ITIL and the itSMF (for example, [1]) is on management. The management skills of supporters need to include an understanding of organizational issues, providing input to the business IT strategy, IT governance, IT risk management, and management of IT and systems to support business change. Recent publications, for example, [18, 19], emphasize the increasing importance of these areas.

- The *interpersonal skills* (sometimes called soft skills) to improve their communication with all the groups, including the other teams of supporters, and to deal sympathetically with people reporting problems to them. One unfortunate thing I have seen is the frustration of some support-line engineers with what they see as stupid questions: "If they just looked at page 123 of the manual, they would find the answer." A good supporter empathizes with the customer's view—maybe if the user can't find the answer, the manual is too complicated or has been written in IT jargon rather than the user's language, or possibly has been badly translated if the software and manual are to be used in many

countries or the supporter's first language may not be the customer's first language.
- We said above that part of the management skills supporters need include strategic planning; this must fit with their customer's *goals and strategy* so that they can focus their technical, measurement, management, and interpersonal skills toward solving the organization's real problems. The links between the customers and the supporters should be very strong.

7.4.2.4 Partnerships and Resources

Supporters operate in a network of partnerships within and outside the organization. These partnerships are in place to help provide the resources managed by the supporters, including the hardware, communications, systems, and software, and the data and information that provide knowledge.

Examples of supporter partnerships are:

- Between groups: with the builders, customers, and measurers to define acceptance criteria for nonfunctional attributes such as reliability, security, performance, to define the problem to be solved, and share information about risks and the fit-for-purpose, user-based quality view.
- Between groups: with the managers to discuss service-level agreements, costs, and value.
- Between groups: with the measurers to understand how operational acceptance criteria can be measured during testing.
- Between groups: with the builders and measurers to understand what resources and environments are required during an SDLC; also with the help-desk team and the trainers to discuss likely training needs and training success.
- Within the supporters group: for example, our supporters at the start of the chapter would benefit from sharing plans and news regularly.
- Outside a particular SDLC, to understand possible conflicts in resource requirements across several projects, or conflicts between the SDLC and BAU.
- Outside the organization: for example, with hardware and equipment suppliers, to plan delivery schedules against capacity and demand forecasts.

7.4.2.5 Processes

Many of the points made in Chapter 5 about builder's processes also apply to supporters. However, one advantage is that there is a globally acceptable definition of the required processes and management for their work in the

IT Infrastructure Library (ITIL) [1, 7–11]. These volumes provide process descriptions and flowcharts, as well getting-started guides and context descriptions of quality standards and excellence frameworks. They also cross-reference each other well. These process descriptions need to be adapted by particular organizations to fit their own requirements.

It is also important to realize that the introduction of new processes will require management of that change. Introduction of new processes or changes into existing working practice can cause motivation problems [15], especially if imposed without consultation and training. It is always worth asking the technical experts to design the processes, based on published standards and their own experience of what is appropriate, then include less-experienced people in the reviews both of the processes and of training material for the processes.

Remember, too, that people do not always follow the processes. Sometimes this means that the process is unworkable; perhaps it cannot be followed in the available time. Sometimes it means they have not understood the reason for the process. I remember one place I worked in many years ago where a small team of builders and measurers working on a minicomputer also had to be their own supporters in certain aspects; we took turns carrying out the daily backup, for example. The process for this was quite clear and written down: a number of tapes were circulated through the daily and weekly backups so that on each day the oldest backup was overwritten. Thus, a set of backups over the previous two weeks was always available. A log was kept of the backups, recording who had done them and so on. I went into the machine room one day to collect something and found the senior programmer, Simon, looking at the tapes in amazed despair. A series of backups had been made over a number of days without circulating tapes properly. We had lost *this week.* as it had been overwritten by *today.* If the computer had failed before today's backup, a week of work would have been lost rather than just today's work. The person who had done the backup was not being deliberately malign, they just did not realize the implication of what they had done. Simon ran a training session explaining not just what must be done but *why it was important* to do it following the process. People are not stupid, and one of the ways they manifest intelligence is by seeing how to "improve" processes. The problem is that if the reason for doing something is not clear, an optimization may remove a safeguard and increase risk beyond what is acceptable.

7.4.3 Results for the supporters

7.4.3.1 Customer Results

All the groups are customers of the supporters because they support the IT systems and software used by all the groups. Their customers will each measure them against their own quality measures—implicit or explicit—and the supporters need to measure their performance for their customers considering those quality viewpoints when setting service-level agreements with customers. We are interested in both the customer perceptions and the actual performance against service-level agreements. Table 7.2 shows some of the possible measures.

The supporters are in a position to collect customer results not just for their own services, but also to allow evaluation of the builders' and measurers' work done during the SDLC. This should be agreed on and used in collaboration with the other groups.

7.4.3.2 People Results

Here, the supporters measure themselves. What is their own reaction to their work and their services? Again, we will measure perception and performance. There are a number of factors that make supporters roles difficult:

- The work can be very reactive, for example, on a help desk or support line, and is therefore paced not by the person but by the frequency of calls. This makes it difficult for people to plan their time and tasks.

- The work is divided between many interlocked and overlapping processes, with many communication points, so it can be complex to control, for example, with ITIL. If we look just at the Service Support book [7] it describes 17 processes, and the Service Delivery book [8] describes another 16 processes; these may be being carried out by one or many teams depending on the size of the organization.

- The quality and attributes of products and services being supported depend on the product delivery team, who may not be involved in the support of the products and services. This means that the supporters do not have control over the products' quality and yet are affected by it.

- The work may involve unsocial hours and shift work because the infrastructure and systems may be in use and need to be supported 24 hours a day. This may involve tedious waiting interspersed with emergencies, which means that concentration cannot be allowed to lapse. I remember visiting some computer operators in a windowless darkened room filled with monitoring screens that had to be watched continuously for abnormal changes in network traffic. It was not a natural or ideal environment for a human.

Table 7.2 Customer Results—What the Other Groups Think of Supporters

	Example of Possible Measures
Perceptions—external to the group—surveys, interviews, compliments, and complaints	Have the supporters got a good image?
	Do other groups report that they find them easy to deal with (for example, are they helpful, flexible, honest, and proactive)?
	Are they seen as reliable, providing good value, providing a good service?
Performance indicators—measures of outcomes	Have we met service-levels agreements for all aspects of service to our customers—service availability, response times, help-line query responses, closure rate on problems, incidents, issues, recidivist problems, service and unavailability?

7.4 Quality framework using the EFQM Excellence Model

For these reasons, careful monitoring of people results for the supporters is important, as is a related rewards and recognition scheme. Examples of the type of results that could be measured are shown in Table 7.3.

7.4.3.3 Society Results

For the EFQM Excellence Model, society means society at large, although we could interpret it as meaning the wider organization. Again, we consider perception and performance indicators. Examples of the type of results that could be measured are shown in Table 7.4.

Table 7.3 People Results—What the Supporters Think of Themselves

	Example of Possible Measures
Perceptions—external to the group—surveys, interviews, compliments, and complaints	Has a motivational study provided positive feedback?
	Are supporters satisfied with their career path, rewards?
Performance indicators—internal to supporters group	Does the supporters group match up to the required qualifications and competencies? For example, do they have appropriate BCS qualifications [13]?
	What are absenteeism and sickness levels compared with other groups? Are overnight operators showing a different absence pattern than IT security staff?
	What is the level of staff turnover compared with other groups and do people want to be recruited into this group? For example, if we advertise a help-desk post internally, is it over- or undersubscribed by internal applicants?

Table 7.4 Society Results—How the Supporters Relate to Society

	Example of Possible Measures
Perceptions—external to the group—surveys, interviews, compliments, and complaints	Are the supporters seen by the organization and wider society as acting ethically?
	Do the auditors and testers check that the IT Infrastructure and systems act properly with regard to health risks, safety hazards, and the environment? This might include checking that the delivered IT service complies with legislation on data protection, availability of services to people with disabilities, or pollution control.
Performance indicators—internal to builders group	Has the group won any accolades, for example, for paper- and energy-saving initiatives, in line with corporate initiatives?
	Has the group been recognized in its efforts to reduce security risks internally and externally, including customer data confidentiality, prevention of spam and virus attacks, and IT governance provisions?
	Is there any consideration in the SLAs of the effect of IT on society, environment, and people? Are there links across the organization so that the management of IT systems, data, information, and knowledge is part of an integrated management system that includes, for example, the overall security, environmental, quality, and financial management?

7.4.3.4 Key Performance Results

As we have seen in earlier chapters, the EFQM Excellence Model divides key performance measures into two areas: financial and nonfinancial measures. Some examples are shown in Table 7.5. It is important to measure the supporter's services against the needs of the organization. For a business, this will mean that the key performance results must reflect the commercial drivers for the organization. For a nonprofit organization, again, the results must support the organization's goals, increasing the efficiency and effectiveness of the services and products provided.

7.5 Communication between supporters and other groups

We will see in Chapters 8 to 12 that supporters are involved in the whole life span of a piece of software, from its conception, through the software-development life cycle (SDLC), during delivery, and postdelivery until decommissioning. We will see that some of the SDLC models encourage supporter involvement and other models do not.

We have seen that supporters communicate with all the other groups, but that they are often reactive in communication by the nature of their work. If this is the case, perhaps the supporters should instigate communications with the other groups so they can find out what is planned, and can become part of the SDLC. As with the customers, the advantage of having little involvement to us as supporters is that while it is being built and delivered we get on with other things. Superficially, it looks as though we are being efficient with our time. The disadvantage is that during the period of the SDLC, things will change; our customers' problems will change, it may be that the underlying infrastructure will change, and, therefore, the solutions we require will change. This means by the time we get the software, it is out of date. The disadvantage of SDLCs with high supporter involvement is that it is time-consuming when we have business as usual to deal with as well as the SDLC. The advantage is that it is far more likely that a useful software solution will be delivered. So we will see in the later chapters that communication between the supporters and the other groups is needed

Table 7.5 Key Performance Results—Financial and Corporate

	Example of Possible Measures
Financial	What is the return on investment (ROI) for the services we have delivered this year (cost of services/money saved/number of new customers/market share gained)?
Nonfinancial	Number of projects/customers who request our team to carry out IT-related work, and the size of these projects
	Cycle times for responding to customer requests and questions
	Innovation by the supporter (e.g., new technology to support time to market with new products)
	How closely have SLAs been met or exceeded?
	How well did the agreed-upon SLAs match the goals of the organization?

throughout the whole life span. The supporters need to communicate with all the other groups (Figure 7.1) because they have information that those groups need.

We will see in Chapters 8 to 12 that from before the SDLC starts until the software is decommissioned, the other groups need the supporters. As things in and around the project develop and change, this may affect the SDLC. I remember a project in which we had decided to focus much attention during system test on performance testing, because the performance of the system after change was assessed as the greatest risk to the success of the project. Part way through the system test, the live environment underwent a hardware upgrade that enhanced the performance of the live systems. It became apparent that our fears about performance had been resolved by this upgrade. We reassessed risk, and as a result discarded our strategy of performance testing, concentrating our efforts on other aspects of the system that were now at higher risk than performance. Without information from the supporters, we measurers would not have known about the environment upgrade, as our environment was not being upgraded, so we would have wasted effort instead of concentrating on the real risks. Table 7.6 lists some of the information that supporter have that other groups need.

Supporters need information from other groups in order to understand the constraints on delivering their wish list. Table 7.7 lists the information supporters need from the other groups

At the end of the postdelivery period, during decommissioning, supporters will be involved to review the decommissioning plans and aid in rehearsal of the decommissioning processes. Supporters will need to assess what parts of the QA and QC library and other data are archived, and what is destroyed. This includes considerations of legal issues with compliance and with data protection.

7.6 Summary of the group

Supporters must communicate well with the other groups if they are to be effective. They have a vital role to play in the success of the organization, in supporting all the groups to get the best from IT. This group has a deep understanding both of the technical risks to systems as changes are introduced and of the real needs of the customer. Having worked with the

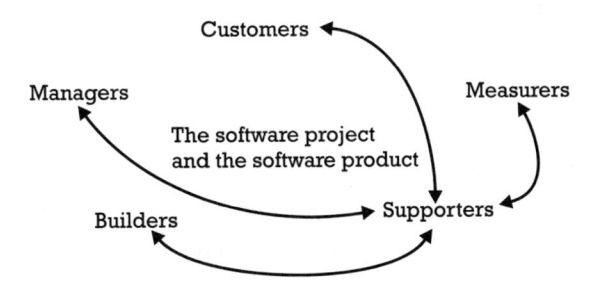

Figure 7.1 Communication between groups.

Table 7.6 Information That Supporters Have That Others Need

Before the SDLC starts and updated throughout the SDLC	Possible solutions to problems/ideas;
	Technical constraints and why these are constraints, for example, in the environment;
	Why this problem/idea (e.g., for a technical problem) is important and the impact on the customers for business as usual;
	Whether proposed aims/indicators are understood;
	Proposed objectives/targets for the solution;
	Whether proposed customer acceptance criteria are SMART (specific, measurable, achievable, realistic, and time-bound);
	Identification of supporter acceptance criteria;
	Technical risks (likelihood of this going wrong) and technical constraints;
	Precision and accuracy of estimates, when refined estimates will be possible;
	Constraints on SLAs postdelivery;
	Scope of supporters' operational acceptance testing.
During the SDLC	Manufacturing/product quality viewpoint—what attributes are of most importance and acceptance criteria for these attributes;
	User quality viewpoint—the operational, fit-for-purpose view of the software, with updated information as this changes over the SDLC;
	Technical impact of proposed changes in scope;
	Review and testing comments on proposed products to measure how closely they meet acceptance criteria, especially for nonfunctional attributes;
	Changes in IT infrastructure, systems, software, and other services that may affect the SDLC plans.
At delivery	Confirmation that the delivery is complete and acceptable.
Postdelivery	Evaluation of the software, how it affects the SLAs, whether it is fit for purpose, number of defects identified, improvements, and optimizations;
	Evaluation of the processes used and how they could be improved;
	Number of defects reported during live use;
	Customer satisfaction with the delivered products;
	Supporter satisfaction with the delivered products;
	Efficiency and effectiveness of quality processes;
	Improvement suggestions for all processes;
	Advice on impact of change.

customers' delivered software, they understand how it stands up to real use. They have knowledge of the risks to the business of software failure and which areas of the software are critical to the organization. They can and must be involved throughout the life span of the software, from conception and through the SDLC, as well as during delivery and use of the system until decommissioning.

7.7 Summary of all the groups

All the groups are important to the success of the IT provision for an organization. We have seen in Chapters 3 to 7 that each group has information

7.7 Summary of all the groups

Table 7.7 Information That Supporters Need from Others

Managers	Organization goals and strategy;
	Changes to the goals and strategy, immediate tactics;
	Problems and issues;
	Forecast requirements for IT and infrastructure;
	Feedback on services provided;
	SLA requirements;
	Customer acceptance criteria.
Builders	Cost and resource constraints and why these are constraints;
	Value quality viewpoint;
	Whether proposed aims/indicators are understood;
	Proposed objectives/targets for the solution;
	Whether proposed acceptance criteria are SMART (specific, measurable, achievable, realistic, and time-bound);
	Nontechnical risks (likelihood of this going wrong) and nontechnical constraints such as resources, time, budget, and people availability;
	Precision and accuracy of estimates, when refined estimates will be possible;
	Feedback on services provided.
Builders	Manufacturing/product quality viewpoint;
	Whether proposed aims/indicators are understood;
	Proposed objectives/targets for the solution;
	Whether proposed acceptance criteria are SMART (specific, measurable, achievable, realistic, and time-bound);
	Technical risks (likelihood of this going wrong) and technical constraints;
	Precision and accuracy of estimates, when refined estimates will be possible;
	Update on progress;
	Environmental requirements for the SDLC;
	Environmental requirements for delivery and live use;
	Feedback on services provided.
Other supporters	Feedback on progress with problems, incidents, and issues;
	Changes in risks;
	Feedback on services provided;
	Supporter acceptance criteria.
Measurers	Manufacturing/product quality viewpoint;
	Whether proposed aims/indicators are understood;
	Proposed objectives/targets for the solution;
	Whether proposed acceptance criteria are SMART (specific, measurable, achievable, realistic, and time-bound);
	Technical risks (likelihood of this going wrong) and technical constraints;
	Precision and accuracy of estimates, when refined estimates will be possible;
	Update on progress;
	Environmental requirements for the SDLC;
	Environmental requirements for delivery and live use;
	Feedback on services provided;
	Advice on acceptance testing;
	Advice on review processes;
	Assurance that QA and QC activities have taken place;
	Results of those activities;
	Aid in using tools and techniques (e.g., regression test packs);
	Aid in using known problem lists and workarounds.

that the others need, and that this information may change throughout the SDLC and the life of the software during use.

Customers provide a user-based, fit-for-purpose view, which changes continuously to meet the changes in the real world. Managers understand the nontechnical constraints on the organization and act as an information conduit between the groups. Builders use their technical knowledge to provide solutions to the customers' problems. Measurers provide information that allow all groups to decide on whether the products are of an acceptable quality for use and optimization over time. Supporters provide an understanding of technical risks to business as usual, together with the supporting infrastructure for all the groups' activities.

In Chapters 8 to 12 we will follow the life of software from its conception to its decommissioning, and we will look at the communication methods and techniques we can use to help these five important but disparate groups understand each other and relate to each other's needs and strengths.

References

[1] IT Infrastructure Library, *Best Practice for Application Management*, London, England: Office of Government Commerce, 2002.

[2] International Standards Organization/International Electrotechnical Commission (ISO/IEC), DTR 9126, Software Engineering—Software Product Quality (Parts 1–4, 2000/2001).

[3] IT Service Management Forum, http://www.itsmf.com, October 2003.

[4] Quagliariello, P., "Introduction to IT Service Management, ITIL, and ITIL Capacity Management," http://www.pultorak.com/home/speaking_engagements/presentations/2003_03_07_cmg.pdf, October 2003.

[5] European Foundation for Quality Management, "EFQM Excellence Model" and "Fundamental Concepts of Excellence," http://www.efqm.org, August 2003.

[6] Malcolm Baldrige model, http://www.quality.nist.gov/index.html, August 2003.

[7] IT Infrastructure Library, *Best Practice for Service Support*, London, England: Office of Government Commerce, 2002.

[8] IT Infrastructure Library, *Best Practice for Service Delivery*, London, England: Office of Government Commerce, 2002.

[9] IT Infrastructure Library, *Best Practice for Security Management*, London, England: Office of Government Commerce, 1999.

[10] The Stationery Office Web site, http://www.tsonline.co.uk/bookshop/bookstore.asp?FO= 1150345, October 2003.

[11] IT Infrastructure Library, *Planning to Implement Service Management*, London, England: Office of Government Commerce, 2002.

[12] IT Service Management Forum, "BS 15000 IT, Service Management," http://www.bs15000certification.com, October 2003.

[13] British Computer Society Qualifications, http://www1.bcs.org.uk/link.asp?sectionID=574, September 2003.

[14] British Quality Foundation, "Recognition and Reward: Keep Your Staff Smiling," *UK Excellence*, August/September 2003 (whole issue devoted to rewards and recognition).

[15] Warden, R., and I. Nicholson, *The MIP Report—Volume 2—1996 Motivational Survey of IT Staff*, 2nd ed., Bredon, England: Software Futures Ltd., 1996.

[16] Beck, K., *Extreme Programming Explained—Embrace Change*, Reading, MA: Addison-Wesley, 2001.

[17] Gilb, T., papers on Evolutionary Delivery on http://www.gilb.com.

[18] The Office of Government Commerce, *How to Manage Business and IT Strategies*, London, England: HMSO, 2002.

[19] The Office of Government Commerce, *How to Manage Business Change*, London, England: HMSO, 2002.

Selected bibliography

IT Service Management Forum, *A Dictionary of IT Service Management: Terms, Acronyms and Abbreviations: Version I*, London, England: The Stationery Office, 2001.

IT Service Management Forum, *A Dictionary of IT Service Management: Terms, Acronyms and Abbreviations: Version I (North America)*, London, England: The Stationery Office, 2001.

IT Service Management Forum, *IT Service Management: A Companion to the IT Infrastructure Library: Version 2*, London, England: The Stationery Office, 2001.

CHAPTER 8

The Life Span of a Software System

Contents

8.1 Life span or life cycle?

8.2 Entry and exit criteria between stages

8.3 Changes in quality viewpoints across the life span of a system

In this chapter I shall:

- Introduce the concept of software life span;
- Describe the stages in a software system's life span;
- Discuss where the quality definitions from Chapter 1 best fit in the stages;
- Introduce the concept of entry and exit criteria between stages;
- Prepare you for the detailed stage descriptions of Chapters 9 to 12.

As a business, we're crippled by our system! My development manager has just told me that removing the annual management charge from our premium account is going to take 50 days' effort. Our competitors do this sort of thing in 5 minutes. Unbelievable!

—Chief operating officer (COO), lamenting those of us who do not think beyond implementation

8.1 Life span or life cycle?

How do we avoid the problems upsetting the irate COO? To help, I am suggesting that we focus on the "life span" of a software system. The dictionary defines life span as "the length of time for which a person or animal lives or a thing functions" [1]. The life span of a *software system* begins when someone identifies a business problem that may be solved with software, continues through build and delivery, and, finally, ends with its decommissioning. The life of a software system includes what is often referred to as the software-development life cycle

(SDLC), which includes the design, build, testing, and delivery of the system. For most systems, the SDLC is a relatively short part of its life span.

Most systems spend the greatest part of their life span in use, being supported and maintained [2]. For example, many of you will remember the worries before January 1, 2000, that systems would not cope with years starting with "20" rather than "19." Some of the systems in question were more than 20 years old and still in use. Many organizations continue to depend on such software. Why replace something that works? Modern systems show the same pattern of a relatively short SDLC, followed by a long life of use and maintenance. Web sites spring to mind: After the initial launch they are continuously used and simultaneously changed.

Thinking about the life span of a software system instead of focusing on its development life cycle forces us to take a wider view of quality. We are more likely to consider the value view. This is surely beneficial, as many organizations struggle with the cost of ownership for their legacy systems. We will also think about the user view: how the customers will deploy the software. We may even identify the requirements of those tasked with supporting it. Understanding the life span of software affects our interpretation of the product and manufacturing views. We may develop tactical software intended to meet a finite need (short life span) very differently from a core system our organization intends to use for many years (long life span). In either case, the software is only there to support other activities. The McCartney report emphasizes that "Delivering IT is only ever part of the implementation of new, more effective ways of working.... Achieving this requires a clear vision of the context in which IT is being implemented" [3].

Because the SDLC is often loosely referred to as the software life cycle, I have chosen to use "life span" to refer to the entire life of a software system, in order to differentiate the initial development from the rest of the software's existence.[1]

The purpose of this chapter is to outline the four main stages I will distinguish throughout the life span of a software system. These four stages I have called *start-up*, *development* (the SDLC), *delivery*, and *postdelivery* (when the customers use the system until it is decommissioned). Maintenance changes are made to the system during postdelivery. You may use different names for these parts of the life span in your organization, or you may find that an SDLC is defined but not start-up, delivery, or postdelivery, or that all four stages are regarded as part of the SDLC. Do not worry about that; the naming and organization of the stages is simply to help us manage our work. The division into four life span stages that I am making is very simple (see Figure 8.1).

---

1. The IT Infrastructure Library refers to the "Application Management Lifecycle," containing Application Development (which includes the SDLC), and "Service Management" for the postdelivery activities. I have decided that for this book, *life span* and *life cycle* are simpler and easier to differentiate [4].

8.1 Life span or life cycle? 155

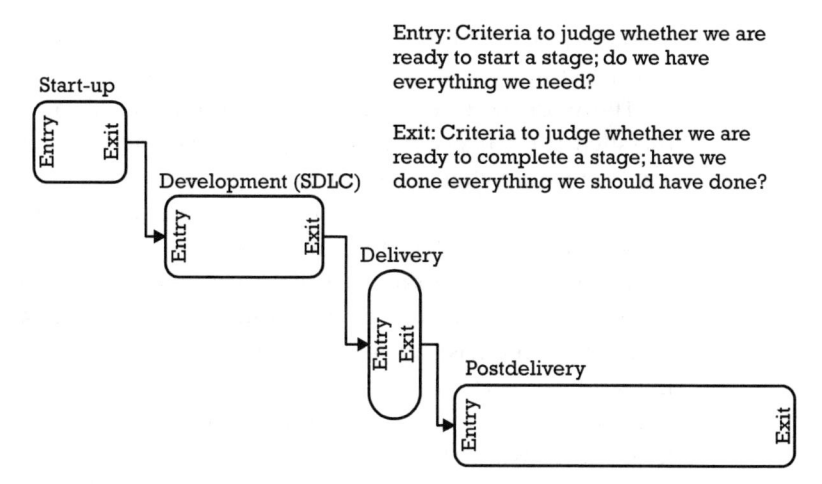

Entry: Criteria to judge whether we are ready to start a stage; do we have everything we need?

Exit: Criteria to judge whether we are ready to complete a stage; have we done everything we should have done?

Figure 8.1 Life span stages.

8.1.1 Start-up

At this stage, members of the customer group realize that they have a problem that needs to be solved. They request the provision of a software solution. I use the word *problem* here; it may, of course, be an *opportunity*, for example, to expand into a new marketplace; or *an outside requirement*, for example, a legislative change, rather than a problem. In a healthy organization where relationships between groups are strong, managers and builders in IT may trigger start-up. IT can *create* opportunities by suggesting technical possibilities unknown to the customers. For example, in a major supermarket group, the customers knew that ordering stock for Christmas was a nightmare, and accepted that they would overorder and run out of products. Surely, that is part of their business, isn't it? The IT director identified a software package that could manage the inventory more effectively, based on predicted demand. The customers were unaware that this was possible, but were delighted when the project had an almost immediate payback.

In start-up, we must understand the problem, and if we do not, explore it more. We need to decide whether a software solution is appropriate, and, if it is, agree on the overall constraints, acceptance criteria, and thus the type of SDLC. If we decide to follow a software solution, we need some formal or informal contract between the groups. This is covered in Chapter 9.

8.1.2 Development

At this stage, a software project is undertaken, through the SDLC. This includes requirement definition, design, build and test activities to bring the software solution from the high-level definition of the start-up stage to a system ready for live delivery. It is important to remember that this is not just code being built by developers. Remember our poor trainer from Chapter 1. People will also be busy designing, building, and testing training, documentation, and support materials. If the software being developed is a package for commercial sale, the support material may include sales and marketing material. For an in-house business system, it may include business process manuals. These are all part of the delivered product.

The work required might include the acquisition of a commercial off-the-shelf (COTS) system, building a custom-made system, tailoring a package, or making changes to an existing live system.

Members of all groups will be involved, directly or indirectly, but the focus is on the builders and measurers.

There are several different life-cycle models for software development. Some of these have been in use for many years, but new models and variations on the models have been developed over the years. The changes to the models have been made as customer problems, perceptions of quality, and the technologies available have evolved. I will look at the main groups of models. We will examine their advantages and disadvantages, and consider how to combine their best aspects to customize a life cycle. This is covered in Chapter 10.

8.1.3 Delivery

This is the point where the completed software solution is moved to live use. It is a time of anxiety for all the groups. The customers take delivery of the software and start to use it. Members of all groups will support the delivery, but their viewpoints will be quite different. The customer and supporters are very engaged at this point. Will the system really work? Will they be able to use it? Will the delivery go well? The builders and managers have quite a different reason for anxiety at this point. Will the project team be able to finish this project and (with more or less relief) move onto a shiny new project? For the measurers, fairly or unfairly, their efforts in assessing quality are now under the microscope. Did they make the right assessment? At delivery, many activities will come together at a single milestone in the project plan. This is a short, intense period of stress, anxiety, and emotions that are a rollercoaster between despair and elation. I will discuss delivery in Chapter 11.

8.1.4 Postdelivery

This is the life of the software while it is being used until it is decommissioned. It is the longest part of a software system's life span [5, 6], and is where the benefits of the software are realized; "A project or program is only successful if it delivers the benefits for which it was initiated" [3]. Customers use the software while supporters maintain and support it. Although the project team has often disbanded, all groups have an interest in quality at this stage (see Section 8.3). Additionally, it is almost certain that the software will undergo maintenance changes. Customers will identify new problems to be resolved and new opportunities to grasp, and will encounter new outside requirements. The system may need to be enhanced, corrected, and adapted to changes in its environment. To aid this, supporters may need to change it to make future support and maintenance easier. So the system will be subject to successive cycles of change, often with many changes taking place in parallel (Figure 8.2). Each maintenance change will have a start-up (SU), development (SDLC/SMLC), and delivery (D), feeding into the post-delivery (PD) system. Figure 8.2 shows new SDLCs, involving the whole cast of characters from before, that could be described as SMLCs (software-maintenance life cycles). This is covered in Chapter 12.

8.2 Entry and exit criteria between stages

Each stage has within it some entry criteria (the criteria for starting that stage) and some exit criteria (the criteria for completing the stage). Some people call these the "quality gates." The entry criteria to a stage must match the exit criteria from the previous stage, like a series of jigsaw puzzle pieces. This may seem obvious, but I have seen projects affected badly by misunderstandings at the hand-over points between stages as confusion arises between people about responsibilities, authority, acceptance criteria, and quality. The reason for entry and exit criteria is to clarify to people how and when a handover can take place, and when it should *not* take place. In a project or program with several parallel activities, a set of exit criteria may feed more than one set of entry criteria, and a set of entry criteria may need exits from more than one previous activity. Long stages, for example the SDLC itself, will have entry and exit criteria to control the steps within the stage. We will see examples of this in later chapters.

Each entry and exit point needs an owner. This is someone who has the knowledge and authority to judge that the criteria are complete, by using a checklist [7] or by best judgment. The former is more objective; if the checklist is complete we move on, otherwise we do not. Using best judgment alone can result in an argument about whether the criteria are fulfilled or not, especially if the ownership and responsibility for the quality gates are not clear. Sometimes, we want to ignore the criteria. For example, during

SU	= Start-up
SDLC/SMLC	= Development (the software development life cycle or the software maintenance life cycle)
D	= Delivery
PD	= Postdelivery

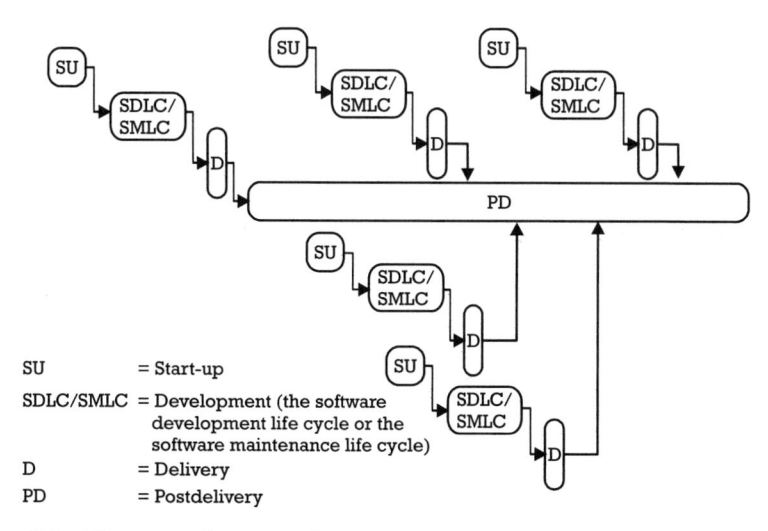

Figure 8.2 Change cycles to a software system.

start-up the project team may want to start work before all the acceptance criteria are set, in the belief that this will save time. If this is the case, we need to examine *why* we set the criteria in a particular way and the risks we take in not fulfilling the criteria. As we will see in Chapters 9 to 12, the precise entry and exit criteria depend on the situation, so checklists will need to be tailored. As well as an owner, identify an escalation authority, to make judgments in borderline cases.

Table 8.1 gives an example of simple entry and exit criteria between stages; we will discuss them in detail within each stage. Typically some type of review is required to check that the criteria have been fulfilled properly; for example, [3] suggests a peer review at "project gateways."

8.3 Changes in quality viewpoints across the life span of a system

Software quality is important throughout the life span of a software system. It can be built in or neglected at each stage of a system's life span. In Chapter 1, we looked at five definitions of quality and at associated quality viewpoints. Now I will consider how these viewpoints change across the life span of the software system.

The dominant group at each stage will dictate the prevailing view (see Table 8.2), but each group will still hold onto its preferred view, sometimes even feeling that their view is being discounted. For example, during development, the easiest view for the project team to use—the manufacturing view—will mean that they concentrate on delivering to specification.

Table 8.1 Example of Entry and Exit Criteria for Stages in the Life Span

	Entry	Exit
Start-up	Problem identified	Contract for SDLC
Development	Contact for SDLC	Acceptance test passed
Delivery	Acceptance test passed	Load to live use complete
Postdelivery	Load to live use complete	Decommissioning complete

Table 8.2 Prevailing Views of Quality Across the Life Span

| Quality View | Stage | | | |
	Start-Up	SDLC	Delivery	Postdelivery
Transcendent view	✓	✓	✓	✓
User view	✓	(✓late)	✓	✓
Value view	✓			✓
Product view		✓		✓
Manufacturing view		✓		✓

✓ is a primary quality view.
(✓) is a quality view that may be taken by some people in this stage.

However, when delivery happens, the user view will prevail. The builders feel pleased that they have delivered to specification, and are then stunned to find the system rejected by the customers.

This happens more often than one might suppose, either because the specification was wrong, or because it was misinterpreted, or because the world has changed so that the specification is out of date by the time the system is delivered.

Once the system is in use, we can measure its effect. The managers will be interested in measures of value for money and return on investment, supporting the value-based view of quality. Supporters, measurers, and builders will be interested in measures of defects reported during use, supporting manufacturing- and product-based views of quality. Customers and supporters engage with the software day to day. They hold a transcendent view of quality ("Are we enjoying this system?") but also the user-based view. They will have a perception of the software as fit for purpose or otherwise.

In the next four chapters, I will describe the quality activities at each stage, showing what people can do as a team at each stage to build in and measure quality, therefore achieving software quality through teamwork.

References

[1] *Compact Oxford English Dictionary,* 2nd ed., Oxford, England: Oxford University Press, 2002.

[2] Hetzel, W., *The Complete Guide to Software Testing,* Wellesley, MA: QED, 1984.

[3] Cabinet Office, *Successful IT: Modernising Government in Action,* London, England: HMSO, 2000.

[4] IT Infrastructure Library, *Best Practice for Application Management,* London, England: Office of Government Commerce, 2002.

[5] Baxter, I. D., and C. W. Pidgeon, "Software Change Through Design Maintenance," *International Conference on Software Maintenance (ICSM '97),* 1997.

[6] Yourdon, E., "Long-Term Thinking," *Computerworld,* October 2000, http://www.computerworld.com/managementtopics/management/story/0,10 801,52398,00.html, accessed January 2004.

[7] Gilb, T., and D. Graham, *Software Inspection,* Reading, MA: Addison-Wesley, 1993.

CHAPTER 9

Start-Up for a Software-Development Project

Contents

9.1 Start-up—description

9.2 Start-up viewpoints

9.3 Entry criteria for start-up

9.4 Start-up—typical activities

9.5 Exit from start-up stage

In this chapter I shall:

- Describe the entry criteria, steps, and exit criteria for the start-up stage;
- Show how to use this stage to decide whether software development is required;
- Identify the quality definitions from Chapter 1 that prevail at start-up;
- Identify how each of the groups identified in Chapter 2 becomes involved at start-up;
- Introduce techniques for analyzing problems and solutions, setting aims and objectives, and defining acceptance criteria and constraints.

Is that what you thought the reason is for this project? That's not why I want it done....
—*The development and business managers discover, several months into the project, that they have opposing goals*

I would have thought it was obvious that we wouldn't want this!
—*Customer rejecting software on delivery*

9.1 Start-up—description

We realize that we have a problem, or an opportunity (for example, to expand into a new marketplace), or an outside requirement such as a legislative change. We must understand it and decide how to resolve it before we launch into delivering a solution. Although many of us see quality as delivering a project excellently, the most important project decision is ensuring that we do the *right* project. If the builders do not understand the problem and the customers' and managers' quality views and their constraints, they may build software that is too costly or not fit for purpose. The cost of making that mistake is huge compared with setting up the project correctly in the first place: One commentator reported that the cost of failed IT projects in the United States was estimated at $84 billion [1]. The cost of finding our mistakes and sorting them out escalates throughout the project [2]. The cost of doing the *wrong project* could be phenomenal; our biggest risk is spending a lot of money and *not* resolving our problem. However, once we identify that we have a problem, our impulse is to start doing something, *anything*, to show that we are taking action. This means that we dive straight into delivery without really knowing what we want to do. Our projects go wrong before they have started! So, in this chapter, I am going to show you how to make the difficult move from a complex and messy business problem to a project that is clear and structured. We will set the foundation for future work, possibly including a software-development life cycle (SDLC) and delivery (see Figure 9.1).

As an SDLC is costly, it is worth spending some time and effort doing this stage well. We might decide that we cannot resolve this problem by a software solution, or that we prefer to use a manual solution, or to do nothing. We must:

- Explore the problem until we understand it.
- Decide whether this problem is worth solving.
- Set general constraints and parameters for the solution.
- Decide how to approach the problem; for example, a software solution may be appropriate.
- Agree on a formal or informal contract of work, with constraints, acceptance criteria, and an outline or high-level plan.

As we see in Figure 9.2, we will not just work our way down the list, checking each off in order; we will find that we need to revisit interrelated tasks as we investigate the problem. We cycle round, investigating the problem until we have enough information to either decide to do nothing, to have a manual solution, or to have a software solution to the problem.

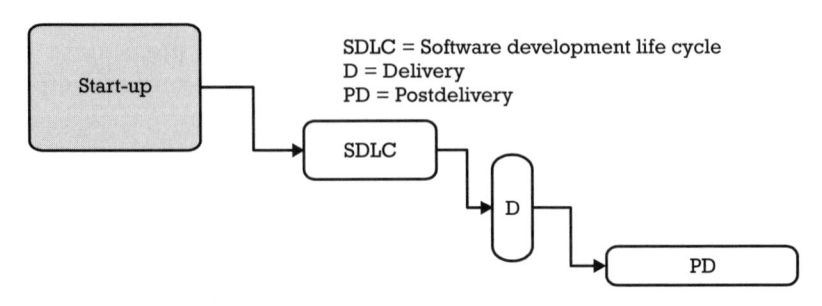

Figure 9.1 Life-cycle stage diagram.

9.2 Start-up viewpoints

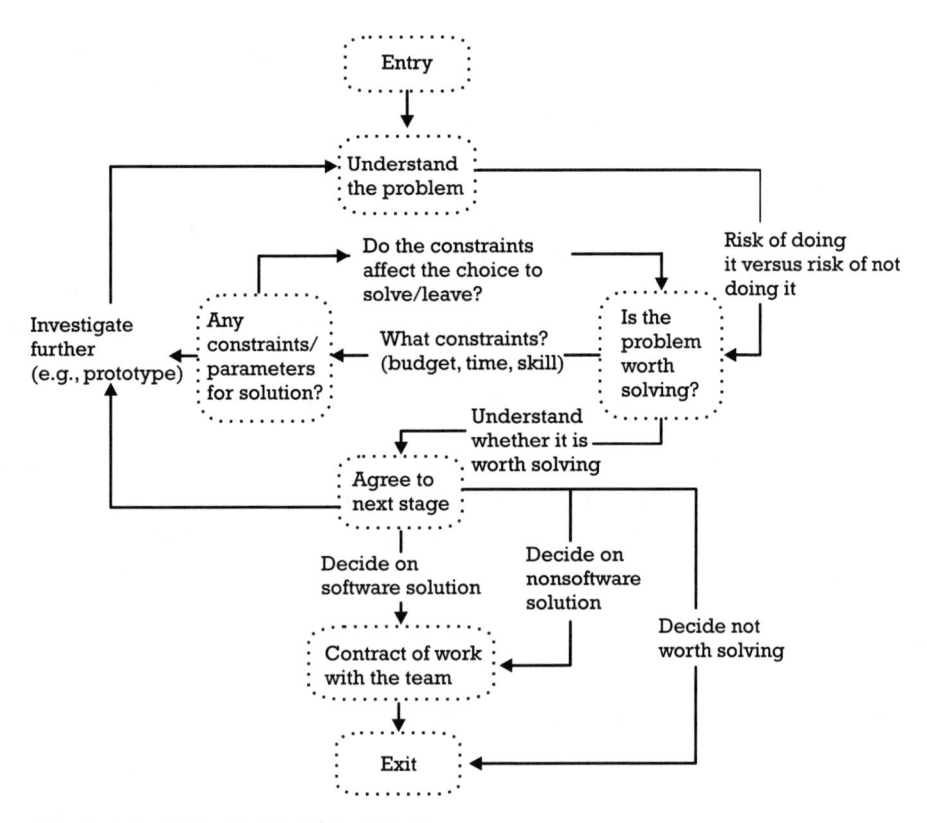

Figure 9.2 Task summary for start-up.

9.2 Start-up viewpoints

A factor I often see contributing to the failure of software projects is that people with useful viewpoints and information are not involved early enough. Often, the only groups that participate in start-up are the customers and managers. Table 9.1 shows the quality views represented.

The team has a biased quality viewpoint, as it lacks either the product or the manufacturing view. Also, because they are not involved, the builders, measurers, and supporters are not being directly exposed to the *value* and *user quality views*. The consequences of this can be severe. In a large transformation program in financial services, a group of consultants found that the IT teams had little understanding of the business cases for their projects. They did not know why they were building, so were unaware of the

Table 9.1 Views of Quality at Start-Up: Simple View

	Groups	
Quality view	Customer	Manager
Transcendent view	✓	✓
User view	✓	
Value view		✓
Product view		
Manufacturing view		

organizational impact of going over budget or missing scope. They delivered software that often failed to meet business expectations.

Table 9.2 shows that involving all the groups covers the quality viewpoints and thus provides wider knowledge of the problem and potential solutions.

Some IT people, including builders, measurers, and managers, express frustration that the customers often do not know what they want, but we must realize that it *is* difficult to understand many problems. Often, when customers call in consultants "All [they know] is that something is not working right and [they] need some kind of help" [3]. In some situations, there is no clear customer group. Suppose your organization builds software packages that are purchased by customers "off the shelf." You may not have direct contact with your "real" customers. Sales, marketing, or market research people could represent the customers or involve customers via market research. In one company producing project management packages, the "key customers" for each release were representatives from group marketing and the customer help desk.

9.3 Entry criteria for start-up

The entry criteria for a stage are the rules or reasons by which we decide we are ready to start that stage. This might include a list of input deliverables or a list of events that have to have happened. For the start-up stage, these are quite simple (Table 9.3); we realize we need something—a problem solved, a change in our processes, a new product supported. We have an idea for an improvement or a change. This may be enough, but in some organizations it

Table 9.2 Views of Quality at Start-Up: Teamwork View

	Groups				
Quality view	*Customer*	*Manager*	*Builder*	*Measurer*	*Supporter*
Transcendent view	✓	✓	✓	✓	✓
User view	✓			(✓)	✓
Value view		✓			
Product view			✓	✓	✓
Manufacturing view			✓	✓	

✓ is a primary quality view.
(✓) is a quality view that may be taken by some people in this group.

Table 9.3 Example of Simple Entry Criteria and Owners for Start-up Stage

Example Entry Criterion	*Example Owner*
System or process problem identified	Change control group
Legislation change identified	Audit and compliance
Idea for new product identified	Marketing
Process improvement identified	Process owner

may be the entry into a suggestion scheme or a change process. When you define entry criteria and steps for your start-up stage, look at your existing scheme, and decide what ideas from this chapter you would like to add to improve it.

9.4 Start-up—typical activities

9.4.1 Understanding the problem/idea

Once a problem or idea has been identified, we can use various methods to analyze it. Remember that I am using "problem" as shorthand for "problem, outside requirement, opportunity, or other reason for wanting to change the status quo." This step is critical, so beware underplaying it. If you get this bit wrong, the project could *already* be doomed to fail! People will have preconceptions about what needs to be done, even if they are using the word "problem," as TQMI[1] [4] identifies:

- *Solution*: "our problem is that we need a new Web-based interface."
- *Symptom*: "our problem is people keep making mistakes in data input."
- *Decision*: "our problem is deciding which supplier to choose."
- *Problem*: "our problem is that it isn't working as we expected."

Involving all groups will help prevent you from confusing the symptom with the cause. Be radical and dig deep until you find the real problem. You will need to consider many possible and underlying causes; for example, a customer complaint might have one or more root causes (Table 9.4).

There are many methods for understanding problems and solutions. Some you will find particularly useful are cause–effect or root-cause analysis, solution analysis, brainstorming, and prototyping (see Table 9.5). You will probably use cause–effect/solution (C-E/S) analysis and brainstorming on your first pass, followed by methods such as prototyping as you start trying to identify possible solutions (see Figure 9.3).

Table 9.4 Severe Customer Complaint Root Causes

Problem	Severe Customer Complaint
Apparent cause	Poor quality products
Possible underlying causes	Product is badly designed/badly built/fails too quickly, and too often.
	Product not matched to customer need/misadvertised/missold.
	Customer expectations not managed against feasible targets/too expensive, late.
	Poor quality service/customer complaints not handled well/customer passed from person to person, multiple calls required to resolve problem.
Root cause in this case	The customer had a minor problem that escalated as multiple calls were required to resolve it.
Solution	Improve customer complaints procedure to ensure a fast resolution to problems.

---

1. Reproduced by permission of TQMI Ltd., from *Problem Solving—Tools and Techniques*.

Table 9.5 Summary of Techniques for Start-Up

Subject Area	Technique Examples	In 30 Seconds… (see Appendix A for more)
Identify problems and root causes, find solutions	Ishikawa fishbones [4, 5]	Use to identify problems, root causes of problems and solutions. On a fishbone diagram, brainstorm problems, their possible causes, their root causes, and, therefore, solutions to the root cause. See Chapter 12 for an example.
Review documents and other products	Walkthrough [6], inspections [2, 6], peer review [6]	Walkthrough is a review with the purpose of increasing understanding of a document. The author introduces the audience to the document and takes them through it, explaining the content. Inspection is a formal review with the purpose of identifying and preventing defects and nonconformities to standards and specifications. Peer review additionally allows discussion.
Improve meetings and improve contributions	De Bono's Six Thinking Hats [7]	Improve meetings by setting rules for behavior. Six "hats" are used. Everyone wears the same color hat at the same time: Blue Hat—meeting structure, Black Hat—pessimistic, Yellow Hat—optimistic, Red Hat—feelings, White Hat—facts, Green Hat—creative ideas. Allows meeting members to move outside their stereotypes and allows time for different, sometimes difficult types of communication.
Helping groups agree on aims, objectives, targets, and indicators	Weaver triangle [8]	On a one-page diagram, the group identifies and agrees on the aim of the project (why it is being done) and associated indicators of success, then on the objectives of the project (what is to be done) and associated targets. They identify where stakeholders have different aims for the project.
Understand/ explore ideas	Prototyping [9, 10]	Not an SDLC! We prototype to try out ideas or, if we are not sure what we want, we build a model of a possible solution(s). Discuss the prototype and review it. Two types of prototyping in software are "lo-fi" and "hi-fi." In hi-fi (high-fidelity), we build screens like those the customer will see. Lo-fi (low-fidelity) prototyping uses paper/white board. In lo-fi there is no danger of believing the prototype is the software.
	Modeling and picturing, stories, metaphors [11–13]	There are a number of modeling and picturing techniques that can be worth exploring with lo-fi prototyping. These include Rich Picturing and Mind Mapping. Sketching a picture of a problem, solution, or idea can clarify it. Use stories, metaphors, and analogy as well; they can help understanding.
Understand whether an idea is worth pursuing	Risk workshop by brainstorming [4, 5]	A brainstorming workshop is run to list all the possible risks people can identify. Risks are sorted into groups, also separate risks (might happen in the future), issues (problems right now) and constraints. Risks are scored for impact and likelihood, and ranked to give a prioritized list.
	Cost–benefit analysis [5]	Cost–benefit analysis is done by calculating the predicted benefits of the proposed change (time, money saved) and setting this against the predicted cost.
Choose which idea to pursue	Pareto analysis [4]	The Pareto principle suggests that 80% of the problems are the result of 20% of the causes. Gather data on the frequency of problems/causes, and then resolve the most frequent.
Team relationships and natural roles/team skills	Belbin team scores [14]	The SDLC can fail because of personal rather than technical factors. Teams need to understand their strengths and weaknesses as a team. A balance of roles/skills is required in the personalities in the team. Example roles: plants have new ideas; completer–finishers want to finish to fine detail. Too many plants and you will never finish anything.

9.4 Start-up—typical activities

Table 9.5 (Continued)

Improve communication— Empathy with others	MBTI [15], Honey & Mumford [16], Kirton [17]	Different people have different personalities and communication styles. People who wave their arms around and talk a lot can annoy people who like to be quiet and think, and vice versa. The Myers-Briggs Type Indicator (MBTI) identifies four contrasting type pairs, e.g., *Introvert/Extrovert*, leading to 16 "types" (e.g. INTJ is *Introvert-iNtuitive-Thinking-Judging*). The Honey & Mumford Learning Styles Questionnaire identifies preferred learning styles (e.g., *Pragmatists vs. Theorists* require different experiences to learn). Kirton identifies preferred problem-solving methods (*Adaptors vs. Innovators*)—do we break the rules or work within them?

If you do not have direct access to your customers, your sales and marketing group may use market research or ethnographical techniques at this stage. This includes observing or interviewing groups of likely or existing customers to help focus understanding of the customer's viewpoint, with use of prototypes. For example, Philips uses their "HomeLab" in Eindhoven to observe how people react to new technology, because it is only by observing people living with the technology that they can identify which ideas are good in practice, as well as in theory [18].

The output from this stage is a problem statement. This does not need to be formal. The aim is to provide a short, clear description of your analyzed problem. I would advise that you get others to have a peer review or a walk-through of the problem statement before you go any further into start-up.

Do not forget that allowing different viewpoints to be heard during discussion of ideas is important. People who are disillusioned may respond negatively to any new idea, including use of new techniques. If people say, "Yes, but…" or "We've tried that and it didn't work…," do not dismiss them. You will need to persist and show people that their contributions are

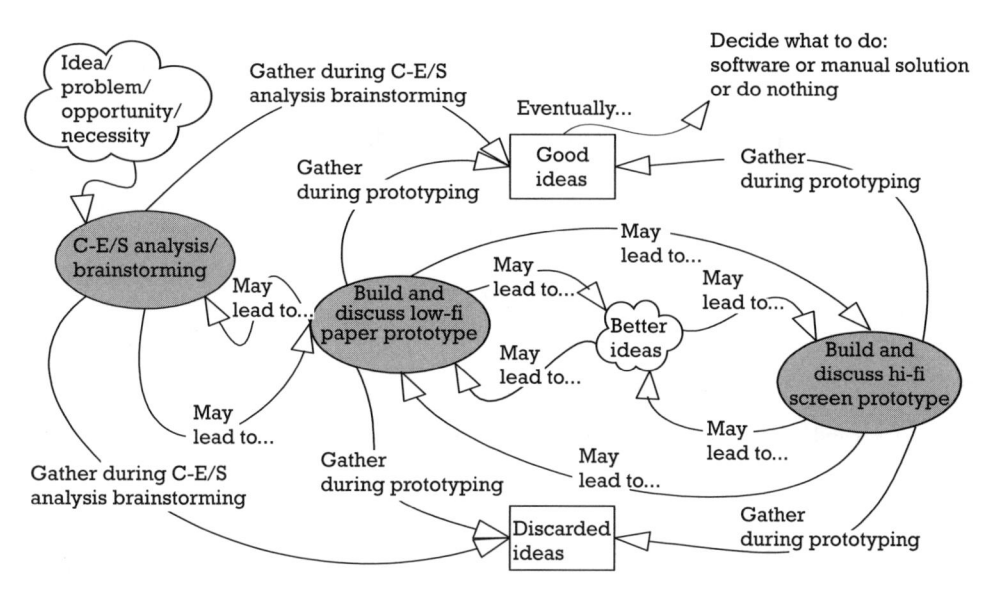

Figure 9.3 Problem and solution analysis cycles during start-up.

listened to seriously. People get into a habit of always reacting in the same way; they consistently either support or condemn suggestions [3]. Using De Bono's Six Hats [7] helps resolve this by encouraging everyone to express positive and negative views (see Table 9.5 and Appendix A). You may also find, as I have, that when you bring the groups together some people are very loud and others reticent. In certain organizational cultures, staff are reluctant to challenge or disagree with their superiors [3]. If you find this, then use techniques to help people express their views. For example, all ideas or comments could be submitted anonymously in advance of the workshop, then discussed "blind" (Frank Johnstone, personal correspondence, April 24, 2003). Technology can help; some organizations use on-line meetings and chat rooms to allow challenges to be presented safely.

Your view of the problem becomes more complete as you look at it from different quality perspectives. Every group should participate in workshops to identify problems and ideas, suggest solutions, build prototypes, and provide examples of similar business situations and how they were solved (Table 9.6).

9.4.2 Decide whether the problem/idea is worth solving

We now have some understanding of our problem or idea. We need to consider whether it is worth doing anything about it, and answering these questions will help us:

- What benefits will we realize by solving this problem?
- What risks are we taking if we do not do this?
- What risks are we taking if we do it and it goes wrong?
- What benefits might we *not* realize if we attempt it but it goes wrong?

Both action and inaction hold risks. For some of the entry criteria examples in Table 9.3, there is no doubt that a software project will be

Table 9.6 Group Contributions to Understanding the Problem

Activity:	Group C = Customer, M = Manager, B = Builder, Me = Measurer, S = Supporter				
Identify problem, idea	All groups				
Provide example of similar problems and solutions	All groups				
Take part in discussions and workshops	All groups				
Identify solutions and build prototypes	All groups				
Review role:	C	M	B	Me	S
Review/test ideas and prototypes against a quality viewpoint: U = User, V = Value, M = Manufacturing, P = Product	U V	V	M P	M P U	U P

undertaken. If a legislative change is required that affects the software systems, then the question is not "is this a good idea?" but "how shall we change the software?" If there is a choice and there may be risks in making changes, it might be better to accept the problem or not implement the new idea, having assessed the risk. For example, not implementing a new product gives us a risk of losing market share because our customers may move to our competitors. Implementing the new product may increase our number of customers and sales, and we should be able to predict the benefit gained. But supposing our infrastructure (warehousing, sales support, and so on) cannot support the increase? We may end up giving poor service to all our customers, and so lose more business than if we had done nothing.

We also need to consider whether there are risks involved with any expectations, for example the target date for getting the new product to market. What is the risk if we miss that date? What is the risk that the date will be too difficult a target for us to meet? You can see that there are two parts to the risk: we need to consider the likelihood that something will go wrong and the impact if it does go wrong. I have generally found that the customers, managers, and supporters have a good understanding of the impact of problems on the existing organization and infrastructure. Builders, measurers, and supporters understand where technical problems are likely to arise; they will understand the technical difficulties in solving the problem and the effect of constraints. Customers and managers understand where business complexity and constraints make problems likely.

The EFQM Excellence Model (see Chapter 1 and [19]) helps structure the way we think about the impact of either not doing something or doing it wrong. Consider the following:

- Impact on our organization's customers—service levels, goods, expectations, continuing delivery;
- Impact on the people in our organization—motivation, staff turnover, attitudes, development, loss of IT infrastructure/support;
- Impact on our partners and resources—support of systems and processes, damage to existing IT and other infrastructure;
- Impact on society—PR, attitudes, legislation, compliance;
- Impact on key performance results—financial, market share.

When we consider the *likelihood* of something going wrong if we *do not* take action and if we *do* take action, we look at our areas of weakness:

- Technical constraints and difficulties, for example, complexity, lack of knowledge of the technical aspects, limits to existing systems;
- Business constraints and difficulties, for example, complexity, lack of business knowledge, product or service delivery constraints;
- Use of, lack of, or misuse of tools, techniques, processes, and standards;
- Constraints, for example, in time, budget, personnel, skill levels, or other resources;

> Measurement of past experience and predictions from that.

The methods you can use were listed in Table 9.5 and are explained in Appendix A. They include risk workshops and cost–benefit analysis. You will probably need to consider risks and benefits along with constraints (see Section 9.4.3) because they will affect each other; if you only have the budget to build a family saloon car, do not expect it to be armor-plated. If you are deciding which of a group of problems to solve to get the greatest cost–benefit ratio, try using Pareto analysis (80% of the problems are the result of 20% of the causes), choosing the most frequent problems/causes to resolve [4].

9.4.3 Set general constraints and parameters for the solution

Some organizations like to keep the risk workshops, constraints definition, and cost–benefit analysis quite separate, but I have found that the constraints will often come out naturally during the risk workshop. You may want use part of the risk workshop specifically to collect constraints. The constraints, risks, and benefits tend to interrelate. If you have a constraint on timescale or budget, you may not be able to do as much as you wanted to do. This might increase your risks, but the risks associated with increased spending may be greater. Someone who took on a course of mine years ago gave me a wonderful analogy—it is like going to buy a washing machine:

> You go into the shop, and ask the sales assistant the price of washing machines. Suppose the assistant says that they range from $800 to $1,500. You only have $15. The assistant will point out that for that money, you can buy a bucket, a washboard, and some soap. You have kept within your budget constraints and avoided the risks associated with getting into debt. However, you are taking some additional risks—the washing will be done at a lower temperature, so it may be not so effective, and you are going to get soap on your skin (risk of "washerwoman's hand").

All the groups will be able to contribute to the discussion of constraints. Customers and managers will know about service level, timescale, budget, and resource and personnel constraints. Builders, measurers, and supporters will know about technical, knowledge, infrastructure, resources, and skills constraints. In particular, the supporters will understand the constraints against current IT service delivery and capacity [20, 21]. While examining the constraints, build prototype plans. Are any of the ideas "runners" within the constraints?

9.4.4 Agree on next stage

We have identified a problem or idea and we have looked at whether it is worth dealing with. Now we need to decide what to do. All the groups have a contribution to make, so consider having a walkthrough of the information gathered so far, encouraging questions, comments, and additions. In a walkthrough, the author of a document takes the meeting through the document step by step, allowing them to ask questions and gather information (see Table 9.5 and Appendix A). This promotes greater understanding and helps find areas of ambiguity and mistakes. Display all the information gathered so that the whole group can see it. I prefer putting everything on the wall to allow everyone to look at it at the same time, standing and walking from chart to chart. It helps the team to discuss and think as a team. Use a data projector and a PC, or flip charts from the workshops. If people are geographically remote, consider on-line review and meeting tools, or videoconferencing.

Once the team has discussed the information, they can make a decision about what to do next. We have four options:

- Do nothing—decide that the problem is not worth solving. Log the decision.
- Do more work on investigating the problem. Perhaps do some prototyping, but check that you have the time, budget, and permission to carry on.
- Decide not to develop software, but to address the problem through your people or processes. For example, the solution might include recruitment, process change, or building a manual solution. Draw up a contract for the work.
- Decide that we need a software solution. Draw up a contract for the work.

9.4.5 Contract for work

Watts Humphrey remarked that one problem with software schedules is that managers view them as contract-like commitments but the software engineers (builders) do not view them as personal commitments: "Too often, software commitments are based on little more than hope" [22]. We need an agreement or contract between the groups. I am not (necessarily) talking about the legal contract between a customer and third-party supplier; it could be a formal or an informal contract between groups within an organization, but it is a commitment. The Personal Software Process (PSP) [22] and the Team Software Process (TSP) [23] emphasize the importance of this commitment, but how do we reach it? It is vital that everyone agrees on:

- The aims and the objectives for the work;
- The constraints for the work—dates, budget, people, resources, technical, and business;
- Acceptance criteria that define how we will know the work has been completed satisfactorily.

Everyone needs to agree on what has been planned and check that it is possible, by contributing to and reviewing the contract. This contract is the basis for the project(s) that will deliver the solution required by the customers, perhaps including an SDLC. Sometimes, it is easy to agree the contract; the problem or idea is well understood. Often, teams find this step difficult; perhaps the customers are not sure what they want, or cannot define it, or sometimes the builders and measurers are not sure they can build and test the software within the constraints. If the team cannot agree on the aims and objectives for the work, plus at least overall constraints and high-level acceptance criteria, it is probably not wise to agree on a contract for an SDLC; the problem or idea is not well enough understood to make a sensible commitment to the work.

There may be reluctance to contribute difficult or controversial ideas in contract negotiation meetings—"If I put my head above the parapet will I get shot?" This is particularly true if different groups disagree about what is *possible* within constraints. To prevent the loudest voice being the only one heard, use the techniques mentioned earlier to control contributions to the discussion.

9.4.5.1 Aims and objectives for the work

A project's *aims* describe why it is being undertaken. They answer the question, "Why are we doing this?" The answer is not "to build a Web site" but "to increase market share." Objectives are what you will do in order to reach an aim: "Our aim is to increase market share, so one of our objectives is to build a Web site." Each aim is associated with one or more objectives, otherwise it will not happen. Every objective must meet one or more aims, otherwise, why do it? Indicators measure the impact that the project has on the business. Did the project make a difference? Were the aims met? Has it realized benefits or mitigated risks? Indicators enable us to assess whether the aims have been met. Targets measure project delivery, monitoring whether the objectives have been achieved. We know whether a requirement is within our scope by testing to see if it aligns with the project aims and objectives.

A useful technique to help define and agree on aims and objectives is a Weaver triangle [8] (see Figure 9.4, Table 9.5, and Appendix A) as it provides a picture of the project on one page. I have used a Weaver triangle with software projects to demonstrate that key people around the project had radically different ideas of the real aim of the project. The reason one project was failing was that there was no agreement about why it was being done. Each team had taken off with different aims, in a different direction.

All the groups participate in defining and agreeing on the aims, objectives, targets, and indicators, remembering to check that they are SMART (specific, measurable, achievable, realistic and time-bound). If the team cannot agree on SMART aims and objectives, do not set the contract. Investigate the problem further.

9.4 Start-up—typical activities 173

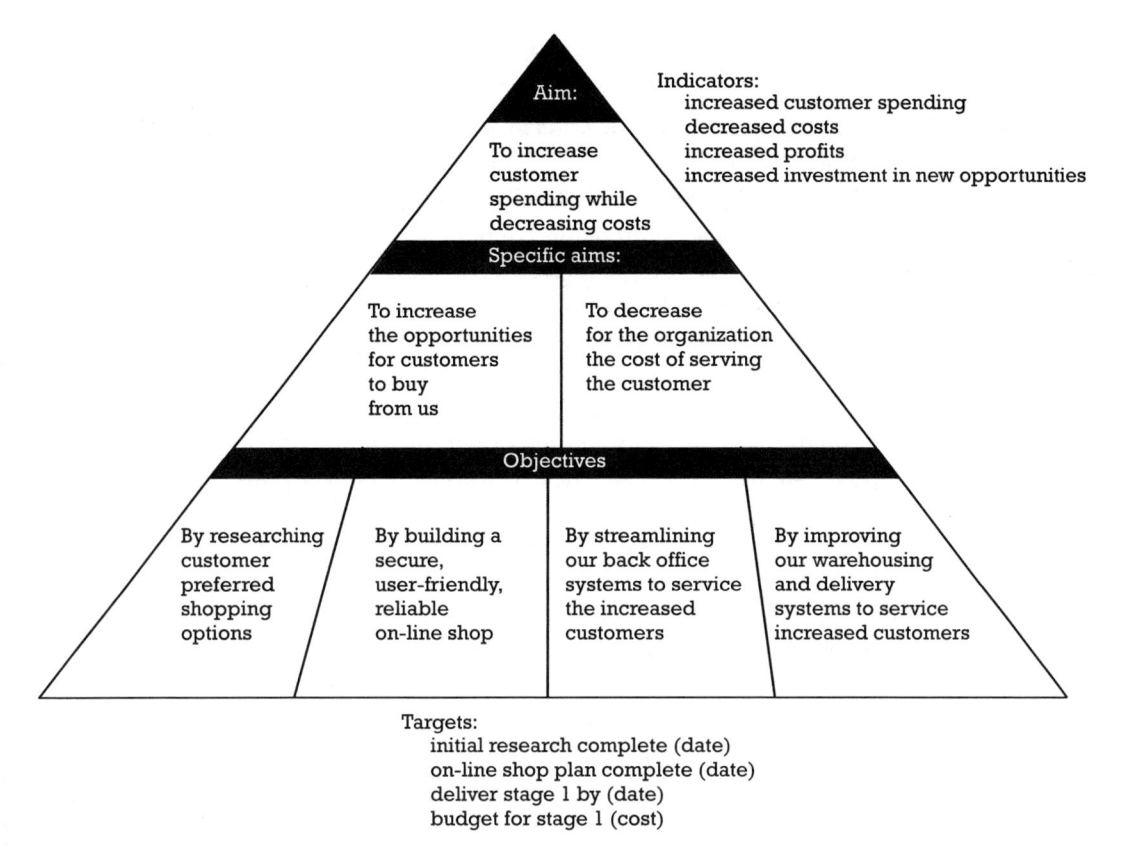

Figure 9.4 Weaver triangle. (*After:* [8].)

Aim: To increase customer spending while decreasing costs

Indicators:
- increased customer spending
- decreased costs
- increased profits
- increased investment in new opportunities

Specific aims:
- To increase the opportunities for customers to buy from us
- To decrease for the organization the cost of serving the customer

Objectives:
- By researching customer preferred shopping options
- By building a secure, user-friendly, reliable on-line shop
- By streamlining our back office systems to service the increased customers
- By improving our warehousing and delivery systems to service increased customers

Targets:
- initial research complete (date)
- on-line shop plan complete (date)
- deliver stage 1 by (date)
- budget for stage 1 (cost)

9.4.5.2 Constraints for the work

We have already looked at gathering the constraints. At this stage, we are confirming that they are correct and complete, and that the project can be delivered inside its constraints. In particular, managers will set date and budget constraints, against value measures. These need to be checked and agreed on by the other groups. As before, the builders, measurers, and supporters identify technical constraints, for example, IT service levels and capacity [22, 23]. These need to be understood and agreed on by the other groups. If the team cannot identify the constraints, at least at a high level, for example, the maximum budget, do not set the contract. Investigate the problem further and prototype the plan to see if it is possible to deliver within reasonable constraints. If there is some leeway in constraints, reflect this in the contract:

- "This date must be met—legal requirement" is mandatory.
- "Marketing have planned a July launch to meet the build up for the holiday market (November/December), latest launch is August" is mandatory with some leeway.
- "Would like to complete work before March next year" is a preferred date and could be renegotiated.

9.4.5.3 Acceptance criteria

Setting acceptance criteria at this stage is very important. The acceptance criteria are the means by which we know if a product or service is acceptable or not. They describe the attributes of a product or service, and the "pass mark" for each attribute for acceptability. If acceptance criteria are not defined or they are vague, we are in danger of building the wrong system. Like the targets and indicators, acceptance criteria must be SMART. Many projects are reasonably good at defining what the software should do (its *functionality*). Very few customers and managers, in my experience, give much thought to *how* the software should function. This is best illustrated by an example. An ATM machine should provide cash—that is its function. *How quickly* should it provide the cash—within 2 hours or within 1 minute? This is a *nonfunctional attribute*—it describes *how* the software works. They are often taken for granted. In the ATM example, it seems obvious that 2 hours is too long to wait for the money. The problem is that people's assumptions about these attributes may differ, so that although one might assume that the nonfunctional attributes are too obvious to mention, they may be interpreted differently by other people in the team. Whether the project includes an SDLC or not, acceptance criteria will be needed, in order that we can check that the project has delivered acceptable products and services.

Software standard ISO 9126 [24] describes attributes of software, and measures for those attributes, but, as you will see, we could adapt some of the attributes for nonsoftware solutions. If we use ISO 9126 to help us define acceptance criteria, we can improve their SMARTness. This increases the likelihood of the right software being delivered.

ISO 9126 breaks down the functional and nonfunctional attributes of software into a series of subattributes, questions and metrics. Some examples are shown in Table 9.7.

Let us take usability as an example. People find it hard to define and measure usability, so "give up" on trying to write acceptance criteria or trying to measure whether the software is acceptable. Look at Table 9.8, and you will see increasing refinement of one aspect of usability until we arrive at measurable acceptance criteria. Statements 1 and 2 are impossible to measure. No attempt is made to define "usability." Statement 3 crudely qualifies what usability means but it will be hard to measure, and it will, therefore, be difficult to design and build software that meets the customers' usability needs. Statement 4 is a little better; we know that some training will be needed but we have no definition of a new user. Is it someone new

Table 9.7 Examples of Attributes, Based on ISO 9126

Example Attribute	Example Subattribute	Example Question or Statement
Functionality	Suitability	Does the function perform tasks that do not conform to specified ones in requirements specifications or user manuals?
Usability	Understandability	Percentage of functions evident to user
Security	Access controllability	Is there any failing to defend against illegal access or illegal operation?

9.4 Start-up—typical activities

Table 9.8 Making Acceptance Criteria Measurable

1.	I assumed you would make it easy to use.
2.	It must be user-friendly.
3.	I want it to be as easy as the current system.
4.	A new user must be able to use it with 30 minutes training.
5.	Based on a sample of 20 typical users, at least 90% must learn to use the system in less than 30 minutes. After training, 100% of the sample users must be able to complete the standard "10 typical tasks" sequence without help, 95% of them completing it without help in less than 5 minutes.

to this particular software or to software in general? Statement 5 (based on ISO 9126 metrics under "Usability" for Learnability, Efficiency and Effectiveness) is measurable. Having more measurable acceptance criteria means it is easier to assess whether they meet other aspects of SMARTness.

The various nonfunctional attributes of software are of interest to different groups, so I would expect all the groups to be involved in setting acceptance criteria. Table 9.9 (based on discussions in 2002–2003 between David Hayman and me) lists attributes and groups. Remember when looking at the table that the customer group includes executives and sponsors as well as the software users.

Table 9.9 Selection of Nonfunctional Attributes and Groups

Attribute	Group Setting Acceptance Criteria and Reason
Performance (e.g., performance, stress, volume, scalability)	Customers—want good response from system
	Supporters—do not want bottlenecks in the infrastructure and systems
Security	Customers—Government and compliance requirements, CIA model (confidentiality, integrity, and accessibility of information)
	Supporters—infrastructure and firewalls
Reliability (e.g., reliability, availability, recovery)	Customers—service levels, product availability, lost sales, compliance, safety, avoid wasted time and lost work
	Supporters—reduce system restarts and help-desk calls, avoid wasted time and lost work
Usability	Customers—attractive system to use and to market, supports users at their skill level—not too easy, not too difficult—efficiency and effectiveness for users completing tasks, avoid wasted time, mistakes, increase productivity
	Supporters—reduce help-desk calls
IT support (e.g., installability, portability, compatibility, conversion, memory management, maintainability)	Supporters—need to support it within the existing infrastructure (e.g., amount of memory required, ease/cost of making changes)
	Managers—cost of changes to infrastructure, cost of making changes
Attribute	Group focus for reviewing acceptance criteria
All attributes reviewed	Measurers: they are testable (specific and measurable)
	Builders and supporters: they can be delivered within the constraints (achievable and realistic)
	Customers: they are what is required (realistic and time-bound)
	Managers: they are within cost/time constraints (realistic and time-bound)

Some of these attributes are specific to software, but others could be applied or adapted to nonsoftware projects. For example, suppose our project is to write some manual business processes. We would still look at attributes and acceptance criteria, for example:

- Usability—people are able to learn and use the new processes to carry out their tasks;
- Maintainability—able to update the business processes;
- Performance—throughput of tasks and business processes bottlenecks.

Just as in Chapter 1, where we saw that there is no "right" definition of quality, there is no "right" set of acceptance criteria. It is situational. Contrast the following:

- Air traffic control system—safety critical, so the emphasis is on reliability, recovery, performance, and security, but usability will also be important.
- Package to improve usability of Web pages for the visually impaired—it is browser-based, so usability and maintainability will be important.
- Software to launch an innovative new product and achieve "first-mover" advantage—marketing may produce a high initial demand and a new user group so stress and usability will be important.

We might believe that in a perfect world we would have no constraints, but this is not reality. For most commercial organizations, it would be unnecessarily expensive to have all the attributes "at 100%." Usually, the customer is best served by balancing the quality viewpoints. This means *planning* to deliver some attributes at a lower standard than what would be achievable in a perfect model. This is necessary to avoid sacrificing the *nonproduct* quality viewpoints. In our project, which of *security, performance, reliability,* and so on are most important to us? What are we prepared to invest in this software? The quality we want to build into the product and the project is a negotiated compromise. In practice, this comes down to identifying the greatest number or level of *attributes* (product-based quality) that:

- We *can deliver* (we have constraints of money, time, resources, and skills);
- To *support the users'* tasks (user-based quality);
- While giving best *cost–benefit ratio* (value-based quality);
- While following *repeatable/quality assured processes within a managed project with minimized defects* (manufacturing-based quality).

The balance that we want to achieve between the quality viewpoints is defined, then formalized in the acceptance criteria that we set for the functional and nonfunctional attributes of the software product and project deliverables (for example, specifications). Our acceptance criteria will prevent conflicts between stakeholders, provide guidance on how we develop the software, and mitigate against failing to meet the customer group's expectations.

Customers can find nonfunctional attributes difficult to conceptualize. As an example, in one project the customers had to set acceptance criteria for performance and response time. Initially they considered 20 seconds response time to be acceptable, even short. It *sounds* short. It *is* short when one is running for a train! However, the customers found it an unacceptable time *for a Web page to load* from the corporate intranet when they saw it live. The builders and supporters must be very proactive in helping the business define the nonfunctional acceptance criteria. Something that helped in the example above was a *performance prototype*; one of the team simply stopped the meeting for 20 seconds, allowing no speaking, no writing, and no movement, to demonstrate "what 20 seconds really feels like." You could also build prototypes and scenarios to help develop availability requirements and acceptance criteria.

Package vendors should note that customers often make purchases based on nonfunctional attributes, where functionality is similar in different products. Poor nonfunctional attributes may mean a product will be rejected [25]. Part of the market and other research for the project should explore this, with acceptance criteria set by the help-desk, support, sales, and marketing teams. Because the attributes are not described in the standard in everyday language, it can be useful to translate them into questionnaires, as suggested by Trienekens and van Veenendaal [26]. For example, asking "Have you an alternative way of carrying out your task if the software is not available?" provides an insight into *reliability* acceptance criteria. The weighting of replies for all the questions gives the priorities for acceptance [27].

The team should agree on the priority for the system attributes, because the most important attributes will be the focus for designing what is built. If the team then cannot set SMART acceptance criteria for the high-priority attributes, or cannot agree on the priority, try some prototyping to help generate ideas. Acceptance criteria should include the measurement of indicators. Indicators (for example, "percentage increase in market share") are measured after the project completes, so acceptance criteria should show which attributes contribute to the aims and, hence, to the indicators.

9.4.5.4 Outline plan

Once the aims and objectives, constraints and acceptance criteria have been agreed on, we can build an outline plan, based on the prototype plans we built before. The reason for doing this is to examine whether it is reasonable to provide a solution within the constraints that meets the aims, objectives, and acceptance criteria. This plan is unlikely to be very accurate or precise; expect to see "ball park" figures, and an allowance for replanning during any project.

9.4.5.5 Reviewing the contract

Any contract for further work should be reviewed by walkthrough, for understanding, and then by an inspection or similar review to identify defects. Whereas the walkthrough is mainly for sharing information and understanding, the inspection is a review that is focused on finding defects (see Table 9.5 and Appendix A) so both are needed to ensure we have the right contract. Each group will bring a different perspective to the review (Table 9.10). Note that a joint customer/supplier contract review is a requirement of ISO 9000, because the contract is the agreement and commitment to the work. It is important that the acceptance criteria for the software are reviewed, both for SMARTness and against the constraints, aims, objectives, targets, and indicators. Use a peer review or an inspection (Table 9.5 and [2, 17]), and ensure that each quality view is covered in the review. If the team cannot set, review, and agree on the contract including the acceptance criteria at least at a high level, then it is too soon to set the contract.

9.5 Exit from start-up stage

The exit from start-up happens either because we have decided to do nothing, or because we have a contract for further work. Examples of exit criteria are shown in Table 9.11. The specific exit criteria you use will depend on your organization. You may be feeding into some other planning process at this stage or you may go straight into a project, for example an SDLC. In some organizations, additional planning and authorization is required depending on the likely cost or risks of a proposed project.

Different organizations use different document names depending on the project management process. You may see the exit decision in a document called any of project idea form, project mandate, initiation document, project approach, or authorization to proceed. The important point is that it should document or refer to the output from all the steps covered in this chapter.

In this chapter, I have shown you some techniques that help you decide whether you need a SDLC and how to improve the contract for the work.

Table 9.10 Review Perspectives at Exit from Start-Up

Group	Quality	Risks	Constraints	Aims, Objectives, Targets, Indicators, Acceptance Criteria, Outline Plan
Customer	User	Impact on organization	Business, service level, time, cost	Realistic, time-bound
Managers	Value	Impact on other projects	Cost, time, skills, resources	Realistic, time-bound
Builder	Manufacturing, product	Likelihood—technical	Technical skills, knowledge, infrastructure	Achievable, realistic
Measurers	Product, manufacturing	Likelihood—previous failures, predictions	Technical skills, knowledge, infrastructure	Specific, measurable
Supporters	User, product	Impact on existing systems	Technical skills, knowledge, infrastructure	Achievable, realistic

9.5 Exit from start-up stage

Table 9.11 Example of Exit Criteria for Start-Up Stage

Example Exit Criteria	Example Deliverables Documented, Reviewed, and Agreed Upon	Example Authorization Owners
1. "Understanding the problem/idea" step complete	Problem statement, prototype assessments	Joint sign-off by representatives of all groups
2. "Decide whether problem/idea is worth solving" step complete	Problem assessment, cost–benefit analysis, risk assessment	Joint sign-off by representatives of all groups
3. "General constraints and parameters" step complete	Project proposal/brief	Joint sign-off by representatives of all groups
4. "Agree on next stage" step complete	Aims and objectives, constraints, acceptance criteria, outline plan	Joint sign-off by representatives of all groups
5. Criteria 1, 2, 3, 4 complete with *decision to do nothing*	Entry in suggestion scheme log	Process owner
6. Criteria 1, 2, 3, 4 complete with *high-level contract for SDLC*	Project mandate	Process owner
7. Criteria 1, 2, 3, 4 complete with *authorization for system change*	Initiation document	Process owner
8. Criteria 1, 2, 3, 4 complete with *authorization for nonsoftware solution*	Project idea form	Process owner

These techniques were summarized in Table 9.5. In the next chapter, I will describe the SDLC.

References

[1] Smith, K., "The Software Industry's Bug Problem," *Quality Digest*, 2003; reproduced on http://www.qualitydigest.com, April 2003.

[2] Gilb, T., and D. Graham, *Software Inspection*, Reading, MA: Addison-Wesley, 1993.

[3] Schein, E. H., *Process Consulting, Vol. 1: Its Role in Organizational Development*, Reading, MA: Addison-Wesley, 1988.

[4] TQMI, *Problem Solving—Tools and Techniques*, Frodsham, England: TQMI, 2001.

[5] Robson, M., *Problem Solving in Groups*, Aldershot, England: Gower, 1995.

[6] IEEE 1028™ Standard for Software Reviews, 1997.

[7] de Bono, E., *Six Thinking Hats®*, New York: Penguin, 1999.

[8] Evans, I., "The Troubled Project—Best Practice from Theory to Reality," *EuroSTAR Conference*, 2001.

[9] Hohmann, L., "Lo-Fi GUI Design," *Software Testing and Quality Engineering*, 1, 5, 24–29, September 1999.

[10] Nance, R. E., and J. D. Arthur, *Managing Software Quality*, New York: Springer-Verlag, 2002.

[11] Freeburn, G., "Mind Mapping 101 for Testers," *EuroSTAR Conference*, 2002.

[12] Buzan, T., *The Mind Map Book*, London, England: BBC Consumer Publishing, 2003.

[13] "Drawing Concerns: A Structured Rich Picturing Approach," http://business.unisa.edu.au/cobar/documents/richpic_colin.pdf, November 2003.

[14] Belbin Associates, "Belbin Team Roles," http://www.belbin.com/belbin-team-roles.htm, October 2003.

[15] Team Technology Web site, "The Mother of Strategic Systems Issues: Personality," http://www.teamtechnology.co.uk/tt/t-articl/news1.htm, October 2003.

[16] Honey, P., "Learning Styles," http://www.peterhoney.co.uk/product/learningstyles, October 2003. PeterHoney.com, 10 Linden Avenue, Maidenhead, Berks, SL6 6HB. Tel.: 01628633946. Fax: 01628633262. E-mail: info@peterhoney.com.

[17] McHale, J., "Innovators Rule OK—Or Do They?" *Training & Development*, October 1986; reproduced on http://www.kaicentre.com/, July 2003.

[18] Johnson, R., "Somebody's Watching You" *Sunday Times*, May 11, 2003.

[19] European Foundation for Quality Management, "EFQM Excellence Model," http://www.efqm.org, August 2003.

[20] IT Infrastructure Library, *Best Practice for Service Delivery*, London, England: IT Infrastructure Library, OGC/TSO, 2001.

[21] IT Infrastructure Library, *Best Practice for Service Support*, London, England: IT Infrastructure Library, OGC/TSO, 2002.

[22] Humphrey, W., *Introduction to the Personal Software Process*, Reading, MA: SEI, 1997.

[23] Humphrey, W., *Introduction to the Team Software Process*, Reading, MA: SEI, 2000.

[24] International Standards Organization/International Electrotechnical Commission (ISO/IEC), DTR 9126, Software Engineering—Software Product Quality (Parts 1–4, 2000/2001).

[25] Watkins, J., "How to Set Up and Operate a Usability Laboratory," *EuroSTAR Conference*, 2002.

[26] Trienkekens, J. J. M., and E. P. W. M. van Veenendaal, *Software Quality from a Business Perspective*, Dordrecht, the Netherlands: Kluwer Bedrijfsinformatie, 1997.

[27] Hendriks, R., E. van Veenendaal, and R. van Vonderen, "Measuring Software Quality," in E. van Veenendaal, *The Testing Practitioner*, Den Bosch, the Netherlands: Uitgeverig Tutein Nolthenius, 2002, pp. 81–92.

Selected bibliography

Belbin, R. M., *Management Teams–Why They Succeed or Fail*, London, England: Butterworth Heinemann, 1981.

Boehm, B. W., *Software Engineering Economics*, Englewood Cliffs, NJ: Prentice-Hall, 1981.

Obeng, E., "Helping Stakeholders to Understand Requirements," *Project Manager Today*, July 2003, pp. 14–17.

CHAPTER 10

Software-Development Life Cycle

Contents

10.1 Software-development life cycle—description

10.2 SDLC viewpoints

10.3 Entry criteria for SDLC

10.4 SDLC—typical activities

10.5 Entry and exit points within the SDLC

10.6 SDLC models

10.7 Quality views and the models—why we might wish to combine models

10.8 Exit from the SDLC

10.9 Conclusion

In this chapter I shall:

- Describe the entry criteria, steps, and exit criteria for the SDLC;
- Outline and compare several approaches for the SDLC, especially for readers who are not software specialists;
- Identify the quality definitions from Chapter 1, which prevail at this stage;
- Identify how each of the groups identified in Chapter 2 become involved at this stage;
- Identify techniques that improve teamwork during the SDLC.

The users are moaning about the software; they say it is doing the wrong thing, but it is functioning according to the specification. When I saw the bug report, I marked it "Not a bug." They're just wasting my time!
—*Irate builder, trying to get on with work*

What do you mean it was not in the specification? You people wrote the specification. It's not my fault if you didn't keep it up to date!
—*Irate customer trying to use the software*

10.1 Software-development life cycle—description

The builders and customers are at loggerheads. Although the builders have developed what was specified, that is not what the customer really needs. Both are right from their own point of view, but they need a way to understand each other better in order that the customer's expectations meet the builder's delivery. The project of building a software system to deliver to a customer is controlled via a software-development life cycle (SDLC). Some SDLCs are formally defined within methodologies. Others are informal but understood by those who use them—"We always do it this way." Regardless of the formality of the definition, all SDLCs are intended to deliver what the customer requires and to avoid the problems of our irate builder and customer.

In this chapter, I will compare models to see how well they do this. I will show you how the models used for the SDLC include detailed specification of what is needed, design of the solution, and the building and testing of products that will deliver what is needed.

In Figure 10.1, we see that the SDLC sits in the software life span between start-up (covered in Chapter 9) and delivery (covered in Chapter 11). During start-up, we identified a problem or idea, investigated it, and decided it was worth building a software solution, so we set a formal or informal contract of work for the SDLC. At the end of the SDLC, if we are successful, the software is delivered. It will be used postdelivery, as it is maintained and supported for the rest of its life span. The SDLC is not building to the moment of delivery, but to postdelivery when the software is used.

10.1.1 Types of software acquisition project

The purpose of an SDLC is to provide a software solution to help the customers solve the problems identified during start-up. The acquisition of the software to resolve a particular problem might be achieved in several ways, for example:

- *Custom-made system:* The whole software system is designed and built to meet a specific customer's requirements; the customer may choose to have the software built by a third-party supplier, that is, another organization, or to use an in-house development team consisting of by people who work for the customer's organization.
- *COTS system:* The customer buys a commercial off-the-shelf (COTS) system or package, sometime referred to as shrink-wrapped software, from a package vendor (a third party who sells COTS packages).
- *Tailored package:* The customer buys a package, but has some tailoring done to it by the supplier; these are changes made to meet specific requirements of the customers.

Any of these would be covered by an SDLC, but the customers will have more or less control over the detailed content of the software depending on the type of system chosen.

The customer may also decide to resolve their problem by requesting a change to an existing system. We will cover these maintenance changes in Chapter 12, but it is worth remarking that the same activities as in an SDLC

10.1 Software-development life cycle—description

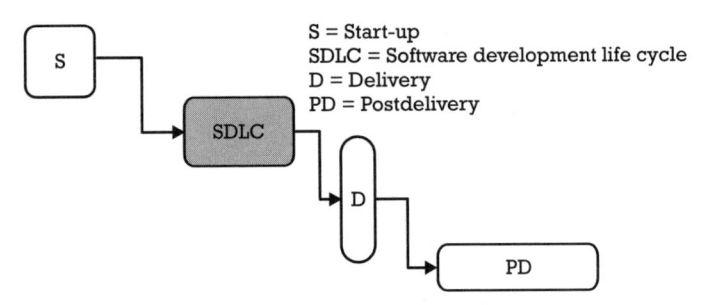

Figure 10.1 Life span stage diagram.

would take place in a maintenance change. The specification, design, build, and test of the change may be quite small activities, or may be equivalent to an SDLC, and, indeed, use the same life cycle model up to the point of delivery.

10.1.2 Identifying the software products

Remember that this is not just code being built by developers; people will also be busy designing, building, and testing training, documentation, and support materials. If the software being developed is a package for commercial sale, the support material may include sales and marketing material. For an in-house business system, it may include business process manuals. These are all part of the delivered product. When I talk about "software" or "product," I mean all of these types of deliverables. The media of delivery might be electronic, paper, on a microchip, or by semaphore signals; it does not matter.

10.1.3 SDLC task summary

There are several different life-cycle models for software development. In this chapter, we are interested in how the SDLC models help us achieve software quality, so rather than describing them fully, I am only going to outline them and give references to further information. The life-cycle models have changed over time to reflect the changes in customer group problems, perceptions of quality, and technologies available. Generally they have been described as development life cycles, but some of them include or may be adapted to maintenance activities. They have a number of steps in common. In some of the models we will see that these are performed once and in others some or all the steps are repeated or broken down into substeps. Put very simply, the fundamental steps are:

- *Planning and monitoring*—we plan what we will do and when we will do it, then track progress against our plan.
- *Managing change*—the real world will change around the SDLC and the deliverables required from the SDLC may need to change to reflect reality.

- *Requirements*—we make a detailed description of what we want.
- *Design*—we design the solution, including the software to meet the requirements.
- *Build*—we build the software based on the designs.
- *Testing*—we test to make sure that the software functions properly.

10.2 SDLC viewpoints

Just as we saw in Chapter 9 that start-up fails if the right people are not involved, during the SDLC we can have problems if we do not make sure that we take account of all viewpoints throughout the project. Sometimes, the customers set the contract, order the software, and then leave the managers, builders, and measurers to get on with it: "It's obvious what we want! Just do it!" This means that the customers are not involved in the SDLC. Similarly, the supporters may not be involved in the SDLC, only being "invited to the party" at delivery. If this happens, it limits the quality viewpoints (see Table 10.1, the definitions in Chapter 1, and assignment to groups in Chapter 2).

We saw in Chapter 2 that the builders and measurers tend to focus on manufacturing and product quality, rather than value or user quality. The manufacturing viewpoint focuses on delivering to specification and removing defects (differences between the product and its specification). The product viewpoint focuses on attributes such as functionality, performance, and security: how they are specified and built. Some builders and measurers, especially user-acceptance testers, do empathize with the user view, adopting a "fit-for-purpose" approach, but often these are people who are involved late in the SDLC, sometimes too late to influence design decisions.

Both builders and measurers hold a transcendent viewpoint ("In my heart I know what is right") that pursues technical excellence or achieving zero defects in software rather than cost-effectiveness or value. One colleague, an excellent tester, said to me when we discussed the value viewpoint, "But we must not sacrifice quality to cost." He was forgetting that although his manufacturing definition of quality focuses on removing defects, in the value view, keeping within costs is a major contributor to quality.

Table 10.1 Views of Quality During SDLC—Simple

	Group	
Quality View	Builder	Measurer
Transcendent view	✓	✓
User view		(✓ can be late in SDLC)
Value view		
Product view	✓	✓
Manufacturing view	✓	✓
✓ is a primary quality view.		
(✓) is a quality view that may be taken by some people in this group.		

When delivery takes place, the user and value viewpoints will prevail. The builders and measurers feel pleased that they have delivered to specification, and are then stunned to find the system rejected or criticized. Perhaps the specification was wrong, misinterpreted, or out of date. Perhaps an overambitious solution had been built, which means that the software has cost more or taken longer than budgeted. The customers, managers, and supporters turn on the others: "How could they have been so careless and extravagant?" The builders and measurers retaliate: "If you hadn't kept changing your minds...," and so on.

Much of this can be avoided by a careful start-up (see Chapter 9) but during the project some things will change (see Table 10.2 for examples) and unless all the groups are represented on the project, the SDLC may proceed without allowing for changes that will be necessary during the SDLC. We can deal with change in the SDLC provided we acknowledge that it is going to happen.

Getting everyone involved in the SDLC team will stop quality views being forgotten during the SDLC (Table 10.3) and will allow the changes in the organization's requirements to be reflected throughout the SDLC.

Table 10.2 Examples of Changes During the SDLC

Real-world changes	The customers' needs, hence the requirements for the software, will change to reflect their changing environment. These might be changes in the marketplace within which an organization operates, or legislative changes that affect how an organization may operate. If the SDLC team are not aware of these changes they will deliver unwanted software. As an example, the McCartney report [1] cites a project at an insurance company in the United States. By the time the project was finished, the company no longer sold the product to be supported by the software being delivered.
IT infrastructure changes	The hardware/network/system on which the software will be used may change, thus changing constraints and risks for the software. In one project I worked on, performance was a critical risk, but a hardware upgrade changed the performance constraints, thus changing the risk focus of the project from performance to other areas.
Existing systems (IT and business) changes	The new system does not "plug in" as anticipated, either because the builders were not aware of the detail of the IT environment and infrastructure or because it changed during the SDLC. The McCartney report [1] cites a government IT project in which changes to the existing systems during the SDLC made integration of the new system into the existing systems difficult.
Skills changes	People with expertise may leave or join the organization or the project, changing the project's capabilities and thus what could be delivered.
Leadership and organization changes	The organization's priorities may change, so the project may become more or less critical than it was, perhaps meaning a change in timescale, budget, people, or resources.
Risk changes	Risks change over time. One mistake project teams often make is to build a risk register at the start of the project and then never reassess the risks. Low risks at the start of a project may grow to come back to bite you later on: "Maybe the worst risk in a project is a lack of an ongoing risk assessment and risk management process" (David Hayman, personal correspondence, March 2003).
Errors made during start-up	We may realize we have made some mistakes during start-up—we are only human and we may have missed something. Building the solution we intended may be harder than we thought, we may have misunderstood an aim, or we may realize that acceptance criteria cannot be met within targets.

Table 10.3 Views of Quality During SDLC—Teamwork

	Groups				
Quality view	Customer	Manager	Builder	Measurer	Supporter
Transcendent view	✓	✓	✓	✓	✓
User view	✓			(✓)	✓
Value view		✓			
Product view			✓	✓	✓
Manufacturing view			✓	✓	

10.3 Entry criteria for SDLC

10.3.1 Entry criteria following a detailed start-up

If we have done everything suggested in Chapter 9, we arrive at the start of the SDLC with a contract and additional information gathered during start-up, which should include:

- Problem/solution analysis—"What problem are we trying to solve?"
- Constraints analysis—"What financial, time, organizational, and technical constraints do we have?"
- Cost–benefit analysis—"What benefits do we expect within our budget?"
- Risk analysis—"What is the likelihood that this will go wrong and the impact if it does or if we do not do it?"
- Aims and objectives for the SDLC—"Why are we doing this? What difference will this project make to the organization?"
- Targets and indicators—"How will we measure progress and whether the project has been worthwhile? Are we making a difference?"
- Acceptance criteria—"How will we know if we have succeeded?"

Table 10.4 Example Entry Criteria and Owners for SDLC

Example of Entry Criteria	Example of Entry Documents	Example of Authorization Owners
1. All start-up steps complete, deliverables documented, reviewed, agreed on, and signed off	Problem statement, prototype assessments, problem assessment, cost–benefit analysis, risk assessment, project proposal/brief, aims and objectives, targets and indicators, constraints, acceptance criteria, outline plan	SDLC project sponsor, process owner, project manager
2. Contract reviewed, agreed, and authorized	Documents from (1) completed, contract checklist completed, all documents received	Project manager
3. System change authorized	Documents from (1) completed and received, change mandate signed	IT support manager
4. Process change authorized	Documents from (1) completed and received, change mandate signed	Process owner

10.3 Entry criteria for SDLC

When we check the entry criteria for the SDLC, we should see all of this information in the contract and associated documents. Table 10.4 shows some simple examples of entry criteria for different projects. You may call some of these things slightly different names in your organization; that does not matter, as long as you have the information indicated.

10.3.2 When no entry criteria have been defined

If no entry criteria have been defined for an SDLC in your organization, you may find that you start work without all the information you need. In this situation, for your current project, whatever its size or status, I would recommend that you try to document something to describe the entry into the SDLC, even on the smallest SDLC. The virtue lies not in the size of the documentation, but in its clear content. At a minimum, take an approach of "on one page" to see if you can capture the essence of the problem in a checklist form like the one in Table 10.5 to give you a basic set of entry criteria. Use the checklist to see which areas you need to investigate more fully; for example, do you have clear acceptance criteria and constraints?

To prevent this problem from recurring, improve the SDLC model that is used in your organization by adding entry criteria to the model.

10.3.3 When entry criteria have not been met

Strictly, if the entry criteria have not been met, we must not start the SDLC. In order that we can be strict, it is important that the entry criteria are:

Table 10.5 Checklist of Entry Criteria Form for a Small SDLC

Project name, date of form completion
Problem/solution analysis—Do we understand what problem are we trying to solve? Is that understanding shared by all parties?
Problem statement:
Constraints analysis—Have the financial, time, organizational, and technical constraints been defined and agreed on?
Constraints statement:
Cost–benefit analysis—Do we understand our expected benefits within our budget?
Cost–benefit statement:
Risk analysis—Have we analyzed the likelihood that this will go wrong and the impact if it does or if we do not do it?
Likelihood:
Impact of doing it wrong:
Impact of not doing it:
Aims and objectives for the SDLC—Do we understand why are we doing this? What difference will this project make to the organization? How will we measure progress against the aims and objectives?
Aim and objectives of the SDLC:
Targets and indicators of success:
Acceptance criteria—How will we know if we have succeeded?

Agreement Signed Date	Customer	Builder	Manager	Measurer	Supporter

- Objective;
- Defined in a way that is SMART (specific, measurable, achievable, realistic, and time-bound);
- Necessary rather than simply desirable.

However, there are occasions when we might decide to waive the entry criteria. This may happen if we decide that the entry criteria are excessive or incorrect, or if we believe we are faced with an emergency. There are also occasions when we may wish to increase the entry criteria, for example, if we see that the SDLC is at a higher risk than our normal projects.

10.3.3.1 We decide the entry criteria are excessive or incorrect

If the entry criteria include items that are desirable rather than necessary, we may wish to redefine them. This requires careful thought; if you do not have all the entry documents or you do not have an authorization to start, what risks are you taking? If the decision is made to bypass or reduce the entry criteria, do we understand the risks we are taking? Is the risk acceptable? I would recommend that you document the reason for deciding that the entry criteria can be reduced or ignored, as part of your project documentation. This might be in the quality plan, which typically documents the quality gates for a project. If the defined entry criteria are incorrect, we should redocument them, again with an explanation, and, if possible, suggest a process improvement that would prevent us from making the same mistake again. Use the checklist in Table 10.5 to help you do this.

10.3.3.2 It's an emergency

As we saw in Chapter 1, in CMM® [2] one of the differences between high-maturity and low-maturity organizations is how the organization reacts to change or crisis. A high-maturity organization holds onto processes during change and crisis, as this helps to manage the problems. A low-maturity organization will discard the processes during emergencies, believing that they add bureaucracy rather than value. This is counterproductive, especially with the entry into an SDLC. The processes should be defined at a suitable level of control without unnecessary bureaucracy; if a metric or a piece of paperwork does not facilitate control, do not have it in the process. Without clear constraints and acceptance criteria, it is difficult to know when to stop work in the SDLC; we have nothing on which to base our exit criteria. In an emergency, this means that we may forget to do something vital. I would recommend that an emergency request still goes through entry criteria, because in an emergency we need processes to support our decisions; we are more likely to make mistakes if we are doing something in a hurry. Some organizations define an emergency SDLC, which encapsulates the spirit of the controls on a single checklist. This can be a useful approach.

10.3 Entry criteria for SDLC

10.3.3.3 We decide the entry criteria are insufficient

If we perceive high risk in the SDLC, we may decide that the defined entry criteria are not stringent enough. In this case, we should add additional criteria, or increase the "pass level" for the entry criteria. We can do this if we allow tailored entry criteria.

10.3.4 Tailoring entry criteria

In several organizations I have observed, project managers have available a number of agreed-on SDLC templates, and they select an SDLC with suitable entry criteria, to meet the specific risk levels for their own projects. Suppose that a particular organization decides on the stringency of the entry criteria for an SDLC based on three factors, the estimated cost of the work, the estimated size in days, and the perceived risk. Each factor is assessed on a score of 1 (low) to 3 (high). The factor scores are multiplied together to give an overall score that will be between 1 ($1 \cdot 1 \cdot 1$) and 27 ($3 \cdot 3 \cdot 3$). The score is used to pick entry criteria levels from a list like the one in Table 10.6.

Table 10.6 Example Tailored Entry Criteria

Cost · Size · Risk Score	Example Entry Criteria / Example entry documents	Example authorization owners
1–5	1. E-mail with request for change from customer, copied to manager, builder, measurer, and supporter 2. Entry checklist in Table 10.5 completed Deliverables: E-mail and acknowledgment, entry checklist in Table 10.5	Customer, builder
6–12	1. As above, plus 2. Request raised at monthly change planning meeting 3. Additional problem statement/assessment, constraints, acceptance criteria documentation completed Deliverables: As above, plus additional notes on problem statement/assessment, constraints, acceptance criteria	Customer, process owner, builder, manager
12–20	1. As above, plus 2. Acceptance criteria prioritized and documented with metrics from ISO 9126 3. Solution prototyping Deliverables: As above, plus additional work on cost–benefit analysis, constraints, acceptance criteria documentation	Customer, process owner, project manager
20–27	1. As above, plus 2. Additional risk management planning carried out by process owner and project manager 3. Project authorization board has discussed and agreed to the change and risk plan Deliverables: As above, plus additional work on problem statement, prototype assessments, problem assessment, cost–benefit analysis, risk assessment, project proposal/brief, aims and objectives, targets and indicators, constraints, acceptance criteria, outline plan, project authorization	Project authorization board, project sponsor, process owner, project manager

10.3.5 When no start-up stage took place

It may well be that you are at the start of an SDLC, or even partway through it, and you do not have a detailed start-up as described in Chapter 9. What do you do?

- *Start of SDLC—Large:* If you are at the start of a large or high-risk SDLC, I would recommend that you carry out the activities in Chapter 9 before proceeding, in order that you can plan the SDLC.

- *Start of SDLC—Small:* If you are at the start of or working on a very small SDLC, you may feel you do not need formal documented entry deliverables, but you will need the information content of the deliverables, documented or in the team's heads. You will need this to plan the project, and to control it, especially when the going gets tough. Use the checklist in Table 10.5 to help you decide whether you have enough information, or whether you should investigate fully.

- *Midway through SDLC:* If you are midway through an SDLC as you read this, you may be wondering how to apply these ideas: "Shouldn't the customer and manager have sorted this out when the contract was signed?" Yes, perhaps so, but if they have not, or if the information you have is not full enough, you may have to revisit the start-up activities. You will need acceptance criteria in order to understand if the software is ready for delivery, for example, and you will certainly need to know your constraints. Use the checklist in Table 10.5 to help you decide what you need to find out, in order to complete the project.

10.4 SDLC—typical activities

10.4.1 Planning and monitoring

It is essential to have a plan for the SDLC. The plan must be based on the information identified during start-up. For most organizations, there will be constraints on cost, time, resources, and skills; we will not have an infinite budget. The acceptance criteria identified at start-up need to be met within the constraints.

The entry criteria give us enough information to start planning. The plan needs to describe how the SDLC will deliver within the constraints, meeting the acceptance criteria and containing the risks, to meet the aims of the project. We will also need to break down the plan into smaller, more detailed plans (bite-sized chunks). One project manager I know assigns responsibility for detailed planning of each chunk to people within the team saying, "Tell me how you will deliver what you need to do within this timescale." This is very effective as it allows each team within the project to understand their constraints and to own their own plan.

Once the plan is put together, it needs to be reviewed and agreed on. The Team Software Process (TSP) [3] recommends a "launch" at the start of the

10.4 SDLC—typical activities

SDLC, where the team goes through the plan and commits to it. A shared planning process followed by a launch meeting allows people to discuss the plan, share causes for optimism and pessimism, understand each other, and so commit to the plan and the SDLC team wholeheartedly.

The plan is used throughout the SDLC to track, measure, and control progress. We inevitably replan during the SDLC as we learn more; it is worth designing replan points into the SDLC and acknowledging those in the contract of work.

Planning and control need to take place at different levels of detail for different people; we need to understand what we do today to be on time at the end of this week for our team, in order to meet that major project milestone in three months. This will match with reporting requirements between the groups, as we saw in Chapters 3 to 7. Managers carry out planning and control with the help of builders, measurers, customers, and supporters. We saw in Chapter 4 that this is needed on a day-to-day basis so that we manage our time to complete tasks today that contribute to meeting an end date months away. We also saw how dependencies between tasks mean they may be on the critical path—if they are not completed on time, then the whole project becomes late. The plan will need to be reviewed; all the groups need to agree that it is a plan to which they can deliver. In particular, there will be intergroup dependencies on the plan—everyone needs to understand and commit to these.

10.4.2 Managing change

During the SDLC, things will change and this will affect the plan and all the activities of the SDLC. One project manager I know regards his plan as "A basis for making changes"; he says "The plan is a description of what will not happen in the future." We saw in Section 10.2 that we will have to deal with changes in circumstance during the SDLC. These types of changes will affect the SDLC in different ways.

We will see later in this chapter that some of the SDLC models are more amenable to managing change than others, but here let us consider which SDLC activities are particularly affected by different types of change. Table 10.7 shows the most affected areas for each type of change. The changes may affect any of the activities; for example, the plan may be

Table 10.7 Example of SDLC Activities Affected by Example Change Type

	Most Affected Areas				
SDLC Activity	Plan	Requirements	Design	Build	Test
Real-world changes			✓	✓	✓
IT infrastructure changes			✓	✓	✓
Existing systems (IT and business) changes			✓	✓	✓
Skills changes		✓	✓	✓	✓
Leadership and organization changes	✓	✓			
Risk changes	✓				✓
Errors made during start-up	✓	✓	✓	✓	✓

affected by any of the changes, and leadership changes may affect any of the areas, but in the table I have indicated the most immediate effects. Some of these cause a chain reaction; we can see that real-world changes may affect the customers' requirements; if these change, then the design, build, and test of the software will also change. Changes to risk will affect the plan and specifically will affect the focus for testing.

If the SDLC model we choose is very rigid, then, superficially, it can appear easier to plan and manage it. However, the rigidity in the SDLC and the contractual arrangements around it make it very difficult to allow changes, whether these have arisen from errors we have made or from real changes in circumstances around the SDLC. This means we are in danger of delivering the wrong solution. We might deliver the wrong product attributes, or deliver solutions with manufacturing defects, at reduced value to the organization, with reduced usefulness, damaging attitudes to the team or the chosen solution.

A more flexible SDLC model, designed to allow for change, removes the problem of rigidity in the solution, but is more difficult to manage because everyone (customer, manager, builder, measurer, and supporter) needs to allow for uncertainty and change in the plans. For example, in the TSP [3], Watts Humphrey suggests a multiphase approach with a "relaunch" meeting for the team at the start of each phase.

10.4.3 Requirements

Some statement of the customers' requirements is needed. The supporters and the managers will also have requirements. The basis of these is the problem/solution analysis and the acceptance criteria defined at start-up. During requirements definition these are explored in much greater depth. The builders will document the requirements; often, this will be done by specialists in analysis. The customers, managers, and supporters all contribute to the acceptance criteria and hence to the requirements (see Chapter 9). The requirements will need to be reviewed. The customers, managers, and supporters will need to review that the builders have a correct understanding of the requirements. The builders, who have not directly been involved in requirements gathering need to know that the requirements have been defined in a way that allow them to design and build the software. The measurers, including testers, want to know that the requirements are testable; that it will be possible to measure whether the requirements have been met. The requirements will include:

- Software/system requirements;
- Infrastructure, operational, and support requirements;
- Training requirements (for software, support and business processes);
- Documentation requirements (for software, support, and business processes);
- Business process requirements (manual processes, for example);

10.4 SDLC—typical activities

- Implementation requirements (for example, media, time constraints, phased or big bang, ability to roll back) [4];
- Data transfer requirements; for a data migration this might include the contents of databases and standing.

All of these will be needed for the solution to be implemented.

10.4.4 Design

The solution will need to be designed. The design is based on the requirements. Some life cycle models divide this into several design areas. You will find that different models and methods have different names for the design stages, but there are three main design steps. An overall business-process design looks at the processes within which the customers will use the system, and would include design of training, documentation, and business processes. System architecture is the design of the overall software system. A detailed technical design covers the design of individual programs within the software. In this chapter, for ease of explanation, I have grouped these together as *design*. Builders will carry out and document the design. These designs will need to be reviewed. The supporters' acceptance criteria directly affect the design, for example, for performance, memory management, and maintainability requirements (see Chapter 9), and so they will want to review those designs. Customers may become involved in reviewing screen and report designs, both functionally and for usability. Builders need to know they will be able to build the software from the designs. Measurers want to know that the designs are testable; that it will be possible to measure whether the design goals have been met. Managers will want to review the designs for cost-effectiveness and value, for example, reduction in future maintenance costs.

The design will include:

- Software/system;
- Infrastructure, operational, and support processes and equipment;
- Training (for software, support, and business processes);
- Documentation (for software, support, and business processes);
- Business processes (manual processes, for example);
- Implementation processes, including rollout and rollback plans;
- Data conversion design.

10.4.5 Build

The solutions need to be built. What is built and how it is built is based on the requirements and design. This includes writing code, but also building all the other software products. Training material, user guides, business process manuals, marketing material, and support manuals all need to be built. All these software products can be reviewed against acceptance criteria.

Supporters review the code and support material. Customers review training, user, process, and marketing material. Measurers will review all the software products for testability and to prepare for testing. Managers will review progress and costs. Builders will take part in those reviews, to cross-check the different types of product and to check adherence to standards.

The build will include:

- Software/system;
- Infrastructure, operational, and support processes and equipment;
- Training (for software, support, and business processes);
- Documentation (for software, support, and business processes);
- Business processes (manual processes, for example);
- Implementation processes, including rollout and rollback plans;
- Data conversion software.

10.4.6 Testing

The software products need to be checked. As with design, there are several types of testing, and they are named differently in different models and in different organizations. Typically, models allow for four levels of dynamic testing. This is testing where code is executed. The lowest level of dynamic testing is often called unit, program, component, or module testing; the building blocks of the system are tested individually as they are built. Next, the building blocks are linked or integrated together, and the links are tested; typically, this is known as integration, link. or string testing. These two levels of testing will be based on the design and the code. Once all the building blocks have been integrated together, system testing takes place; the system as a whole and the processes using it are exercised. This level of testing is based on the requirements and the design. It may also be necessary to test how this system interacts with other systems. Finally, acceptance testing takes place; this checks the system against the acceptance criteria to decide whether it can be delivered. Various types of tests are run at each level, to check functional and nonfunctional attributes (see Chapter 9). Specialist testers will be jumping up and down at this point and shouting, "Testing is not just done at the end of the SDLC!" That is absolutely true; we have opportunities to test statically as well. This is testing done without executing the code. It includes all the review activities we did during start-up, planning, review, design and build, plus static analysis, by which we examine the code for flaws without executing it. These are all measurement activities. As we saw in Chapter 6, people from any of the groups may join the measurers group on a temporary basis. The test designs and the test results should be reviewed. The choice of people to carry out the review depends on the level of testing; any of the groups might be involved.

Depending on the scope of the project, the test stages might include testing of:

- Software/system (reviews of products, component, integration, system, and acceptance);
- Infrastructure, operational and support processes and equipment (reviews of products and operational acceptance);
- Training (reviews of products, trial runs, and walkthroughs);
- Documentation (reviews of products, trial runs, and walkthroughs);
- Business processes (review of products, walkthroughs, acceptance testing);
- Implementation processes, including rollout and rollback plans (review of products, walkthroughs, acceptance testing);
- Data conversion process and software (conversion software testing, data checks, dry runs).

10.5 Entry and exit points within the SDLC

There are entry and exit points between the steps; sometimes, these are called quality or project gates. Depending on the SDLC model that the project uses, these may appear at different points. As we will see, some life-cycle models have a strict cutoff between steps. In others, steps are omitted, repeated, or overlapped. The strictness of the criteria depends on the level and type of risk for the project as well as the skill set of the people on the team. In some SDLC models, particular handover points are regarded with significance and very formal entry and exit points are used. These are sometimes referred to as quality gates or project gates [1]. They are often used where control of the work is handed from one team to another, to ensure that all the deliverables have been handed over and are fit for purpose.

An example of a simple SDLC is found in Figure 10.2, showing the minor entry and exit points, indicated by an arrow between activity rectangles, and the major quality gates, indicated by the rounded rectangles. For a simple situation, if no training material, business processes, or infrastructure changes are required, this may be enough. Figure 10.3 shows a more detailed SDLC. Here the major quality gates are shown, and the activities between them explicitly include all the products and activities types, as well as differentiation between possible exit routes—to deliver a product or cancel the project, for example.

10.6 SDLC models

People talk about big bang, phased, iterative, and incremental approaches, but not everyone uses the words in the same way. In what follows, I will use building a model village as an analogy for how the terms are used in the descriptions below. The steps taken in building this village are set in italics. First, I will give an outline of the models, with the advantages and

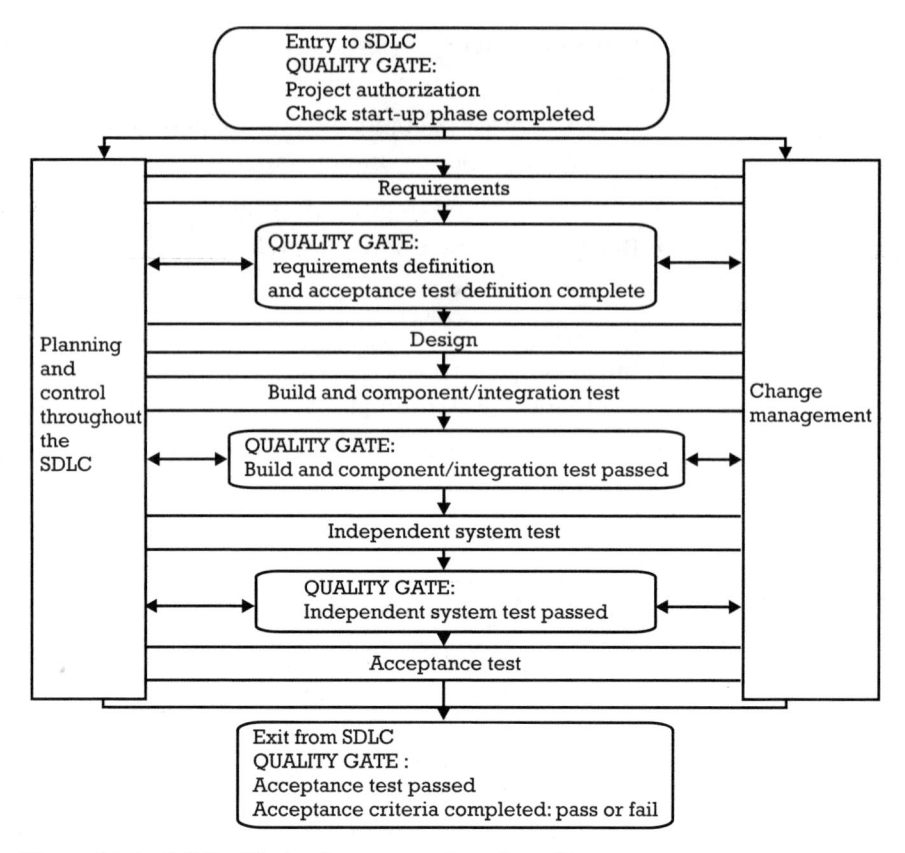

```
┌─────────────────────────────────┐
│ Entry to SDLC                   │
│ QUALITY GATE:                   │
│ Project authorization           │
│ Check start-up phase completed  │
└─────────────────────────────────┘
            │
┌───────────┼───────────────────────────────────┬───────────┐
│           ▼                                   │           │
│         Requirements                          │           │
│           ▼                                   │           │
│   ┌───────────────────────────────────┐       │           │
│   │ QUALITY GATE:                     │       │           │
│   │ requirements definition           │       │           │
│   │ and acceptance test definition    │       │           │
│   │ complete                          │       │           │
│   └───────────────────────────────────┘       │           │
│ Planning         Design                       │           │
│ and                ▼                          │ Change    │
│ control   Build and component/integration test│ management│
│ throughout         ▼                          │           │
│ the       ┌───────────────────────────────┐   │           │
│ SDLC      │ QUALITY GATE:                 │   │           │
│           │ Build and component/          │   │           │
│           │ integration test passed       │   │           │
│           └───────────────────────────────┘   │           │
│                    ▼                          │           │
│           Independent system test             │           │
│                    ▼                          │           │
│           ┌───────────────────────────┐       │           │
│           │ QUALITY GATE:             │       │           │
│           │ Independent system test   │       │           │
│           │ passed                    │       │           │
│           └───────────────────────────┘       │           │
│                    ▼                          │           │
│             Acceptance test                   │           │
└───────────────────┬───────────────────────────┴───────────┘
                    ▼
┌─────────────────────────────────────────────┐
│ Exit from SDLC                              │
│ QUALITY GATE :                              │
│ Acceptance test passed                      │
│ Acceptance criteria completed: pass or fail │
└─────────────────────────────────────────────┘
```

Figure 10.2 SDLC with simple entry, exit, and quality gates.

disadvantages of each model listed in Table 10.8. Then I will show how to tailor the SDLC models. The published SDLC models I have looked at in writing these outlines are listed in Table 10.9.

10.6.1 Waterfall model (big bang or phased)

This is the most traditional of the models. It is used on either a big bang or a phased project. The requirements are set at the start of the project, and all subsequent designs, code, and other products are based on those defined requirements (see Figure 10.4). Each step has a clear cut off; the requirements are agreed on and frozen, then the design, and so on; water only goes one way down a waterfall. An example of a defined waterfall model SDLC from DoD-STD-2167 is in [5].

10.6.1.1 Big bang waterfall

A project may be run with a "big bang" approach. *All the work is delivered at one time; all the houses, roads, and gardens must be ready at the same time for the village to open.*

At the start of the SDLC we can make a clear statement of what we need. Customer: "These are our requirements." Manager: "I will need three

10.6 SDLC models

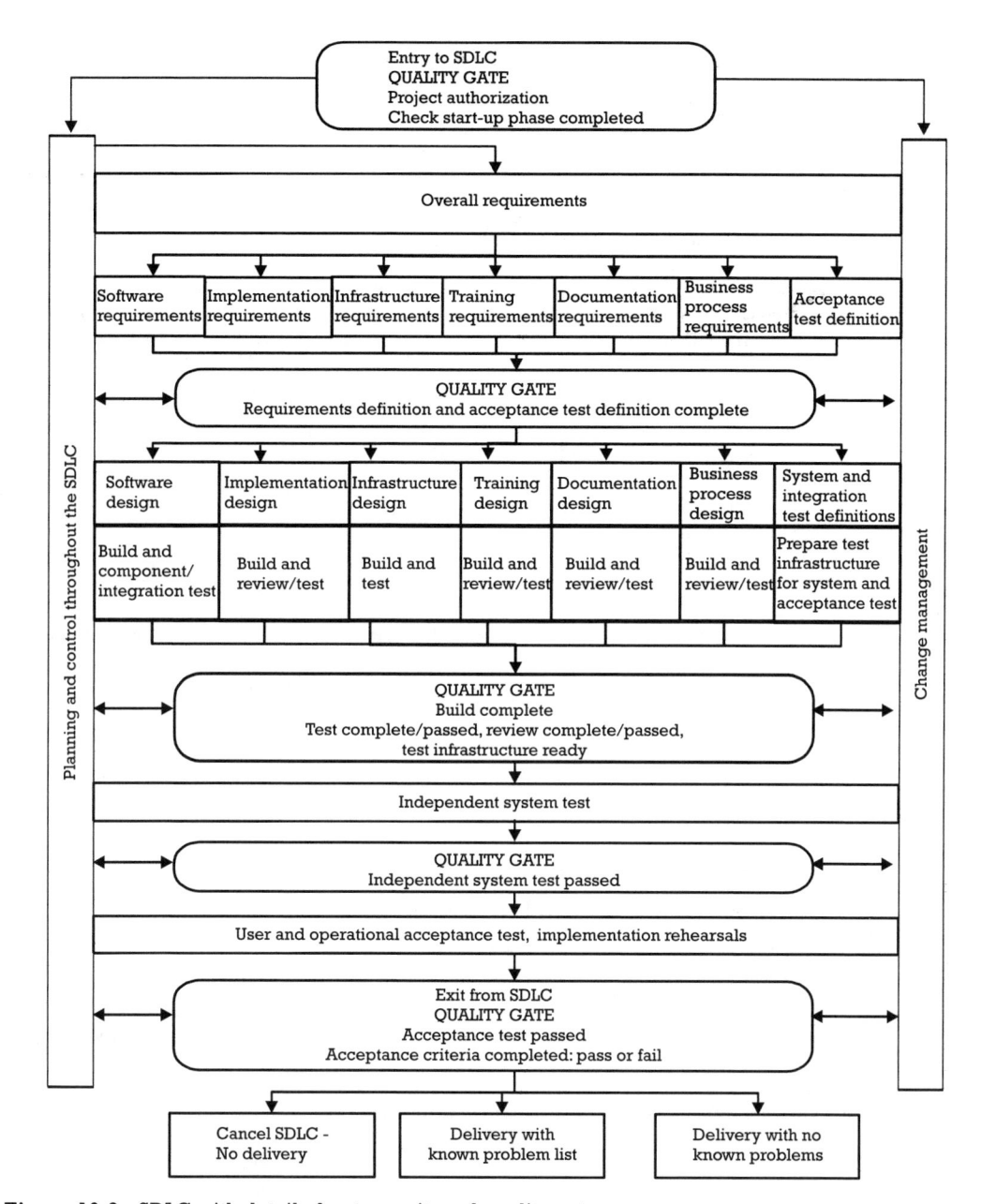

Figure 10.3 SDLC with detailed entry, exit, and quality gates.

analysts for 6 weeks, then five designers for 10 weeks, then 15 programmers for 10 weeks, then five testers for 6 weeks." After the requirements sign-off, measurers, customers, and supporters do not become involved again until testing.

10.6.1.2 Phased waterfall

In a project that has a "phased" approach, the work is grouped into separate chunks and delivered at intervals perhaps by different teams. *The village is*

Table 10.8 Advantages and Disadvantages of the Models

Life Cycle	Advantages	Disadvantages
Waterfall—phased or big bang	Clear-cut steps make project management and resource management easier. Audit trail. ISO 9000 compliant	One chance to get it right, mistakes in requirements and design are not found until testing; costly to repair. Does not allow for changing requirements.
Incremental	Enables larger problems to be tackled in small chunks by one team.	Does not, unless combined with iteration or spiral or evolutionary, solve the waterfall problems.
Iterative/spiral	Allows for change and high customer involvement Can be time-boxed (value view—cut losses if not productive). Some practitioners say it is easy to manage time. Allows refinement of plans and ideas. Testing earlier—faults found earlier. Do important areas first.	Time for test and regression test increases. Long time between start and going live. Some practitioners say not so clear-cut for management by stages, could be harder to control time and costs, less clarity on milestones.
Evolutionary	As iterative/spiral, plus bite-sized milestones, short time between start and going live, deliver important areas first.	As iterative/spiral, plus risk of faults going live sooner if insufficient testing.
V-model	Easy to manage; clear contract sign-off points, meets ISO 9000:1994. Test is continuous and cost-effective as defects found and fixed earlier.	Resourcing different, early weight to life cycle can seem bureaucratic. Can feel costly early in the life cycle.

Table 10.9 SDLC Models Referred to in This Chapter

Example of the SDLC Model	Comment
Boehm's Spiral Model [5, 6]	Uses prototyping and replanning with reassessment of risks and constraints with each prototype.
Team Software Process (TSP) [3]	Emphasis on clearly defined team roles and goals, checklists of activities, measurement, use of CMM® Level 5 processes. Phased or iterative approach.
Giddings Domain-Dependent Life Cycle [5]	Waterfall model with feedback loops, and experimentation or prototyping.
Rational Unified Process (RUP) [7]	Based on the spiral model, uses iterations within increments, with testing happening throughout the SDLC. Emphasis on defining, building, and testing the most important parts of the software first.
eXtreme Programming (XP) [8]	Incremental approach, relies on continuous (automated) testing by builders, on oral rather than written communication, and close collaboration.
Dynamic Systems Development Method (DSDM) [9]	Phased or incremental approach, with strong emphasis on people, their skills, and their ability to work in teams.
Gilb's Evolutionary Model [10]	Incremental or phased approach with delivery at the end of each increment.
DOD-STD-2167 Model [5]	Classic waterfall model.
V- and W-model [11, 12], Component Test Process Life Cycle [13], STEP (Systematic Test and Evaluation Process) [11]	Life cycles that emphasize the place of and control of software testing; these may be considered as fitting with the other life cycles. In this chapter, I have concentrated on the V-model and how it might fit in the SDLC models.

10.6 SDLC models

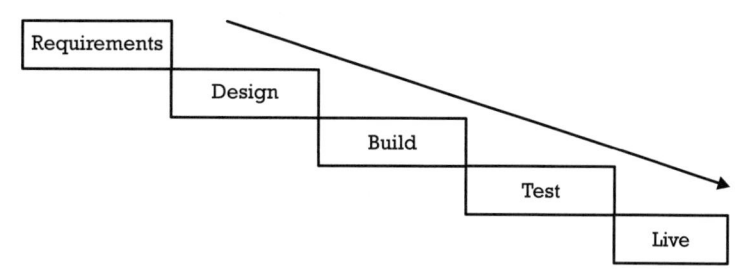

Figure 10.4 Waterfall model—big bang.

divided into four sectors (N, S, E, and W) that are worked on as separate projects. The whole of a sector is delivered together as one project, but each sector might be ready on a different date. It is possible to divide a waterfall style into phases, which run in parallel, provided that the work can be divided into distinct chunks, each being smaller, more manageable miniprojects with its own team.

10.6.1.3 When to use the waterfall method

The waterfall is a good model to use if:

- The contract for the work is complete, correct, and unambiguous.
- The requirements and acceptance criteria are complete, correct, and unambiguous.
- The work can be completed within the constraints.
- No change is expected in the requirements or design—the customers' world is static.
- The problem and solution are well understood and clearly defined.
- No one is going to make mistakes in the requirements or design.

It is very rare (I am tempted to give a probability of approaching zero) for all these to be true for a software development; software is too complicated, the world is constantly changing, and people are fallible. We need something better.

10.6.2 Spiral, incremental, and iterative models

There is a large family of incremental and iterative models that were developed from the 1980s onwards as a response to the problems of the waterfall model. These include increments in miniwaterfalls and in iterative or spiral models, as well as evolutionary models.

10.6.2.1 Incremental

In an incremental project (Figure 10.5), the work is chunked in a different way from a phased model. *The work is divided into houses, roads, and gardens. The roads are put in place, then the houses, and, finally, the gardens. The*

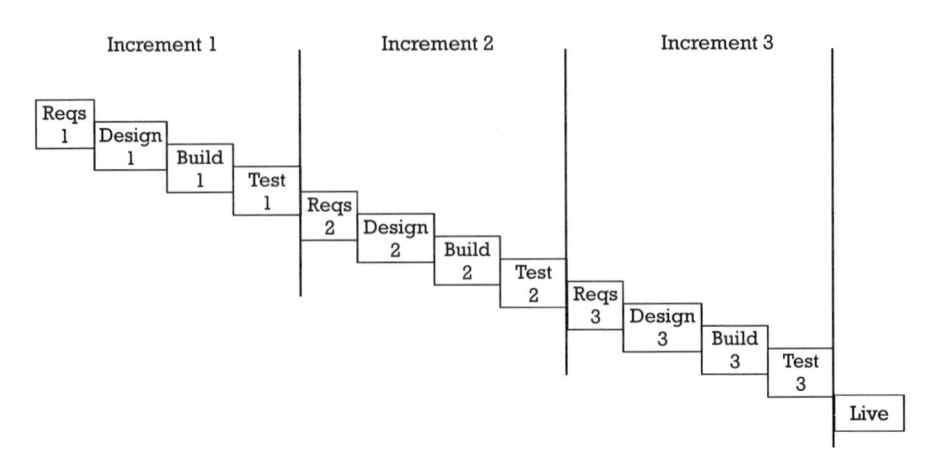

Figure 10.5 Incremental model.

incremental model is similar to the phased model, but one team can work on all the increments, whereas in the phased model, separate teams deal with each phase in parallel. This approach is useful if:

- The problem is too large for the team to tackle at one time, so building in stages is sensible
- The solution must to "go live" all at once

10.6.2.2 Iterative and spiral models

In an iterative approach (see Figure 10.6), steps in the project are repeated (iterated) allowing work to be revisited and refined. *The most important roads, with houses and gardens, are put in place first. As new houses are built, additional roads and gardens are added, and existing structures may be altered to fit with the new areas.*

The spiral model [5, 6], as shown in Figure 10.7, uses a series of prototypes, and through the prototyping refines our understanding of what we

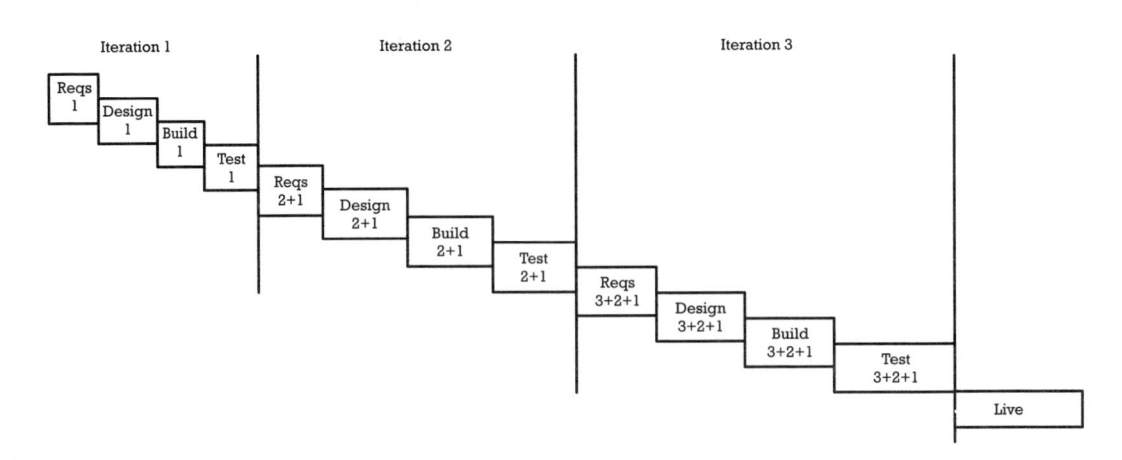

Figure 10.6 General iterative model.

10.6 SDLC models

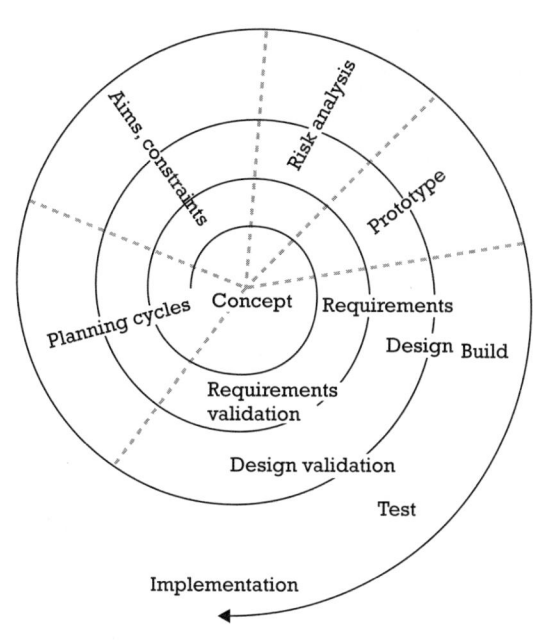

Figure 10.7 Spiral model. (*After:* [5].)

want to build, and our understanding of the risks, constraints, and so on. With each circuit of the spiral, we refine our plans against our improved understanding. *We build a paper plan of the village, then a cardboard scale model, then a full-scale model. As a result, we refine our understanding of what is required in each house, garden, and road, and we are able to cater for changes in requirements.*

The iterative and spiral models are more exploratory than the other models; they suggest that the same areas of requirements, design, build, and test are revisited repeatedly during the project, in order to correct errors, refine understanding, and introduce changes. However, each iteration will take more effort and time, to ensure that changes to existing structures are defined, made, and tested properly, and that unchanged areas have not been adversely affected. This is known as retest and regression test. The ability to change requirements may be useful for the customer, but is difficult for managers and builders if a fixed-price contract is agreed. As a colleague remarked to me, "Changing requirements can be an advantage and a disadvantage. If you have bid a project very thinly in a competitive tender process, the last thing you want to do us allow the customer to change requirements. It can make the difference between making money on the project or losing it." In particular, the spiral model encourages the use of prototyping (see Table 10.10 and Appendix A) as a technique to clarify what is required and to try out different ideas. It is useful because it acknowledges that we may not know everything we need to know, particularly about timescales and budget, at the start of the SDLC. Additionally, validation (does the specification describe what the customer needs?) and verification (have we met the specification?) take place at each step. In the TSP [3], for example, a "relaunch" of the plan is carried out at the start of each iteration.

Table 10.10 Summary of Techniques for Teamwork During the SDLC

Subject Area	Technique Examples	In 30 Seconds... (see Appendix A for more)
Team relationships and natural roles/team skills	Belbin team scores [14]	The SDLC can fail because of personal rather than technical factors. Teams need to understand their strengths and weaknesses as a team. A balance of roles/skills is required in the personalities in the team. Example roles: plants have new ideas; completer–finishers want to finish to fine detail. Too many plants and you will never finish anything.
Improve communication—empathy with others	MBTI [15]	Different people have different personalities and communication styles. People who wave their arms around and talk a lot can annoy people who like to be quiet and think, and vice versa. The Myers-Briggs Type Indicator (MBTI) identifies four contrasting type pairs (e.g., Introvert/Extrovert), leading to 16 "types" (e.g., INTJ is Introvert-iNtuitive-Thinking-Judging).
	Honey & Mumford [16]	The Honey & Mumford Learning Styles Questionnaire identifies preferred learning styles (e.g., Pragmatists and Theorists require different experiences to learn).
	Kirton [17]	Kirton identifies preferred problem solving methods (Adaptors versus Innovators)—do we break the rules or work within them?
Improve meetings	De Bono's Six Thinking Hats [18]	Improve meetings by setting rules for behavior. Six "hats" are used. Everyone wears the same color hat at the same time: Blue Hat—meeting structure, Black Hat—pessimistic, Yellow Hat—optimistic, Red Hat—feelings, White Hat—facts, Green Hat—creative ideas. Allows meeting members to move outside their stereotypes and allows time for different, sometimes difficult types of communication.
Identify problems and root causes, find solutions	Ishikawa fishbones [19, 20]	Use to identify problems, root causes of problems and solutions. On a fishbone diagram, brainstorm problems, their possible causes, their root causes, and, therefore, solutions to the root cause.
Review documents and other products	Reviews [21, 22]	There are five types of review: management review, technical review, inspection, walk-through, and audit—all of which are relevant throughout the SDLC. Specialist testers regard them as a form of testing because they are used to find and prevent defects in products and processes.
Understand/ explore ideas	Prototyping [5, 23]	Not an SDLC! We prototype to try out ideas or, if we are not sure what we want, we build a model of a possible solution(s). There are two types of prototyping in software, "lo-fi" and "hi-fi." In hi-fi (high-fidelity), we build screens like those the customer will see. Lo-fi (low-fidelity) prototyping uses paper/white board. Discuss the prototype and review it. There is no danger of believing it is the software.
	Modeling and picturing, stories, metaphors [24–27]	There are a number of modeling and picturing techniques that can be worth exploring with lo-fi prototyping. These include Rich Picturing and Mind Mapping. Sketching a picture of a problem, solution, or idea can clarify it. Use stories, metaphors, and analogy as well; they can aid in understanding.
Understand whether an idea is worth pursuing	Risk workshop by brainstorming [19, 20]	A brainstorming workshop is run to list all the possible risks people can identify. The risks are sorted into groups, separating risks (might happen in the future) from issues (problems right now) and constraints. The risks are scored for impact and likelihood, and ranked to give a prioritized list.
	Cost–benefit analysis [19]	Cost–benefit analysis is done by calculating the predicted benefits of the proposed change (time, money saved) and setting this against the predicted cost.
Track progress	Earned value [28]	Not only is it possible to track cost against budget, but also what the cost so far was supposed to achieve compared with what actually has been done.

One problem that has occurred with the use of the iterative models is the commonly held belief among managers and customers that testing is reduced, for example, by removing test levels or by reducing the time to test. This is not the case. A colleague notes: "The clear implication of iterative methods is that you start testing earlier and test more often through the life cycle, not to mention the regression testing of all the earlier work; ergo, you do more testing." For example, in eXtreme Programming (XP) [7], the SDLC has two levels of testing (programmer and user) instead of four. I have received mixed reports of how well this works; XP enthusiasts say it works well and streamlines the project, but some testers are reporting differently:

> The theory is very plausible-plan and design test before development. Simplified roles and responsibilities, simplified testing phases. The reality ... is very different. In practice, testing seems to fare even worse under an XP project than a traditional one (in terms of being neglected or done poorly).

10.6.3 Evolutionary model

We can see that the incremental, iterative, and spiral models all still suffer from the problem of the length of time from the start of the SDLC to delivery of software for use by the customers. The evolutionary model (Figure 10.8) was developed, for example, by Gilb [8], because it helps to break down the software into chunks that can be delivered earlier to the customer; this means that the real-life problem is at least partly resolved more quickly. According to Tom Gilb (at a seminar on Evolutionary Delivery, London, England, September 20, 2003), two characteristics that mark an evolutionary delivery as opposed to either an incremental or a phased delivery are the very large number of small increments and deliveries and the emphasis on feedback loops at each delivery so that continuous improvement is built into the SDLC. *The first deliveries of the village put dirt roads in place, plus some houses with basic rooms complete and the gardens laid to grass, in order that the first families can move in. In the later deliveries, the roads are asphalted, additional road furniture is installed (benches, night and security lighting), play and garden rooms are added, spare bedrooms fitted out in the existing houses, and new houses are added. As deliveries progress, each provides some new improvement: gardens are relaid according to individual requirements for flower beds and paths, garden sheds are installed, water features and other refinements are added to the gardens, and the kitchens are refurbished.*

10.6.4 V-model

The V-model and its close relation the W-model [12] were developed by testers who wanted to emphasize the cost-effectiveness of early testing. V-model SDLCs explicitly describe review activities as early testing. They expect that specialist testers are involved from requirements definition onward. *In the village, buildings inspectors are involved from the planning stage onwards, as are representatives of the people who will "accept" the village as suitable*

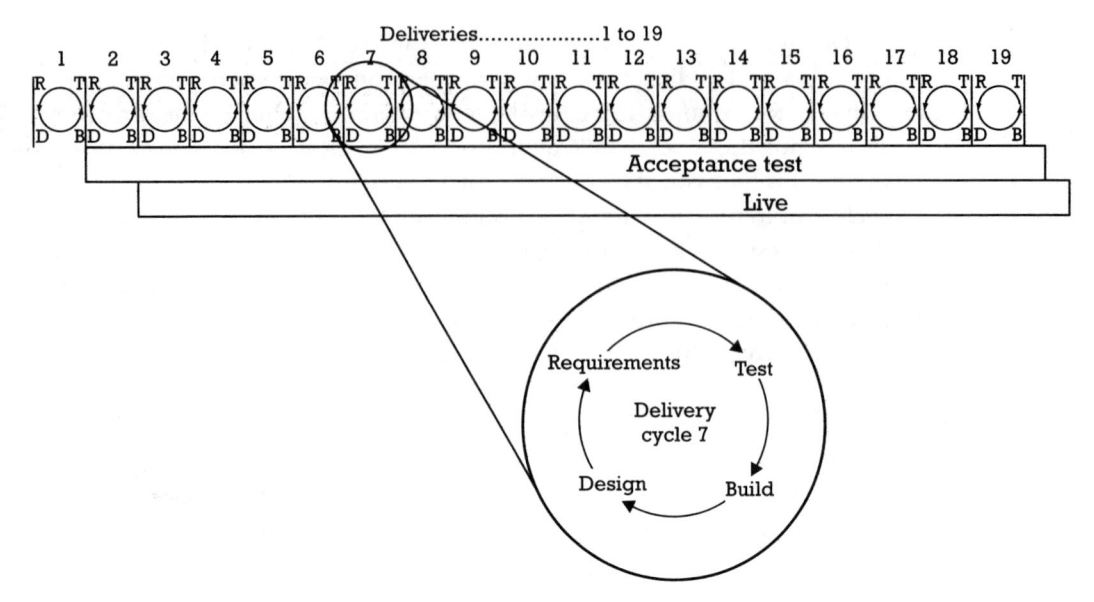

Figure 10.8 Evolutionary model in incremental SDLC.

to live in. They look at and comment on the plans and decide what checks they will do during building. At each step in the early part of the SDLC, products are built that relate to the dynamic stages of testing. Therefore, three things can happen together, as shown in Figure 10.9. Different V- and W-models may show these three steps in slightly different ways but, in essence, what is happening is that:

- A product is built (for example, the requirements, the designs, the code).
- The product is reviewed, by peer review, inspection or walkthrough, to show it matches the products at the previous stage, to show it meets a particular standard, and to show that it can be used as input to the next step.
- Test designs are built that will be used later to run dynamic tests that apply to this product and that demonstrate whether the product is testable.

10.6.5 Advantages and disadvantages of the models

The models each have advantages and disadvantages. These were summarized in Table 10.8.

10.7 Quality views and the models—why we might wish to combine models

We can see in Table 10.11 that the models favor particular quality views, because of which groups are involved in the SDLC.

10.7 Quality views and the models—why we might wish to combine models

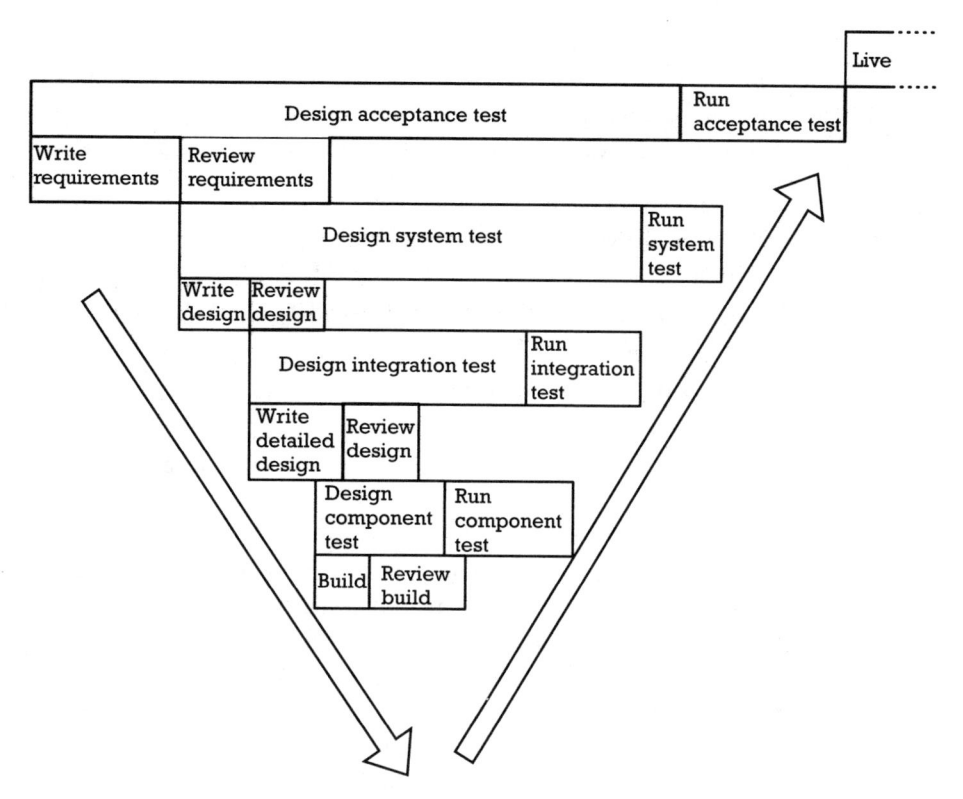

Figure 10.9 V-model.

The models I have shown are generic models. You will find off-the-shelf models and variations described in different companies' standards as well as in books and methodologies (see Table 10.10). You will also see variations on the themes in the models. It is perfectly reasonable to tailor the models to fit what your organization needs, and use published models in a "pick and mix" fashion. However, I do recommend that having looked at the models you settle on a tailored model and a few variations for your organization, with suitable additional tailoring rules. No model is perfect; you will need to use common sense and experience to tailor the model to specific projects, but if you allow a complete free-for-all, chaos will quickly ensue. I have seen situations in which each project is using its own terminology, methods, and measurements, resenting any "outside" ideas. The outcome is that

Table 10.11 Quality Views and the Models

| | Life Cycle | | | |
Quality View	Waterfall	Spiral/Iterative/ Evolutionary	V-Model	Combined
Transcendent	✓	✓	✓	✓
User view		✓		✓
Value view		✓		✓
Product view		✓		✓
Manufacturing view	✓		✓	✓

projects cannot be compared, people cannot easily transfer between projects, hostility between projects emerges, and organizations fail to learn from experience because projects guard their own outcomes.

Let us try an example. We look at our organization and assess that:

- Involvement of real customers will help us get the requirements right, and acknowledgment of changing requirements means we want to involve the customer right through the SDLC.
- Appropriate level of control and processes—we do not have very experienced people, but time to market is important so we need to have control without too much bureaucracy.
- Early testing to focus on areas of importance will help us deliver against risks. Maybe static testing (static analysis and reviews) might help us.

From this, we might choose to pick aspects of evolutionary delivery to get important functionality to the customers early, but combine it with some aspects of XP. Because our team is not mature, we would not use the whole of XP, but we might adopt the principle of continuous retest by the programmers and continuous customer involvement. From the V-model, we could use early reviews of requirements and designs, early test design, and static analysis on code. This would be useful if we could involve one of our experienced testers to check the requirements and design for testability, plus to set some detailed entry and exit criteria for steps in which we know we have particular technical weaknesses. To reduce time to market, we might take the risk of combining test levels or removing the formal entry and exit criteria except for high-risk steps. We now have a life cycle like the one in Figure 10.10, tailored to the risks and constraints for our situation [29].

I have seen tailored SDLCs introduced with a marked positive effect, not just on manufacturing quality, but across the quality definitions and groups. For example, in one organization, a framework with entry and exit criteria for the SDLC and for steps within the SDLC gave project teams the ability to tailor for large and small projects. They could split or combine steps and deliverables. The control of the SDLC was through authorization on the

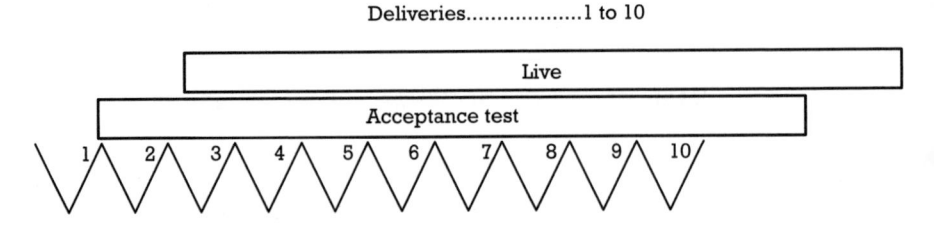

Evolutionary delivery gives us frequent deliveries to live
V-model gives us reinstatement of test levels lost from
XP, plus entry and exit criteria at key points

Figure 10.10 Evolutionary, XP, and V-model combined.

entry and exit criteria at each mandatory quality gate within the SDLC. An example of this is shown in Table 10.12, showing an SDLC tailored to a one-page form that describes a particular project. The customer has made a request for what looks like a fairly small and simple piece of work. With the manager and a senior builder, the checklist in Table 10.5 has been completed, and an assessment of the likely cost, size, and risk has been made, to give the Cost · Size · Risk calculation of less than nine. However, the feasibility of providing a simple enough solution is not clear, so a waterfall model would not be suitable. The team believes it will be necessary to produce a prototype to demonstrate that the proposed solution is possible within the constraints of time and budget. A small team of relatively experienced people is available. This suggests that an SDLC tailored to combine some steps is possible, especially as some of the team members are highly experienced in this application area. The team involved will consist of:

- Tom Customer (TC), who has made the request for work to be done, will be involved throughout to help in defining requirements, test prototypes, and test delivered software (user-acceptance test or UAT).
- Mary Builder (MB) (a senior software engineer) and Fred Builder (FB) (a programmer in training) will help TC define requirements, design the solution, build prototypes and deliverables, and carry out their own testing during each iteration.

Table 10.12 Tailored SDLC for the XYZ Project

Iteration and Step	*People During Step, Delivering*	*Exit Review Team*	*Authorize to Move On*
Iteration 1 planning	TC, DM—Plan for iteration 1, based on entry checklist, C · S · R 9	TC, MB, JS, DM, JM, FM	TC
Requirements/ design/build/test	TC, MB, FB—build and test prototype	TC, MB, FB, JS, JM	TC MB
Iteration 2 planning	TC, DM, MB—Refined plan for iteration 2, based on prototype, test results, actual effort, and cost *or* no-go decision	TC, MB, JS, DM, JM, FM	TC, DM
Requirements/ design/build/ initial test	TC, MB, FB—Refine requirements and interface design, first build of solution. JM builds tests, environment for independent test.	TC, MB, FB, JS, JM, FM	TC, MB
Independent test	JM—perform independent test of first build	TC, JM, MB	TC, DM
Iteration 3 planning	TC, DM, MB, JM—Refined plan for iteration 3, based on test results, actual effort, and cost *or* no-go decision	TC, MB, JS, DM, JM, FM	TC,DM
Requirements/ design	TC, MB, FB—Refined requirements and interface design, TC, JS, JM build tests, two environments for independent tests (UAT and OAT)	TC, MB, JS, DM, JM, FM	TC, MB, JS
Build/test	MB, FB—build of solution	MB, FB, JM, TC, JS	TC, JS, JM
	JM—Independent test of build in environment 1		
Independent test	TC, JS—Operational and user-acceptance test (OAT and UAT) in like-live environment 2 leading to decision:	TC, JS, JM, MB, FB, DM	TC, JS
	Solution ready for delivery to live use *or* no-go decision		

- Jenny Supporter (JS) will review the design at each iteration for implications around the infrastructure and existing systems, and will run an operational acceptance test (OAT) as part of iteration 3.
- Dave Manager (DM) will aid with planning and decision making, check that the work is staying within time/budget constraints, and be an escalation point for all team members.
- Joe Measurer (JM) is a specialist tester who will carry out reviews of the requirements and design at each stage, review test results at each iteration, and plan and carry out independent testing in iterations 2 and 3.
- Fiona Measurer (FM) is a quality and process specialist who will review that the SDLC tailoring and the plans are suitable for the level of risk, cost, and size of project.

The team decides to tailor the life cycle. They want to combine the flexibility, replanning, and prototyping of the spiral model, the idea of early tester involvement and reviewing from the V-model, and a three-iteration SDLC. Some of the activities will not have formal exit criteria; effectively they are combined into single steps. The entry criterion for each step is the completion of the previous step plus any preparation activities. Exit reviews and authorization to move on are done formally at significant points given the size of the project.

10.8 Exit from the SDLC

10.8.1 Exit criteria following a detailed acceptance test

If the SDLC completes after an acceptance test based on SMART acceptance criteria like those defined in Chapter 9, it is easy to make the go/no-go decision for taking the software to live use. Either the acceptance criteria have been met or they have not. In Table 10.13, we see simplified example exit criteria for different projects. Notice that the exit from the SDLC may be to deliver software for use, or the SDLC may be stopped and nothing delivered for use. The acceptance test, by which the customer and the supporter decide whether they are prepared to run the software for real, live use may have several outcomes:

- The test passes completely; no problems are identified during the test.
- Some tests have failed but the software is sufficiently fit for purpose that it can be accepted and used with workarounds planned for identified problems.
- The acceptance test fails and the software needs changing; these mean the software will have to be tested again.
- The acceptance test fails and it is judged that the cost and risk of fixing the problems is too great. Nothing is delivered for live use; fixing software is difficult, and prone to cause chain-reaction problems. The SDLC is stopped.

10.8 Exit from the SDLC

Table 10.13 Example of Exit Criteria for SDLC Stage

Example of Exit Criteria	Example of Deliverables Documented, Reviewed, and Agreed Upon	Example of Authorization Owners
Acceptance test completed and passed in all aspects; software will move to delivery.	Acceptance test summary report, including acceptance of the implementation/rollback plan, infrastructure, training, documentation, processes, and software.	Process owner, support manager
Acceptance test completed and failed; users and supporters willing to accept as is with documented work rounds.	Acceptance test summary report including acceptance or otherwise of the implementation/rollback plan, infrastructure, training, documentation, processes, and software. Cost–benefit analysis Known problem and workaround list.	Process owner, support manager
Acceptance test completed and failed; rework software and rerun tests.	Acceptance test summary report including acceptance or otherwise of the implementation/rollback plan, infrastructure, training, documentation, processes, and software. Cost–benefit analysis. Rework and rerun plan.	Process owner
Acceptance test completed and failed; cancel project.	Acceptance test summary report including acceptance or otherwise of the implementation/rollback plan, infrastructure, training, documentation, processes, and software. Cost–benefit analysis. Definition of alternative solution.	Process owner

10.8.2 When no exit criteria have been defined

If you have not defined exit criteria from the SDLC, how will you know when to stop? It might be that you make the decision to go live because you have run out of time or budget, or because you have completed all the planned tests, or because our manager will get angry if we do not deliver soon. Any of these could be the right or the wrong reason for stopping. If we think of the quality definitions and the groups, each group will have a preferred quality reason for stopping or continuing:

- Customers may be desperate for the new software, and they will go with fit-for-purpose rather than perfect, or, indeed, what is in the specification, but may be less sanguine once defective code is delivered.

- Managers will be watching the time and cost of the SDLC—they want to ensure the organization gets a proper return on investment and does not spend excessively.

- Builders want to ensure that they have implemented all the features and attributes from the specification.

- Measurers can become excessively focused on defect identification and removal at the expense of time and budget constraints.

- Supporters will go with fit-for-purpose rather than perfect, or, indeed, what is in the specification, but may be less sanguine once defective code is delivered.

If no exit criteria are defined and agreed on between the groups, the differing viewpoints will mean that the team argues about whether the software is ready for delivery or not. If you are approaching the end of an SDLC without agreed exit criteria, then I suggest you attempt to document and agree on some criteria for acceptance (see Section 10.8.5). You also need to identify the circumstances under which the software would not be accepted and the actions to be taken in that case.

To prevent this problem from recurring, improve the SDLC model that is used in your organization by adding exit criteria to the model.

10.8.3 When exit criteria have not been met

As with the entry criteria, if the exit criteria have not been met, we must not exit the SDLC. In order that we can be strict, it is important that the exit criteria are:

- Objective;
- Defined in a way that is SMART;
- Necessary rather than simply desirable.

However, there are occasions when we might decide to waive the exit criteria. This may happen if we decide that the exit criteria are excessive or incorrect, or if we believe this is an emergency. There are also occasions when we may wish to increase the exit criteria, for example, if we see that the SDLC is at higher risk than our normal projects. Exactly the same lessons apply as we discussed in Section 10.3.3, so I will not repeat them here. It suffices to say that the exit from the SDLC should match to the entry to delivery (Chapter 11).

10.8.4 Tailoring exit criteria

Exit criteria will be similar for different SDLC models, but there may be differences for specific projects or pieces of work. As with the entry criteria, tailoring against cost, budget, and risk measures may help teams to choose appropriate exit criteria for a particular project. Table 10.14 shows some examples.

10.8.5 When no acceptance criteria have been set

However late it is in the SDLC, if we do not have acceptance criteria, we should try to set some. For the acceptance criteria, it may well be too late to do anything about attributes the team has not considered. Use Table 9.8 in Chapter 9 to help you build a checklist of attributes to consider as acceptance criteria.

To prevent this problem from occurring in the future, improve the process to include a detailed start-up for the SDLC.

Table 10.14 Example of Exit Criteria Tailored to Projects

C · S · R Score	Example of Exit Criteria / Example of Exit Documents	Example of Authorization Owners
1–5	1. E-mail with notification of change completion and request to move code to live from builder to supporter, and customer, copied to manager and measurer Deliverables: E-mail and acknowledgment, code standards checklist complete by builder, customer test results	Customer, supporter
6–12	1. As above, plus 2. Request raised at monthly change management meeting 3. Tests completed by independent tester and by customer/supporter Deliverables: As above, plus acceptance criteria completion report, evidence from testing. and known fault list	Customer, process owner, supporter builder, manager
12–20	1. As above, plus 2. Acceptance criteria metrics from ISO 9126 completed and reviewed 3. Separate unit, system and acceptance test stages complete Deliverables: As above, plus acceptance criteria documentation, evidence from all testing stages and known fault/workaround list	Customer, process owner, project manager
20–27	1. As above, plus 2. Additional risk assessment on delivery carried out by process owner and project manager 3. Implementation planning, including contingency planning completed 4. Project authorization board has discussed and agreed to the implementation and risk plan for delivery Deliverables: As above, plus additional work on risk assessment, achievement of aims and objectives, targets and indicators, constraints, acceptance criteria, implementation plan, project authorization to complete	Project authorization board, SDLC project sponsor, process owner, project manager

10.9 Conclusion

No single SDLC model is perfect. What we choose depends on our definition of quality, our constraints and our risks. All the life cycles have similar steps, and we must tailor SDLC models to fit the risk level and constraints within a particular project.

There are more deliverables that just the software systems. We must also plan for delivery of:

- Infrastructure, operational, and support processes and equipment;
- Training (for software, support, and business processes);
- Documentation (for software, support, and business processes);

- Business and manual processes;
- Implementation processes, including rollout and rollback plans;
- Data, for example, during a data migration, both databases and standing data.

It is worth having some pretailored SDLC models, associated with different levels of risk and different types of projects. All SDLCs need some start-up beforehand; you cannot be successful with any SDLC unless you have fulfilled the entry criteria. All SDLCs require good communication between all groups. All are aimed at delivery, which we will look at in Chapter 11.

References

[1] Reid, S. C., "Software Testing Standards—Do They Know What They Are Talking About?" http://www.testingstandards.co.uk/publications.htm, August 2003.

[2] Software Engineering Institute, "Capability Maturity Model®," http://www.sei.cmu.edu, July 2003.

[3] Humphrey, W., *Introduction to the Team Software Process*, Reading, MA: SEI, 2000.

[4] IT Infrastructure Library, *Best Practice for Service Management*, London, England: Office of Government Commerce, 2002.

[5] Nance, R. E., and J. D. Arthur, *Managing Software Quality*, New York: Springer-Verlag, 2002.

[6] Boehm, B. W., "A Spiral Model of Software Development and Enhancement," *IEEE Computer*, Vol. 21, No. 5, 1988, pp. 61–72.

[7] Kruchten, P., *The Rational Unified Process*, Reading, MA: Addison-Wesley, 1999.

[8] Beck, K., *Extreme Programming Explained*, Reading, MA: Addison-Wesley, 2001.

[9] DSDM, DSDM, http://www.dsdm.org, April 2003.

[10] Gilb, T., papers on Evolutionary Delivery on http://www.gilb.com, including "Competitive Engineering: A Handbook for Systems and Software Engineering," http://www.gilb.com, September 2003.

[11] Craig, R. D. and S. P. Jaskiel, *Systematic Software Testing*, Norwood, MA: Artech House, 2002.

[12] Gerrard, P., and N. Thompson, *Risk Based E-Business Testing*, Norwood, MA: Artech House, 2002.

[13] BSI, BS7925-2:1998, Software Testing—Part 2: Software Component Testing, BSI 1998.

[14] Belbin Associates, "Belbin Team Roles," http://www.belbin.com/belbin-team-roles.htm, October 2003.

[15] Team Technology Web site, "Working Out Your Myers Briggs Type," http://www.teamtechnology.co.uk/tt/t-articl/mb-simpl.htm, October 2003.

[16] Honey, P., "Learning Styles," http://www.peterhoney.co.uk/product/ learning styles, October 2003.

10.9 Conclusion

[17] Kirton, "Adaptors and Innovators Defined," KAI Web site, http://www.kaicentre.com/, July 2003.

[18] de Bono, E., *Six Thinking Hats®*, New York: Penguin, 1999.

[19] Robson, M., *Problem Solving in Groups*, Aldershot, England: Gower, 1995.

[20] TQMI, *Problem Solving—Tools and Techniques*, Frodsham, England: TQMI, 2001.

[21] IEEE 1028™ Standard for Software Reviews, 1997.

[22] Gilb, T., and D. Graham, *Software Inspection*, Reading, MA: Addison-Wesley, 1993.

[23] Hohmann, L., "Lo-Fi GUI Design," *Software Testing and Quality Engineering*, Vol. 1, No. 5, September 1999.

[24] "Drawing Concerns: A Structured Rich Picturing Approach," http://business.unisa.edu.au/cobar/documents/richpic_colin.pdf, November 2003.

[25] Rose, J., "Soft Systems Methodology as a Social Science Research Tool," http://www.cs.auc.dk/~jeremy/pdf%20files/SSM.pdf.

[26] Buzan, T., *The Mind Map Book*, London, England: BBC Consumer Publishing, 2003.

[27] Freeburn, G., "Mind Mapping 101 for Testers," *EuroSTAR Conference*, Edinburgh, Scotland, 2002.

[28] Pavyer, E., "An Introduction to Earned Value Management," *Project Manager Today*, Vol. 11, April 2003.

[29] Evans, I., "The Risks We Take with Testing," *British Quality Foundation IT&T Group Meeting*, February 2003.

Selected bibliography

Belbin, R. M., *Management Teams—Why They Succeed or Fail*, London, England: Butterworth Heinemann, 1981.

Belbin, R. M., *Team Roles at Work*, London, England: Butterworth Heinemann, 1995.

Gilb, T., *Principles of Software Engineering Management*, Reading, MA: Addison-Wesley, 1988.

Gnatz, M., et al., "The Living Software Quality Process," *Software Quality Professional*, June 2003, pp. 4–16.

Honey, P., and A. Mumford, *The Learning Styles Helper's Guide*, Maidenhead, England: Peter Honey Publications, 2002. PeterHoney.com, 10 Linden Avenue, Maidenhead, Berks, SL6 6HB. Tel.: 0162863946. Fax: 01628633262. E-mail: info@peterhoney.com.

Kroeger, O., J. M. Thuesen, and H. Rutledge, *Type Talk at Work: How the 16 Personality Types Determine Your Success on the Job*, New York: Bantam Doubleday Dell, 2002.

McHale, J., "Innovators Rule OK—Or Do They?" *Training & Development*, October 1986, http://www.kaicentre.com/.

Sticky Minds Web site Roundtable, facilitator Craig, R., "What Is Software Quality and How Do You Measure Its Value?" http://www.stickyminds.com/s.asp?F=S6540_ROUND_46, August 2003.

CHAPTER 11

Delivery and Support When Going Live

Contents

11.1 Delivery—description

11.2 Delivery viewpoints

11.3 Entry criteria for delivery

11.4 Delivery—typical activities

11.5 Exit from delivery

11.6 Conclusion

In this chapter I shall:

- Describe the entry criteria, steps, and exit criteria for delivery;
- Identify the quality definitions from Chapter 1 that prevail at this stage;
- Identify how each of the groups identified in Chapter 2 become involved at this stage;
- Introduce techniques that aid teamwork at this stage.

It's 10 p.m. on Sunday; either we complete the implementation and work around the defects, or we roll back now. We cannot wait any longer, or there isn't time to roll back and be ready for Monday.

—*Customer makes an assessment of the path of least damage during a flawed implementation*

11.1 Delivery—description

11.1.1 Delivery considerations

Delivery is the point in the life span of software after the software-development life cycle (SDLC) has completed when products are moved to live use. It is a (relatively) short but anxious period of time, but it is highly importance; many activities will come together at a single milestone in the project plan. Delivery is not always a success; sometimes the implementation fails and we have to roll back by removing the software and restoring the systems to their predelivery state. "Postponement of a system's implementation is painful and often very costly. The implementation of a poor system, however, is much more costly and also much more painful" [1]. The roots of a failed delivery are found in the entry and exit criteria for the SDLC, which I discussed in Chapters 9 and 10.

Delivery comes between the SDLC and the postdelivery period when the software is used (Figure 11.1). As with the earlier stages, all the groups have a significant contribution to make but they do not always realize their part. In this chapter, I will discuss the activities carried out during delivery, and how all the team can contribute to making it a success. Specific activities need to be planned and managed leading to the delivery point if the delivery is to be achieved without problems.

There are things to consider when planning the delivery, depending on the type of software, the other deliverables that come with the software solution, and the type of customer:

- *Installation team:* The installation of the software plus any other products may be done by the customer, or by a team from the support group (operations or help desk) or by the build team themselves.

- *Method of delivery:* Delivery and installation of the software might be by different media (download from Internet/intranet, by transfer within a configuration management system, by use of removable media such as diskettes, tapes, or CDs). Delivery of other products such as training and support may be face to face, via documentation, or via other media such as video and CD.

- *Time period for installation:* Delivery and installation may be a short process, taking minutes, or it may be an extended process. In the latter case, it may take place overnight, over a weekend, or over a longer period. For a large installation, it may be phased in geographically or in some other way, or there may be a pilot project.

- *Urgency of the delivery:* Sometimes, emergency changes to systems are required, and in this case the change may require a special process in order to speed up the delivery without losing control.

- *Support around the delivery:* A small delivery may not require particular support; perhaps the minimum would be a release notice with a known problem list. Larger deliveries may be supported by training, which

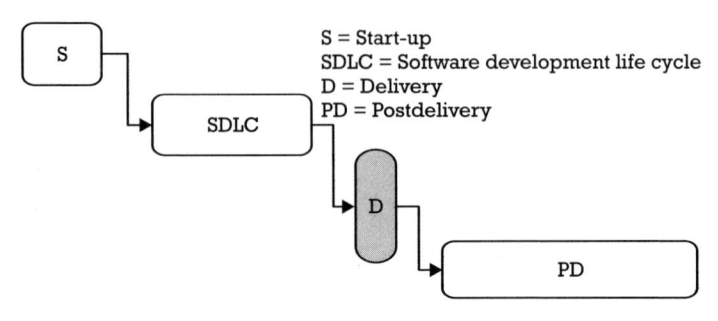

Figure 11.1 Life span stages.

would then be a deliverable in itself. Other support to a software delivery might include expert teams to work on support lines or with the software users. The need for additional support depends on how transparent the delivery is to the people using the IT systems.

- *Quality measures of the deliverables:* The release notice will typically list any known problems and workarounds for the deliverables. The quality measures for the deliverables will affect the decision to make the delivery or not. This includes an assessment of the known problems and whether the exit criteria for the SDLC were met.
- *Size of delivery:* Different delivery strategies may be required for new "green field" systems, small and large changes to existing systems, single changes, and groups of changes.

11.1.2 Identifying the delivery

A delivery will consist of one or more of the following deliverables, built and tested during the SDLC:

- Software;
- Infrastructure, for example new hardware, communications equipment, systems software, plus operational and support processes;
- Training material and delivery of training for software, support, and business processes;
- Documentation for software, support, and business processes, for example, user and support guides;
- Business and other processes as well as process changes, for both manual and IT processes;
- Implementation processes, including rollout and rollback plans;
- Data, for example, during a data migration, both databases and standing data.

The delivery plan should identify all the deliverables, each identified with its version number and status, under a configuration management system. A configuration management system is used to make sure we deliver the right version of each deliverable; this is because as we build and test deliverables, they will go through many revisions. It is an easy human error to deliver the wrong version. The group of deliverables to be released together may be identified with a release ID [2]. This is updated for later deliveries of changes to an existing system so that the size and type of the delivery is identified in the release ID: for example, if the first release into live use is identified as "V1":

- "V2" is a major release that contains significant changes to V1.
- "V1.1" is a minor release of small changes to V1.
- "V1.1.1" is an emergency fix to the system.

In an SDLC that takes place as part of an organization or business transfer, the point of delivery might also be the point at which the business is responsible for transferred customers and staff. Although this would not normally be considered as part of the SDLC delivery, the introduction of these people to the new organization would need to be managed as part of an overall business delivery process, including introductions and induction training.

11.2 Delivery viewpoints

Each group has a view of when the point of delivery happens, and of what is included in the delivery. For the builders, they may only be interested in the deliverables for which they have direct responsibility. For example, within the build group, developers will be interested in the delivery of their code, trainers will be interested in the delivery of the training, and technical authors in the delivery of the user guides. It is interesting to note that in *Introduction to the Team Software Process* [3], the final step in the software engineering project is the *postmortem*, which comes immediately after the system test; the implication is that the software engineers hand over the code at this point, before the acceptance test, so the user-acceptance test would be carried out by the customers, leading into the delivery, to be carried out by customers and supporters. From the viewpoint of the supporters, the delivery covers code and the infrastructure to support it. For example, in the IT Infrastructure Library (ITIL) manual *Best Practice for Service Support* [2] under Release Management, the main components of a release for delivery are identified as:

- Application programs, developed in-house or externally, including packages;
- Utility software;
- Systems software;
- Hardware and hardware specifications;
- Assembly instructions and documentation, including user manuals.

Notice how this includes everything in which the supporters will be interested, but not training or business processes, which some IT people would regard as outside the SDLC. Yet, from the customer viewpoint, without the business processes and training, it may not be possible to take delivery of the software successfully.

Thus, we see that if we take a simple view of the point of delivery, we may forget to deliver something needed by one of the groups. Some projects may see the delivery as being the responsibility of the customers and the supporters, with the managers, builders, and measurers simply handing over tested code and no other material. The managers, builders, and measurers have taken the system to the end of either system test for handover to

11.2 Delivery viewpoints

the acceptance test, or have supported it to the end of the acceptance test. At acceptance, the project is complete. The deliverables are handed over, and the customer and supporter proceed on their own. The supporter perhaps carries out the installation of the software, and the customer prepares to use it, perhaps by reading the user guide. In other projects, such as the delivery of a commercial off-the-shelf (COTS) package, the customer may not even have a supporter to carry out the installation. For example, in a one- or two-person company, the acquisition of a desktop computer, with word processing and accounting software, may only require a purchase order and a visit to the local computer store, with the person using the PC carrying out the entire installation themselves.

As we see in Table 11.1, if only the customer and supporter are involved, this results in a limited quality viewpoint, which may or may not matter depending on the size and complexity of the delivery.

If the SDLC has been carried out with a viewpoint limited to the builder, measurer, and manager (see Table 10.1 in Chapter 10) we may quickly find that the customer and supporter views of whether they have received a quality system is at odds with the others' views of whether they have delivered quality.

In many large projects, particularly for custom-made or tailored systems, the builders, measurers, and managers will aid in the delivery, and may well have a team to support the customers and supporters as the customers take delivery of the software and start to use it. Although members of all groups will support the delivery, their viewpoints will be quite different (Table 11.2):

Table 11.1 Views of Quality at Delivery—Simple

	Groups	
Quality View	*Customer*	*Supporter*
Transcendent view	✓	✓
User view	✓	✓
Value view		
Product view		✓
Manufacturing view		

Table 11.2 Views of Quality at Delivery—Teamwork

	Groups				
Quality View	*Customer*	*Manager*	*Builder*	*Measurer*	*Supporter*
Transcendent view	✓	✓	✓	✓	✓
User view	✓			(✓)	✓
Value view		✓			
Product view			✓	✓	✓
Manufacturing view			✓	✓	

✓ is a primary quality view.
(✓) is a quality view that may be taken by some people in this group.

- Customers are very engaged at this point. Will the system work for real? Will they be able to use it? Will the delivery go well? From the user quality viewpoint, will the system be fit for purpose?
- Supporters are also very engaged; they will be rolling out the system and starting to support it. Their questions and viewpoint are similar to that of the customer, with the addition of a product viewpoint that looks at the effect of attributes in the system as a whole; for example, how does the new software affect performance of the overall system?
- Managers have quite a different reason for anxiety at this point. Will the project team be able to finish this project and (with more or less relief) move onto a shiny new project? Using the value quality viewpoint, did the project come in within budget and time scale, and can any delays in delivery be prevented?
- Builders will be pleased to have completed the project; they will want to see a clean sign-off against the delivery. From their manufacturing and product quality views, is the delivery defect free and does the software have all the specified attributes?
- Measurers will share the builders' views and, in addition, will be worried about their efforts in assessing quality from the manufacturing view. They will be focused on defects identified during delivery that were not identified earlier.

For a release of any complexity, it is likely that many people will be involved. It may be useful to have a *responsibility matrix* [2] to show who is involved and with what responsibilities for the different types of SDLC and projects. This might be arranged by size and risk, as well as by technical content of the delivery; for example, whether the delivery is of a bought package, a customized package, database changes, hardware changes, or custom-made software. For example, in contrast with our one- or two-person company above, in a large organization, depending on its processes, the purchase and installation of a PC with word processor and accounting software may require involvement from a logistics group, the desktop support group, the change management team, IT security, an electrical equipment safety team, and so on. The authority and responsibilities for delivery tasks would be included in the responsibility matrix, which could be incorporated with the entry and exit criteria for delivery.

In particular, the support of builders and measurers will be needed to aid in resolving any problems that arise during the delivery. Managers need to be involved to make cost–benefit analysis for any change of plan during the delivery.

The period around the delivery needs to be managed carefully because change is taking place. The unfamiliar system requires a learning curve from the customers and supporters. There also may well be "teething problems" as the system is first used. The enthusiasm for the new software may drop significantly if benefits from the delivery cannot be realized right away. Enthusiasm for the system may not be regained until significant benefits have been demonstrated for the system. This is referred to as the "Silver Bullet Life Cycle" [2]. Managing the relationships and communication between the groups is vital in order that the team works through the delivery taking account of changes in attitude and confidence as well as the technical activities. Using the teamwork techniques listed in Table 11.3 and described in Appendix A will help to manage the communications.

11.3 Entry criteria for delivery

The entry criteria for delivery must include all the exit criteria for the SDLC, but may include additional tasks required for the delivery into live use, if these tasks have not been defined as part of the SDLC. Table 11.4 shows some example entry criteria for which preparation for delivery in terms of an implementation and rollback plan has been completed within the SDLC, but other aspects of infrastructure and service support have not been included.

As the SDLC may not include consideration of release and rollout plans, the entry criteria for delivery should explicitly mention completion of tasks beyond simply the delivery of the software. The specific entry criteria will depend on the type of organization and the type of delivery. In particular, evidence of acceptance testing of a delivery should include testing not just the functionality of the software, but ascertaining that it can be installed and backed out (deinstalled) [2].

Apart from use of the software, there are a number of services that are needed postdelivery, and I will discuss them in Chapter 12. We should not need to carry out detailed planning and delivery of these services for every SDLC; these activities should be in place in order that we can support software systems. For a project in which we are acquiring a new system on a new infrastructure, we would plan and set them up as part of the whole IT infrastructure, so our entry criteria would include checking that all the support and infrastructure is in place to support the live system. For a project in which we are delivering new software to an existing infrastructure, we would need to review whether changes were needed in any of these areas to support the delivery and use of the software. The completion of these changes would become part of the entry criteria for delivery for that particular project. A very good description of the type of infrastructure activities required and checklists for reviewing delivery plans are in the ITIL Service Delivery and Service Support Manuals [2, 4].

11.4 Delivery—typical activities

The activities that take place during delivery depend on the size and complexity of the project. This is best illustrated by some examples.

Table 11.3 Summary of Techniques for Teamwork in Delivery

Subject Area	Technique Examples	In 30 seconds... (see Appendix A for more)
Delivery	Pilot projects [5, 6]	A limited delivery to a small area, which enables the customers and suppliers to test delivery and use of the proposed system before rollout to a large number of sites.
Delivery	Release management [2, 4, 7]	"Release management builds the final customer solution, which also includes instantiation of the developing and testing environment. In a product-line context, release management includes the release of core assets to product developers. When shopping for CM tools, make sure the one you buy can help you build releases." [7]
Delivery	Build management [2, 4, 7]	"Build management enables developers to create a version of a product, which can be anything from a single component to a complete customer solution for the purpose of testing and/or integration." [7]
Team relationships and natural roles/team skills	Belbin team roles [8]	The SDLC can fail because of personal rather than technical factors. Teams need to understand their strengths and weaknesses as a team. A balance of roles/skills is required in the personalities in the team. Example roles: plants have new ideas; completer–finishers want to finish to fine detail. Too many plants and you will never finish anything.
Improve communication—empathy with others	MBTI [9]	Different people have different personalities and communication styles. People who wave their arms around and talk a lot can annoy people who like to be quiet and think, and vice versa. The Myers-Briggs Type Indicator (MBTI) identifies four contrasting type pairs (e.g., *Introvert/Extrovert*) leading to 16 "types" (e.g., INTJ is *Introvert-iNtuitive-Thinking-Judging*).
	Honey & Mumford [10]	The Honey & Mumford Learning Styles Questionnaire identifies preferred learning styles (e.g., *Pragmatists vs. Theorists*) require different experiences to learn.
	Kirton [11]	Kirton identifies preferred problem solving methods (*Adaptors vs. Innovators*)—do we break the rules or work within them?
Improve meetings	De Bono's Six Thinking Hats [12]	Improve meetings by setting rules for behavior. Six "hats" are used. Everyone wears the same color hat at the same time: Blue Hat—meeting structure, Black Hat—pessimistic, Yellow Hat—optimistic, Red Hat—feelings, White Hat—facts, Green Hat—creative ideas. Allows meeting members to move outside their stereotypes and allows time for different, sometimes difficult types of communication.
Identify problems and root causes, find solutions	Ishikawa fishbones [13, 14]	Use to identify problems, root causes of problems and solutions. On a fishbone diagram, brainstorm problems, their possible causes, their root causes, and, therefore, solutions to the root cause.
Review documents and other products	Reviews [15, 16]	There are five types of review: management review, technical review, inspection, walkthrough, and audit—all of which are relevant throughout the SDLC. Specialist testers regard them as a form of testing, because they are used to find and prevent defects in products and processes.
Understand whether an idea is worth pursuing	Risk workshop by brainstorming [13, 14]	A brainstorming workshop is run to list all the possible risks people can identify. The risks are sorted into groups, separating risks (might happen in the future) from issues (problems right now) and constraints. The risks are scored for impact and likelihood, and ranked to give a prioritized list.
	Cost–benefit analysis [13, 14]	Cost–benefit analysis is done by calculating the predicted benefits of the proposed change (time, money saved) and setting this against the predicted cost.

11.4 Delivery—typical activities

Table 11.4 Example Entry Criteria for Delivery

Example of Entry Criteria	Example of Entry Documents	Example of Authorization Owners
1. Acceptance test completed and passed in all aspects; software will move to delivery	Acceptance test summary report, *including acceptance of the implementation/rollback plan, infrastructure, training, documentation, processes, and software*	Process owner, support manager
2. Acceptance test completed and failed; users and supporters willing to accept as is with documented workarounds	Acceptance test summary report, *including acceptance or otherwise of the implementation/rollback plan, infrastructure, training, documentation, processes, and software* Cost–benefit analysis Known problem and workaround list.	Process owner, support manager
3. Hardware change: Either 1 or 2 completed, plus hardware delivery complete	Hardware implementation test complete and accepted	Infrastructure manager
4. Additional support line/help desk required: Either 1 or 2 completed, plus support plan implemented	Support policies and processes complete and agreed on Support line/help-desk infrastructure (hardware, communications, and software tools) complete and accepted Support personnel trained and ready	Support line/help-desk manager
5. Change to business processes required: Either 1 or 2 complete plus business process changes agreed on, tested and accepted, and business training complete	Business processes agreed on Business personnel trained and ready	Process manager, customer services manager

11.4.1 Person buys PC and software for self-installation

The builders, measurers, managers, and supporters will work for the PC and software vendors. They must prepare the product with everything the customers will need to support them through delivery and into use of the system. The level of intervention by a specialist with technical knowledge of PCs will need to be reduced by improving the installation process itself, perhaps by automation, but also by providing step-by-step instructions not just for the installation of the software but including steps to take before and after the installation. Additionally, supporting documentation should be written in the customer's terminology, not in IT terminology. The delivery activities that might be typical here would be for the customer to:

- Check all the delivered components against a supplied parts checklist.
- Assemble hardware following a step-by-step guide
- Boot up system and follow on-screen initialization steps.
- Customize system.
- Back up system.
- Install purchased software package, following steps in the installation guide.

- Check that the installed software works as expected.
- If it does work, make a backup of the system.
- If it does not work, deinstall following the manufacturer's deinstallation instructions.

Of course, at the point where the customer finds that the software does not work, they may want to take a number of actions: following the troubleshooting guide supplied by the manufacturer, ringing the help line, looking at on-line help, or asking for their money back [17].

11.4.2 Single-site delivery of software

For a delivery of new software or an upgrade to an existing system, the steps within delivery need to protect processes or people using the system from unexpected changes. The delivery steps might include:

- Awareness, education, and training prior to the delivery—people are made aware that a change will be made and given any training they will need, plus details of additional support such as additional help-line numbers.
- Carry out normal day's processing on system.
- Carry out end-of-day processes on system.
- Back up system.
- Overnight, install new software, following steps in the installation procedures.
- Check that the installed software works as expected.
- If it does work, make a back up of the system and make ready to go live.
- If it does not work, deinstall following the deinstallation instructions and make ready to go live with the old system.

If the installation was not successful, the team may chose to go live with the changes anyway; the exit criteria for the delivery would need to define the acceptance levels.

11.4.3 Multisite rollout of new software to existing infrastructure

The steps will be similar to the single-site delivery but will be repeated at each site, and there may be a delay in the rollout or installation to allow the people using and supporting the system to become used to it. For a multisite installation a phased approach is easier to manage and less prone to error than a "big bang" approach [6]. For new software, for example taking on a software tool that replaces manual activities with a radical change in process, a pilot project may be useful. In fact, pilots are useful when the customer for the delivery is the IT group itself; for example, when taking on a new testing tool, piloting the use of the tool in a small group and then rolling out to the rest of the IT teams is generally recommended [7]. The steps might include:

- Choose pilot and make a draft implementation rollout plan for remaining sites.
- Awareness sessions for the pilot and release plan.
- Implement on the pilot system, as a single-site process, including education and training.
- Monitor and evaluate the pilot, confirm or update rollout plan.
- If proceeding, roll out to the next site, as a single-site process, including education and training.
- If not proceeding, roll back.
- Monitor and evaluate the site, confirm or update rollout plan.

If the pilot is not successful, a decision needs to be made about how to proceed, so the pilot needs its own acceptance and exit criteria. For a with problems, we might decide to go ahead with the implementation rollout anyway, or to implement it only in certain areas, or to change/rework the software and repilot, or roll back and look for a different solution.

Once the pilot is complete, if a part of the rollout is not successful the next move is more difficult; this means that rollback plans should be considered in detail at each stage. If the pilot and the first phase of rollout have been accepted, but the second phase fails, should we roll back just the second phase or to the first phase and pilot as well? Will it still be possible to roll back if data on the systems relies on the new software? Will formats still be compatible? The implication of rollout and rollback must be considered in the delivery planning.

11.4.4 Data migration project software and hardware changes

In this type of project, the delivery is more complex. The project might require making changes to the target system to ready it for the new data, removing data from the source system, perhaps converting its format, loading it to the target system, and checking that all the data has been moved. The delivery may take place over several days, and activities on different systems may be taking place in parallel:

- Prior to the migration, deliver the software and hardware changes to the target system (see Section 11.4.3).
- Carry out final day's processing on source system.
- Carry out end-of-day processes on source system.
- Back up source system.
- Extract source data.
- Final day's processing on target system.
- Carry out end-of-day processes on target system.

- Back up target system.
- Convert data.
- Load converted data.
- Check that all data has loaded.
- If all data has loaded successfully, go live on target system.
- If data has not loaded successfully, restore to backup on source and target.

If the data migration was not successful, the team may chose to go live anyway; the exit criteria for the migration delivery would need to define the acceptance level for the data. Migrations may be carried out as a big bang or with a phased approach. As with the multisite approach, the delivery plan must consider the implications of rollout and rollback.

11.5 Exit from delivery

Exit from delivery takes place when the exit criteria for delivery have been met. This will either be:

- When the release activities have completed successfully and the system is ready for live use; it will then move into the postdelivery stage (Chapter 12);
- When the release is declared unsuccessful and the release has been rolled back.

Table 11.5 lists some examples of exit criteria for delivery.

11.6 Conclusion

The delivery requires involvement of all groups, whether it results in a successful rollout or in a rollback. There are standard IT infrastructure processes that support the delivery.

Table 11.5 Example of Exit Criteria from Delivery

Example of Exit Criteria	Example of Deliverables Documented, Reviewed, and Agreed Upon	Example of Authorization Owners
Installation and release complete, ready for live use	Delivery checklist complete and reviewed	Process owner, IT infrastructure manager
	Updated IT service	
	Updated configuration management system (new software, live version)	
	Decommission checklist complete	
	Known defect list	
	Resolved defect list	
Release rollback complete	Deinstallation checklist complete and reviewed	Process owner, IT infrastructure manager
	System restore to preinstallation back up complete	

References

[1] Pol, M., and van E. Veenendaal, *Structured Testing of Information Systems*, Deventer, the Netherlands: Kluwer BedrijfsInformatie, 1998.

[2] IT Infrastructure Library, *Best Practice for Service Support*, London, England: Office of Government Commerce, 2002.

[3] Humphrey, W., *Introduction to the Team Software Process*, Reading, MA: Addison-Wesley, 2000.

[4] IT Infrastructure Library, *Best Practice for Service Delivery*, London: Office of Government Commerce, 2002.

[5] Craig, R. D., and S. P. Jaskiel, *Systematic Software Testing*, Norwood, MA: Artech House, 2002.

[6] Fewster, M., and D. Graham, *Software Test Automation*, Reading, MA: Addison-Wesley, 1999.

[7] Software Engineering Institute, "A Framework for Software Product Line Practice," v4.1, Software Engineering Institute Web site, http://www.sei.cmu.edu.

[8] Belbin Associates, "Belbin Team Roles," http://www.belbin.com/belbin-team-roles.htm, October 2003.

[9] Team Technology Web site, "Working Out Your Myers Briggs Type," http://www.teamtechnology.co.uk/tt/t-articl/mb-simpl.htm, October 2003.

[10] Honey, P., "Learning Styles," http://www.peterhoney.co.uk/product/learning styles, October 2003. PeterHoney.com, 10 Linden Avenue, Maidenhead, Berks, SL6 6HB. Tel.: 01628633946. Fax: 01628633262. E-mail: info@peterhoney.com.

[11] Kirton, M. J., "Adaptors and Innovators Defined," see KAI Web site, http://www.kaicentre.com/, July 2003.

[12] de Bono, E., *Six Thinking Hats®*, New York: Penguin, 1999.

[13] Robson, M., *Problem Solving in Groups*, Aldershot, England: Gower, 1993.

[14] TQMI, *Problem Solving—Tools and Techniques*, Frodsham, England: TQMI, 2001.

[15] IEEE 1028™ Standard for Software Reviews, 1997.

[16] Gilb, T., and D. Graham, *Software Inspection*, Reading, MA: Addison-Wesley, 1993.

[17] Kaner, C., *Bad Software*, New York: Wiley, 1998.

Selected bibliography

Belbin, R. M., *Management Teams—Why They Succeed or Fail*, London, England: Butterworth Heinemann, 1981.

Honey, P., and A. Mumford, *The Learning Styles Helper's Guide*, Maidenhead, England: Peter Honey Publications, 2002. PeterHoney.com, 10 Linden Avenue, Maidenhead, Berks, SL6 6HB. Tel.: 01628633946. Fax: 01628633262. E-mail: info@peterhoney.com.

Kroeger, O., J. M. Thuesen, and H. Rutledge, *Type Talk at Work: How the 16 Personality Types Determine Your Success on the Job*, New York: Bantam Doubleday Dell, 2002.

McHale, J., "Innovators Rule OK—Or Do They?" *Training & Development*, October 1986, http://www.kaicentre.com/.

CHAPTER 12

The Life of a System Postdelivery

Contents

12.1 Postdelivery—description

12.2 Delivery viewpoints

12.3 Entry criteria for postdelivery

12.4 Postdelivery—typical activities

12.5 Exit from postdelivery

12.6 Conclusion

In this chapter I shall:

- Describe the entry criteria, steps, and exit criteria for the postdelivery stage;
- Identify the quality definitions from Chapter 1, which prevail at this stage;
- Identify how each of the groups identified in Chapter 2 become involved at this stage;
- Introduce the types of support activities carried out at this stage, especially for readers who are not support specialists, including the different types of maintenance changes to the delivered system;
- Introduce techniques that aid teamwork at this stage.

My team has been given the assignment of picking up after this latest "wow project." We need to run several manual batch jobs each day and I'm getting beaten up because the support cost has gone up by 30% since implementation. I think the project team got a bonus for this mess!
   —*Cynical application maintenance manager wondering why no one involves supporters until after delivery!*

12.1 Postdelivery—description

Postdelivery covers the life of the software from when it is first delivered and while it is being used until it is decommissioned. It is the longest part of a software system's life span. During this time, customers use the software while supporters maintain and support it. It comes after the delivery stage covered in Chapter 11 (see Figure 12.1).

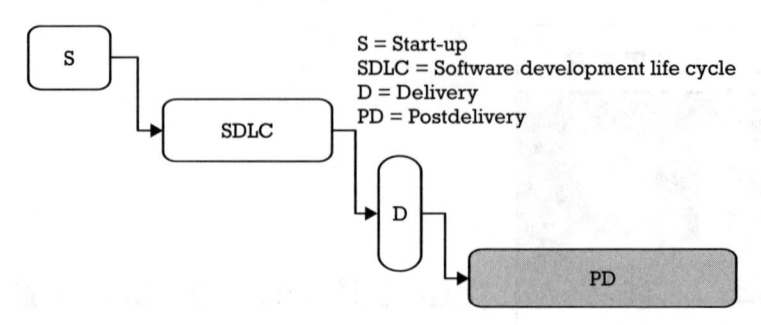

Figure 12.1 Life span stage.

12.1.1 Postdelivery for different types of software acquisitions

Postdelivery activities will be different for different types of customers, systems, and software. Let us look at some examples.

12.1.1.1 Commercial off-the-shelf (COTS) package installed by customer

The customer installs the software and uses it. Postdelivery, if the software does not work as expected, they might deinstall and replace it by something else, contact the vendor's help line for assistance, or find a workaround by themselves. The vendor may advertise *patches* that fix reported bugs, and these may be delivered to the customer on request for the customer to install. If the vendor produces a new version of the software, with enhancements, the customer may choose to install the upgrade or to continue using the existing system without the upgrade. The postdelivery activities are:

- Use of the software;
- Customer applying patches and upgrades when they are ready, if wanted;
- Deinstallation.

12.1.1.2 System developed in-house

The software system is likely to be used during office hours by the user group (customers). There may be overnight batch processing run on behalf of the user group by the operations team (supporters). From time to time maintenance changes will be applied. These may be requested by the users themselves, or they may be required by the IT infrastructure team to improve support of the system. During the postdelivery period, the IT infrastructure activities will include monitoring and evaluating the system, and proposing changes. Eventually, the system will be decommissioned, and in the lead-up to that point, data might be migrated to a new system. Activities postdelivery include:

- Use of the software;

- Development and installation of maintenance changes;
- Monitoring of the system infrastructure and service levels;
- Deinstallation and decommissioning.

12.1.1.3 Third-party developed system

The third party who developed the software will have a contract with the customer that describes the scope of their responsibility. It may be that they complete their responsibility when the acceptance test is complete, or when delivery is complete, or when some agreed-on period of time has passed (a warranty period), or they may have a long-term support contract. The activities might be the same as the COTS package, but perhaps in a larger organization the IT infrastructure group (supporters) would provide support for installation and a service/support line. It might be that the source code has been delivered and the supporters will carry out maintenance changes, or the third-party suppliers may make the maintenance changes. The activities would include:

- Use of the software;
- Development and installation of maintenance changes;
- Monitoring of the system infrastructure and service levels;
- Deinstallation and decommissioning.

12.1.1.4 System with periodic updates

Some software is delivered with an assumption of periodic updates; a good example is a virus checker. Here the vendor will supply upgrades at regular intervals; for example, monthly by mail or weekly via a download to the customer system. Typical activities include:

- Use of the software;
- Development and installation of upgrades;
- Deinstallation and decommissioning.

12.2 Delivery viewpoints

Once we have installed the software and it is in use, we will evaluate it. By "we," I mean any one who has an interest in the delivery. We ask: Does it help the customers? Are they happy with it? However, if only the views of the customers are considered in evaluating the software, we will find that we have not considered all the quality views (see Table 12.1).

In fact, a true evaluation of the software can only be made by involving all the groups, because although the project team has disbanded, all groups have an interest in quality at this stage. It is almost certain that the software will have maintenance changes, and these may involve work from the

Table 12.1 Views of Quality at Postdelivery—Simple

Quality View	Group Customer
Transcendent view	✓
User view	✓
Value view	
Product view	
Manufacturing view	

original development team as well as from maintainers working within the supporters group. Even with a COTS system installed by the customer, the builders, measurers, managers, and supporters at the vendor will have a view on the quality of the software.

For the evaluation, managers will be interested in measures of value for money and return on investment, supporting the value-based view of quality.

Supporters, measurers, and builders will be interested in measures of defects reported during use, supporting a manufacturing- and product-based view of quality. It is only once the software is live that we can evaluate the effectiveness of our defect prevention, identification and removal activities, including inspection, review, and testing activities. For example, test effectiveness could be measured by comparing the number of problems found in live use of the software with the number found during testing, and a similar measure could be made for reviews and inspections [1, 2]. If many more defects are found during QC processes such as testing and review than during live use, our quality measurement processes may be considered effective. We may additionally want to measure where we have made mistakes and introduced defects, in order to introduce improvements to reduce defects in future, as the fewer defects introduced, the better our planning and build processes were. A very simple example might help:

- Suppose we find 30 defects during our testing and reviews. In the first 6 months after delivery, we find another 20 defects. The total number of defects is 50. The efficiency of our defect finding processes is 30/50 = 60%.

- We analyze the 50 defects. Fifteen were introduced at the point where we gathered the requirements and were caused by misunderstandings between the customers and builders. We introduce some training and process changes to improve communication between the groups during requirement gathering, and set an expectation or target for a reduction in these types of defects in the next project. When we analyze the defects from that project, we will measure and compare to see if our process changes resulted in reduced defects.

Of course, that is a very simplified example. You would need to take onto account the other variables such as comparative size and complexity of the projects, and you might want to measure the cost rather than the number of defects. Of course, there may still be defects we have not found yet. Perhaps we would want to measure again after 12 months. All I want to indicate here is that it is possible to make measurements and use them to evaluate what work has been done as well as to drive improvement initiatives for the future.

Customers and supporters engage with the software day to day. They hold a transcendent view of quality ("are we enjoying this system?") but also the user-based view. They will have a perception of the software as fit for purpose or otherwise. They will evaluate whether the software has solved the problem they identified (Chapter 9) during start-up.

Involving all the groups gives a wider view of the quality of the system in use (Table 12.2).

12.3 Entry criteria for postdelivery

Postdelivery can only be entered if the delivery itself has been successful. If the delivery was rolled back or canceled, then the new software is not in operation. Example entry criteria are shown in Table 12.3.

12.4 Postdelivery—typical activities

12.4.1 Use of the system

This is the whole reason for the work up to the point of delivery. A software solution has been defined, designed, built, tested, and delivered. Finally, the

Table 12.2 Views of Quality at Postdelivery—Teamwork

Quality View	Groups				
	Customer	Manager	Builder	Measurer	Supporter
Transcendent view	✓	✓	✓	✓	✓
User view	✓			✓	✓
Value view		✓			
Product view			✓	✓	✓
Manufacturing view			✓	✓	

Table 12.3 Example Entry Criteria for Delivery

Example of Entry Criteria	Example of Entry Documents	Example of Authorization Owners
Installation and release complete, ready for live use	Delivery checklist complete and reviewed, updated IT service, updated configuration management system (new software, live version), known defect list, resolved defect list	Process owner, IT infrastructure manager

customers can use the software that will, we hope, resolve the problem or opportunity identified during start-up. The customers will use the software to carry out their tasks.

As we saw in Chapter 11, when software is first delivered, there may be problems, either with the delivery or with the delivered product. These will need to be resolved during the delivery period, either by fixing the problem or by working around it. Additionally, the users of the system will be new to it, and will need to learn how to use the system efficiently. This means that during the immediate postdelivery period, the customers may feel disillusioned. For example, I have recently taken delivery of a new laptop computer. My pleasure in unpacking the parcel with the shiny new machine had dissipated by two days later as I was still trying to install all the software, migrate my data, learn a slightly different keyboard layout, and get the laptop settings as I wanted. I was quite ready to throw it out of the window!

Once the bedding in of the software has been accomplished and the initial learning curve has been climbed, customers should start to gain benefits from the use of the new software. The organization as a whole will want to monitor that the cost of the software is outweighed by the benefit of using it. This should be measured over a period of time, taking into account the dip in enthusiasm (Figure 12.2 and [3, 4]).

Over time, the customers will require changes to the software, to correct problems, or to enhance the facilities available or to meet some change in requirements. They need to make a request for a change, and the change would be planned using the start-up activities we saw in Chapter 9. I will discuss changes to software in Section 12.4.3.

12.4.2 IT infrastructure and service management activities

The activities postdelivery include use of the software, monitoring of the system, evaluation of the system, maintenance and update of the system, and infrastructure support. The activities needed to support an organization's IT provision are covered in a number of best-practice guides, codes of practice, and standards, as we saw in Chapter 7; see, for example, those in [3–12]. If we talk to the supporters, we will find typically that they carry out

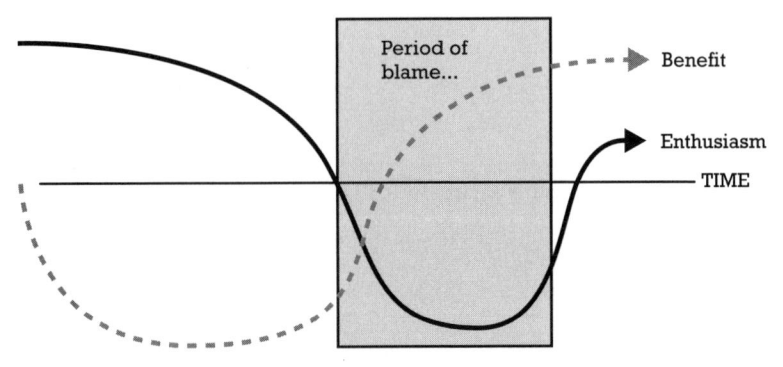

Figure 12.2 Silver bullet life cycle. (*From:* [3]. © 1998 DISC PD 0005:1998. Reprinted with permission.)

12.4 Postdelivery—typical activities

activities based on the recommendations of the IT Service Management Forum [7], which is an international center of expertise for IT service management. For example, the IT Infrastructure Library (ITIL), [4, 6, 8] and BSI Code of Practice for IT Service Management [3] identify activities for IT infrastructure management, service support, and delivery that focus on the customer's access to services that support the business functions, and the level and costs of those activities. These include:

- The *service, support, or help desk* is the customer's first port of call if something goes wrong; they rely on the other activities in this group.
- *Incident management* is intended to restore normal service as quickly as possible and minimize impact.
- *Problem management* seeks to minimize the impact of incidents and prevent recurrence of incidents.
- *Configuration management* identifies relationships between items that make up a system.
- *Change management* controls changes made to the configuration.
- *Release management* controls packages of changes as identified releases.
- *Service-level management* is about understanding, agreeing on, and monitoring the level of service provided by the IT system, perhaps by measuring against service-level agreements.
- *IT financial management* controls running costs for the IT systems, budgeting, accounting, and charging for services.
- *Capacity management* covers the monitoring and tuning of existing services, plus forecasting future requirements.
- *IT service-continuity management* is a subset of business continuity and defines a minimum set of IT provision for business continuity; for example, looking at whether during a change or release recovery/rollback is possible.
- *Availability management* looks at the factors from a customer viewpoint that are concerned with availability and reliability of the IT services.
- *Security management* defines and monitors the security of the IT systems and the software.
- *Infrastructure management*, including network service management, operations management, computer installation and acceptance, and systems management will continue throughout the life of the software and the IT system as a whole.

Note: If you are new to this subject area, or just need an overview, [9–11] are quick guides to the subject.

During the life of the software, changes to the overall system and the infrastructure will be needed. The supporters may need to upgrade hardware or software components that support the software the customers actually use. A start-up activity to analyze the problem would be needed, followed by a project to provide a solution, which might be paper-based, software-based, hardware-based, or use some other media, or a mixture of these.

Many of the techniques we discussed in Chapter 9 for identifying and analyzing problems, for example, the Ishikawa fishbone, are specifically mentioned in ITIL [4] as tools to use postdelivery. Figure 12.3 shows an example of a partially completed fishbone diagram for customer complaints about the help desk; the complaints have been grouped under suitable headings, showing some of the underlying reasons (root causes) for the problems. In this example, the customers have complained that the help-desk staff are unaware of new software. During the session to discuss the complaints and put together the fishbone diagram, the help-desk team realized that they did not receive a known problem list for the new software. They did not know that the software had been delivered!

12.4.3 Making changes to an existing system

During the life of the software postdelivery, customers will identify new problems to be resolved and new opportunities to grasp, and will encounter new outside requirements. The system may need to be enhanced, corrected or adapted to changes in its environment. To accomplish this, supporters may need to have it changed to make future support and maintenance easier.

When changes are made to existing software, this is called software maintenance. It takes place in a software-maintenance life cycle (SMLC). Most software projects are SMLCs rather than SDLCs, because software spends most of its life in the postdelivery stage, being used and changed. Often, when people say they are working on a SDLC, they are actually working in software maintenance. So the system will be subject to successive cycles of change, often with many changes taking place in parallel (Figure 12.4). In fact, these are new SDLCs, involving the whole cast of characters from before, and could be described as SMLCs (software-maintenance life cycles).

There are four main types of maintenance changes to software systems:

- Corrective;
- Enhancement;
- Perfective;
- Adaptive.

12.4.3.1 Corrective maintenance

These are maintenance changes to rectify problems identified in products; making fixes to software, and correcting typographical or factual errors made in documents.

Corrections may be high-priority, even emergency, changes that need to be done at speed. Many corrections are not high priority or emergency, and can be built and released in groups or with other maintenance work.

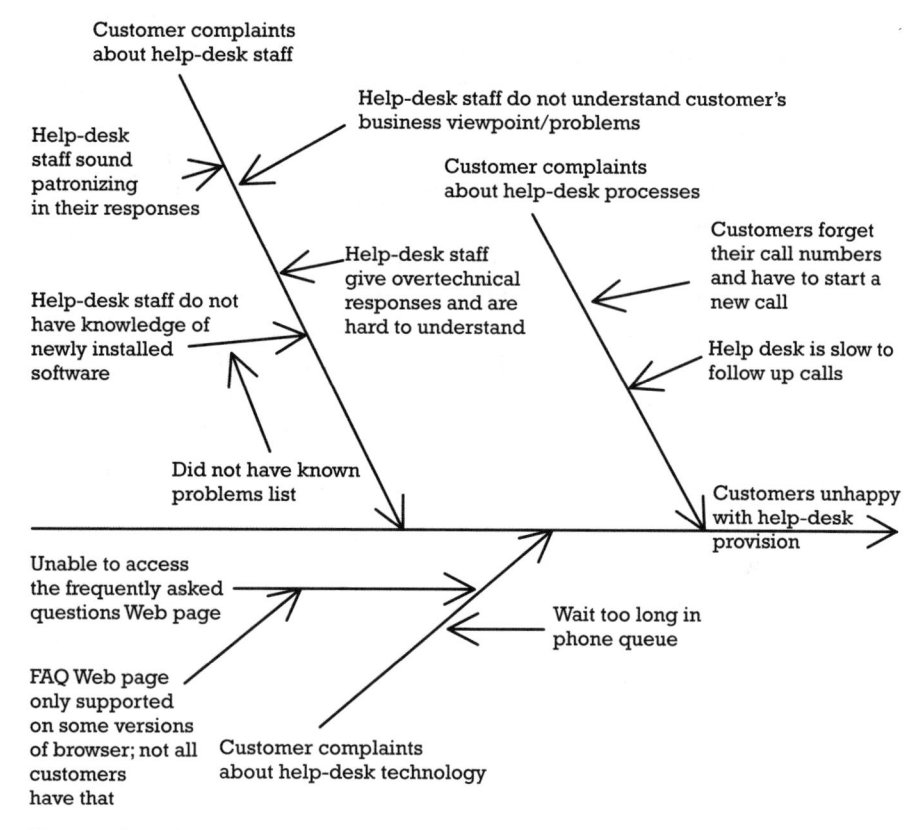

12.4 Postdelivery—typical activities

Figure 12.3 Example of an Ishikawa fishbone.

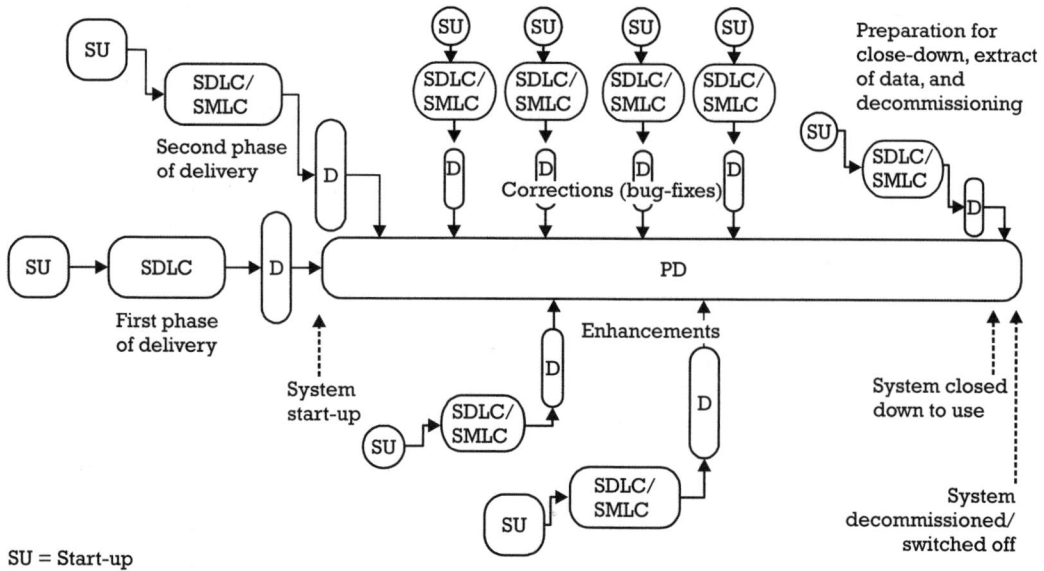

Figure 12.4 Parallel changes during postdelivery.

SU = Start-up
SDLC/SMLC = the software-development life cycle or the software-maintenance life cycle
D = Delivery
PD = Postdelivery

Even emergency changes that take place overnight need to be controlled within the life span structure I suggest. Suppose for example, that the overnight batch run stops unexpectedly, or that the company e-commerce Web site becomes unavailable. The maintenance to restore the service must take place as quickly as possible.

Despite the need for speed, the emergency change will require a start-up (problem and solution definition), some SDLC/SMLC activities, including requirements, design, build and test, and delivery. Because it is an emergency, a well-understood process with a suitable level of control and follow up is vital; it is during an emergency that we make mistakes. An SMLC designed as an "on one page" form with suitable checkpoints, tests, and sign-off may well be appropriate. It is important that the actions taken are documented. I am reminded of a notice I saw over a nurses' station in a hospital recently, "If it isn't documented, it didn't happen." Once the emergency is over, it is easy to forget what steps we took, and these might cause a chain reaction, resulting in other problems. Also, following the first-aid fix to the emergency problem, we may wish to revisit the changes, and perhaps even rework them to improve the fix.

Nonemergency fixes may be grouped and worked on in an agreed-upon timescale. Depending on the size of the fixes, it may be appropriate to use a tailored rather than a full SDLC, as we saw in Chapter 10.

12.4.3.2 Enhancements

Here the change is to enhance or improve some attribute of the software, either functional or nonfunctional. A group of minor enhancements would lead to a minor release and one or more major enhancements may lead to a major release, as we saw in Chapter 11. Enhancements and nonemergency fixes are often treated together; grouped according to priority, for example, and released in groups, in an agreed-upon timescale. Depending on the size of the changes, it may be appropriate to use a tailored rather than a full SDLC, as we saw in Chapter 10.

If we build and implement many small enhancements at one time, this might in itself be a major release in terms of risk; the size of the whole set of changes must be considered, as well as the impact of individual changes on "business as usual" and the possible interaction of changes.

One important point to consider is that there can be critical disagreement about whether changes are enhancements or correction of defects. This can be a contractual, even a legal issue. If a supplier organization has to absorb the cost of correcting defects within a fixed-price contract, it may resist accepting requirements problems as defects. The relationship between groups at this stage can deteriorate as arguments rage about whether a required change is a correction or an enhancement. If the customers are charged for enhancements but not for corrections, the argument from the builders and measurers may be that the software has been delivered to meet its specification, and if the customers require a change, this must be an enhancement. However, the customers may have interpreted the specification differently, or the specification could be wrong. If we carry out the activities we discussed in Chapters 9 and 10, we should find that these differences of opinion are reduced. It is also important to have an agreement between all parties that defines what is considered a correction and what is considered an enhancement.

12.4.3.3 Perfective maintenance

This is work done to make the software more maintainable in future. This is important to reduce support and maintenance costs. Typical problems with software that is changed frequently and used over a long period of time include:

- The people who know the software and who know the reasons why it has a certain structure leave, taking knowledge with them.
- The documentation that describes the system (requirements documents, design specifications) is not updated with the software, so it is out of date and does not describe the software.
- The code becomes increasingly complicated as it is changed over time, and, eventually, it is not possible to tell what is affected by a change.
- The complexity and lack of definitive information make it increasingly difficult to test the changes to the software, especially as software tends to become more complex as it is changed over time.

In one organization, I remember that a package had been customized for particular clients, but each client's software was built on some central code. One of the programmers, in making a change to a client area of the code, changed code that affected all the clients, without realizing it. It was so difficult to understand the code that this mistake was not surprising; the software had grown almost organically over the years, and was not structured for easy maintenance. It was also impossible to know that the testing had covered the changes and the rest of the software sufficiently. The software needed to be completely restructured to make it possible to maintain and test it.

The activities in perfective maintenance include rewriting code to improve its structure (reengineering the code) and writing specification and design documents that describe the existing system (retrodocumentation).

12.4.3.4 Adaptive maintenance

These maintenance changes are made to support changes in the software's environment; for example, it may be necessary to upgrade hardware or systems software, or other supporting parts of the IT infrastructure. The software may need to be changed—adapted—to work properly in its new environment. This may include "porting" software or migrating data to a new infrastructure, in which case the software or the data or both may need to be adapted. An example would be my new laptop; moving my databases onto the new laptop was easy—copy to and from removable media. However, in order to use the data in the database, I had to make a choice either to allow the upgraded database software to reformat the data, in which case I would not be able to use it on the older laptop, or to use it as read-only. The new software was going to carry out adaptive maintenance on the data to change its format.

12.4.3.5 Who gets involved in a change?

All the groups have an interest in the changes made:

- *Customer:* How will this change affect me? What is its impact? What are the implications for my normal work? Will it affect business as usual? Will it benefit me? What are the risks? Do I want this change?
- *Supporter:* How will this change affect me? What is its impact? What are the implications for the IT infrastructure and for service management? Will it benefit me? What are the risks? Do I want this change?
- *Manager:* What are the cost implications of making the change and of not making the change? Will there be a cost–benefit trade-off? If we do this work, what other work has to be halted? What is the priority of this change compared with others?
- *Builder:* Will I be asked to make the change? Do I want to make the change? Do I understand the change?
- *Measurer:* Will I be asked to test the change? What else needs testing? Can I test the change?

Whatever the size of the change we want to make, we need to involve all the groups and go through the activities described in Chapters 9, 10, and 11. For a small change we would do a "cut-down" version of the activities—the checklist approach we have looked at in the earlier chapters. For a large change we would take a more detailed approach. Even an emergency fix requires involvement from the different groups, to get an understanding of the impact of the problem and the proposed fix. In one organization, the overnight call went not just to the analyst/programmer who would implement the change, but also to a senior business user who would assess the impact on business as usual of the proposed fix, compared with the impact of the problem itself.

12.4.3.6 Testing changes to software

Testing changes to existing systems is difficult. Because it is easy to make changes that have an unexpected effect on software, we want to make sure that the change works, and that other parts of the software have not been changed. The assessment of the impact of any proposed changes must be made both in terms of what products are effected—"If this screen is changed, the user documentation and the training material also need changing"—and also in terms of what measurement and assessment is needed—"If this screen is changed, I need to test that the change is correct in all those products, and also to check that these other related parts of the software and other products have not changed." This is known as *regression testing*; we need to check that we have not changed anything we should not have changed. The need for regression testing means that changes that look simple may be expensive; the requirements, design and build part of the SMLC may be easy and cheap to do, but the testing, including a regression test, may take a long time and be difficult to plan and execute. I do not want to get into the detail of regression testing here, but it must be considered when considering the impact of a change:

> You are right to emphasize the testing task. I remember one major bank saying that whenever they had made significant changes to their core banking system, they always had to run a regression test that cost several million dollars, and took several weeks to complete. (Richard Warden, personal communication, July 2003)

There is no reason to suppose the burden will decrease with Web site and e-commerce work; continuous change will mean continuous regression testing of very public functional and nonfunctional attributes.

12.4.4 Monitoring and evaluation

During the postdelivery period, we can monitor the use of the software and collect information that will help us measure the success of the original SDLC and of subsequent SMLCs. We can also monitor and evaluate the service management and infrastructure management services.

Because the postdelivery period of the software is the longest part of its life span, we will want to look for improvements in the software itself and in the surrounding support services. ITIL [4], for example, suggests use of the *Deming Cycle*, proposed by W. Edwards Deming [13]. The cycle has four stages, sometimes called the Plan, Do, Check, and Act cycle and sometimes the Plan, Do, Review, and Improve cycle (see Figure 12.5). Here, we plan what to do, and we do it. Then we review what we did. Was it successful? Did it go as planned? What should we improve? We then put improvements in place and plan the next cycle of activities.

12.4.4.1 Evaluation of the SDLC/SMLC

A formal evaluation of each SDLC/SMLC is important; this should involve representatives of all the groups. The evaluation needs to be timed sensitively, and may need to be a series of evaluations over a period of time. I remember one project manager saying, "Never have the end-of-project party until six months after the software's been installed!" Table 12.4 shows some possible timings for evaluation and the advantages and disadvantages of each.

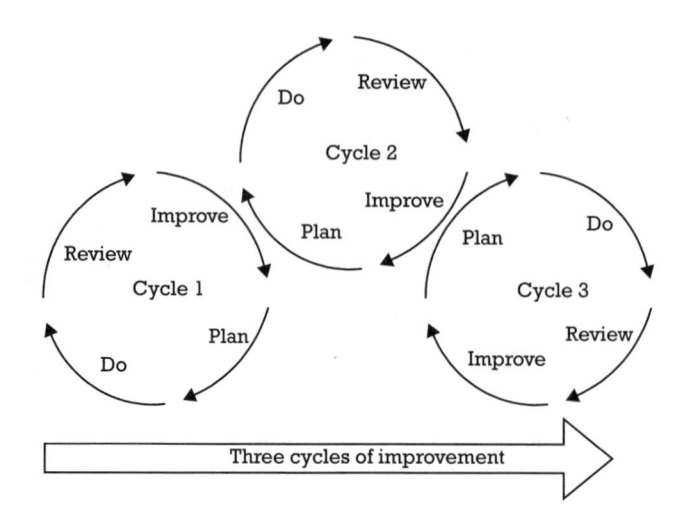

Figure 12.5 Plan, Do, Review, and Improve cycle. (*After:* [13].)

Evaluation meetings need to be managed carefully, so take into consideration of some of the team and communication techniques we have discussed in earlier chapters. Use the Six Hats [14] technique described in Appendix A, for example, to help participants look for good points as well as bad points for the evaluation (Table 12.5).

12.4.4.2 Ongoing monitoring and evaluation of software

Part of the service delivery work will include monitoring the software and surrounding services, including numbers of problems reporting to the help desk or support lines. These should be used to analyze whether:

- SDLC/SMLC software/code products could be improved, for example, if problems are being reported that could be resolved by better design, or might have been found with improved testing.
- Other SDLC/SMLC products could be improved, for example, if a task is described in the on-line help or user guide, but customers cannot find

Table 12.4 Timing the Postdelivery Evaluation of the SDLC/SMLC

Time After Delivery	Advantage	Disadvantage
Immediately	Will not have forgotten the good and bad points of the SDLC/SMLC.	Too soon to tell if the software works in reality.
During the immediate postdelivery period	Will not have forgotten the good and bad points of the SDLC/SMLC.	May be too busy. May be too soon to assess.
During low point of period of blame (Figure 12.2)	Will not lose information about the problems and areas for improvement.	Will be only focused on bad points. Evaluation meeting likely to be unpleasant.
Six months after delivery	Can do cost–benefit analysis against a period of use. Successes and problems seen against perspective of real use.	Too late to influence the following projects. Team now focused on other projects. May have forgotten both problems and what was done well.

12.4 Postdelivery—typical activities

Table 12.5 Techniques Used to Aid Teamwork Postdelivery

Subject Area	Technique Examples	In 30 Seconds… (see Appendix A for more)
Team relationships and natural roles/team skills	Belbin Team Scores [15]	Support of the software can fail because of personal rather than technical factors. Teams need to understand their strengths and weaknesses as a team. A balance of roles/skills is required in the personalities in the team. Example roles: plants have new ideas; completer–finishers want to finish to fine detail. Too many plants and you will never finish anything.
Improve communication—empathy with others	MBTI [16] Honey & Mumford [17] Kirton [18]	Different people have different personalities and communication styles. People who wave their arms around and talk a lot can annoy people who like to be quiet and think, and vice versa. The Myers-Briggs Type Indicator (MBTI) identifies four contrasting type pairs, e.g., *Introvert/Extrovert*, leading to 16 "types" (e.g., INTJ is *Introvert-iNtuitive-Thinking-Judging*). The Honey & Mumford Learning Styles Questionnaire identifies preferred learning styles (e.g., *Pragmatists vs. Theorists*) require different experiences to learn. Kirton identifies preferred problem-solving methods (*Adaptors vs. Innovators*)—do we break the rules or work within them?
Improve meetings	De Bono's Six Thinking Hats [14]	Improve meetings by setting rules for behavior. Six "hats" are used. Everyone wears the same color hat at the same time: Blue Hat—meeting structure, Black Hat—pessimistic, Yellow Hat—optimistic, Red Hat—feelings, White Hat—facts, Green Hat—creative ideas. Allows meeting members to move outside their stereotypes and allows time for different, sometimes difficult types of communication.
Identify problems and root causes, find solutions	Ishikawa fishbones [4, 19]	Use to identify problems, root causes of problems and solutions. On a fishbone diagram, brainstorm problems, their possible causes, their root causes, and, therefore, solutions to the root cause.
Review processes	Reviews [2, 20]	For processes use audit. For checking process documents use walkthrough, peer review, or inspection.
Understand whether an idea is worth pursuing	Risk workshop by brainstorming [19, 21]	A brainstorming workshop is run to list all the possible risks people can identify. The risks are sorted into groups, separating risks (might happen in the future) from issues (problems right now) and constraints. The risks are scored for impact and likelihood, and ranked to give a prioritized list.
	Cost–benefit analysis [4, 21]	Cost–benefit analysis is done by calculating the predicted benefits of the proposed change (time, money saved) and setting this against the predicted cost. An example of a worked cost–benefit analysis for service support is in [4], a general worked example is in [21], and there is also an example in Appendix A.

the information, it does not mean they are foolish; it means the user guide and on-line help should be improved.

- SDLC/SMLC software/code and other products are not deteriorating over time; for example, as changes are made to code, it can become more complex, until it is far too expensive to change and test successfully. Tools are available for measuring software complexity, so this can be monitored over time. Additionally, other products can become out of step with the code, and this can be monitored through configuration management if it is applied to all products and not just the code.

- Service support and delivery could be improved. For example, if customers find they are waiting too long for a response from the help desk, what could be done to improve call turnaround?

12.4.4.3 Monitoring and evaluating the postdelivery processes

This can be done by carrying out process audits [20] to check that the defined processes are being followed and that they are suitable. ITIL suggests use of the EFQM Excellence Model or its U.S. equivalent, the Baldrige criteria [4, 22, 23]. As we saw in Chapter 1, EFQM would expect evaluation of measured performance and perceptions of the postdelivery services from the viewpoint of the *Customers. Society* results measure what the organization is achieving in relation to local, national and international society, where appropriate—the wider customer group. It would also expect measurement of *People* (those who are employed to carry out the work, in this case, the builders, measurers, supporters, and managers). EFQM expects measurement of the *Key Performance Results*, including financial measures such as return on investment, which will interest the managers and customers.

12.5 Exit from postdelivery

We only exit from postdelivery when the software is deinstalled (removed) or the system closes down. This may never happen; some software is more than 20 years old, and if it is still working, there is no real reason to remove it. Some systems and software are deinstalled or decommissioned. The exit from postdelivery will generally take place when the replacement software is available. Typically, a full SDLC (Chapter 10) and delivery will have completed successfully before the old software is removed and the old infrastructure decommissioned. It may be that the old and new software are run in parallel for a while; the same tasks being carried out on both until the customers and supporters are satisfied that the new software and system has been delivered correctly. In Table 12.6, we see examples of exit criteria for postdelivery.

12.6 Conclusion

In Chapters 8 to 12, we have followed a software system through its life span, from start-up, through the SDLC, into delivery, and so into the activities of postdelivery, including repeated SMLCs. In summary the activities are:

- *Start-up:* We explore the problem until we understand it, decide whether it is worth solving, set general constraints and parameters for

12.6 Conclusion

Table 12.6 Example of Exit Criteria from Postdelivery

Example of Exit Criteria	Example of Deliverables Documented, Reviewed, and Agreed Upon	Example of Authorization Owners
System ready to decommission: new system accepted, data migrated	Acceptance criteria sign-off list. Accepted new system (SDLC exit and delivery exit). Data migration controls sign-off. Parallel run sign-off.	Business process owner, infrastructure manager
System decommission complete	Data migration complete. Parallel run complete. Software and data back up and archive complete. Software close-down checklist complete. Hardware close-down checklist complete.	Business process owner, infrastructure manager

the solution, decide how to approach the problem, for example, a software solution may be appropriate, and agree on a formal or informal contract of work, with constraints and acceptance criteria and an outline or high-level plan.

- *SDLC:* We plan the SDLC in detail and monitor the activities, we manage change, we define the requirements in detail, we design products, including the software code, we build the software based on the designs, and we test to see that the software and other deliverables are OK.
- *Delivery:* We install the software and check that it has installed correctly.
- *Postdelivery:* We use the software, carry out service delivery and support activities, carry out IT infrastructure activities, make changes to the software, and monitor and evaluate the postdelivery activities to look for improvements.

At each stage, all the groups must contribute; at each stage customers, managers, builders, measurers, and supporters help enable software quality to be built into the software and to be confirmed. We saw in Chapters 3 to 7 that each group holds its own view of quality, and that all these views are reasonable and must be considered.

No single standard will help right through the software life span. The EFQM Excellence Model [22] will provide a framework for all activities, and with techniques like Balanced Scorecard [24], enable a strong alignment between the goals of IT and its customers, perhaps in one integrated management system. Within that elements of CMM® [25] and its relations, such as the Team and Personal Software Processes [26, 27], ISO 9000 [28] will enable us to control our work during the SDLC and help us decide which SDLC model we use, whereas the ITIL [4] will provide a structure during the deployment and optimization of the software as it is being used and changed.

Teamwork and communication is fostered by clear processes, which encourage involvement from all the groups, and recognize their different viewpoints. Clear entry and exit points agreed on by all the groups will help this. I mentioned W. Edwards Deming earlier; he distilled his philosophy of quality management into 14 points [13]. In the ITIL [4], a number of these points are highlighted, and at the top of their list is a key point: "Break down barriers—improve communication between departments" [4, 13].

Let me take this further: Break down barriers between people; communication and team work are key to achieving software quality. It is not my responsibility, and it is not your responsibility. It is our responsibility, together.

References

[1] Fewster, M., and D. Graham, *Software Test Automation*, Reading, MA: Addison-Wesley, 1999, pp. 211–219.

[2] Gilb, T., and D. Graham, *Software Inspection*, Reading, MA: Addison-Wesley, 1993, pp. 386–388.

[3] British Standards Institute, DISC PD 0005:1998, *Code of Practice for IT Service Management*, 1998 (PD0005).

[4] IT Infrastructure Library, *Best Practice for Service Support*, London, England: Office of Government Commerce, 2002.

[5] IT Service Management Forum, "BS 15000 IT Service Management," http://www.bs15000certification.com, October 2003.

[6] IT Infrastructure Library, *Best Practice for Service Delivery*, London, England: Office of Government Commerce, 2002.

[7] IT Service Management Forum, "IT Service Management Forum," http://www.itsmf.com, October 2003.

[8] IT Infrastructure Library, "IT Infrastructure Library"; see the ITIL Web site http://www.itil.co.uk or the TSO Web site http://www.tsonline.co.uk/bookshop/bookstore.asp?FO=1150345, October 2003.

[9] IT Service Management Forum, *A Dictionary of IT Service Management: Terms, Acronyms and Abbreviations: Version 1*, London, England: The Stationery Office, 2001.

[10] IT Service Management Forum, *IT Service Management: A Companion to the IT Infrastructure Library: Version 2*, London, England: The Stationery Office, 2001.

[11] IT Service Management Forum, *A Dictionary of IT Service Management: Terms, Acronyms and Abbreviations: Version 1 (North America)*, London, England: The Stationery Office, 2001.

[12] British Computer Society, BCS Qualifications, http://www1.bcs.org.uk/link.asp?sectionID=574, September 2003.

[13] The W. Edwards Deming Institute, "Deming's Teachings," http://www.deming.org/theman/articles/articles_gbnf04.html, November 2003.

[14] de Bono, E., *Six Thinking Hats®*, New York: Penguin, 1999.

[15] Belbin Associates, "Belbin Team Roles," http://www.belbin.com/belbin-team-roles.htm, October 2003.

[16] Team Technology Web site, "Working Out Your Myers Briggs Type," http://www.teamtechnology.co.uk/tt/t-articl/mb-simpl.htm October 2003.

[17] Honey, P., "Learning Styles," http://www.peterhoney.co.uk/product/learning styles, October 2003. PeterHoney.com, 10 Linden Avenue, Maidenhead, Berks, SL6 6HB. Tel.: 01628633946. Fax: 01628633262. E-mail: info@peterhoney.com.

[18] Kirton, M. J., "Adaptors and Innovators Defined," KAI Web site, http://www.kaicentre.com/, July 2003.

[19] TQMI, *Problem Solving—Tools and Techniques*, Frodsham, England: TQMI, 2001.

[20] IEEE 1028™ Standard for Software Reviews, 1997.

[21] Robson, M., *Problem Solving in Groups*, Aldershot, England: Gower, 1995.

[22] European Foundation for Quality Management, "EFQM Excellence Model," http://www. efqm.org, August 2003.

[23] Malcolm Baldrige model, http://www.quality.nist.gov/index.html, August 2003.

[24] Kaplan, R. S., and D. P. Norton, *The Balanced Scorecard*, Boston, MA: Harvard Business School Press, 1996.

[25] Software Engineering Institute, "Capability Maturity Model®," http://www.sei.cmu.edu, July 2003.

[26] Humphrey, W., *Introduction to the Team Software Process*, Reading, MA: SEI, 2000.

[27] Humphrey, W., *Introduction to the Personal Software Process*, Reading, MA: SEI, 1997.

[28] International Standard Institute, ISO 9000:1994 and ISO 9000:2000 Quality Systems.

Selected bibliography

Belbin, R. M., *Management Teams—Why They Succeed or Fail*, London, England: Butterworth Heinemann, 1981.

Deming, W. E., *Out of the Crisis*, Cambridge, MA: MIT Press, 2000.

Honey, P., and Mumford, A., *The Learning Styles Helper's Guide*, Maidenhead, England: Peter Honey Publications, 2002. PeterHoney.com, 10 Linden Avenue, Maidenhead, Berks, SL6 6HB. Tel: 01628633946. Fax: 01628633262. E-mail: info@peterhoney.com.

IT Infrastructure Library, *Best Practice for Application Management*, London, England: Office of Government Commerce, 2002.

IT Infrastructure Library, *Best Practice for Security Management*, London, England: Office of Government Commerce, 2002.

Kroeger, O., J. M. Thuesen, and H. Rutledge, *Type Talk at Work: How the 16 Personality Types Determine Your Success on the Job*, New York: Bantam Doubleday Dell, 2002.

McHale, J., "Innovators Rule OK—Or Do They?" *Training & Development*, October 1986, http://www.kaicentre.com/.

Quagliariello, P., "Introduction to IT Service Management, ITIL and ITIL Capacity Management," http://www.pultorak.com/home/speaking_engagements/presentations/ 2003_03_07_cmg.pdf, October 2003.

Appendix A

Techniques and Methods

This appendix is summary of the techniques mentioned in the chapters, with additional information and resources for you to follow up ideas that interest you. If you start a literature or Internet search for any of these topics you will find much more information and other related or similar techniques. This appendix is intended to introduce you to ideas and resources rather than to be a complete compendium of the techniques available.

A.1 Communication, team dynamics, and meeting behavior

We all carry with us *taken-for-granted* assumptions about the world and other people—what is normal and how people should behave—and it these assumptions that allow us to build trust between individuals within groups and organizations [1]. Although many taken-for-granted assumptions are shared, there will be differences between cultures, organizations, and family/friendship groups. Just because you "always do it that way" it does not mean it is the right way. One of our assumptions can be that others will share our taken-for-granted assumptions. If we discover that other people have different core beliefs, we are surprised and may dismiss their views as wrong—it is hard to see other people's view. We may also assume that other people communicate in the same way as we do, that they share our sense of humor, use body language in the same way, and share our preference for written, pictorial, or verbal messages. I recently had a discussion with a colleague because we could not understand each other. It turns out that we used two key phrases in opposite ways, both equally correct but meaning the opposite of each other:

- I had used "I think" to mean "I am not sure" but my colleague had used "I think" to mean "I am certain."
- My colleague had used "I feel" to mean "I am not sure" but I had used "I feel" to mean "I am certain."

These communication differences are increased by cultural differences between organizations, and between colleagues from different types of organization, and from different countries. We need to be careful of our own taken-for-granted assumption, and be aware of other people's without dismissing them. This section is an introduction to some of the techniques and ideas people have developed to help understand and bridge communication gaps.

In this appendix, I will introduce a number of ways of examining communication preferences. It is very important that to get the most from these techniques, you use this as just a taster. I have suggested search words to help you find out more from the Internet, and there are books, journals, and Web sites in the references and selected bibliography. Be aware also that you will not get the most from some of these techniques without the help of specialists; psychometric tests are not to be played with.

For this section, the Internet/Web search words are: taken-for-granted assumptions, communication skills, team work, ethnomethodology, sociology, team dynamics, body language, transactional analysis, personality types, culture, Garfinkel, Busco, emotional intelligence, and Goleman.

A.1.1 Belbin Team Roles

Whether teams are drawn from all the groups (customer, manager, builder, measurer, supporter) or from a single group, work can fail to be successful if people in the group do not understand their strengths and weaknesses as team members. This means we may fail to deliver and support software successfully because of personal rather than technical factors. Teams need to understand their strengths and weaknesses *as a team*. Belbin [2–4] defined a number of roles that people take when in a team. These are summarized in Table A.1.

A balance of roles/skills is required in the personalities in the team if it is to be successful. For example, *plants* have new ideas whereas *completer–finishers* want to finish to fine detail. If you have too many *plants* in the team you will never finish anything, but if you only had *completer–finishers*, you might not have so many new ideas. Each person in the team takes an assessment, and this provides a picture of the strengths and weaknesses of the team as a whole. All the roles are needed, so if one is missing, either the team fails or some team members take on secondary roles. I have certainly observed that people will change roles depending on the particular team, but they may not be comfortable. Most people will score to show a mix of the team roles.

Assessment is by a questionnaire that is administered and marked by a Belbin assessor. Details of how to get a Belbin assessment for a team can be found on their Web site [4]. Assessments may be on-line or by mail. They also provide training for certification in use of Belbin assessments. It is best to use qualified people to administer these types of tests.

The earlier work by Belbin [2] has been updated, and the latest thinking is in [3, 4].

A.1 Communication, team dynamics, and meeting behavior

Table A.1 Belbin Team Roles

Team Role	Contribution	Allowable Weakness
Plant	Creative, imaginative, unorthodox	Ignores incidentals
	Solves difficult problems	Too preoccupied to communicate effectively
Resource investigator	Extrovert, enthusiastic, communicative	Overoptimistic
	Explores opportunities	Loses interest once initial enthusiasm has passed
	Develops contacts	
Coordinator	Mature, confident, a good chairperson	Can be seen as manipulative
	Clarifies goals, promotes decision making, delegates well	Offloads personal work
Shaper	Challenging, dynamic, thrives on pressure	Prone to provocation
	The drive and courage to overcome obstacles	Offends people's feelings
Monitor Evaluator	Sober, strategic and discerning	Lacks drive and ability to inspire others
	Sees all options	
	Judges accurately	
Teamworker	Cooperative, mild, perceptive and diplomatic	Indecisive in crunch situations
	Listens, builds, averts friction	
Implementer	Disciplined, reliable, conservative and efficient	Somewhat inflexible
	Turns ideas into practical actions	Slow to respond to new possibilities
Completer–finisher	Painstaking, conscientious, anxious	Inclined to worry unduly
	Searches out errors and omissions	Reluctant to delegate
	Delivers on time	
Specialist	Single minded, self-starting, dedicated	Contributes on only a narrow front
	Provides knowledge and skills in rare supply	Dwells on technicalities

In this section the Internet/Web search words are: Belbin, team, team dynamics, and team roles.

A.1.2 De Bono's Six Thinking Hats

Sometimes in meetings, we either find that the same people always contribute the in the same way—"Joe's always so pessimistic and negative" or "Mary never acknowledges there might be problems"—and sometimes the meeting dissolves into acrimonious chaos, with people no longer on speaking terms. Can we do anything about this? Edward de Bono [5] decided that we could, and the Six Thinking Hats was the result. I first came across it as an idea for improving software projects from Jens Pas' EuroSTAR presentation and workshop [6] as a means of introducing emotional intelligence to rationally biased software projects; in other words, allowing fact-based people an opportunity to also express emotional views.

Use of de Bono's Six Hats at a meeting encourages people to take different roles at the meeting, and to categorize their communication and thus improve it. This means that it is acceptable to express emotion, for example, but we separate those communications from the other communications, such as collection of facts. The six hat colors and their meaning are summarized in Table A.2.

By using the hats, we set rules for behavior. Everyone wears the same color hat at the same time, and the hats are not associated with particular

Table A.2 Six Hats at a Meeting

Hat Color	When we ask everyone to wear this color hat, it means the meeting will focus on
White	Providing facts—what information do we have? Do we know it is fact, or is it opinion?
Red	Adding to the White Hat thinking by expressing our feeling about the situation we are discussing and working from intuition, hunches, opinion—what do we feel? What is our "gut reaction"? Can we identify sensitivities?
Black	Identifying what could go wrong—should we be cautious about this? What risks are there? What have we overlooked? What if?
Yellow	Looking for the positive things—what benefits are there? What new proposals do we have? How can we make this happen? What if? Leading to ...
Green	Creating new ideas—supposing we tried...? We could do it this way instead!
Blue	Thinking about the process of the meeting itself—was that what we meet to cover? Which hat would be useful now? Have we spent long enough in *Black Hat*?

people. This allows meeting members to move outside their perceived stereotypes and allows time for different, sometimes difficult types of communication. De Bono discussed the order and way the hats are used; it depends on the meeting and the problem, as well as the team's experience in using the techniques. Suppose we have a meeting to discuss a design for an interface. We might have a meeting agenda like this:

- Blue Hat to set the scene—why are we here and what do we want to achieve?
- White Hat—what facts do we have about the design that every one can agree on?
- Red Hat—do we like or dislike the design—what is our gut feel about it?
- Yellow Hat—what are the good things about the design?
- Black Hat—what disadvantages can we see in the design?
- Green Hat—can we identify new ideas to help us overcome the black hat points?
- Red Hat—how do we feel now about this design?
- Blue Hat to close the meeting—what are the next steps?

The advantages that de Bono identifies [5] are:

Powerful, focused working which is

- *Time saving* because the meeting is not run as a series of confrontational arguments, thus
- *Removing of ego* by removing confrontation allowing the meeting to deal with
- *One thing at a time.*

All the ideas from all the people at the meeting at treated as parallel rather than confrontational—once a complete picture has been arrived at using the Six Hats then it is easier for people to agree a solution or make a decision. We can use the hats to change the focus of the meeting: "It looks like with the Yellow Hat thinking we have identified some real advantages to the approach we're discussing. Let's just try some Black Hat thinking—what are the disadvantages?"

You can find more information about de Bono's work on thinking, including the Six Thinking Hats, on his Web site [7].

In this section the Internet/Web search words are: de Bono, Six Hats, Meetings, and team work.

A.2 Communication styles

In order to improve communication with others, we need to understand their points of view and communication styles. We need to empathize with others. I do not intend to pigeonhole people by discussing these indicators of communication styles, but I think it is useful to consider that our own preferences are not "right"—they are just preferences. My observation of people is that their preferences will change with mood, context, and group mix.

A.2.1 Myers-Briggs Type Indicators

The work of Myers and Briggs, described, for example, in [8–11], suggested that different people have different personalities and communication styles. To put it at its simplest, people who wave their arms around and talk a lot can annoy people who like to be quiet and think, and vice versa. Myers and Briggs built the *Myers-Briggs Type Indicator* (MBTI), which identifies four contrasting type pairs:

- *E and I:* *E*xtroversion (e.g., prefers social interaction) versus *I*ntroversion (e.g., quiet and private)
- *S and N:* *S*ensing (e.g., experience and practicality) versus i*N*tuition (e.g., prefers novelty and aspiration)
- *T and F:* *T*hinking (e.g., prefers analytic or critical approach) versus *F*eeling (e.g., prefers sympathizing and appreciative approach)
- *J and P:* *J*udgment (e.g., prefers firmness and control) versus *P*erception (e.g., prefers flexibility and spontaneity).

There are other factors which make up the pairs, as you see if you look at [8–11]. These four pairings give rise to 16 "types" (e.g., INTJ is Introvert-iNtuitive-Thinking-Judging), as summarized in Table A.3.

We discussed briefly in Chapter 5, how these communication preferences might affect the communication between builders and other groups. Conflicts arise between any two people, regardless of group. You can see

Table A.3 Myers-Briggs Type Indicators: The 16 Types

ESTJ	ESTP	ESFJ	ESFP
ENTJ	ENTP	ENFJ	ENFP
ISTJ	ISTP	ISFJ	ISFP
INTJ	INTP	INFJ	INFP

that if two people have preferences at different ends of the table, there is real potential for them annoying each other.

Research [10] has shown that more IT people tend to be INTJ than in the general population, where a larger proportion tend to be ESTJ or ESFJ:

> INTJs represent just 2% of the population, yet form about 10% of computer staff. The other main types in computing are ENTJ, ISTJ, and ESTJ. (The latter two feature highly in many jobs, as they represent a large part of the male population). ESTJ is a likely culture of the business units you are supporting. [10]

The communication preferences of these groups may be radically different.

If you are going to look at MBTI, beware of stereotyping! It is worth noting that just because someone is in a particular job, it does not mean they are a particular type, and just because someone appears to be a particular type does not mean they will be a success in an apparently related job. Remember, if 10% of computer staff are INTJ, then 90% are *not* INTJ. Similarly, being a woman does not mean you *cannot* be an ESTJ.

As with all of these types of test, make sure it is administered by someone who is suitably trained and can interpret the results properly.

In this section the Internet/Web search words are: Myers-Briggs Type Indicator and MBTI. Also try searches on particular types such as INTJ and ESFJ, since there are Web sites and discussion groups for some of the types.

A.2.2 Honey and Mumford Learning Styles

When we want to impart new information, we design user guides, help messages, wizards, training sessions, and presentations to help us put our message across. We need to think about the communication styles of our audience, and as part of that we need to understand that *different people learn in different ways* and there is not one *right way* to teach or to learn. Honey and Mumford's work identified people's preferred learning styles [12, 13]. There are four styles identified by Honey and Mumford, and you will find the learning styles concepts adopted by education and training organizations, for example, [14]. The learning styles identified are:

- Reflectors like to collect data and think about it, reflect, and observe, but are not so happy working spontaneously without time to prepare.

A.2 Communication styles

- Activists like to do things, work in teams, and try things out, but they learn less from teaching by lectures or reading on their own.
- Theorists like new ideas and enjoy adapting and integrating observations into complex and logically sound theories, but they do not enjoy situations that emphasize emotion and feelings, or unstructured activities with poor briefing.
- Pragmatists like training that is related to their immediate job or problem, where they have a model to follow, but they do not like training with no apparent payback to the learning, or if they see the event or learning is "all theory."

This means that when we need to get new ideas across to people, we need to think about two things:

- Who needs to know about what and can we identify their preferred learning style? For example, not everyone will learn from a slide presentation.
- Who would be good at delivering the information in that style? For example, not everyone is comfortable with teaching a role play/group work session.

If we are implementing a large, new system affecting many people we may need to offer several different ways for people to learn about the system itself, when and how it will be implemented, and how to get help and further information. We may even want to consider how we organize QA and QC measurement activities using these ideas; activists and pragmatists may find that a review of a working prototype, perhaps with a role play rehearsal, helps them to identify potential problems, and perhaps theorists and reflectors may get more from an inspection process.

The importance of learning and creativity in management is being increasingly recognized and other theories have been advanced, but as there is evidence that the Honey and Mumford approach links with the MBTI we discussed in Section A.2.1, and it is designed specifically to link to organizations and management [15], I have just described this one approach.

The Learning Styles Helper's Guide and *The Learning Styles Questionnaire 80 Item Version* (containing the questionnaire) are copyrighted by and available from Peter Honey Publications. The questionnaire is also available on-line at http://www.peterhoney.com or from Peter Honey Publications Limited, 10 Linden Avenue, Maidenhead, Berks SL6 6HB. A description of the learning styles is reproduced by permission of Peter Honey [13].

In this section the Internet/Web search words are: Honey, Mumford, learning styles, reflector, activist, theorist, pragmatist, and training styles.

A.2.3 Kirton adaptors and innovators

Kirton's work on *adaptors* and *innovators* looks at two groups of characteristics that each of us have to a greater or lesser degree; we are a mix. Adaptor characteristics are those of discipline, efficiency, and resolving problems within the existing rule set and with an eye to maintaining the team's cohesion. Innovators challenge the rules, and may appear to adaptors to be insensitive to needs of the team; they enjoy radical change and challenging the accepted rules. This theory is not about ability; it assumes all people are creative and instead asks "Will someone prefer to be creative within the rules or by breaking the rules?" We all find ourselves somewhere on the continuum between extreme adaptor and extreme innovator:

> The beauty about the KAI is that it makes no negative evaluations about people. Whatever point you find yourself on along the continuum, you will find advantages and disadvantages associated with being there. Indeed, what will be useful and appropriate (advantageous) in one situation might cause problems in another. Armed with this insight, it then becomes possible for people to make informed choices about how they cope with the situations they find themselves in. [16]

The KAI characteristics are measured by a short test; information about this is on the KAI Web site [17]. Again, it needs to be properly administered and interpreted by a trained and certified KAI administrator.

In this section the Internet/Web search words are: KAI, Kirton, adaptor, innovator, and creativity.

A.2.4 Motivation studies

"We have sent them on a training course, we have bought them new PCs and we paid them a bonus—and they are still miserable! What's wrong with these people?" That director of a software company had motivational problems in his teams, and just could not solve them. What was wrong?

I have mentioned in a number of chapters the work on motivation done by Warden and Nicholson [18], which is based on the Job Characteristics Model of Motivation [19]. The job diagnostic survey provides a comprehensive set of motivational measures. As a process model, it can diagnose problems with motivational dynamics caused by poor job design. Psychometric measurement techniques do not provide this capability.

A number of other studies into what motivates people have been carried out; see [11, 20] for some examples. One commonly used is based on work by Maslow in the mid-twentieth century [21], which developed into the *Maslow Hierarchy of Needs,* described in many books and Web sites, for example, references [22–24]. Maslow's original levels of need may be described as:

- *Physiological*—food, water, sleep;
- *Safety*—freedom from danger;
- *Love*—need to belong to a group, friendship;
- *Esteem*—reputation beyond family and friends;
- *Self-actualization*—self-fulfillment.

The model has developed over the years, by different authors, so if you look at this, particularly by Internet searches, you may see the hierarchy extended or detailed added to explicitly mention cognitive, aesthetic, and spiritual needs as well as the need to help others.

Until someone's basic needs (for example, food and shelter) are met, this may be all they are interested in. Once they have enough at one level, then other motivators become more important —however much more food you give them, they will not be any happier. The cutoff point for moving from one point in the hierarchy to another is different for different people, so for some people "enough" at one level is different from another person's need at that level.

When we look at these two studies together with the personality traits we have examined above, we can see that there may be many reasons why our director's teams might still be unhappy and *fed up*. Interestingly, this originated as a term in falconry—when you overfeed a hawk, it sulks until it has finished digesting; it had enough food and is described as a *fed-up falcon*. The many people in the organization may have

- Conflicting communication and learning styles—they may not understand each other and the director;
- Different needs from their jobs—some will want to follow a process, some will want to "fly free";
- Jobs that are too stressful, too boring, or just badly designed—some people will want less stressful job, some will work best under pressure;
- All the fulfillment they need at a particular level, so reward and recognition at that level may not work—they may prefer a sabbatical to a pay raise, for example;
- Become irritated by what they see as "gestures" by the director, when they see other causes for their problems.

Motivation is not simple. People are not simple. Each person is an individual, with likes, dislikes, preferences, moods, and a life outside the team.

In this section the Internet/Web search words are: motivation, Maslow, hierarchy of needs, Motivation Improvement Programme, Mayo, Hawthorne, McGregor on Theory X and Theory Y, Likert on Exploitative, Benevolent, Consultative and Participative management of organizations, McClelland on achievement motivation, Argyris on bureaucratic, pyramidal versus humanistic, and democratic organizations.

A.2.5 Transactional analysis

We discussed transactional analysis in Chapter 4, based on Wagner's work [25], which itself refers to earlier work by Berne, for example, [26]. Wagner's book is useful to us here because it concentrates on work relationships rather than personal relationships or family situations.

The idea of transactional analysis as described by Wagner is that we are all six people rather than just one and that some of these six "inner people" are effective in dealing with others, but some of the "inner people" are not so useful. The six inner people or *ego states* Wagner identifies are:

- *The natural child*—an effective ego state that acts spontaneously, expresses feelings, and has need for recognition, structure and stimulation.
- *The adult*—an effective ego state that is logical and reasonable; it deals in facts rather than feelings.
- *The nurturing parent*—an effective ego state that is firm with others, but also understanding, sensitive, and caring.
- *The critical parent*—an ineffective ego state that uses body language, gesture and tone of voice to "tell others off," perhaps by sarcasm, pointing the finger, or a raised voice.
- *The rebellious child*—an ineffective ego state that gets angry and stays angry, is very negative, does not listen, may deliberately forget things, or procrastinate.
- *The compliant child*—an ineffective ego state that blames itself, uses a soft voice and whines, and is very careful and self-protective.

As we saw in Chapter 4, communication between the effective ego states is generally useful. We can create and play if we are both in "natural child." We can exchange facts clearly in adult to adult communication, and our nurturing parent ego states mean we can empathize and help each other. If we cross into the ineffective ego states, we will argue, whine, and blame without communicating or changing anything; in fact, we may make things worse. We need a way to move out of the ineffective states into effective states, and the de Bono Six Hats [5–7] that we discussed in this section allow us to do that, by providing a formal behavior pattern that acknowledges feelings as well as facts.

As Wagner discusses [25], the use of TA is not just in personal relationships in the family. Looking at our own behavior whether as a manager or in reacting to our managers and colleagues is useful, as supervising, delegating, making decisions, resolving conflict, and hiring or firing people may all cause unexpected behavior, and this may be caused by ineffective ego states.

A related study area is emotional intelligence. You will find checklists on these "soft skill" areas on the Chartered Management Institute Web site.

In this section the Internet/Web search words are: transactional analysis, "games people play," scripts, ego states, Berne, Wagner, and emotional intelligence.

A.3 Techniques to identify and classify problems and assess ideas for solutions

A.3.1 Cause–effect, root cause, and solution analysis

Cause–effect analysis helps us look for the root causes of problems, using *cause and effect diagrams*, sometimes called *fishbone diagrams* because of their shape, or *Ishikawa diagrams* after the person who first developed them, but now widely used in identifying quality and other problems [27, 28]. The diagram is simply a means of helping us think about and classify the causes of problems and their underlying root causes.

The first step is to draw a fishbone diagram with the effect (which is the problem or symptom noticed) on the head of the fish. Then, label the ribs of the fishbone to show typical areas of root cause. You can choose your labels. Typical ones are the 4 Ms—Manpower, Machines, Materials, Methods [27], or the "PEMPEM" labels, which gives People, Environment, Methods, Plant, Equipment, Materials [28], or you could make up your own labels. Figure A.1 shows a fishbone at the start of a meeting, as it was drawn up on the whiteboard. There had been a series of complaints about the help-desk provision. These have been divided into three groups, and each group placed on a separate arrow. A fourth arrow has been added for "other complaints" in case we have forgotten anything.

If you were in the team discussing this, you would now use discussion and brainstorming to generate causes for the effect. Try to group the ideas on the fishbone to show how they relate to each other. The next step is to allow the ideas to incubate. Robson [28] suggests putting the diagram on a public board so other people can see, comment, and add to it, and so that the people can suggest other causes. We discussed this example in Chapter 12, so you will see the completed fishbone in Figure 12.3.

Having identified some root causes, we may want to "reverse" the fishbone, to go from a problem to a solution [27, 28]. To do this, we draw the diagram in reverse, write our proposed solution in the box, and then under our fishbone headings discuss whether the proposed solution will work:

Fishbone diagram before start of discussion about customer complaints

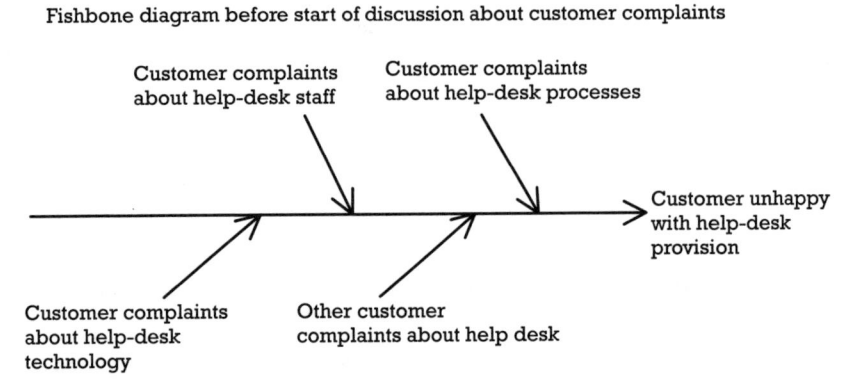

Figure A.1 Ishikawa fishbone diagram—empty at start of discussion.

- What actions do we require under the 4 Ms or PEMPEM or our own titles to make sure the solution works? (Note: whichever titles you use, make sure you have a place to look at time, money and staffing which will all constrain the solution.)
- What advantages or positive effects will the solution have?
- What disadvantages or negatives can we identify?

TQMI [27] suggest using different color pens for the advantages and disadvantages, so you could match pen colors to the de Bono Six Hat's colors, using yellow for optimistic and black for pessimistic views (see Section A.1.2). Figure A.2 shows an example solution analysis fishbone. We can see here that the initial thought is that a new IT system for the help-desk staff might solve the problems. However, the constraints of time, budget, and staffing, as well as the observation that a new system will only solve some of the problem, leads to rejection of a new IT system. Instead, the solution analysis will continue by looking at possible staff training and process changes to improve the service to customers.

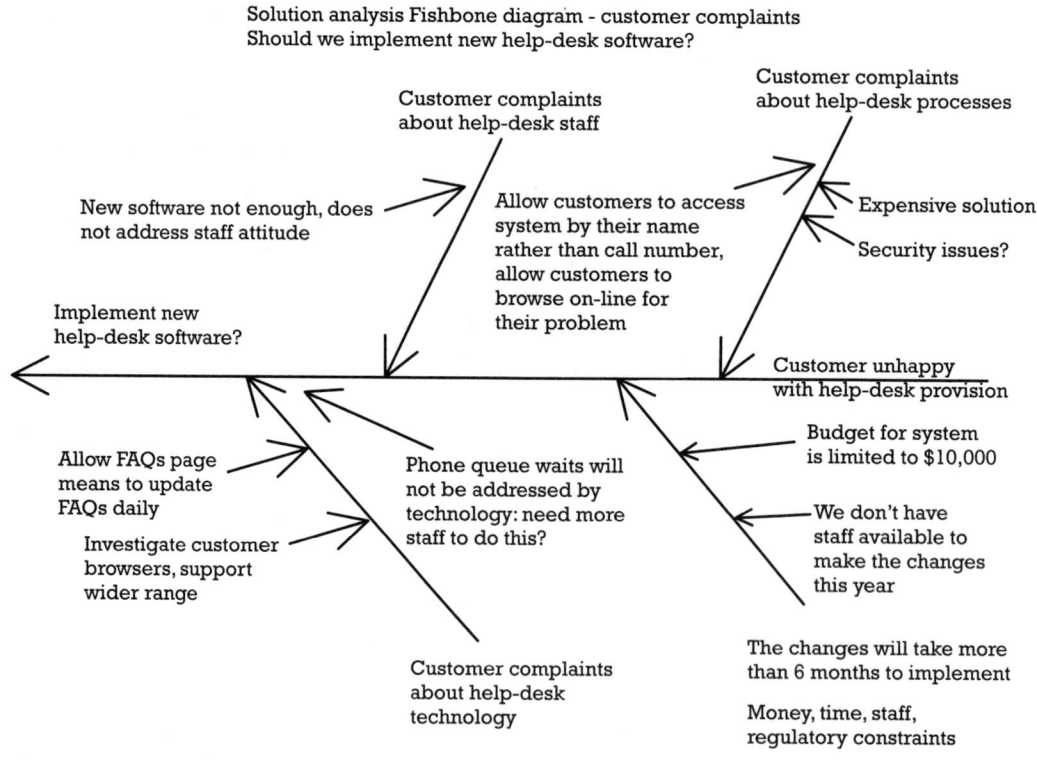

Solution analysis Fishbone diagram - customer complaints
Should we implement new help-desk software?

Customer complaints about help-desk staff
- Allow customers to access system by their name rather than call number, allow customers to browse on-line for their problem
- New software not enough, does not address staff attitude

Customer complaints about help-desk processes
- Expensive solution
- Security issues?

Implement new help-desk software?

Customer unhappy with help-desk provision

Customer complaints about help-desk technology
- Allow FAQs page means to update FAQs daily
- Investigate customer browsers, support wider range
- Phone queue waits will not be addressed by technology: need more staff to do this?

- Budget for system is limited to $10,000
- We don't have staff available to make the changes this year
- The changes will take more than 6 months to implement
- Money, time, staff, regulatory constraints

Conclusion from discussion so far:
- A new help-desk system will not solve the problems within budget or a reasonable timescale.
- Consider another solution, for example, look at staff training and processes, with addition of a FAQs page to the intranet this year.
- Log the other suggestions for consideration when help-desk software is upgraded in 3 years.

Figure A.2 Example of a solution analysis fishbone.

In these methods, brainstorming is a useful technique for gathering ideas. When using brainstorming, it is worth marking the start of the brainstorm session by agreeing or reminding ourselves of some rules [27, 28]. The precise rules may vary between organizations, so it is worth clarifying them. Typical rules include:

- All ideas are allowed.
- All ideas are documented.
- There is no discussion or evaluation during ideas gathering.
- Be relaxed.
- Do not criticize other's ideas.

In this section the Internet/Web search words are: Ishikawa fishbone, root cause analysis, solution analysis, and brainstorm.

A.3.2 Prototyping and ideas modeling

Prototyping is not an SDLC. It is a method of exploring a problem and potential solutions in order that the right solution can be selected. Prototyping is not just used in software; it is used in many fields to test design ideas. For example, if you make clothes, you may choose to use ready-made patterns as bought, or to alter ready-made patterns to fit your particular shape. Alternatively, you might build clothes against a general design but measured for a specific person (for example, a custom-made suit), or you could design your own clothes with unique patterns.

In all cases, you can use a prototype, called a *muslin, toile,* or *form,* which you use to try out the pattern. Using a cheap material, such as muslin, you build the garment from the pattern, in order to see if it turns out as you expect. Does the garment fit? Does it fall well? Does it flatter you? We do this to check our ideas and ability to understand what we need to do without cutting into the expensive cloth that we will use for the final garment.

Particularly if we are designing clothes rather than using an off-the-shelf pattern, a prototype is essential to try out new ideas.

Keen sewers will use a muslin to check out a new pattern; they are using the prototype to try out their understanding of *and adjustments to* "off-the-shelf" solutions. *You only use the prototype to try out ideas—you will not be wearing it in reality.*

If you want to see a good example of prototyping using muslin, look at a sewing publication, for example, *Threads* magazine [29], where user testing of sewing pattern software is done by making a set of prototype patterns for different sized and shaped people. The authors built prototypes to explore commercial off-the-shelf pattern fitting programs and decide which one to recommend.

In software, we can use prototypes in the same way. We can try out ideas if we are not sure what we want. In that situation, we do not want to build the real software. Instead we want to build a model of it, in order that we can explore the problem and potential solutions.

There are two types of prototyping in software, "lo-fi" and "hi-fi" [30, 31]. In hi-fi (high-fidelity) prototyping, we use software to build screens like those the customer will see. This can lead to people believing that the prototype is an almost complete system. "If the screens are ready," managers and customers may argue, "what else can be going on in the system that is so complicated? Why can't we have the system now?" But, as the builders, measurers, and supporters will tell you, the guts of the system are where the complexity lies. This is a big problem for software development and support. Think of our muslin; we were not expecting to wear it, so it is tacked together relatively roughly and not in a material we were expecting to wear or clean or alter; the muslin is not worn but thrown away. The same thing will be true of the software; are you really expecting to use it once and throw it away? I thought not; you will want to maintain and change it, so the rough and ready prototype, however polished on the surface, cannot be the system we deliver. An exception to this is the idea of evolutionary prototyping [31], which means that even the early prototypes must be built to be supportable and maintainable.

For this reason, many people prefer lo-fi (low-fidelity) prototyping. Here we do not build a prototype in software. We might use paper and pen, or sticky paper, or a presentation, or a whiteboard. We can still discuss the prototype and review it, but there is no danger of believing it is the software.

As we saw in Chapter 9, in Figure 9.3, whether we use the hi-fi or lo-fi approach or both, prototyping involves generating and discussing ideas and building a succession of models. As we do this, we gather good ideas and discard bad ideas. Eventually, we can decide what we want to do: develop some software, have a manual solution, or do nothing.

There are a number of related modeling and picturing techniques that can be worth exploring with lo-fi prototyping. These include Rich Picturing [32, 33] and Mind Mapping [34, 35]; both are ways of capturing ideas in an easily communicated and condensed way. In Graham Freeburn's workshop on the final day of EuroSTAR 2002 [35], for example, he summarized "What we learned at the conference" (3 days), with the participating audience contributing to one mind map on one slide, in 45 minutes. Sketching a picture of a problem, solution, or idea can clarify it. Using stories, metaphors, and analogy also helps in understanding problems, and this is why they are used in newer IT analysis methods such as UML [36], and there is no reason why they should not also be useful in more traditional approaches such as SSADM.

In this section the Internet/Web search words are: prototyping, rich picturing, mind mapping, use cases, and Buzan.

A.3.3 Assessing whether an idea is worth pursuing

Not all the ideas we generate are worth pursuing. We need to decide which are possible and cost-effective. Pareto analysis, risk analysis, and cost–benefit analysis are some of the techniques that help us to decide.

A.3 Techniques to identify and classify problems and assess ideas for solutions

Pareto analysis [27, 28] is based on the "Pareto principle," which suggests that 80% of the problems are the result of 20% of the causes. This means that if we can identify solutions to those 20% of the problems, we should get a better, more effective payback from our chosen solution. To decide which problems to solve, identify which are the most frequent. To do this, gather data on the frequency of problems and the underlying causes. The most frequent problems and causes are candidates for resolving, so the ideas that address those problems may be worth pursuing.

In risk analysis, we use techniques such as brainstorming to list all the possible risks people can identify. Risks are sorted into groups, by topic area. We may find we have identified some issues (things that are problems now) and constraints (known limits to any solution we suggest) as well as risks. Risks have not yet happened, but may happen (turn into an issue or problem) in the future. When we assess a risk we need to know its likelihood of turning into a problem, as well as the impact if it does. There is therefore an element of forecasting in risk assessment. When we are assessing possible solutions to problems for their risk, we are asking whether the risk of pursuing a solution is greater or less than the risk of an alternative solution or doing nothing:

- If we do nothing, what could go wrong?
- If we adopt this solution and it goes as we expect what chain-reaction problems might we have?
- If we adopt this solution and it goes wrong, what problems arise from wrong delivery or nondelivery?

In each case we need to:

- List potential problems (risks).
- Identify the likelihood of each risk becoming a problem and use some scoring system.
- Identify the impact of each risk if it does become a problem and use some scoring system.
- Multiply impact by likelihood to get a risk score.
- Rank the risks.
- Identify what you can do to reduce risk or remove it.
- Decide whether the probable consequences of adopting or discarding the solution.

You will see variations on this theme in different people's work. For example, Hans Schaefer's work on risk assessment for software testing looks at the impact of failure as criticality of system, frequency of usage, and visibility of the problem [37]; whereas in TQMI's Failure Prevention Analysis [27], *probability* and *consequence* are used to calculate an overall rating for each possible failure's root cause, and these are used to rank to possible failures.

Cost–benefit analysis [28] is done by calculating the predicted benefits of the proposed change and setting this against the predicted cost. The steps in making a cost–benefit analysis, at its simplest are:

- Identify the financial costs of the solution—for example, direct costs of the solution in equipment, resources, and loss of time on revenue earning activities if staff are diverted to the project.
- Identify the nonfinancial costs of the solution. These may translate into financial costs but you may find it easier to start by listing them and then attempt to translate them. Examples might be adverse publicity, staff dissatisfaction with the change, and customer complaints.
- Identify the financial benefits of the solution—money saved by efficiency increases, additional sales, and customers.
- Identify the nonfinancial benefits of the solution. Again, these may translate into financial benefits but you may find it easier to list them first and put a price on them afterward. Examples might be improvements to staff morale, greater effectiveness in serving the customer, and improved image of the organization.
- Use this information to workout the "payback" over a number of years (see Table A.4). We can see that with the accumulated costs of the original implementation and support year by year, we will not get a payback until year 6.

When you look at the cost–benefit of an idea, you will need to look at how the benefits of the idea match to the organization's goals. This will give you an insight into whether the idea helps the organization's goals—a benefit—or whether it detracts from the organization's goals—a cost. You may well find that financial and nonfinancial targets have been set with the goals, and your cost–benefit discussion needs to reflect these targets. For example, if your organization uses a Balanced Scorecard, as we saw in Chapter 4, financial goals will be balanced against customer, process, and innovation costs and benefits. This information will help put together a cost–benefit discussion in terms familiar to senior management showing how their goals will be affected by your idea.

You may also wish to look at *earned value management* or *budgeted cost of work performed* measures [38], which allow you not only to track cost and budget, but also what the cost so far was supposed to achieve compared

Table A.4 Cost, Benefit, and Payback (in Dollars)

Year	Cost This Year	Benefit This Year	Accumulated Cost	Accumulated Benefit	Benefit Minus Cost
1	100,000	0	100,000	0	−100,000
2	2,000	25,000	102,000	25,000	−77,000
3	2,000	25,000	104,000	50,000	−54,000
4	2,000	25,000	106,000	75,000	−31,000
5	2,000	25,000	108,000	100,000	−8,000
6	2,000	25,000	110,000	125,000	15,000

with what actually has been done. To put it simply, we may have saved budget, but we have not delivered. In Table A.5, we see that although we are apparently under budget, we are behind in delivery, and therefore in earned value. We have, in fact, overspent compared with what we have delivered.

In this section the Internet/Web search words are: Pareto, 80–20 rule, failure prevention analysis, risk, impact, likelihood, probability, consequence, exposure, risk tree, risk-based testing, Schaefer, cost, benefit, payback period, financial planning, cash flow forecasting, profit and loss forecasting, business financial planning, balanced business scorecard, balanced scorecard, Kaplan and Norton scorecard, earned value management (EVM), and budgeted cost of work performed (BCWP).

A.4 Understanding aims and objectives

We saw in Chapter 9 (Figure 9.4) that we need to set aims, objectives, targets, and indicators. One useful technique is the Weaver triangle. This was originally developed by Jayne Weaver for use with nonprofit organizations, and, with her help, I then adapted it for use in IT and business projects [39] On a one-page diagram, the group identifies and agrees on the aim of the project (why it is being done) and associated indicators of success, then the objectives of the project (what is to be done) and associated targets. This helps identify where stakeholders have different aims for the project. The form is used to encourage teams to focus in one an overall aim or goal, and to show pictorially how the aims and objectives fit together. Some ground rules are:

- The aim should answer the questions "why are we doing this?" and "what difference will this make?"
- The specific aims should break down the overall aim in some detailed aims, but avoid having more than three to five of these, or you will get confused.
- Each specific aim also answers a "why?" and "what difference?" question.
- In order for the aims to be achieved, something needs to be done—these are the objectives—so each specific aim must be associated with at least one objective.
- The objectives each answer the question "What do we need to do in order to meet the aim?"

Table A.5 Earned Value Calculations

Budgeted Cost to Date	Planned Delivery to Date	Actual Costs to Date	Actual Delivery to Date	Earned Value
$1,000	Five documents (earned value $200 per document)	$800 (under budget)	Three documents (behind schedule)	$600 (this is $400 behind the expected earned value)

- There will be several objectives, which may be projects within a program or parts of a project, depending on their size.
- Each objective must be focused on achieving at least one of the aims, otherwise there is no in point doing it.
- Aims are measured by indicators that measure whether we are making the difference we intended.
- Objectives are measured by delivery targets such as savings, number of people affected, delivery dates, and budget.
- Indicator and target measures should be linked to measures used generally in the organization; for example, you could show how these measures link to the organization's balanced scorecard.
- Consensus is required between the stakeholders; this is not done by the managers and told to everyone else; it requires contributions and discussion from all the groups.

In this section the Internet/Web search words are: target, indicator, Gilb and Planguage, Seddon, and systems thinking, which will show alternative views about target setting and methods. There is none for Weaver triangle, as this is newly published.

A.5 Review techniques

There are five types of review [40]: management review, technical review, inspection, walkthrough, and audit, all of which are relevant during start-up, throughout the software-development life cycle (SDLC), and during delivery, as well as during the software-maintenance life cycles (SMLC) in the postdelivery period. Specialist testers regard them as a form of testing, because they are used to find and prevent defects in products and processes, but they can be used by any of the groups. Further, they may be used as an opportunity for communication between the groups. The review types have different purposes:

- The management review is carried out to check progress against plans.
- The technical or peer review has the purpose of identifying conformance to specification and finding defects in a document.
- An inspection is a formal review with the purpose of identifying and preventing defects, based on a sample from a document.
- A walkthrough is a review with the purpose of increasing understanding of a document.
- Audits are used to check process conformance rather than products.

We saw in Chapter 3 how useful taking part in reviews can be for the customer, and that the review process need not be complicated. Gilb and

Graham provide a full description of the Inspection process, with example forms [41], and the standard [40] provides an overview of each of the review processes. To get the best from reviews, it is best for people to have some training to understand how to review, and to have a process to follow. For all the reviews, it is good to:

- Set a policy for reviews. Decide what must be reviewed and which type of review is needed. Also decide what should be reviewed but could be left in an emergency, what could be reviewed if there is time, and what will not be reviewed, perhaps based on the risks associated with errors in the products or processes under review.
- Plan to have reviews. Allow time and resource for the activities as we saw in Chapter 4, and use a project review and audit plan structure like the one in Appendix B.
- Plan each particular review—its goals, who should be involved, and what specifically you want them to check, write, or improve the preparation checklists. An example of an audit checklist is in Appendix B.
- Communicate with everyone who will take part to explain what will happen and why the review will be done.
- Train reviewers so they know *how* to prepare—it is not enough to just read a document. Try to use it, or to match it against a related document such as standards, policy, or another product document.
- Ensure that each reviewer has prepared properly—do not hold the review unless everyone has prepared. A review where a reviewer is ill-prepared is just a waste of time and money because you will not find so many defects and you will not gain the same understanding.
- Make sure the review is of the product or process *not the person*—it needs to be objective and helpful not accusing. Some of the communication techniques in this appendix may help.
- Follow up the review. Improve this product and this iteration of the process, but also put in place improvements for the future to prevent future problems.
- Measure the reviews cost–benefit (time/money spent and faults removed/failures prevented) ratio and suggest improvements to the efficiency and effectiveness of the review process itself.

In this section the Internet/Web search words are: software review, technical review, inspection, and Fagan inspection statistical process control.

A.6 Improving graphics in reporting

I thoroughly recommend Edward Tufte's books [42–44]. Not only are they packed with useful information, but they are also a delight to handle and to read, being their own example of good information design. In Chapter 4, I showed an example of a distorted graphic (Figure 4.7) and the equations proposed by Tufte that allow us to measure the distortion of data in a graphic [42].

The *lie factor*, which we saw shown in Chapter 4, Figure 4.7, gives a measure of the exaggeration of data in a graphic. The *data ink ratio*, shown in Figure A.3, is a measure of how much of the graphic provides information and how much is decorative. The data density, Figure A.4, compares the number of data items with the size of the graphic. In summary, the equations are as shown in Figure A.5.

In this section the Internet/Web search words are: Tufte, information design, and graphics press.

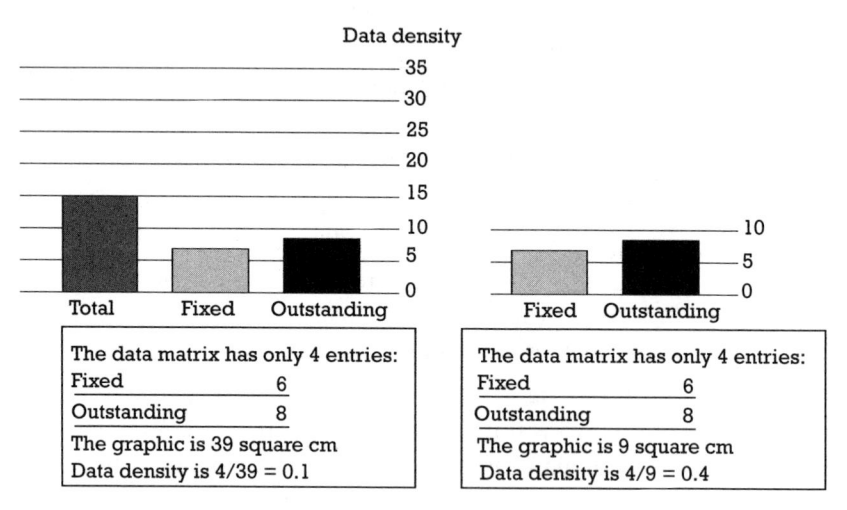

Figure A.3 Data ink ratio in graphics. (*After:* [42].)

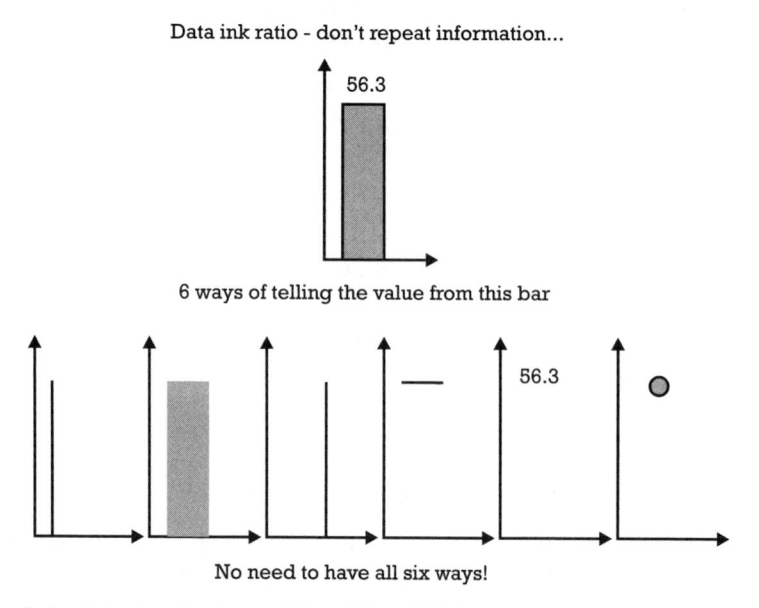

Figure A.4 Data density in graphics. (*After:* [42].)

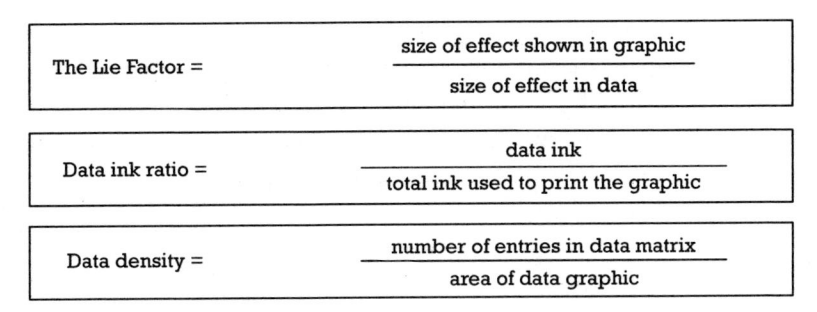

$$\text{The Lie Factor} = \frac{\text{size of effect shown in graphic}}{\text{size of effect in data}}$$

$$\text{Data ink ratio} = \frac{\text{data ink}}{\text{total ink used to print the graphic}}$$

$$\text{Data density} = \frac{\text{number of entries in data matrix}}{\text{area of data graphic}}$$

Figure A.5 Tufte's data graphics equations (*From:* [42]. © 1983 Graphics Press. Reprinted with permission.)

A.7 Useful sources and groups

This section is just a starting list of useful further information and groups. There are many quality techniques and standards that I have not covered in this book. New ideas for improving IT provision are always coming to light. The list in Table A.6 and the following Internet/Web search words are just a starting point for your future research.

Table A.6 Some Sources for QA and QC Standards, Frameworks, and Best Practice

The National Strategy to Secure Cyberspace	http://www.whitehouse.gov/pcipb/
IT Governance Institute	http://www.itgi.org
Information Systems Audit and Control Association	http://www.isaca.org
The Institute of Internal Auditors	http://www.theiia.org/
Institute of Quality Assurance	http://www.iqa.org/
American Society for Quality	http://www.asq.org
Testing Standards Working Party	http://www.testingstandards.co.uk
Sticky Minds	http://www.stickyminds.com
BSI	http://www.bsi.org.uk
ISO	http://www.iso.ch
IEEE	http://www.ieee.org
TickIT	http://www.tickit.org/international.htm
National Institute Standards	http://hissa.ncsl.nist.gov
Office of Government Commerce	http://www.ogc.gov.uk
Successful IT: Modernizing Government in Action	http://www.ogc.gov.uk/index.asp?docid=2632
Six Sigma and robust design	http://www.isixsigma.com
Juran articles	http://www.juran.com
Tufte articles	http://www.edwardtufte.com
Deming articles	http://www.deming.org/
Acronyms expanded	http://www.acronymfinder.com/
Technical terms explained	http://whatis.com
EFQM—European Foundation for Quality Management	http://www.efqm.org
BQF—British Quality Foundation	http://www.quality-foundation.co.uk
SEI—Software Engineering Institute	http://www.sei.cmu.edu
ESI—European Software Institute	http://www.esi.es/
FORTEST—formal methods and testing	http://www.fortest.org.uk/
BCS Industry Structure Model	http://www.bcs.org.uk
BCS Special Interest Groups	http://www.bcs.org.uk
BSC Qualifications	http://www.bcs.org.uk
International Software Testing Qualification Board	http://www.istqb.org
Chartered Management Institute	http://www.managers.org.uk
For an alternative view of quality models...	http://www.lean-service.com
Balanced Score Card Group	http://www.bscol.com
Software Quality Professional	Journal
Better Software (previously STQE)	Journal
Project Manager Today	Journal

In this section the Internet/Web search words are: quality, excellence, quality improvement, governance, audit, standards, software engineering, Crosby, Juran, Deming, CMM®, TMM®, process improvement, patterns, exploratory testing, agile methods, agile manifesto, key process, software testing, verification, validation, continuous improvement, Just In Time, Six Sigma, Taguchi, and Sarbanes-Oxley Act.

References

[1] Busco, C., et al., "When Crisis Arises and the Need for Change Confronts Individuals: Trust for Accounting and Accounting for Trust," http://www.cimaglobal.com/downloads/research_enroac_busco.pdf, November 2003.

[2] Belbin, R. M., *Management Teams—Why They Succeed or Fail*, London, England: Butterworth Heinemann, 1981.

[3] Belbin, R. M., *Team Roles at Work*, London, England: Butterworth Heinemann, 1995.

[4] Belbin Associates, "Belbin Team Roles," http://www.belbin.com/belbin-team-roles.htm, October 2003.

[5] de Bono, E., *Six Thinking Hats®*, New York: Penguin Books, 1999.

[6] Pas, J., "Emotional Intelligence as the Key to Software Quality," *EuroSTAR Conference*, Stockholm, Sweden, 2001.

[7] de Bono, E., "Edward de Bono's Web," http://www.edwdebono.com/, October 2003.

[8] Kroeger, O., J. M. Thuesen, and H. Rutledge, *Type Talk at Work: How the 16 Personality Types Determine Your Success on the Job*, New York: Bantam Doubleday Dell, 2002.

[9] Team Technology Web site, "Working Out Your Myers Briggs Type," http://www.teamtechnology.co.uk/tt/t-articl/mb-simpl.htm, October 2003.

[10] Team Technology Web site, "The Mother of Strategic Systems Issues: Personality," http://www.teamtechnology.co.uk/tt/t-articl/news1.htm, October 2003.

[11] Mullins, L. J., *Management and Organisational Behaviour*, 5th ed., New York: Financial Times/Pitman, 1999, p. 313.

[12] Honey, P., and A. Mumford, *The Learning Styles Helper's Guide*, Maidenhead, England: Peter Honey Publications, 2002, http://www.peterhoney.com. PeterHoney.com, 10 Linden Avenue, Maidenhead, Berks, SL6 6HB. Tel.: 01628633946. Fax: 01628633262. E-mail: info@peterhoney.com.

[13] Honey, P., "Learning Styles," http://www.peterhoney.co.uk/product/learningstyles, October 2003. PeterHoney.com, 10 Linden Avenue, Maidenhead, Berks, SL6 6HB. Tel.: 01628633946. Fax: 01628633262. E-mail: info@peterhoney.com.

[14] Campaign for Learning, http://www.campaign-for-learning.org.uk/aboutyourlearning/whatlearning.htm, October 2003.

[15] Hicks, L., "The Nature of Learning," in L. J. Mullins, (ed.), *Management and Organisational Behaviour*, 5th ed., New York: Financial Times/Pitman, 1999, pp. 344–375.

A.7 Useful sources and groups

[16] McHale, J., "Innovators Rule OK—Or Do They?" *Training & Development*, October 1986, http://www.kaicentre.com/.

[17] Kirton, "Adaptors and Innovators Defined," KAI Web site, http://www.kaicentre.com/, July 2003.

[18] Warden, R., and I. Nicholson, *The MIP Report—Volume 2—1996 Motivational Survey of IT Staff*, 2nd ed., Bredon, England: Software Futures Ltd., 1996.

[19] Hackman, J. R., and G. R. Oldham *The Job Diagnostic Survey: An Instrument for the Diagnosis of Jobs and the Evaluation of Job Redesign Projects*, Technical Report No. 4, New Haven, CT: Yale University, Department of Administrative Sciences, 1974.

[20] Accel-team.com, http://www.accel-team.com/human_relations, October 2003.

[21] Maslow, A., *Motivation and Personality*, New York: Harper and Row, 1954.

[22] Maslow, A., *Motivation and Personality*, New York: Harper and Row, 1970.

[23] Gywnne, R., "Maslow's Hierarchy of Needs," http://web.utk.edu/~gwynne/maslow.HTM, November 2003.

[24] Accel-team.com, "Maslow's Hierarchy of Needs," http://www.accel-team.com/human_relations/hrels_02_maslow.html, October 2003.

[25] Wagner, A., *The Transactional Manager—How to Solve People Problems with Transactional Analysis*, Denver, CO: T.A. Communications, 1981.

[26] Berne, E., *Games People Play*, New York: Grove Press, 1964.

[27] TQMI, *Problem Solving—Tools and Techniques*, Frodsham, England: TQMI, 2001.

[28] Robson, M., *Problem Solving in Groups*, Aldershot, England: Gower, 1995.

[29] Neukam, J., and J. Sauer, "Pattern-Drafting Software," *Threads*, May 2003, pp. 42–49.

[30] Hohmann, L., "Lo-Fi GUI Design," *Software Testing and Quality Engineering*, Vol. 1, No. 5, September 1999, pp. 24–29.

[31] Nance, R. E., and J. D. Arthur, *Managing Software Quality*, New York: Springer-Verlag, 2002.

[32] "Drawing Concerns: A Structured Rich Picturing Approach," http://business.unisa.edu.au/cobar/documents/richpic_colin.pdf, November 2003.

[33] Rose, J., "Soft Systems Methodology as a Social Science Research Tool," http://www.cs.auc.dk/~jeremy/pdf%20files/SSM.pdf.

[34] Buzan, T., *The Mind Map Book*, London, England: BBC Consumer Publishing, 2003.

[35] Freeburn, G., "Mind Mapping 101 for Testers," *EuroSTAR Conference*, Edinburgh, Scotland, 2002.

[36] Fowler, M., and K. Scott, *UML Distilled*, Reading, MA: Addison-Wesley, 1997.

[37] Schaefer, H., "Testing—The Bad Game and the Good Game," *BCS SIGiST Conference*, Edinburgh, Scotland, 1997.

[38] Pavyer, E., "An Introduction to Earned Value Management," *Project Manager Today*, Vol. 11, April 2003.

[39] Evans, I., "The Troubled Project—Best Practice from Theory to Reality," *EuroSTAR Conference*, Stockholm, Sweden, 2001.

[40] IEEE 1028™ Standard for Software Reviews, 1997.

[41] Gilb, T., and D. Graham, *Software Inspection*, Reading, MA: Addison-Wesley, 1993.

[42] Tufte, E., *The Visual Display of Quantitative Information* (Equations from p. 57, the Lie Factor; p. 93, The Data Ink Ratio; p. 162, Data Density), Cheshire, CT: Graphics Press, 1983.

[43] Tufte, E., *Visual Explanations*, Cheshire, CT: Graphics Press, 1990.

[44] Tufte, E., *Envisioning Information*, Cheshire, CT: Graphics Press, 1997.

Selected bibliography

Crosby, P., *Quality Is Free*, New York: Penguin, 1980.

Garfinkel, H., *Studies in Ethnomethodology*, Englewood Cliffs, NJ: Prentice-Hall, 1967.

Handy, C., *Understanding Organizations*, New York: Penguin, 1993.

Hofstede, G. H., *The Game of Budget Control*, London, England: Tavistock, 1968.

Humphreys, W., "Pathways to Process Maturity: The Personal Software Process and Team Software Process," http://interactive.sei.cmu.edu/Features/1999/June/Background/Background.jun99.htm, August 2003.

Northcott, D., *Capital Investment Decision Making*, San Diego, CA: Academic Press, 1992.

Ould, M., *Managing Software Quality and Business Risk*, New York: Wiley, 1999.

Perry, W. E. and R. W. Rice, *Surviving the Top Ten Challenges of Software Testing: A People-Oriented Approach*, New York: Dorset House, 1997.

Winant, B., "Visual Requirements," *STQE*, June 2003, pp. 34–42.

Appendix B

Quality Planning Documents and Templates

B.1 The document family

As we saw in Chapter 4 (see Figure 4.1), the quality planning required for a particular project will be based on the organization's standards, including its policies and chosen methods of work. Within an individual project, once the aims, objectives, risks, and constraints for the project are understood, we can develop a family of documents which describe how *for this project* we will carry out our work. We have seen that quality planning for the SDLC should involve all the groups. This activity should be part of project planning. There are a number of documents that might be needed; on a small project I would have these as paragraph headings in the project plan, whereas on a large project, you might need a series of documents, with levels of detail from a strategy through detailed plans. Table B.1 lists the levels of quality planning documents.

Table B.1 Quality Planning Documents

This is what we do as an organization	Policy documents organization level, brief, part of organization QMS
This is how we will do it as an organization	Standards and processes organization level, descriptive, steps "how to", organization Quality Management System (QMS) for all activities, not just QA/QC activities
This is what we will do for this SDLC	Project QMS or quality plan
	Program/project level, documents tailoring decisions based on risk and constraints, choice and tailoring of SDLC (see Chapter 10), may include policy, standards, and processes, where these differ from the organization level documents, for QA, QC, management, and build activities
This is how we carry out QA/QC activities for this SDLC	QA: Audit and review strategy and overall plan
	QC: Document review strategy and overall plan
	QC: Testing strategy and overall plan
	Project/program level, responsibilities, overall approach based on tailored QMS, which groups will contribute to which QA/QC activities
This is how we will carry out this particular QA/QC activity	Detailed plans for each particular audit, review, document review, test level, stage within SDLC, specific, detailed approach, detailed task plan, specific responsibilities

In an organization with a documented Quality Management System (QMS) there will be a documented policy for both QA and QC activities, describing at a high level what is expected for any SDLC. Even if the organization does not have written policies, there will be unwritten, taken-for-granted assumptions: "We always do it this way." The policies will be backed up by process descriptions, procedures, and standards. Again, in some organizations these will be documented, but in others they are based on word of mouth, individual expertise, and training. Some important questions to think about are:

- Have we chosen the appropriate standards/methods/tools and techniques to carry out our work?
- Do they need adapting for this project?
- Are there specific expectations or rules from our customers about how we do the work—do we need to follow a particular standard or method?
- Are we doing the right QA/QC activities bearing in mind the risks and constraints?
- Are the QA and QC activities sufficient to meet any external or internal requirements?
- Does everyone agree that these QA and QC activities are needed?
- Have they been defined in a way that will allow measurement of product and process?

In order to allow these questions to be considered, I think it is useful to have a written QMS that contains the policies, processes, and standards, but, importantly, has a rule that "the processes and standards can be tailored to suit the risks and constraints for the particular project" We have seen some examples of tailoring in Chapter 12. In Figure B.1, we can see an example document family. Remember this is just an example; you may choose to have fewer documents by combining some of them.

We see in the figure that the documents we developed during start-up (Chapter 9) plus the company policies and standard drive what appears in the project documents. The documents in the project that address quality include the project plan itself, the risk-management plan, the configuration-management plan, and the quality plan. These documents—or project plan parts in a small project—need to be developed together; they are a complementary set. Each may be the parent for a document family. In this figure, we will develop the quality branch. The quality plan divides into three main parts in this project: an audit plan, a plan for which documents to inspect or review, and an overall plan for testing. Each of these branches has a similar structure, so let us just look at the audit branch. There will be several audits, and each will need a plan. This is not a large document; it just means that we need to agree on the time and place for each audit, who will be involved, book rooms and so on. It might be just a checklist or an e-mail to confirm

B.2 Why we use document templates 275

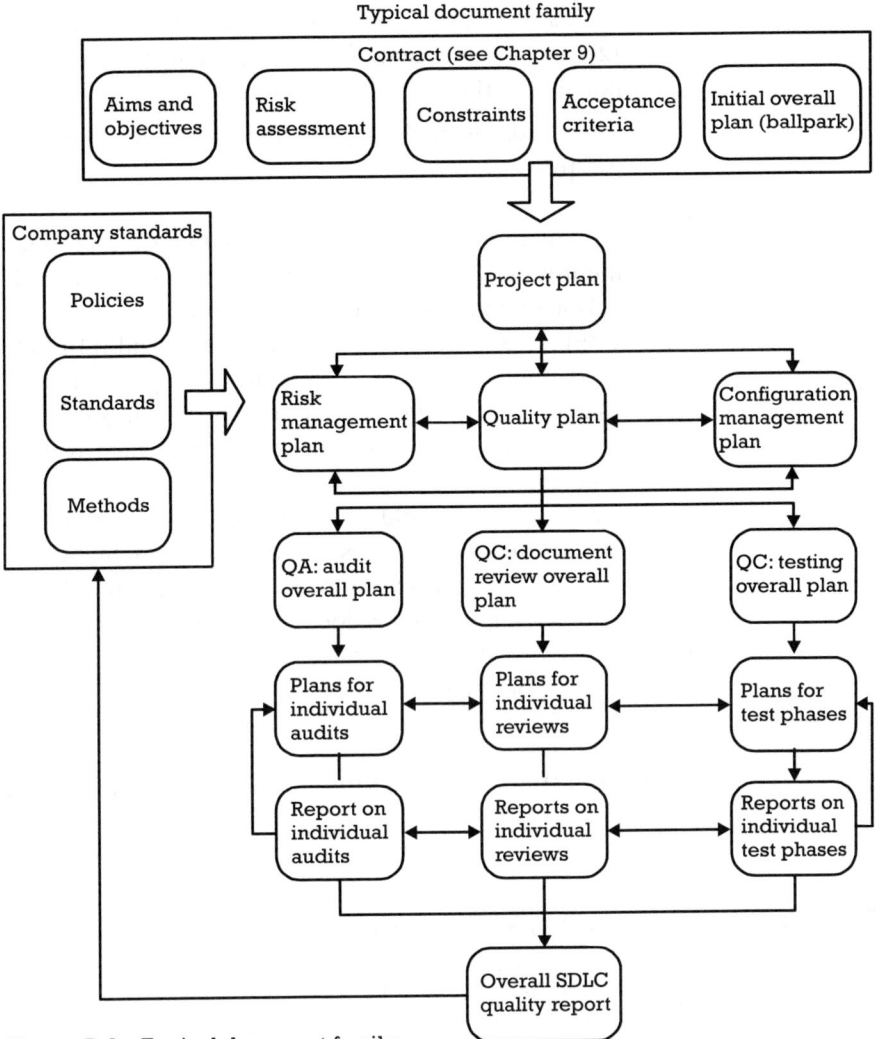

Figure B.1 Typical document family.

what the auditor and team being audited have agreed. After each audit, a short report is needed, just the good points and areas for improvement in a list, with priorities. Do not write much, but do share it with the team you have audited and get their feedback. Finally, all the quality activities feed into an overall quality report, which helps all the groups decide on the outcome of the project, but also feeds improvements to the company standards.

B.2 Why we use document templates

We need to know which documents we have to write, why we write them, and what their contents should be. To save everyone time deciding what is needed, it is useful to have a set of standard document templates. There are a number of standards that provide document templates, for example:

- IEEE standards, including standards for project plans [1], quality plans [2], test documentation [3], requirements documents [4], and user documentation [5];
- BSI standards, including standards for documenting component testing [6].

The standard bodies update these documents, and so it is best to consult the standards bodies for the latest versions. For example, IEEE 829™ [3] is the Test Documentation standard. If you look on the IEEE Web site [7], you will see IEEE 829:1983, which is superseded, and IEEE 829:1998, which at time of writing is the current standard, but you will also see IEEE P829, which is a project to revise the standard by bringing it into line with current thinking, and other, more recent standards, which will result in the 1998 version being superseded.

These standards should be your source for deciding on the content of your own document templates, but almost inevitably, you will find that you want to adapt the standards in some way. Tables B.2 through B.5 are deliberately not a complete set of documents, so that you are encouraged to find out what the standards bodies are offering, and to obtain the latest standards for each type of document. Sources of information are:

- IEEE [7];
- BSI [8], including the BSI Software and Systems Quality Framework (SSQF) [9];

Table B.2 Example of a Project Plan Template

Project plan	Not just the schedule. To allow discussion of whether the project is possible—using tools and techniques like PERT (see Chapter 4), we can model the project. Loosely based on [1], tailored over use.			
Project plan for project:	Author	Date	Status	Version
Reference	To higher level documents—do not repeat information from higher level documents in this document; just document differences, new information, and exceptions (e.g., project authorization, terms of reference)			
Introduction	Overview			
Deliverables	List of all the deliverables			
Evolution	Change control			
Vocabulary	Definitions and acronyms on this project			
References	Documents that will expand on the information in this document if required (e.g., quality plan, configuration management plan, risk management plan)			
Organization	Process model, organizational structure, organization boundaries and interfaces, project responsibilities, managerial process, objectives, and priorities			
Risk	Assumptions, dependencies and constraints, risk management, monitoring and controlling mechanisms			
People	Staffing plan, staffing needs, staff available, training and induction plans, rewards and recognition plans, teams, team dynamics			
Methods	Technical processes, methods, tools and techniques, software documentation, project support functions			
Schedule	Work packages, dependencies, resource requirements, budget and resource allocation, schedule			

B.2 Why we use document templates

Table B.3 Example of a Quality Plan Template

Quality plan	Document approach, specifically exceptions to policy and standards, help you consider and plan for QA/QC activities, evidence of decisions, rule book for actions, checklist for QA/QC activities. Loosely based on [2], tailored over experience.
Quality plan for project:	Author — Date — Status — Version
Reference	To higher-level documents—do not repeat information from higher-level documents in this document; just document differences, new information and exceptions (e.g., project authorization, terms of reference, project plan)
Quality objectives	Summary, list of items subject to the quality plan, features of interest, items not subject to the quality plan, specific quality objectives
Approach	General approach, selection of methods including QA/QC Methods, pass and fail criteria, sign off procedures, suspension and resumption, corrective actions
Exceptions	List of differences from policies and standards, adaptations made to templates, other changes to normal process
QM tasks and deliverables	QM deliverables, QM, QP, QA, QC tasks, test, inspection, examination and audit programs
Scheduling/ resourcing	Environmental needs, responsibilities and authorities, resources required and resources available, staff and training needs, schedule, budget
Risks	Specific risk areas, float available, contingency plans
Review	Change control on this plan, review points on this plan
Other	What else might we need to think about?
Lower-level documents	List documents which will expand on this information if required (e.g., configuration management plan, risk management plan, test plan)

Table B.4 Example of a Risk Management Plan Template

Risk management plan	Gain agreement from all parties on control of risk, define management processes for RM. This template is experience-based; there is an IEEE standard in [10].
For Project:	Author — Date — Status — Version
Reference	To project plan, risk assessment, risk register
Introduction	Purpose, Scope, Definitions/mnemonics
Management	Responsibilities and authorities, escalation
Activities	Risk reassessment cycles—timing, responsibilities
	Risk identification and assessment activities
	Risk containment measures—criteria for deciding whether a risk is to be treated by prevention, mitigation, or contingency plans, or is to be accepted
	Relationship to quality plan—QA and QC activities related to risk
Review	Change control on this plan, review points on this plan
Other information	What else might we need to think about?
References	Quality plans, including audit plans, review plans, test plans
Approvals	Who needs to approve? Who needs to buy in? Who needs to know?

- ISO [11];
- Testing Standards Web site [12], including Reid's paper comparing testing standards [13];
- ITIL [14];
- itSMF [15].

Table B.5 Example of a Configuration Management Plan Template

Configuration management plan	Gain agreement from all parties on control of changes, define management processes for CM
	Loosely based on [16], tailored from experience.
For Project:	Author · Date · Status · Version
Reference	To higher level documents—do not repeat information from higher level documents in this document; just document differences, new information and exceptions
Introduction	Purpose
	Scope
	Definitions/mnemonics
Management	Organizations, SCR responsibilities, Interface control, status accounting, audits, CC board
Activities	Configuration identification, configuration control, configuration status accounting, audits and reviews, tools, techniques and methodologies, supplier control, records collection and retention
Review	Change control on this plan, review points on this plan
Other Information	What else might we need to think about?
References	List documents which will expand on the information in this document if required
Approvals	Who needs to approve? Who needs to buy in? Who needs to know?

B.3 Using the document standards to provide your own templates

Put together a set of templates as a starting point for all projects, and have two or three "sizes"—perhaps an "emergency" template, an "agile" template, and a "high-risk" template, as we discussed in Chapter 10—and set the policy for projects by adapting these. Make sure these templates provide enough information for anyone who needs to understand or take on aspects of the work. For example, do the supporters need additional information because they will take on the maintenance of the system after delivery?

B.4 Auditing considerations

Consider whether you will be audited, who by, and if there is an expectation that you adhere to particular documentation standards. If so, you need to understand whether you are allowed to adapt the published standard; for example a customer may require you to provide "test documentation written to meet the IEEE 829 Test Documentation Standard" [3]. What does this mean? To which date standard are they referring? Can you adapt it? If you can adapt, document the adaptation and make it clear how it meets the standard.

B.5 The team's information needs

The team size and experience may affect how much you document. For a small project team, with membership from all the groups and good communication skills, who have worked together before and who are working on a fast track project, you need to use these documents as checklist of things to remember. Maybe you only have to document the exceptions to rules you have previously developed. However, if you have a large team of people, and perhaps working together for the first time, perhaps from different organizations, you need to find a way to communicate and agree how things will be done. Try using the document headings as an agenda for a discussion meeting. Then document and review the outcome to check that you all have a common understanding. Remember to communicate the information; I remember seeing a very good test strategy that was only known to its author; no one else had read it, yet the development manager and the operations group both needed information from that document.

B.6 Adapting templates

If you adapt document templates for a particular project, when you start your next project, go back to the original templates. Otherwise you will forget why you adapted the template in a particular way, and perhaps miss something important from the original template. Expect the document templates to change over time. When you make changes to the templates, go back to the standards and think about *why* each section is there and whether you will be missing something if you change it (see Tables B.2 through B.5).

B.7 Keep it brief—do not repeat or copy information

Try to evolve a family of documents, with the lower-level documents only adding information, not repeating information from higher up the family tree. An example family tree is shown in Figure B.2. You will see that we may not need the detailed plans on all the branches of the tree.

As a general rule, just document any changes and exceptions. Discourage people from copying chunks from one document to another; repeated information makes update harder.

Do not allow people to pick up completed documents, copy them, and alter them; they may stop thinking about the content of the document and producing it may become a chore done for no purpose. The important thing about these documents is that they help us think and solve problems.

B.8 Do you need a document at all?

We write documents to communicate and to reach agreement. You may not need a set of text documents on paper; that may not be the best way to communicate or to reach agreement. You may be better off with a Web site, a presentation, a notice board, diagrams, a spreadsheet, a video of the discussion meeting, a video of the project sponsor—you decide what is best.

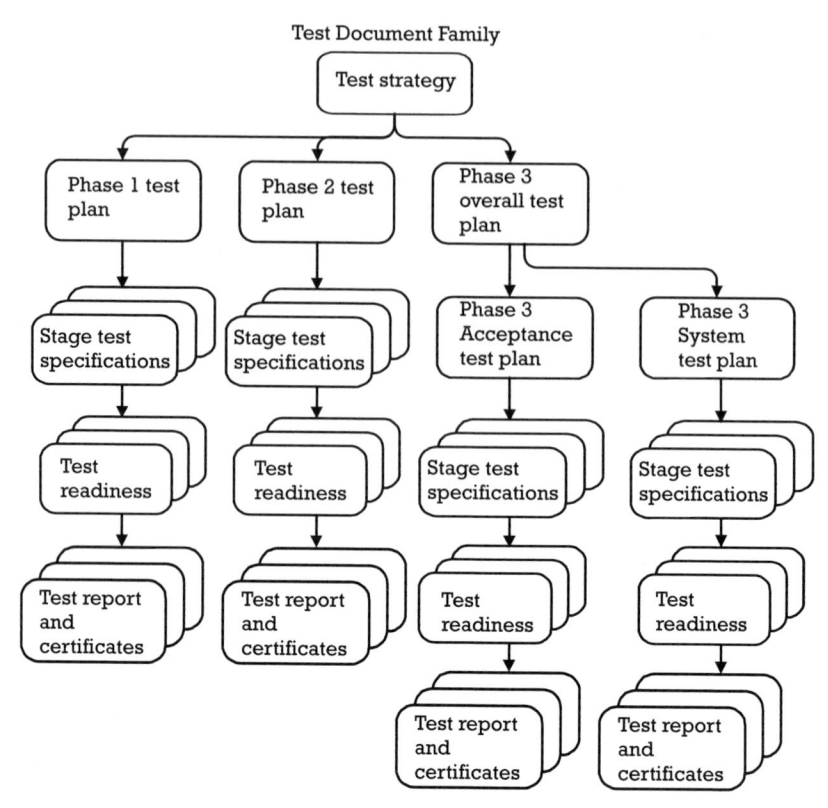

Figure B.2 Typical test documentation family. (*After:* [3].)

B.9 Simple project audit plan and report templates

These documents are ones I have developed based on the test and quality documentation [2, 3], and then tailored. For each planned audit, for example, in a spreadsheet, collect the following information, initially for planning and then for tracking:

- For *Planning* the headings are: Topic area, Topic detail, Audit planned month, Audit team, Audit place, Audit goal.
- For a *Detailed plan for one audit*: Audit checklist or reference to it.
- For *Tracking against plan* the headings are: Audit done date, Audit outcome, refer to Audit report, All issues resolved?

For a particular audit, the audit detailed plan may be a checklist. An example audit checklist that the auditor has started to develop for code maintainability might look like Table B.6.

The report for audits may be a text report, or it could be a spreadsheet of positive observations and areas of concern, or you may wish to log nonconformances to standards in the same way and place that you log inspection and test defects—in the defect logging system—or you might wish to use the audit primarily to identify risks, in which case log them in the risk register. For each point identify:

B.9 Simple project audit plan and report templates

Table B.6 Example of an Audit Checklist (Maintainability Audit)

For Project:	Topic area	Audit team	Date	Status	Version
	Code quality—Maintainability				
Logistics and planning	Speak to team leader of the area to be audited and explaining what will happen				
	Identify who will be interviewed				
	Set times for a start meeting, interviews and a closing meeting				
	Book rooms if required				
Review goal	Establish whether the project deliverables will be acceptably maintainable				
Initial Questions	What are the maintainability acceptance criteria for the project?				
	Are these set at a level which meets the customer's needs?				
	What analysis of maintainability is being carried out by the team?				
	How complex is the code?				
	How internally consistent and correct is the code?				
	Does the code have areas that cannot be executed?				
	How does the team check that data is defined and used correctly across interfaces?				
	What static analysis tools being used to support maintainability measures?				
	Which factors does the chosen tool address?				
	How easily will changes be made to the delivered code?				
Metrics	Number of programs checked/number of programs				
	For each program checked:				
	Program size: Lines of code or number of programs or number of objects				
	Code complexity: as measured using the ABC tool set				
	Developer assessment (perception measure) of maintenance ease: predicted number of hours to make changes (see example of changes set), predicted number of faults, perception of "trickiness"				
	Note: Check whether they are using ISO 9126 [17] for any Maintainability measures				
Method	Static analysis of code using tools and inspection				
	Interview of project members				
	Interview development manager				
	Inspect coding standards				
Audit date	Refer to audit report				

- The specific point for example by audit name/number/date;
- Auditor name (person who raised the point);
- Review area;
- Reference to document or source of information;
- Description of area of concern or positive observation;
- Metric used and measurement;
- If this is an area of concern, identify risks associated (likelihood of problems arising and impact of those problems if they arise);
- If this is a reaudit, assessment of changes in risk since last audit;
- Prediction of outcome;
- Suggested resolution;
- Comment from audited team/team leader;

- Actual resolution;
- Date resolved
- Sign-off by audited team/team leader;
- Sign-off by auditor/audit team leader.

References

[1] IEEE™ 1058:1998 Standard for Software Project Management Plans.

[2] IEEE™ 730:1989 Standard for Software Quality Assurance Plans.

[3] IEEE™ 829:1998 Standard for Software Test Documentation.

[4] IEEE™ 830:1998 Recommended Practice for Software Requirements Specifications.

[5] IEEE™ 1063:2001 Standard for Software User Documentation.

[6] British Standards Institute, BS7925-2:1998 Software Testing, Part 2 Software component testing.

[7] IEEE Web site, http://www.ieee.org.

[8] British Standards Institute Web site, http://www.bsi.org.uk.

[9] British Standards Institute, PD0026:2003, "Software and Systems Quality Framework—A Guide to the Use of ISO/IEC and Other Standards for Understanding Quality in Software and Systems," May 2003.

[10] IEEE 1540-2001™ Standard for Software Life Cycle Processes—Risk Management.

[11] International Standards Organization Web site, http://www.iso.ch.

[12] Testing Standards Working Party Web site, http://www.testingstandards.co.uk.

[13] Reid, S. C., "Software Testing Standards—Do They Know What They Are Talking About?" http://www.testingstandards.co.uk/publications.htm, August 2003.

[14] IT Infrastructure Library, Web site http://www.itil.co.uk.

[15] IT Service Management Forum, http://www.itsmf.com, October 2003.

[16] IEEE 828:1998™ Standard for Software Configuration Management Plans.

[17] International Standards Organization/International Electrotechnical Commission (ISO/IEC) DTR 9126 Software Engineering—Software Product Quality (Parts 1–4, 2000/2001).

About the Author

Isabel Evans has 20 years of experience in the IT industry, mainly in quality management, testing, training, and documentation. She has helped organizations in the development of procedures, standards, and methods to aid in the testing of software during development and maintenance projects. She has managed test groups and performed testing design and development for the acceptance and system testing of packages and bespoke systems. Ms. Evans has also provided quality assurance support, release management, and customer support for IT organizations. She has worked independently since 1992, running her own company, IE Testing Consultancy Ltd. After working closely with Testing Solutions Group (TSG) since 2002, Ms. Evans joined the company in January 2004.

Ms. Evans writes and presents courses; for TSG, these include courses for beginners, the ISEB Foundation, and Practitioner Certificates in Software Testing and specialist courses in testing and quality methods. In the past she has provided training and tutorial material in quality management, project management, and documentation skills. While she has a sound theoretical basis for testing and quality, her own experience as a tester and as a quality consultant provides a practical approach and real-life experiences.

As well as presenting seminars and training courses to clients, Ms. Evans has spoken on software quality, testing, and test management at conferences in the United Kingdom, Europe, and the United States, including EuroSTAR, PSST, Quality Forum, BCS SIGIST, and the Year 2000 and EURO Summit. She regularly attends conferences, courses, and meetings in her interest areas. Ms. Evans has been a member of various working parties and groups to contribute to improvement in software quality and testing, including the Quality Forum Testing Metrics Forum, the Customer Satisfaction Measurement working party, and the BCS SIGIST Test Standards Working Party, currently developing nonfunctional testing standards.

Index

A

Acceptance criteria, 174–77
  maintainability, 176
  measurable, making, 175
  performance, 176
  reliability, 177
  setting, 174
  SMART, 177
  usability, 176
Adaptive maintenance, 239–40
Aims and objectives, 172–73, 265–66
Audits
  considerations, 278
  defined, 266
  external, 122
  internal, 122
  plans, 280–82
  project, 112
Availability management, 235

B

Belbin
  team roles, 250–51
  team scores, 27
Big bang waterfall, 196–97, 199
Budgeted cost of work performed (BCWP), 265
Builders, 77–97
  buy-in, 91, 92
  change involvement, 240
  communication responsibility, 95
  communication with other groups, 95–96
  corrections and changes, 82–83
  criticism, 78
  customer results, 92–93
  delivery and, 220
  EFQM Excellence Model and, 86–87
  EFQM Excellence Model enablers for, 87–92
  EFQM Excellence Model results for, 92–95
  group, 19, 21
  group members, 79–80
  group summary, 96–97
  information needed by, 97
  information that others need, 97
  introducing, 77–79
  key performance results, 95
  leadership, 87–88
  manufacturing-based view, 80
  measurers and, 84, 125
  partnerships and resources, 90–91
  people, 89–90
  people results, 93–94
  policy and strategy, 88
  processes, 83, 91–92
  product-based view, 81
  quality framework, 86–95
  quality viewpoint, 80–86
  SDLC and, 80
  society results, 94
  as suppliers, 87
  transcendent view, 81
  See also Groups

C

Capability Maturity Model® (CMM®), 7, 11–12
  Integration® (CMMI®), 11–12
  intergroup relationships, 24–25
  levels, 11
  People (PCMM®), 12, 13
  software development, 11
Capacity management, 235
Cause–effect analysis, 259–61
Change management, 183, 191–92, 235
Change(s), 236–41
  adaptive maintenance, 239–40
  builders and, 82–83
  corrective maintenance, 236–38
  cost of, 83–84
  enhancements, 238–39

285

Change(s) (continued)
    impact, 83
    involvement in, 240
    managing, 183
    parallel, during postdelivery, 237
    perfective maintenance, 239
    testing, 240–41
Commercial off-the-shelf (COTS)
        customers, 36–38
    delivery, 219
    home/hobby users, 37
    large organizations, 37
    niche users, 37
    relationship management, 36
    small businesses, 37
    See also Customers
Communication(s)
    builders and other groups, 95–96
    customers and other groups, 45–47
    fostering, 246
    improvement techniques, 26, 27
    managers and other groups, 68–73
    measurers with other groups, 125–28
    poor, cycles of, 70
    supporters with other groups, 146–47
Communication styles, 253–58
    Honey and Mumford learning styles, 254–55
    Kirton adaptors and innovators, 255–56
    motivation studies, 256–57
    Myers-Briggs Type Indicator (MBTI), 253–54
    transactional analysis, 257–58
Corrective maintenance, 236–38
Cost–benefit analysis, 264
Critical paths, 64
Customer results
    for builders, 92–93
    for customers, 43
    defined, 9
    for managers, 65–66
    for measurers, 123
    for supporters, 143–44
    See also Results
Customers, 2, 31–48
    "awkward," 17
    change involvement, 240
    communication with groups, 45–47
    complaint root causes, 165
    customer results, 43
    delivery and, 220
    EFQM Excellence Model and, 39–40
    EFQM Excellence Model enablers for, 40–43
    EFQM Excellence Model results for, 43–45
    of end users, 32
    focus, 6
    group, 19, 20
    information needed by other groups, 47
    information needed from other groups, 48
    in-house, 33–35
    introducing, 31–32
    IT specialists as, 38
    IT system, 32
    key performance results, 44–45
    leadership, 40
    organizational, 33
    partnerships and resources, 43
    people, 41–42
    people results, 43–44
    policy and strategy, 41
    processes, 43
    quality framework, 39–45
    quality viewpoint, 38–39
    results, 9
    society and government as, 33
    society results, 44
    third-party custom-made system, 35–36
    third-party package/COTS, 36–38
    types of, 32–33
    See also Groups
Custom-made system customers, 35–36

D

Data migration delivery, 225–26
De Bono's Six Thinking Hats, 251–53
    advantages, 252–53
    colors, 252
    defined, 27, 215
    use of, 251
Defects
    analyzing, 232
    found, 232
    prevention, 103–5
    propagation and removal, 104
Delivery, 156
    activities, 221–26
    conclusion, 226
    considerations, 215–17
    COTS package, 219
    data migration, 225–26
    description, 215–18
    entry criteria, 221
    entry criteria example, 223
    exit criteria example, 226
    exit from, 226
    identifying, 217–18
    in life span stage diagram, 216
    method, 216
    multisite, 224–25
    planning, 216–17
    quality measures, 217
    release for, 218

Index

self-installation, 223–24
single-site, 224
size, 217
support around, 216–17
teamwork techniques summary, 222–23
urgency, 216
viewpoints, 218–21
See also Software system life span
Deming cycle, 5, 56
Design, 184
    defined, 193
    elements, 193
    See also Software development life cycle (SDLC)
Development stage. *See* Software development life cycle (SDLC)
Distorted data representation, 72
Document templates, 275–78
    adapting, 279
    configuration management plan example, 278
    creating, 278
    project plan example, 276
    quality plan example, 277
    risk management plan example, 277
    See also Quality planning documents

E

Earned value management (EVM), 264, 265
EFQM Excellence Model, 7–10, 13–15
    builders and, 86–87
    continuous learning, innovation, improvement, 6
    customer focus, 6
    custom organization and, 39–40
    defined, 5, 7
    enablers, 7–9
    enablers for builders, 87–92
    enablers for customers, 40–43
    enablers for managers, 57–65
    enablers for measurers, 114–22
    enablers for supporters, 138–43
    as framework, 13
    fundamental concepts, 6–7
    illustrated, 8
    intergroup relationships, 25–26
    key performance results, 10
    leadership, 6, 7–8
    management by processes and facts, 6
    measurers and, 113–14
    models in, 13–15
    partnership development, 6
    people development and involvement, 6
    public responsibility, 6
    results, 9–10
    results for builders, 92–95
    results for customers, 43–45
    results for managers, 65–68
    results for measurers, 123–25
    results for supporters, 143–46
    results orientation, 6
    supporters and, 136–38
Ego states, 258
Enablers, 7–9
    for builders, 87–92
    for customers, 40–43
    leadership, 7–8, 40, 57–58, 87–88, 114, 138–39
    for managers, 57–65
    for measurers, 114–22
    partnerships and resources, 8–9, 43, 60, 90–91, 119, 142
    people, 8, 41–42, 59–60, 89–90, 115–19, 139–42
    policy and strategy, 8, 41, 58–59, 88, 114–15, 139
    processes, 9, 43, 61–65, 91–92, 119–22, 142–43
    for supporters, 138–43
    See also EFQM Excellence Model
Enhancements, 238–39
European Foundation for Quality Management. *See* EFQM Excellence Model
Evaluation
    SDLC/SMLC, 241–42
    timing, 242
Evolutionary model, 198
    advantages/disadvantages, 198
    defined, 203
    illustrated, 204
    See also SDLC models
Excellence concepts, 5–7
EXtreme Programming (XP), 203

F

Fed-up falcon, 257
Feedback
    MBTI, 34
    personality types and, 34
    supporter problem, 140
    for testers, 118

G

Games programs, 38
Graphics
    data density, 268
    data ink ratio, 268
    equations, 269
    improving, 267–69

Graphics (continued)
    lie factor, 268
Groups
    attitudes, 18
    builders, 19, 21, 77–97
    customers, 19, 20, 31–48
    EFQM Excellence Model and, 25–26
    interaction between, 22–27
    intergroup relationships, 24–26
    list of, 19
    managers, 19, 20–21, 51–74
    measurers, 19, 21, 101–26
    motivation, 24
    nonfunctional attributes and, 175
    organization, 26
    problems attributed to people outside, 23–24
    quality views across, 22
    summary, 148–50
    supporters, 19, 22, 131–50
    See also Teams

H

Hawthorne effect, 105
Help-desk team, 137
Honey and Mumford
    learning styles, 254–55
    Learning Styles Helper's Guide, 255
    Learning Styles Questionnaire, 27, 255

I

ICT specialists, 133–34
Ideas
    modeling, 261–62
    pursuing, 262–65
    start-up and, 165–70
Incident management, 235
Incremental model, 199–200
    advantages/disadvantages, 198
    defined, 199–200
    example, 198
    illustrated, 200
    See also SDLC models
Influence leaders, 87
Infrastructure management, 235
In-house customers, 33–35
    group relationships, 33
    technical team dialog, 34
    See also Customers
Inspections, 266
Inspectors, 111
Installation
    self, 223–24
    team, 216
    time period for, 216

    See also Delivery
Ishikawa fishbones, 237
    defined, 27, 259
    diagram illustration, 259
    solution, 260
ISO 9000:1994, 10
ISO 9000:2000, 10
ISO 9126, 174
Iterative/spiral model, 200–203
    advantages/disadvantages, 198
    examples, 198
    exploratory nature of, 201
    iterative, illustrated, 200
    spiral illustrated, 201
    use problems, 203
    See also SDLC models
IT Infrastructure Library (ITIL), 136–37
IT service–continuity management, 235
IT Service Management Forum, 235
IT specialists
    as customers, 38
    security, 134

K

Key performance results
    for customers, 44–45
    defined, 10
    for managers, 67–68
    for measurers, 124–25
    for supporters, 146
    See also Results
Kirton adaptors and innovators, 255–56
    characteristics, 256
    defined, 27

L

Leadership, 6, 7–8
    for builders, 87–88
    for customers, 40
    defined, 6
    influence, 87
    for managers, 57–58
    for measurers, 114
    poor/undetermined, circle of, 88
    for supporters, 138–39
    See also Enablers
Lie factor, 72, 268

M

Maintainability, 176
Maintenance
    adaptive, 239–40
    corrective, 236–38

Index

enhancements, 238–39
perfective, 239
types of, 236
See also Change(s)
Malcolm Baldrige model, 5, 10, 14
Management review, 266
Managers, 51–74
    change involvement, 240
    cliché, 53
    communication cycles and, 68–70
    communication with other groups, 68–73
    consistency of behavior, 59
    customer results, 65–66
    customer strategy awareness, 56
    delivery and, 220
    EFQM Excellence Model and, 54–57
    EFQM Excellence Model enablers, 57–65
    EFQM Excellence Model results, 65–68
    focus, 51
    group, 19, 20–21
    group summary, 73–74
    information needed from others, 73
    information others need from, 73
    inspiration ability, 57
    introducing, 51–52
    key performance results, 67–68
    leadership, 57–58
    learning to be, 61–62
    monitoring, control, measurement of progress, 64–65
    negotiations, 68
    partnerships and resources, 60
    people, 59–60
    people results, 66
    people who are, 52
    planning/estimating for quality activities, 63–64
    policy and strategy, 58–59
    processes, 61–65
    quality framework, 54–68
    quality viewpoint, 53–54
    reporting process, 70–73
    society results, 66–67
    as villains of SDLC, 51
    See also Groups
Manufacturing-based quality view
    builders, 81
    definition, 3
    measurers, 107
Maslow Hierarchy of Needs, 256
    defined, 27
    list of, 256
Measurement(s)
    framework, 119–20
    improvement and, 120–22
    processes, 120
    reporting process, 122
    techniques, 141
Measurers, 101–29
    builders and, 84, 125
    change involvement, 240
    clichéd observation, 108
    communication with other groups, 125–28
    customer results, 123
    defect prevention, 103–5
    delivery and, 220
    EFQM Excellence Model and, 113–14
    EFQM Excellence Model enablers for, 114–22
    EFQM Excellence Model results for, 123–25
    fault/failure focus, 106–7
    group, 19, 21
    group members, 106
    group summary, 128–29
    as improvers of quality, 102–3
    information needed from others, 128
    information that others need, 127
    introducing, 101–5
    key performance results, 124–25
    leadership, 114
    manufacturing-based view, 107
    measurement framework, 119–20
    motivation and appreciation, 118–19
    nonspecialist, 115–16
    partnerships and resources, 119
    people, 115–19
    people results, 123
    policy and strategy, 114–15
    processes, 119–22
    product-based view, 107
    quality framework, 113–25
    quality impacts, 111
    quality viewpoint, 106–13
    reporting process, 122
    society results, 123–24
    specialist, 115–16
    team organization, 117–18
    transcendent view, 107
    types of, 116
    See also Groups
Mind Mapping, 262
MIP, 27
Monitoring/evaluation, 241–44
    evaluation timing, 242
    ongoing software, 242–44
    process, 244
    SDLC/SMLC evaluation, 241–42
    See also Postdelivery
Motivation studies, 256–57
Motivation Survey, 87

Multisite delivery, 224–25
Myers-Briggs Type Indicator (MBTI), 253–54
    16 types, 254
    contrasting pair types, 253
    defined, 27
    feedback, 34
    See also Communication styles

N

Nonfunctional attributes, 174
    delivery planning, 176
    importance of, 175
    selection of, 175

O

Operational Acceptance Test (OAT), 141
Organization, this book, xx–xxii
Outline plan, 177

P

Partnerships
    development, 6
    organizational, 60
Partnerships and resources, 8–9
    for builders, 90–91
    for customers, 43
    defined, 8–9
    for managers, 80
    for measurers, 119
    for supporters, 142
    See also Enablers
People, 8
    for builders, 89–90
    communication improvement techniques, 26, 27
    for customers, 41–42
    defined, 8
    for managers, 59–60
    for measurers, 115–19
    for supporters, 139–42
    See also Enablers
People CMM® (PCMM®), 12, 13
People results
    for builders, 93–94
    for customers, 43–44
    defined, 9
    for managers, 66
    for measurers, 123
    for supporters, 144–45
    See also Results
Perfective maintenance, 239
Performance, 176
    acceptance criteria, 176
    prototype, 177
    See also Key performance results
Personal Software Process (PSP), 11, 12
    defined, 12
    development, 12
    intergroup relationships, 24–25
    process emphasis, 24
PERT charts, 64
Phased waterfall, 197–99
Policies
    building activities, 88
    defined, 58
    managers setting, 58
    rules translation, 139
Policy and strategy
    for builders, 88
    for customers, 41
    defined, 8
    for managers, 58–59
    for measurers, 114–15
    for supporters, 139
    See also Enablers
Postdelivery, 156–57, 229–46
    activities, 233–44
    change making, 236–41
    conclusion, 244–46
    COTS package (customer installation), 230
    defined, 229
    description, 229–31
    entry criteria, 233
    entry criteria example, 233
    exit criteria example, 245
    exit from, 244
    IT infrastructure and service management activities, 234–36
    in life span stage diagram, 230
    monitoring/evaluation, 241–44
    system developed in-house, 230–31
    system with periodic updates, 231
    teamwork techniques, 243
    third-party developed system, 231
    viewpoints, 231–33
    See also Software system life span
Problem management, 235
Problems
    analysis cycle, 167
    group contributions to understanding, 168–70
    likelihood, 169
    sketching pictures of, 262
    solution decision, 168–70
    solutions parameters/constraints, 170
    statements, 167
    understanding, 165–68
    view of, 168

Index

Processes
    for builders, 91–92
    for customers, 43
    defined, 9
    for managers, 61–65
    for measurers, 119–22
    for supporters, 142–43
    See also Enablers
Product-based quality view
    builders, 81
    definition, 3
    measurers, 107
    supporters, 135
Project audits, 112
Prototyping, 261–62
    types of, 262
    uses, 261

Q

Quality
    activities damaging quality, 110
    builder viewpoint, 80–86
    costs, 110
    customer viewpoint, 38–39
    defining, 1–5
    delivery viewpoints, 219–21
    human factors and, 2
    impacts, 85
    importance, 1–15
    improvers of, 102–3
    management, 5, 56
    managers, 112
    manager viewpoint, 53–54
    manufacturing-based definition, 3
    measurers viewpoint, 106–13
    planning for, 55
    postdelivery viewpoints, 231–33
    product-based definition, 3
    SDLC viewpoints, 184–86
    stakeholders for, 79
    start-up views, 163
    supporters viewpoint, 134–36
    transcendent view, 13
    user-based view, 3
    value-based view, 3–4, 13
    viewpoint differences, 22–24
    views of, 14
Quality assurance (QA)
    activities, 55
    carrying out, 103, 105
    experts, 64, 103
    external audit, 122
    internal audit, 122
    need for, 101–2
    rules of thumb, 121
    sources, 269
    tasks, 63, 103
    team independence, 117
    teams, 21, 106
    training requirements, 115
Quality control (QC)
    activity timing, 103
    carrying out, 103, 105
    checks, 55
    experts, 64, 103
    forms of, 102
    need for, 101–2
    processes, 5
    rules of thumb, 121
    sources, 269
    tasks, 63
    team independence, 117
    teams, 21, 106
    training requirements, 115
Quality framework
    builders, 86–95
    customers, 39–45
    managers, 54–68
    measurers, 113–25
    supporters, 136–46
Quality Management System (QMS), 274
Quality planning documents, 273–75
    brevity, 279
    families, 275
    list of, 273
    templates, 275–78
    test, 280

R

Reliability, 177
Reporting
    graphics, improving, 267–69
    planning, 71
    process, 70–73, 122
    templates, 280–82
    See also Communications
Requirements
    definition errors, 105
    QA/QC training, 115
    SDLC, 184, 192–93
Responsibility matrix, 220
Results, 9–10
    for builders, 92–95
    customer, 9, 43, 92–93, 123, 143–44
    for customers, 43–45
    key performance, 10, 44–45, 95, 124–25, 146
    for managers, 65–68
    for measurers, 123–25
    people, 9, 43–44, 93–94, 123, 144–45

Results (continued)
    society, 9–10, 44, 94, 123–24, 145
    for supporters, 143–46
    See also EFQM Excellence Model
Return on investment (ROI), 53
Reviews
    audits, 266
    guidelines, 267
    inspection, 266
    management, 266
    technical/peer, 266
    techniques, 266–67
    training, 267
    walkthrough, 27, 266
    work contract, 178
Rich Picturing, 262

S

Scorecards
    defined, 67
    illustrated, 68
    measures, 67–68
    quality balanced, 69
    variations, 67
SDLC entry criteria, 186–90
    checklist, 187
    excessive, 188
    incorrect, 188
    insufficient, 189
    not defined, 187
    not met, 187–89
    tailoring, 189
    See also Software development life cycle (SDLC)
SDLC exit criteria, 208–11
    example, 209
    following detailed acceptance test, 208
    not defined, 209–10
    not met, 210
    not set, 210
    tailored, example, 211
    tailoring, 210
    See also Software development life cycle (SDLC)
SDLC models, 195–204
    advantages/disadvantages, 198
    evolutionary, 198
    examples, 198
    incremental, 199–200
    iterative/spiral, 200–203
    quality views and, 204–8
    V-model, 203–4
    waterfall, 196–99
    W-model, 198, 204

See also Software development life cycle (SDLC)
Security management, 235
Self-installation, 223–24
Service-delivery specialists, 133
Service-level agreements (SLAs), 138
Service-level management, 235
Silver bullet life cycle, 234
Single-site delivery, 224
SMART acceptance criteria, 177
Society results
    for builders, 94
    for customers, 44
    defined, 9–10
    for mangers, 66–67
    for measurers, 123–24
    for supporters, 145
    See also Results
Software
    acquisition of, 182
    deployment, 132
    games, 38
    optimization, 133
    products identification, 183
    protection, 132
    purpose of, 31
    supportable, 134–35
    as tool, 32
    updates/changes, 133
Software and Systems Quality Framework (SSQF), 14, 113
Software development life cycle (SDLC), 35, 155–56, 181–212
    activities, 190–95
    build, 184, 193–94
    builders and, 80
    change examples, 185
    change management, 183, 191–92
    conclusion, 211–12
    customer involvement and, 45
    defined, 154, 181–82
    definition of, 182
    description, 181–84
    design, 184, 193
    entry/exit points within, 195
    evaluating, 241–42
    exit from, 208–11
    in life span stage diagram, 183
    managers as villains, 51
    no start-up stage and, 190
    planning and monitoring, 183, 190–91
    purpose, 182
    requirements, 184, 192–93
    in software system life span, 154
    task summary, 183–84

Index

teams, 185, 191
teamwork techniques, 202
testing, 102, 184, 194–95
viewpoints, 184–86
See also SDLC entry criteria; SDLC exit criteria; SDLC models
Software engineers. *See* Builders
Software-maintenance life cycles (SMLCs), 140, 236
    evaluating, 241–42
    software projects as, 236
Software-maintenance specialists, 134
Software quality. *See* Quality
Software system life span, 153–59
    change cycles, 157
    delivery, 156, 215–26
    development, 155–56, 181–212
    entry/exit criteria between stages, 157–58
    postdelivery, 156–57, 229–46
    quality importance, 158
    quality viewpoint changes across, 158–59
    stages, 154
    stages illustration, 155
    start-up, 153, 155, 161–79
SSADM, 262
Start-up, 153, 155, 161–79
    activities, 165–78
    constraints/parameters setup, 170
    description, 161–63
    entry criteria, 164–65
    exit criteria, 179
    exit from, 178–79
    in life-cycle stage diagram, 162
    next stage agreement, 170–71
    problem/idea solution decision, 168–70
    problem/idea understanding, 165–68
    task summary, 163
    teamwork view, 164
    techniques summary, 166–67
    viewpoints, 163–64
    work contracting, 171–78
    See also Software system life span
Strategies
    for managers, 58
    for measurers, 114–15
    See also Policy and strategy
Supporters, 131–50
    change involvement, 240
    communication with other groups, 146–47
    customer results, 143–44
    delivery and, 220
    EFQM Excellence Model and, 136–38
    EFQM Excellence Model enablers for, 138–43
    EFQM Excellence Model results for, 143–46
    group, 19, 22
    group composition, 133–34
    group summary, 147–48
    information for other groups, 148
    information needed by others, 149
    interpersonal skills, 141–42
    introducing, 131–33
    key performance results, 146
    knowledge, 132
    leadership, 138–39
    management skills, 141
    measurement techniques, 141
    partnerships and resources, 142
    people, 139–42
    people results, 144–45
    policy and strategy, 139
    problem view, 140
    processes, 142–43
    product-based view, 135
    quality framework, 136–46
    quality viewpoint, 134–36
    service-support specialists, 133
    skills, 141
    society results, 145
    too little involvement, 132
    transcendent view, 136
    user-based view, 135–36
    See also Groups

T

Taken-for-granted assumption, 249
Teams
    defining, 19–22
    in disunity, 17–19
    help-desk, 137
    information needs, 278–79
    installation, 216
    organization, 117–18
    personalities, 250
    plan layout, 62
    QA, 21
    QC, 21
    roles, 250–51
    SDLC, 185, 191
    strengths/weaknesses, 250
Team Software Process (TSP), 7, 11, 12
    defined, 12
    development, 12
    intergroup relationships, 24–25
Teamwork
    fostering, 246
    start-up view, 164
    techniques during SDLC, 202
    techniques in delivery, 222
    techniques to aid postdelivery, 243

Technical/peer review, 266
Test automation specialists, 112
Testers
　feedback for, 118
　skill variety, 118
　types of, 116
　See also Measurers
Testing, 102
　changes, 240–41
　code execution, 194
　elements, 195
　SDLC, 184, 194–95
　user-acceptance, 112
　without written specification, 109
Test managers, 112
Third-party customers, 35–38
　custom-made system, 35–36
　package/COTS, 36–38
TQMI, 165, 260
Transactional analysis, 257–58
　defined, 258
　ego states, 258

U

Usability, 176
User-acceptance testing, 112
User-based quality view
　builders and, 81
　definition, 3, 81
　measurers and, 108
　supporters, 135–36

V

Value-based quality view
　builders and, 81–82
　definition, 3–4, 81–82
　measurers and, 108
V-model, 203–4
　advantages/disadvantages, 198
　defined, 203
　example, 198
　illustrated, 205
　See also SDLC models

W

Walkthroughs, 27, 266
Waterfall model, 196–99
　advantages/disadvantages, 198
　big bang, 196–97, 199
　examples, 198
　phased, 197–99
　when to use, 199
　See also SDLC models
Weaver triangle
　defined, 27
　illustrated, 173
　uses, 172
W-model, 198, 204
Work
　acceptance criteria, 174–77
　aims/objectives, 172
　constraints for, 173
　contracting, 171–78
　contract review, 178
　outline plan, 177

Recent Titles in the Artech House Computing Library

Achieving Software Quality through Teamwork, Isabel Evans

Action Focused Assessment for Software Process Improvement, Tim Kasse

Advanced ANSI SQL Data Modeling and Structure Processing, Michael M. David

Advanced Database Technology and Design, Mario Piattini and Oscar Díaz, editors

Agent-Based Software Development, Michael Luck, Ronald Ashri, and Mark d'Inverno

Building Reliable Component-Based Software Systems, Ivica Crnkovic and Magnus Larsson, editors

Business Process Implementation for IT Professionals and Managers, Robert B. Walford

Data Modeling and Design for Today's Architectures, Angelo Bobak

Developing Secure Distributed Systems with CORBA, Ulrich Lang and Rudolf Schreiner

Discovering Real Business Requirements for Software Project Success, Robin F. Goldsmith

Future Codes: Essays in Advanced Computer Technology and the Law, Curtis E. A. Karnow

Global Distributed Applications with Windows® DNA, Enrique Madrona

A Guide to Software Configuration Management, Alexis Leon

Guide to Standards and Specifications for Designing Web Software, Stan Magee and Leonard L. Tripp

Implementing and Integrating Product Data Management and Software Configuration, Ivica Crnkovic, Ulf Asklund, and Annita Persson Dahlqvist

Internet Commerce Development, Craig Standing

Knowledge Management Strategy and Technology, Richard F. Bellaver and John M. Lusa, editors

Managing Computer Networks: A Case-Based Reasoning Approach, Lundy Lewis

Metadata Management for Information Control and Business Success, Guy Tozer

Multimedia Database Management Systems, Guojun Lu

Practical Guide to Software Quality Management, Second Edition, John W. Horch

Practical Insight into CMMI®, Tim Kasse

Practical Process Simulation Using Object-Oriented Techniques and C++, José Garrido

A Practitioner's Guide to Software Test Design, Lee Copeland

Risk-Based E-Business Testing, Paul Gerrard and Neil Thompson

Secure Messaging with PGP and S/MIME, Rolf Oppliger

Software Fault Tolerance Techniques and Implementation, Laura L. Pullum

Software Verification and Validation for Practitioners and Managers, Second Edition, Steven R. Rakitin

Strategic Software Production with Domain-Oriented Reuse, Paolo Predonzani, Giancarlo Succi, and Tullio Vernazza

Successful Evolution of Software Systems, Hongji Yang and Martin Ward

Systematic Process Improvement Using ISO 9001:2000 and CMMI®, Boris Mutafelija and Harvey Stromberg

Systematic Software Testing, Rick D. Craig and Stefan P. Jaskiel

Systems Modeling for Business Process Improvement, David Bustard, Peter Kawalek, and Mark Norris, editors

Testing and Quality Assurance for Component-Based Software, Jerry Zeyu Gao, H. -S. Jacob Tsao, and Ye Wu

User-Centered Information Design for Improved Software Usability, Pradeep Henry

Workflow Modeling: Tools for Process Improvement and Application Development, Alec Sharp and Patrick McDermott

For further information on these and other Artech House titles, including previously considered out-of-print books now available through our In-Print-Forever® (IPF®) program, contact:

Artech House
685 Canton Street
Norwood, MA 02062
Phone: 781-769-9750
Fax: 781-769-6334
e-mail: artech@artechhouse.com

Artech House
46 Gillingham Street
London SW1V 1AH UK
Phone: +44 (0)20 7596-8750
Fax: +44 (0)20 7630-0166
e-mail: artech-uk@artechhouse.com

Find us on the World Wide Web at:
www.artechhouse.com

TUNED OUT

Engaging the 21st Century Learner

PEARSON

PEARSON

Copyright © 2011 Pearson Canada Inc., Toronto, Ontario.

All rights reserved. This publication is protected by copyright and permission should be obtained from the publisher prior to any prohibited reproduction, storage in a retrieval system, or transmission in any form or by any means, electronic, mechanical, photocopying, recording, or likewise.

Portions of this publication may be reproduced under licence from Access Copyright, or with the express written permission of Pearson Canada Inc., or as permitted by law. Permission to reproduce material from this resource is restricted to the purchasing school.

The information and activities presented in this work have been carefully edited and reviewed. However, the publisher shall not be liable for any damages resulting, in whole or in part, from the reader's use of this material.

Brand names and logos that appear in photographs provide readers with a sense of real-world application and are in no way intended to endorse specific products.

Permission to reprint copyright material is gratefully acknowledged. Every effort was made to trace ownership of copyright material, secure permission, and accurately acknowledge its use. For information regarding permissions, please contact the Permissions Department through www.pearsoncanada.ca.

Feedback on this publication can be sent to editorialfeedback@pearsoned.com.

Pearson Canada Inc.
26 Prince Andrew Place
Don Mills, ON M3C 2T8
Customer Service: 1-800-361-6128

ISBN-13: 978-0-13-802013-2

Vice-President, Publishing:
Mark Cobham

Vice-President, Marketing and Professional Field Services:
Anne-Marie Scullion

Research and Communications Manager:
Chris Allen

Managing Editor:
Joanne Close

Project Editor:
David MacDonald

Senior Production Editor:
Lisa Dimson

Copy Editor: Kate Revington

Proofreader: Linda Szostak

Senior Production Coordinator: Louise Avery

Composition: David Cheung

Permissions Research:
Indu Arora

Photo Research:
Jamie Whittla

Cover and Interior Design:
Alex Li

Illustrator: David Cheung

Cover Image Credit:
© Digital Vision/
Getty Images

e-Learning Team

Publisher, e-Learning:
Hélène Fournier

Managing Editor, e-Learning: Kelly Ronan

e-Learning Resource Developer: Dalton Miller

Videographer: SpaceRace

1 2 3 4 5 TCP 14 13 12 11 10
Printed and bound in Canada.

Contents

Acknowledgments   vii
Reviewers and Case Study Contributors   ix
Credits   x

About This Book and Website   xi

Seeking   1

1 Terms of Engagement   2
Defining Engagement   5
Measuring Engagement   6
What We Know About Student Disengagement   8
What We Know About Teacher Disengagement   12

2 15 300 Hours   15
A Mission Statement for the 21st Century   20
Visions Aren't Just for Psychics   24
Rough Waters Ahead   26

Competence   29

3 Below the Surface   30
Life in the Real World   31
Opposites Thinking   35
The Roots of Engagement   37
21st Century Needs   41
Competent Teachers   44
Students (and Their Teachers?) Need…   46

4 Developing Learners 51

Reward Less, Celebrate More 52
Help Students Set Personal Goals 54
Connect Effort and Success 58
Focus on Relevance 62
Broaden Your Definition of Intelligence 66
Sometimes Let Them Choose 70

Creativity 75

5 Searching the Haystack 76

On the Job 78
Creative Teachers 82
Beliefs 84

6 Practical Creativity 87

It's Not That There Are No Rules 88
Not Just for English Class 90
5 Ways to Get Lots of Ideas 94
Solving the Tough Ones 96
Worth a Thousand Words 100
Put It on Paper 104
In Your Mind's Eye 106
Hands-on Learning 108
Interdisciplinary Study 110

Community 117

7 A Bundle of Sticks 118

Networked Teens 120
Relating to Adolescents 123
The Classroom Community 125
Professional Learning Communities 127

8 Webs of Relationship 129

Vanquish Fear and Negative Stress   130
Checking In   134
Koinonia   138
Demise of the Lone Ranger   144
Just Beyond the School Walls   148
Online Communities   152

Context 157

9 21st Century Rat Parks 158

Workplaces and Schools   162
Adolescents, Adults, and Technology   163
Technology in Our Schools   165
Technology, Engagement, and Learning   166
The Future Is Around the Corner   171
"Digital Immigrant" Teachers   173

10 Environments for Learning 175

Predictable Classrooms   176
Intervening with At-Risk Students   178
ICT Literacy   180
Your Professional Learning Network   184
A Tale of Two Districts   186
School Design   190

Challenge 195

11 Hard Fun 196

Flow   197
Video Games and Challenge   199
The Purpose of Sustained Engagement   202
Engaging Instruction   203
You Get What You Expect   205
Change-Challenged Brains   207

12 Minds-on Learning 209

Change of Plans 210
Release Gradually 214
En Route to Expertise 218
If It's Good Enough for Medical Students... 220
Curious Minds 226
Differentiating for Success 230
The Power of Ideas 232

Finding 239

13 Courageous Together 240

Collaborative IQ 241
Wrestling Alligators 245
The Messenger Matters 248
Crafting a Vision 250

14 The Road Ahead 253

References 261
Index 268
About the Author 275

Acknowledgments

I bought an iPhone around the time I was thinking about what to write in these acknowledgments. I signed up for a cell phone plan that allows unlimited free phone calls to be placed to and from my choice of five numbers. If you have one of those plans, you know you have to think carefully about who you are going to choose. This is especially true if you travel a lot, as I do, and want to remain connected to people whose company you really enjoy—people who make a positive difference in your life.

Two of the five phone numbers on my favourites list belong to David MacDonald, Project Editor for this resource, and Joanne Close, Managing Editor of Professional Learning at Pearson. David has stellar editorial skills and even better ideas. After having had the pleasure of working on four books together, I can't imagine writing a book for which David isn't the editor. Joanne provided unflagging support and advocacy—both of which were particularly important as the three of us worked to create a book and website that we hope you will find fresh, inspiring, and useful, regardless of your role in education. This resource is different from my previous books, in large part because David and Joanne are creative people who enjoy new challenges. It was great fun to work on this book and website together.

There are many other people at Pearson who played an important role in the development of this resource, including Chris Allen, Research and Communications Manager for Professional Learning, and Mark Cobham, Vice-President of Publishing. *Tuned Out* is a better resource because of their understanding of the needs of educators who will use it. Thanks are also extended to Marty Keast, President of Pearson's School Division, and Allan Reynolds, President and CEO of Pearson Canada. Although I wasn't involved with them on a daily basis, this resource would not have been possible if Marty and Allan weren't leaders with a keen interest in 21st century learning and enthusiastic supporters of my work.

In this, my sixth professional book, I want to offer a special thank you to Anne-Marie Scullion, Vice-President, Marketing and Professional Field Services. It was Anne-Marie who saw the potential in my first book—*Start Where They Are: Differentiating for Success with the Young Adolescent*—when it was little more than a title and an idea. Anne-Marie inspires, challenges, and encourages me. I value her insight, intelligence, and friendship.

Production editor Lisa Dimson worked on my last three books and I was delighted when she signed on for this one—once again, she was an invaluable part of the team. To copyeditor Kate Revington and proofreader Linda Szostak, I extend my thanks for their meticulous work.

Tuned Out is both a book and a website. The design, production, and website development teams did a fantastic job, for which I am grateful.

Following these acknowledgments, you will find a list of reviewers and case study contributors. Good reviewers provide an author with feedback that improves the final product, and this group certainly did that. The case study contributors whose stories are in these pages were generous with their time and honest in their reflections about what worked well in their classrooms, schools, and districts, and what didn't. My sincere appreciation is extended to all of these educators for sharing their work.

Last, but far from least, my parents have a permanent "top dog" spot both on my "fave five" phone list and in my heart. I have been engaged in learning all my life because of their influence.

Reviewers and Case Study Contributors

Reviewers

Karen Bauer
Secondary English Teacher
School District 2, Riverview, New Brunswick

Cindy Coffin
Assistant Superintendent—Learning Services
Greater Saskatoon Catholic Schools, Saskatchewan

Risha Golby
Vice Principal—Student Support Services
School District 42, Maple Ridge—
Pitt Meadows, British Columbia

Dr. Jean Hoeft
Executive Director
Calgary Regional Consortium, Alberta

Patricia Jamison
Coordinator of Curriculum and Instruction
Saskatoon Public School District, Saskatchewan

Lynn M. Landry
Consultant, Literacy Assessment & Reporting
Halifax Regional School Board, Nova Scotia

Michael Muise
Vice Principal
Algonquin and Lakeshore Catholic District
School Board, Ontario

Maureen Taylor
Superintendent of Schools
Saskatchewan Rivers School Division, Saskatchewan

Jerry Thibeau
Facilitator, Curriculum Implementation
Halifax Regional School Board, Nova Scotia

Dan Trainor
Principal
Niagara Catholic District School Board, Ontario

Case Study Contributors

Annalee Adair, Ottawa, Ontario

Sherron Burns, Battleford, Saskatchewan

Maggie Boss, Mississauga, Ontario

Eric Boutin, Longueuil, Québec

Zoe Branigan-Pipe, Hamilton, Ontario

Cheryl Carr, Scarborough, Ontario

François Couture, Longueuil, Québec

Jason Crean, Western Springs, Illinois

Jeannie Everett, Calgary, Alberta

Rebecca Frise, Cobourg, Ontario

Melanie Greenan, Mississauga, Ontario

Jonathan Lewis, Maple, Ontario

Bernie Ottenheimer, St. John's, Newfoundland and Labrador

Joanna Panagiotakakos, Toronto, Ontario

Mike Poluk, Sault Ste. Marie, Ontario

Mavis Sacher, Rocky Mountain House, Alberta

Cindy Sargeant, Peterborough, Ontario

Leyton Schnellert, Richmond, British Columbia

Karen Sinoski, Prince Albert, Saskatchewan

Tania Sterling, Maple, Ontario

Susan Strutz, Baraboo, Wisconsin

David Vandergugten, Maple Ridge—
Pitt Meadows, British Columbia

Dr. Steven Van Zoost, Windsor, Nova Scotia

Graham Whisen, Brampton, Ontario

Nicole Widdess, Richmond, British Columbia

Carmella Wilson, Burlington, Ontario

Marla Zupan, Toronto, Ontario

Credits

1 photo: © iStockphoto/AVTG; **5** excerpt (Willms et al.): Reprinted by permission of Canadian Education Association via Access Copyright; **9** graph, figure, and quote: Reprinted by permission of Canadian Education Association via Access Copyright; **10** graph: Reproduced with the permission of the Minister of Public Works and Government Services, 2010, and courtesy of Human Resources and Skills Development Canada; **16** excerpt (Wood): Reprinted with permission from Heinemann Publishing; **25** Reprinted (Wood) with permission from Heinemann Publishing; **29** photo: © iStockphoto/Mark Evans; excerpt from poem: Reprinted with permission from Dundurn Press Ltd. Copyright 1979; **43** photo: © imagesource/First Light; **63** photo: © Gregory G. Dimijian, M.D./First Light; **66** figure: Permission granted by Mensa International Ltd. on behalf of Dr. Abbie Salny. Material copyright Dr. Abbie Salny; **72** photo: Dean Mitchell/Shutterstock.com; **73** photo: © Gemstone Images/First Light; **75** photo: © iStockphoto/ryasick; **79–80** From Tapscott, D. (2009). *Grown up digital: How the net generation is changing your world.* (pp.160–69). Toronto: McGraw-Hill. Reprinted by permission of McGraw-Hill Companies; **80** quote: From Tapscott, D. (2009). *Grown up digital: How the net generation is changing your world.* (p.159). Toronto: McGraw-Hill. Reprinted by permission of McGraw-Hill Companies; **81** photo: © ERIN SIEGAL/Reuters/Corbis; **83, 93, 94** excerpt, figure, and quote: From A WHACK ON THE SIDE OF THE HEAD by Roger von Oech. Copyright © 1983, 1990, 1998 by Roger von Oech. By permission of Grand Central Publishing; **94, 95, 98, 104** excerpts: From THINKERTOYS: A HANDBOOK OF CREATIVE-THINKING TECHNIQUES 2ND EDITION by Michael Michalko, copyright © 1991, 2006 by Michael Michalko. Used by permission of Ten Speed Press, an imprint of the Crown Publishing Group, a division of Random House Inc.; **103** photo: National Archives of Canada (PA-139073)/The Canadian Press; **113** photo: © NitroCephal 2010 Used under license from Shutterstock.com; **114** photo: Justin Wonnacott; **117** photo: © iStockphoto/Daniel Fowler; **120** photo: © iStockphoto/Andrey Prokhorov; **154** photo: © imagesource/First Light; **155** photo: ©Toria 2010 Used under license from Shutterstock.com; **157** photo: © iStockphoto/Dirk Freder; **159–160** (Willms et al.) Reprinted by permission of Canadian Education Association via Access Copyright; **161** From Tapscott, D. (2009). *Grown up digital: How the net generation is changing your world.* (p.148). Toronto: McGraw-Hill. Reprinted by permission of McGraw-Hill Companies; **164** photo: © iStockphoto/RickBL; **180, 181** quote and chart: *Redefining literacy 2.0.* 2nd ed, D.F. Warlick. Copyright © 2009 by Linworth Books. Reproduced with permission of ABC-CLIO, LLC.; **190** quote (Wood): Reprinted with permission from Heinemann Publishing; **191** excerpt: From *Curriculum 21: Essential Education for a Changing World* (pp. 63, 70, 78), by Heidi Hayes Jacobs, Alexandria, VA: ASCD. © 2010 by ASCD. Reprinted with permission. Learn more about ASCD at www.ascd.org; **195** photo: © iStockphoto/nicholas belton; **200** photo: © Charlie Chu/courtesy Jenova Chen; quote (Willms et al.): Reprinted by permission of Canadian Education Association via Access Copyright; **204** figure: Copyright © 1998 Mihaly Csikszentmihalyi. Reprinted by permission of Basic Books, a member of the Perseus Books Group; **214** poem: *From No Voyage and Other Poems* (published by J. M. Dent and Sons, Ltd., London, in 1963; published by Houghton Mifflin in 1965) by Mary Oliver, copyright 1959, 1960, 1961, 1962, 1963, 1964, 1965 by Mary Oliver. Reprinted by permission of the author; **224** excerpt: From Goodlad J. (2004). *A place called school* (20th anniversary ed.) (p. 230). Toronto: McGraw-Hill. Reprinted by permission of McGraw-Hill Companies; **232** *High School II* is available from Zipporah Films at www.zipporah.com; **233** excerpt: From Goodlad J. (2004). *A place called school* (20th anniversary ed.) (p. 229). Toronto: McGraw-Hill. Reprinted by permission of McGraw-Hill Companies; **239** photo: © iStockphoto/Aimin Tang; **242, 247** excerpts and figure: From *Educators as Learners: Creating a Professional Learning Community in Your School* (pp. 36, 42), by Michael S. Castleberry & Penelope J. Wald, Alexandria, VA: ASCD. © 2000 by ASCD. Reprinted with permission. Learn more about ASCD at www.ascd.org; **243** photo: © iStockphoto/Damir Cudic; **260** photo: © Bartlomiej K. Kwieciszewski 2010 Used under license from Shutterstock.com.

About This Book and Website

There are seven sections in this resource. The first section defines the term *engagement* and considers the issues of both student and teacher disengagement. The last section offers practical tips for achieving a classroom, school, or district where engagement is a characteristic shared by all.

The first and last sections bookend the five remaining sections. Each of these sections deals with an aspect of schooling where, I believe, we can make a positive difference to student engagement.

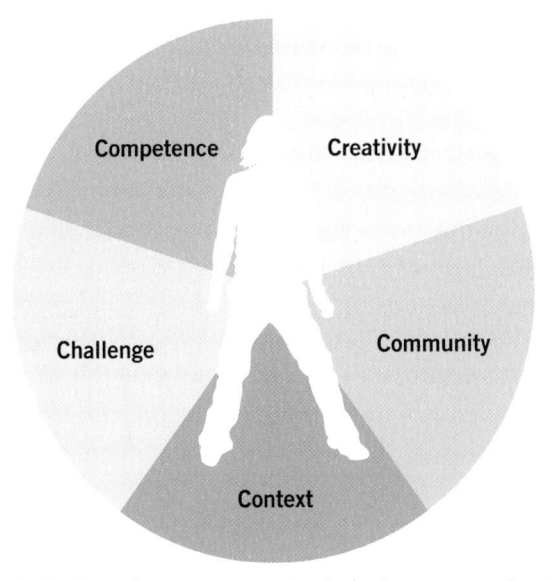

The actions we take in these five areas promote student engagement and achievement.

The first chapter in each of the five middle sections will help you clarify the results you are working toward. I describe ways in which students and the world are different in the 21st century, and ways in which they are just the same as always. We will look at the implications of these changes to your beliefs and your professional practice.

A central premise of this resource is that if something is necessary to student engagement, it is equally important to teacher engagement.

Therefore, for each aspect of schooling that affects student engagement, there is a corresponding focus on actions you can take to maintain and enhance teacher engagement.

The second chapter in each of the five middle sections offers suggestions for actions you can take in your classroom, school, or district. Some of these actions are for your students, some are for classroom teachers, and some are for facilitators of adult learning—school administrators, consultants, and teacher leaders. (The icon shown in the margin indicates material of particular interest to facilitators of adult learning.)

The *Tuned Out* website (www.pearsoncanada.ca/tunedout) offers a wealth of useful material, along with an electronic version of the text. To access the website, use your personal access code, provided inside the front cover of this book. (The access code is not provided in the e-text.)

Throughout the book, watch for icons that alert you to related content in one of the following three sections of the website:

Conversations

Conversation icon—a blog where I share some of my thoughts and experiences, and invite you to respond to topics in the book. Brief "Video Bytes" introducing the five sections of the book that deal with aspects of schooling are also provided.

Resources

Resources icon—a variety of resources, including reproducible line masters. For a summary of all activities, see the *Tuned Out* Activity Summary in Chapter 2 of the Resources section.

Research

Research icon—book reviews, research, and useful web resources

Under each icon, you'll find the title of the related website material. To locate this material on the website, do the following:

1. Click on the section of the website identified by the icon.
2. On the menu of items in that section, click on the title given under the icon in this book.

If you are reading the electronic version of the text, click on an icon to go directly to the relevant website content.

Seeking

Two roads diverged in a wood, and I—

I took the one less travelled by,

And that has made all the difference.

—*From "The Road Not Taken" by Robert Frost*

1 Terms of Engagement

We teachers are a hard-working and dedicated bunch. We devote countless hours to meeting the challenge of crafting lessons that are content rich and pedagogically effective, as well as relevant and engaging. Then, we plan how to deliver those lessons with energy, enthusiasm, and that hard-to-define but key ingredient: personal style.

But what happens when all our efforts are met with blank stares and disinterested faces? The more resistant and disengaged students are, the more we pull out all the stops. These are the times when professional entertainers have nothing on us. Like comedians in front of an apathetic audience, we are prepared to do whatever it takes to get some kind of response—a glimmer of interest, or even just a laugh. When we succeed in engaging students, we surf the wave of an adrenaline high. When our best efforts fail, we are left feeling physically and emotionally wrung out.

The problem is that teaching as performance art is not sustainable class after class, day after day. This reality is especially true when the best of who we are and what we have to offer is not enough. Through their indifference, disdain, and disrespect—or through their absences—students tell us that we have been judged and found wanting.

©2004 ZITS Partnership. Distributed by King Features Syndicate.

In the last few years, I have worked with thousands of teachers in professional learning workshops. Whether I've been asked to speak on differentiated instruction, assessment and evaluation, or some other topic, it's clear that teachers are hoping I'll provide solutions to the problems they face with student disengagement. In conversations before, during, and after workshops, the same questions come up with increasing frequency: *What on earth is going on with today's students? And what can I do about it?*

To address the significant challenges posed by highly disengaged, resistant, and struggling learners, we need to choose an approach, a direction, a path. I am reminded of Robert Frost's poem "The Road Not Taken," in which a traveller has to decide which of two roads to take. As in the poem, the road we choose can make "all the difference."

So, what choices do we have?

One road is to accept the argument that students have changed, but not for the better. Proponents of this position tell us that students today can't read, can't write, and can't think; that they lack basic skills as well as basic values, including respect and any kind of work ethic. The solution, according to this perspective, is to hold the line on the erosion of civilization; to demand that students reach our high and exacting standards. We should support students who want to learn and insist that students who resist learning be held accountable for their decisions. Students must learn to defer immediate gratification for a future that we can see and they cannot. The slogan for this position might be, "Trust us because we are your teachers."

Another road is to accept the argument that students have changed, but their teachers have not. Proponents of this position often make us feel, quite unintentionally, that we are antiquated, out of touch, and blinded by a determination to enact schooling exactly as it was experienced by us and other successful people from the last 200 years. The solution, according to many proponents of this perspective, is nothing less than wholesale change, often beginning with the embracing of new technologies. If only we did all of our teaching through blogs, wikis, and iPods; if only our students were engaged in collaborative social justice projects with people from around the globe, all would be well. The slogan for this position might be, "Get with the times—or get out of the way."

> The test of a first-rate intelligence is the ability to hold two opposing ideas in mind at the same time and still retain the ability to function. One should, for example, be able to see that things are hopeless yet be determined to make them otherwise.
>
> —*F. Scott Fitzgerald*

These positions may be extreme, but I don't think they are overstated. On any given day, an interaction with a disengaged and reluctant learner can leave us feeling frustrated with the student (the first road) or ineffectual (the second road).

I am disheartened by these extreme positions. When I was growing up my dad always said, "When faced with two choices, look for the third." In the case of student engagement, I believe that we can use our creativity and imagination, our knowledge and integrity, to forge a third road: the road of moderation.

Moderation is often viewed as a compromise position, what some call "the best bad choice available." But I'm not interested in compromise. I want nothing less than for all learners—students *and* teachers—to demonstrate sustained engagement in challenging and meaningful intellectual work. For teachers and students alike, the ideal is to be creative, flexible learners who know how to make necessary changes in the manner and at the pace that works for them as individuals.

To entice you to travel this road of moderation, I am going to do my best to convince you that while students may have changed and the world is certainly different from when many of us attended school, neither our students nor the world are unrecognizable. We possess the knowledge, experience, wisdom, and heart to embrace all learners where they are and to engage them in learning that honours the best of the past, prepares them for the future, and yet remains relevant today.

Conversations
Choosing a Road

The Road Less Travelled

Do you agree with my descriptions of the two roads, or am I overstating the case? How would classrooms be different if more teachers and students ventured down the perhaps less-travelled road of moderation? You might want to discuss this question face to face in your local book-study group or online in the blog on the *Tuned Out* website. (For information about accessing the website and an explanation of margin icons, see page xii.)

Resources
Blank Frayer Diagram

Before You Go On

Frayer diagrams are a useful and quick form of pre-assessment. By having students complete a Frayer diagram for a key concept, you will be able to quickly ascertain their understanding of that concept. A blank Frayer diagram appears in the Resources section of the website, if you'd like to try your hand at defining student engagement before you read further. You can then check a completed Frayer diagram for *student engagement* in the website's Research section.

Research
What Is Student Engagement?

Defining Engagement

Think about common uses of the word *engagement*. You can be engaged to be married, engaged to fulfill the terms of a contract, or engaged in battle with an enemy. In all of these examples, engagement is about interaction. The same is true of student engagement.

Consider, for example, this definition of student engagement:

> *The extent to which students identify with and value schooling outcomes, have a sense of belonging at school, participate in academic and non-academic activities, strive to meet the formal requirements of schooling, and make a serious personal investment in learning.*
>
> (Willms, Friesen, & Milton, 2009, p. 7)

Each descriptor in this definition describes an interaction between a student and a person, structure, or activity. When we speak of student engagement, we are always talking about *relationship* to someone or something. Motivation, while a related concept, differs from engagement in that it describes a student's internal processes, such as reasons for behaving a certain way.

Although the terms and descriptions vary, researchers are in general agreement that there are three dimensions to engagement:
- school (behavioural/processes/academic)
- heart (emotional/belonging/connection/social)
- mind (intellectual/cognitive)

In the early days, most studies of engagement focused on behavioural compliance, which was often measured through time on task. Behavioural engagement is now referred to as *school process engagement* (Chapman, 2003) or *academic engagement* (Willms et al., 2009). It concerns such things as attending class, following the teacher's instructions, and submitting assigned work.

Social engagement (Willms et al., 2009), also known as *emotional engagement*, refers to a student's sense of belonging or connectedness to the school and the people in it. This dimension of engagement is concerned with issues such as the extent to which students feel that their peers and their teachers like them, and the degree of student participation in curricular and extracurricular activities of the school.

Intellectual engagement is concerned with a student's investment in learning. One report describes it like this:

> [Students] select tasks at the border of their competencies, initiate action when given the opportunity, and exert intense effort and concentration in the implementation of learning tasks; they show generally positive emotions during ongoing activity, including enthusiasm, optimism, curiosity, and interest.
>
> (Skinner & Belmont, 1993, p. 572)

Intellectual engagement is the dimension that researchers have found most difficult to describe in ways that can be consistently measured. However, many researchers—and perhaps most teachers—find it the most useful dimension of engagement to develop in school. Although we will consider all dimensions of engagement in this book and website, intellectual engagement will be our main focus.

No matter how engagement is defined or which dimension is considered, research confirms this truism of education: *The more engaged you are, the more you will learn*. As Adena Klem and James Connell point out, "Regardless of the definition, research links higher levels of engagement in school with improved performance" (2004, p. 262).

Measuring Engagement

Researchers find *engagement* challenging to define and even more challenging to measure. For teachers, doing so is less of a problem—with just a little classroom experience, many of us are confident that we can accurately determine whether a student is engaged or disengaged, virtually at a glance. (*Note*: Throughout this book I use the term *disengagement* to refer to the opposite of engagement. Some researchers prefer the term *disaffection*, meaning the feeling of being alienated from other people.)

Make a Prediction

On the website, you will find a list of observed student behaviours. How successfully can you sort the behaviours according to whether they show engagement or disengagement? Make a prediction before you give it a try.

Use the "curiosity gap theory" to engage students by having them make predictions. Find out more on the website.

Resources
Sorting Student Behaviours

Observation can help us identify a student as being at a particular place on a continuum from highly engaged to highly disengaged. We must, however, remember two things:
- We are making inferences based on observations, and these inferences are subjective, coloured by our own beliefs and values.
- Engagement is always about *relationship* with a person, situation, or activity—and relationships are difficult to analyze. Determining what about a relationship produces the resulting behaviour can be challenging.

We are teachers, not psychologists. It is reasonable to decide that we do not have the time or the need for a nuanced understanding of every student action. What we do need is enough information to inform our next steps, often with the class as a whole rather than with an individual student.

To gather information about engagement without having to rely on observations and inferences, researchers often have students self-report through surveys and questionnaires. A variety of questions are posed for each dimension of engagement being assessed, and students are invited to respond using a rating scale that provides indicators ranging from "strongly agree" to "strongly disagree." This information is anonymous so that students are comfortable giving honest responses. The compiled results are therefore "big picture," representing an entire class, department, school, or system.

Research
- WDYDIST Survey
- Sample Survey Questions

Resources
- Creating Surveys
- Interviewing Students
- Conducting Student Focus Groups
- Debriefing with Students

Oral self-reporting—listening to students share their points of view—is a more time-consuming process than surveys and does not offer students anonymity, but it has the significant benefit of increasing student ownership in the learning. This form of self-reporting can be accomplished through individual interviews, classroom debriefs, or focus groups led by staff or students. More information about each of these processes can be found on the website.

Research
Meaningful Student Involvement

What We Know About Student Disengagement

When Do Students Disengage?
While you may know a disengaged 6-year-old and a highly engaged 14-year-old, the general finding is that disengagement is a particular issue for adolescents, especially those in Grades 7 through 10 (Gallup, 2009; Willms et al., 2009; Yazzie-Mintz, 2007).

> K–3 > 4–6 > 7–9 > 10–12

Who Is Disengaged?
A disproportionate number of disengaged students are found in the following groups.

Who Is Disengaged?
- Boys
- Members of ethnic minorities (but not Asians)
- Aboriginal students
- Students living in poverty
- Students from single-parent families
- Students who are not in advanced programs
- Students with identified special needs

Research
HSSSE Report

Sources: Boys—Willms et al., 2009 (for intellectual engagement); Yazzie-Mintz, 2007; Aboriginal students—Mendelson, 2006; students from single-parent families—Willms et al., 2009; all others from Yazzie-Mintz, 2007

Attendance

Regular school attendance decreases as students progress through the grades. In secondary school, boys skip classes more often than girls.

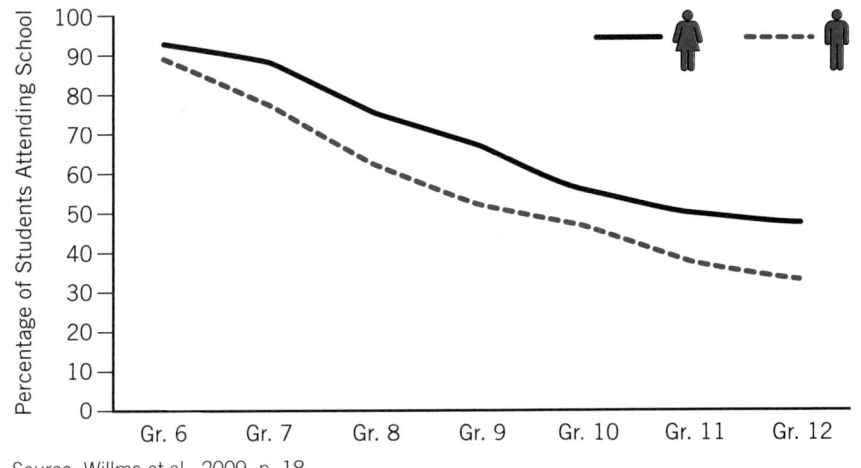

Source: Willms et al., 2009, p. 18

Sense of Belonging

The percentage of students who report a positive sense of belonging through the middle and secondary school years stays relatively constant (Willms et al., 2009).

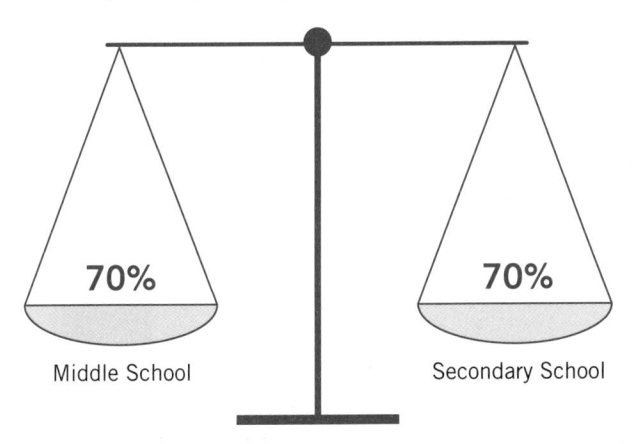

Middle School: 70%
Secondary School: 70%

> "The longer students remain in school, the less likely they are to be intellectually engaged."
> —Willms et al., 2009, p. 31

Terms of Engagement 9

> # Students Need Confidence and Challenge
>
> Students who are not confident of their skills in language arts and math have lower levels of engagement across all dimensions. When students are not confident *and* not challenged, the chances of them being engaged are even lower. Results are similar for students who are confident but not challenged (Willms et al., 2009).

Ultimate Disengagement

Students who drop out of school before attaining their high school diploma often cite school factors as the reason for their departure (Ferguson et al., 2005).

Research
- Dropout Statistics
- Spotlight on *Early School Leavers*

Good news! The percentage of Canadians ages 20 to 24 who are not attending school and have not graduated from high school has steadily decreased.

Source: HRSDC, 2007

Of the students who do leave school early, 40 percent leave by age 16 with a Grade 10 education or less (Ferguson et al., 2005).

Analyze It!

Conversations
Analyzing Disengagement Data

What do you notice? Is there anything in the data on these pages that surprises you? What pieces of data stand out from the rest? What questions do you have? Share your thoughts with colleagues in your school or online through the blog on the website.

Seeking

What Don't We Know?

Research is still needed to determine the following:

- the relationships among different measures of engagement for a single student (For example, as Willms and colleagues (2009) point out, we can't say for certain that a student who feels a sense of belonging also has good attendance.)
- how to accurately measure degrees of engagement (Different researchers use different cut-points, meaning that distinctions between high and low levels of engagement vary from study to study.)
- the impact of other conditions on student engagement (For example, what impact do the culture and climate of the school have?)
- how to accurately track changes in the level of engagement within a lesson or across a day
- how to interpret some of the results (For example, is a decline in participation in extracurricular activities always a sign of disengagement, or is it sometimes a sign that a student has an after-school job?)

What's Your POV?

Psychologists have realized that you don't learn much about positive situations by studying the corresponding negative ones. For example, you don't learn about happiness by studying people who are depressed, and you don't learn about mental health by studying mental illness. Each of the two states is qualitatively different; they are not just opposite sides of the same coin.

What about engagement? Can we learn what it takes to engage students by studying the disengaged? What is your point of view?

What We Know About Teacher Disengagement

Work satisfies more than the need to earn a living. It also provides us with opportunities for personal and professional growth, social interaction, creativity, and meaningful challenge. For many teachers, the pleasure of influencing the achievement of young people and the enjoyment of staying involved with a particular discipline are added benefits.

> Teaching is a strategic act of engagement.
> —*James Bellanca*

Teaching, like engagement, is all about relationship. Teachers are in relationship with students, colleagues, parents, subject matter, and the conditions present at their school and in the profession. When any of those relationships are damaged, it makes sense to think that a teacher might experience a decrease in engagement—with a specific relationship in particular and perhaps with teaching in general.

While relatively few teachers are disengaged to the point of burnout, many different aspects of work life can contribute to varying degrees of disengagement for any teacher. These aspects might include the following:

- limited opportunities for professional learning (Baylor & Ritchie, 2002)
- lack of influence and control over working conditions (Shen, 1997)
- administrators who don't provide support and encouragement (Weiss, 1999)
- unsafe school climates and student misbehaviour (Geving, 2007)
- unfair distribution of workload (Reyes & Imber, 1992; cited in Leithwood & Beatty, 2008)
- number of different courses taught (Klusmann et al., 2008)
- difficult relationships with parents and the community (Buckley, Schneider, & Shang, 2005)
- fear of being judged by students, and found wanting (Palmer, 1998)
- number of years in the profession (According to Huberman (1993), mid-career teachers generally experience the highest levels of satisfaction and engagement.)

> Teaching is a hard job when students make an effort to learn. When they make no effort, it is an impossible one.
> —*William Glasser*

What Matters to You?

Have any of the aspects of work life listed on the previous page affected you? Are there others that should be added to the list? You will find the rest of this book more helpful if you take a few minutes now to reflect in writing about the conditions under which you feel engaged and the ones that make you feel disengaged.

Principals Matter

"[W]hen individual teacher factors were controlled, schools with a more supportive principal had more engaged teachers" (Klusmann et al., 2008, p. 145). The support, according to the researchers, is "in pedagogical matters." Discuss with a colleague or individually reflect in writing about the ways in which you currently show pedagogical support.

Structuring for Engagement

Review staff teaching assignments. Are teachers with the least experience working with the most challenging students? In Grades 7 and 8 classrooms, where students don't necessarily benefit from a different teacher for every subject, are student timetables built with a focus on student needs or teacher preferences?

Talk with colleagues about whether your school's timetable and teaching assignments are structured for student engagement, teacher engagement, or both. What evidence supports your point of view?

The Chicken and the Egg

In his book *A Passion for Teaching*, Christopher Day has this to say about teacher engagement:

> *Teacher commitment is closely related to job satisfaction, morale, motivation and identity, and is a predictor of teachers' work performance, absenteeism, burnout, and turnover as well as an important influence on students' achievement in attitudes towards school.*
>
> (2004, p. 63)

How would you define teacher commitment? Do you agree that your commitment influences students' attitudes towards school, or do students' attitudes have more of an impact on teacher commitment and morale? Discuss with colleagues your responses to these questions before reading the next page.

On the website, you can read my thoughts about burnout.

> Teaching has been a career in which the greatest challenges and most difficult responsibilities are faced by those with the least experience—a strange state of affairs indeed.
>
> —*Carl Glickman, Stephen Gordon, and Jovita Ross-Gordon*

Conversations
It's Not All Fun and Games

What Don't We Know?

Unlike student engagement, there are few quantitative studies of teacher engagement, and there is much we don't know. Questions worthy of further research include the following:

→ Does student engagement stimulate teacher engagement?

→ Does engagement as a general concept make a difference to student achievement, or does it need to be a specific kind of engagement, such as engagement with subject matter?

→ Do teachers who exhibit lower levels of work satisfaction and engagement have students who make lower achieved gains and have higher levels of absenteeism? If so, how do we determine which came first?

→ Do we know how to recognize an engaged teacher from a disengaged one? What are the critical attributes of each?

Summary of Chapter Website Content		www.pearsoncanada.ca/tunedout
Conversations	**Resources**	**Research**
• Choosing a Road • Analyzing Disengagement Data • It's Not All Fun and Games	• Blank Frayer Diagram • Sorting Student Behaviours • Creating Surveys • Interviewing Students • Conducting Student Focus Groups • Debriefing with Students	• What Is Student Engagement? • WDYDIST Survey • Sample Survey Questions • Meaningful Student Involvement • HSSSE Report • Dropout Statistics • Spotlight on *Early School Leavers*

2   15 300 Hours

Students who attend half-days of Kindergarten and then full days in Grades 1 through 12 spend approximately 15 300 hours in school. While every teacher makes a significant contribution to the quality of those hours, teachers in Grades 6 to 12 are vital because they work with students at a particularly crucial time in their development. We know that young adolescents and adolescents are changing in every conceivable way, including physically, socially, emotionally, morally, and cognitively. Their brains are restructuring, pruning some neural connections and strengthening others. Students in Grades 6 through 12 are in the final stages of the process of becoming who they are always going to be.

There is only one other period in the human lifespan when individuals undergo such dramatic change, and that is between birth and age two. As teachers of adolescents, we bear the weighty responsibility of contributing to the development of young people who are soon to take their place in adult society. What's more, we encounter these students at a time in their lives when the opportunity to have a positive influence on them is unparalleled.

Teachers are not alone in carrying responsibility for guiding adolescent development; we share with others the opportunity to have a significant impact on young people's lives. The 15 300 hours students spend in school represents approximately just 13.5 percent of their time on the planet. Family, friends, and the larger community all have a role to play. Even so, the role you play in your students' lives may seem a daunting responsibility. Remember, though, that you do not bear it alone. Within the 15 300 hours of school, students will have a number of teachers before you and, depending on the grade you teach, several more after you. If you teach high school or middle school on a rotary timetable, you might spend 150 hours a year with a particular student—if that student attends every day. These 150 hours represent just under 1 percent of a student's total time in school. Just how much influence can you have?

> Educators play a special role in society because their role is to play life forward.
>
> —*Noah Ben-Shaye*

> Without a commitment to mission, we don't really have a school; we just have a home for freelance tutors of subjects.
> —*Grant Wiggins and Jay McTighe*

The answer, surprisingly, is "quite a lot," as long as you accept two basic premises:

1. You work in a school, and not just in a classroom. The largest influence comes from constancy of purpose and consistent implementation of actions directed towards that purpose across the entire school and, ideally, in the surrounding community.

2. Your focus remains firmly on your circle of influence (what you can control), as opposed to your circle of concern (circumstances beyond your control).

The obvious questions become "What do you want for students during the thousands of hours they spend at your school?" and "What aspects of their lives do you want to influence?"

These questions used to be unnecessary. Schools once had the clear purpose of sorting students according to ability. Achievement by the end of high school, for those who made it that far, would to a large extent determine what kind of job a student would acquire as an adult. Many young people stayed in school because the alternative was work in a factory or on a farm. Engagement wasn't an issue. George Wood, a high school principal, puts it bluntly:

> *School was a ticket out of hard labour, and kids would tolerate almost anything to get that ticket punched. Today, high school prevents kids from playing. So we should not be surprised when old structures and methods fail to hold kids. Actually, what should be surprising is that, faced with this new reality, we still seem unwilling to let our schools catch up with the times.*
>
> (2005, p. 151)

Society's requirements have changed. Now, instead of leaving lots of children behind, the goal is "No child left behind." The sentiment of that slogan, created in the United States, is shared by industrialized countries around the world. I suspect you'll find a version of it in your school's mission statement.

Do you remember mission statements? These declarations of an organization's purpose were all the rage in the late 1980s. Ideally, the mission statement for a school answers the question "What aspects of students' lives do we want to influence during the thousands of hours they spend at our school?" and focuses attention on a few key priorities.

If you were teaching in the late 1980s, you were likely involved in creating a mission statement for your school. If your teaching career began more recently than that and you want to know your school's mission statement, check for a plaque near the main entrance, or some inspiring words about potential and lifelong learning on your school's letterhead, agendas, newsletters, or website.

If I seem a touch cynical, I am guilty as charged. The vast majority of schools got as far as creating and displaying a lofty-sounding mission statement, but few have stayed focused on achieving it. Rare is the staff member or administrator who remembers those words, and rarer still is the one who uses a mission statement to guide daily decisions.

Mission statements should be useful. It just makes sense that a clear statement of purpose would save time and energy wasted on activities that don't address that purpose. Yet mission statements have not had this effect in education. Why?

The reality is that schools are expected to be all things to all people. A mission statement cannot help us address priorities if everything is a priority.

> There is no one more hopeful than a cynic waiting to be proved wrong.
> —*Kris Kristofferson*

"That's our new mission statement."

Consider this list of what schools have historically said is their purpose:

- → Academic excellence and intellectual preparation for higher education
- → The development of mature habits of mind and attitudes
- → Artistic and aesthetic ability and sensitivity
- → Health, wellness, and athletic development
- → Character—mature social, civic, and ethical conduct
- → Personal skill development and professional direction

(Wiggins & McTighe, 2007, p. 11)

Mission Impossible

Compare the list above to the mission statement in your school or district. Which items are emphasized in the mission statement? Which items does the mission statement not address? If you were to rewrite the mission statement, which items from the list would you address, and which would you leave out? Why? Which items do you imagine would promote student engagement? Which would discourage it?

Tough Decisions

As an interesting experiment, ask everyone in your group or on staff at your school to individually prioritize the six purposes in the list above. Reassure them that you realize that a school can and does achieve a wide variety of outcomes, but ask that they make some tough decisions and determine, at minimum, the most important item and the one they find least important. To get a sense of people's priorities, ask them to record and submit their responses, perhaps anonymously. Alternatively, you might have your group or staff meet with like-minded colleagues to discuss their choices. Try the same activity with parents and other members of your local school community. The results will inform your next steps (see page 22).

Wood (2005) suggests that if a person from the early 20th century used a time machine to travel to their hometown in the present, the local high school is one of the few institutions where that person would feel at home—and not simply because the building probably hasn't changed much. Images like Wood's are often used to illustrate that high schools have not kept pace with changes in society, which may well be true. When it comes to purpose, however, schools have long been holding fast to a noble calling: to prepare students to succeed in the world they live in. Since that purpose is comprehensive (or vague) enough to require that attention be paid to every item on the above list provided by Wiggins and McTighe, teachers and administrators have been willing to tackle them all.

Project managers will tell you that successful project teams begin by identifying what is "out of scope"—what they are *not* going to do. Jim Collins, author of the bestseller *Good to Great*, says the "stop doing" list is vital to the success of any business. In *Made to Stick*, authors Chip Heath and Dan Heath explain that a key characteristic of an idea with staying power (a "sticky" idea) is that it is simple and essential. (You will find a review of this terrific book on the website.)

Research
Spotlight on *Made to Stick*

Many teachers feel that there is little point talking about a school's purpose because they see their individual purpose as getting through the mandated curriculum. But the map is not the territory. Curriculum documents are typically lists of content objectives, means to the end of achieving educational purposes, not the purposes themselves:

> Coherent and effective schooling requires that all educational decisions be considered from a vantage point outside of the content. Only then do we have a way to make decisions about what to keep and what to cut, how learning should be structured and how not.
> (Wiggins & McTighe, 2007, p. 20)

A designer knows he has achieved perfection not when there is nothing left to add, but when there is nothing left to take away.
—*Antoine de Saint-Exupéry*

Inevitably, there are significant differences between the curriculum as it appears on the page and the curriculum we teach. Even if we intend to address every curriculum objective, we give more emphasis to some than to others. The objectives we emphasize and the manner in which we teach those objectives reveal the educational purposes we value.

Through the Lens of Purpose

Choose any curriculum objective. Working alone or with others who teach the same content, identify the aspects of the objective that might be emphasized and/or the ways in which the objective might be taught according to different purposes. A sample is provided on the worksheet in the Resources section of the website.

Resources
Curriculum and Purpose

A Mission Statement for the 21st Century

An increasing number of corporate and educational groups are urging a reconceptualization of schools in the 21st century. Their argument is that the confluence of the following three major influences necessitates significant changes to all levels of schooling:
- globalization, which increases global interdependence and competition
- technological innovations that promote greater engagement in teaching and learning, and that provide 24/7 access to content and people
- new research on how people learn

(Apple, 2008)

There is no doubt that we live in a time of incredible, rapid change. For example, consider the last 3000 years in the history of communication. All the major developments since Gutenberg's printing press took place in the last 550 years or so, and most of them far more recently than that. To get a sense of how recent these developments are, see the stopwatch animation on the website.

Research
Stopwatch Animation

As Yogi Berra said, "the future ain't what it used to be." How should schools prepare students for a future that is difficult to anticipate? Will the societal and technological changes of the 21st century change the purpose of schooling, or just the tools through which an existing purpose is achieved? Responses to this question vary widely; for example:
- Twenty-first century rhetoric represents old wine in new bottles—the importance of so-called 21st century skills, such as critical thinking, has been recognized since Plato.
- A few significant and well-placed alterations to current practice will do the trick.
- Nothing less than wholesale change will work; it is now time to reimagine schools from the ground up.

Do schools need to serve the same purposes in the 21st century as they did in the 20th century? Are any items on Wiggins and McTighe's list (see page 18) more or less important than they were just 20 years ago? Do any new items need to be added?

As you work with the material in this book and on the website, you will read some of my responses to these questions and, more important, have plenty of opportunity to explore your own thoughts and beliefs. However, I recommend that you take some time now to record a few of your ideas at this point. Whether you do this as a school community, a staff, a department, or a book study group, you can collaboratively work towards a clarified and focused mission statement for the 21st century. Even if you are working on your own, thinking through your priorities at this early stage will help you determine which of the practical suggestions provided throughout this book will allow you to most efficiently and effectively achieve your purpose.

A caveat: Before doing any of the following activities, all participants need to agree to focus solely on the purpose of school for students. This is not the place for parents to be advocating for their children's particular needs, for teachers to be thinking about what subjects and classes they prefer to teach, or for anyone to be talking about curriculum mandates or budget limitations.

Visions of the 21st Century Learner

A number of organizations and individuals have listed what they consider to be important attributes of the 21st century learner. You will find some of these lists in the Research section of the website. Again, I don't recommend adopting what someone else has created—some of the lists provided are a bit overwhelming, while others are specific to the mission of the organization that developed them. Compare the lists to your own thinking, noting where you agree or disagree.

Research
Profiles of the 21st Century Learner

A Mission Statement for the 21st Century – continued

Indirect Truths

Resources
Third Things

Parker Palmer (2009) talks about the value of approaching a topic through a "third thing"—a song, poem, story, or image. He calls these "third things" because they represent a voice separate from the voice of the facilitator or the voices of any participants. Third things allow people to come at concepts indirectly, much like Rorschach inkblot tests invite individual interpretations.

Use one or more of the third things provided in the Resources section of the website to talk about the purpose of schooling. If the conversation veers away from the third thing, bring it back by anchoring what you say to a word, line, or part of an image.

Top 10 for Grads

What attributes should your school support students in developing by the time they graduate? Provide the people in your group with sticky notes and invite them to individually brainstorm and record their ideas.

If more than a dozen people are doing this activity at one time, have them next meet in small groups, share their sticky notes, and reach a consensus on their top 10.

Ask participants to post on the wall the top 10 from each group (or all notes if the group is small enough) and arrange them in categories. Assign groups (or individual participants for small groups) the responsibility for further developing a particular category by

- choosing the attributes they feel it is most important for the school to develop
- writing a paragraph in support of their position

Pass the Popcorn

Conversations
21st Century Learner Videos

Resources
Watching Videos

View some of the online videos suggested in the Resources section to start a great conversation about the needs of the 21st century learner. Before you do this, you might want to make a prediction about the prevailing theme(s) you will encounter in these videos. You could also check out my blog post on 21st century learner videos.

Mission Prep

Before beginning to craft a mission statement, you may want to develop your own thoughts about the purpose of school. To get started, take a look at the list below—it contains goals that a Harvard Business School professor suggests many people share.

1. Maximize human potential.

2. Facilitate a vibrant, participative democracy in which we have an informed electorate that is capable of not being "spun" by self-interested leaders.

3. Hone the skills, capabilities, and attitudes that will help our economy remain prosperous and economically competitive.

4. Nurture the understanding that people can see things differently—and that those differences merit respect rather than persecution.

(Christensen et al., 2008, p. 1)

Keep Reading!

In the first chapter of each of the next five sections in this book, I review the changes we are seeing in society and in our students. By reading and discussing these chapters, and engaging in the suggested activities, you will be considering the 21st century realities that may need to inform your mission statement. For an overview of activities provided in the book, see the list on the website.

Resources
Tuned Out Activity Summary

Visions Aren't Just for Psychics

A mission statement alone is not sufficient—you also need to have a vision.

Think of a mission statement as a skeleton, and a vision as the meat on the bones. Or consider the mission statement as a destination and the vision as the variety of routes that will take you there.

In practical terms, a mission statement is a slogan that states an intended result, while a vision is a lengthy narrative that provides indicators of success. A vision statement is where you answer the question "What will it look like if we are living our mission every day?"

Visions aren't limited to psychics and school boards. Most people create visions all the time—when they picture the life they'll lead after retirement or imagine how great their home office will be once they've finally had a chance to get everything organized. Whenever you create a picture of the future, you're creating a vision. In some cases, it might be a broad vision, and in others, it might be quite detailed.

Vision statements are always unique to a particular situation. They are important to the change process because they

- → clarify direction and provide a road map for the change, while remaining flexible enough to allow for some individual variation in approach.

- → provide indicators that can be used as benchmarks of success in achieving the purpose.

- → provide such a clear and engaging view of a desired future that people are willing to put forth the effort required to achieve that future.

> Creating commitment is in part a matter of setting a clear, compelling vision that engages people's hearts and minds.
> —*Ben Levin*

Vision Options

Individually or in a group, list the pros and cons of receiving a vision from your district office or borrowing a successful vision from another school. Then compare your thoughts with the information on the website.

Resources
5 Ways *Not* to Get a Vision

Ask Some Questions

Principal George Wood shares four questions that his staff worked through when they were making some significant changes to the organizational structures and teaching practices at his school. The questions help us to focus on key elements of learning that need to be considered in a vision statement. Any of them have the potential to generate a great conversation.

1. *What are the conditions under which you learn best? How does the way we organize our school resemble those learning conditions?*

2. *How do you know when you really know something? Does the way we assess students in our school tell us whether or not our kids have really learned something?*

3. *What are the most important things we could teach our kids? Is the school organized in such a way as to show students that we value these things?*

4. *If you were a student here, what would you really like about our school? What things would make it hard for you to learn? What would make you unhappy here?*

(Adapted from Wood, 2005, pp. 152–153)

I invite you to share your response to the first question above in the online blog.

Conversations
The Best Learning

Chart Your Course

Working with your group, use several sheets of flip-chart paper to make a large "If/Then" chart. On the first page (the "If" page), list the main components of your mission statement. Write one of the following labels on each of the next four pages: Students, Teachers, Administrators, Parents. These pages become the "Then" pages, which will describe what each of these groups will do to help achieve each of the components on the "If" page. For example, let's say you list the following goal on the "If" page: "Students will be aware of their responsibilities as citizens, and will respond accordingly to both local and global issues." On the next pages, you will list what each group will do to contribute to achieving that goal.

Ideally, students, teachers, administrators, and parents will be involved in completing their respective parts of the chart. Since all these groups are affected by the school's vision, encourage their participation in creating it.

Leadership is ultimately about creating new realities.

—*Peter Senge*

Rough Waters Ahead

If you are a leader in your school or district, the suggestions on these two pages may prove to be particularly helpful.

I think mission and vision statements are good ideas that were often poorly executed the first time around. If the lofty slogans we developed in the 1980s had been more often accompanied by detailed narratives explaining what achievement of those commitments would look like in our classrooms and schools, our slogans would have been less lofty and our actions more meaningful.

I believe that now is the ideal time to revisit this process and do a better job. We have two compelling reasons: the rapidity of change we have been experiencing since the dawn of the 21st century, and the significant problem of student disengagement and its demoralizing impact on teachers.

Compelling reasons to engage in a challenging process certainly help, but most of us are seasoned enough to realize that re-visioning a classroom, school, or school system is not an easy task. All manner of roadblocks, difficulties, and tensions will arise. Here are a few, along with suggestions for how to deal with them:

→ **"It's déjà vu all over again."**

School systems and schools are not blank slates waiting to be written on by leaders. They are composites and collections of previous, often long-forgotten "solutions" to problems that other people thought were compelling at one time or another.

(City et al., 2009, p. 40)

Research

Spotlight on *Made to Stick*

- Make sure you create a persuasive and easily understood "story" about the new vision. You will find help for doing so on pages 142–143 and in *Made to Stick*, a book by Chip Heath and Dan Heath. If you haven't done so already, see my review of this book on the website.
- Constantly talk about the new vision. Teacher leaders should be referring to it in department and division meetings; new staff, students, and parents should be familiarized with it

immediately; and the mission and accompanying vision should be displayed prominently and referenced often.

→ **"Life gets in the way."**

The challenge of imagining a new and different future for your school is a bit like trying to build a plane while flying it. During the process, you need to maintain all of the day-to-day responsibilities of managing a school or classroom.

- Try to keep the new work in the forefront of your mind by talking about it constantly (see previous page) and by occasionally conducting an "environmental scan," where you assess whether the stated purpose or the old routines are receiving most of people's time and attention. You won't always be able to focus on the new, but putting it off for a quieter time probably won't work either.

→ **"Our mission will need to wait until I'm finished with the district's/this school's 10 other new initiatives."**

We…know from bitter experiences that even the highest level of commitment is rarely impervious to a stupid system. In schools and school systems, we face the difficult yet important challenge of aligning the various elements of the system.

(Levin, 2008, p. 127)

- Align what you can. Evaluate your school's procedures and policies, and get rid of the ones that don't connect with the school's mission.
- Show people in the school and at the district office how the vision aligns with current initiatives, rather than being another add-on.
- Identify the aspect of the vision that will be either easiest to implement or so significant that there is great potential for improvement. Focus on achieving that aspect first.

Rough Waters Ahead – continued

→ **"I attended a school just like this one, and look how well I turned out."**

Teachers, like everyone else, are typically blind to the power of unthinking routines—a situation made worse by our isolation from other adults and trusted critical friends and a firm belief in our noble intentions.

(Wiggins & McTighe, 2007, p. 258)

- Read *Tuned Out* in a book study group. Each section of the book offers practical suggestions for working with students, as well as practical suggestions teachers can use to identify and change any unthinking routines or limiting beliefs.
- Provide release time so teachers can "shadow" a student for a day, attending all of the student's classes and doing everything the student is asked to do. George Wood tells the story of a principal who provided this opportunity in her school. Of the eight teachers who participated, four had begged off before the end of lunch and none made it to the end of the day. Our memories of our own school experiences are coloured by time and our adult perspective. Reliving the experience instead of remembering it can be enlightening.

Summary of Chapter Website Content		www.pearsoncanada.ca/tunedout
Conversations	**Resources**	**Research**
• 21st Century Learner Videos • The Best Learning	• Curriculum and Purpose • Third Things • Watching Videos • *Tuned Out* Activity Summary • 5 Ways *Not* to Get a Vision	• Spotlight on *Made to Stick* • Stopwatch Animation • Profiles of the 21st Century Learner

Competence

You thought you knew me
before I walked in.
You looked at my grades,
you knew my brother,
also my sister,
and last year's teacher.
You think you know me very,
very well.
What can I do to
make you change your mind?

—From "Dear Teacher" by Mary-Ruth C. Mundy

3   Below the Surface

Conversations
"Competence"
Video Byte

*C*ompetence is a term with specific meaning in the business world. Individuals are considered competent when they display behaviours (referred to as *competencies*) that contribute to effective performance and success. The desired behaviours are identified by analyzing a task to determine which behaviours must be in place for the task to be performed successfully (these are called *basic competencies*), and which behaviours differentiate high performers from low performers (called *performance competencies*).

It is understandable why determining the competencies required for success in a particular job is critical to any organization. Doing this is the corporate version of backward planning (see page 161)—knowing exactly what success looks like makes all the difference in determining which people to hire, and how to train and support new employees so they will make the maximum contribution to the workplace.

Teachers also look for observable competencies. Perhaps we notice that students who do well in our classes are persistent or ask questions when they are confused. If we are reflective practitioners, we can ascertain which behaviours are likely to lead to success, and we can encourage those behaviours in our students. With some fine-tuning we can even distinguish among levels of performance and put them on a rubric. We recognize *degrees* of success.

Competencies, like the 10 percent of an iceberg that is above water, can be seen. They are what we *do* and their specifics are relative to our situation. For example, if you are at a staff party, your social competencies, such as your ability to mingle and be at ease when talking with your administrator's spouse, are what matter. Your academic competencies in this situation are less important, unless you're on the faculty at one of those universities where small talk is a thinly veiled opportunity for academic one-upmanship.

It all sounds so simple and straightforward, at least in the workplace: Determine the competencies you need, find the individuals who possess them, and then provide training and on-the-job experience to fill any gaps or to turn an adequate employee into a high-performing one.

But there's a problem when attention is devoted exclusively to what can be seen. The observable behaviours by which we judge an individual's competence are just the tip of the iceberg. Underneath these behaviours lie all kinds of things—attitudes, beliefs, experiences, interests, learning preferences, knowledge, skills. These are often unseen and difficult to measure; they can also be even harder to influence.

Life in the Real World

Teachers often caution students that life is going to be different when they get out in the "real world." Although I find the phrase mildly annoying—I think school is as much a part of the real world as any other institution—I understand the sentiment behind the warning. It is difficult to imagine any profit-driven organization tolerating the unexcused absences, lacklustre efforts, or attitude of entitlement that we observe in some of our students.

Certainly, if some of the worst adolescent behaviours were played out in corporate offices, the individuals responsible would soon be looking for other employment. But since many of the most egregious behaviours are part of the developmental stage of adolescence, and because most students do not take on full-time work until they are adults, this is less of an issue than we might imagine. Furthermore, just as students behave differently at school than they do at home, many students will behave differently, and better, at work than they do at school.

For everything short of wanton disregard for company policies and severely limited or non-existent demonstration of competence, workplaces have much less flexibility of response than we might think. There are several reasons:

1. When members of the baby-boom generation retire en masse during the next decade, young people will be in the driver's seat when seeking employment.

2. Both hiring and firing employees cost money. Estimates of the cost of employee turnover, even for relatively new employees, range from 38 percent to 200 percent of the employee's annual salary, depending on whether all the costs of recruitment, training, dismissal, lost productivity, and impact on customers and remaining staff are included in the calculation.

3. Managers are hesitant to fire an employee they hired. Not only does it reflect poorly on their judgment, but it puts them in the position of hiring again, and hiring is always a risky business. Many of the specific competencies of a particular workplace can be acquired only through on-the-job training followed by experience, and it's difficult to predict which applicants will be able to develop these competencies. So, managers prefer to invest time and effort in ensuring the success of a new employee, rather than firing someone and taking the risk of hiring again.

If businesses can't guarantee success in hiring a competent workforce, and they can't just continue to replace people until they arrive at the perfect (and probably unsustainable) team, what do they do?

Businesses, like schools, are realizing that they need to pay increased attention to the individual behind the performance—to the unseen 90 percent that creates the observable competencies. This shift in focus is supported by research from Gallup (2008), which shows that there are measurable differences between engaged and disengaged employees in terms of productivity, number of safety incidents, absenteeism, and profitability.

> The hardest thing for your competitors to match is the most unique aspect of your organization—the hearts and minds of your employees.
> —*Lee Colan*

Recognizing the importance of engagement, workplace leaders try to determine the conditions under which an individual will be motivated to do his or her best work, and they endeavour to create and sustain those conditions. Motivation and engagement, therefore, are far from abstract theoretical concepts in the workplace; they have real implications for a company's success, just as they do for a teacher's success in instructing students and a student's success in school.

The Workplace of School

Leadership expert Lee Colan defines the best managers as those who engage both the hearts and minds, or passion and performance, of employees. This information is also critical for district and school leaders. Teachers who are passionate about working with students but who lack instructional skills will struggle with effective teaching. Teachers who are skilled in instruction but not passionate about their work may find it difficult to come up with a creative solution to an instructional challenge or to make an extra effort when needed.

Talk with colleagues about the conditions and supports that you believe need to be in place to engage teachers in their work. Research about these conditions and their implications for schools is provided at the end of this chapter.

Although there are undoubtedly exceptions, I imagine that most adults begin their work lives engaged. That is certainly the case for teachers. Individuals become teachers for a wide variety of reasons, many of them quite noble. Even when that is not the case, the lengthy preparation period required to qualify as a teacher, as well as the poor pay that is provided in some regions, indicates that teaching is an active career choice, not usually a fallback position. William Ayers suggests that

> ...people teach as an act of construction and reconstruction, and as a gift of oneself to others. I teach in the hope of making the world a better place.
> (2001, p. 8)

That statement, however, is followed immediately by this one:

> While practically every teacher I have known over many years came to teaching in part with this hope, only a few outstanding teachers are able to carry it fully into a life of teaching. What happens?
> (2001, p. 8)

What happens, indeed? The same question can be asked of our students. Every one of us begins life highly engaged, but many of us don't stay that way. While disengagement is most prevalent in Grades 6 through 10, some students are disengaged as early as their primary school years.

Engaged with Life

This is Cole, the son of friends of mine. Every time I look at Cole, I am reminded of the joie de vivre, the insatiable curiosity and drive, the intrinsic motivation that every young child possesses.

Engagement is a given for all infants and toddlers. Children come into the world dependent on others to meet their basic needs, but by the time they are three years of age, they are autonomous individuals. In the first three years of life, children explore the world through their senses, begin to understand cause and effect (for example, a hot stove burns), and learn to classify objects and solve problems. Young children embrace some tough challenges, including learning to walk and talk, and they don't give up.

Good parents encourage a child's innate curiosity about the world by providing a range of experiences in a safe and secure environment. They pay attention and are responsive to their child's needs and preferences. This is certainly the case for Cole. He is growing up in a home where he is loved unconditionally. His early experiences don't include poverty, prejudice, or abuse. His parents value learning.

There are never any guarantees, but there's a pretty fair likelihood that Cole is going to do well in school and beyond. Yet despite Cole's advantages, statistics suggest that he will also experience periods of disengagement at school, starting around Grade 6. There will be times, perhaps long stretches of time, when his innate curiosity and enthusiasm will be nowhere to be found.

Dial Back

Think about any early work experience—a part-time job when you were in high school or university, or maybe your first teaching assignment. Describe the work to a colleague. If you felt engaged, what was it about the experience that engaged you? Identify the indicators of your engagement in the work.

Did you disengage over time on the job, or was there someone in the workplace who did? If so, what was it about the experience that might have caused this disengagement?

Dial Way Back!

Once when my niece was eight, I gave her a hard time about something she had done. She looked at me and said, "But Aunt Karen, I've only been on the planet for eight years!"

When I'm working with a disengaged student, I try to remember two things: (1) They've been on the planet a short while, and they need time and help to get it right; (2) They didn't begin life as passive and apathetic. Doing the following activity will likely provide you with some insight:

1. Choose a disengaged student you teach. If you don't have a student who will view your interest as genuine and supportive, rather than intrusive, you could use a family member who was disengaged at school for some period of time. (We all have them!)

2. Work with that person to find out everything you can about their first five years of life. Look at photographs and baby books; listen to their stories of early passions, and share some of your own. If you have chosen a student, review the Kindergarten intake notes and drawings in the student's record.

Whether you have chosen a student or a family member, understanding the points at which engagement turns to disengagement can inform future teaching decisions and actions. For a whole-class variation of this activity, see my blog post on the website.

Opposites Thinking

Thinking about competencies, opposites, and mindsets can help us understand why students and adults disengage.

Student Sorting

Read through a class list, writing the letter "C" beside the names of students you consider academically competent.

Then, make a two-column chart. In the first column, record common characteristics of the students you have coded as academically competent. In the second column, record common characteristics of students who are not academically competent. Are the characteristics you listed in the first column matched by their opposites in the second column? For example, does your chart include contrasting pairs, such as "motivated/unmotivated," "engaged/disengaged," "excelling/struggling," and "succeeding/failing"? Save your chart for future reference.

Conversations
Dr. Seuss and Me

Simba, you are more than what you have become.
—*Mufasa in* **The Lion King**

Resources
My History as a Reader

> There are two kinds of people in the world: those who believe that everything can be divided into two categories—and the rest of you.
>
> —*Joke*

It is human nature to view life in terms of opposites or contrasting pairs. We discriminate one concept from another by attending to differences, and nowhere are differences more apparent than with opposites. In society and in our personal lives, we teach young children the difference between friends and strangers, talk of hard versus soft sciences, value either logic or emotion, and revel in joy because we have experienced despair.

In our teaching lives we work with adolescents, students in a developmental stage where every generalization we make reminds us that we've also seen its opposite, often in the same individual. For example: "José is self-centred and lazy, but he worked hard to raise money for the local animal shelter" or "My students are insolent in class, but they were so thoughtful and respectful when we visited the retirement home."

It is easy to fall into the habit of thinking in terms of opposites. Carol Dweck (2006) classifies people as falling into the opposite categories of having a "growth mindset" or a "fixed mindset." She found that people with a "growth mindset" believe intelligence can be built throughout life, while people with a "fixed mindset" believe they have to work with whatever intelligence they have because it can't be increased.

How do these categories relate to students? Growth mindset learners see working harder as a way to improve. When given a novel challenge, they persist and try a wide variety of solutions. Fixed mindset learners, on the other hand, resist novel challenges if they can't succeed immediately—they view every new challenge as an opportunity to be judged as a winner or loser, smart or dumb, cool or nerdy.

Thinking in terms of opposites has some benefits, but it isn't always advisable. It saves us time by removing the need to treat every situation as new and unique. But thinking of ourselves or others in terms of opposites also leads to classifying and labelling, which can be dangerous:

> *We classify at our peril. Experiments have shown that even the lightest touch of the classifier's hand is likely to induce us to see members of a class as more alike than they actually are and items from different classes as less alike than they actually are. And when our business is to do more than merely look, these errors may develop during the course of our dealings into something quite substantial.*
>
> (James Britton, cited in Robinson, 2001, p. 183)

The problem with opposites thinking in our classrooms is threefold:

1. Declaring that a student is "unmotivated" or "disengaged" can have us searching for a targeted solution to the problem, or it can be a way of blaming the student and absolving ourselves of any responsibility.

2. Having decided on a category, the characteristics of that category come to the foreground, and we often fail to notice other aspects of the individual.

3. The categories we create are accompanied by different expectations for the individuals in them. (See the website for an activity about the significance of teacher expectations.)

Resources
Teacher Expectations

The Roots of Engagement

Since engagement is key to success in school and in life, it would be helpful to have a more nuanced understanding of this term, rather than simply saying that a student is engaged or disengaged. We need look no further than a metaphor offered by Lee Colan, who suggests we think of engagement as "more like a dimmer switch than an on/off switch" (2009, p. 26).

There are at least three clear points on a continuum of engagement: engaged, disengaged, and actively disengaged.

> **Engaged** people are happy to be at work or school. They generally enjoy what they do, even on bad days. At work, they feel that their energy and passion make a difference to their company or to society. Engaged students believe that what they do is important, that it matters in their lives now or will in the future. Engaged workers and students are rarely absent.
>
> **Disengaged** people are physically present at work or school, but there is a sense that their "real lives" are happening elsewhere. Energy and passion are missing. Disengaged workers and students concentrate on the task rather than the goal. They wait to be told what to do and go through the motions once they are told. This state Colan refers to as "I quit but forgot to tell you" (2009, p. 26).

Actively disengaged people are a problem—for themselves, their bosses, their teachers. They don't just refuse to participate; they undermine what others are accomplishing. The actively disengaged make sure that everyone around them knows they are unhappy. Employees and students who are actively disengaged are absent more frequently than either the engaged or the disengaged.

Gallup's Findings

Research

Employee Engagement Index

Gallup surveyed adults across the United States, asking them a dozen questions to determine their level of engagement in their work. The results are in the Research section of the website, but before you look, please predict the answers to the following:

1. What percentage of workers are engaged? disengaged? actively disengaged?

2. What aspect of a work environment is the best predictor of whether or not an employee is engaged?

3. In an average organization, the ratio of engaged workers to actively disengaged workers is _____:1.

4. In a world-class organization, the ratio of engaged workers to actively disengaged workers is _____:1.

5. Approximately how much does the lower productivity of actively disengaged workers cost the United States economy in one year?

6. Each year over a period of 10 years, Gallup is surveying approximately 70 000 students in Grades 5 to 12 to determine their level of engagement. What is the percentage of students who are engaged? disengaged? actively disengaged?

For all the similarities between employees and students in the categories on the engagement continuum, there is at least one significant difference. Students fluctuate between categories far more frequently than do employees. During any given day—from class to class or even moment to moment—students can jump from one category to another. For example, Sasha is consistently engaged in math class, but she's disengaged in the day's physical education class because the teacher is making the class practise basketball drills, and she hates drills. When a game is played in the last 20 minutes of class, Sasha re-engages.

Engagement is a prerequisite for competence. To be academically competent, students need to engage with the curriculum; to be socially competent, they need to engage with other people. What causes students to engage or disengage?

Motivation is the precursor to engagement. But asking what you can do to motivate a student or an employee is asking the wrong question. Motivation is an internal process beyond external control, although knowing that doesn't stop us from trying to control!

Teachers, administrators, parents, and employers have a long and eventful history of using external motivators of reward to encourage compliance, and punishment to demand it. This practice is based on the stimulus-response theory—the theory of carrots and sticks, of believing that rewarding a behaviour means you will see more of it, while punishing a behaviour means you will see less of it.

Stimulus-response theory appeals to the strict taskmaster who uses a "produce or get out of my classroom" approach to teaching. It does work, but only in the short term and only for menial tasks. The long-term motivation needed to develop competence in any area of life must be intrinsic—it must come from within the individual. Extrinsic motivators not only don't work in these situations, but they actively undermine the development of intrinsic motivation. (For alternatives to extrinsic motivators, see pages 52–53.)

www.cartoonstock.com

Intrinsic motivation theory says that all human beings are genetically driven to achieve a handful of basic needs and that "all of our behaviour is always our best attempt at the time…to satisfy one or more of these basic needs" (Glasser, 1986, p. 14). The basic needs are

- **survival**—both physical (food, shelter, safety) and emotional (order, security)
- **connection**—belonging and love
- **power/competence**—feeling important; being good at something
- **freedom**—making choices and being free of fear, negative stress, and disrespect
- **fun**—play, enjoyment, creativity

> Disengagement is simply the result of unfulfilled needs.
> —*Lee Colan*

This list of needs comes from psychologist William Glasser. Unlike Abraham Maslow, who believed that needs always had to be achieved in a specific order, beginning with the most basic need first, Glasser believes that people will always choose to fulfill whatever need is most unsatisfied at a particular time.

Glasser argues that according to his "choice theory" (formerly "control theory"), the majority of students begin school with a positive mental image of learning, but failure or excessive criticism damages this image. When students aren't developing academic competencies, they give up on academics as a way of achieving power or competence in their lives and search for another way to meet this need for competence. Glasser's theory is supported by the finding that failing grades or subjects is a key indicator of a student being at risk of dropping out of school (Ferguson et al., 2005; Hammond, Smink, & Drew, 2007).

Some students achieve their need for competence through sports, music, visual art, or theatre programs, which speaks to the importance of these programs both within the school curriculum and as extracurricular activities. Some students find other, far more detrimental, ways to achieve power in their lives—gang membership, drug abuse, violence, or sexual behaviour.

Needs or Nonsense?

A school can become a "Glasser Quality School" if after students and teachers are taught to use choice theory, it meets the following criteria:

- Students do better on state proficiency tests.
- All students do some quality work each year.
- All other work reflects competence.
- Students, parents, and administrators say there is a joyful atmosphere in the school.

(Sullo, 2007, p. 26)

Conversations
Needs or Nonsense?

If all of the students and teachers in your school were taught choice theory, would the criteria for a Glasser Quality School be within the realm of possibility?

What do you think of Glasser's choice theory? Does it explain not only your students' behaviour, but your own? Is it a theory that will allow you to build the competence (and the required engagement) of increasing numbers of students, or is it yet another justification for lowered expectations and too much student control?

Your beliefs about what motivates student behaviours will dictate the actions you take in your classroom to improve student performance. I urge you to take the time to reflect on the beliefs you hold and to record your thoughts either privately or by responding to my blog post on the website. By the way, can you guess how many Glasser Quality Schools there are in the world? I'll tell you in my blog.

21st Century Needs

Are some needs more pressing than others, depending on the conditions present in society at the time? Glasser says, for example, that survival needs dominated until shortly after the Second World War, when a more affluent lifestyle and the advent of television allowed people to focus on meeting needs for belonging, freedom, and fun.

Although it does not specifically deal with choice theory, a book titled *The Ego Boom* by Steve Maich and Lianne George (2009) makes a strong case that 21st century North Americans, particularly those under the age of 35, are prioritizing the needs for freedom and fun above all others.

The argument is that baby-boomer parents (born between January 1946 and December 1964) were the first generation to experiment on a large scale with two-income households, divorce, and blended families. In a desire to have more for themselves and more for their children, many boomer parents worked long hours, put off having children until they were in their 30s or 40s, and were guilty of being too indulgent, too affirming, and too involved with their children.

This focus on self-regard, on having your individual needs met no matter what, has developed to such an extent that "You" (the individual) has become a force to be reckoned with in the market, and at the same time a media darling. In 2006, "You" was *Time's* Person of the Year, "the consumer" was named Ad Agency of the Year by *Advertising Age*, and "You!" topped *Business 2.0*'s list of "The 50 Who Matter Now."

According to the authors of *The Ego Boom*, parents, marketers, and society at large have created a generation or more of young people who believe they are

- → **fascinating**—There are roughly 65 million blogs on the internet and the number is growing. "Underlying the current practice of archiving one's life is the belief that everything a person does is worthy of documentation" (Maich & George, 2009, p. 53).

- → **special**—A Pew Research Center study found that 64 percent of 18- to 24-year-olds believe that they belong to a unique generation, that they have inherited a golden age, and that it is reasonable that their highest ambition is to be rich (81 percent) or famous (51 percent).

- → **unique**—A 30-second ringtone for your cell phone may be a little thing, but when the money spent on ringtones surpasses $4.4 billion, as it did in 2006, ringtones become a bellwether of the demand for being seen as a unique individual.

The danger is if the focus on the individual replaces any concern for community—if "I" is always more important than "we." The findings in this regard are inconsistent. Some researchers argue that today's young people are not disillusioned or discontented with political systems and community activity, but rather are simply disengaged. They focus on personal gratification and become, as a result, increasingly isolated from the community's concerns.

On the other side of the coin, there are those who argue that it is the form of community engagement that is changing, with students more involved in online activism and volunteerism that isn't confined to the local neighborhood but rather reaches around the world.

Your PC, Your Way

At Dell's North Carolina plant, a "custom-built" desktop computer comes off the assembly line every three seconds or less. The process is referred to as "mass customization"—every individual is treated as a market of one. Instead of saving money by eliminating choices, Dell gives the opportunity to specify the size, colour, and capabilities of each machine produced.

Dell began the move away from personal computer to personalized computer, and made a lot of money doing so—$56 billion in 2008. Other computer manufacturers quickly shifted their own marketing strategies to match. Sony's 2008 tagline for their laptop computers was "This Laptop is Me." Microsoft didn't take long to jump on the bandwagon by promoting the idea that Windows has become a personalized operating system through a series of ads in which happy Windows users declare, "I'm a PC and Windows 7 was my idea." A long-time PC user, I recently purchased a Mac, in part because of the way my needs were addressed by the "concierge" and my "personal shopping assistant" at the Apple store, as well as the reassurance that my unique needs would be met through the purchase of a "One to One" assistance plan.

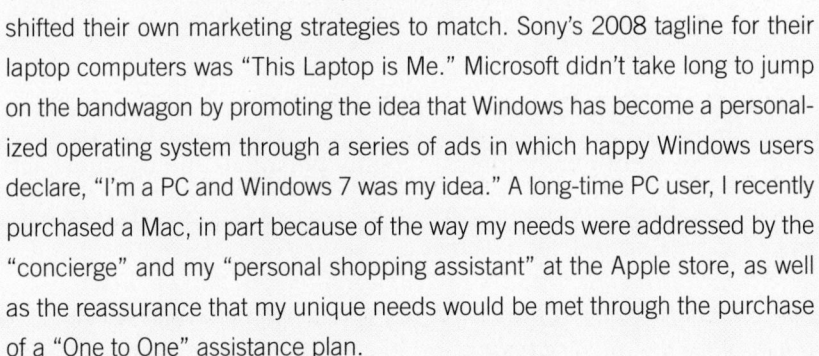

The internet makes mass customization possible because people can be reached with marketing messages targeted to their needs. Unlike the early days of mass production where you could have any colour car you wanted as long as it was black, or even the recent days of segmented markets where you could purchase from a wide variety of car models and colours, the marketing messages of computer mass customization feed "the notion that no computer could ever really live up to your expectations unless you were guiding its very creation" (Maich & George, 2009, p. 64). Of course, you're not really guiding. You are making choices from a limited range of pre-set options. Nevertheless, Dell and companies like it have proven that there is "spectacular profit potential awaiting companies that manage to drill into their customers' desire to feel special, to get involved, and to be treated like individuals" (Maich & George, 2009, p. 63).

> The average teenager still has all the faults his parents outgrew.
> —*Author Unknown*

Your Classroom, Your Thoughts

Adults have been complaining about young people since the beginning of time:

> *I see no hope for the future of our people if they are dependent on the frivolous youth of today, for certainly all youth are reckless beyond words. When I was a boy, we were taught to be discreet and respectful of elders, but the present youth are exceedingly wise and impatient of restraint.*
>
> —Hesiod, 8th century BCE

> Adolescents are not monsters. They are just people trying to learn how to make it among the adults in the world, who are probably not so sure themselves.
> —*Virginia Satir*

Write a statement that summarizes what you think about the future, based on the young people of today. Underline any parts of your statement that you think are unique to conditions in our 21st century society. Circle any parts of your statement that refer to specific characteristics of adolescents.

If you are working in a group, post on a wall the statements from all members and review them. Compile phrases from the statements on two pieces of chart paper—one for conditions unique to the 21st century, and one for characteristics of adolescents.

Discuss the information recorded on both lists. Examine each statement to determine whether it is a fact or a belief (see pages 84–85), and to consider the implications of each for the development of your school's mission and vision statements.

Competent Teachers

Teaching is an emotionally intense, highly personal, and dynamic act:

> *Teaching is not something one learns to do, once and for all, and then practises, problem-free, for a lifetime.... Teaching depends on growth and development, and it is practised in dynamic situations that are never twice the same. Wonderful teachers, young and old, will tell of fascinating insights, new understandings, unique encounters with youngsters, the intellectual puzzle and the ethical dilemmas that provide a daily challenge. Teachers, above all, must stay alive and engaged with all of this.*
>
> (Ayers, 2001, pp. 122–123)

Research
Teacher Competencies

That said, lists of competencies and professional standards are provided by any number of groups, including provincial teacher accreditation organizations in Canada and the National Board for Professional Teaching Standards in the United States. For a summary of some of the most frequently cited teacher competencies, see the Research section of the website.

The competency that I suggest underlies all others is self-awareness. In my experience, teachers who are aware of the 90 percent that is below the surface of their own observable behaviours also tend to be aware of the following:

- → the individual characteristics of their students
- → the times when it's appropriate to change direction in instruction and assessment
- → the assumptions and beliefs that might inappropriately guide thinking and action
- → the need to consider and evaluate a variety of responses to a problem

Self-awareness results in learning and, when accompanied by self-efficacy, leads to positive change. *Self-efficacy* refers to the extent to which an individual believes he or she has the resources, ability, and power to achieve a goal. Belief in your own ability to change, to keep growing and learning, is essential for teachers—if you don't believe in your own ability to learn and change, it's difficult to believe that the same is possible for your most challenging students.

Research
A "Self" Glossary

Recent research suggests that even when your individual sense of efficacy is lacking, significant progress can be made if collective or group efficacy is in place in your school.

Collective efficacy refers to the belief that the staff, as a whole, possesses the ability to achieve the goal of increased student achievement. When collective efficacy is present, an optimistic school climate is created—one where "there is a high level of social expectation that [all teachers] will do what is necessary to achieve success" (Leithwood & Beatty, 2008, p. 55).

Although the research base on collective efficacy is still quite small, sources of this optimistic state seem to be similar to those required for individual efficacy. Leithwood and Beatty (2008) suggest that these include the following:

- past experiences of success or failure, both individually and as a staff
- opportunities to observe teachers being successful in similar situations
- encouragement and persuasion by trusted colleagues
- the levels of self-efficacy experienced by colleagues

Resources
Reflection Methods

Reflection Preferences

Self-awareness develops through individual and collaborative reflection. See the website for more information about the value of reflection and some suggestions for reflection methods that suit your learning preferences.

Students (and Their Teachers?) Need...

According to researchers, if students are to develop academic competence and to be engaged in schoolwork, they need

- a positive, committed connection to an adult who has high expectations and provides appropriate support, feedback, and recognition
- understanding of a task's purpose and relevance to their lives
- challenging work
- autonomy, where possible, in how the work is to be completed
- confidence that they can be successful

Throughout this book and website, you will find suggestions for creating and sustaining the conditions that support competence and engagement in your classroom.

©2003 ZITS Partnership. Distributed by King Features Syndicate.

They Aren't Engaged If You Aren't

With the possible exception of the rare student who has a keen interest in a topic, I would guess that you have seldom been in a situation where your students were more engaged in a lesson than you were. If you aren't engaged, chances are your students won't be either.

> Teachers' enthusiasm about teaching has been shown to positively affect students' enthusiasm about learning.
> —*Edward Deci*

Teachers need to be engaged to promote student success and, like employees in other fields, need to be engaged in order to become competent and develop additional competencies. In order to become and stay engaged, do teachers have the same needs as students? A version of the list of needs on the previous page, slightly modified to address teachers' needs, is provided in the Resources section of the website. Take a minute to drag and drop the items to create a prioritized list of your own needs. If you are working with a group, compare your priorities with those of other group members and discuss why you ranked items the way you did.

Resources
I Need…

Take a look at the online list of teachers' engagement needs (see icon beside the paragraph above). Which one of these teacher needs, once realized, will most positively influence student achievement? You will find the answer in the Research section of the website, along with a review of an interesting book about the impact of leadership actions on teacher engagement and competence.

Research
- A Leader's Responsibility
- Spotlight on *Leading with Teacher Emotions in Mind*

Individual teachers will prioritize their engagement needs differently, depending on their personality and work environment. The findings of researchers such as Carol Dweck, William Glasser, and Gallup suggest that people of all ages are engaged, productive, competent, and satisfied when their needs for connection, sense of purpose, challenge, and autonomy are met.

Below, briefly, are some of the research findings, their implications for our teaching lives, and the chapters in this book where you will find more information. For a summary of the limited research into leader efficacy, see the website.

Research
Leader Efficacy

Connection (See Chapters 7 and 8.)

Finding: Gallup's Employee Engagement survey is based on more than 30 years of research with more than 12 million employees. This research has identified 12 core elements that best predict employee performance. Workplace relationships were determined to be so important that 4 of the 12 elements address the quality of these relationships.

Finding: In a study of four exemplary Grade 9 teachers (Ross et al., 1997), the opportunity to collaborate with others was the single most important contributor to a successful destreaming effort (putting students achieving at different levels together in a class).

Implication: Teachers should take advantage of the opportunity to build professional relationships through structures such as professional learning communities, learning teams, and working with others to provide or receive instructional coaching.

Finding: A teacher's relationship with the school principal has a significant impact, positive or negative, on a teacher's level of engagement and development of competence (Leithwood & Beatty, 2008). Trust is central to this relationship because it creates a safe environment for the risk taking necessary for continued learning (Tschannen-Moran, 2004).

Implication: Teachers and administrators need to work together to build trusting relationships. Trust is a two-way street, but since administrators have evaluative power over teachers, administrators bear the greatest responsibility for building trust. To be perceived as trustworthy, administrators must be consistent, able to maintain confidences, and committed to not using those confidences against a teacher during a performance review.

Sense of Purpose (See Chapter 2.)

Finding: The greatest satisfaction is experienced by people who see their work as a calling and perceive it as meaningful and having a higher purpose, such as making a contribution to society, or even to the individual's personal growth. This sense of purpose is unrelated to the specific nature of the work, the prestige of the occupation, or financial compensation (Wrzesniewski, McCauley, Rozin, & Schwartz, 1997).

Implication: Teachers need to be clear about the purpose of their work so they can rely on this purpose as a touchstone when making decisions, and so they can contribute their sense of purpose to a collective mission and vision developed by the school.

Finding: A review of research (Dannetta, 2002) identified a significant connection between a shared perception of purpose and commitment to that purpose. "When most teachers in a school believe that, together, they can be successful in teaching their students, there is a high level of social expectation that they will do what is necessary to achieve success" (Leithwood & Beatty, 2008, p. 55). In contrast, when teachers don't accept the value of pursuing school-wide goals, they disengage.

> Living a satisfying life requires more than simply meeting the demands of those in control.
> —*Daniel Pink*

Implication: Leaders need to constantly articulate the shared purpose of the school; they also need to provide their teachers with opportunities to collaboratively solve problems in order to achieve that purpose.

Challenge (See Chapters 11 and 12.)

Finding: Work becomes tiresome when tasks are always at the same level of challenge. Studies have confirmed that challenge is a key source of intrinsic motivation and one of the primary factors in job satisfaction (Csikszentmihalyi, 2003). A study of 11 000 industrial scientists and engineers found that the desire for intellectual challenge was the best predictor of productivity (Pink, 2009).

> Human beings have an inherent tendency to seek out novelty and challenges, to extend and exercise their capacities, to explore, and to learn.
> —*Edward Deci*

Implication: Unlike people in careers where mastery of a skill set may result in changing jobs in order to take on new challenges, teachers and administrators work in such complex environments that new challenges are always available. It is a matter of stepping forward to meet them.

Autonomy (See Chapter 4.)

Finding: Autonomy (the opportunity to make choices or to have control over one or more aspects of work—task, time, technique, or team) is as important to teachers as to any other employee group (Dannetta, 2002). For example, superior results were obtained when professional learning about computers in the classroom was differentiated according to individual teacher needs, thus giving teachers choice and control over how they were taught (Ross, Hogoboam-Gray, & Hannay, 2001).

Implication: Teachers need a degree of autonomy in their work. Scripted lessons, while they may ensure consistency of approach, remove this autonomy. Leaders need to promote and defend teacher autonomy, and support it by involving teachers in school decisions, providing choice over how they do their work, seeing issues from the individual's point of view, and providing meaningful and individualized feedback. Note, however, that being autonomous doesn't necessarily mean working alone. There are advantages to being autonomous and interdependent, as the research on collective efficacy indicates (see page 45).

> If you put fences around people, you get sheep.
> —*William McKnight*

Teacher Lee Shulman has this to say when reflecting on 30 years in the profession:

> *Classroom teaching...is perhaps the most complex, most challenging, and most demanding, subtle, nuanced, and frightening activity that our species has ever invented.*
>
> (2004, p. 504)

I believe that teaching is all of these things and more because of the 90 percent that lies underneath our students' and our own observable competencies; it is this 90 percent that makes us unique. Developing the self-awareness to understand our motivations and the sense of self-efficacy to persist in learning will result in increased engagement and achievement for both students and their teachers.

Summary of Chapter Website Content		www.pearsoncanada.ca/tunedout
Conversations	**Resources**	**Research**
• "Competence" Video Byte • Dr. Seuss and Me • Needs or Nonsense?	• My History as a Reader • Teacher Expectations • Reflection Methods • I Need...	• Employee Engagement Index • Teacher Competencies • A "Self" Glossary • A Leader's Responsibility • Spotlight on *Leading with Teacher Emotions in Mind* • Leader Efficacy

4 Developing Learners

Reward Less, Celebrate More 52

Help Students Set Personal Goals. 54

Connect Effort and Success 58

Focus on Relevance. 62

Broaden Your Definition of Intelligence 66

Sometimes Let Them Choose 70

Reward Less, Celebrate More

Since even those with the loftiest of motives wouldn't likely be in the teaching profession without regular rewards, both financial and intangible, trying to engage disengaged students through rewards ranging from stickers to free time to marks seems to make sense.

There is, however, a difference between using rewards with employees and with students. Rewards for learning may have the following unintended consequences:

- → **setting parameters of effort**—If the reward is for completing two out of a set of activities, most students will stop at two even if they have time to complete more.

- → **signalling that learning has no intrinsic value**—A homework pass, for example, sends a clear message that the reward for hard work and learning is not having to do more of it.

- → **damaging trust**—Learners, particularly disengaged learners, may feel that rewards are being used to manipulate them and that they're considered too stupid to recognize it.

Research suggests that the expectation of a reward, not the reward itself, has the most negative impact on intrinsic motivation. For a summary of related research, see the website.

There is one condition when it's fine to have students expect and receive a reward: when the task is dull. "Rewards do not undermine people's intrinsic motivation for dull tasks because there is little or no intrinsic motivation to be undermined" (Deci, Koestner, & Ryan, 2001, p. 14). For everything else, move away from rewards by using ideas from the following list.

Positive Alternatives to Rewards

A caveat: If alternatives are to support motivation and engagement in building academic competence, they must be grounded in authentic accomplishment.

> Do rewards motivate people? Absolutely. They motivate people to get rewards.
> —*Alfie Kohn*

Research
The Problem with Rewards

> Careful consideration of reward effects reported in 128 experiments lead to the conclusion that tangible rewards tend to have a substantially negative effect on intrinsic motivation.
> —*Edward Deci, Richard Koestner, and Richard Ryan*

- √ Celebrate. Everything from team cheers to pizza lunches work when they are unexpected and happen after the learning.

- √ Praise students for their efforts and the strategies they use, not their intelligence. (See page 58.)

- √ Teach students to set goals (see page 56), identify action steps, and regularly assess their progress. Accomplishing even a few small action steps can build intrinsic motivation to continue.

- √ Provide an appropriate challenge and stand back. A natural reward for learning is the endorphin high that comes with accomplishing something meaningful.

- √ Share positive news with parents. Parents are a primary source of a student's sense of belonging, even though adolescents may deny it. To make contact easy, consider sending a brief postcard or an email addressed to both student and parents.

- √ Teach students that self-talk is the way we encourage or discourage ourselves when we work. Use think-alouds and metacognitive questions to show students how to talk themselves through day-to-day problems. See the website for some ideas.

- √ Involve students in self- and peer assessment. Ask them to identify a strength and a next step before submitting work to you. Feedback is one of the best sources of intrinsic motivation, no matter who it comes from (Jensen, 1998). For this technique to work, you will need to explicitly teach students how to give helpful feedback (see the website). You will also need to provide clear success criteria through detailed rubrics and (if possible) work samples, so students can be accurate in their feedback.

If you work in a leadership capacity in your school or district, see the website for information about using celebrations to sustain teacher engagement.

> Celebrate what you want to see more of.
> —*Thomas J. Peters*

Resources
Positive Self-Talk

Resources
Feedback That Works

Resources
Celebrations and Adult Learners

Help Students Set Personal Goals

The Marshmallow Test was started back in the 1960s by Stanford psychologist Walter Mischel. Four-year-old children were taken one at a time to a room where a marshmallow was sitting on a table. The children were told they could eat the marshmallow whenever they wanted to, but if they waited while the researcher ran an errand, they would get two marshmallows when the researcher returned.

The results of the test aren't particularly surprising—one-third of the children ate the marshmallow right away, one-third waited a short while, and one-third waited the 15 to 20 minutes it took for the researcher to return.

The Marshmallow Test was part of a longitudinal study (Sethi & Mischel, 2000). Years later, the differences between the group who waited for the researcher to return and the group who ate the marshmallow right away included the following:

Characteristics of Children Who Waited	Characteristics of Children Who Didn't Wait
• Positive, self-motivating, and persistent in the face of difficulties • Able to delay gratification when pursuing their goals • Reported successful long-term marriages, good health, and high career satisfaction	• Troubled and mistrustful • Indecisive • Unable to delay gratification and unable to achieve goals • Easily distracted from goals by more pleasurable activities • Reported less successful marriages, poorer health, and lower career satisfaction

The children who waited for the researcher's return were exhibiting goal-directed behaviour, which requires the following:

→ self-discipline to delay immediate gratification in return for a greater reward

→ self-monitoring skills to recognize where one stands in relation to the goal's achievement

→ perseverance to stay the course

Goal-directed behaviours are vital to success. One study shows that goal-directed behaviours in students with learning disabilities were more predictive for life success than either school grades or IQ (Raskind et al., 1999).

"Just Right" Goals

Analyze a learning goal by comparing it to the criteria for an effective goal as identified in Robert Marzano's review of research (Marzano et al., 2001):

- The goal is specific enough that it establishes a direction for learning.
- The goal is not so specific that students will ignore related information that wasn't mentioned in the goal statement.
- The goal can be personalized by adapting it to individual needs, perhaps by setting sub-goals or relating it to an area of personal interest.

Shared Goals

The short-term goals necessary for achievement of your school's vision need to be owned by every person on staff (see page 16). Ensuring that this happens requires the courage to have sometimes difficult conversations about school-wide goals. Before or after looking at the tips on the website, work with colleagues to role-play your response to the following scenario:

At a staff meeting, most teachers agree that the school should set the goal of all students passing a standardized literacy test. However, a few people urge the group to set a much lower goal of 50 percent for the year. "The goal can be increased when we have better students," they say. How will you respond?

©2004 ZITS Partnership. Distributed by King Features Syndicate.

> The key to a self-directed and self-modifying learner is the ability to set meaningful goals…and create the work plans that will help them fulfill [goal] requirements.
> —*Arthur Costa and Bena Kallick*

Resources
Difficult Conversations

Help Students Set Personal Goals – continued

Helping Students Work with Goals

How many of your students would have passed the Marshallow Test? For all students, try the following tips for working with goals:

- √ **Teach the difference between a goal and a fantasy.** By devoting himself to hockey from the age of two, Sidney Crosby made a professional hockey career a goal rather than a fantasy. A goal has specific action steps; a fantasy relies on luck.

- √ **Make goals relevant now.** A student's sense of time and future doesn't develop until age 15 or 16 (Feinstein, 2004), so telling students that a task will be relevant when they're in the workplace has little impact. While immediate relevance can't always be established, trying to find a connection to an area of interest has been shown to be especially important to students with attention deficit hyperactivity disorder (Willis, 2007). Older students may be inspired by having you make a connection to a larger purpose or long-term goal. For more on relevance, see pages 62–65.

- √ **Be involved when students personalize classroom goals.** Disengaged students need considerable teacher support to set challenging yet attainable goals, but this support is worth the effort. Achieving a challenging goal enhances competence and sets the stage for continued success.

- √ **Focus on short-term goals.** Short-term goals have action steps that can be achieved immediately or in the near future. Achieving these steps allows students to experience some success and keeps them motivated. For more about the relationship between effort and success, see pages 58–61.

- √ **Teach students to visualize.** Visualizing primes the neural circuits that will be used to perform the task; it also aids recall of strategies that led to success in the past and activates the positive emotions connected to success. For tips on teaching students to visualize, see page 107.

- √ **Set interim achievement targets.** Research by Dan Ariely (2008) at the Massachusetts Institute of Technology showed that even with highly motivated students, interim deadlines increased academic success. This kind of support isn't coddling; it is a project management skill practised daily in the workplace.

- √ **Explicitly teach goal-setting techniques.** Goal setting is not innate; it needs to be taught. See the website for some support in writing SMART goals.

Resources
Writing SMART Goals

- √ **Encourage students to keep track of goals visually.** Rubrics and checklists help students see the steps leading to a goal. Graphs and progress charts can be helpful in tracking progress and achievement of some goals. Recording goals on sticky notes and leaving them on the corner of their desks also will help students (and you) keep a goal in mind. Finally, some students will make a deeper commitment when a goal is written down, as in a learning contract, and signed by everyone involved. A learning contract template is provided on the website.

Resources
Learning Contract Template

Knowing Where You're Going

Think about something you will be teaching and decide which of the following statements best describes your thoughts:

- ❏ My goal is to teach the material and have students learn it.
- ❏ My goal is to define the outcome or expectation in a way that shows students what success looks like.
- ❏ My goal is to get through the material in the time I have available.
- ❏ My goal is to identify the characteristics of success for an essential understanding or skill that addresses a number of outcomes or expectations.
- ❏ My goal is to achieve the outcome stated in a curriculum document.

After you've made your selection and perhaps discussed it with colleagues, check out and consider responding to my blog post.

Conversations
My Goal-Setting Soapbox

Connect Effort and Success

Carol Dweck (2006) did studies involving hundreds of young adolescents. She gave each a set of 10 problems from a non-verbal IQ test. Most students did quite well with these challenging problems, so she praised them. Some students were praised for their ability ("You got x correct. You must be smart at this"), and some for their effort ("You got x correct. You must have worked really hard").

In subsequent tasks, students' engagement changed according to whether they were praised for ability or effort.

When Students Were...	Students Praised for Ability...	Students Praised for Effort...
asked if they'd like to try a challenging task they could learn from	• rejected the offer so as not to do anything that would call their intelligence into question	• embraced the new challenge
given more difficult problems where they didn't experience as much success	• thought they weren't so smart after all	• thought they should work harder
asked about the experience	• said they enjoyed the first set of problems, but after the difficult problems, the activity wasn't fun anymore	• said they enjoyed all of the problems, and many said that the hardest problems were the most fun
given a new set of easier problems	• did worse than when they started because they had lost faith in their ability	• found that their work on the harder problems had sharpened their skills

Dial Way Back, Part II

Thinking about the individual you identified in Chapter 3 (see page 35), use the chart above and the information on pages 36–37 to determine whether the person has a fixed mindset (focused on ability) or a growth mindset (focused on effort). Individually or with a colleague, think about the impact of this mindset on the individual's experiences at school.

Mindsets often vary according to the nature of the task. If the individual you selected usually demonstrates a fixed mindset, search for at least one situation where there is evidence of a growth mindset. You can do this by talking with the individual or speaking with other teachers or the student's parents. The growth mindset may not be evident at school. Look beyond the curriculum to extracurricular activities or personal interests, such as playing video games.

Use the example of the growth mindset to talk with the person about the relationship between effort and success.

Disengaged and actively disengaged students often don't realize that there is a relationship between effort and success. By the time they are adolescents, many disengaged students have had repeated experiences of academic struggle and failure. They protect themselves from more of the same by refusing to make an effort. These adolescents don't believe anything they do in school will make any difference to their success, so they go looking elsewhere to achieve their need for competence.

> You don't drown by falling in the water; you drown by staying there.
> —*Edwin Cole*

Danger, Will Robinson, Danger!

It is not easy to forge the connection between effort and success with adolescents who have experienced a lot of failure and who are intensely concerned with saving face in front of their peers. Aware of this, teachers of adolescents face the dilemma of what to do about the situation. Once again, responses can be described as two roads.

One road is the belief that there is nothing we can do. Some proponents of this road believe that adolescents need to take responsibility for their own learning, and some students will need to experience the "school of hard knocks" before they will make a serious effort. Others believe that years of failure are either impossible to overcome or are a sign that these students are not capable of success.

Conversations
Avoidable or Inevitable Failure?

The other road is the belief that self-esteem and confidence need to be enhanced before a student can learn. Proponents of this road believe that adolescents need large doses of success, even if that success comes from lowered expectations or an exclusive focus on building a relationship with the student, independent of academics.

Where do you stand? What do you believe? This is a highly sensitive issue that should be discussed only in groups where there is a great deal of trust and some processes in place for handling difficult conversations. If that does not describe your situation, I encourage you to reflect on this topic privately, ideally in writing so you can look back on your thoughts as you work with the material in this book. If you'd like to join the public conversation at any time, please see the website blog.

Resources
Difficult Conversations

Connect Effort and Success – continued

Ways to Connect Effort and Success

√ Guarantee success by asking for small things first. Notice and praise tiny actions that are steps in the right direction.

√ Build on incorrect or partially correct answers. Stay with the student who provided the answer, identifying what is right about it or the helpful strategies the student used.

√ Allow students to complete activities in a way that works for them. This may ultimately involve choice (see pages 70–71), but until your students understand who they are as learners, you will likely need to make process decisions for them, based on your understanding of their learning strengths.

√ Provide timely feedback. Getting to a student before he or she has given up is critical, as is identifying something positive in the work before requiring improvement.

√ Short-term goals make clear the relationship between effort and success. Recognizing this relationship has been shown to have more impact on goal attainment than does the teaching of time management techniques (Van Overwalle & De Metsenaere, 1990).

√ Improvement is a clear sign of effort, but it's not an option if students don't have opportunities to revise or redo their work, or retake a test. Admittedly, some students use redo opportunities to avoid making effort on their first attempt, but this problem can be minimized by specifying what needs to be improved and how long a student has to make the improvement.

√ Model appropriate self-talk for students. For example, if a student claims to be too stupid to solve a math problem, counteract this learned pessimism by talking your way through the problem, demonstrating that setbacks are temporary and failure is overcome by perseverance. Guide students to see that sweeping generalizations about their abilities are always inaccurate.

√ Tell students personal stories about times when you succeeded at a task or achieved a dream because you persisted.

Above all, believe that all students are capable of academic success, and support them in achieving it. Disengaged students need every ounce of your energy and support.

One More Try

If you or your colleagues don't believe in providing opportunities for students to redo work, read and discuss the following quotation:

> Pilots can come around for a second attempt at landing. Surgeons can try again to fix something that went badly the first time. Farmers grow and regrow crops until they know all the factors to make them produce abundantly and at the right time of the year. People mark the wrong box on legal forms every day only to later scribble out their earlier mark, check the correct box, then record their initials to indicate approval of the change.
>
> Our world is full of redos. Sure, most adults don't make as many mistakes requiring redos as students do, but that's just it—our students are not adults and as such, they can be afforded a merciful disposition from their teachers as we move them toward adult competency.
>
> (Wormeli, 2006, p. 136)

Consistency Helps

Students and their parents appreciate a consistent policy on redoing work. To develop your school's policy, consider these questions:

- Should students be allowed to redo small assignments? large projects? tests?
- Should they be allowed to redo a task only once a term? multiple times?
- Should the opportunity to redo work be available for any reason, or only for serious extenuating circumstances, such as illness or a death in the family?
- If the work in question is to be evaluated for a report card grade, what mark should the student receive? The new mark? A set mark such as 50 percent?
- What are the signs that a student is taking unfair advantage of the opportunity to redo work? How will this be handled?

Focus on Relevance

The next time you are standing in line at the photocopier or grocery store, politely ask the person in front of you if you can move ahead. Research suggests that 60 percent of people will say yes. That's not bad, but if you really want to move up, give a reason—"I have only five copies to make (or items to purchase)"—and 94 percent of people will allow you to jump the line. Even if your reason doesn't make a lot of sense—"I need to make copies" or "I need to pay for my groceries"—93 percent of people will acquiesce.

These results come from a single study of waiting in line at a photocopier (Langer, 1989), so they may not be replicable. (And if your colleagues have read this section of the book, I can guarantee they won't be!) However, regardless of replicability, providing reasons strengthens the effectiveness of telling students what to do, and providing reasons about the relevance of the learning is best of all. One study found that even if a task was boring or tedious, identifying its relevance resulted in increased student engagement (Assor, Kaplan, & Roth, 2002).

> If we expect students to find meaning, we need to be certain that today's curriculum contains connections to their past experiences, not just ours.
> —*David Sousa*

Relevance requires both connection and importance. Connection is established when new learning is built on something already known. New learning, according to brain researchers, must activate a learner's existing neural networks. The more relevance or connection, the greater the meaning. Research studies show that personally relevant material more readily transfers from short- to long-term memory (Poldrack et al., 2001) than do facts and skills learned in isolation.

Importance refers to work that students see as having either immediate value or leading to something of value in the longer term. Remember that young adolescents have difficulty thinking of the future (see page 56). Try to find immediate benefits for the learning wherever possible.

Irrelevant from the Get-Go?

Conversations
Is Anybody Listening?

Given the appealing options available to students outside of school, is it inevitable that what teachers have to offer will be seen as irrelevant? Discuss your thoughts with colleagues, or with a larger network of educators, by responding to my blog post on the website.

62 ■ Competence

©P

Case Study: Impact on Engagement: Relevance Through Real Work in Genetics

Name: Jason C. **Subject:** Biology **Grades:** 9–12

Genetics is a major topic in today's society, and in all four grade levels of the biology courses my colleagues and I teach. We wanted our students to see the relevance of what they were learning, so we developed a two-part investigation.

In our laboratory exercise, students assembled a karyotype by cutting out chromosomes, pairing them, and fixing them to a card after having compared them to a set of known samples. Next, students received a DNA sequence and, with the prescribed set of restriction enzymes, "cut" the sequence into fragments, filling in a table that would give them a banding pattern unique to their species. These unknown patterns were also compared to a set of known patterns.

By doing this work, students were able to determine the species to which their individual belonged. We used data on owl monkeys (genus *Aotus*) from the work of Dr. Jean Dubach, animal geneticist, who has done a great deal of zoo and conservation genetics research. One of her projects looks at different species of owl monkeys, which may look similar but are genetically distinct; we were able to give each student in a group their own unique set of samples based on these different genetic profiles.

Impact on Engagement

Tarik had been struggling academically for some time before this activity. I expected he would be engaged because he found the topic interesting, but I wasn't sure if that interest would be enough to keep him working. As a result of dividing the investigation into two parts so that students would not be overwhelmed by the procedure, and giving each student in a group a different sample set and responsibility for contributing their results to the work of the group, I found that Tarik stayed engaged and successfully completed the activity.

Resources
Aotus Activity

Focus on Relevance – continued

Resources
Determining Student Interests

> There is no human competence which can be achieved in the absence of a sustaining interest.
> —*Sylvan Tomkins*

Relevance Through Student Interests

Making connections to a student's interests builds new learning on prior experiences, which supports achievement and addresses the need for competence, which supports engagement. To determine student interests, use any of the activities suggested on the website.

One of the following activities might serve double duty in your classroom, encouraging students to demonstrate a competency to their peers and addressing one or more of your curriculum outcomes.

- √ **Make a Zine**—Zines are online or print magazines circulated within small groups of people. They have a counterculture feel to them; they are not intended to be polished, balanced, and tidy. Zines might include full-colour original art, black-and-white sketches or cartoons, photos from home, and pictures from magazines.

- √ **Teach and Tell**—Invite students to teach the class about something that is important to them. Jonathan Erwin (2004) says this idea is a favourite in his Grade 12 English classes.

- √ **FedEx Day**—Try this classroom version of Google's "20 percent" time (see page 80). Invite students to come to class with a problem to solve or a project to tackle. They can work alone or with their choice of classmates. Support students by helping to collect information and supplies they might need. Make sure they know that the day is called FedEx Day because, like the courier company, they have to deliver.

As I mentioned earlier (see page 46), your engagement often sets the bar for student engagement. So show your passion! Many of us have grown to love a subject because we had a teacher who loved it. Be that person for your students.

Case Study: Impact on Engagement: Relevance Through Personal Connection

Name: Karen S. **Subjects:** Social Sciences, English **Grades:** 6/7

Parents, Elders, and the school division's Aboriginal consultant participated in joint planning of an inquiry unit developed around the essential question, "How can we know where we are going by reflecting on our past?" The inquiry was planned using the backward design approach to ensure a strategic alignment from outcomes to assessment to learning activities.

We planned activities using multiple entry points to learning (see page 69), which allowed students to learn and to demonstrate their understanding in a wide variety of ways. Students began by individually creating family trees which they used throughout this unit to understand the different perspectives that could be taken during any learning activity. Activities were chunked into meaningful, manageable pieces dealing with ancestors, culture, language, values, and lifestyle. Many of the lessons were presented by parents, grandparents, Elders, and community members—essential and valuable resources because 27 of my 28 students had First Nations, Métis, or Inuit backgrounds.

Impact on Engagement

Russell was a student with identified special needs. He had fetal alcohol syndrome and was often violently resistant to participating in classroom activities when he felt he couldn't measure up to other students. My hope was that this unit would optimize engagement for Russell, yet not compromise standards.

Throughout the unit, Russell was indeed an equal! He was totally connected and engaged, working cooperatively with two other students and smiling during the process. Russell and his classmates worked diligently to complete the performance task and presented it with honour and pride.

Resources
Performance Task

Broaden Your Definition of Intelligence

Intelligence is a capacity, a potential. "It is the usable potential to learn, to profit from experience, to deal with problems and solve them, to improve one's own life and those of others, to speculate on the unknown, and to chart new worlds and explore new horizons." So says Marilyn vos Savant (1990, p. 20), arguably the smartest person alive. On the Stanford-Binet intelligence test, where a score of 100 is normal, Marilyn scored 230.

Mind Your Mindset

Research
Mensa Workout

It probably won't come as a big surprise to learn that Marilyn vos Savant is a member of Mensa—the elite group open only to people whose IQ score is in the top 2 percent of the general population. Information about Mensa and a link to a Mensa "workout" or pretest appear in the Research section of the website.

Here is a question from the Mensa Workout for you to try:

Which of the figures in the bottom line of drawings best completes the series?
Source: www.mensa.org/workout

I included this question because I failed it. To be honest, I failed it because I didn't even try. As soon as the question appeared on the screen, I pushed the "Next" button. When I sought feedback at the end of the test and read through the explanations for any of my incorrect answers, I skipped right past the explanation for this question. Not only did I not answer the question, I wasn't even interested in finding out the answer! (By the way, the correct answer is the last figure.)

My lack of effort indicates a fixed mindset when it comes to visual pattern recognition questions on intelligence tests. However, when the questions test my knowledge of proverbs or whether I can make new words out of existing words, I have a growth mindset. Even if I don't answer a question correctly, I know I can learn.

Make a two-column chart. In one column, list the kinds of questions and activities for which you have a fixed mindset, and in the other column, list those for which you have a growth mindset. Challenge yourself to come up with at least 20 entries for your chart. You might include activities in categories such as leisure (perhaps doing crossword puzzles), physical (playing tennis), social (giving a dinner party), and work (preparing a teaching plan).

Keep your chart for use in the next activity, "Asking the Right Question."

Howard Gardner was once introduced at a conference as the man who changed the world by adding the letter "s" to the word *intelligence*. I'm not sure that Gardner would agree that he changed the world—30 years after developing his theory of multiple intelligences, Gardner wrote this:

> *While I am pleased that my theory has had some impact, I can also say that I have assembled a massive amount of data about how difficult it is to change people's minds about what intelligence is, how it operates, and how to assess it.*

(2006, p. 30)

Nevertheless, most educators have considerable experience with the fact that students think and learn in a variety of ways. As a result, many of us have been quick to embrace either Gardner's theory of multiple intelligences or Robert Sternberg's theory of triarchic intelligences.

Gardner's theory is that we each have nine different intelligence potentials that we use to varying degrees and in different combinations. These potentials may be categorized as shown below:

Multiple Intelligences		
Based on Material Objects	**Based on Symbols**	**Personal**
• visual-spatial • bodily-kinesthetic • naturalist *Associated more with skills*	• verbal-linguistic • musical-rhythmic • logical-mathematical *Associated more with concepts, stories, theories*	• interpersonal • intrapersonal • existential *Associated more with knowing humans*

Broaden Your Definition of Intelligence – continued

Sternberg's theory of successful intelligence is that we use all three intelligences—analytical, creative, and practical—but have a preference for one.

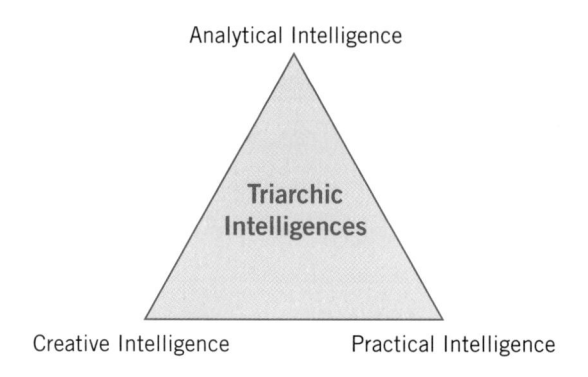

```
            Analytical Intelligence
                    /\
                   /  \
                  /    \
                 / Triarchic \
                / Intelligences \
               /_____\
        Creative Intelligence   Practical Intelligence
```

Asking the Right Question

Resources
- Multiple Intelligences Inventory
- Triarchic Intelligences Inventory

Gardner's and Sternberg's theories encourage us to change the question we ask of ourselves and our students from "How smart are you?" to "How are you smart?" Use the inventories provided on the website to answer this question for yourself. Add the information to the appropriate columns on the two-column chart you created in the previous activity, "Mind Your Mindset."

Gardner's and Sternberg's theories serve a noble purpose by reminding us that there are more ways to learn than just through linguistic, mathematical (Gardner) or analytical (Sternberg) intelligences. Our task as educators is to show students that they can be successful and develop academic competencies in a variety of ways.

One More Time

Take one more look at your two-column chart from the activities "Mind Your Mindset" and "Asking the Right Question." Put a check mark beside each entry that translates into something you do in your classroom. For example, I enjoy wordplay so I routinely engage students in work with idioms, palindromes, and clever definitions for obscure words. On the other hand, I dislike and am terrible at visual pattern recognition. I never give students opportunities to solve visual puzzles.

What do the check marks on your chart tell you? If, like me, you are sometimes guilty of teaching only in the way that works for you, consider using some of the ideas in the following lists to engage students with learning strengths different from your own.

Multiple Intelligences in the Classroom

√ From time to time, allow students to work in cooperative groups and structure the groups so that various learning preferences are represented in each group.

√ Teach concepts through a variety of entry points that roughly map onto the multiple intelligences. See the Resources section of the website.

Resources
Multiple Entry Points

√ Involve students in mentoring and apprenticeship activities where they are able to see intelligence potentials applied in workplaces.

√ Sometimes, allow students choice in how they demonstrate their understanding. Provide choices that reflect the various intelligence potentials.

√ Use and teach students to develop metaphors and analogies that represent a concept in a variety of ways. (See pages 90–93.)

Triarchic Intelligences in the Classroom

Triarchic teaching is easy to do. The main principles are simple:

1. Some of the time, teach analytically, helping students learn to analyze, evaluate, compare and contrast, critique, and judge.

2. Some of the time, teach creatively, helping students learn to create, invent, imagine, discover, explore, and suppose.

3. Some of the time, teach practically, helping students learn to apply, use, utilize, contextualize, implement, and put into practice.

4. Some of the time, enable all students to capitalize on their strengths.

5. Most of the time, enable all students to correct or compensate for their weaknesses.

6. Make sure your assessments match your teaching, calling upon analytical, creative, and practical as well as memory skills.

7. Value the diverse patterns of abilities in all students.

(Sternberg et al., 2000)

Sometimes Let Them Choose

The hypothalamus is the part of the brain responsible for what is referred to as our "primitive" emotions—anger, fear, and aggression. The hormones associated with puberty often increase activity in the hypothalamus, supporting research that suggests the hypothalamus is at its most active during adolescence. Additionally, adolescents are strongly influenced by peers, and peers are often exhibiting hypothalamus behaviours. If you sometimes have the feeling that one student's emotions and behaviours are controlling everyone else's, you may not be far wrong.

One of our needs, according to William Glasser, is our need for autonomy—control over aspects of our environment. Brain researchers would agree. As Kathie Nunley suggests,

> ...one of the easiest ways to engage the hypothalamus of anyone is to take away their perception of control. When people are backed into a corner and feel that they are powerless or have no control whatsoever over their situation, the hypothalamus becomes engaged. Once that happens we see destructive, angry, and aggressive behaviours.
>
> (2003, p. 51)

I wonder how many actively disengaged students and adults deliberately undermine others in an effort to achieve their need for autonomy when they feel they have none. How many disengaged students and adults refuse to work to their potential just to prove that they can refuse?

Choice addresses our need for autonomy. It is important in the classroom for different aspects of teaching and learning:

- → **differentiated instruction**—It allows students to sometimes choose to work in an area of personal strength.
- → **assessment**—Providing choice of assessment tasks will give you a more accurate picture of student understanding.
- → **behaviours**—Choice helps students learn to make their own decisions and not follow the crowd.
- → **preparation for 21st century realities**—When presented with an increasingly wider range of choices, consumers need to understand how to make good decisions. Initiative and self-direction, two important 21st century skills, develop through choice.

> Choice is a critical ingredient. Students are more likely to want to do schoolwork when they have some choice in the courses they take, in the material they study, and in the strategies they use to complete tasks.
> —*National Research Council*

Appealing Options

In an experiment by Sheena Iyengar and Mark Lepper (2000), arrays of exotic jams were displayed in a busy gourmet food store. People were invited to sample the jams and received a coupon for a dollar off a jar. In one variation on the experiment, six varieties of jam were available for tasting; in another, 24 varieties were available. Regardless of the number of varieties provided for tasting, all 24 varieties were available for purchase.

Research
Choosing Jams

Discuss your responses to the following questions with colleagues, giving reasons for your answers.

1. Which array of jams (6 or 24) attracted the most people?

2. Was there a difference between the number of jams sampled in each variation? If so, in which variation did people sample more jams?

3. Were more jams purchased by people who were at a display with six choices or by those at a display with 24 choices?

After the discussion, check the website to learn the results of the experiment.

Choice in Your Classroom

On the website you'll find a list of differentiated instruction structures that you can use to provide students with choices. Share your experiences using these structures with your colleagues. If there's one that you haven't used but would like to try, get some pointers from a colleague or perhaps work together to develop the necessary material.

Resources
DI Structures

Choice is as powerful a motivator for adults as it is for students. When working with adults, clearly define the goal and then allow people to achieve it in a variety of ways. Setting the standards and then giving people the freedom to meet them in whatever way they choose results in higher quality implementation and more engaged participants.

Sometimes Let Them Choose – continued

Case Study: Impact on Engagement: Mind Map and Choice Board

Name: Rebecca F.   **Subject:** English   **Grade:** 11

What motivated the main character? That's the question I asked my students as they read The *Curious Incident of the Dog in the Night-time* by Mark Haddon. It wasn't an easy assignment—the novel's main character is a boy who has Asperger Syndrome. In order to help students answer the question, I had them complete a short research assignment where they investigated Asperger Syndrome and reported their findings to the class.

I began with a mind map created using SMART Ideas software. The map contained four questions that students needed to answer, such as "What behaviours are exhibited by people with Aspergers?" In addition, there were four blanks where students were able to ask and answer their own questions. Students were given one 75-minute period in the library to complete the research component of the assignment online.

I made the research portion of the assignment highly structured because it was the first such assignment of the semester. I also thought that structure would support the students in my class, some with identified special needs and some who were actively disengaged.

After completing their research, students chose a question from the mind map and shared their answer with the class. They were given a choice of creative options for sharing their responses.

Impact on Engagement

This was the first time I had allowed students to identify and pursue areas of interest related to a topic. I noticed that our class discussions of the novel were rich and that my usually disengaged students took part. All students clearly felt they had something unique to contribute. I will definitely encourage students to pursue personal interests in the future!

Given the number of bodily-kinesthetic learners in my class, I was surprised and a bit disappointed to find that the majority of students chose to write an information paragraph to demonstrate their learning. When asked, they told me that it was the most straightforward option and would require the least amount of effort. In the future, I will offer fewer choices, and I may remove the paragraph option.

Case Study: Impact on Engagement: RAFT

Name: Cindy S. **Subject:** English **Grade:** 10

"Do we HAVE to do this?" This was the question that greeted me every single day in my locally developed Grade 10 English class. The students were a disinterested, unmotivated group, and I was trying to engage them by finding relevant reading materials for them and creating innovative assignments.

I'd done well with relevance. We had just finished reading the novel *Tom Finder* by Martine Leavitt and my students had really connected with it. We even emailed the author to tell her we'd loved her novel, and she graciously answered our many questions. I now needed an innovative culminating task.

Looking around my classroom, I noticed that every last student was plugged into an MP3 player. I decided to use a RAFT for the final assignment and have each student take on the role of one of the novel's characters, complete a short writing task, and then create a podcast. Since my students were also big fans of the "Idol" TV singing competitions, we'd listen to each student's podcast and choose a "Podcast Idol."

The assignment hooked every one of my students, except Zack. An 18-year-old with few graduation credits to his name, Zack vehemently refused to do the assignment. Deciding not to argue, I allowed him to do a different task while students recorded their podcasts.

Zack lasted 30 minutes before approaching me and asking if he could do the assignment. I happily handed him a headset and microphone, and he was soon hard at work and completely engaged.

Prior to this assignment Zack had the lowest mark in the class, but when the podcasts were shared he was chosen as "Podcast Idol." His oral reading was excellent, and he had added sound effects to enhance his presentation. He beamed when we applauded him and presented him with his prize—his very own headset and microphone.

Resources
- *Tom Finder* RAFT
- The Winning Podcast

Sometimes Let Them Choose – continued

Resources

Classroom Choice Checklist

Choice is certainly beneficial for student engagement, but it doesn't always result in meaningful learning that has an impact on student achievement. Effective choices meet the following criteria:
- All choices address the same learning outcome.
- All choices are engaging and respectful.
- All choices take approximately the same length of time to complete.

For maximum effectiveness, use the tips on the website when providing choice.

Summary of Chapter Website Content		www.pearsoncanada.ca/tunedout
Conversations	**Resources**	**Research**
• My Goal-Setting Soapbox • Avoidable or Inevitable Failure? • Is Anybody Listening?	• Positive Self-Talk • Feedback That Works • Celebrations and Adult Learners • Difficult Conversations • Writing SMART Goals • Learning Contract Template • *Aotus* Activity • Determining Student Interests • Performance Task • Multiple Intelligences Inventory • Triarchic Intelligences Inventory • Multiple Entry Points • DI Structures • *Tom Finder* RAFT • The Winning Podcast • Classroom Choice Checklist	• The Problem with Rewards • Mensa Workout • Choosing Jams

Creativity

Albert Einstein was once asked about the difference between his intelligence and everyone else's. After giving the question some thought he said, "When other people go looking for a needle in a haystack and find it, they stop looking. I keep looking—for second, third, fourth, and fifth needles."

5 Searching the Haystack

Conversations

"Creativity" Video Byte

What comes to mind when you think of Albert Einstein? Scientist? Towering intellectual giant? $E=mc^2$? Or, as one of my students once suggested, "that guy with all the bad-hair days"?

Did the word *creative* come to mind? Probably not. Yet Einstein's contributions to the world, as well as his response to the question about intelligence (see previous page), confirm that he was highly creative.

Creative is a word that carries a lot of connotative baggage. Many people are quick to reject the idea that they are creative because they associate the term exclusively with people who work in fields such as advertising, architecture, fashion, fine art, performing arts, and publishing. For those of us who would like to become more creative, we might hamper our own efforts by comparing ourselves to the greats within these industries. If we can't be Coco Chanel, Tom Thomson, Martha Graham, James Joyce, or any other creative person we admire, we may wonder whether we should strive to "be creative" at all.

What, if anything, does creativity have to do with your day-to-day responsibilities as a teacher? with student engagement? with learning in the 21st century? My answer to these questions is "Quite a lot"—though *my* answer is irrelevant. What matters is what you believe.

Belief Check

What do you believe about creativity and education? Please check all statements below that apply.

❏ 1. Creativity is not valued in the world of work.

❏ 2. Creativity is different from intelligence.

❏ 3. In school, creativity "belongs to" teachers of the arts.

❏ 4. I don't have a creative bone in my body.

❑ 5. For students, creativity is advisable only after they have mastered the content and rules of a discipline.

❑ 6. It doesn't matter what I think about creativity. If it's not in my curriculum, I don't have time to teach it.

❑ 7. Creativity is a solitary process.

❑ 8. Creativity helps me solve the problems I encounter in my teaching.

Creativity Myths

Several of the "Belief Check" statements represent popular myths about creativity. On the website, you will find a comment on each of these statements. Try to dispassionately observe your reaction when you read a comment that contradicts your belief. You might find yourself arguing with it, giving an example that proves your case, or ignoring the comment altogether. Such responses are normal. Beliefs are highly resistant to any evidence that contradicts them.

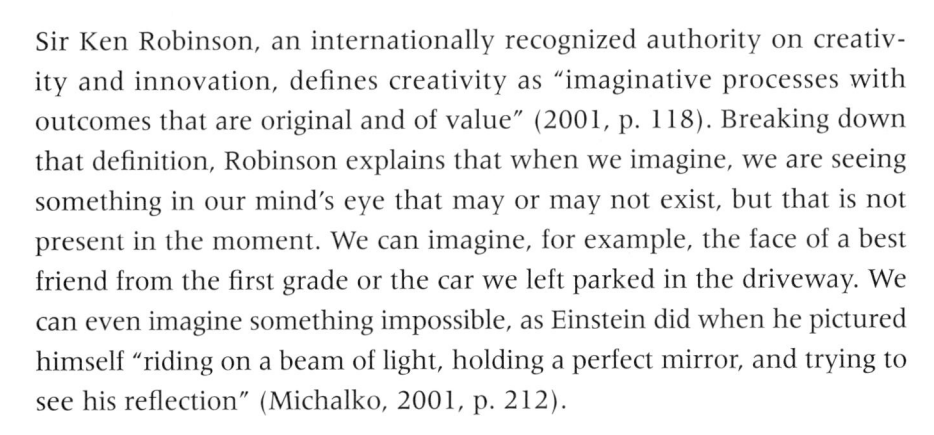

Research
Belief Statements

Sir Ken Robinson, an internationally recognized authority on creativity and innovation, defines creativity as "imaginative processes with outcomes that are original and of value" (2001, p. 118). Breaking down that definition, Robinson explains that when we imagine, we are seeing something in our mind's eye that may or may not exist, but that is not present in the moment. We can imagine, for example, the face of a best friend from the first grade or the car we left parked in the driveway. We can even imagine something impossible, as Einstein did when he pictured himself "riding on a beam of light, holding a perfect mirror, and trying to see his reflection" (Michalko, 2001, p. 212).

Creativity involves imagining new possibilities, but it goes beyond simple imagining by having a focus on action and on original results that have value. If Einstein had relaxed in his easy chair, imagining his interstellar travels but never doing anything with that image, we wouldn't have the theory of relativity and we wouldn't say he was creative.

Mihaly Csikszentmihalyi (1996) uses the term *"capital c" creativity* to refer to people like Einstein—people who produce work that others in the same field recognize as innovative, and that sooner or later has a significant impact on subsequent work in the field.

Fortunately, we don't all have to be Einsteins who produce results that have never been seen before and that benefit all of humanity. We are also being creative when we produce results that are original and valuable to us (such as a new theme for a daughter's birthday party) or to a particular community (such as creating a new system for helping the school track expenses). These are examples of *"small c" creativity*—personal achievements that are important because they contribute to a rich and fulfilling life. As Csikszentmihalyi (1996, p. 344) reminds us, "Even though personal creativity may not lead to fame and fortune, it can do something that from the individual's point of view is even more important: make day-to-day experiences more vivid, more enjoyable, more rewarding."

On the Job

Applied creativity, or innovation, is the defining characteristic of success in today's globally competitive marketplace:

> [N]ew products, new techniques, new services, and new solutions to old problems...mark the difference between a company that will thrive and one that will soon be deader than the eight-track tape.
>
> (Brown, 2009, p. 134)

Research

Data Storage Capacity

It is a myth, however, to believe that a handful of brilliantly creative individuals are out there propping up the world's economy for the rest of us. The Renaissance woman or man who is an expert in multiple domains is a rarity today. Rather, the 21st century is an age of increasing specialization; it cannot be otherwise. Our store of knowledge is doubling every 10 years and, thanks to the internet and increases in data storage capacity, we have instant access to much of it. To put this in a personally meaningful context, consider what you did when preparing to write an essay during high school or university. If you were at school in the early days of the internet or before, as I was, perhaps you shared my habit of first surrounding yourself with every relevant book and journal article you could find, trying to ensure you would have all the applicable knowledge at hand before beginning to write. If that was a fool's game then, what is the experience like for students who try to do the same today?

In the last few decades, the knowledge of experts has become increasingly specialized. Mathematicians may fully understand only a handful of 50 papers presented at a mathematical conference, as there are now about 236 subspecialties in this field. By the end of the 1960s, Michael Polanyi had already noted this trend in science: "[A]ny single scientist may be competent to judge at first-hand only about a hundredth of the total current output of science" (Polanyi, 1969, cited in Robinson, 2001, p. 170).

How is such specialized knowledge useful outside the realm of pure research? Innovation comes from project teams, the pre-eminent organizational structure of the 21st century workplace (see also page 110). These teams, whose members may work in the same office or around the globe, usually consist of individuals with specialized knowledge *and* the flexible thought processes that allow them to relate disparate ideas from multiple domains to their own experiences and knowledge. People with this combination of specialized expertise and the creative ability to see connections between disparate ideas are highly prized in the 21st century workplace.

> Creativity thinks up new things; innovation does new things.
> —*Michael Gerber*

Corporations prefer to hire people who already have expertise and creative thinking ability, rather than trying to develop these qualities on the job. Young people with the necessary skills have tremendous opportunities—because of baby-boomer retirements there is a shortage of talented workers who are ready to step into management positions. (See "Talent Wars" on the website.)

Research
Talent Wars

Employers are finding that talented young people are entering the workforce with expectations quite different from the ones their parents had. In their careers, young people today are looking for

- **freedom**—to work outside the office; to have a flexible schedule rather than working from 9 to 5; to have a balance between work and personal life; to have the opportunity to gain experience in a variety of different jobs within a company
- **customization**—to be seen as individuals; to be provided with individualized job descriptions and professional development opportunities; to receive frequent informal feedback that recognizes specific contributions to the organization

> Adapt to the NetGen ways of doing things and win their loyalty—and the War for Talent. Or stick to the old ways and lose.
> —*Don Tapscott*

- **scrutiny**—to work for companies with a culture that embraces sharing business plans, new-product ideas, and financial data with all employees
- **integrity**—to be employed by companies that are honest, considerate, and willing to live by their commitments
- **collaboration**—to work in a job with a problem or dilemma no one knows how to solve, and lots of great people to work with
- **entertainment**—to be engaged in work that is enjoyable; to have the freedom to use social networking sites when taking a break
- **speed**—to have opportunities for rapid advancement; to be able to deal directly with people who can provide answers and help them take action, rather than working through a chain of command or bureaucratic red tape
- **innovation**—to be allowed or encouraged to find new ways of accomplishing a job, and new ways to contribute to the organization's success

(Adapted from Tapscott, 2009, pp. 160–169)

Seeing Red

Conversations
Desires of the Net Generation

Young people's desire for collaborative and innovative work environments seems a good fit to the needs of the 21st century workplace, but am I the only one who seethes when I read the rest of the expectations of the Net Generation? In my blog, I try to figure out if my irritation is based on legitimate concerns, jealousy, or fear. I invite you to contribute your thoughts to the blog or share them in your book study group.

While many companies haven't made significant changes in decades, an increasing number are providing models of the kind of 21st century workplace young people are looking for—and these are proving to be highly successful. Google's 2008 revenue of $20 billion came from innovation. "Google *requires* employees to innovate. It's part of the job. It's how workers are valued. It's how Google grows" (Jarvis, 2009, p. 111). Engineers are asked to spend 20 percent of their work time on projects of personal interest to them, and they have freedom to choose their team, the resources they'll need, and the approach they'll take. Gmail and Google News both resulted from personal interest projects.

Relaxing into Productivity at Google

At the Google complex in Mountainview, California, there's a rock-climbing wall as well as a company pool, beach volleyball pit, gymnasiums, and nap pods (shown in photo). Bicycles and scooters are available for travel between buildings in the complex. There are flexible work hours, wide-open time to play volleyball or IM friends, and few solo offices. Google relaxes its 20 000 staff members into productivity and innovation—and it works.

Google's name is a play on the word *googol*, which is the mathematical term for 1 followed by 100 zeros. The company's founders, Larry Page and Sergey Brin, chose the name to represent both the immensity of information that exists in the world and Google's mission to organize all of that information and make it accessible. Google doesn't report how many servers it runs to keep the world's information accessible to us—estimates are in the millions.

Google is well on its way to realizing its mission. There are more than 150 Google domains, in addition to the well-known search engine. You can read digitized books, translate from one language to another, share your calendar with others, and collaborate with others in writing anything from a business plan to a novel. All of Google's domains and applications come from staff members who were hired for ability rather than experience, and who work in an environment built for cross-team collaboration.

Google's corporate culture accepts, even welcomes, mistakes. After moving too quickly and making an error that cost the company millions of dollars, one Google executive was praised for making fast decisions and was told, "If we don't have any of these mistakes, we're just not taking enough risk" (Jarvis, 2009, p. 94).

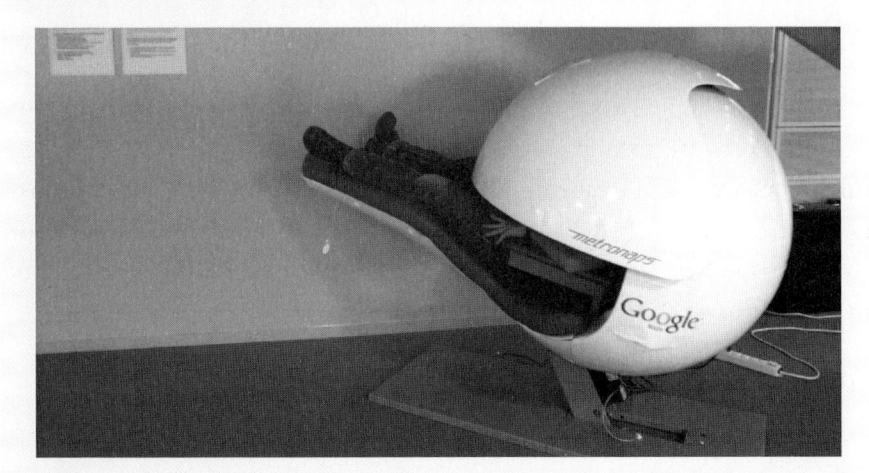

> We are currently not planning on conquering the world.
> —*Sergey Brin*

Companies such as Google, Facebook, craigslist, and Amazon are arguably in a league all their own. Nevertheless, there is considerable evidence to support author Daniel Pink's idea that as a result of increasing affluence, technology, and globalization, we are now moving from the Information Age, with its focus on knowledge, to the Conceptual Age, which puts a focus on creation.

Creative industries are growing by leaps and bounds relative to other industrial sectors. In the United States today, for example, more Americans are working in arts, entertainment, and design than in law, accounting, and auditing (Pink, 2005). This growth is occurring in part because people in creative industries are able to connect with and extend the creativity and innovation coming from other fields, such as math, science, and technology.

A Fascinating Read

Research
Spotlight on
A Whole New Mind

Every year, I'm lucky enough to read at least one book that stays with me and shifts the way I think. One of those books is *A Whole New Mind: Why Right-Brainers Will Rule the Future* by Daniel Pink. Pink describes the shift from the Information Age, with its focus on left-brain skills, to the Conceptual Age, a time of right-brain creativity. You'll find my undeniably biased endorsement and the reasons for it in on the website.

Creative Teachers

Our students clearly need both specialized knowledge and flexible thought processes if they are to be successful. If we accept Tapscott's characteristics of the Net Generation, students also need opportunities to be flexible and innovative in order to feel engaged. Unfortunately, there is often a significant disconnect between what is offered at school and what is desired by students and society. Fortunately, the problem is easily resolved.

I would suggest that when it comes to the classroom, flexible thought processes are less about creativity, as defined by Robinson, and more about creative thinking processes or a creative outlook on life, as encouraged in leading-edge businesses around the world. Roger von Oech describes creative thinking in this way:

Creative thinking requires an outlook that allows us to search for ideas and play with our knowledge and experience. With this outlook, we try different approaches, first one, then another, often not getting anywhere. We use crazy, foolish and impractical ideas as stepping stones to practical new ideas. We break the rules occasionally, and explore for ideas in unusual outside places. And, in the end, our creative outlook enables us to come up with new ideas.

(2008, p. 14)

Check Your Beliefs

Please refer back to the "Belief Check" statements on pages 76–77, substituting *creative thinking* every time you read the words *creative* or *creativity*. Do any of your responses change? Why? What does this tell you?

My guess is that for many teachers there is greater familiarity with creative thinking than with creativity. Most of us have taken part in creative thinking activities in various workshops we have attended. We might have brainstormed a list of ideas without censoring our thoughts, diagrammed our thinking with images and key words in a mind map, combined seemingly unrelated concepts, created a metaphor, or examined a situation from a variety of perspectives. All of these actions are among the tools of creative thinking—thinking that encourages us to be curious, question assumptions, and break with habitual patterns of thought.

> Creative thinking may simply mean the realization that there is no particular virtue in doing things the way they have always been done.
>
> —*Rudolph Flesch*

We should not assume, however, that familiarity equals comfort. In my experience, creative thinking activities in professional development workshops are appreciated by some teachers and barely tolerated by others. It makes perfect sense that people respond differently—we are individuals, each with a unique profile of learning preferences. Furthermore, some of those creative thinking activities really do put us out on a limb—we feel foolish if we don't have any wacky ideas...or if we do!

There are many ways to incorporate creative thinking processes into teaching so that the work is meaningful and not forced or artificial. I will share a number of them in Chapter 6. However, I recommend that you begin by applying creative thinking processes to some of the practices you use now and considering how these practices relate to your beliefs. New insights become possible when we have the courage and flexibility of mind to look for more than one needle in the haystack. In education, we can do that by first unearthing and examining the beliefs we hold about our students, ourselves, and our role as teachers.

Beliefs

Beliefs come from our experiences. They are generalized understandings we have of others, of ourselves, and of the world around us. Educator Theodore Marchese (1998) explains it well:

> [W]e develop, at quite early ages—as five-year-olds, for example—basic sets of ideas about how the world works, what's dangerous, who's friendly, about right and wrong, what to like and how to behave, and so on. The scary part is that these childhood versions of reality tend to get pretty hard-wired into the brain and prove quite resistant to change. Once we think we've figured out some corner of the world, we tend to see what we want to see and hear what we want to hear, bending subsequent experience into confirmation. I say "scary" because the existence of prior beliefs can be a major impediment to subsequent learning. The beliefs, after all, may be objectively wrong, or bigoted, or dysfunctional, and block fair and open encounter with the new or different.

It is often said that parents and other members of a community consider themselves experts on schooling because they once were students. It is equally true that most of what we know about teaching we learned from our own experiences as students.

Belief or Fact?

Conversations
Disengaging Beliefs

How can you decide whether a thought is a belief or a fact? Judith Yero (2002) suggests that if you can think of a situation where a statement is not true, it most likely represents a belief rather than a fact. For example, "Students are motivated by grades" is a belief statement because it is not true of all students.

For each of the statements in "Belief Check" (see pages 76–77), ask yourself if there is a situation in which the statement might not be true. Are there any facts in the list? On the website I have identified some beliefs that I think are problematic for student engagement. Do you agree? Are there others you would add?

Let's consider an example of how beliefs can limit response. On any given day, in any high school classroom in North America, chances are good that a teacher is working with only 50 to 80 percent of the students on his or her roster. The rest of them didn't show up. Discount the students who are absent because of illness, the need to work or to care for a younger sibling, or some other excusable reason. There are still students who simply chose not to attend. Unless you are a teacher who is fortunate enough to work at a school where attendance is not an issue, addressing the problem of chronically absent students may be one of the biggest challenges of your career.

"We can't engage students who aren't there," we tell our colleagues, our administrators, anyone who will listen. "Furthermore," we continue, "when these students do show up, they expect us to get them caught up during class time, which is almost impossible to do because the class has moved on. When we ask them to submit overdue work, they just shrug and say they don't have it done."

If you are a classroom teacher, you probably found it impossible to read the preceding two paragraphs dispassionately. How do you explain chronic absenteeism? What actions should be taken to correct it? If you closely examine your responses, you'll see that they reveal your beliefs about what is *really* going on.

> I have always thought the actions of men the best interpreters of their thoughts.
> —*John Locke*

A belief has three components:

1. *Cognition*—the logical argument you would provide in support of the belief
2. *Feeling*—the emotion that comes from the value you hold or the need you have and underlies the belief
3. *Behaviour*—what you do in response to the situation, and what motivation or reason you assign to the student's behaviour

(Yero, 2002)

What's Going On?

Here is a list of some possible reasons why students skip school. Which ones do you believe are true?

Resources
Analyzing a Belief

Our students are skipping school because...

- the learning isn't relevant to their lives
- they aren't held accountable for their actions through failure or suspension
- they don't feel that their teachers care about them
- they haven't ever been taught a work ethic
- administrators aren't doing their jobs

- parents aren't doing their jobs
- they have to check all of their technology at the door
- school isn't as challenging as video games

For each statement you believe to be true (or for any new statements you would like to add), complete a copy of the "Analyzing a Belief" chart provided on the website. If you are working with colleagues, each person could select a different statement to analyze. (You might find it helpful to use or adapt the chart for use in situations such as a PLC or department meeting when discussing issues for which analyzing underlying beliefs is beneficial.)

Our beliefs lead us to conceptualize a problem in a particular manner and then to seek a solution to *the problem we have identified*. This approach is reasonable. But what if our solution doesn't work? What should we do then?

This is the dilemma we face when considering significant issues of student disengagement, such as student truancy. But this dilemma presents us with the opportunity to use creative thinking processes for our own purposes—to solve problems of practice so we can better deal with the relentless changes in today's educational landscape.

Getting Ready to Talk

If truancy is an issue in your school, the creative thinking processes described in Chapter 6 may help you develop some possible solutions. It's important to do these activities with colleagues you trust, and to be open to having your beliefs challenged. The "Belief Quotes" activity on the website can be used to help a group establish process agreements before they begin to work.

Resources
- Working with Quotes
- Belief Quotes

Summary of Chapter Website Content		www.pearsoncanada.ca/tunedout
Conversations	**Resources**	**Research**
• "Creativity" Video Byte • Desires of the Net Generation • Disengaging Beliefs	• Analyzing a Belief • Working with Quotes • Belief Quotes	• Belief Statements • Data Storage Capacity • Talent Wars • Spotlight on *A Whole New Mind*

6 Practical Creativity

It's Not That There Are No Rules 88

Not Just for English Class 90

5 Ways to Get Lots of Ideas 94

Solving the Tough Ones 96

Worth a Thousand Words 100

Put It on Paper 104

In Your Mind's Eye 106

Hands-on Learning 108

Interdisciplinary Study 110

It's Not That There Are No Rules

> When forced to work within a strict framework the imagination is taxed to its utmost—and will produce its richest ideas. Given total freedom the work is likely to sprawl.
> —*T.S. Eliot*

There are writers, musicians, artists, and inventors whose work is so breathtakingly original it seems they have created their own world, invented their own rules. That is rarely the case. It is more likely that the individuals have thoroughly mastered the rules of their domain and achieved superb technical control of their medium. It is not freedom but rather the tension between wide-open thinking and clearly defined parameters that breeds superior results.

Your Creative Thinking IQ

Give yourself exactly two minutes to list uses for a coat hanger. Then give yourself one point for each idea. A score of 8–10 is the global average; 16 is a good "brainstormer" level; 24 is exceptional and rare; 32 is genius level (Buzan, 2005).

Improving Your Creative Thinking IQ

> There are no tests that provide a reliable picture of a person's creative capacities.
> —*Sir Ken Robinson*

Here's a second test (Buzan, 2005). This time, find uses and associations between a coat hanger and each of the following: golf ball, snow, knife, money, music, circus, plant. Take as much time as you need, and work with others if you want to. Ready? Go!

You may have found that thinking creatively is much easier when the task has some parameters. When your brain is given two items, it will always search for and find a link between the two.

"Thank you for calling Creative Business Seminars. If you'd like to become a more creative problem solver, press 1 without touching any part of your telephone."

©Randy Glasbergen/glasbergen.com

Involving your students or yourself in creative thinking or creative work of any kind does not mean abandoning all standards and accepting anything offered. I recommend that you follow these "rules" of the creative process, and teach them to your students:

"Rules" of the Creative Process

→ *Recognize where you are in the process.* There are different models of creativity, but they all describe a process of focus, withdrawal, and breakthrough (Robinson, 2001). Creative thinking can have the same phases but it is most often described in terms of generating ideas, followed by evaluating and executing the best ideas.

→ *Know what to expect of a phase.* Don't expect "good copy" when students are drafting their thoughts. When stuck on a problem, don't assume that you can force a breakthrough. You will quite likely need to allow a solution to incubate in your mind while you do other things for a while.

→ *Don't try to be in two phases simultaneously.* Walt Disney avoided this problem by taking three different perspectives when he worked. On the first day he was the dreamer; on the second, the realist; and on the third, the critic (Michalko, 2006).

→ *Learn the technical and process skills necessary for success.* A visual arts student needs to be taught the domain-specific skill of attaching handles to a clay dish in such a way that they are strong as well as aesthetically appealing. A student in any subject area needs to be taught the flexible thinking skills that are necessary for generating ideas.

→ *Relax and have some fun!* Creativity and creative thinking are opportunities to be fully alive in the classroom—to recognize and enjoy the unique ability all humans have to look at the world with fresh eyes and open minds.

> Making mistakes is not the same thing as being creative, but if you are not willing to make mistakes, then it is impossible to be truly creative.
>
> —**Garr Reynolds**

Creativity Without Rules

I took my class to an art gallery for a session with a well-known art critic (who shall remain forever nameless). In my blog post I tell what happened and invite your thoughts. Specifically, was I wrong in interpreting the event as I did?

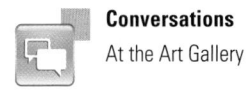

Conversations
At the Art Gallery

Not Just for English Class

Which of these explanations of nerve cells is easier to understand?

a. Dendrites serve as stimulus receptors for the neuron, but they respond to a number of different types of stimuli. Some receptors respond to chemical neurotransmitters, some to electrical stimuli. Nerve cells function asynchronously when at rest.

b. Your brain is like an orchestra. "Each nerve cell has an instrument and each nerve cell is a virtuoso performer. When they are all sitting waiting for the conductor, they are doing things independently of each other. One of the tuba players might be tuning his tuba. The third horn is talking on her mobile....your brain in the resting state is exactly like this....your nerve cells are just bumbling along perfectly content in their own space."

(Curran, 2008, p. 36)

While some details, not to mention specialized vocabulary, are lost in the translation, if you don't know much about nerve cells it is likely you found that the second option is easier to understand.

> The unexpected connection is more powerful than one that is obvious.
> —*Heraclitus*

Learning happens through connection. We make sense of new information by forging connections to something we already know. Connections that are unusual or unexpected can lead to creative insights that result in new ideas. For example, William Harvey discovered that blood circulates when he made a connection between the heart and a pump.

The understanding of existing ideas and the creation of new ones rely on making connections—recognizing and comparing similarities and differences across concepts. Three forms of figurative language are most often used to fulfill this function:

- *metaphor*—This word from old Greek literally means "to carry" or transfer ideas from one set of concepts to another. Example: *The cell is a factory*.
- *simile*—A simile is a metaphor that uses *like* or *as* in the comparison. Example: *Your eyes are like a camera*.

- *analogy*—This form is the most challenging because it involves comparison of two sets of relationships. Example: *Furs were to North American Aboriginal peoples what cash is to today's consumer*.

When Carl Sagan wanted to interest U.S. taxpayers in spending money on asteroid research, he wrote a three-page article that contained 58 metaphors and similes. Why should metaphors matter to educators who don't teach English? "The subject of asteroid research is roughly equivalent to the unfamiliarity of many subjects we present to students every day" (Ruef, 1996, p. 61).

Teaching with Metaphor and Analogy

√ If you are providing the comparison, choose one that is relevant to your students. If you can't find a relevant comparison, that's a sign that students don't have the background knowledge they need for the new concept. You will have to explicitly build that knowledge.

√ Have students identify similarities and differences between concepts. Doing so will reinforce that all metaphors have their limitations; it will also help students isolate the critical attributes, or essential differences, between one concept and another.

√ Teach students to evaluate the quality of a comparison. The more characteristics the two concepts share, the stronger the metaphor or analogy. Recognizing why a metaphor or analogy doesn't work is as revealing of student understanding as creating one that does.

Kinesthetic Learning Through Metaphor and Analogy

√ Post in each corner of the room a picture of something that can serve as a metaphor for a concept you are teaching. Ask students to go to the metaphor that best matches their thinking and to discuss with the other students in that corner why they chose that metaphor. Each group then summarizes their thinking for the class. *Tip*: Use images that involve action. For example, students

Not Just for English Class – continued

might compare a concept to cooking a gourmet meal or putting out a fire. Action images invite fertile metaphors (von Oech, 2008).

√ Have students create collages using magazine images that metaphorically represent a concept or some aspect of it. They can label each image with a word or phrase and then complete the sentence, "My concept is a lot like _____ because it...."

√ Take students on a 20-minute walk, looking for objects and situations that make interesting metaphors for concepts you are studying. Students can take photographs or make lists. When they return to the classroom, have them choose one image or list item and fully develop it as a metaphor. Share results in a gallery walk.

Case Study — Impact on Engagement: *The Private Eye*

Manuel's interests were girls, cars, and cartoons, in that order. Putting thoughts on paper threatened Manuel's image so he refused to do it. "I have zero interest in writing," Manuel would say. "ZERO."

Poetry scored a –27 on Manuel's scale of acceptable classroom activities—until the day he was given a loupe and told to examine his finger. Peering through the loupe, which blocked out all distractions, Manuel stared at his magnified fingertip.

Manuel had to ask himself the following questions ten times, jotting down an answer each time: "What else does it remind me of? What else does it look like?" (Ruef, 2003). The final step was to choose one or more of the comparisons and write a poem.

Manuel wrote a poem that day. Why? Was it because the activity was novel and the close-up view of his finger intrigued him? Because the comparisons were his own so he couldn't get them wrong? Or maybe because the comparisons themselves sounded poetic, so Manuel figured he could successfully use them to write a poem? Who knows. What is certain is that Manuel willingly wrote a poem that day, he made sure his friends and family read it, and he referred to it proudly—and often—as his best work of the year.

You'll find Manuel's poem on the website, along with a link to the website for *The Private Eye* (the book that was the source for this activity).

Resources
Thinking Through Analogy

Metaphors are not just for student learning. The metaphors we work with as adults extend or limit our thinking and reveal our perspectives, guiding how we see the world.

> *If we change the metaphor in which a concept is expressed, we change the frame, making it possible for the concept to be understood differently. It is precisely this change of perspective that allows us greater choice in how we perceive and act upon the world.*
>
> (Owen 2008, p. xv)

Your Mind on Twitter

Roger von Oech (2008) suggests that a given century's prevailing metaphor for the mind is related to technological advancements of the time.

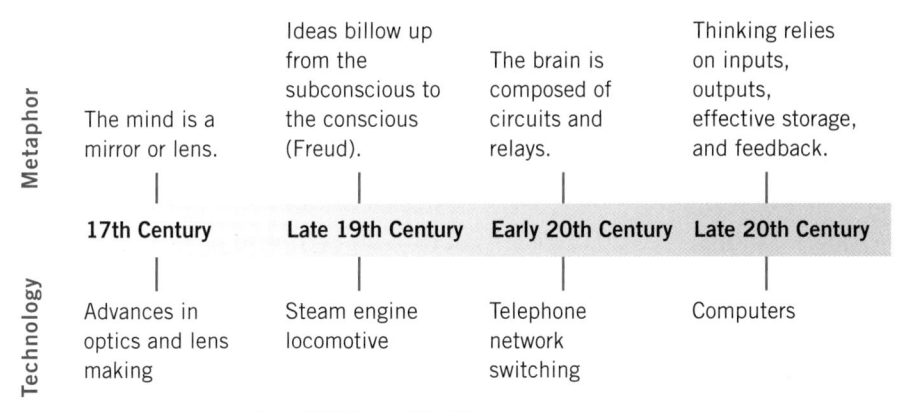

	17th Century	Late 19th Century	Early 20th Century	Late 20th Century
Metaphor	The mind is a mirror or lens.	Ideas billow up from the subconscious to the conscious (Freud).	The brain is composed of circuits and relays.	Thinking relies on inputs, outputs, effective storage, and feedback.
Technology	Advances in optics and lens making	Steam engine locomotive	Telephone network switching	Computers

Source: Adapted from von Oech (2008), pp. 56–57

What metaphor for mind do you think is appropriate for the 21st century?

Circular Thinking

Think of an issue related to student disengagement and write it in a circle in the centre of a page. Draw a larger circle around the central one—that's your frame. Inside the frame write whatever words related to your issue that come to mind. These words reflect your frame of reference—the beliefs through which you view the issue. What metaphor do the words you wrote suggest? How does your circle map (what it includes and what it doesn't) reflect your beliefs about the issue? What can you learn from your metaphor?

> You don't see something until you have the right metaphor to let you perceive it.
>
> —*Thomas Kuhn*

5 Ways to Get Lots of Ideas

> Sometimes searching for ideas is like being a mosquito in a nudist colony. You know what you want to do but don't know where to begin.
> —*Michael Michalko*

When our focus is on arriving at the first "correct" response, thinking stops after the answer is found. When people are encouraged to have lots of ideas, everyone can contribute without fear of being wrong. Give the following approaches a try, and don't be surprised when creative, interesting ideas come from the most unlikely, otherwise disengaged, participants.

1. Brainstorm

Brainstorming is a familiar process for most teachers and students, but it doesn't always work. The classroom community may not be supportive of new ideas or of all members, individuals may be unwilling to offer or unable to think of new ideas, or students may be tired of being asked to brainstorm. It's a good idea to be prepared with some other options for generating ideas.

2. Brainwrite

> If you have only one idea, you don't have anything to compare it to. You don't know its strengths and weaknesses.
> —*Roger von Oech*

Clarify the problem to be solved or issue to be addressed. Divide students into groups. Give each student a stack of index cards or sticky notes. Students record one idea per card and put completed cards in the centre of the table. When people need an idea, they look at the cards.

3. Do a Gallery Walk

Each participant stands in front of a sheet of chart paper posted to the wall. After the issue has been described and clarified, individuals take a specified amount of time to write or draw a response. When the time is up, participants do a gallery walk, making notes of anything on other people's sheets that might be helpful to their own work. At the end of the walk, individuals return to their sheets and refine or add to their ideas.

4. Reclassify

Changes in context create changes in thinking. Roger von Oech (2008) provides the example of a ball bearing, which we might first think of as something that reduces friction. Reclassifying the ball bearing as something shiny and pretty opens up possibilities for it as an object for jewellery or art.

Reclassifying probably works best with objects, but you can use it for issues if you first list the features and characteristics of the issue, and then reclassify one or more of them.

> Nothing is more dangerous than an idea when it's the only one we have.
> —*Émile Chartier*

5. SCAMPER

SCAMPER is a set of questions that can make a big difference, whether you're developing a product or solving a problem. The questions come from Alex Osborne, the advertising executive who created brainstorming. (The SCAMPER acronym is attributed to Bob Eberle.)

On the website, you'll find one set of questions for use when solving problems and another set that can help you when creating.

Resources
- Solving Problems with SCAMPER
- Creating with SCAMPER

Reasons to Look Beyond the First Idea

→ One of the alternative ideas may solve your problem.

→ An alternative idea may help you rearrange the components of your problem, thereby solving it indirectly.

→ An alternative might prove to be a better starting point.

→ One alternative might be a breakthrough idea that has nothing to do with the problem at hand.

→ You may generate a number of alternatives and then return to your original idea. Instead of being chosen because it seems the only option, it is chosen after it becomes apparent that it is the best one.

(Michalko, 2006, p. 73)

Solving the Tough Ones

Dar um jeito is a Brazilian expression. Loosely translated, it means "No problem is unsolvable and no barrier is too great to cross."

Dar um jeito is a great sentiment, but it may not seem overly realistic when we're talking about one of the most challenging issues of student disengagement—student truancy. Truancy is one of those problems that never seem to get solved; it just becomes more entrenched.

If you want to solve a truancy problem in your school, or any other problem, try this sequence of steps that combines the best of creative and logical thinking.

1. Decide

The first step in solving a really tough problem is to decide if it's worth pursuing. Make a long list of the direct and indirect benefits to solving the problem, and make sure they are worth the effort required. Some of the benefits of solving a truancy problem might include the following:

→ increase in the number of productive, contributing citizens as a result of a decrease in the number of high school dropouts

→ faster progress through curriculum because less time is spent helping students who have been absent get caught up

→ greater job satisfaction for teachers because they are free to focus on teaching rather than motivating or policing

2. Commit

If the benefits are worth the effort, commit to accepting the challenge of solving the problem. The greater your commitment, the more likely you are to achieve an innovative and workable solution.

3. Define

How you define a problem is important because your definition limits the range of possible solutions. For example, defining a truant student

> The first requisite of success is to apply your physical and mental energies to one problem without growing weary.
> —*Thomas Edison*

as one who is absent from school for at least *x* number of full days per month may direct you towards solutions that include attendance counsellors, social workers, and alternative programs for teen parents.

Defining a truant student as one who is in the school building but cutting classes may speak to the need for teacher mentors, more academic supports, and the creation of a strong, positive learning environment.

Think about whether you are trying to move away from the problem of truant adolescents or towards increased student engagement. When you are moving away from something, motivation to continue may decrease with each small victory. Design to achieve success rather than to avoid failure.

Gather and review all of the data you have about the problem, and compare different data sets. Determine what else you need to know and how you will gather that information. For a list of data sources to consider for the issue of student truancy, and for a book that will help you with the process, see the website.

As you talk with others about the data, always be careful to separate the processes of analysis and interpretation. Data analysis answers the question "What do the data say?" while interpretation answers the question "What do the data mean?" The sense you make of a particular piece of information is based on your beliefs and experiences. If you identify your beliefs, you will do a better job of defining a problem's parameters and will have an easier time solving the problem.

Break down the problem in as many ways as you can. Try these tips for effective problem definition:

- √ Substitute synonyms for key words.
- √ Ask questions—Who? What? Where? When? Why? How?
- √ List attributes of the problem, and determine the relationships among the parts.
- √ Draw the problem.

Resources
Data Sources

Research
Spotlight on
The Evidence-Based School

To spell out the obvious is often to call it in question.
—*Eric Hoffer*

Solving the Tough Ones – continued

> The greatest challenge to any thinker is stating the problem in a way that will allow a solution.
> —**Bertrand Russell**

√ Write about the problem from several different perspectives (e.g., yours, a student's, a parent's) and then combine them into a single statement of the problem.

Word your final statement of the problem as a question; for example, it might begin like this: "In what ways might we...?" By writing the problem as a question rather than as a statement, you'll be less likely to look at it from a single perspective (Michalko, 2006).

4. Explore

Use creative thinking to generate a range of solutions (see pages 94–95). Remember to focus on generating ideas, not on evaluating.

Research
Responses to Student Truancy

After you have generated some new ideas on your own, look at how others have solved the same or a similar problem. Since many schools struggle with student truancy, there are plenty of possible responses to be found. See the Research section of the website for a list.

Identify the solutions that appeal to you. Before adopting them, determine the beliefs or assumptions on which they are based.

> *Whenever Thomas Edison was about to hire a new employee, he would invite the applicant over for a bowl of soup. If the person salted his soup before tasting it, Edison would not offer him the job. He did not hire people who had too many assumptions built into their everyday life. Edison wanted people who consistently challenged assumptions.*
> (Michalko, 2006, pp. 44–45)

Test each belief by taking these four steps:

1. Confirm whether you're dealing with a belief or a fact by asking if it is always true.

2. Determine the opposite belief and question it. Asking new questions can give you new answers.

3. Pay attention to any idea that causes an emotional reaction.

4. Challenge yourself or allow others to challenge you.

(Yero, 2002)

See the Resources section of the website for an example using the four steps listed on the previous page.

Resources
Check Your Beliefs

5. Plan and Implement

Decide which solution to the problem has the best chance of working. If you are focusing on the problem of student truancy, your choice needs to be one that can be employed across the school.

Use the force field organizer on the website to list the forces in your school and school community that can be marshalled to support your solution, as well as those forces that will work against your solution. Consider what you can do to emphasize the positive forces and minimize the negative ones.

Resources
Force Field Organizer

Develop a clear and detailed picture of what success will look like. (Some of these descriptive details can serve as indicators of success throughout the process.)

Commit to timelines and responsibilities. Celebrate progress along the way.

Please Share!

The *Tuned Out* website is a perfect place to share your experiences, puzzlements, and—I hope—solutions to the problem of student truancy. Please take a look at my blog post on this issue and consider giving an online response to my questions. If we address this problem together and with creativity, I am certain we can solve it.

Conversations
Solving the Truancy Problem

Creative School Cultures

Tough issues are easier to solve in schools and districts that support creativity and creative thinking. Complete the online assessment to see how your workplace scores on the identifiable and observable characteristics of creative cultures.

Resources
Creative Culture Assessment

Worth a Thousand Words

Numerous research studies confirm this finding: "Text and oral presentations are not just less efficient than pictures for retaining certain types of information; they are way less efficient" (Medina, 2008, p. 234). This is called the Pictorial Superiority Effect (PSE). It means that the more visual the input, the greater the recognition and the recall. PSE may not hold true for all kinds of information—for example, we don't know whether an abstract concept such as freedom is better communicated through image or narrative—but it's a solid and important research finding nevertheless.

Computer developers have taken full advantage of PSE research. Using a personal computer is visual and intuitive. Tools to perform different functions are based on pictorial analogies to ordinary objects, such as a file folder, wastebasket, or printer. It is easy to quickly adjust aspects of images that are known to grab our attention—motion, colour, orientation, and size (Medina, 2008).

> Images are the missing link between the mind and the body.
> —*David Hunt*

Using and working with visuals in teaching has significant impact beyond recognition and retention of information. Visuals also do the following:

- → help students with a visual preference understand subject matter
- → function as a universal language for English Language Learners
- → mirror the increasingly visual orientation of today's society
- → inspire creativity by helping us focus on details that are often missed when we don't have an image to refer to

> A visually literate person should be able to read and write visual language.
> —*Dr. Anne Bamford*

A visually literate individual is able to

- → visualize internally
- → interpret and understand the meaning of visual messages
- → make judgments about the accuracy and worth of images
- → apply the basic principles and concepts of visual design when communicating

→ produce visual messages using computers and other technologies

→ use visual thinking to conceptualize solutions to problems

Some of these visual literacy skills develop automatically; some, such as the higher order skills of analysis and evaluation, require direct teaching.

Presenting

Motion, colour, orientation, and size are the four aspects of images that grab our attention. Use this knowledge to support your instruction no matter where you are on the following continuum of comfort with technology:

Research
Interactive Whiteboards

No Technology	PowerPoint/Other Presentation Software	Interactive Whiteboards	Computer Animations
• Write and draw concepts on a flip chart or board. Use colour markers to emphasize important points. • Post visuals to the wall to support the concepts you teach.	• Avoid "death by PowerPoint" by considering what information you are representing in words that could be replaced with a photograph (Reynolds, 2008).	• Use presentation tools provided with interactive whiteboard software to manipulate text and images.	• Create simple two-dimensional animations. "Studies show that if the drawings are too complex or lifelike, they can distract from the transfer of information" (Medina, 2008, p. 238).

Visual Chit Chat

Pecha Kucha (pronounced *pe-chak-cha*; Japanese for *chatter*) is an event that was devised in Tokyo in 2003 to provide young designers with the opportunity to network with others and share their work. The rules of Pecha Kucha are that you project 20 visuals for 20 seconds each, telling your story as the visuals play. When the screen goes blank, the presentation is over. Try developing your next PowerPoint or Keynote presentation following the rules of Pecha Kucha. For examples of Pecha Kucha presentations, see the website.

Research
Pecha Kucha

Worth a Thousand Words – continued

Interpreting

In our increasingly visual culture, students are surrounded by images of all kinds—photographs, fine art, webs, computer animations and simulations, scientific notations, logos, graphs, and cartoons, to name just a few.

Visual literacy involves recognizing that all images are created and that decisions are made, consciously or unconsciously, according to the creator's understanding of the image's purpose and audience.

Being visually literate means being able to "read" an image—not just the content, the meaning of which may change according to culture and context, but also the composition or syntax of the image. The visually literate reader notices a number of features, such as the relative size of different items, the uses of light and shadow, layering of various elements, flow of movement, and perspective.

Consider discussing the images in your subject textbook *before* students read the print. Use the questions provided in the Resources section of the website to get the conversation started.

Resources
Talking About Images

Connecting

When students make connections between a written text and an image, they are practising the skill of transfer—applying knowledge or information gained in one context to another context. Transfer is the ultimate evidence of student understanding.

Support students in learning how to transfer knowledge by using ideas such as the following:

Resources
Image Sources

√ In English class, ask students to find a painting or sculpture that corresponds to the style or content of a piece of literature. They could write an explanation of the connections.

√ In Art class, invite students to create artwork based on a poem or other text.

√ In History class, suggest that students use an image, such as Margaret Bourke-White's photograph "Nuremberg After Allied Bombing" and assume the role of historical writer. They could explain the scene in the image and what led to it, and then make connections between the consequences of the event and today's society (Walling, 2005).

Case Study ⇒ Impact on Engagement: Images and Artifacts

Name: Marcus T.   **Subject:** History   **Grade:** 7

My normally talkative students fell silent as I placed the items one by one on the table in the centre of our circle of chairs—the collar of an old dress, a baby's sock, an old letter, a noose, an 1886 portrait of Louis Riel, a photograph from Riel's trial, a political cartoon, and a poem Riel had written.

I had been looking for a way to bring Métis leader Louis Riel to life for my students when I stumbled across Kathy Gould Lundy's interesting book, *What Do I Do About the Kid Who…?: 50 Ways to Turn Teaching into Learning*, and decided I'd try an activity she suggested.

I passed the items and images around the circle, giving everyone a chance to take a close look.

I then had students get into groups and I asked them to reorder the list of artifacts to match the order in which they would have appeared in the Métis leader's life. After that, each group took the responsibility of sharing the story of Riel's life and death through artifacts and images alone. They were required to add or substitute three artifacts or images, all of which had to be created with art materials.

Impact on Engagement

Students were highly engaged, beyond anything I have ever seen in a History class. When we debriefed afterwards, I asked what had helped them to be successful. Many said that using artifacts and historical images made them feel as if they were detectives assembling the pieces of Riel's life so they could make sense of them.

Put It on Paper

Drawing

Did you know…?

- Insights often come from drawing because you notice features that might not otherwise have been apparent. This fact explains why it's useful to have students illustrate the steps in a math problem.
- Doodling, rather than being a distraction, may help some students attend to the content of a lesson.
- Objects can be easier to draw if you squint. When you limit your field of vision by squinting, you will find that you focus on an object's shape and form.
- Symbols are an effective shorthand form of communication, so encourage students to use them. Have students create their own symbols for reading strategies, scientific processes, or key vocabulary terms in any subject.

> Drawing is putting a line round an idea.
> —*Henri Matisse*

The Martians Have Landed

Drawing can support and extend thinking in all subject areas, but it can be intimidating if viewed as art. To overcome concerns about your own drawing skills, work with a group to try this variation on an activity from Michael Michalko:

Imagine that a delegation of Martians has just landed on your school's parking lot. You welcome them inside. They do not understand any Earth languages—only graphic symbols. They are curious about your school and about you.

1. Each person creates a short "speech" composed entirely of graphic symbols to welcome the Martians and explain something about the school. Choose a common topic, such as explaining the role of a teacher, the structure of the school, or the purpose of extracurricular activities.

2. Tape the visual speeches to the wall and have everyone review them.

3. Select the speech you would present to the Martians (optional).

(Michalko, 2006, p. 308)

Mapping and Webbing

Graphic organizers are visual representations of the relationships among ideas. They can be used at all stages of learning—before (as advance organizers to help learners connect new knowledge with existing knowledge), during (for taking visual notes), and after (to summarize, analyze, and synthesize understanding).

Mind maps and word webs are two forms of organizers frequently used for generating ideas. Both enable people to see connections among ideas that are not as obvious through outlining or note taking (Wolfe, 2001).

The only difference between word webs and mind maps is that maps use symbols as well as words to show the connections among ideas. Here are the seven steps to mind mapping, from the originator of the technique:

1. Start in the centre of a blank page turned sideways. This gives you the freedom to spread your ideas in all directions.

2. Use an image for your central idea. This will keep you focused and help you concentrate.

3. Use colours throughout. Colours are as exciting to your brain as images.

4. Connect your main branches to the central image, and second- and third-level branches to the first and second levels, and so on. Your brain works by association. Links will help you understand and remember.

5. Make branches curved rather than straight. Curved branches are more riveting to your eye.

6. Use one key word per line. Single key words generate an array of associations and connections in a way that phrases and sentences do not.

7. Use images throughout. Each is worth a thousand words.

(Buzan, 2005, pp. 17–18)

In Your Mind's Eye

Temple Grandin is a renowned expert on cattle psychology and behaviour. She has designed one-third of all livestock-handling facilities in the United States. Grandin is also autistic. In her aptly titled book *Thinking in Pictures*, she describes her amazing visualization skills:

> *Today, everyone is excited about the new virtual reality computer systems in which the user wears special goggles and is fully immersed in video game action. To me, these systems are like crude cartoons. My imagination works like the computer graphics programs that created the lifelike dinosaurs in Jurassic Park. When I do an equipment simulation in my imagination or work on an engineering problem, it is like seeing it on a videotape in my mind. I can view it from any angle, placing myself above or below the equipment and rotating it at the same time. I don't need a fancy graphics program that can produce three-dimensional design simulations. I can do it better and faster in my head.*
>
> (2006, p. 5)

Visualizing allows Grandin to invent new and more humane ways of handling cattle, and to make corrections to a design before construction. Visualization also allowed Niels Bohr to determine what goes on inside an atom, and Benoit Mandelbrot to invent fractal geometry. "[S]ome of the most original thinkers in fields ranging from physical science and mathematics to politics and poetry have relied heavily on visual modes of thought" (West, 2009, p. 23).

Recent studies of the early growth patterns of the human brain have shown that there is tremendous diversity in brain structure. While not all students who struggle with the highly verbal nature of the classroom are going to turn out to be creative geniuses, there is increasing awareness that strong visual skills are essential to creativity and innovation in the 21st century. You may well have students in your classroom who do their thinking in pictures.

What makes visualizing such a powerful tool? The answer lies in how the brain works. Let's say you follow a specific sequence of steps to sink a basketball and score the game-winning point. That sequence of steps forms a neural pathway in your brain. So what happens in your brain if you just visualize scoring that winning point? Even then, a neural pathway is formed. Here's the surprising part: Your brain can't tell the difference between a neural pathway created by doing an action and one created by visualizing it.

There are differences between visualizing an event and a text. When athletes are visualizing their moves on the basketball court, for example, they are reconstructing the original neural networks formed during practice, and they are imagining themselves in the situation. In contrast, when readers are visualizing a text, they are bringing words on the page to life by attending to description and creating what amounts to a mental movie of the text (Keene & Zimmerman, 1997). Both event visualization and text visualization improve ability to problem-solve before, during, and after learning (Antonietti, 1999).

> Words are only postage stamps delivering the object for you to unwrap.
> —*George Bernard Shaw*

Teaching Visualization in Skill-Based Classes

√ Instruct students to break a skill down into small parts and visualize each part separately.

√ Show students what a skill looks like in slow motion. Talk about any nuances they might have missed at normal speed.

√ Encourage students to include all five senses and emotions in their visualization. The greater the sensory involvement, the more real the visualization.

√ Visualizing requires concentration. Help students determine the right time and place for them to visualize. In competitive situations, visualizations often last one minute or less.

√ Provide frequent opportunities for students to practise visualizing—without practice, visualizations will not be available when needed.

√ Encourage students to visualize key moments. These can be either positive (what the student is going to do well) or negative (how the student will handle a potential problem).

For ways to teach visualization of text, see the website.

Resources
Visualizing Text

Hands-on Learning

I have rarely read an academic report as straightforward as this one:

> *The motivation for change in engineering education at the University of Colorado at Boulder is driven by the understanding that traditional, strictly theoretical, engineering education does not engage or adequately educate engineering students. The small number of American students in the natural sciences, mathematics and engineering (SME), notably only 4.5% of 24-year-olds in the United States, is well documented. Attrition from the SME fields is...a function of the learning environment common to the SME fields not matching the learning preferences of 95% of the population.*
>
> (Schwartz & Dunkin, 2000, p. 218)

Hands-on learning refers to the active involvement of students in manipulating objects to gain knowledge or understanding (Haury & Rillero, 1994). Also referred to as "learning by doing" or "kinesthetic learning," hands-on learning has been the teaching approach in auto mechanics, woodworking, and arts classes for years. In the last 40 years it has also become a mark of effective teaching in science and math.

Hands-on learning can be meaningful or superficial. Meaningful learning is "minds-on" as well as hands-on. Students are challenged, they receive feedback, and they are required to articulate what they are learning.

This type of learning benefits all students. For kinesthetic learners, students with special needs, and English Language Learners, hands-on learning is essential.

Benefits of Hands-on Learning

- → makes some concepts more visible and explicit
- → enhances cooperative behaviour as students work together to meet a common goal
- → permits creative responses that often result in a tangible and satisfying product
- → increases skill proficiency
- → provides an additional entry point to learning (see page 69)

- → increases motivation to learn and engagement in learning
- → builds teacher awareness of student learning preferences and skills

Brain researcher and teacher Eric Jensen believes that hands-on learning is especially beneficial for students who are highly disengaged:

> *If you have a student who is unresponsive...the solutions require positive activity. At school, meaningful movement can mean being involved in crafts, design, building, dramatic arts, fixing things, athletics—almost anything where there is active cause and effect....All of these movements force an individual to make choices that matter: You fix it or it stays broken, you build it or you never get to own it, you stand or fall, you catch the ball or get hit in the face....*
>
> (2001, p. 87)

The research into what's happening in the brain when students are engaged in hands-on learning is still in its infancy. Nevertheless, the benefits for some students are so immediately apparent that neuroscientists such as Joaquin Fuster (2003) are proposing new theories of learning that make action central to all learning except for simple memorization.

In Fuster's theory, education should be focused on building rich neuronal connections in the brain. He argues that the richest connections come from experiences that engage both mind and body in the context of an enriched learning environment where students have multiple exposures to the same information over an extended period of time.

Apprenticeship programs in the trades are an adult example of hands-on learning. Apprenticeships also confirm the importance of hands-on learning being equally minds-on. Learning comes not just from having an experience but from also actively processing what that experience is teaching.

Coaching Hands-on Learning

Consider a hands-on or learning-by-doing experience in which you have been involved. Describe for colleagues the ways in which the activity was minds-on as well as hands-on. What did the instructor do and what did you do to actively process the experience? I share a slightly embarrassing math story on the website.

> Brain activity and working with our hands are so interdependent, so synergistic and complex, that no single brain theory can adequately account for it.
>
> —*Eric Jensen*

Conversations
Math Basics

Interdisciplinary Study

The problem with increasing specialization (see page 78) is that we risk losing the connections across disciplines that lead to innovation. Losing these connections is an issue for any society that wishes to stay competitive in our global world, and an issue for adolescents who need to see how the information they are learning and the skills they are developing fit together and affect their lives.

In schools and workplaces alike, "new ideas often come from the dialogue between different disciplines, through which specialists in different fields make their ideas available to each other and create the opportunity for new interpretations and applications" (Robinson, 2001, p. 182).

Interdisciplinary instruction requires that teachers collaborate to plan work that is coherent and relevant for students, while still honouring the deep understandings that need to be developed in each subject area. For maximum effectiveness it is important that teachers be highly knowledgeable about their subject matter and that the school leaders arrange for additional planning time as well as flexible scheduling when the interdisciplinary work is underway.

Community Scan

Interdisciplinary experiences can be provided by teachers within a school, teachers across a district, or teachers working with community artists, businesspeople, or parents with the necessary skill sets and expertise.

If you have an idea for an interdisciplinary experience you'd like to create, find the people who can help you realize your vision by conducting a community scan. Call the arts organizations in your community, check with your school office for the names of potential partners, and talk with students and their parents.

To generate ideas for an interdisciplinary project, assemble a team and see pages 94–95.

A few interdisciplinary programs are already in place in many secondary and some middle schools. These programs are often in the field of technology and focus on students achieving practical products and solutions. Design technology, for example, might bring together, art and design, craft, home economics or family studies, and technology.

> Creativity comes from unlikely juxtapositions. The best way to maximize differences is to mix ages, cultures, and disciplines.
> —*Nicholas Negroponte*

Case Study: Impact on Engagement: Design Technology Business Simulation

Name: Susan S. **Subjects:** Family/Consumer Studies, Social Studies, Math, Art **Grade:** 7

The bank manager arrived yesterday to help students create business plans for their new company, Stitchin T-Birds. The first order of business after the banker left was to have the class choose a CEO for the company, based on the qualities of a good leader identified through class discussion.

I read aloud the novel *The Toothpaste Millionaire* by Jean Merrill to help students understand the advantages and disadvantages of a business that designs something unique versus a business that produces something that already exists. The class-appointed CEO then assisted the class in creating a list of possible projects to sew and sell. Students had learned to sew a number of simple items in the first few weeks of class, so they knew what they could handle. Typical products included shopping bags, iPod covers, stuffed animals, and small pillows.

From the master list created, the class chose three products for Stitchin T-Birds to produce. The CEO then directed students to choose which of the three products they wanted to work on. Students who chose the same item became members of a product division, and a manager was chosen for each division.

Each division manager worked with his or her group to create a prototype, which was reviewed by the CEO. Managers also conducted a personal skills inventory of each employee and used this information to determine the divisional structure—assembly line or individually created products. Although all students participated in initial product creation, some students in each division later chose to work on marketing or accounting for their particular product, making use of learning from social studies (advertising techniques and ethics), art (video advertisements), and math classes (spreadsheets).

The products were sold to other students and to parents. Half of the money from the sale was put aside for the next company simulation, while the other half was donated to charity.

During the time students worked for Stitchin T-Birds, they received "paycheques." At the end of the business simulation, students were able to use their paycheques to "purchase" a variety of small items I provided.

Reasons for Simulation

- Students completed short assignments where it quickly became evident that they were unable to define financial terms, or to fill out a balance sheet. Testing in our state of Wisconsin often involves word problems with scenarios that are similar to the ones presented in the assignments.

Practical Creativity 111

Interdisciplinary Study – continued

- A county workforce skills survey indicated that current adolescent employees needed improvement in the areas of decision making, conflict resolution, organization, and customer service.

- Interdisciplinary units of study are a school goal.

- An online career activity showed that many students had very unrealistic expectations about the costs associated with living on their own. To address this, the paycheques students received during the simulation had realistic deductions for such things as medical benefits and income tax.

Impact on Engagement

Prior to developing this simulation activity three years ago, many students failed to complete any of the sewing projects. In this simulation, students enjoyed the opportunity to make a contribution based on their individual strengths, and all students were keen to be involved. They also appreciated being able to make a real contribution to a local charity and were excited to see how much money they could raise.

> Work in the arts is not only a way of creating performances and products; it is a way of creating our lives.
> —*Elliot Eisner*

Research
The Arts and Highly Disengaged Adolescents

The arts are another well-tested and frequently used source of interdisciplinary work. Intrinsically engaging, the arts are a place where students have the opportunity to engage both mind and body in experiences that often allow them to showcase individual strengths, imagine their future selves, and actively process new learning through the full range of senses.

Multiple research studies show that the arts are particularly powerful in reaching those students who are most highly disengaged. For a summary of this research, see the website.

Case Study → Impact on Engagement: The ArtsSmarts Model

Name: Annalee A. (National Director)   **Subjects:** All   **Grades:** All

ArtsSmarts is a national arts organization that generates and sustains innovative school partnerships centred around the arts.

The ArtsSmarts model is interdisciplinary in that a teacher and an artist from the local community come together to co-plan a unit of study where concepts in any subject area will be taught and students will demonstrate their understanding through the arts.

In the 10 years since the inception of ArtsSmarts, research and the experiences of students, artists, and educators has transformed the ArtsSmarts model from a focus on arts integration to a focus on creative inquiry. (See pages 220–225 for an extensive discussion of teaching and learning through inquiry.) Research has shown that this model results in increased student engagement and success.

ArtsSmarts defines *creativity* as the act of producing new ideas, approaches, or actions. Students take on problems that spring from their own curiosity, from a teacher's challenge, or from the pressing needs of the world around them. Students take ownership of their projects and take the risks necessary to answer compelling questions, solve problems, and make their learning visible through different art forms. To do this, ArtsSmarts projects model the creative process—a series of four interrelated stages of learning:

→ *inquiry*—definition of a big idea, question or problem

→ *design*—observation and study of main issues and goals

→ *expression*—the emergence of new ideas

→ *reflection*—implementation and review

The ArtsSmarts approach creates the conditions for learning in six interrelated dimensions that lead to important outcomes for all learners in all grades and subject areas. For a graphic of these six dimensions and further information about ArtsSmarts, see the website. For examples of ArtsSmarts projects, see the case studies on the next page and on page 194.

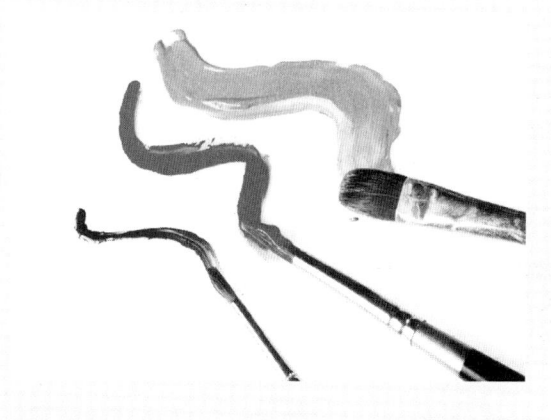

Resources
ArtsSmarts

Practical Creativity

Interdisciplinary Study – continued

Case Study: Impact on Engagement: Our Voice, Our Land

Name: Sherron B.   **Subjects:** History, Art   **Grades:** 9–12

"**What does it mean for us *all* to be Treaty people?**" That was the essential question that led to First Nations and non-First Nations students, teachers, and artists gathering for two days at Fort Battleford, Saskatchewan.

Fort Battleford was established in 1876 to house the NorthWest Mounted Police. They were charged with working with First Nations people to support the creation and implementation of treaties that the federal government believed were necessary before settlement could commence.

Over time, the relationship between the North-West Mounted Police and First Nations gradually deteriorated. Treaty promises were repeatedly broken and complaints to the government about the mistreatment of First Nations peoples went unanswered. These tensions led to the North-West Rebellion in 1885, as well as to the public hanging of eight First Nations people at Fort Battleford for their role in the rebellion. This history has created anger and tension that today's First Nations adolescents have inherited.

The two-day ArtsSmarts project began with Traditional Knowledge Keeper Judy Bear teaching students about treaties and the history of the relationships formed. She also introduced students to various concepts about the First Nations worldview.

Students then worked in four different groups based on artistic media. Using theatre, visual arts, filmmaking, or music, students told stories about their culture and imagined people of long ago. Students had brought with them a stone each had selected from a place they considered special. They were asked to think about a story they could share, using their stones as a connection. These stones were incorporated into the arts projects.

Students did not deal with issues of race or historical wrongs, but shared their own stories about who they were and how they connected to the land. For many, the experience was transformational. As one student concluded, "This project helped me with my treaty background….It taught me lots about our relationships with others and now I think differently about things."

Case Study: Impact on Engagement: Integrated Arts and Technology

Name: Maggie B. (consultant)   **Subject:** Arts Integration District-Based Professional Learning

Teams of classroom teachers, special education resource teachers, and administrators in Maggie's district meet once a month in professional learning networks of 25 to 35 people, drawn from a geographically cohesive "family" of schools. There are seven of these networks. Monthly network workshops follow a consistent format:

1. Teachers are taught a new technology, such as how to use an interactive whiteboard to share high-resolution artwork from a virtual gallery. The technologies taught are ones that are available in all schools.

2. There is discussion of the technology and its connection to the arts. *The Arts as Meaning Makers* by Claudia Cornett and Katharine Smithrim is used as a launching point for the discussion.

3. Teachers work in interdisciplinary project teams to apply new learning to curriculum expectations in History, Geography, English, Religion, and the Arts, and to develop activities for use in the classroom.

4. Teachers perform the activities they have developed. All work is designed to be experienced by the teacher in the professional learning situation and then recreated in the classroom.

Reasons for Arts Integration Focus

- Differentiated instruction has been a focus for many of these teachers. Arts integration addresses a wide variety of learner preferences and needs.

- The province of Ontario has developed a new Arts curriculum.

- Provincial testing indicates a need for a continued focus on students' literacy skills.

- An integrated approach allows the efficient achievement of a broad range of curriculum requirements.

- Available technology needs to be used to meaningfully enhance instruction.

- The district believes that technology and the arts are powerful tools of engagement for both students and teachers.

Impact on Engagement: Sample Teacher Responses

"After a photography lesson students received constructive criticism and begged me to allow them to redo the assignment because they thought they could do better. This approach has made my students more reflective and willing to take risks so they can learn. It has allowed for more creativity and laughter from my students."—N.P.

Interdisciplinary Study – continued

"The new technology has been a huge motivator for my students. They look forward to me returning from each workshop, as they know I will have something new and exciting to share."—L.G.

"As a special education resource teacher I have witnessed the excitement and enthusiasm of the classroom teachers in the Integrated Arts Initiative. The students are totally focused and engaged in the activities. The kids are curious and showing that they want to learn. We need to grab that and run with it."—B.S.

"I have learned that integrated arts lessons have huge payoffs when it comes to motivating students."—C.A.

"With the integrated arts I have a renewed passion for teaching. I'm becoming a better teacher and my students are learning more as a result."—J.C.

Summary of Chapter Website Content		www.pearsoncanada.ca/tunedout
Conversations	**Resources**	**Research**
• At the Art Gallery • Solving the Truancy Problem • Math Basics	• Thinking Through Analogy • Solving Problems with SCAMPER • Creating with SCAMPER • Data Sources • Check Your Beliefs • Force Field Organizer • Creative Culture Assessment • Talking About Images • Image Sources • Visualizing Text • ArtsSmarts	• Spotlight on *The Evidence-Based School* • Responses to Student Truancy • Interactive Whiteboards • Pecha Kucha • The Arts and Highly Disengaged Adolescents

Community

"Take this stick and break it," the old man says to the young boy.

The boy easily breaks the stick.

"That's an individual," says the old man. "Now, take this bundle of sticks and break it."

The boy tries but can't.

"That's a community," says the old man.

—Based on a fable by Aesop

7 A Bundle of Sticks

Conversations

"Community" Video Byte

Three teachers happen to be in the staff washroom at the same time. "Oh my goodness," jokes one. "We must be having a professional learning community meeting."

Our weariness with terminology is understandable. As a profession, teaching is notorious for co-opting terms, applying them all over the place, and eventually rendering them meaningless. *Community* is one such term.

Considering Community

Resources

Community Images

View the photos depicting community on the website and respond to the questions provided. You will end up selecting two photos. Share and discuss your selections with colleagues and then on your own create a Venn diagram to show similarities and differences between adolescent and adult perceptions of community.

> We are in community each time we find a place where we belong.
>
> —*Peter Block*

At its most basic, a community is a group of people interacting together in a common location. That common location can now be virtual, which explains why some refer to Wikipedia contributors as members of an "online community." To be robust enough to encourage student or teacher engagement, however, a community must be so much more than three teachers in a washroom, a few dozen people contributing to an online project, or 30 students and a teacher in a classroom. What is needed is a "sense of community" (McMillan & Chavis, 1986), which develops when individuals in a group feel that they

- → belong and matter to one another
- → can safely be themselves
- → have influence over what happens in the group
- → will have their needs met if they support the group as a whole

When people feel connected to others through community, the basic human need of "belonging" is met. A sense of belonging in a community has been linked to "increased engagement in school activities, lower rates of student burnout, class cutting and thoughts of dropping out, and a higher likelihood of feeling bad when unprepared for class" (Bluestein, 2001, p. 100). Some researchers refer to this need for connection as the "contact urge" (Gopnik, Meltzoff, & Kuhl, 1999). They argue that this urge is an inborn survival mechanism because it is impossible to care for ourselves when young, to procreate, or to raise children without any help from others.

In contrast, the absence of this sense of belonging in adolescents—of connection with both peers and adults who accept, value, and care about them—is considered at least partially responsible for many of the worrying traits we see more and more in young people: aggression, poor self-image, inability to defer gratification, resentment towards authority, and delinquency (Bluestein, 2001). Some research also suggests that students with fewer social connections are much more likely to become addicted to drugs and alcohol (Restak, 1995).

> Call it a clan, call it a network, call it a tribe, call it a family: Whatever you call it, whoever you are, you need one.
> —*Jane Howard*

We all belong to a number of different communities, some of which provide a stronger sense of community than others. For many adolescents, the strongest sense of community comes through interaction with their peers. This has always been so—it's how adolescents try out and form their identities—but some people suggest that social networking sites have accentuated this process. Don Tapscott, for example, calls the adolescents of today "the relationship generation" (2009, p. 89). Adolescents want and need to stay connected to their friends and they do so in droves—in 2008, 60 percent of Canadian teens were daily visitors to online social networking sites, such as Facebook, MySpace, and Twitter (Bricker & Wright, 2009).

Connecting on Facebook

Facebook was launched in 2004 by Mark Zuckerberg and two fellow students from Harvard University. Named after the book of staff and student photos given to incoming first-year students, Facebook was originally intended to provide an online network exclusively for Harvard. Its popularity quickly grew. By the end of 2004, Facebook membership was extended to all Ivy League schools. In

> We're just getting started on our goal of connecting everyone.
> —*Mark Zuckerberg*

2005, membership was opened to high school students if they were friends of people already on the site, as well as to university alumni and the staff of a few large corporations. By 2006, membership was available to anyone with a valid email address. At the time of this book's publication, there were more than 500 million active users on the site. (An active user is someone who has logged on in the last 30 days.)

With more active users than the combined populations of Canada and the United States, Facebook tries to emulate "real-life" connections by structuring networks around corporations, schools, and geographic regions. These networks are made up of Facebook users and their "friends," who must also have Facebook accounts. The average user has 130 friends on the site; there is a limit of 5000 friends per user.

Over time, Facebook has broadened the range of activities that can be conducted on the site. Programmers have created applications to make it easier for users to share photos, videos, and multimedia content.

Networked Teens

Research
Teens and Social Networking

According to researchers who conducted a three-year ethnographic study of the digital habits of 800 adolescents, teen uses of social media fall into three distinct categories. Ito and colleagues (2010) named the categories in the title of their book—*Hanging Out, Messing Around, Geeking Out: Living and Learning with New Media*. Links to their study and others can be found on the website.

Here are brief explanations of the three categories:

→ *Hanging Out*—The majority of adolescents use online networks to stay connected to the friends they already have in their "offline" lives. Teens hang out online by instant-messaging each other, browsing social network profiles, listening to and sharing music, playing online games (boys more than girls), watching TV shows on YouTube, and chatting on cell phones.

Hanging out is characterized by "ongoing lightweight social contact that moves fluidly between online and offline environments" (Horst, Herr-Stephenson, & Robinson, 2010). Increasingly, it is happening simultaneously in both. For example, teens may be interacting with some friends in person while instant-messaging others to find out what's happening in their lives at that moment or to make plans for the future.

→ *Messing Around*—Adolescents are messing around when they are pursuing a topic of personal interest they've come across through random internet surfing, customizing profile pages and gaming activities, or acquiring new technology skills.

Messing around is self-directed learning based on a lot of trial and error to figure things out. Because of this, most messing around activities occur among high school students with free time who live in technology-rich homes with parents who are willing to grant some autonomy over how that time is used online, or among college-age students who are out on their own for the first time.

Messing around is interest driven rather than friendship driven. It allows students to connect with others who are not in their immediate social group. Adolescents who mess around online are often in a transitional phase between hanging out and geeking out (Horst et al., 2010).

"I need more time. Unlimited minutes aren't enough!"

→ *Geeking Out*—The main difference between messing around and geeking out is intensity. Adolescents who geek out are driven to develop some form of technological expertise, often in a particular aspect of media production, because of their passionate interest in it. They are not satisfied, for instance, with simply playing an online game with friends (hanging out) or even discovering an existing but hidden code (messing around). Rather, they want to create their own online games, write new code that will change an existing game in a significant way, or find a way to download a new game before it is available to the public.

Students who geek out are often those who have been marginalized by their peers in school. They find their tribe—their community of interest—online with others who have specialized knowledge and who share their passion. This online community differs from the other two by including adults who are accepted by young people as simply more experienced peers.

In addition to addressing the need for belonging, communities teach. Sociocultural theory (Vygotsky, 1986) suggests that it is impossible to understand either learning or human development solely by studying the individual because we live in a social world where we are always in interaction with people, objects, and events that cause learning and inform development.

The very idea that people learn through interaction makes some parents and teachers nervous about adolescents' involvement with social media. *What* are they learning?

Helpful, Harmful, or Somewhere in Between?

Conversations
Social Networks and Learning

Talk with colleagues about what students might be learning in each category—hanging out, messing around, and geeking out. Consider whether any of the categories include activities that are

- important to adolescent development
- useful for classroom learning
- problematic for classroom learning

In my blog post I share some of my thoughts as well as some parent and teacher responses from the *Hanging Out, Messing Around, Geeking Out* study.

Fess Up

If you already participate in a social network, talk with colleagues about your experiences. What attracted you to your chosen network site? What's keeping you there? If you have developed a sense of community through your online activities, what specific features or actions made that possible?

If you are interested in social networking sites for people who share a specific interest, see the website. If you don't participate in a social network and would like to give it a try, the website provides information on creating a profile.

Whether you participate or not, make a prediction: Is there a difference between the online social network habits of adolescents and those of adults? Check the website for some information that might surprise you.

Resources
- Social Networking Sites
- Creating a Profile

Research
Adults and Social Networking

Relating to Adolescents

Social networking sites allow teens to keep friends at their fingertips 24/7. Adolescents are able to share interests and support one another through the traumas and dramas that we adults may consider trivial. It is hardly surprising, therefore, that many parents and teachers feel that social networking sites are exacerbating the generational divide—the rejection of adult authority that is a hallmark characteristic of the developmental stage of adolescence.

Separation from adults may be necessary as the adolescent works to forge his or her identity but, as one parent suggests, that understanding doesn't make the rejection any easier to take:

> *Even if I know this separation is necessary, it breaks my heart. And even if my heart is broken, I can't just skulk off and lick my wounds, because the little infidels still need me to love them, still want that tiny dot in the distance that used to be the whole world to receive them warmly on their occasional visits. All I can do is find some cooler place to stand, some way to let go but not leave, so I can continue the task of caring about people who are conducting a vigorous multi-year exorcism of me.*
> (Winik, 2005, p. 222)

Being Rejected

Teachers are not immune to adolescent rejection, especially by disengaged students. Like parents, we can understand cognitively that disdain of an authority figure is a typical and necessary part of adolescence; however, this understanding does not erase the affective component, which is our emotional reaction.

Conversations
Michelle Made Me Crazy

A Bundle of Sticks

Rather than pushing emotions aside by telling myself, "I shouldn't take this personally," I have found that analyzing my emotional reaction can help me uncover the beliefs that lie behind it. For an anecdote that illustrates this, have a look at my blog post "Michelle Made Me Crazy."

Research
Spotlight on
I Wanna Be Sedated

I encourage you to respond with your own experiences or to discuss them with supportive and trustworthy colleagues. For more about having great conversations with colleagues, see pages 138–143. See the website for my review of *I Wanna Be Sedated*, which contains some hilarious and heartrending experiences in parenting teens.

Despite issues with disengaged adolescents, teachers are generally in a privileged place when it comes to connection with students. There isn't the strong emotional tie that teens have with their parents, so there isn't the same intensity of conflict. Our relationship with students presents us with the opportunity to make a positive difference. A large longitudinal study found that connection to a positive adult at school and to a positive adult outside of school were the two most significant factors in preventing negative outcomes for students (Schaps, 1999). Teachers are often able to serve as the significant role models and mentors that adolescents need.

The brain is the only organ in the body that sculpts itself from outside experience.
—*Pat Wolfe*

"Role model" might be a more accurate job title for teachers than we once thought. Mirror neurons are brain cells whose activity reflects their surroundings. These neurons were first discovered in research with monkeys, but have since been identified in humans as well. Mirror neurons are responsible for simple behaviours, such as when a baby imitates you when you stick out your tongue. Research going on now suggests that humans of all ages mirror others. Children and teens mirror the modelling they receive from parents, siblings, peers, and teachers. Adults mirror co-workers to learn the habits, practices, and language of chosen careers (Hurley & Charter, 2005).

While we don't yet know if mirror neurons are responsible for more than the simplest imitative behaviours, we do know that experiences change our brains (Begley, 2007). By modelling appropriate interactions and working to build a strong classroom community where students feel a sense of belonging with us and with their peers, we can override less effective patterns of interaction learned in other environments and create new opportunities for students.

Using Your Influence

There is little hope of engaging students if they do not relate to their teacher as well as to their peers. What do you think a teacher's relationship with students should look like in a classroom community where students are both engaged and learning?

This relationship is the place where the two roads I described on page 3 tend to be most evident. Here's an example of the hold-the-line-against-the-erosion-of-civilization perspective:

> Young people need mentors not to go with the youth flow, but to stand staunchly against it, to represent something smarter and finer than the cacophony of social life. They don't need more pop culture and youth perspectives in the classroom. They get enough of those on their own. Young [people] need someone somewhere in their lives to reveal to them bigger and better human stories than the sagas of summer parties and dormitory diversions and Facebook sites.
>
> (Bauerlain, 2009, p. 199)

> Relation, except in very rare cases, precedes any engagement with subject matter.
> —*Nel Noddings*

A get-with-the-times position might look like this:

For students to feel they belong, they need mentors who understand their lives. Good teachers watch the same YouTube videos as their students, listen to the latest hit songs, participate in sites like Facebook, and keep up with teen lingo. Their students see them as friends and allies.

Discuss these two approaches with your colleagues, and consider what a third road—a road of moderation—might look like. What specific actions do you take in your classroom to promote a sense of belonging? What new actions might you take, based on your discussion? Share your thoughts with your colleagues.

The Classroom Community

Creating a sense of belonging and connection is necessary but not sufficient. A classroom community that promotes intellectual engagement and student achievement is a community focused on learning.

Here is how Roland Barth describes a learning community:

> ...*a place where students and adults alike are engaged as active learners in matters of special importance to them and where everyone is thereby encouraging everyone else's learning.*
>
> (1990, p. 9)

Other authors provide similar descriptions, for example:

> *...a cultural setting in which everyone learns, in which every individual is an integral part, and in which every participant is responsible for both the learning and the overall well-being of everyone else.*
>
> (Myers & Simpson, 1998, p. 2)

Some find these descriptions more idealistic than realistic. Nevertheless, the Partnership for 21st Century Skills identifies similar attitudes, behaviours, and skills as ones that students should be learning and practising within classroom communities in order to be successful in life.

The Partnership's list includes the following:
- Act responsibly with the interests of the larger community in mind.
- Demonstrate ability to work effectively and respectfully with diverse teams.
- Exercise flexibility and willingness to be helpful in making necessary compromises to accomplish a common goal.
- Assume shared responsibility for collaborative work, and value the individual contributions made by each team member.
- Respect cultural differences and work effectively with people from a range of social and cultural backgrounds.
- Communicate effectively in diverse environments (including multilingual).
- Respond open-mindedly to different ideas and values.
- Leverage social and cultural differences to create new ideas and increase innovation and quality of work.

Source: www.p21.org

Two interrelated conditions of 21st century life make these particular attitudes and skills especially important. The first is that technology has made it possible for diverse work teams to assemble from countries around the globe, complete their assignments, disperse, and reassemble with new team members for new projects. The second is that this diversity demands skills of collaboration and communication that used to be expected only of university graduates and international tour guides.

In the next chapter I suggest a variety of actions you can take to build a classroom community that is focused on and supportive of learning.

> "We cannot always build the future for our youth, but we can build our youth for the future."
> —*Franklin Delano Roosevelt*

> "As knowledge-based services and intellectual capital become more central to corporations, improving the way people work together will be a major way to leverage intellectual capital, making a critical competitive difference."
> —*Daniel Goleman*

Professional Learning Communities

Margaret Wheatley tells this story:

> Solidarity in Poland began with conversation—less than a dozen workers in a Gdansk shipyard speaking to each other about their despair, their need for change, their need for freedom. In less than a month, Solidarity grew to 9.5 million workers. There was no email then, just people talking to each other about their own needs, and finding their needs shared by millions of fellow citizens. At the end of that month, all 9.5 million of them acted as one voice for change. They shut down the country.
>
> (2002, p. 22)

Setting aside the political action, I have to ask: When was the last time your professional learning community had this kind of energy?

I believe that professional learning communities play an important role in our schools. They provide us with an opportunity to look at school data, analyze and interpret that data, and plan actions we will take as a result. To me, professional learning communities are an invaluable way of creating change by encouraging a focus on collaborative reflection and action in the midst of the busy and often isolating environment of a school.

However, precisely because our work environment is so busy, I believe that we need to allot time in our meetings for simple conversation—for telling the stories about our experiences. It seems to me that doing this is especially necessary in the face of significant problems of student disengagement. Parker Palmer describes an all too common occurrence:

> Day after day, year after year, we walk into classrooms and look into younger faces that seem to signal, in ways crude and subtle, "You're history. Whatever you value, we don't—and since you couldn't possibly understand the things we value, we won't even bother to try to tell you what they are. We are here only because we are forced to be here. So whatever you have to do, get it over with, and let us get on with our lives."
>
> (1998, p. 48)

When we don't have the opportunity to talk about our experiences with others, we create shorthand comments that can be shared in two minutes in the staff workroom between one class and the next—comments like "I think Tony's mission in life is to get under my skin."

> There is no power equal to a community discovering what it cares about.
>
> —*Margaret Wheatley*

When we don't have the opportunity for conversation, we lose the chance to have others help us examine our beliefs and look at an event through a different lens (see pages 84–86). Palmer continues:

> *That is how we sometimes interpret the signals our students send when, in truth, they are usually signals of fear, not disdain. Until I learn to decode that message, I will be quick to cast too many of my students in the role of the Student from Hell—and I will never learn to decode it until I understand my own fear of the judgment of the young.*
>
> (1998, p. 48)

Mindful of the educator's predilection for turning something simple into a complicated set of techniques, I continue to remind myself that conversations have been around since the beginning of language. We don't need to invent ways to talk. There are, however, different levels of conversation. Simply venting our frustration to friends often serves to embed us even deeper in our misery and indignation.

> There is more than a verbal tie between the words *common, community,* and *communication.*... Try the experiment of communicating, with fullness and accuracy, some experience to another, especially if it be somewhat complicated, and you will find your own attitude toward your experience changing.
>
> —*John Dewey*

While I'll give specific suggestions in Chapter 8, here are a few understandings that will help to make any conversation safer and more powerful for all:

√ Deliberately slow down so there is time to think and reflect (Wheatley, 2002).

√ Remember that this is just a conversation. You do not need to convince anyone of anything. Be open to other points of view.

√ Conversation is natural. We all know how to do it. That doesn't mean it will be easy. Expect it to get messy (Wheatley, 2002).

Great Conversations

What basic understandings would need to be in place for you to feel comfortable being part of an open and honest conversation? You could reflect on this individually in a journal or in discussion with one or more colleagues.

Summary of Chapter Website Content		www.pearsoncanada.ca/tunedout
Conversations	**Resources**	**Research**
• "Community" Video Byte	• Community Images	• Teens and Social Networking
• Social Networks and Learning	• Social Networking Sites	• Adults and Social Networking
• Michelle Made Me Crazy	• Creating a Profile	• Spotlight on *I Wanna Be Sedated*

8 Webs of Relationship

Vanquish Fear and Negative Stress 130

Checking In 134

Koinonia 138

Demise of the Lone Ranger 144

Just Beyond the School Walls. 148

Online Communities. 152

Vanquish Fear and Negative Stress

Emotions affect both motivation and learning. Motivation and attention are related—we pay more attention to things that motivate us, and we are motivated by what we attend to. The amygdala (the part of the brain that helps to create and maintain emotions) pays more attention to information or events that are emotionally charged than to those that are emotionally neutral. The specific aspect of the information or event that draws attention varies with the individual, making it important to present new information in a variety of ways (see pages 66–69).

Once the amygdala has connected emotion to a piece of information or an event, it will be remembered for a long time and with great accuracy. Molecular biologist John Medina explains why:

> *The amygdala is chock-full of the neurotransmitter dopamine, and it uses dopamine the way an office assistant uses Post-It notes. When the brain detects an emotionally charged event, the amygdala releases dopamine into the system. Because dopamine greatly aids memory and information processing, you could say the Post-It note reads "Remember this!" Getting the brain to put a chemical Post-It note on a given piece of information means that information is going to be more robustly processed.*
>
> (2008, pp. 80–81)

In the teenage brain, the amygdala is developing faster than the frontal cortex (the area responsible for abstract thinking, language, and decision making). This fact explains why adolescents are more often reactive than reflective, and why they so frequently answer questions about their feelings or behaviour with such responses as "Whatever" or "I don't know." Fortunately, adults do most of their thinking with the frontal cortex, not the amygdala, so if we stay calm we are usually able to de-escalate any confrontations and model appropriate responses.

What we may not be aware of is that adolescents also have difficulty interpreting facial expressions and body language. In one study, only 50 percent of teens were able to accurately interpret the facial expression of a woman as fear; others looked at the photograph and saw either anger or shock (Baird et al., 1999). In contrast, 100 percent of adults read the facial expression correctly. Research suggests that the inability to identify another person's emotions drops by as much as 20 percent at puberty and does not recover until approximately age 18 (McGivern et al., 2002). Since "the key to intuiting another's feelings is the ability to read nonverbal channels: tone of voice, gesture, facial expression, and the like" (Goleman, 2006, p. 96), the fact that adolescents often misinterpret non-verbal signals has a significant impact on their relationships with peers and adults.

Memorable Moments

Think of a memorable school experience. Are you able to remember the details of any significant school experience that wasn't related to an emotion, positive or negative?

Alternatively, tell a colleague the story of trying to learn something new when your dominant emotion was fear. How did fear affect the learning?

Emotions are necessary to both motivation and learning, but given the heightened activity in the adolescent's amygdala, teachers need to be careful that the emotions attached to learning are positive. Eric Jensen makes the following recommendation:

> *Start by removing threats from the learning environment. No matter how excited you are about adding positives to the environment, first work to eliminate the negatives.... There is no evidence that threats are an effective way to meet long-term academic goals.*
>
> (1998, p. 30)

Learning is diminished when adolescents feel threatened by any of a number of situations, such as the following:

→ anything that embarrasses them or makes them stand out

→ unrealistic deadlines and expectations

→ a belief that the teacher doesn't like them

→ a belief that no matter what they do, they cannot be successful

→ criticism

→ assessments used to "catch" them for not doing the work or not understanding

→ one-size-fits-all teaching and assessing

> The people who influence you are people who believe in you.
>
> —*Henry Drummond*

Vanquish Fear and Negative Stress – continued

Threats cause people of all ages to focus on protecting themselves. Blood flows to the extremities rather than the brain, readying us to fight or flee (LeDoux, 2003). Prolonged or severe threats cause a negative stress on our brains that has been shown to affect short- and long-term memory, skills in math and language, concentration, and our ability to transfer information from one setting to another (the key indicator of true understanding). "In almost every way it can be tested, chronic stress hurts our ability to learn" (Medina, 2008, p. 178).

Chronic stress can come from outside the classroom as well as inside. Marital stress within a student's family—that is, stress caused not by divorce but by overt conflict—"can negatively affect academic performance in almost every way measurable and at nearly any age" (Medina, 2008, pp. 184–185).

There are threats outside and inside the classroom that you can do nothing about. As a classroom teacher you can do nothing about marital stress in a student's family, for example. Threats you might inadvertently create are also beyond your control—a student interprets the look of surprise on

Case Study → Impact on Engagement: Relevance Through Storytelling

Name: Carmella W.   **Subjects:** Social Studies, English   **Grade:** 6

Jefferson had amazingly creative ideas he was quite willing to share orally, but he balked at any request to put those ideas on paper. That started to change when I invited professional storyteller Cathy Miyata to our classroom.

After listening to Mrs. Miyata share several Aboriginal legends, Jefferson and his classmates were inspired to write legends they could then share orally with their peers and with other classes in the school.

Jefferson made multiple revisions to his story as a result of the supportive feedback he received from peers. He developed a strong sense of voice and demonstrated an excellent understanding of what makes a good storyline. Although his attitude towards writing didn't change completely, Jefferson's later writing had a spark that hadn't been there before. He became a more confident writer.

your face as anger. However, since academic success is tied to a sense of emotional safety, it's vital that you do what you can to create a classroom community of mutual respect, caring, and support.

Low-Threat Classrooms

Check all of the boxes that apply in the following self-assessment of your classroom environment. Remembering Eric Jensen's caution that we need to remove threats before adding positive elements, consider which of the boxes you've left unchecked represent a threat in your classroom, and work to address them. See pages 210–213 for help with making necessary changes.

In my classroom…

- ❏ I use positive, inviting language with all students; for example, "You can do it" and "I won't give up on you."

- ❏ I either don't use sarcasm or I use it cautiously because I know that students can easily misinterpret it.

- ❏ I provide my students with meaningful choices whenever possible, so they achieve their need for autonomy and feel in control of their work (see pages 70–74).

- ❏ I actively work to build and maintain a positive relationship with each student (see pages 123–125).

- ❏ I use a variety of activities to ensure that my students know one another by name and are comfortable working together (see pages 144–146).

- ❏ I use plenty of partner and group activities so students can interact socially while learning (see pages 144–146).

- ❏ I instruct and assess in a variety of ways to meet the varying needs, interests, and preferences of my students in order to support everyone's success (see pages 66–69 and 230–231).

> Laughter need not be cut out of anything, since it improves everything.
>
> —*James Thurber*

Checking In

When students are asked about the qualities of good teachers, caring is always at or near the top of the list. Caring is evident when teachers "check in" with students through actions that include the following:

- √ Walking around the room talking to everybody to see how they are doing and to answer questions
- √ Helping with school work
- √ Noticing and inquiring about changes in behaviour
- √ Recognizing different learning styles and speeds
- √ Seeking to know students as unique human beings
- √ Showing respect for students by having one-on-one conversations with them in a quiet voice or in private
- √ Doing a good job of explaining the content, making sure that all students understand
- √ Encouraging students to improve

(Bosworth, 1995, pp. 691–692)

You Know and Do More Than You Realize

The following activity is one I've used in many workshops. You can do it alone, but it will inspire good conversation if you talk about your results with others.

1. Get a sheet of paper and a pen. Think of the largest class you teach or, if you are a leader working with adults, think of a large group such as everyone who works on your floor of the building.

2. Set a timer for 90 seconds. In that time write down the first names of people in your class or group. You can do this in the form of a list, map, or graphic organizer.

3. At the end of 90 seconds, look over the names you've recorded. Take another 30 seconds to add any names you might have missed.

4. Talk with others about how you recalled names (for example, visualizing the classroom or friendship groupings, or remembering an alphabetized list) and how you recorded them (perhaps in a seating plan, graphic organizer, or list).

> The meeting of two personalities is like the contact of two chemical substances: if there is any reaction, both are transformed.
> —*Carl Jung*

These responses speak to your natural learning preferences. They're important for you to be aware of because people commonly teach the way they learn best. Recognizing that, you can sometimes vary what you do so you reach students with learning preferences different from your own.

5. Put a check mark beside the name of every student or adult for whom you can identify a personal interest. For example, if you know that Jasper plays hockey, put a check mark by his name.

6. Discuss how you became aware of individual interests. (Student interests often come to light through the process of checking in with students to see how their day is going.)

7. As a final step, turn the check mark into an X if you have said or done something in the last 30 days to let a person know that you are aware of his or her interests. For example, perhaps you asked Jasper how his team did in the last game or brought in a complimentary newspaper article about the team to share with the class. It is this final step of connecting that allows the student to identify you as a caring teacher.

Try any of the following ideas to check in and keep tabs on how your students are doing:

Greet Them—Stand by the door and greet all students by name as they enter. Adolescents may not be good at reading body language (see pages 130–131), but you are, and you will easily pick up on tensions or concerns, some of which you may be able to alleviate simply by making this quick connection.

"How's It Going?" Journals—This strategy has worked well for me. When I was too busy to check in personally with each student, I'd ask everyone to take a few minutes and respond in writing to the question "How's it going?" Students could talk about anything they wanted, knowing that I would maintain their confidence, provide a written response, and work with them to address any issues they raised.

2 x 10—Spend two minutes a day for 10 consecutive days with a disengaged student. These interactions might happen in various places, such as in class, at the student's locker, and in the cafeteria. Talk about anything

Checking In – continued

except the student's lack of engagement. The idea is for you and the student to get to know each other without the pressure of expectations. Behaviour expert Allen Mendler says he has recommended this approach for years because he has found that it gets good results: "It is common toward the end of the cycle to see many students begin to behave more acceptably and complete more of their work" (2000, p. 52).

Resources
Conducting Student Focus Groups

Host a Focus Group—Businesses routinely conduct focus groups to help them make important decisions, and focus groups are now becoming increasingly common in schools. You'll find detailed information about how to conduct a focus group on the website. For the purpose of checking in with students, a group would be a maximum of five students from a class. If you want general feedback, select students who cover the range from engaged to actively disengaged. If you want to use the focus group for problem solving, choose students who demonstrate the same level of engagement.

Attend Extracurricular Events—There's no question this recommendation is asking a lot of busy teachers, but acting on it can make a world of difference to disengaged or actively disengaged students. They'll know that you care enough to support them by attending events outside the classroom. It's also reassuring and informative to see these students in an environment where they are capable and engaged.

> The most powerful narcotic in the world is the promise of belonging.
> —*Kalle Lasn*

George's Book—I attended a workshop years ago where a teacher named George told us that he selected five students to focus on in each class. He made a point of noticing and recording positives about each student in a class notebook. By the end of the week, George had made positive jot notes about every student in class. I remember that George's notes were heartwarming and inspiring, that his students loved reading the notebook, and that his awareness of his students' unique strengths had an enormous impact on the engagement and achievement of students who were dealing with a variety of serious challenges. (I can't remember George's last name or where he was from, so I'm honouring his great idea by referring to it as "George's Book.") I tried this approach in my own classroom but couldn't keep it up. Nevertheless, I saw benefits in my classroom in the two weeks I was able to maintain my George's Book. It's an idea worth trying.

Debrief with Students—Class meetings or community circles are well worth the time and effort. Use meetings at the beginning of the year to help students get to know each other and to establish the processes and ground rules of meetings. Use meetings throughout the year to solve classroom problems. Class meetings give you a way to check in with all of your students, and they build students' commitment to community. Some ground rules to establish for class meetings include offering a positive comment before saying anything negative, refraining from assigning blame, and focusing on solutions rather than problems. Have students take turns as leaders, with you participating as a group member.

Resources
Debriefing with Students

My Life in Six Words—Legend has it that when Ernest Hemingway was challenged to write a novel in six words, he wrote, "For Sale: Baby shoes, never worn." Larry Smith, editor of the online magazine *Smith*, picked up on this idea in 2006 and invited readers to submit their life story in exactly six words. In the first two months Smith received 15 000 replies, the best of which were published in a *New York Times* bestselling book titled *Not Quite What I Was Planning*.

In an environment where text messaging limits students' writing, you might find that they will be enthusiastic if you occasionally check in with them by inviting them to tell you how they are doing, using exactly six words, such as "I have not accomplished much…yet".

Resources
Six Words

You will find links to more information, as well as more examples of six-word memoirs, on the website.

Webs of Relationship ■ 137

Koinonia

Socrates and his colleagues so fervently believed in the power of the group to advance thinking that they established principles of conversation that would maintain a sense of community. These principles were referred to as *Koinonia* which means "spirit of fellowship" (Michalko, 2001).

Here are the three Koinonia from Socrates' time, and a fourth I've added for the 21st century:

1. Establish Dialogue

Peter Senge (1994) identified a four-point continuum of the types of conversations most likely to occur in organizations:

Raw Debate   Polite Discussion   Skilled Discussion   Dialogue

> At the core of every successful conversation lies the free flow of relevant information.
> —*Kerry Patterson et al.*

All types of conversation have their advantages. For example, raw debate is useful to the extent that it identifies people's stands on issues. Dialogue, however, is far more useful because meaning flows freely between two or more people, creating a pool of shared meaning that enriches the group's thinking and the quality of any decisions made (Patterson, Grenny, McMillan, & Switzler, 2002).

> The void created by the failure to communicate is soon filled with poison, drivel, and misrepresentation.
> —*C. Northcote Parkinson*

Senge defines skilled discussion as a balance of advocacy and inquiry. This type of discussion is considered highly effective and efficient in a school setting, but it's relatively rare. Far more frequent is polite discussion, in which participants mask their true feelings and responses. Engaging in polite discussion may signify passive refusal to commit to the work, which may ultimately lead to problems implementing any decisions made.

Try Dialogue

The basic rules of dialogue for the Greeks were "Don't argue," "Don't interrupt," and "Listen carefully" (Michalko, 2001). Do the conversations you have in your school qualify as dialogue, discussion, or debate?

Discussion is more common than dialogue because "people find it easy to express their opinions and to bat ideas back and forth with others, but most of the time they don't have either the motivation or the patience to respond empathically to opinions with which they may disagree or that they find uncongenial" (Yankelovich, 1999, p. 44).

Use the process page provided on the website to help people experience dialogue. This process involves dialogue with a partner, but note that dialogues are not limited to two people. The word *dialogue* means "through" (*dia*) "meaning" (*logos*) or "talking through" an idea. Conceivably, an entire staff could have a dialogue.

Dialogue takes time and isn't always necessary. For information about when to use dialogue and when not to bother, see the website.

Resources
Practising Dialogue

Research
Dialogues and Decisions

> I pin my hopes to quiet processes and small circles, in which vital and transforming events take place.
> —*Rufus Jones*

2. Clarify Your Thinking

Socrates and his friends recognized that thoughts and opinions were based on beliefs. They treated all beliefs as untested assumptions and tried to suspend their assumptions during dialogue. For more information about the significance of beliefs to teaching and learning, see pages 84–86.

Listen & Ask

The next time you are engaged in a conversation of any kind, try these approaches:

To identify your own beliefs, listen for what surprises or disturbs you. "If what you say surprises me, I must have been assuming something else was true. If it disturbs me, I must believe something contrary to you" (Wheatley, 2002, p. 36).

Webs of Relationship 139

Koinonia – continued

In her book *Talk About Teaching!* (2009), Charlotte Danielson suggests that using plural forms, paraphrasing comments, and probing for more information are all useful strategies for conversations. Below, I apply these strategies and one other to examining our own and others' beliefs during conversation.

To help others clarify their beliefs:

- √ Use plural forms in your questions to signal that there is no one correct answer, and encourage analysis by asking questions where one situation is compared with another. For example, "What factors do you think might have affected Rhonda's motivation to excel on this task when she has failed so many others?"

- √ Paraphrase by repeating a person's statement in a slightly different manner so the speaker can hear what was said and can correct any mismatch between what was heard and what was intended.

- √ Probe by asking, "Could you say more about that?" or by allowing 5 to 10 seconds of silence. Wait time helps adults and students explain their thinking.

- √ Encourage people to share their thinking with a partner, in a small group, or through individual written reflection before they engage in conversation with a large group. These approaches are responsive to individuals' learning preferences and will help to create an environment where people feel safe to share their thinking.

3. Be Honest

Michael Michalko explains this principle as, "Say what you think, even if your thoughts are controversial" (2001, p. 256). That's easier said than done, but here are some tips from Kerry Patterson and his colleagues (2002) that will help make any conversation safer (see also pages 127–128):

- √ *Establish a mutual purpose*—Doing this is a basic condition of both dialogue and skilled discussion. When we share a common goal, it's much easier to care about what others think and value. Debate is one sign that mutual purpose is at risk; other signs include defensiveness, hidden agendas, accusations, and a return to the same topic over and over again.

- √ *Commit to mutual respect*—Conversations are derailed when power differences exist and when people's needs are not being met. It is important for facilitators and leaders to deliberately create the environment for a good conversation (see the website for more information). Anger is a key indicator that an individual is feeling disrespected.

- √ *Recognize your personal signs of disengagement*—Look for the cues that indicate your brain is disengaging and the conversation is deteriorating. These cues vary with the individual but might include physical responses (dry eyes, tight or upset stomach); emotional responses (feeling scared, hurt, or angry and either reacting impulsively or repressing these feelings); and behavioural responses (raising your voice, withdrawing).

Resources
Safe Environments for Conversation

Contentious Groupings

When, if ever, should students be grouped according to their abilities? Is it a problem for high school students to be in "streamed" or "tracked" classes? Are those classes a way of effectively and efficiently differentiating our instruction so we meet student needs?

I hesitated before deciding to address ability grouping on the website. The question of ability grouping is enormously contentious among educators, which means that it is activating a number of our beliefs. As we know, issues that activate core beliefs about who we are as people and as teachers are best dealt with through face-to-face dialogue, where we can read each other's body language and work together towards a common pool of meaning. But in a dialogue on this topic, the chances of people losing their goodwill seem to me quite high.

However, since I have discussed uncovering and working with beliefs in previous chapters (and talk about taking risks in subsequent chapters), I feel compelled to model what I recommend. I invite you to read my blog post on the website and to discuss your thoughts either with colleagues or online with all of us. Further information about grouping students is available on pages 144–146.

Conversations
Group by Ability?

Webs of Relationship

Koinonia – continued

> There have been great societies that did not use the wheel, but there have been no societies that did not tell stories.
>
> —*Ursula K. LeGuin*

4. Tell Stories

This seems a strange principle to add for the 21st century since storytelling has been around since the beginning of humankind; however, as Daniel Pink suggests, we need stories now more than ever:

When facts become so widely available and instantly accessible, each one becomes less valuable. What begins to matter more is the ability to place these facts in context and to deliver them with emotional impact.

(2006, p. 103)

Psychologists sometimes refer to stories as being "psychologically privileged," meaning that they are treated differently in memory than other forms of input. Cognitive psychologist Daniel Willingham (2009) suggests that stories are considered not only the oldest, but also the most effective form of teaching because they are

→ *easy to understand*—We are familiar with narrative structure.

→ *interesting*—A well-told story requires that we make inferences.

→ *easy to remember*—Making inferences throughout requires thinking about the story's meaning as you listen, which aids memory. Additionally, narrative structure makes it likely that if you remember one part of the plot, you'll remember the next thing that happened because it was caused by the event you remembered.

The story structure is helpful for teaching in all subject areas. It is also, as Nick Owen suggests, tremendously helpful in professional conversations:

Like putting on different pairs of glasses, stories allow us to look at life and experience in ways that can shift our perspective, range, and focus. Different lenses in the frames allow stories to zoom in, or take a distant view, on their subject. Filters can be attached to a lens to change colour, mood, and energy levels. At their most magical, stories can challenge and disturb our existing frames of reference, our accustomed map of the world, and shift us away from our limited thinking towards new learning and discovery.

(2008, p. xiii)

Tell Your Stories

The difference between giving an example and telling a story is the addition of emotional content and added sensory details in the telling.

(Simmons, 2006, p. 31)

Read my blog post and talk with your colleagues about what makes this post a story rather than an example. Then, please consider sharing a story of your own, either in writing (perhaps on the website blog) or orally with colleagues. One suggestion is to tell a story of a teacher or other adult who inspired you to be the kind of teacher you are today. Another is to tell the story of a disengaged student and an experience that showed you were making a difference in the student's life.

Conversations
The Boys in Basic English

Your School Story

Successful leaders must have teachable points of view about ideas, values, energy, and edge. It is through stories, however, that they tie them together and energize others to move from the present into a winning future.

(Tichy & Cohen, 1997, p. 42)

Tell a colleague from another school or district a story that exemplifies one of the best qualities of your workplace.

Next, tell a story about your school or district four years into the future. Your story might be about one day in the life of a student or teacher, or it might be a series of stories that show your vision of a 21st century workplace where students, teachers, and parents are engaged in learning.

If you are telling your story aloud, ask someone to write down some of the key words you use. If your story is in writing, circle these words. Reflect on whether these words clearly communicate your vision and, if necessary, revise them so they do. For more information about storytelling as an organizational practice, see the links on the website.

Research
Storytelling for Learders

Stories have a job to do. They can't just lie around like lazybone dogs. They have to teach you something.

—*Lloyd Jones*

Webs of Relationship 143

Demise of the Lone Ranger

Under the right conditions, both students and teachers find that working with others is more engaging than working alone. Considering only the research conducted on adolescents, benefits of working with others include increases in the following areas:

- academic achievement—Two studies (Bowen, 2000; House, 2005) found that working with others improved achievement in science.
- motivation to learn (Slavin, 1990)
- social competencies of cooperation, altruism, and empathy (Aronson, 2000)
- relationships among students (Gillies, 2008)
- self-understanding (Hogan, Nastasi, & Pressley, 1999)

A longitudinal study of more than 10 000 high school students surveyed 10 years after graduation found that students who had been rated by their teachers as easily able to relate to others had higher levels of postsecondary education and a higher annual income than those who rated lower on social skills. This finding held true regardless of the student's intellectual abilities (Lieras, 2008).

Dents in the Universe

Research
Spotlight on *Organizing Genius*

Steve Jobs told the team that created the Mac personal computer that great groups "make a dent in the universe." Although it's unlikely that many of us have worked at the level of creativity and dedication exemplified by Jobs and his team, a terrific experience working with a partner or group makes a dent in our little corner of the universe. Tell a partner or your book study group the story of a positive experience of working together. After you have listened to each other's stories, identify any common characteristics that seem to be required for a partner or group effort to be successful.

If you want to be inspired by stories of some world-class groups, see the review on the website of one of my all-time favourite books, *Organizing Genius: The Secrets of Creative Collaboration* by Warren Bennis and Patricia Ward Biederman (1998).

When Groups Aren't Great

When conditions are right, working together is great; when they are wrong, few experiences are more frustrating and potentially demoralizing. Once again, please share a story—this time of an experience working in a group that wasn't successful—and look for commonalities among the stories offered.

Given the importance of social interaction to learning, self-concept, and our students' future success, we need to ensure that the conditions are right for adolescents to experience all of the benefits of working with others. The following chart provides some suggestions.

Resources
- Random Pairs
- Creating Diverse Groups

If…	Then…
• You have established group norms, but students persist in problematic behaviours such as refusing to help each other	√ Spend more time modelling what helping each other looks like. Remember the research on mirror neurons (see page 124); students will do what they see you doing, not what you tell them to do. √ Take time for groups to develop written agreements about how they will work together.
• Some students have limited opportunity to contribute	√ Check group size and task structure. Groups of four tend to work well. The task needs to require "positive interdependence." In other words, everyone must make a contribution if the group is to be successful.
• The task doesn't require a contribution from everyone	√ Don't use groups. Have students work alone or with a partner.
• Some students are "hitchhikers" or "social loafers," relying on others to do the work	√ Identify the problem and then have students suggest solutions (see page 235), choose a solution to try, and then report back on the results.
• Students in a group are not becoming a cohesive team	√ Increase the challenge of the task. The "Survivor" television show is based on the idea that success is possible only if people work together. (For specific examples of cooperative learning structures that support students working at a high level of challenge, see pages 63 and 111–112.) √ Increase the sense of urgency by shortening the time available to complete the task.

Demise of the Lone Ranger – continued

If...	Then...
• Students seem lost or the quality of work is not to your satisfaction	√ Make sure students are aware of the learning goal and what successful achievement of that goal looks like. √ Check for understanding. If there are significant gaps, return to direct instruction and guided practice before continuing with group work.
• Frequently absent students make it difficult to create balanced groups	√ When planning your groups, add frequently absent students last, increasing group size to five or six. These students will then have a group they can join when present, but the ongoing group remains stable and balanced regardless.
• Students want to work only with their friends	√ Make students more comfortable working with a variety of classmates by frequently using random pairings of students. See the Resources section of the website for ways to create these pairings. √ Stress diversity of strengths, learning preferences, and gender, whether you are constructing groups or allowing students to choose their groups. For a variety of ways to construct diverse groups, see the website.

©2004 ZITS Partnership. Distributed by King Features Syndicate.

146 ■ Community

Case Study: Impact on Engagement: Geocaching Teams

Name: Cheryl C.   Subject: Geography   Grade: 9

I prepared 15 caches, using plastic film canisters filled with small trinkets, and hid them in various places outside the school. For each location, I recorded the latitude and longitude using a GPS (global positioning system), and wrote a clue. For example, one cache was hanging from a pine tree outside the school library. The clue read, "If you 'hang around,' you can read all about this plant on the other side of the window."

Students were assigned to random groups, and each group was given a GPS unit and a paper with the latitude, longitude, and clue for their cache. As a group, they entered the coordinates into their GPS unit and set off in search of their cache. When all caches were found, students returned to the classroom to debrief and discuss problems and suggestions for other hiding locations. If there was time, students prepared and hid caches for another class.

Impact on Engagement

Geocaching is a high-tech treasure hunt, making it appealing to students who would rather be playing video games than sitting in a classroom. The use of technology, the concept of a game, and the fact that facility with English isn't essential mean that a wide variety of students can be successful at this activity. In fact, I found that my students really began to value peers who may not have been successful in traditional terms, but who were often much more likely to think creatively about where a film canister might be hidden.

The ultimate sign of engagement was that geocaching activities led to students convincing their families to purchase an inexpensive GPS and then signing up to become geocachers, hiding their own caches for others to find.

(For Cheryl's recommendations on geocaching and links to useful resources, see the website.)

Resources
Geocaching

Just Beyond the School Walls

Parents and local community members are a vital and all too often untapped resource in encouraging the engagement of all students. Terrence Deal and Kent Peterson write about the methods and the benefits of connecting with parents and community organizations:

Successful cultures try to find ways to increase

> Trying to educate children without the involvement of their family is like trying to play a basketball game without all the players on the court.
>
> —*Bill Bradley*

- → **Convening**—Bring parents and community members into the school to meet staff and students; proximity breeds understanding.
- → **Conveying**—Use multiple sources of communication with parents. Visit their homes, send email, call, and send short positive notes; communication sends signals of engagement.
- → **Collaborating**—Include parents in planning, decision making, and implementing new ideas; empowerment fosters respect.
- → **Conspiring**—Work with parents to increase school funding, pass referenda, and gain resources from the district and local businesses; conspiring encourages dialogue.
- → **Co-creating**—Use the creative juices of parents and community organizations to produce television shows and podcasts, develop the arts, and add dazzle to the school's appearance; joint creating fosters close ties.
- → **Celebrating**—Recognize and commemorate parents, but also support the celebration of school staff by parent groups; mutual appreciation breeds trust and branding.

(2009, p. 186)

Re-engaging Parents

While parents are often keenly involved in the educational activities of young children, their involvement typically decreases as their children become adolescents. (Reasons for this can be found on the website.) As a staff, discuss the difference supportive parents make to the engagement of adolescents, and determine one or more actions that could be taken to increase parental involvement in your school. Use the list of suggestions above, creative thinking ideas from Chapter 6, and accounts of what some parent groups are achieving. Be sure to see the link to the article about Club 2012 on the website.

Research
- Parents of Adolescents
- Club 2012

Cooperative Education

Cooperative education programs allow students to gain credits towards graduation while they are involved in a work experience with a local community business or organization. These experiences, in settings of interest to students, allow community partners to collaborate with the school to develop students' knowledge and skills in a relevant context. At their best, when students are guided towards increasing involvement in the work, cooperative education programs are a form of cognitive apprenticeship where the relationship between the expert and the student drives engagement and learning.

> Think of the entire community as an extension of the classroom, filled with skilled and knowledgeable residents with teaching and learning agendas and capacities of their own.
> —*Anne Lewis and Anne Henderson*

Service Learning

Service learning allows students to give back to their community through volunteerism or social justice initiatives that are tied to curriculum objectives. Whether students are working at a soup kitchen, the local animal shelter, or the hospital, the benefits are as much to the students as to the community. Disengaged students, in particular, can achieve their need for power or competence through serving as a needed and valued volunteer, or by bringing attention to an issue through online activism.

> Giving back is a powerful 'hook' for all youth, especially for those not used to thinking of themselves as successful.
> —*Bonnie Benard*

Place-Based Learning

Place-based learning uses the local community to achieve curriculum objectives. (This type of community-based approach is central to Aboriginal cultures.) Social research in the community is a form of place-based learning, as is environmental research in the ponds, swamps, and landfills of the area. No matter what subject you teach, there is likely a way to integrate place-based learning. For some disengaged students, the novelty of working outside the school can reignite curiosity and motivation.

Just Beyond the School Walls – continued

Case Study: Impact on Engagement: Making a Difference

Name: Mike P.   **Subjects:** Social Studies, English   **Grades:** 5/6

I want my students to know they have the power to affect real change in the world if they learn to problem-solve and think creatively. After sharing an online example of a young student who demonstrated global citizenship, I asked students to make jot notes of the positive differences they could make in the four categories of home, school, community, and world. I encouraged them to start small and local, suggesting that the momentum established through success would ultimately let them take on the world!

The next step was for students to use their notes to write an introduction to their personal plan for making a difference. I spent considerable time modelling and teaching students how to write an engaging introduction, and found that made a significant difference to the quality of student writing.

Once the introductions were written, students used Audacity software to record their work. Audacity allows students to make revisions to an audio file without re-recording the entire piece. When satisfied with their work, students added music. Each file was published to our classroom podcast.

Impact on Engagement

All students enjoyed recording their introductions and were strongly motivated to produce quality pieces because their work would have an audience beyond the classroom. One of my reluctant writers asked me if his work would be heard around the world. Pointing to the world map of our podcast audience, I replied that it could be heard by anyone with an internet connection. His response: "I need to re-do this!"

Research
"Make a Difference" Podcast

Case Study: Impact on Engagement: Place-Based Learning

Name: Steven V. **Subject:** English **Grade:** 12

I was apprehensive about one student's lack of engagement with a dead poet. My class had been studying the work of Alden Nowlan, a writer who had been born and raised in the same county as our high school. After three weeks of reading Nowlan's work, we decided to visit his birthplace in Stanley, Nova Scotia, a 20-minute drive from the school. We took camping chairs, our favourite pieces of Nowlan's work to share, our testimonies of how his work helped and/or challenged our thinking, and food, including an apple crisp made by a retired secretary of the school.

Nowlan's birthplace is marked by a cairn in remembrance of his early life in the community. Students were surprised to learn that Nowlan had come from a rural community with no stop signs, stores, or cell phone service.

After returning to the school, students looked up Stanley, Nova Scotia, on Wikipedia and decided to enrich the one-line description provided. Using a wiki (a collaborative writing tool) in a Moodle (an online learning environment) to communicate and post work, my students co-wrote a description of Stanley, which I posted on Wikipedia.

Impact on Engagement

Students in my Advanced Grade 12 English class were predominantly from rural homes, often a 60- to 90-minute bus ride from the school. Nowlan was an appropriate choice for these students because his work references his rural background. The students in this class were engaged with Nowlan because he was local and successful, and his writing was accessible to them. Our field trip became a common point of reference and a happy memory for our classroom community.

The student I was worried about read a passage from a Nowlan poem at Nowlan's birthplace. He decided that the poet really did have something relevant to say to him, after all.

Resources
Stanley, Nova Scotia

Webs of Relationship

Online Communities

In the case studies provided below, you'll read about the experiences of four teachers who combined our human need for belonging with social networking tools and meaningful content to promote both intellectual and social engagement in their classrooms.

Case Study ⇒ Impact on Engagement: Ning

Name: Graham W.   **Subject:** Science   **Grade:** 10

David required more processing time than some of my other students and he was reluctant to offer ideas that he thought might be wrong. While he was academically competent, I worried that David and a few others like him were disengaging socially and emotionally from life in the classroom.

To address this issue, I started a Ning in my Grade 10 science class. Ning is a service that allows anyone to create a social network on any topic. Within the Ning, students can share videos and photos, participate in discussion forums, write comments to each other, and maintain their own blogs. Each of these features has multiplied my opportunities to interact with students and to have them interact with each other. By being involved online on a daily basis, I was able to subtly model for students appropriate responses and the skills of positive interaction. I noticed that both the frequency and quality of response improved with my involvement. Additionally, because this online community is focused on science, I was able to assess my students' knowledge, thinking, application, and communication skills in an informal setting.

Impact on Engagement

Students made connections between science and their lives in ways I hadn't anticipated. David's contributions were among the most prolific. He began a number of discussions, and frequently commented on other students' blogs. The social network allowed David and others to express themselves without the social pressures and time restrictions of the classroom.

Resources
Student Science Blog

152 ■ Community

©P

Case Study → **Impact on Engagement: Blogs**

Name: Marla Z.   **Subject:** Media Literacy   **Grade:** 7

Whispers of "Wow, I get my own website?" greeted my introductory lesson about student blogging. Why did I choose blogging? Although my students were chatting and texting daily with their friends, their critical thinking skills were not developing through their interactions, and their written assignments were short, perfunctory, and lacking in detail. I'd hoped that combining technology with purposeful writing would engage students so they would make an effort to develop their skills.

Student blogs were all linked to my teacher blog for easy access within our classroom community. After developing strict rules around online posting, students were given some autonomy over the content of their blogs and were supported with opportunities to use the school's computer lab to write new posts or respond to their friends. There was an expectation that each student would post a blog entry at least once a week.

I blogged on a regular basis, posting homework assignments, reminders of supplies needed for class, and notes of appreciation for students.

Impact on Engagement

Students loved designing their blog pages and creating their profiles. They appreciated being able to blog about topics of personal interest, and I found that they gradually started to include positive comments to each other in response to my modelling.

Next Steps

Next time I'll try a wiki, since that will allow for more collaboration among students. First, though, I'll need to explicitly teach information literacy skills so my students are able to make meaningful contributions to our online discussions.

Resources
Grade 7 Blogs

Online Communities – continued

Case Study → Impact on Engagement: VoiceThread

Name: Jonathan L. **Subject:** English (Reading) **Grades:** 7/8

A number of boys in my class tended to disengage as soon as they were required to read anything other than a high-interest book of their choice. I also had several students who had been overexposed to reader response journals, literature circles, and various activities for recommending books to classmates. I wanted to create an assignment that would allow all students to interact with their classmates and with technology—two aspects that were very appealing to my adolescent learners—as they discussed books.

VoiceThread is an online application similar to Facebook in that students have a profile and the opportunity to post a wide variety of file formats. Because students would be working online, I purchased an educational subscription to VoiceThread, which provides a secure environment.

Before using VoiceThread, I spent significant time discussing good book choices with students. Their challenge was then to present a book in an interesting manner, through VoiceThread, so others would be enticed to read it. After each thread was started, students were able to respond to each other's recommendations and provide and respond to peer feedback.

The variety of mediums through which students could share their recommendations and respond to their classmates was key to engagement.

Students were able to upload the cover of the book they were reading and highlight specific areas that would lead to predictions or inferences. Responses from classmates or the teacher could be uploaded as text files, typed directly into the thread, recorded with a microphone, or videotaped with a web cam.

Impact on Engagement

All students were keenly engaged in this task. Although some had initially participated only to be part of an online social network, they ended up engaging in in-depth discussions of books they normally wouldn't have touched. Furthermore, all students took time to ensure that their work was of high quality because they were sharing it in what they considered a "public" forum.

Case Study → Impact on Engagement: Professional Learning Network

Name: Zoe P.   **Subjects:** All   **Grade:** 6

I found myself smiling—feeling satisfied and proud that many of the resources I use in my classroom had been fed to me from my personal/professional learning network via Twitter and RSS.

In a single week in my classroom, students used the following technologies:

- Skype to read Shel Silverstein poems to Grade 1 students

- Google Docs to collaboratively write and edit PowerPoint presentations

- Wikispaces to post information and assignments related to a social sciences unit

- Scratch to create advertisements for a media literacy unit

- VoiceThread to post comments, reflections, and connections to a novel

- Smories (videos of students reading their stories) to respond to prompts and write and produce their own stories on video

I learned to use each of these technologies by connecting online to colleagues around the world. For example, Jenny from Australia inspired me to use iPods in my classroom so my students can blog and read news and events from their homelands in their own languages. And Andy, from Ontario, helped me with every technology question I ever asked.

Impact on Engagement

The use of technology inspired my students to take more ownership of their learning. The same is true for me. I have learned that sharing a single idea with my online community will result in many more ideas coming back to me. Technology has provided opportunities, tools, and choices. Most of all it has provided access—the opportunity for me to listen, write, and collaborate with innovative teachers and to never feel alone.

Online Communities – continued

Teachers and Principals Who Blog

Resources
Educator Blogs

Zoe, the teacher in the case study on the previous page, is one of a growing number of educators who have created an online professional learning community through blogging. (See also pages 184–185.) If you have never read an educational blog (other than the one on the *Tuned Out* website), I encourage you to take 10 minutes to sample just a few of the many educational blogs available through the link on the website.

Summary of Chapter Website Content		www.pearsoncanada.ca/tunedout
Conversations	**Resources**	**Research**
• Group by Ability? • The Boys in Basic English	• Conducting Student Focus Groups • Debriefing with Students • Six Words • Practising Dialogue • Safe Environments for Conversation • Random Pairs • Creating Diverse Groups • Geocaching • Stanley, Nova Scotia • Student Science Blog • Grade 7 Blogs • Educator Blogs	• Dialogues and Decisions • Storytelling for Leaders • Spotlight on *Organizing Genius* • Parents of Adolescents • Club 2012 • "Make a Difference" Podcast

Context

"No sensible decision can be made any longer without taking into account not only the world as it is, but the world as it will be."

—Isaac Asimov

9 — 21st Century Rat Parks

Conversations
"Context" Video Byte

A number of soldiers who returned from the Vietnam War were addicted to heroin or morphine and yet, once home, many were able to stop using these substances. Canadian psychologist Bruce Alexander and colleagues (1980) wanted to know why some veterans were able to stop taking the drugs, since numerous studies had recently proven that both heroin and morphine were highly addictive to rats—animals with a nervous system similar to our own.

When reviewing the scientific studies, Alexander realized that all of the lab rats had something in common other than drug addiction—they all lived in cages. Knowing that humans aren't terribly fond of life behind bars, Alexander wondered if the same might be true of rats. Perhaps environment had an impact on addiction.

To test his hypothesis, Alexander constructed a rat park—a rat's version of the perfect environment. Some lucky rats got to live in the rat park, while a control group stayed in cages. Rats in both conditions were provided with two bottles of water—one untreated; the other laced with sugar (a favourite of rats and humans) and morphine.

Can you predict the results? The rats in the cages chose the water with morphine and quickly became addicted. The rats in the rat park overwhelmingly chose the plain water. Under some conditions, the caged rats consumed 20 times as much morphine as the rats in the rat park.

Alexander upped the ante by further sweetening the morphine-laced water. The rats in the rat park rejected it. He then put a few drops of Naloxone into the morphine water—Naloxone counteracts the intoxicating effects of a drug. The rats in the rat park drank a little bit, but quickly returned to the plain water.

For the final step in confirming his hypothesis that environment matters, Alexander took the caged rats and put them in a rat park. They immediately cut back on the amount of treated morphine water they were drinking, even though that meant they experienced the horrible symptoms of withdrawal.

Rat Parks for Learners

Environment—what I'm referring to as "context"—matters to humans just as it does to rats. Before you read further, I encourage you to take some time to describe, with colleagues, the ideal learning environment or "rat park" for 21st century learners. If you had the ability to construct the perfect conditions for students and teachers of this century to be engaged in learning, what would you include?

Note that this is a good activity for drawing your ideas. Choose whether you will focus on a classroom, a school, or perhaps an entirely new, even virtual, environment, and create a map of that space. Remember, however, that we are talking about more than the physical environment, so be sure to include your thoughts about aspects of classroom and school climate—for example, use of time and the nature of the student–teacher relationship.

The researchers who developed the "What Did You Do in School Today?" survey (Willms, Friesen, & Milton, 2009; see page 7) measured four aspects of classroom and school climate that have been shown to have an impact on student achievement, added one of their own (instructional challenge), and examined the relationship of each measure to student engagement.

Brief descriptors of the five measures, as well as references to the chapters in this book where further information appears, are as follows:

→ **effective learning time**—efficient use of class time, extent to which important concepts are taught and understood, degree to which course outcomes are aligned with homework assignments and evaluation procedures (See Chapter 10.)

→ **teacher–student relationships**—students' perceptions of how teachers treat them (A broader view of teacher–student relationships is discussed throughout *Tuned Out*.)

→ **classroom disciplinary climate**—extent to which students internalize and conform to classroom norms (See Chapter 10.)

> **expectations for success**—teachers having high expectations for all students and valuing academic achievement (See Chapter 12.)

> **instructional challenge**—the extent to which teachers challenged students in language arts and math classes, and whether students felt confident about their skills in these subjects. (See Chapter 11.)

(Adapted from Willms et al., 2009, p. 13)

The three measures discussed in this section—effective learning time, teacher–student relationships, and classroom disciplinary climate—were all shown to have an impact on students' emotional and intellectual engagement.

Resources
New Technology Terms

Although the ideal rat park you developed in the activity above probably included various aspects relating to classroom and school climate, I'm more confident in asserting that you undoubtedly included extensive reference to technology. Even if you aren't a teacher or leader witnessing adolescent and adult uses of technology on a daily basis, the term "21st century" has become synonymous with "technology," especially the newer forms. For a quiz to self-assess what you know about the newer forms of technology frequently used in classrooms, see the website.

If you have read the chapters in this book sequentially, perhaps you have noticed I haven't spent a lot of time extolling the virtues of technology. If you are into wikis, blogs, Moodles, or _____ (name your passion), you might even be disappointed that I haven't directly equated your favourite form of technology with long-term student or teacher engagement, especially since it has worked so well for you.

In this section on context, I will relieve the disappointment of some by talking almost exclusively about technology in this chapter and quite a lot in the next—after all, rapid advances in technology will continue to be a defining and inescapable characteristic of 21st century life. At the same time, I will make some people happy (and will annoy others) by asserting that I do not believe that more technology in our schools, or even more use of the technology we have, is the magic bullet that will solve the problem of our disengaged and underachieving students.

I don't deny that new technology engages. Engagement is about relationship—between people or between a person and a structure, activity, or idea. Many of our students have committed relationships with their iPods and cell phones. But our concern with student engagement in school is with the relationships students form *in the service of learning*—relationships that will help them to become "educated members of society," however that term is defined. Giving students more time on computers or buying interactive whiteboards for every classroom are actions that, in themselves, will not result in sustained intellectual engagement.

Technology, in my view, is a suite of tremendously useful tools that can help us engage students in learning, but these tools are meaningless and even detrimental to that learning without a predetermined worthwhile purpose (see activity below) and some form of social interaction (see page 119).

I agree with Don Tapscott's view of learning in the 21st century:

> *Focus on the change in pedagogy, not the technology. "Learning 2.0" is about dramatically changing the relationship between a teacher and students in the learning process. Get that right and use technology for a student-focused, customized, collaborative learning environment.*
>
> (2009, p. 148)

> Technology does not necessarily improve education. Take a simple innovation like the pencil: One can use it to write a superlative essay, to drum away the time, or to poke out someone's eye.
>
> —*Howard Gardner*

A Secret Hidden in Plain Sight

Backward design (Wiggins & McTighe, 2005) is a three-step planning process that begins with setting a clear purpose or goal for learning, followed by determining what evidence we need to gather before, during, and after the learning to ascertain where students are in relation to achievement of that purpose or goal. Choosing the activities and resources we will use in pursuit of the goal is the *final* step in backward design, not the first.

Backward design is therefore quite different from getting a new piece of technology, such as an interactive whiteboard, and asking ourselves, "How can I use this whiteboard to engage students and achieve my curriculum objectives?" In my blog post, I talk about these differences and why I consider backward design to be a secret hidden in plain sight. Before reading that post, I encourage you to determine the differences through reflection or discussion with colleagues.

Conversations
Benefits of Backward Design

Workplaces and Schools

Built to produce a workforce to staff and operate assembly lines, schools of the early 1900s mimicked the structure of the factory.

Factories	School
Divided day into segments of work and break time, with the start of each segment signalled by a bell	Divided day into classes of equal length, with the start of each class and each break signalled by a bell
Structured so individuals performed the same task all day long	Structured so teachers taught the same subject all day long, with students circulating from one teacher to the next
Managed by bosses who kept workers on task	Managed by principals who kept teachers on task and teachers who kept students on task
Expected workers to comply with predetermined expectations of bosses and the company	Expected teachers to follow procedures developed by principals and later by textbook publishers, with teachers expecting all students to learn the preset curriculum at the same pace when taught in the same way
Evaluated employees by their daily production of tangible results and the time they spent on task to achieve those results	Evaluated teachers by their ability to maintain order and follow procedures, with teachers evaluating students on recall of a fixed set of concepts and time on task

Schools in the Industrial Age sorted students, according to their performance in school and score on an intelligence test, into one of three forms of education that matched the three basic roles in industrial life—managers and leaders, skilled workers and merchants, and manual labourers.

> Why should any employer anywhere in the world pay [North] Americans to do highly skilled work—if other people, just as well educated, are available in less developed countries for half our wages?
> —*Thomas Friedman*

Today, in what Daniel Pink (2006) refers to as the "Conceptual Age," automation has significantly reduced the need for manual labourers, and legions of highly skilled workers are found at half the cost in countries such as China and India. For example, approximately 350 000 engineers graduate from India's colleges and universities each year. As I have discussed in previous chapters (see pages 20, 41–42, 78–80, and 126), schools are preparing students for the demands of workplaces that are markedly different from those found in the Information Age, never mind the Industrial Age.

Susan Brooks-Young takes a strong stand on what she sees as our responsibility as educators in this new age:

> *I often hear educators say their time is limited and too many demands are already placed on them. It's absolutely true that your workload is far greater now than it was in the past. However, it's also true that your job is to prepare today's students for their future, not your past. To do this, you must use the kinds of tools and learning experiences that will help students develop marketable 21st-century skills. It's doubtful this can be accomplished in a technology-free environment.*
>
> (2007, p. 46)

Adolescents, Adults, and Technology

I suspect that even in the early 1900s, the schools described in the table on the previous page were likened to a cage by more than a few demoralized and disengaged students and teachers. Certainly, such schools today would be a far cry from the ideal learning environment for 21st century adolescents and their teachers. As Brooks-Young suggests and as the following statistics make clear, this ideal environment needs to include technology for both students and teachers.

Canadian statistics from Darrell Bricker and John Wright (2009) of the polling company Ipsos-Reid indicate that age-related differences in the frequency of technology use are decreasing. Consider these statistics:

- Eighty-seven percent of adults over 55 say they communicate regularly online, as compared to 90 percent of 18–34 year-olds. "In the language of opinion polls, that counts as a tie" (p. 201).
- Ninety-nine percent of Canadian teens (13 and older) have internet access at home, as do 70 percent of Canadians over the age of 55. (Note that this statistic does not apply to people living in remote communities.)
- When teens were polled in 2004, they were found to spend about 13 hours per week online, in contrast to adults, who were online 10 hours each week. When polled in 2008, the number of hours for teens remained constant while the hours for adults increased to 19 per week. The researchers explain the increase in adult hours online as due to requirements at work, and the maintenance of teen hours as due to parents limiting their children's computer time. BlackBerries and iPhones that permit web accessibility may change those numbers in the next opinion poll.

> The average Canadian receives 200 emails per week, including unsolicited emails.
>
> —*Darrell Bricker and John Wright*

"Broadcast Yourself"

The heading above is YouTube's tagline, and it's an apt description of the service the site provides. YouTube allows users to upload video files to the web so they can be viewed by anyone, free of charge. Developed in 2005 by three employees of PayPal, YouTube was originally used by people who wanted to share home videos with friends and family. Some of those videos caught on with viewers—an early one called "The Evolution of Dance" is still online and, at the time of this book's publication, had been viewed more than 150 million times.

YouTube is a form of social media in that users who upload must have created a profile, and a video can be made public or restricted to people selected by the person who uploaded it. Videos are tagged so they can easily be accessed through a keyword search, or users can browse a particular category. Because all YouTube videos are shared through a single format (Flash), they can easily be embedded in other web pages, such as blogs.

Within a year of YouTube's launch, Google purchased the company for $1.65 billion. The exorbitant price tag wasn't because of YouTube's profits (there weren't any) or its infrastructure—the founders were already running into trouble because users were posting copyright-restricted material on the site. Rather, the purchase was seen by many as Google's bold statement about the future of the media business. As it turned out, they were right.

According to Ian Jukes, an estimated 13 hours of video are uploaded to YouTube every minute of every day. That is the equivalent of 780 years of video content being uploaded each year. About 70 000 videos are viewed each and every day. How many people are watching these videos? In May 2010, YouTube achieved a staggering 2 billion views a day.

YouTube now has thousands of licensing deals with everyone from major cable channels to teenagers with digital cameras. It provides an experience that is reminiscent of and yet quite different from television. Viewers can not only create content, but can give their opinions about videos, influence the standing of the video in "most-viewed" lists, and follow links to view related content.

For a variety of materials related to YouTube, see the website.

> We need to pay careful attention to YouTube—it's the canary in the coal mine indicating the major trend that video is rapidly replacing email, texting, and blogging for the younger generation.
> —Ian Jukes

Resources
YouTube in the Classroom

Research
More Online Video Stats

Your Tech IQ

Frequency of usage statistics are the tip of the iceberg when it comes to understanding the details of how teens use technology. Can you do the things that many of your students can do? Check all that apply.

Many adolescents know how to

- ❏ instant-message using mobile phones
- ❏ operate digital still and video cameras
- ❏ create a blog
- ❏ set up a Facebook or MySpace profile
- ❏ use a cell phone to upload pictures to Flickr or another photo-sharing site
- ❏ make a podcast and post it on iTunes
- ❏ download and remix music
- ❏ participate in virtual reality games
- ❏ contribute to a wiki
- ❏ edit a video and upload a clip to YouTube

> Technology is anything that wasn't around when you were born.
> —*Alan Kay*

Your students routinely engage in more than one media activity at a time. For information about what's happening in their brains when they listen to music *and* watch YouTube videos while doing homework, see the website. Before you read the research, make a prediction: Who is better at multitasking—adults or adolescents?

Research
The Truth About Multitasking

Technology in Our Schools

Don't be too hard on yourself if you are challenged by any, or even many, of the actions in the "Your Tech IQ" quiz. After all, recent advances in technology have been absolutely mind-boggling. To put the developments in perspective, Ken Robinson suggests that if the technology of cars had developed at the same rate as the technology of computers, your family car would be able to travel at six times the speed of sound, would average 100 miles to the gallon, and would cost under $2 (Robinson, 2001).

Technology has progressed a long way from the 16 mm film projectors that brought educational media to the classroom in the 1960s. That technology was replaced by televisions in the late 1970s, after the cost of VCRs decreased. Have you been teaching long enough to remember 30-minute training sessions on how to insert and rewind videotapes? Certainly, few among us who were teaching in the 1980s will ever forget our first classroom computer—with a pulsing cursor and green screen that revealed words one letter at a time, 30 to 60 seconds after we'd typed them. That computer took ages to "boot up" and came with no educational software to speak of, yet somehow we were supposed to use it in our teaching.

Now in our classrooms and schools we have dozens of computers equipped with powerful operating systems, sophisticated software, and web-based applications, not to mention internet access. Decreases in the cost of computer-projection systems allow students in many classrooms to view images and text from the computer on a large screen. Increasingly, that screen is an interactive whiteboard where students and teachers can manipulate and work with whatever is projected.

Research
- Interactive Whiteboards
- Response Technology and Engagement

A wireless mouse and keyboard gives teachers freedom to move around the classroom as they share material on the screen with students, and these items—as well as wireless tablets and student-response systems—allow students to be active, contributing participants in computer-based lessons. For a summary of research on the impact of response technologies on student engagement, see the website.

A Tech Inventory

As a staff, conduct an inventory of all technology available in your school (including anything on loan from your district office). Partner with a colleague to share information about how a particular technology can be used in the classroom.

Technology, Engagement, and Learning

The standard argument, as mentioned earlier, is that technology equals engagement and, by extension, learning.

Research evidence suggests that technology is indeed engaging, but there is uncertainty about just what aspects of technology make it so. Some possibilities include the following:

→ Technology promotes active rather than passive learning. There's a "hands-on" feel to it, and adolescents regularly report that they prefer hands-on activities.

- → Students are often collaborating with others when they use technology.
- → Technology provides greater opportunity for creativity and experimentation.
- → Use of technology often involves meaningful and authentic challenge. Students may solve a problem or design and create a product. Frequently, the product gains additional meaning and relevance through being shared with an audience, often one from beyond the classroom.

In a study of 32 elementary and secondary teachers whose students had constant access to Apple computers, researchers (Sandholtz, Ringstaff, & Dwyer, 1994) found that technology had an enduring impact on student engagement only if four conditions were met:

1. Computers were used only if they were the most appropriate tool for achieving a particular outcome, not just because they were available. Teachers used a variety of instructional approaches in their classrooms, and students did not become overexposed to computer activities.
2. Computer skills were developed in the context of purposeful learning, rather than in "computer classes," where the purpose was to learn how to use the technology.
3. Teachers emphasized use of applications, such as desktop publishing software, rather than drill-and-practice programs. Students were more engaged when they were permitted to explore and experiment.
4. Teachers differentiated technology use according to students' interests and readiness. Students were challenged at individually appropriate levels.

As for impact on learning, study after study has demonstrated that technology enhances student achievement, as long as the chosen technology is appropriate to the purpose of the learning and the technology is used at an appropriate point in the learning. For example, using computers in simulation activities improved math test scores of students in Grades 4 and 8, but using computers to drill math skills for the same test had a negative impact on achievement (Wenglinksy, 1998). The thinking is that students can learn both concepts and skills while solving the problems in a simulation, but if they over-practise skills in a drill situation without a focus on understanding, they will have a difficult time applying those skills to new situations on a test.

Tech aficionados point out that computers and various other technologies (such as digital still and video cameras, MP3 players, and cell phones) engage students and affect their achievement by doing the following:

- personalizing instruction and providing immediate feedback
- increasing relevance—for example, through video-based problems or connecting students with experts
- involving students in learning-by-doing through use of modelling software and simulations
- addressing a variety of learning preferences
- helping students construct new knowledge
- providing visual representations of challenging concepts
- fostering collaboration among students
- strengthening connections between school and home—for example, through homework support sites and online school calendars

Yet despite these advantages, technology has remained *on the verge* of revolutionizing schools for the last 30 years. Christensen and colleagues make the following observations:

> *If the addition of computers to classrooms were a cure, there would be evidence of it by now. There is not. Test scores have barely budged.*
>
> (2008, p. 3)

> *Classrooms look largely the same as they did before the personal computer revolution, and the teaching and learning processes are similar to what they were in the days before computers.*
>
> (2008, p. 72)

Teetering on the Brink

If we consider only computers as capable of revolutionizing schools, rather than all educational media, 30 years is a bit of an overstatement. It wasn't until the late 1980s that mass production brought costs down and made computers accessible for school and district budgets. Furthermore, it wasn't until the creation of operating systems by Microsoft and Apple that software developers were able to create applications that were useful in schools. And it wasn't until 1995 that the World Wide Web became available to the general public.

Still, whatever date we choose, years have passed and, with few exceptions, computers continue to be used in a limited range of ways in our classrooms—in the early grades as an activity centre where students practise skills by playing games such as *Math Rabbit*, and in middle and high schools for word-processing, searching the internet for research material, and playing games—only a small percentage of which are educationally related (Christensen et al., 2008). For more information about the impact of computers on classroom practice, see the website.

Research
Computers in Classrooms

Although your classroom is perhaps an exception, do you agree that computers have generally had limited impact on teaching and learning? If so, work with colleagues to generate a list or create a mind map of possible reasons (see pages 94–95 for a variety of ways to brainstorm ideas). If you disagree, talk with colleagues about the evidence that supports your opinion, and try to identify the particular event or aspect of technology that started the revolution.

According to many researchers and proponents of technology in the classroom, a major reason that computers haven't revolutionized teaching and learning is because teachers like me think of technology as a tool. We typically use tools to help us do the things we've always done, albeit a bit more efficiently. This thinking not only means that computers are being used in ways that simply maintain current practice but also, because students are using technology in a wide variety of ways outside of school, we are widening the gap between their school experiences and the rest of their lives.

> This focus on doing the same old thing a bit more efficiently is a major cause of the disconnect between teacher use of technology and student use of technology.
> —*Susan Brooks-Young*

"How can I trust your information when you're using such outdated technology?"

The solution, according to some, is to think of technology the way we think of books: as extensions of our minds. Students who were born into a technologically enriched society do this naturally, but thinking that way can be challenging for those of us who wrote our university papers on electric typewriters, even if those typewriters had a high-tech erase button.

Tools or Extensions of Mind?

Using technology as a tool is referred to in the research literature as "adaptation." For example, having students make a PowerPoint slide show to accompany an oral presentation is an adaptive use of technology, as is making a poster on the computer as opposed to drawing it by hand.

In contrast, a transformational use of technology changes the learning experience. Using Google Docs to write an essay is an example of transformation because although a student initially uses the computer as a word processor (an adaptive use), being able to work with peers to edit and revise the essay in Google Docs changes the writing experience from individual to collaborative.

To determine where you are in your current practice, sort the technology opportunities you provide for students into two groups—adaptive and transformational. If you are unclear as to where an activity belongs, refer to the checklists on the website.

Resources
Technology Use: Checklist

Remember that there's nothing wrong with using adaptive activities in your classroom. Sometimes they are all that is needed. Other times they are an important step on the path to transformational activities. In Chapter 12 (see pages 210–213), we will consider how you can use change processes for a transition from adaptive to transformational technology activities in your classroom.

From Adoption to Invention

If you are a leader in your school or district, consider what uses teachers are currently making of technology. How do you know? The rubric provided on the website will give you actions to look for during classroom visits, along with suggestions for next steps you can take to support teachers.

Resources
Technology Use: Look-Fors

Changes are occurring so quickly that more than 33 percent of Canadian adults complain they can barely keep up with the speed of technological advance, and a further 20 percent see themselves as falling way behind (Bricker & Wright, 2009, p. 199). Perhaps the continuing evolution of technology, along with young teachers who are products of the digital age, will make the "technology revolution" in classrooms more reality than rhetoric.

The Future Is Around the Corner

We are in the second iteration of the World Wide Web and about to embark on the third.

Link directories such as Yahoo! allowed users of Web 1.0 to navigate to web pages, but all people could do was read the content.

The current Web 2.0 is a "read-write" social web. Users can read, but they can also contribute their own content through sites such as YouTube, Flickr, and Wikipedia, or to any blog or discussion forum. Social networking sites encourage online connections.

According to education futurist Stephen Wilmarth, Web 3.0 "will fundamentally change our understanding of the potential of the Internet to create and deliver new knowledge" (2010, p. 88). The impact of Web 3.0 will be comparable to the difference between life before the World Wide Web and life now.

Web 3.0 is the semantic web, the web of data. Kevin Kelly (2006) provides an explanation in an interesting article he wrote about the online library that will result from the digitization of music, movies, and books:

> *Turning inked letters into electronic dots that can be read on a screen is simply the first essential step in creating this new library. The real magic will come in the second act, as each word in each book is cross-linked, clustered, cited, extracted, indexed, analyzed, annotated, remixed, reassembled and woven deeper into the culture than ever before. In the new world of books, every bit informs another; every page reads all other pages.*

> [I]n the 21st century, it will become increasingly commonplace for overwhelming developments of enormous power to appear suddenly.
> —*Frank Kelly, Ted McCain, and Ian Jukes*

Web 3.0 may sound fantastic and far-fetched, but it is already in the works. Kelly reports that nearly 100 percent of contemporary recorded music has already been digitized, as have many movies. Copyright issues and the time required to scan a book mean that digitization of books is a relatively slow process, but at the time of Kelly's article in 2006, one million books a year were being scanned by corporations and libraries around the world.

The complexity of the semantic web will demand new and intelligent search capabilities that more accurately mimic the way we naturally use language and that reflect our individual preferences. The semantic web will allow each of us to have our own personalized web. Here is how Google CEO Eric Schmidt explains it:

> *Search is so highly personal that searching is empowering for humans like nothing else...it is the antithesis of being told or taught. It is empowering individuals to do what they think best with the information they want.... Search is the ultimate expression of the power of the individual; using a computer, looking at the world, and finding exactly what they want, everyone is different when it comes to that.*
>
> (Friedman 2005, p. 156)

Considering the Implications

Why might Web 3.0 have an impact on teaching and learning when other technological advances have not? What will that impact look like in our classrooms? If you don't think Web 3.0 is going to change teaching and learning, what will? Do we need more computers? more engaging software for a variety of learners? Discuss your thoughts with colleagues or online in response to my blog post.

Conversations
Web 3.0 Possibilities

"Digital Immigrant" Teachers

It is a tall order to ask those of us who didn't grow up with digital technology to think of it as an extension of our minds. In fact, I don't think it can be done. Marc Prensky agrees—he calls us "digital immigrants" and says we are destined to always retain our accent, our "foot in the past" (2001, p. 2). Even if we are enthusiastic about learning new technologies, our accent shows in little actions such as reading the manual for a program—not because that's our genuine learning preference, but because we think the program won't teach us how to use it.

> One thing is crystal clear. The advance of technology makes constructing new and richer contexts for teaching and learning ever more tenable and more necessary.
> —*Dave Kinnaman*

While we may never lose our accent, Prensky believes there is hope, at least for some of us:

> Smart adult immigrants accept that they don't know about their new world and take advantage of their kids to help them learn and integrate. Not-so-smart (or not-so-flexible) immigrants spend most of their time grousing about how good things were in the "old country."
>
> (2001, p. 3)

> Nostalgia is like a grammar lesson: You find the present tense and the past perfect.
> —*Unknown*

Those of us who are digital immigrant teachers learning about technology need considerably more than a single workshop where we are taught how to calibrate an interactive whiteboard or use a piece of software. We need time and opportunity to talk and plan with colleagues, either in our immediate environment or online with educators in other locations, as well as ongoing technical support. Everyone benefits if we are also willing to learn from our students. We are reminded of the pleasures and frustrations of learning something new, and students are delighted to be in a redefined teacher–student relationship where they are the experts.

Researchers from an early study in the Apple Classrooms of Tomorrow—Today project (Sandholtz, Ringstaff, & Dwyer, 1994) found that in classrooms where teachers were willing to relinquish the role of "dispenser of knowledge," many moved from curriculum-centred to student-centred instruction, with a corresponding student change from passive to active learning. These researchers came to the following conclusion:

> *We believe that fundamental instructional changes such as these will have an impact on student engagement far more lasting than that of any technological tool in and of itself.*
>
> (Sandholtz et al., 1994, p. 21)

In Chapter 10 we will consider ways, with and without technology, to create a context for learning that will be an ideal rat park for our 21st century learners.

Summary of Chapter Website Content		www.pearsoncanada.ca/tunedout
Conversations	**Resources**	**Research**
• "Context" Video Byte • Benefits of Backward Design • Web 3.0 Possibilities	• New Technology Terms • YouTube in the Classroom • Technology Use: Checklist • Technology Use: Look-Fors	• More Online Video Stats • The Truth About Multitasking • Interactive Whiteboards • Response Technology and Engagement • Computers in Classrooms

10 Environments for Learning

Predictable Classrooms 176

Intervening with At-Risk Students 178

ICT Literacy 180

Your Professional Learning Network 184

A Tale of Two Districts 186

School Design 190

Predictable Classrooms

> Smooth well-running classrooms where time, space, and materials are used effectively maximize the opportunities students have to engage.
>
> —*Carolyn Evertson and Catherine Randolph*

Novelty provokes curiosity, which can be helpful to both engagement and learning when it is used in conjunction with an academic task (see pages 226–229.) There is, however, a place where novelty is detrimental to engagement and learning, and that is in the creation and maintenance of an effective learning environment. All students benefit from the predictability of consistent procedures and routines. Lack of predictability requires students to attend indiscriminately to everything happening around them, while sufficient predictability means that students feel safe and are free to focus their attention and energy on their work.

To ensure that you provide the safety and security of predictability, develop procedures for managing the following:

	Examples
Movement	moving furniture, leaving the room
Resources	distributing supplies, storing materials
Interactions	assigning students to groups, adjusting noise level
Work	distributing assignments, knowing what to do if help is needed or work is finished, handing in completed work

Predictable Procedures

Conversations
This Works for Me

Some teachers believe they shouldn't waste time teaching procedures to adolescents because their students have been in school for many years and should know how to behave appropriately. Adolescents, however, work with a number of different teachers, each using their own procedures and their own definition of "appropriate."

Meet with colleagues to compare notes about the procedures you use, and work towards a common set of expectations for the procedures you consider most important to student success. Ideally, you will have consistency across your school, but if that isn't immediately achievable, you should still notice improvements in your students' behaviour if there is consistency across a grade level or department.

Please consider sharing some of your surefire classroom procedures in the website blog.

Managing Technology Use

Classroom management issues sometimes develop around the use of technology. You may find the following tips helpful:

- √ Reinforce that technology is serving a learning purpose by having students complete preparatory work, such as developing a storyboard before they videotape. Students will know what they are going to do and can get to work right away.

- √ Give each student a coloured sticky note. Anyone who is having difficulty with a task can quietly signal you by putting the sticky note on the top corner of the monitor or desk.

- √ When you are giving instructions, have students turn off their computer monitors or put down their hand-held devices.

- √ Actively monitor student use of the technology. Walk around the classroom, looking over students' shoulders to check such things as windows that have been minimized at the bottom of the computer screen. It's good to trust your students, but they need to know that you expect them to be focused on learning.

Case Study → Impact on Engagement: Creating Healthy School Climates

Name: Bernie O. (Consultant)   **Grades:** K–9

Teachers and administrators began the professional development day brainstorming words related to a healthy school climate. From that point on, they were engaged in a variety of activities dealing with the development of safe and caring classrooms, such as differentiated instruction, classroom organization, and character education.

Impact on Engagement

By involving participants in hands-on experiences, opportunities for collaboration, and time for reflection, I hoped teachers would experience the engagement they could provide to their students by using similar activities. Teachers indeed found that the session was informative and the activities were ones they could use in their classrooms.

Intervening with At-Risk Students

In educational terms, a student who is at-risk is a student who is in danger of academic failure, especially of failure to graduate on schedule. However, the factors that lead to academic risk may be outside the influence of educators. Pregnancy, drug or alcohol abuse, family turmoil, and the mental health concerns of the student or a family member are among possible factors.

The disengagement of at-risk students who are dealing with serious personal or family issues is difficult to manage. To avoid becoming overwhelmed by the needs of at-risk adolescents in our schools, it is often helpful to think of a three-tiered system of interventions.

Tier 1 contains the universal supports that are put in place for all students to help prevent intellectual and emotional disengagement. These include many of the ideas discussed in this book.

Tier 2 is the first step of intervention for at-risk students. In tier 2 you are dealing with smaller numbers of students, often in group settings. An example of a tier 2 academic intervention is providing intensive support in reading or mathematics to a small group for some duration of time. An example of a tier 2 intervention for emotional engagement is a small group, rather than an individual, counselling session. Some therapists find that adolescents, in particular, benefit from learning that they are not alone in having problems and from having the opportunity to receive support from peers as well as group leaders.

Tier 3 interventions—the most intensive—are necessary in most schools for just a small number of students. They are provided to students on an individualized basis according to need. These interventions often include access to community services.

Case Study: Impact on Engagement: Distance Learning with a Twist

Name: Mavis S. (Principal)   **Grades:** 7–12

The award-winning Sunchild E-Learning program has been recognized nationally and internationally for its work with Aboriginal learners.

Sunchild E-Learning offers more than 70 high school courses, accredited by Alberta Education, to students in an online environment. In addition, the program offers adult literacy and numeracy courses to prepare adults for the high school program. Sunchild has also worked with a corporate partner to offer a Gas and Oil Production Operators Level 1 course, allowing students in remote areas to receive this certification.

Using synchronous software, students and teachers interact online, in real time, with no limits on distance or time. As concepts are introduced, various multimedia components, such as videos, archives of previous classes, PowerPoint presentations, and interactive activities, are embedded into the lesson. Teachers assess student work weekly in order to catch problems early and provide timely intervention.

Impact on Engagement

Over the past six years, the Sunchild model has demonstrated an unprecedented level of high school graduation and academic success among First Nations, Métis, non-status, and Inuit students. One measure of the program's success is that students have been re-entering the school system and staying in school. Take, for example, Andrew, who initially enrolled in the Sunchild Adult Literacy program and was soon able to begin high school upgrading courses. Although he'd known hard times, including life on the street, Andrew was so motivated to work on his own personal development that he quickly became an inspiration to other students, using the microphone in his virtual classroom to "talk his truth." For a link to the Sunchild website and a video about the program, see the website.

Research
Sunchild E-Learning

ICT Literacy

The word *literacy* once referred to the ability to read print texts—textbooks, reference books, newspapers, magazines, novels, and the like—and to write. In the 21st century, *literacy* still refers to the ability to read and write more traditional text forms, but it now includes reading (or interpreting) and writing (or creating) a much broader range of texts, both print and visual. Videos, websites, blogs, Nings, and other new and emerging technologies are among them.

The reading aspect of 21st century literacy requires that we teach students the skills to "find, navigate, access, decode, evaluate, and organize information from a globally networked information landscape" (Warlick, 2009, p. 17); the creating aspect requires that students learn and be able to apply the rules of film, graphics, and music (Daly, 2004).

> Information and communication technologies, or ICTs, are the quintessential tools of the 21st century.
> — **Bernie Trilling and Charles Faber**

Together, these requirements for reading and creating texts form 21st century Information and Communication Technology (ICT) literacy.

Adolescents often seem so comfortable accessing the internet and various forms of visual media that it can be easy to forget that we need to explicitly teach ICT literacy skills. Media literacy professor David Considine offers this caution:

> *While more young people have access to the Internet and other media than any generation in history, they do not necessarily possess the ethics, the intellectual skills, or the predisposition to critically analyze and evaluate their relationship with these technologies or the information they encounter. Good hand/eye coordination and the ability to multitask are not substitutes for critical thinking.*
>
> (Cited in Baker, 2010, pp. 138–139)

Research
ICT Literacy Standards

A number of organizations offer lists and continuums of ICT literacy standards, as well as extensive teaching suggestions for helping students to achieve these standards. A few suggestions are offered below, but for more information, be sure to take a look at the website.

Decide

Pre-assess students to find out what aspects of ICT literacy they may have mastered. Use the pre-assessment results to decide who will teach which skills. Ideally, you will have students doing some of the teaching. Regardless of who is teaching, all instruction should involve modelling of the skill, followed by student use in authentic situations.

Decide the keywords and search phrases that will be used for a topic. English teacher Sara Kajder (2003) recommends you model this and then engage students in guided practice by having everyone initially work with the same topic. Conduct a test run before class to ensure that the keywords used will not result in inappropriate hits.

Search

Use a model such as S.E.A.R.C.H., developed by David Warlick (2009, p. 39), to teach students how to search the net:

Start	Small and Simple. It may not be helpful to start with Google, which could deliver millions of hits on the first search. Start with a small, indexed search engine such as Yahoo! Examine a sampling of hits, identifying words common in the relevant resources and words common in the less than relevant pages.
Edit	Use the words identified in the previous step to Edit your search phrase. Use Boolean or Search Math as the grammar of your search phrase.
Advance	Advance to a large database search engine, such as Google. Enter the edited search phrase and examine a sampling of hits, identifying more words that are common in pages that help you solve your problem and pages that are not relevant.
Refine	Refine your search phrase using the words identified in your Advance search.
Cycle	Cycle back and advance again.
Harvest	Harvest the resources that were identified during your searches. This is an ongoing process.

Resources
- Search Engines
- Editing Search Terms

ICT Literacy – continued

Warlick also recommends that we ensure students think about their searching by asking them to maintain a search log. They keep track of which search tools they use and what search phrases they enter. Students also record comments on how many hits they get, as well as whether or not those hits seem relevant.

You probably won't be able to get students to maintain a search log for long—it's a tedious process—but if they do it at least once when you are teaching them to search, they will realize that they can improve their search skills.

Resources
RSS Feeds

To learn how to get relevant information to come to you, see the website.

Evaluate

Resources
- Hoax Sites
- Website Evaluation

Your students may spend as little as two seconds on a website before clicking to another site. Since students need to "analyze information about authorship, content, navigability, point of view, purpose, and related links" (Kajder, 2003, p. 60), it's important to get them to slow down. Using hoax websites to model how to evaluate a site, you might teach students to either ask themselves a series of questions when they are reviewing sites or have them complete a website evaluation form.

Your doubts are the strongest asset you bring to the Internet.
—*Paul Gilster*

Create

Successful communications are those that compel us to take notice of the information being shared and, often, to think or act differently as a result. Compelling communications are essential in all walks of life, but unfortunately they are all too frequently the exception rather than the rule. Movie director George Lucas has this to say about the misuse of visual communications in the workplace:

> *You often see very educated people—doctors and lawyers and engineers—trying to make presentations, and they have no clue about how to communicate visually and what happens when you put one image after another. So their lectures become very confused because, from a visual perspective, they're putting their periods at the front of their sentences, and nobody understands them.*

(Daly, 2004)

There are three steps to creating successful communications:

1. **Determine purpose and audience.**
   Messages have to compete for attention in our information-saturated world, and they aren't successful unless they achieve their specific purpose with the target audience. Classroom assignments are more likely to be authentic and relevant if students stay mindful of purpose and audience. For assistance in designing authentic assignments, see the website.

2. **Choose the medium most appropriate for delivering the message and/or reaching the target audience.**
   Technology gives students opportunities to develop their writing and creating skills in a wide variety of ways. Different forms of technology can easily be combined to deepen impact through a multimodal presentation.

3. **Apply format conventions of the chosen medium.**
   Encourage students to format the message to maximize its effectiveness. In this step they might determine font sizes and layout, crop and layer visuals, or focus on pacing in video productions.

Anecdotal evidence suggests that teaching video production and digital publishing to at-risk students can improve their prospects after school by giving them marketable skills (Lau & Lazarus, 2002).

Classroom teachers and facilitators of adult learning also need to be in the business of creating compelling presentations. Two books by Garr Reynolds—*Presentation Zen* (2008) and *Presentation Zen Design* (2010)—offer inspiring suggestions for creating powerful visual presentations. See my reviews of these books on the website.

Resources
Authentic Assignments

> We must accept the fact that learning how to communicate with graphics, with music, with cinema, is just as important as communicating with words. Understanding these rules is as important as learning how to make a sentence work.
>
> —*George Lucas*

Research
- Spotlight on *Presentation Zen*
- Spotlight on *Presentation Zen Design*

Your Professional Learning Network

> Transforming schools into 21st century learning communities means recognizing that teachers must become members of a growing network of shared expertise.
> —*Kathleen Fulton, Irene Yoon, and Christine Lee*

Adult learners are unique. We have varied interests, learning preferences, and readiness to learn new concepts. Preferences for professional learning, therefore, run the gamut from face-to-face interaction only, to online interaction only, to distributed learning—a blended combination of the two.

Since both engagement and learning happen through interaction with other people, resources, and ideas (see page 5), the real challenge of professional learning, regardless of the form, is finding ways to make that interaction work for all learners. Doing this requires developing a sense of community (see page 118) where people feel safe, trust that their needs will be met, and take responsibility for supporting the group as a whole.

Face-to-face learning offers the distinct advantage of being able to read participants' non-verbal language, which provides immediate feedback about how our messages are being received and makes it easier to feel that we know people. The disadvantage is that there is less opportunity for in-depth discussion because of the small number of people involved.

In online learning, you can have access to people on the other side of the world, everyone can speak at once, and discussions can be rich and extended. Many people also feel less inhibited online than they might in a face-to-face setting, so will be more likely to contribute. However, it can be more difficult to develop trust and a sense of belonging and importance in an online environment. Furthermore, since online communication is still primarily through written text, the quality of the interaction is quite dependent on the quality of the writing.

One big advantage to online discussion is that it is easier for everyone to see artifacts of student learning, such as work samples, photos, and video clips, than it is in a face-to-face environment. These artifacts anchor conversation around real classroom practices and results. Additional benefits to online learning through Web 2.0 tools are noted by Harvard professor Chris Dede:

> ...Web 2.0 tools—social bookmarking, video sharing, social networking, wikis, all the things that let people create and share knowledge—are really very powerful for professional development because they reinforce the

message that we want professional development to be an experience where everybody learns from everybody else. And we're also modelling what we want teachers to do with students, which is to create active learning situations, where everybody learns from everybody else. So the medium is reinforcing the message.

(2010, p. 14)

Get What You Need

Talk with colleagues about your experiences with various forms of professional learning. Which ones really worked for you? Which ones didn't? What do your experiences suggest about your learning preferences?

You will find an account of my early online experiences in my blog post on the website.

Conversations
Chatting with the Gurus

Digital Junkies, Unite!

Bill Ferriter is a teacher and self-avowed digital junkie. He believes that only by developing his own 21st century skills through participation in online networks can he show his students the power of networking for learning. He wants his students to develop the skills of making their thinking transparent, accessing information from co-learners beyond the borders of the school, and creating shared content. Ferriter says, "I consider experimenting fearlessly with digital connections to be part of my job as a teacher" (2009, p. 86).

Do you agree? Talk about Ferriter's point with colleagues. If you have experience with online networking, describe any skills you have developed online that couldn't be developed through face-to-face interaction.

Skill Check

If you are involved in facilitating online professional learning sessions, use the checklist from the website to self-assess your facilitation skills and determine a next step for your own professional growth.

Resources
Online Facilitation Checklist

A Tale of Two Districts

District and school leaders need to ensure that all necessary conditions are in place to support the kinds of technology use that can make a real difference in student engagement and achievement. When that doesn't happen, large sums of money are wasted, teachers are demoralized, and student engagement and achievement quickly return to previous levels.

However, when infrastructure supports are in place and consistently maintained, the impact can be astonishingly powerful, as the following case study proves.

Case Study → Impact on Engagement: Wireless Writing Program

Name: David V. (Director of Instruction) **Subject:** Writing **Grades:** 6–7

Our goal was to improve writing. The technology wasn't an end in itself—it was a tool we could use to help kids be successful in school. And they have been successful beyond our expectations.

The Wireless Writing Program, the first of its kind in Canada, began 11 years ago in the Peace River North School District in northern British Columbia. After a successful 18-month pilot project, the district leased an Apple laptop for every one of the 1150 Grades 6 and 7 students and their 37 teachers in 17 schools.

From the beginning, the program was carefully conceived, developed, and tracked. A 1:1 laptop program was a new and risky venture—we knew we needed a single focus so our efforts and attention wouldn't be scattered. We chose writing because of its importance across the curriculum and throughout life, and because we had a variety of assessment measures we had used for several years that would give us helpful longitudinal data.

Furthermore, British Columbia writing performance standards would serve as a set of common expectations for writing instruction and assessment, while still allowing teachers to use a variety of resources and instructional approaches.

Meetings were held with everyone: parents and the British Columbia Teachers' Federation, to gain their support; teachers, on a monthly basis for professional development in how to help students achieve writing performance standards and to provide them with opportunities to work with colleagues; and school administrators, to apprise them of the specific support teachers needed at various points along the way.

Classroom assessment was built into the program. Software was configured so that student-friendly versions of the British Columbia writing performance standards were attached to every document students produced. Students then used software highlighters to self-assess their writing assignments against these performance standards before electronically submitting the assignments to their teachers.

An external researcher was hired to help with the creation of a research plan, as well as analysis and interpretation of attitude surveys, district test achievement data, and samples of student writing.

Classroom observations, as well as formal and informal interviews with teachers, parents, and students, were conducted. The results of provincial reading and writing assessments completed in May were also analyzed. (Statistical results are available on the website.)

The district chose wireless technology for the program to avoid the cost of retrofitting classrooms for new networks. They chose Apple laptops because they were intuitive to use and easily configured by non-technical staff. The District Technology Resource Centre provided consistent and timely technical support, to the extent that students were guaranteed they wouldn't be without a working computer for more than one hour of class time.

Impact On...

Engagement

- → Responses to all writing attitude survey questions were more positive after implementation of the Wireless Writing Program. The greatest gains were in student pride (measured by responses to the survey statement "I like to save things I have written") and sense of competence (measured by responses to "I am a good writer"). Grade 7 students were slightly less enthusiastic than Grade 6 students. This result was interesting because many students were in combined Grade 6/7 classrooms, so all of those students had the same experiences. Some of the novelty may have worn off for Grade 7 students (who were in their second year of the laptop program), students may have been experiencing some of the malaise that sometimes accompanies adolescence, or perhaps some other factor was involved.

- → In the 2007 survey, 92 percent of students reported that they enjoyed having a laptop; 81 percent reported that having a laptop improved their attitude towards writing; 55 percent reported that having a laptop improved their attitude towards school, and 74 percent reported that having a laptop was important to their success in school (Jeroski, 2007).

Writing

- → Teachers reported that they had to establish maximum word counts for written assignments, even though they used to have to pressure students to achieve a minimum.

A Tale of Two Districts – continued

- Provincial, district, and classroom assessments showed substantial increases in the number of students who met or exceeded writing expectations.

- Gaps in literacy performance decreased between males and females (from 21 percent in 2003 to 8 percent in 2004), and between Aboriginal students and the total population (from 17 percent in 2003 to 5 percent in 2004).

- Teachers of Grade 8 (the first year of high school) reported that they immediately recognized who had been involved in the Wireless Writing Program because of the strength of their writing. Random sampling of Grade 8 student work suggested that improvements were sustained over time.

- Noticeable improvements were made in developing, organizing, and expressing ideas. These improvements were significantly greater than any improvements in use of conventions, which led us to believe that changes were happening at a deep rather than at a superficial level.

Classroom Climate

- Teachers were able to spend less time on class management and more on teaching and individual feedback because students were happily engaged in their work.

- Students often worked in self-selected groups to create projects. In some instances, students who had gone on holiday continued to log in so they could work with their group while away.

- Some students who were quiet or reluctant participants in face-to-face situations seemed to be much more comfortable communicating with peers either online or face to face when they had a computer in front of them.

Teachers

- By 2007, 81 percent of teachers reported that they felt confident using computers in teaching, as compared to 51 percent in 2003.

- Teachers who accepted that their role had changed from dispenser of knowledge to that of coach transformed their classroom practice towards more project-based learning.

- Teachers were collaborating freely and often. In particular, monthly meetings were highly beneficial because all teachers were using Apple laptops with the same software. They had all of their teaching content on their laptops, making it easy to share ideas and plan with colleagues.

Parents

- → Students were allowed to take their laptops home. That levelled the socioeconomic playing field, making it possible for all parents and other family members to collaborate with students.

- → Parents consistently reported that the program was highly beneficial. They wanted to purchase the laptops, wanted their children to continue to use laptops in their learning, and wanted other children in the family, especially high school students, to have access to the program.

Next Steps

Peace River North School District has continued their focus on writing in the 1:1 wireless laptop program. I have relocated to Maple Ridge–Pitt Meadows, a school district just east of Vancouver. My new district adopted the Wireless Writing Program five years ago after seeing our work in Peace River North.

Maple Ridge–Pitt Meadows District has recently reframed the wireless program around 21st century skills, with the goal of improving literacy and communication skills while teaching critical thinking and creative problem-solving.

Students are provided with opportunities to develop and extend these skills through a variety of activities throughout the year. Many activities are developed by individual teachers or, more often, through group collaboration during regularly scheduled professional learning and planning sessions. As the year progresses and students' skills develop, students have greater opportunity to create their own assignments.

Students are given choice in how they present their assignments. Options include making a movie, recording a podcast, putting together a PowerPoint presentation, creating a group wiki, or writing a report.

We are developing rubrics that will allow teachers and students to self-assess their work on 21st century skills. External research plans are being developed.

Teacher collaboration continues to be vital. In keeping with our focus on 21st century skills, we have added Twitter to our menu of options for collaboration. So far, approximately 30 percent of teachers have maintained online collaboration.

Research
Wireless Writing Stats

School Design

Heidi Hayes Jacobs (2010) identifies the following four essential elements we need to consider as we redesign schools for the 21st century:

1. Schedules for Learning

For students to experience the sense of community necessary to engagement, they need to feel that they are known by their teachers. Many high schools already offer four 70-minute classes per semester instead of the old structure of eight 42-minute classes all year long. The new structure limits the number of teachers students have in a single semester, providing the opportunity for teachers and students to get to know one another better during the semester. Longer classes also increase the time available for in-depth work, which is important in classes where the emphasis is on inquiry, technology use, or interdisciplinary studies.

Some other options that could be considered include the following:
- three semesters with three two-hour classes per day
- one full-day class per semester, taught by interdisciplinary teams
- the existing schedule with periods of several weeks at different times in the year devoted to sustained interdisciplinary work, such as the creation of digital products

Short-term scheduling involves the use of time during a class period. Brain researcher John Medina (2008) strongly advises teaching in 10-minute modules, each module beginning with an essential single concept that can be explained in one minute and then elaborated on for the remaining nine minutes. He recommends that teachers explicitly link concepts from one module to the next so students can focus on meaning rather than trying to figure out how ideas fit together.

At the end of every 10-minute module, when students' attention may begin to wane, Medina suggests that we regain their attention by using emotionally powerful stimuli such as a brief relevant story. Another option is to pause and have students make connections between a concept and their own lives.

> We tend to devote years to studying what to change and little if any time to actually making change. In the meantime, kids continue to go through our schools without the benefit of the programs we know we should run.
>
> —*George Wood*

2. Grouping Learners

A central tenet of differentiated instruction is that learners will work in a variety of short-term flexible groupings according to their needs. Jacobs (2010) offers the following reminder about groupings:

Students in any class, whether it is Advanced Placement Physics or Basic Biology, will always display a range of skill levels. In short, to some extent all classes are heterogeneous, and the wrong question is being raised. Rather than asking whether homogeneous or heterogeneous is the best generic grouping, the question should be, "What type of grouping would best support learning for a specific group of students to address specific objectives?"

(p. 70)

In schools where multiple classes are working on the same concept, it's worth considering team teaching so students can be grouped as needed.

Another option for student grouping is reducing the size of large high schools by dividing students into schools or houses within the school. A growing body of evidence points to the benefits of smaller schools (perhaps around 400 students). These schools tend to be safer, and they also have higher attendance rates, better participation rates in a range of school activities and, at the high school level, lower dropout rates. Small schools are repeatedly found to benefit students' level of engagement, their sense of belonging, and their achievement (Jackson & Davis, 2000).

©1991 ZITS Partnership. Distributed by King Features Syndicate.

School Design – continued

3. Grouping Teachers

Classrooms in schools are most often grouped by grade level or department. Although this structure lends itself to easier communication and team teaching between like-grade or like-subject teachers, other groupings may also be beneficial. For example, teachers in a K–8 school could sometimes be grouped vertically to consider the development of an essential concept over the grades, and teachers from a variety of disciplines in a secondary school could be grouped to consider essential concepts from a range of perspectives, thereby increasing their relevance for learners.

Whatever the choice of teacher groupings, provide opportunities for both individual and common planning times, and keep teams together for an extended time. Research shows that schools engaged in teaming teachers for five or more years had higher frequencies of desirable instructional practices and team interactions than those engaged in teaming for shorter periods of time (Flowers et al., 2000).

4. Creating and Using Space

Although technology may enable "anytime, anywhere learning," our students still spend their days in a physical plant known as a school. The physical spaces in which we work can go a long way towards encouraging or discouraging student and teacher engagement.

A Physical Space Inventory

Use the inventory on the website to determine which design elements supportive of 21st century learning are either in place or possible for your school.

If you aren't in a new school, it's likely that your physical environment will be missing a few or many of the design elements listed on the inventory. That doesn't need to stop you. Choose one element that you consider especially important to student engagement and learning. Work with interested students, staff, parents, and community members to determine what changes can be made. To be inspired by design possibilities, see the case studies below and the website.

Resources
Physical Space Inventory

Research
Award-Winning School Designs

Case Study

Impact on Engagement: School Design for the 21st Century

Name: Jeannie E. (Principal)   **Grades:** 5–8

The goal was to create a new school that would meet the needs of adolescents today and in the future. Teachers were hired with the expectation that they would work together in a professional learning community focused on engaging students in learning through the use of inquiry questions (see page 228) correlated to relevant career and technology studies outcomes. Grade level teams had common daily preparation times and were required to meet and engage in analysis of student work every two weeks.

The school facility was designed to support inquiry. A two-storey Learning Commons provided access to print resources, as well as a rich online library. Additional facilities included a large main gymnasium, auxiliary gym, dance studio, fitness centre, band room, art room, and drama space.

Classrooms were configured in pods, each with many smaller break-out spaces for flexible groups to support student learning. Each pod has a large foyer connecting four classrooms. Between each classroom are sliding glass walls to facilitate flexible instructional groups. As additional grades are incorporated into the school, portable classrooms will be attached to the building.

Teachers and students were provided with a rich digital environment and were expected to explore this to its fullest to enhance student engagement in learning. Available tools included laptops, interactive whiteboards, iPods, digital cameras, response systems, document cameras, video conferencing capabilities, and an extensive range of software.

Impact on Engagement

It has been impossible to find a disengaged student or teacher in our new school. Technology coupled with an inquiry approach to teaching and learning has allowed teachers to differentiate their instruction so every student has been able to access the curriculum and demonstrate their learning in a wide variety of ways.

School Design – continued

Case Study: Impact on Engagement: School Design for the 21st Century

Names: François C., Eric B.   **Subjects:** Français, Math, Social Sciences, Arts   **Grades:** 5–6

Students worked with an industrial designer who helped them understand the use of space and the types of spaces needed for a classroom. They made perspective drawings of their ideal classroom, and used Google SketchUp to create an animated view. Then they turned their plans into reality by redesigning the old classroom furniture and repainting the room to better represent their values and interests. All of this work and its impact on our students was shared with others in the school through a podcast radio program.

Impact on Engagement

Our school is located in a low socio-economic area of our district. Additionally, many of the students in our two classes have identified special needs. We wanted our students to realize that they had the power to transform their environment, and the skills to do so through design rather than words.

The project was a huge success. Students who were often reluctant participants in other situations were fully involved in decision making and highly motivated to attend school on the days when the artist was there to work with them.

Summary of Chapter Website Content		www.pearsoncanada.ca/tunedout
Conversations	**Resources**	**Research**
• This Works for Me • Chatting with the Gurus	• Search Engines • Editing Search Terms • RSS Feeds • Hoax Sites • Website Evaluation • Authentic Assignments • Online Facilitation Checklist • Physical Space Inventory	• Sunchild E-Learning • ICT Literacy Standards • Spotlight on *Presentation Zen* • Spotlight on *Presentation Zen Design* • Wireless Writing Stats • Award-Winning School Designs

Challenge

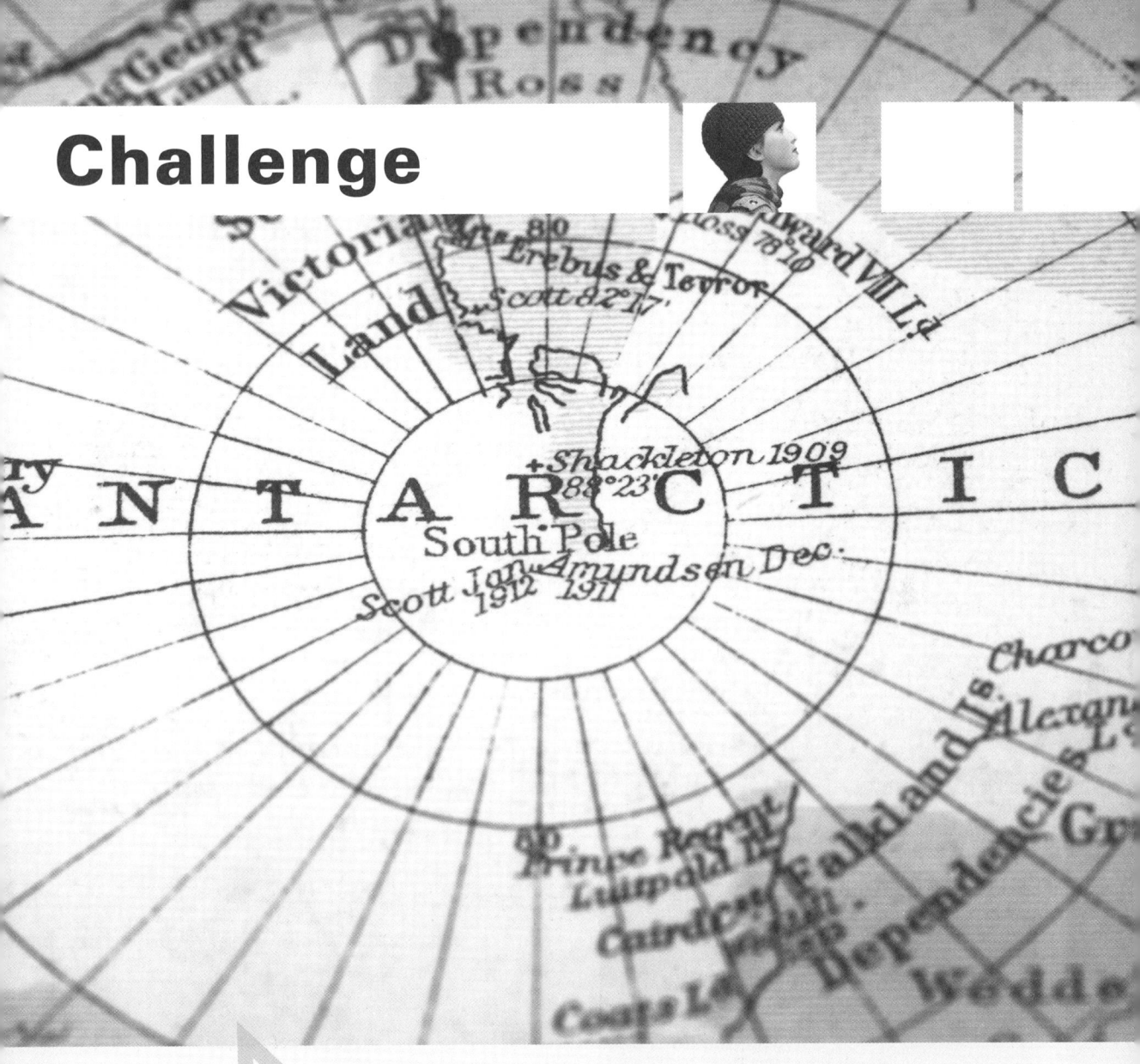

> **Men wanted for hazardous journey. Low wages, bitter cold, long hours of complete darkness. Safe return doubtful. Honour and recognition in event of success.**
>
> —Sir Ernest Shackleton

Shackleton reputedly placed this newspaper ad to find men for his 1914 Imperial Trans-Antarctic Expedition. While the ad is likely apocryphal, we do know that a letter Shackleton published in a London newspaper prompted 5000 replies from eager potential participants. Shackleton sorted these replies into three categories: "mad," "hopeless," and "possible."

11 Hard Fun

Conversations
"Challenge" Video Byte

Research
Video Game Pros and Cons

What would prompt so many people to respond to Shackleton's letter (see previous page) when the journey would so clearly be both difficult and dangerous? The current popularity of video games may provide us with the answer.

In the ongoing debate about the educational value of video games, many teachers and parents are quick to choose sides. To some, games are a ridiculous waste of time—responsible for increased aggression, shortened attention spans, even tooth decay. To others, games allow students to develop skills in problem solving, collaboration, and manual dexterity. Proponents on either side of the debate cite the titles of specific games and newspaper headlines to bolster their arguments. (See the website for arguments on both sides of the debate.)

In the midst of this raging debate, it is easy to lose track of an essential question: Why, according to Amanda Lenhart and colleagues (2008), do anywhere from 94 to 99 percent of adolescents play video games?

I suggest that a large part of the answer can be found in the concept of "hard fun." This term was coined by mathematician and educator Seymour Papert (2002) when he was visiting an elementary school where students were learning to program computers using LOGO, the computer language Papert developed. One student was overheard to say that the work was hard and fun, which Papert understood to mean that the task was fun *because* it was hard.

The concept of hard fun may have its roots in the biology of the brain. As psychiatrist Gregory Berns explains:

> Much of what is known about motivation has to do with the neurotransmitter dopamine, which, until the mid-1990s, many scientists thought of as the brain's pleasure chemical....Actually, dopamine is released prior to the consummation of both good and bad activities, acting more like a chemical of anticipation than of pleasure. The most parsimonious explanation of dopamine's function suggests that it commits your motor system—your

body—to a particular action. If this idea is correct, then satisfaction comes less from the attainment of a goal and more in what you must do to get there.

The most effective way to keep your dopamine system humming, says Berns, is "through novel, challenging experiences" (p. xiv).

Flow

Psychologist Mihaly Csikszentmihalyi (pronounced *chik-sent-me-high-ee*) would agree. Csikszentmihalyi developed the concept of "flow" (1990) by studying people who were doing things for enjoyment rather than for rewards of money or fame. He found that respondents described the quality of their experiences in similar terms, regardless of their culture, gender, socioeconomic background, age, or the nature of the activity in which they were engaged. After years of interviewing almost 10 000 people in all walks of life, Csikszentmihalyi (2003) found that there are eight salient characteristics to a flow experience.

1. **The goals are clear**. Csikszentmihalyi is talking about step-by-step goals, not just the final outcome. Paying too much attention to the outcome will prevent the flow experience and interfere with performance.

2. **Feedback is immediate**. Feedback may be provided by peers or supervisors, but ideally, it comes from the activity itself.

3. **There is a balance between opportunity and capacity**. When a challenge is too far beyond our capacity, we feel anxious; when our skills exceed the challenge, we are bored. Csikszentmihalyi argues that flow is the ideal state for learning because "skills are fully involved in overcoming a challenge that is just about manageable" (1997, p. 30). This argument echoes Lev Vygotsky's view (1978) that learning takes place in the zone of proximal development, where work is just a bit tougher than students can handle on their own.

4. **Concentration deepens**. When in flow, "the distinction between self and activity disappears" (Csikszentmihalyi, 2003, p. 47). There are no distractions, not even the awareness of being in flow. Indeed, if someone gained that awareness, it would destroy the flow.

5. **The present is what matters**. Concentration on the task at hand excludes any thoughts of the past or of anything further ahead than the most immediate future.

6. **Control is no problem**. When in flow, we experience a sense that we can control our performance because we have the skills necessary to meet the challenge. This sense does not extend to a belief in the ability to control other people or even totally control the outcome. Rather, we experience a calm confidence that we have what it takes to handle the situation.

7. **The sense of time is altered**. Focused attention means that time may seem to speed up, slow down, or stand still. The way in which the sense of time is altered depends on the needs of the activity.

8. **There is a loss of ego**. When we are at one with an activity, thoughts of how we present ourselves to the rest of the world disappear. After a flow experience, the sense of self returns and self-esteem soars.

The arts and sports provide what Csikszentmihalyi describes as "almost pure examples of flow, uncontaminated by other motives" (2003, p. 58). However, Csikszentmihalyi's research shows that any experience can become a flow experience. In a study of 75 adolescents, Csikszentmihalyi and Larson (1984) found that students sometimes experience flow when learning, though the experience more frequently occurs during active involvement in a favourite activity, such as a sport. In contrast, people rarely experience flow when engaged in passive activities such as watching television or relaxing.

Life in the Zone

If you have ever had a flow experience, describe it to colleagues and discuss to what extent it matches the eight characteristics of flow listed above. Note that not all characteristics need to be experienced to the same degree, or at all, for an experience to qualify as flow.

If you have never had a flow experience, tell your colleagues about a challenge you have faced that made you feel strong, regardless of whether or not you succeeded. Identify what made the challenge so satisfying and also what was missing and thereby prevented it from being a flow experience.

Video Games and Challenge

In a study of 647 adolescents in British Columbia (*Video Game Culture*, 1998), researchers found that over 80 percent of the teenagers experienced video games as pleasant, exciting, challenging, and interesting. They asserted that good games are realistic and unpredictable, and that they offer good weapons, an interesting storyline, and plenty of player control.

James Gee (2007) is a professor of Literary Studies and an expert in the learning potential of video games. He points out that since gamers won't accept short and easy games, good video games are long and hard. However, difficult games wouldn't sell if learning to play them was too onerous a task. Therefore, a good video game has excellent principles of learning built into its design. Gee argues that schools would benefit from applying those same principles of learning to classroom instruction.

Many of Gee's 36 principles of learning benefit both engagement and learning, and are discussed in *Tuned Out*. Some of the key words and phrases in these learning principles include the following:
- invites participation with others who share similar interests/goals
- develops self-knowledge of strengths and potentials
- supports risk-taking where consequences are minimized
- provides ongoing feedback customized to learner's level and effort
- offers lots of practice in a context that isn't boring

> [T]he theory of learning in good video games fits better with the modern, high-tech, global world today's children and teenagers live in than do the theories (and practices) of learning that they sometimes see in school.
> —*James Gee*

The best video games make use of Dynamic Difficulty Adjustment (DDA)—a design concept that allows a game to be dynamically responsive to the player's skills and performance. Since game designers can't read minds, this responsiveness is challenging to achieve. If, for example, a player deliberately performs a suicidal stunt in Grand Theft Auto, it doesn't mean that the player's skills are low. Dynamic Difficulty Adjustment is therefore achieved by creating play at a number of different levels and giving the player choice, either directly or intuitively, in the experience he or she will have. During the game, the difficulty level increases, ensuring that there is a constant tension between mastery and challenge. There is also ongoing feedback—every 7 to 10 seconds according to one game designer—for the player's decisions.

flOw

Video games don't have to involve weapons, car chases, and avatars in order to be engaging. Designer Jenova Chen developed the game of *flOw* as part of his thesis research for a Master of Fine Arts degree. Chen wanted to experiment with Dynamic Difficulty Adjustment to see if allowing players to intuitively make choices within a game would allow them to experience flow while playing.

There are 20 levels to the game, and in each level the player guides a micro-organism through the ocean so it can eat other organisms and evolve. In *flOw*, there's no need to complete one level before progressing to the next. Players control the level through their choice of various foods to eat. If they are unsuccessful in one level of the game, they "die" and return to the previous level. This flexibility of levels makes it possible for non-gamers, casual gamers, and hard-core gamers to all experience a challenge that can be mastered. Chen (2006) reports, "By swimming closer to or farther away from other organisms, and eating different types of food, players subconsciously balanced their flow experience."

Released free of charge in 2006, *flOw* was downloaded 350 000 times in the first two weeks and more than 600 000 times by the time Chen's game company website was launched. It has garnered a shelf full of awards and led to a three-game development deal with Sony. To try *flOw* for yourself, see the link on the website.

Resources
Play *flOw*

> If academic learning does not engage students, something else will.
> —*John Goodlad*

When students' perceptions of video games are compared to their perceptions of school, the differences are sobering. A full 50 percent of students in one U.S. study of high school student engagement reported that they were bored at school every day, and a further 17 percent reported being bored in every class (Yazzie-Mintz, 2007). The Canadian picture is equally depressing: "Our first year of data clearly indicates that intellectual engagement decreases steadily and significantly from Grade 6 to Grade 12. The longer students remain in school, the less likely they are to be intellectually engaged" (Willms, Friesen, & Milton, 2009, p. 31).

It can be difficult to hear that as teachers we are neither as interesting nor as challenging as an electronic game. For some of us, the first response to this criticism is to assert that we are not going to try; that our students need to wake up and recognize that success at video games won't take them anywhere near as far as success at school. However, since we know that learning doesn't happen without sustained engagement, we need to consider what video games can teach us about developing our students' capacity to engage intellectually with important content and skills.

A novel experiment is being conducted at Quest to Learn (Q2L), a newly opened school for 12- to 18-year-olds in New York. The brainchild of Katie Salen, a game designer and professor of design and technology, Q2L is not teaching through video games, but rather is applying to curriculum the characteristics that make video games appealing. The hope is that this approach to curriculum will be engaging and meaningful to 21st century students.

Teaching at Q2L is inquiry based, with technology integrated when its use will make a difference to student learning. The focus is on higher-order thinking tasks and problem solving from a variety of perspectives.

Q2L's school day is divided into four 90-minute blocks devoted to the study of domains such as Codeworlds (a combination of math and English), The Way Things Work (math and science), and Being, Space, and Place (English and social studies). In a domain, students take on the role of a relevant character such as a scientist or historian. Their work in the domain concludes with a two-week examination called a "Boss Level," a term commonly used by gamers. During the two weeks, students apply the knowledge and skills they have developed to propose solutions to complex real-world problems.

Research
Q2L

Step Back

Should teachers make use of video games? Working in a group of at least three people, use the avatar cards provided on the website to explore a variety of perspectives on this issue. Then, please take a minute to share your point of view in response to my blog post.

Resources
Avatar Cards

Conversations
Video Game Viewpoint

The Purpose of Sustained Engagement

If a school simply renamed traditional experiences using game terms, there would be no change or perhaps a negative change in student engagement. For intellectual engagement to happen, students must be presented with real and achievable challenges that they find both interesting and important. Although students will have widely varying views of what is interesting and important, there is growing consensus among adults as to what today's students need if they are to succeed in their lives after school. The lists are long and there are variations in terminology and emphasis, but many 21st century learning organizations and authors agree on the importance of the following:

→ **The need to teach both content and skills.** While it is true that information can be looked up and there is no value in memorizing an assortment of discrete facts, background knowledge makes new information easier to understand. In one study (Recht & Leslie, 1988), effective readers and struggling readers were given a story about baseball. Their knowledge of baseball proved more important in determining how much they understood of the story than did their reading skills

> An expert is an individual who, after a decade or more of training, has reached the pinnacle of current practice in her chosen domain.
> —*Howard Gardner*

Skills are equally important to teach. Roger Martin defines a skill as "the capacity to carry out an activity so as to consistently produce the desired result" (2007, p. 100). Some skills are specific to a particular discipline and are intertwined with content knowledge. It is this intertwining of excellence in skill and knowledge that defines an expert. Experts, as I noted earlier (see page 79), are sought after in the interdisciplinary project teams that are increasingly important in global 21st century workplaces.

→ **The need to teach thinking skills.** All students need to learn to analyze and evaluate arguments and evidence, solve a variety of problems, and interpret information to draw conclusions. There is nothing uniquely 21st century about the importance of developing thinking skills, but there may be a more universal need for these skills than there was in the past. Teacher Ted McCain suggests that 21st century businesses have reorganized work so that all individuals, not just managers, need to "evaluate the relative importance of information and make judgments based on that evaluation" (2005, p. 8). Howard Gardner makes a particular case for synthesis skills, stating, "Individuals without synthesizing capabilities will be overwhelmed by information and unable to make judicious decisions about personal or professional matters" (2008, p. 18).

→ **The need to teach critical literacy skills.** Because students are exposed to huge amounts of information, which has been developed for a variety of purposes and audiences, all students need to learn not only how to access that information efficiently, but also how to judge its worth.

→ **The need to teach for transfer.** Educated individuals are able to transfer their learning to a variety of settings, issues, and problems—those that are similar to the situation in which they learned (called "near transfer") and those that are dissimilar (called "far transfer"). Transfer, the most reliable indicator of understanding, is vital in our rapidly changing world where we need to recognize the similarities between situations in order to be effective.

Microscope or Telescope?

Are any of the four needs in the list above important only for students who will be attending university? attending college? going directly to the workplace? Do any of these groups of students have unique learning needs that are not listed? Discuss these questions with colleagues or online in response to my blog post.

Conversations
Not Just in Training

Engaging Instruction

Jeff Wilhelm doesn't mince words:

> *Traditional information-driven approaches zap the energy of teaching and learning, and undermine the capacity of students to apply what they learn to their lives in ways that will continue to increase their competence.*
>
> (2007, p. 153)

Effective instruction involves the student as a mentally active participant. The qualifier "mentally active" is important. Engagement is not about being busy; it's about being involved in meaningful and important intellectual challenges. These challenges have intellectual rigour and are connected to the world outside the classroom; they require and develop deep thinking and immerse the student in disciplinary inquiry (Newmann & Wehlage, 1993).

When education is understood as the construction of meaning, rather than merely the transmission of knowledge, the primacy of the student's engagement in the process becomes self-evident.

—*William Garrison*

Some specific aspects of effective instruction are described in greater detail in Chapter 12. The challenge, of course, is that many of us know what great teaching is supposed to look like, but we don't know what to do when our students refuse to engage—when they tell us that doing nothing is preferable to demonstrating curiosity and interest in anything we are teaching.

I don't think it is an exaggeration to say that all teachers of adolescents understand that the word *bored*, when uttered by a teenager, could have a number of different meanings. In the U.S. study of high school student disengagement referenced earlier (see page 7), the 50 percent of students who said they were "bored" every day and the 17 percent who said they were "bored" every class selected the following reasons for their boredom:
- Material wasn't interesting—75 percent.
- Material wasn't relevant to me—39 percent.
- Work wasn't challenging enough—32 percent.
- No interaction with teacher—31 percent.
- Work was too difficult—27 percent.

(Yazzie-Mintz, 2007)

> Engagement is not a goal; it is a feeling that accompanies important ongoing activity.
> —*Paul Goodman*

I have addressed the importance of interest (see pages 64–65) and relevance (pages 46, 62–65, and 110–114), as well as the significance of the relationship between teacher and student (pages 46, 124, and 134–137). Given what we know about the essential role of challenge in engagement, it is equally important to address the wide range of skills and knowledge evident in every classroom.

The diagram below can be used to determine what needs to happen to engage students of various skill levels in learning.

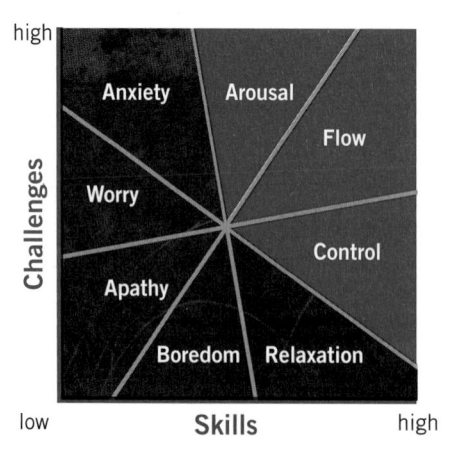

Source: Csikszentmihalyi, 1997, p. 31

As you can see, a student with a low level of skill who is given an equally low challenge will not be engaged, but rather will experience apathy or boredom. Increasing the challenge without increasing the student's skills will cause worry or anxiety. The solution is to develop the student's skills so he or she feels in control of the challenge that is being presented.

Similarly, the student who finds the work too easy is at best relaxed (not a good place for learning) and at worst apathetic. The challenge must be increased if the student is to be engaged in learning.

Motivation to learn is seriously damaged when tasks are consistently too easy or too difficult for a student. Intellectual engagement requires that students are given challenges they can master. One of the most effective ways of doing this is to provide differentiated instruction for the most important content and skills you teach. Information on how you can differentiate for student readiness is provided in Chapter 12.

> The major factor in whether or not people achieve expertise is not some fixed prior ability but purposeful engagement.
> —Robert Sternberg

Personalize It

Deepen your understanding of the diagram on the previous page by doing one of the following:

- √ Think of a student whose lack of engagement concerns you and plot that student's position on the diagram for a few different activities. After reading Chapter 12, determine one action you could take that might alter one of those positions and give it a try.

- √ Think about your own experiences as a learner (either as a student or as an adult), and plot your position on the diagram for a few different activities. Assess whether the descriptions of the responses according to the intersection of skill and challenge are accurate for you.

You Get What You Expect

Although I am a passionate advocate for differentiated instruction and I consider it a powerful approach in promoting both engagement and achievement, I am also well aware that some adolescents enter our classrooms with years of academic failure (or perceived failure) weighing them down and making them unwilling to try, no matter how much we differentiate instruction.

Resources
Assessing Academic Expectations

There is no question that teachers find this problem hugely demoralizing and difficult, but we really can't afford to give up. Research confirms that while our initial assessments of students are usually accurate, if we engage in behaviours that maintain our students' sense of failure and our low expectations for them, students may fail to make progress (Cotton, 1989). When this happens, it is almost always because we have been unaware that we are treating some students differently, based on our expectations of success for these students. (For a self-assessment to determine whether you are treating students differently based on your expectations, see the website.)

The Heath brothers tell the true story of Jefferson County High School in Louisville, Georgia, where 80 percent of the students lived in poverty and only 15 percent had continued on to college. Teachers at this school felt defeated. They had come to the painful conclusion that they were going to have to accept that some students simply couldn't be successful and that their job as teachers was to be there for the ones who could go on to college.

A new principal abolished the vocational stream at the school and put everyone into the college track, whether they would be going to college or not. Students were matched with teachers who would serve as their advisors for their four years at the school. And, perhaps most significantly, the grades of "D" and "F" were replaced by the grade "NY"—"Not Yet." Students had come to view failing grades as the easy way out, and the school had become embedded in a culture of failure. After the grade "Not Yet" was implemented, and tutorial programs and more frequent assessments for learning were put in place, substantial changes occurred. The Heath brothers report:

> *The school was reborn. Students and teachers became more engaged, the school's graduate rate increased dramatically, and student test scores went up so much that remedial courses were eliminated.*
>
> (2010, pp. 174–175)

While Jefferson County High School is only one example, and its transformation may sound more reminiscent of a "feel-good" Hollywood movie than of an everyday school, such examples of expectations making a huge difference proves that these kinds of changes are possible.

Reach for the Stars

School and district leaders can give survey statements similar to those provided on the website to teachers, support staff, parents, and students. Survey results will allow leaders to gather perceptions of the degree to which high expectations for academic achievement are evident in a school.

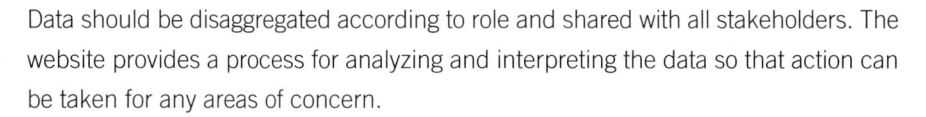

Data should be disaggregated according to role and shared with all stakeholders. The website provides a process for analyzing and interpreting the data so that action can be taken for any areas of concern.

Change-Challenged Brains

The human brain makes changing our teaching practice (or anything else) really tricky. Although we now know that we don't ever have to stop learning and that we can forge new neural pathways until the end of our lives, two things the brain does make changes difficult. Our brains are always "on," always working, so to work more efficiently we tend to spend a fair bit of time on autopilot—doing the same things over and over again. The term for this is "habituation." We also have a tendency to look for patterns—to match current experiences to experiences from the past, and to generalize from small samples, sometimes as small as a single prior event.

To complicate matters even further, it seems that overconfidence that we are above average is part of the human condition, making us susceptible to all kinds of errors of judgment, from purchasing gym memberships we are never going to use, to not recognizing our own limitations and weaknesses in our work (Hallinan, 2009). For example, a full 25 percent of people believe they are in the top 1 percent in terms of their ability to get along with others (Heath & Heath, 2010). If we believe we are better than we are, where's the impetus for change?

Resources
- Expectations Survey
- Working with Data

Almost everyone is overconfident—except the people who are depressed, and they tend to be realists.
—**Stefano DellaVigna**

Copyright Grantland Enterprises. All rights reserved. www.grantland.net

> The easier it is to be good, the harder it is to be great.
> —*Henry Ford*

Of course, teachers are as susceptible to change-challenged brains as anyone else. The very vagueness of the terms we use support overconfidence. If there are many ways to be a "good teacher" (and there are), who is to say that one way is better than another?

By this point in the book, I hope I have established my conviction that teaching is the most important profession in the world and that its practitioners are among the most dedicated, thoughtful, and caring people on the planet. So I trust that the following comment will be taken in the spirit in which it is intended: *If your students are disengaged, you need to change what you are doing*. It's not about blame, or wishing that things were different. It's about our recognition that engagement is required for learning and that we have the professional responsibility of ensuring that learning happens.

In Chapter 12, you will find suggestions for ways to make changes, whether in your teaching practice or in any other aspect of your life.

Summary of Chapter Website Content		www.pearsoncanada.ca/tunedout
Conversations	**Resources**	**Research**
• "Challenge" Video Byte • Video Game Viewpoint • Not Just in Training	• Play *flOw* • Avatar Cards • Assessing Academic Expectations • Expectations Survey • Working with Data	• Video Game Pros and Cons • Q2L

12 Minds-on Learning

Change of Plans 210

Release Gradually 214

En Route to Expertise 218

If It's Good Enough for Medical Students... 220

Curious Minds 226

Differentiating for Success 230

The Power of Ideas 232

Change of Plans

> It is a capital mistake to theorize before one has data. Insensibly one begins to twist facts to suit theories, instead of theories to suit facts.
> —*Sir Arthur Conan Doyle*

Checklists can make a big difference to successful implementation of a change. They help us remember the important information and guide our thinking according to relevant categories so we can avoid blind spots.

Consider using the following checklist of ideas to support any change you are considering in your professional life. (You might also find the checklist useful for making changes in your personal life.)

❏ **Get the Facts**

Make a conscious, deliberate effort to search for facts related to the proposed change. Discriminating between facts and interpretations is easier said than done. Each of us sees what we expect to see in a situation, and we quickly apply our own stories, assumptions, and beliefs to data, often concluding that we know the facts when what we really know are only our own interpretations.

❏ **Make a Choice**

If you believe you can't make a particular change, try altering your language to say that you "won't" make the change. When you substitute *won't* for *can't*, it is easier to recognize that all actions and non-actions are choices. Feeling in control of our choices sometimes makes it easier to make new ones. (Ryan, 2009)

❏ **Understand Change**

Research about change confirms what many of us have experienced—if we wait to make a change until *after* we are 100 percent convinced of its merits, we will be waiting a long time. Our beliefs change after we have made a change and experienced positive results, not before.

Experiences are helpful in ensuring that the change we choose will lead to positive results. These experiences can be personal (for example, being coached by another teacher who is successfully implementing the practice you are considering) or vicarious (watching a video clip or hearing a colleague's story).

❏ **See the Destination**

Authors Chip Heath and Dan Heath describe the importance of what they call a "destination postcard—a vivid picture from the near-term future that shows what could be possible" (2010, p. 76). While SMART (specific, measurable, achievable, realistic, time-bound) goals may be necessary to school improvement plans, the Heaths argue that they don't inspire the emotional commitment needed for change. That comes from a clear vision of a compelling destination.

❏ **Plan Your Moves**

Determine the specific actions that will lead to your destination. Whether you refer to them as "critical moves" (Heath & Heath, 2010) or as "vital behaviours" (Patterson, Grenny, Maxfield, McMillan, & Switzler, 2008), the idea is that you need to decide which actions are going to result in success. For example, rather than saying, "I'm going to get better at engaging students in their work," you might say, "After I talk about a concept, I will give students time to work with the idea through small-group activities."

> It is not enough to do your best; you must know what to do, and THEN do your best.
> —*W. Edwards Deming*

❏ **Shrink the Change**

When I am speaking with groups, I encourage people to choose and make a single change, preferably in an area where they are already experiencing some success. The idea is that small changes are achievable and therefore motivating, whereas huge changes are difficult and overwhelming. As the Chinese proverb says, "A journey of a thousand miles is accomplished one step at a time."

> If you think small things don't matter, try spending the night in a room with a mosquito.
> —*The Dalai Lama*

❏ **Set Your Intention**

Researcher Peter Gollwitzer (1999) gave college students the option of earning extra credit by writing a paper about how they spent Christmas Eve. The catch was that the paper had to be submitted by December 26. Many students said they intended to write the paper, but only 33 percent did. However, among a second group of students who had to say where and when they would write the

Change of Plans – continued

paper, 75 percent completed the task. Gollwitzer refers to this as an "implementation intention." He suggests that adopting this approach is a useful way of overcoming inertia and procrastination, at least for tasks we seriously want to achieve.

❏ **Expect a Dip**

A designer at IDEO, a product design firm, sketched a "project mood chart" that predicted how people would feel during a change. The graphic is a simple U-shaped curve. The word *hope* is at the top left; the word *confidence* is at the top right, and in between the two peaks is "a negative emotional valley labelled 'insight'" (Heath & Heath, 2010, p. 169). The take-away message is "Expect failure and tough times, but think of them as insights or learnings experienced en route to success."

❏ **Tweak the Environment**

If you've ever tried dieting by putting your food on a smaller plate, you've experienced tweaking the environment—finding ways to make the right behaviours a little easier and the wrong behaviours a little more difficult.

The Heath brothers (2010) give a wonderful example of tweaking the environment that is appropriate to the topic of this book. They tell the story of two male high school students who persistently arrived late to class and then sat at the back, laughing and disrupting the learning for everyone. Nothing teacher Bart Millar did to resolve the problem worked. Millar decided that his "critical move" (see "Plan Your Moves" on page 211) would be to get the two students into their seats before the class started. If he could do that, he reasoned, he'd stand a chance of next doing something about the disruptive behaviours.

Millar tweaked the environment by buying a used couch and putting it at the front of the classroom. Most students immediately decided that this was the cool place to sit. So did the two boys, who began arriving early to class so they could get good seats.

> There are three kinds of men, ones that learn by reading, a few who learn by observation, and the rest of them have to pee on the electric fence and find out for themselves.
>
> —*Will Rogers*

- **Imitate Others**

    A huge body of research says we take our cues about how to behave from the people around us. So, in the case of a change, hang around the people who are doing the things you'd like to be doing.

    M. J. Ryan (2009) has another idea that's quite clever. She recommends creating an avatar, an alter ego, and thinking about what your avatar would do in a particular situation. If, as Ryan suggests, you imbue your avatar with characteristics such as innovation and imagination, you'll think of ideas you didn't know were in you.

- **Doublethink**

    Novelist George Orwell coined the term *doublethink* to describe the concept of holding two opposing beliefs in your mind and accepting both. Researchers have found that just as we need to identify compelling reasons for making a change, we also need to recognize the obstacles in our way if we are to succeed (Oettingen & Gollwitzer, 2002).

    Determine a practice you would like to change. Then, spend a few minutes visualizing what your classroom will be like when the change is achieved. Follow that with a visualization of your most significant obstacle and the ways you will deal with it. If you have multiple reasons and obstacles, go through the process as many times as necessary, pairing a reason and an obstacle each time.

- **Go Public**

    The idea here is simple—you're more likely to achieve your goal if you tell someone about it. This idea is especially true if your colleague will gently but firmly hold you accountable.

> Find out what is working. Do more of it.
> —*Steve de Shazer*

Release Gradually

The summer I was 10, I taught myself to swim by propping open a book on the dock at a friend's cottage and imitating the actions I saw in the illustrations. I came away from that experience with a bad case of sunstroke, the ability to float in no less than four different ways, and a conviction that I could learn anything I ever needed to learn by reading.

What I didn't develop (and haven't to this day) is the ability to swim more than a few strokes or the confidence to be in water higher than my waist without fear of drowning.

The Swimming Lesson

Feeling the icy kick, the endless waves
Reaching around my life, I moved my arms

And coughed, and in the end saw land.
Somebody, I suppose,
Remembering the medieval maxim,
Had tossed me in,

Had wanted me to learn to swim,
Not knowing that none of us, who ever came back
From that long lonely fall and frenzied rising,
Ever learned anything at all
About swimming, but only
How to put off, one by one,
Dreams and pity, love and grace,—
How to survive in any place.

—Mary Oliver

Deep Water Memories

Tell a colleague the story of how you learned to swim or, if you don't swim, how you learned to ride a bike, ski on snow or water, or drive a car. As you tell your story, be sure to include the specific details of who was involved, what you did, how you felt at the time, and your facility with the skill now.

After you and your colleague have told your stories, contrast your experiences with that of the narrator in Mary Oliver's poem. If you are working in a book study group, consider beginning your discussion of the poem through "walk around reading" (Lundy, 2004). To do this, people read the poem aloud as they walk around the room—stagger the starting times so you are not reading in unison. Upon reaching the end of the poem, each person starts again. At an agreed-upon signal, people stop reading, silently choose their favourite line, phrase, or word, and take turns saying it out loud, creating a new reading of the poem that speaks to the participants' viewpoints. Walk around reading is a powerful way to begin discussion.

The gradual release of responsibility model of instruction (Pearson & Gallagher, 1983) is based on the premise that powerful learning happens when there is a slow and purposeful transfer of responsibility from teacher to student for completing a cognitive task.

The gradual release model is often described by the catch phrase "I do it/We do it/You do it." Educators Douglas Fisher and Nancy Frey (2008) suggest that this model misses one key element that should take place right before student independence. They describe this element as "we do it together" or "collaborative learning," where students work with partners and in small groups but complete work individually.

Two things about gradual release need to be kept in mind. There is no set amount of time required—gradual release may take place over a day, week, month, year, or longer. It is also important to recognize that learners may not proceed through the stages in a lockstep, sequential manner. Learning is a dynamic, not a linear, process.

The Frayer diagrams on the following two pages provide details for each step of gradual release.

> Knowing when to offer a steadying hand, and when to withdraw it, is truly the art and science of teaching.
> —*Douglas Fisher and Nancy Frey*

Release Gradually – continued

Modelling
"I do it."

Purpose—Establishes the purpose of the learning and provides a model of the thinking and skills required for success

Looks Like—A brief whole-class session (5–10 minutes) with a single focus, perhaps structured around four questions (Anderson, 2002): What am I trying to accomplish? What strategies am I using? How well am I using the strategies? What else could I do?

Doesn't Look Like—Lecturing that doesn't let students in on your thinking; asking questions of students

Check for Understanding—Have students summarize either orally with a partner or in writing, perhaps using a strategy such as QuickWrite.

Guiding
"We do it."

Purpose—Provides directed support, according to student need, for the single focus that was modelled

Looks Like—Meeting with small groups created according to predetermined need; providing frameworks, such as graphic organizers, to scaffold student work

Doesn't Look Like—Long-term ability groups or random groups

Check for Understanding—Provide targeted feedback as students work with you in a small-group setting.

Purpose—For students to consolidate thinking in interaction with peers	**Looks Like**—Students working together in formats such as literature circles, learning stations, labs, and simulations while you guide a small group
<td colspan="2" align="center">**Collaborating** *"We do it together."*</td>
Doesn't Look Like—New information being learned; group products created as result of group work	**Check for Understanding**—Each student is responsible for an independent product, which you assess formatively.

Purpose—For students to apply and extend new learning	**Looks Like**—Authentic tasks; writing in response to prompts; learning stations; independent reading
<td colspan="2" align="center">**Independence** *"You do it."*</td>
Doesn't Look Like—A stack of worksheets; a demand for skills and knowledge that haven't been taught	**Check for Understanding**—Assess formatively through metacognitive prompts and summatively through a full range of assessment tools, such as performance tasks and tests.

One Step at a Time

Talk with a partner about the extent to which your learning of a physical skill such as how to drive a car mirrors the gradual release of responsibility model. Discuss why I asked you to consider a physical skill rather than new conceptual learning, and what this says about any difficulty you might have in using the gradual release model. I say more about this in my blog post on the website.

Conversations
Abrupt Release

En Route to Expertise

Cognitive scientist Daniel Willingham summarizes the capabilities of experts as follows:

> They see problems and situations in their chosen field functionally rather than at the surface level. Seeing things that way enables them to home in on important details among a flood of information, to produce solutions that are always sensible and consistent (even if they are not always right), and to show some transfer of their knowledge to related fields. In addition, many of the routine tasks that experts perform have become automatic through practice.
>
> (2009, p. 105)

Research
The 10-Year Theory

Although you are not going to be able to move students from novice to expert in their time with you (see the website for more information), the following instructional actions will help your students learn more efficiently and more effectively.

Background Knowledge

Determine the background knowledge that students will need to have in order to understand new material. Be selective in choosing information that is central to future understanding rather than factual information that can be easily explained. Organize the information into conceptually similar chunks to make it easier for transfer to take place. This is how experts work, while novices usually try to memorize sequences of information (Atkinson, Catrambone, & Merrill, 2003).

> When students don't have background knowledge, new content seems overwhelming and learning tasks make them feel incompetent. Taken together, this has to dampen motivation.
> —*Douglas Fisher and Nancy Frey*

Misconceptions

Identify the common misconceptions of your subject matter. Pre-assess to determine which misconceptions, if any, your students hold, then deal explicitly with those misconceptions by providing experiences that challenge them. Research tells us that if misconceptions are not addressed, they will limit learning.

Research
Misconceptions

Patterns

Explicitly teach students the strategies they need in order to be able to recognize patterns, such as how texts in your subject are structured and the kinds of evidence necessary for proof in a discipline.

Metacognition

Experts develop their problem-solving strategies by thinking about what they do and do not understand. You can develop reflective skills in your students by using a variety of metacognitive prompts. Sample prompts are provided on the website.

Resources
Thinking about Thinking

Purpose

The more specifically you set the purpose for the learning, the more focused students will be. In one fascinating experiment (Pichert & Anderson, 1977), students were asked to read a short text about a house. One group of students were to read it as if they were potential home buyers, one group was told to take the perspective of a burglar, and one group was not given a perspective. Not only did both the home buyer and burglar groups demonstrate better comprehension of the text, but they paid attention to different aspects of the information according to their roles.

Practice

The knowledge you needed in order to become a teacher resided only a little in books and a lot in practice—the most important knowledge comes from learning-by-doing in the company of more experienced practitioners (Brown, Collins, & Duguid, 1989). Give students plenty of opportunity to learn and practise in authentic situations with your support.

Strategies are the patterns in people's thought processes. There are effective strategies and ineffective strategies. Effective strategies will always succeed in getting you the results you want.

—*Nick Owen*

Transfer

A key characteristic of an expert as well as a key determinant of understanding is the ability to transfer learning from one context to another. Help students recognize commonalities between problems presented in different contexts, and give them frequent opportunities to apply their learning to new situations.

If It's Good Enough for Medical Students...

Instructors in the medical school faculty at Canada's McMaster University are reputed to have been the first to use Problem-Based Learning (PBL). They began using this approach in the late 1960s to prepare students for life after graduation, when they wouldn't have access to more knowledgeable physicians every time they made a diagnosis.

> Wonder, inquiry, scepticism, and doubt—the pillars of our civilization, the promise of our future on the planet.
> —*John Barell*

Now, problem-based learning is used not only by a number of medical schools around the world, but also by law schools, business schools, faculties of education, departments of engineering, and in university and college courses from criminal justice to biochemistry and physics.

Problem-based learning is just one of many approaches to teaching and learning that fit under the broad approach known as *inquiry*.

Varieties of Inquiry

Case learning	Involves inquiry if used when the case study is problem based, but not if it serves as a review of previously taught concepts presented in narrative form
Challenge-based learning	Inquiry into problems of global importance; solutions must be locally applicable, and products created to share the learning must make use of new technologies (Johnson, Smith, Smythe, & Varon, 2009).
Expeditionary learning	Inquiry that includes exploration of the natural world and/or the community through students going out into the world and experts coming into the school
Group investigations	Inquiry that is divided among small groups, with each group conducting its own investigation of an aspect of the question or problem. Groups work interdependently to share results and come to conclusions.
Literature circles	Inquiry through small, peer-led reading discussion groups, using any text form (Harvey & Daniels, 2009)
Problem-based learning (PBL)	Inquiry based on a problem that is presented so students recognize they need to learn new knowledge in order to solve the problem

Project-based learning	Inquiry that results in the construction of a performance or artifact. Note that not all student-created products are the result of inquiry.
Simulations	Involve inquiry when they provide a way for students to discover a variety of perspectives, such as through role-play
WebQuest	A structured form of inquiry conducted online

Case Study: Impact on Engagement: Residential Schools

Name: Joanna P.   **Subject:** Canadian History   **Grade:** 10

"Stop complaining and work harder. Life isn't fair." That's what I told the half of my class who were angry that they had been set up to fail in a spelling bee competition.

My Grade 10 history students had completed a unit of study about Aboriginal life when they were in Grade 9, and many thought they knew everything they needed to know. I wanted them to feel the injustices experienced by Aboriginal students who were put in residential schools, and I wanted them to engage with this question: "Did the residential school system help destroy Aboriginal culture?" To do this I used small simulation activities under the headings associated with culture—beliefs, norms, behaviours, and values. For example, in discussion of norms I had students experience the difficulty of learning a new language by requiring that they tell a partner about another class without using the letter *e*.

Debriefs that followed the activities helped students connect their simulated experiences to the harsh reality of life in residential schools.

Impact on Engagement

Experiencing discrimination, even in small ways, had an impact on my students that extended well beyond understanding a time of discrimination in Canadian history. In supported opinion paragraphs that students wrote, it was evident that students who spoke fluent English were able to understand the difficulties that English Language Learners might be having in the classroom, and that boys and girls saw one another in a different light (see the student paragraphs on the website).

Resources
Student Paragraphs

If It's Good Enough for Medical Students... – continued

Similarities outweigh the differences among the approaches to learning described in the chart on pages 220–221. All share the following characteristics of inquiry-based learning:

> Nobody is bored when trying to make something that is beautiful, or to discover something that is true.
> —*William Inge*

→ The inquiry begins with an essential question or problem that is central to the discipline being studied. The question or problem requires students to work towards developing the conceptual understanding, knowledge, and skills of experts in that discipline.

→ The question or problem is complex and is not easily solved by reference to a single expert or resource. A number of perspectives are possible and are considered.

→ The student's role is to research, investigate solutions and, above all, think.

→ The teacher's role is to monitor, coach, and co-investigate, not to provide answers.

Not Like the Others

Resources
Inquiry or Not?

On the website you will find various scenarios. Sort them according to the degree to which they are good examples of inquiry. Then, choose one scenario and determine how you would change it to make it more inquiry based.

11 Good Reasons to Teach Through Inquiry

1. Students are engaged because they are being challenged with relevant questions and issues that don't have easy answers.

2. Teachers are engaged—inquiry restores intellectual excitement.

3. Inquiry mirrors the approach to learning that students will experience across a wide variety of disciplines in university.

4. Inquiries apprentice students in the patterns of thinking and specific strategies used by experts in the discipline being studied.

5. Metacognitive skills are developed in context as students make choices in the strategies they will use to research the question or problem, generate and test hypotheses, and share their methods and conclusions with others.

6. Robust questions and problems encourage the use of all three intelligences defined by Robert Sternberg (2001)—analytical, creative, and practical.

7. Learning is deeper because of the focus on meaning making. Students are involved in applying and integrating knowledge, rather than simply collecting and recalling facts.

8. Inquiry-based learning makes meaningful use of technology during the research and product creation phases.

9. Inquiry provides opportunities to easily differentiate for student readiness, interests, and learning preferences.

10. The grouping of diverse learners, which commonly occurs in the inquiry process, is also common in the project team approach that is central to 21st century workplaces. Students have meaningful opportunities to develop skills of collaboration, personal responsibility, and respect for different approaches to a problem.

11. Inquiry approaches to teaching are superior to more traditional approaches in developing the skills that some argue are especially important in the 21st century. These include the following:
    - critical thinking
    - problem-solving
    - transfer of knowledge to new situations
    - synthesis and evaluation

> I lectured for years, but there is something so powerful in PBL. You're never quite sure what's going to happen, but attendance is 100%, the students are motivated, working on problems. It has restored the intellectual excitement for faculty who said they had been burned out.
> —*Barbara Duch*

> He who questions much, does and discusses much, shall learn much.
> —*Sir Francis Bacon*

If It's Good Enough for Medical Students... – continued

Conversations
Why Inquiry?

Resources
Inquiry Checklist

Compelling Reasons

Compelling reasons can spell the difference between success and failure of a change in teaching practice (see pages 48–49). Considering the list provided on pages 222–223, identify one or two reasons for inquiry-based teaching and learning that you find most compelling. Share your reasons with a colleague or online in response to my blog post, explaining what problems of practice their implementation would help you resolve.

Maintaining Status Quo

Given the long list of benefits to teaching and learning through inquiry, it may seem surprising that more of us aren't doing it. But we aren't. More than two dozen years ago, John Goodlad summarized the prevailing mode of instruction in more than 1000 classrooms. In the foreword to the 20th anniversary edition of Goodlad's book *A Place Called School*, educator Ted Sizer notes, "There is a sad, almost eerie relevance to the detailed specifics of Goodlad's critique" (2004, p. xx):

> *The two activities, involving the most students, were being lectured to and working on written assignments (and we have seen that much of this work was in the form of responding to directives in workbooks or on worksheets). When we add to the time spent in these learning modes the time spent on the routines of preparing for or following up instruction, the extraordinary degree of student passivity stands out. The amount of time spent in any other kind of activity (e.g., role-playing, small group planning and problem solving, constructing models) was miniscule....*
>
> (2004, p. 230)

Before you read further, brainstorm with colleagues reasons why inquiry-based learning hasn't developed more of a following among teachers.

8 Not Necessarily Good Reasons Why We Don't Teach Through Inquiry

1. *Assessment*—Standardized tests assess what is easiest and therefore least expensive to assess, namely, content knowledge. If student achievement is measured through standardized tests, inquiry-based teaching doesn't show well. Students who learn through inquiry do very well on assessments of understanding and critical

thinking, but those skills aren't often measured by standardized tests or classroom assessments.

2. *Time*—Inquiry-based learning takes more time than traditional instruction; it is an inefficient way to learn lots of facts.

3. *The Question or Problem*—It isn't easy to develop a good inquiry question or problem that is authentic and open-ended, one that doesn't appear to have a straightforward answer that we are stubbornly refusing to share with our students.

4. *The Discipline*—The question or problem needs to be crafted so that students will learn what they need to learn, which means we must know the core concepts, patterns of thought, and strategies used by experts in the discipline.

5. *Behaviour*—Students need to be explicitly taught process skills, such as how to work in a group, research, solve problems, manage time, and create products in various forms. If these skills are not explicitly taught, the best we can hope for is a lot of wasted time; the worst is a class management nightmare.

6. *Flexibility*—While flexibility is often considered a virtue of inquiry-based teaching and learning, inquiry doesn't have a set of easily transferable techniques in the same way that cooperative learning does. Although models of inquiry and some classroom examples exist, the approach can look quite different depending on grade level, question or problem, and student characteristics.

7. *Resources*—A wide range of print, visual, digital, and human resources is needed in an inquiry-based classroom. Although these resources are almost always available through school and public libraries and the internet, they require time, effort, and advance planning to compile.

8. *Fear*—Most of us weren't taught through inquiry and many haven't experienced it. We don't have a mental picture of what our role looks and sounds like in an inquiry classroom. Given the small number of teachers who use the inquiry approach, we likely don't have colleagues who can guide us.

Curious Minds

When you are a kid you have your own language, and unlike French or Spanish or whatever you start learning in fourth grade, this one you're born with, and eventually lose. Everyone under the age of seven is fluent in ifspeak; *go hang around with someone under three feet tall and you'll see. What if a giant funnel-web spider crawled out of that hole over your head and bit you on the neck? What if the only antidote for venom was locked up in a vault on the top of a mountain? What if you lived through the bite, but could only move your eyelids and blink out an alphabet? It really doesn't matter how far you go; the point is that it's a world of possibility. Kids think with their brains cracked wide open; becoming an adult, I've decided, is only a slow sewing shut.*

(Picoult, 2004, p. 299)

> The cure for boredom is curiosity. There is no cure for curiosity.
> —*Dorothy Parker*

Curiosity is a defining characteristic of creative thinkers and an essential component of inquiry. Curious people tend to have greater analytic ability, problem-solving skills, and overall intelligence (Kashdan, 2009). Curious people are also more engaged in their work than others because curiosity sparks imagination and wonder, and also challenges our deepest assumptions.

You can recognize a curious and creative person by the questions they ask, and by their willingness to remain uncertain while they search for answers.

Make a Question Generator

Resources
- Question Deck
- Critical Literacy Question Generator

Open-ended questions provide learners with opportunity for creative responses, and teachers with opportunity to engage learners' curiosity. The next time you are asking questions of your students, encouraging them to ask questions of themselves, or working with other adults on any topic or issue in your school, use the Question Deck on the website. If you are near a computer when you are working, you can use the Critical Literacy Question Generator in the Resources section of the website.

Whichever approach you use, you will get responses that are more thoughtful and creative if you ask the same question several times rather than immediately moving on to another.

Ponder This!

Good questions feed curiosity. The following are some great questions for you and your students to ponder. As you do, challenge students to identify the characteristics of good, curiosity-provoking questions.

- If 0 degrees is a temperature, is 0 centimetres a height?
- If you believe your own lies, are they lies?
- If you don't run over the squirrel darting across the road, have you saved its life?
- Is the future closer than it was this time last year?
- Is it ever possible to learn nothing?

(Gilbert, 2008)

> The whole art of teaching is only the art of awakening the natural curiosity of young minds for the purpose of satisfying it afterwards.
> —*Anatole France*

Because good questions promote and detect student achievement, questioning is the most extensively studied of all instructional strategies. Less frequently studied but just as important is the power of good questions to motivate students to engage with the ideas of the curriculum.

Norah Morgan and Juliana Saxton (2006) have developed a Taxonomy of Personal Engagement that teachers can use in a sequential manner as they develop questions to promote student engagement and sense of ownership and control over learning. See the website for a summary of the taxonomy.

Resources
Questions to Engage

Another way to engage students through questioning is to get them to ask the questions. Putting students in this active role is particularly engaging for adolescent learners because it gives them choice and control over their learning. You may wish to post this quotation from Neil Postman and Charles Weingartner in your classroom:

> *Once you have learned to ask questions—relevant and appropriate and substantial questions—you have learned how to learn and no one can keep you from learning whatever you need to know.*
>
> (1969, p. 23)

For a variety of ways to give students practice in asking a range of meaningful questions, see the website.

Resources
Students Ask Questions

Curious Minds – continued

Questioning the Mission

While developing new mission and vision statements for your school or district (see Chapter 2), you probably considered several essential questions, such as "What is the relationship between a good education and a good human being?" and "What is the role of technology in preparing students for an unknown future?" Use the strategies suggested on the previous two pages to explore these and other questions with teachers, students, parents, and other members of the community.

Case Study: Impact on Engagement: Asking Essential Questions

Names: Leyton S. (consultant); Nicole W. (teacher)   **Subjects:** English, Science   **Grades:** 6/7

We found that asking questions that spark student interest affected motivation, engagement, and success. We took this approach when co-teaching a unit about ecosystems. Beginning with two broad questions for the unit—"How are humans impacting the environment?" and "What can we do to sustain the environment?"—we structured each week's work around a smaller inquiry question students could explore. We identified the key ideas we wanted students to develop through their exploration, the thinking skills they would need in order to be successful, and the teaching strategies we would use to support their learning.

Impact on Engagement

Students were engaged with our teaching because our mini-lessons were providing them with the skills and strategies they needed to answer their inquiry questions. They enjoyed being able to explore their questions through a combination of research and hands-on experiences. We noticed a significant increase in focused talk about the inquiry and in the use of science-specific vocabulary among English Language Learners.

Case Study ⇒ **Impact on Engagement: Mathletes Solve Problems**

Name: Tania S.   **Subject:** Mathematics   **Grades:** 7/8

Jessica didn't see the value of math beyond school and resisted efforts to help her develop her skills and engage in the work.

Jessica's responses changed when I began each lesson with an open question about a big idea with a rich problem to solve.

The activity was posted the day before class in our "Mathletes" Moodle. The role of the scribe of the day was to come to class prepared to lead the discussion by posing further guiding questions. The scribe displayed the question on the interactive whiteboard, read it aloud, and reminded classmates to begin solving the problem on their own.

Students reflected on previous experiences and used notes, problems, diagrams, calculators, and manipulatives as they jotted down ideas. Wherever possible, they were encouraged to make connections between the strands and big ideas taught thus far. Next, the scribe of the day directed students to work in teacher-selected groups of three students to unpack the problem collaboratively. As I circulated, I recorded anecdotal observations about individual student use of mathematical reasoning.

Using the interactive whiteboard, students then took turns proposing their solutions to the class. This whole-group sharing helped students discover the wide variety of approaches that can be used to solve a problem. After everyone had shared their responses, one person from each group was responsible for synthesizing the group's thinking and posting a well-supported answer to the "Minds On" activity in the Moodle for the next day. Having this electronic archive of my students' thinking provided valuable evidence to support formative assessment.

Impact on Engagement

Inevitably, the "Minds On" activity from one day gave rise to the next day's question or problem. Therefore, part of the job of the "Minds On" scribe was to post the next day's question for the following lesson, and the process continued.

My students, Jessica included, were engaged in solving problems using technology and in answering authentic questions.

Minds-on Learning ■ 229

Differentiating for Success

Differentiated instruction makes learning possible for all students, not by making it easier but by providing appropriately pitched challenges that will help all students succeed to the same high standard on a curriculum outcome.

Differentiation can be based on student interests (see pages 64–65), learning preferences (see pages 66–69), or readiness. When differentiating by readiness, you are attending to a student's background knowledge, skill level, and understanding relative to a concept or skill you are teaching.

Readiness is determined through pre-assessment and usually results in a decision that a student is working at grade level, striving to do so, or excelling at the concept or skill you will be teaching. It's important to recognize that this determination means either thinking of or placing students in three short-term, flexible groups. Differentiated instruction is not individualized instruction, and it shouldn't be overwhelming for teachers or students.

To create good differentiated activities based on student readiness, make sure that they share the following characteristics:

→ All differentiated activities address the same outcome and are assessed using the same rubric or other assessment structure.

→ All differentiated activities require about the same time to complete and present a similar degree of complexity.

→ All activities are equally engaging and equally respectful.

Assess the DI

Use the list of characteristics above to assess differentiated instruction activities you provide in your classroom. If an activity falls short in one or more of the three characteristics, determine the alterations that would be required to make it an example of effective differentiation.

When differentiating for student readiness, start by first creating the task that will be appropriate for students working at grade level. Doing so will ensure that you are clearly targeting appropriate learning outcomes for your grade. Then, consider what you can do to support those learners who are not yet working at grade level, as well as those who require extra challenge. Some examples of aspects of a task that can be differentiated are provided in the following chart.

Sample Considerations for Differentiation Through Readiness		
Striving	**Working at Grade Level**	**Needing Extra Challenge**
Examples provided are concrete.	Examples provided are mostly concrete, with some abstraction.	Examples provided are abstract.
A minimal number of steps are required to complete an assignment.	More steps are required to complete an assignment.	Assignment can be more open-ended, with decisions about how to complete it left to the student.
Reading level is appropriate for students; may be below grade level.	Reading level is at grade level.	Reading level is above grade level.

None of the considerations in this chart suggest that students who are striving should be given lower order thinking questions and activities. All students need the opportunity and support to work at higher order thinking skills, and all students are able to do so. The variable that you need to attend to is not complexity, but difficulty. Difficulty refers to the amount of energy that needs to be expended within a level of complexity. For example, having students copy a map of Canada from the textbook is a low-complexity task—"recall" at best on Bloom's taxonomy—with a high level of difficulty. Asking students to use the map of Canada in their textbook to rank three cities or towns of their choice according to their access to natural resources that can sustain primary and secondary industries is a high-complexity task requiring analysis and evaluation, but its level of difficulty is low.

The Power of Ideas

In a documentary about the highly successful Central Park East Secondary School, an alternative school in New York's Spanish Harlem, director Frederick Wiseman (1994) captures founding principal Deborah Meier sharing her inspiring vision for life and for her school:

A good life is to be everlastingly involved, either internally or externally, with a terrific conversation for which you need to know more and more in order to make that conversation go somewhere. It is certainly at the heart of what a powerful citizenry and a powerful democracy would be, and that is citizens who are in a position to carry on that public dialogue about the nature of their society, its purposes, and ways in which it could be improved.

That's the idea that we're struggling with—how to create a school that's powerful enough to turn kids on to the possible power of ideas in their lives.

Meier's powerful conversations can happen in our schools through inquiry at the unit level (see pages 220–225) and through inquiry at the lesson level. Both uses of inquiry are based on the following:

→ recognizing the importance of talk in the classroom

→ creating a supportive environment for meaningful talk

→ asking effective questions

→ teaching students to think

The Importance of Talk

Learning is a social phenomenon where students use talk to engage with ideas, create meaning, and accomplish tasks. Developing students' skills of analysis, synthesis, and evaluation often happens through talk—we ask essential questions and model for students how to use those questions to generate hypotheses, reason logically, combine ideas, and appraise the quality of our own and other people's arguments. To paraphrase Prof. James Britton, "Learning floats on a sea of talk."

> [W]hen students all over the country are saying they have no time to discuss ideas or learn to think critically, one worries about the big mistakes we are making.
>
> —*Anne Lewis*

However, knowing that talk is important to learning does not necessarily mean that we find it easy to make time for meaningful talk—teacher Ted McCain provides a case in point. McCain now uses simulation activities in his teaching that are so creative and captivating that I yearn to be a student in his class or try out his ideas with a group of adolescents. (See my review of his book *Teaching for Tomorrow* on the website). Nevertheless, McCain spent many years teaching in a way that fell a little (or a lot) short of his espoused values. He writes:

> *Even though I had great visions of high-level thinking activities taking place in my classes, the reality was that when the door was closed and I was left all alone with thirty students staring at me, I stood up in front of the class and told them everything I thought they needed to know.*
>
> (2005, p. 19)

Research
Spotlight on *Teaching for Tomorrow*

Not All Talk Is Created Equal

In his study of 1000 classrooms, John Goodlad writes,

> *We observed that, on the average, about 75% of class time was spent on instruction and that nearly 70% of this was "talk"—usually teacher to students. Teachers out-talked the entire class of students by a ratio of about three to one. If teachers in the talking mode and students in the listening mode is what we want, rest assured that we have it.*
>
> (2004, p. 229)

More damning even than the amount of teacher talk is the nature of that talk. Goodlad found that teacher talk is almost exclusively "telling," with less than 1 percent of this talk inviting students to reason or give an opinion. A study of students in lower track classes found that classroom dialogue was so rare there wasn't even enough of it to conduct valid research (Applebee, Langer, Nystrand, & Gamoran, 2003).

Use the checklist on the website to determine the nature of the talk in your classroom. Whatever the results, take pride in the courage you demonstrated by your willingness to find out what's really going on.

Resources
Classroom Talk Checklist

Minds-on Learning

The Power of Ideas – continued

Creating the Environment

In our defence, many teachers have had the experience of allowing—even encouraging—talk in the classroom only to find that the talk is entirely social and has nothing to do with learning.

To set the conditions for purposeful, learning-focused talk in your classroom, consider the following:

√ *Physical Arrangement*—Whether the conversation is small group or whole class, all students should be close enough to hear one another, to make eye contact, and to interpret one another's body language. If your classroom furniture doesn't allow for the easy clustering of desks or tables, consider leaving a portion of the room permanently open and providing a stack of chairs nearby that can be quickly arranged in a semicircle

√ *Participation*—Talk for learning requires everyone's involvement, but that can be difficult to achieve in whole-class conversations. Use lots of partner and small-group discussions so everyone has a chance to participate, and then sometimes use whole-class conversations to hear reports of the small-group discussions and extend the talk. See the website for suggestions of ways to increase student participation.

√ *Classroom Climate*—Students need to know that their opinions and tentative forays into reasoning will be treated with respect. Work to establish an atmosphere in your classroom that shows you are prepared to wait for students to think and that you will support their efforts through clarifying questions. Make it clear that you won't rescue by providing all of the answers. The goal is getting students to talk to one another, building on and challenging one another's ideas respectfully. Model this process during whole-class sessions and monitor it during partner and small-group sessions. As Jeff Wilhelm reminds us, "If you sit at your desk and grade papers, small-group work can blow up pretty quickly" (2007, p. 104).

Resources
Increase Student Participation

Teach Thinking Skills

When we ask students questions or give them assignments that require them to consider a variety of perspectives, provide evidence for their point of view, determine bias, or put forth a hypothesis, we are teaching them *how* to think. In contrast, asking questions or giving assignments that require students to fill in the blanks with preconceived correct answers teaches students *what* to think. (For a link to a glossary of thinking terms, see the website.)

If you believe your students need more than just information to be successful, you will need to teach them how to think. Good thinking improves student achievement. It also promotes student engagement because it removes the mystique associated with success. When asked how he managed to solve the problem that won him the Nobel Prize in physics, scientist Richard Feynman reportedly joked, "You write down the problem. You think very hard. Then you write down the answer."

Teaching your students to think shows them they can influence their own learning. For a variety of ways to engage students while teaching thinking skills, see the website.

Research
Thinking Terms Glossary

Even in the increasingly high-tech world of the 21st century, what students need first and foremost are effective thinking skills.
—*Ted McCain*

Resources
Engagement Through Thinking

©1999 ZITS Partnership. Distributed by King Features Syndicate.

Minds-on Learning ■ 235

The Power of Ideas – continued

Case Study: Impact on Engagement: A Thinking Matrix

Name: Melanie G. (Vice-Principal) **Subjects:** All **Grade:** 8

"The blog is fun because you can see everybody else's perspective." That comment, and many others like it, became the norm when the students at our school were taught thinking skills and encouraged to apply them in the context of a digital environment.

Our work commenced when we were given two months to pilot an Apple computer project that provided our two Grade 8 classes with 10 MacBook laptops, 10 iPod touches, a video camera, and a still digital camera. Our challenge was to figure out the best way to use the technology within the curriculum to have the greatest impact on student learning in a relatively short time.

As a staff, we first agreed to a common vision. We wanted to use the technology authentically, not simply as a way of having students present appealing final products to their classmates. We wanted to target curriculum outcomes that required higher order thinking skills—outcomes that included extending understanding, analyzing texts, responding to and evaluating texts, and considering multiple perspectives.

To achieve our goals we used backward design to plan a unit of study on conflict and change. Students consulted a variety of research sources to develop answers to this question: "Was Louis Riel a hero or a rebel?"

As research efforts extended beyond the class textbook to include text, images, and videos found on a variety of websites, students quickly realized that each source provided a single and therefore limited perspective. Reviewing multiple sources made it easy for students to evaluate texts and form tentative opinions, but two problems quickly became apparent. We needed to find a way to capture the discussion; we also needed a way to help students take a more thoughtful and careful approach to their work.

A class blog provided the forum for student thinking and learning to become transparent. Students posted their opinions in response to the inquiry question, read each other's responses, and posted again in an ongoing written dialogue. Teachers approved all student entries before posting. They provided timely feedback as students learned to respond to their classmates with constructive comments (using appropriate phrases such as "Have you thought of...?" or "Did you consider...?").

As the work progressed, we developed a thinking matrix (see the website for a copy) and taught students to identify the nature of the response required by different kinds of questions.

Impact on Student Engagement

Our school had been chosen for the Apple pilot project because 74 percent of our population is English Language Learners, many of them newcomers to Canada facing challenging economic circumstances.

We found that the inquiry approach to learning and the explicit teaching of thinking skills allowed students to make deep and meaningful personal connections to their work regardless of varied backgrounds. Students also gained the support they needed to express and defend their opinions. All students were intellectually engaged, so much so that absenteeism was minimal and discipline issues were virtually non-existent.

The use of technology enhanced the engagement of our students, particularly the boys. All students handed in all assignments during the unit. They also stayed at school late and worked during their breaks. The opportunity to create final products, such as iMovie monologues, certainly inspired many, but even something as simple as editing and revising blog posts through cut-and-paste functions on a computer strengthened our students' motivation to do their best work.

Impact on Teacher Engagement

We gained as much as our students did from this technologically enriched inquiry. Because our students were so engaged, they were self-directed, and we were able to serve as facilitators and become co-learners. Having time to spend with students who needed us had a significant, positive impact on student achievement.

We also enjoyed the opportunity to engage in collaborative planning and moderated marking. As we participated in the project and discussed our work, we found that we became consciously competent—aware of the advantages of teaching higher order thinking skills in the context of a meaningful inquiry question. We also had a lot of fun learning to make blogs, podcasts, and iMovies—sometimes from the Apple educational consultant and sometimes from our students!

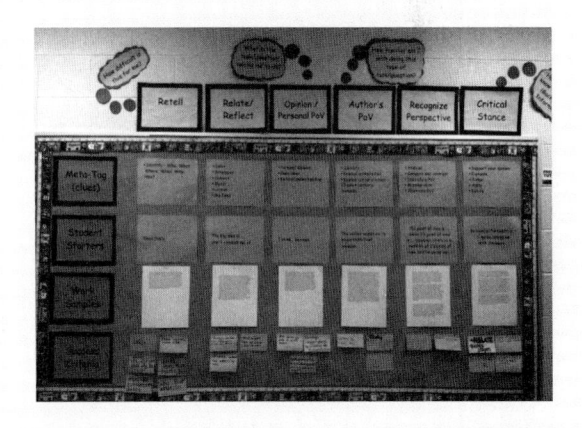

Resources
- Curriculum Map
- Thinking Matrix

The Power of Ideas – continued

Summary of Chapter Website Content
www.pearsoncanada.ca/tunedout

Conversations	Resources	Research
• Abrupt Release • Why Inquiry?	• Thinking About Thinking • Student Paragraphs • Inquiry or Not? • Inquiry Checklist • Question Deck • Critical Literacy Question Generator • Questions to Engage • Students Ask Questions • Classroom Talk Checklist • Increase Student Participation • Engagement Through Thinking • Curriculum Map • Thinking Matrix	• The 10-Year Theory • Misconceptions • Spotlight on *Teaching for Tomorrow* • Thinking Terms Glossary

Finding

One evening an old farmer was walking along a country lane. He looked into a field and saw a group of young women bathing naked in a pond. The women noticed him at about the same time as he noticed them.

One woman shouted, "We're not coming out till you leave."

The farmer replied, "Oh, I'm not here to watch you ladies swimming naked, or running around in the meadow with nothing on.

"I'm just here to feed the alligator."

—Owen, 2007, p. 103

13 Courageous Together

The story on the previous page may seem a strange one to use near the end of this book, particularly when the final section is titled "Finding" and is intended to provide an inspiring picture of what 21st century classrooms and schools might look like when filled with engaged students and teachers. But I value our profession and your contribution to it far too much to pretend that there are no alligators. In fact, there are few ponds in education that don't contain at least one alligator lurking about somewhere. I've made a point of drawing attention to a few of them throughout this book and website. They are necessary to creating cognitive dissonance and encouraging change.

What is the nature of the alligators that continue to threaten your engagement as a teacher? For some of us, it is the speed of change, particularly technological change. Our concern is that we can't meet the demands of these changes—or that we don't feel any desire to. If we don't see a value in actions that are touted as the way of the present or the future, we can feel out of step and misplaced.

For others, the alligator is having our beliefs about teaching and learning challenged by the research cited in this book. If, for example, you believe that students should be spending most of their time sitting quietly and working independently, or if you consider today's adolescents to be lazy, unmotivated, unintelligent, and unredeemable, the ideas discussed in this book will definitely create cognitive dissonance and be more than a little threatening.

A Reflective Moment

Take the time to reflect individually about all of the ideas shared in the *Tuned Out* book and website, and to identify the alligators that remain in your pond. The processes discussed in this chapter may help to slay them once and for all.

> It is the business of the future to be dangerous.... The major advances in civilization are processes that all but wreck the societies in which they occur.
> —*Alfred North Whitehead*

Collaborative IQ

In Chapter 2, I said that you can have quite a lot of influence over the students you teach, as long as you accept two basic premises:

1. You work in a school, not just in a classroom. The largest influence comes from constancy of purpose and consistent implementation of actions directed towards that purpose across the entire school and, ideally, in the surrounding community.

2. Your focus remains firmly on your circle of influence (what you can control), as opposed to your circle of concern (circumstances beyond your control).

Throughout this book, I have talked about change primarily from the perspective of the individual. Even when I write about professional learning communities and powerful conversations, or urge collaboration with book study partners, my focus tends to be on you and your role in those gatherings.

My emphasis on the individual has been deliberate. I think that change and learning are, if not synonymous terms, closely related. I have always liked Heraclitus' statement that "You cannot step twice into the same river, for other waters are continually flowing on." I believe that learning changes us; if we allow it, we are made different as a result of new ideas. Since our strongest circle of influence is in the arena of our own beliefs, thoughts, and actions, focusing on change at the level of the individual makes sense.

However, the greatest influence comes from the collective, not the individual. This makes sense, especially in the context of our discussion about engagement. It is relationship—with ideas, structures and, perhaps especially, with others— that keeps us engaged, and it is engagement that makes change possible.

Collaborative IQ is the idea that all of us together are more intelligent, more powerful, and more capable than any of us on our own. Schools and districts with high collaborative intelligence enjoy many benefits not experienced in environments where a few individuals are shouldering all of the responsibility for change.

Individuals in highly collaborative environments

- → feel a strong sense of connection and belonging
- → achieve goals through relationships rather than politics
- → experience less negative stress because they are able to share problems and develop solutions with colleagues who understand and don't judge
- → engage with the group because the work is meaningful and important

> The only happy people I know are the ones who are working well at something they consider important.
> —*Abraham Maslow*

The last characteristic in the list above reinforces the importance of developing a sense of purpose together and of capturing that purpose through powerful statements of our mission and vision. Just as students need to see the relevance of what they are asked to do, adults are most willing to engage with others when their participation addresses a meaningful purpose. For students, that meaningful purpose is often provided by a performance task or a required product. For educators, the meaningful purpose is a sense of mission, a response to this question: "Why do we exist?"

Your Purpose

Educators Penelope Wald and Michael Castleberry offer us an important reminder:

> *It is the work of every school community to discover its unique purpose—a purpose that reflects its ideals, its soul, its essence.*
>
> (2000, p. 36)

Resources
Wordle

As a staff, revisit the work you have done to determine the purpose of your school or district, beginning with the activities on pages 18 and 22–23 of Chapter 2. You might want to consolidate your sense of purpose by answering this question: "What would happen if our program, our school, or our service ceased to exist?" (Wald & Castleberry, 2000, p. 36)

If individuals or small groups of people generate a number of purpose statements, as suggested in the activities in Chapter 2, you can begin to consolidate them by inputting all of the text to create a "Wordle." For information about Wordle, see the website.

Once a clear purpose has been established, it should be written in the form of a mission statement. A mission statement is not a SMART goal; it is a distillation of an organization's purpose, meant to inspire and direct future actions. Some examples of mission statements from businesses include the following:

- Apple Computer—We want to educate the world.
- Google—We will organize the world's information and make it universally accessible and useful.
- Southwest Airlines—We are in the business of freedom.
- Walt Disney—We want to make people happy.
- 3M—We will solve unsolved problems innovatively.

Mission statements, like the ones listed above, are often on a very grand scale, yet they are still specific enough to provide a clear sense of what the business does and does not do. Here are a couple of historical examples of grand yet specific mission statements:

- Ford (early 1900s)—Ford will democratize the automobile.
- Sony (early 1950s)—Sony will become the company most known for changing the worldwide poor-quality image of Japanese products.

Mission statements are one of the writing tasks where staff members who spend time on Twitter will really have a chance to shine! Likely more than one member of your school community fits the bill.

Tweet, Tweet

At age 15, Jack Dorsey was working for a bike courier company. He was intrigued by the way dispatchers were able to direct couriers all around a city, gathering and dispensing information in real time. That experience, years later, informed Dorsey's creation of Twitter—an online service that is part microblog, part social network, and part instant message.

Twitter, like other social networking sites, requires users to create an account and a personalized profile page. Then, as in microblogging and instant messaging, people create short text messages—"tweets" of no more than 140 characters. This length makes it possible for tweets to be sent through any online environment, including mobile phones.

Twitter was invented to allow people to share in real time the details of their lives. Originally, the status question asked of users was "What are you doing?"—which invited tweets about the minutiae of daily life: "I'm trying to find the ketchup" or "I'm walking down the street."

However, the status question has changed from "What are you doing?" to "What's happening?" While trivial details are still being shared, Twitter is increasingly being used in a wide variety of ways, from Barack Obama campaigning for the presidency to the Red Cross sharing minute-by-minute information during natural disasters. In April 2009, a search bar and a sidebar of hot topics were added to Twitter, making it possible for Twitter to function as a place where important issues can be identified simply because so many people are talking about and pointing to them through their tweets.

The success of Twitter has been phenomenal. Even major news organizations such as CNN have been quick to incorporate tweets into broadcasts. While Twitter remains secretive about usage statistics, a Wikipedia account reports 4 billion postings in the first quarter of 2010—double the number of posts made in the final quarter of 2009.

For information about Twitter's use among educators, see the website.

Research
Twitter for Educators

Your Mission

Your mission statement is the touchstone that guides the development of the longer and more involved vision statement. Because it is short, the mission statement tends to be shared with the school community, posted on letterhead and walls and, ideally, referred to when decisions are being made.

Take the purpose you identified in the previous activity (see "Your Purpose" on page 242), and turn it into a clear and concise mission statement. Doing any of the following activities, alone or in a group, may prove helpful:

- √ Write the statement in 140 characters or less. Or, even better, get online and tweet it. If you tweet it, you won't have to count characters, and everyone can take part in developing, reviewing, and revising.

- √ Set a dollar value (perhaps $8), and assign values to different parts of speech (for example, nouns are 50 cents, verbs are a dime). Challenge people in the group to write mission statements that come close to the maximum but don't exceed it.

- √ Circle the nouns and verbs in your statement of purpose. Use a thesaurus to find synonyms for these words, and write your mission statement using the synonyms.

Please consider posting your completed mission statement to the website.

Conversations
Share Your Mission

No matter how hard you try to make your mission statement unique, chances are good that others will have statements that sound much like yours. There are a limited number of inspiring, education-related words that you can use in a mission statement. Fortunately, coming up with a statement that is unique isn't important. What is important is that you have worked together to identify a limited number of priorities. Shared purpose is what unites a school or district staff with high collaborative IQ.

Wrestling Alligators

I recognize the danger in asking you to work with others to determine your purpose and craft your mission statement while there may still be alligators lurking in your pond. Signs that alligators are present include experiencing feelings of depression, irritation, or cynicism while working on the activities offered so far in this chapter. Although those feelings may seem to be related to the alligators mentioned earlier—technology, today's adolescents, or characteristics of effective teaching and learning—any one of them may signal your concern that you don't have the resources, ability, or power to create change.

I have been in this position, and I understand how awful it feels. My personal experience is that only two things help, and they are related. One is having a strong sense of purpose; the other is collaboration with others who share that sense of purpose.

> The indispensable first step to getting the things you want out of life is this: Decide what you want.
> —*Ben Stein*

Erik Erikson identified "purposefulness" as a defining characteristic of productive adult life. Recent studies of aging have shown that a key indicator of health and well-being in old age is whether or not a person remains purposeful after retirement (Baltes, Lindenberger, & Staudinger, 2006). And researcher Daniel Kahneman (2000) has found that happiness comes not from attaining things for ourselves, despite our conviction that a lottery win would solve all of life's problems! Rather, happiness is the result of engagement in something we find challenging and compelling, particularly when it makes a contribution to a larger purpose.

There is a ready-made purpose in education. Although it can be difficult to remember when we are caught in challenging situations, many of us became educators because we are concerned with the well-being of future generations. We are what researchers call "generative" adults—highly dedicated to our work and to mentoring young people (McAdams, 2001).

Oftentimes, our students will remind us of our purpose. I hope we have all had the experience of having a really bad day turned around by a student's insightful remark or humorous action. Our students remind us daily why we chose to teach adolescents, and they help us sustain our engagement and sense of purpose, just as we help them do the same.

©2005 ZITS Partnership. Distributed by King Features Syndicate.

We also need the support of other adults. Geese flying south for the winter often serve as a metaphor for strong teams. The metaphor is apt because as each goose flaps its wings, it creates uplift for the bird that follows. By flying in a V formation, the flock has at least 71 percent greater flying range than each bird would have on its own. When one bird falls out of formation, it loses the power of the flock and experiences tremendous drag and resistance (Cherry & Spiegel, 2006).

When the staff of a school or a district is making significant changes in practice, there is a predictable sequence of events. Business leader Jim Collins describes it as a flywheel:

> *Like pushing on a giant, heavy flywheel, it takes a lot of effort to get the thing moving at all, but with persistent pushing in a consistent direction over a long period of time, the flywheel builds momentum, eventually hitting a point of breakthrough.*
>
> (2001, p. 186)

Wald and Castleberry (2002, p. 42) give us the image of a roller coaster of change:

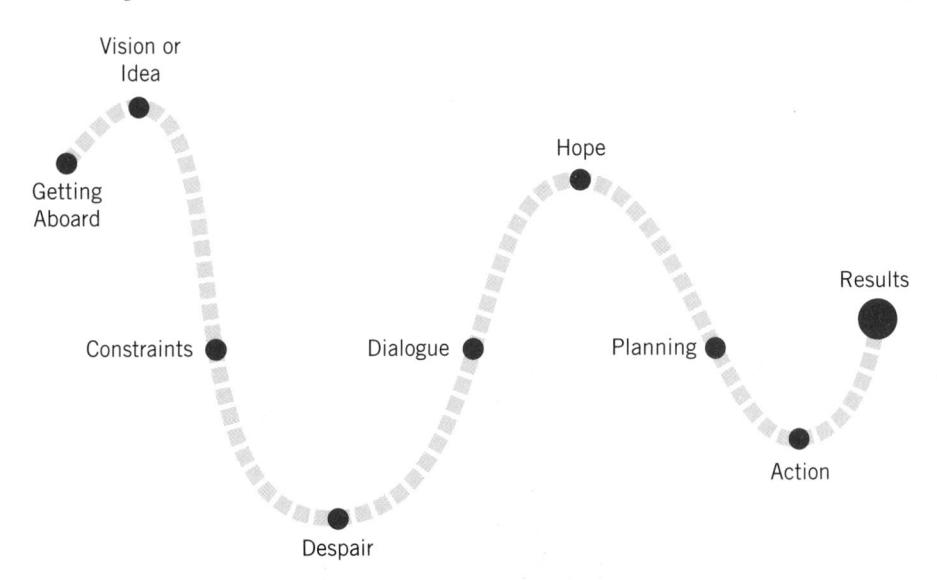

Getting Aboard → Vision or Idea → Constraints → Despair → Dialogue → Hope → Planning → Action → Results

Regardless of the metaphor used, drag and resistance are inevitable travelling companions in the early stages of any change. To succeed, it is important to identify and make use of a specific group of people who can help a staff to overcome early difficulties.

The Messenger Matters

Stanley Milgram (1963) is a psychologist who was mystified by Hitler's ability to compel German soldiers to kill innocent people. In an effort to determine if there is a particular type of person capable of these acts, Milgram conducted an experiment that would never get past an ethics review board today, but that has taught us a great deal that we'd rather not know about human behaviour.

In Milgram's experiment, research subjects were told that they would play the role of "teacher" in a study about the impact of negative reinforcement on learning. Their task was to deliver electric shocks of increasing intensity to a learner who was unsuccessful at recalling words. With each failure, the research subject was instructed to increase the voltage, delivering ever more powerful shocks to a maximum of 450 volts.

Before Milgram's study was conducted, fellow psychologists predicted that 1.2 percent of the population would be willing to deliver shocks at the maximum voltage. Their prediction seems reasonable—after all, the research subject had met the learner and had a friendly conversation with him, not realizing he was part of the research team. Furthermore, the learner had made it known that he had a heart condition, and each research subject had experienced a 45-volt shock and knew that it hurt.

However, Milgram's experiment is famous in part because the prediction of 1.2 percent was so wrong. Although the learner was never harmed, the research subjects didn't know that, and fully 65 percent of them administered 450-volt shocks. They didn't want to do it—they resisted and complained and worried—but when the researcher told them the experiment must continue, they did as they were told.

While Milgram's experiment is both fascinating and disturbing, what is of interest to us in our discussion of collaboration is the data Milgram provided in a second report (1974). In an experiment to determine which aspect of the environment most influenced people's behaviour, Milgram found that it was the presence and behaviour of another person that had the greatest impact.

In his study of over 1000 participants, Milgram found that when he planted a confederate who would give a shock of 450 volts just before a research subject had a turn at the machine, the percentage of people who administered 450-volt shocks soared from an already alarming 65 percent to a staggering 90 percent. Conversely, if the confederate refused to administer the full shock, the research subject who heard this refusal also refused, and the percentage of subjects who administered 450-volt shocks plummeted from 65 percent to 10 percent.

The take-away lesson, says Kerry Patterson and colleagues (2008, p. 143), is that "it took just one person to turn the tide of compliance."

In any change effort, the behaviours of individuals influence the group's likelihood of success. But when it comes to influence, not all individuals and all behaviours are created equal. Patterson and colleagues report,

> *To harness the immense power of social support, sometimes you need to find only one respected individual who will fly in the face of history and model the new and healthier vital behaviours.*
>
> (2008, p. 143)

Researcher Everett Rogers (1983) is credited with determining which people in a group will be most influential. After obtaining a Ph.D in sociology and statistics, Rogers was hired to encourage Iowa farmers to use new and improved strains of corn. His research, however, had either no impact or a negative impact on the farmers who considered him an ivory tower intellectual with no practical experience to support his claims.

So Rogers found one farmer who would try the new corn. The farmer was "a rather hip fellow who actually wore Bermuda shorts and drove a Cadillac. He had a proclivity for embracing innovation, so he tried the new strains of corn and enjoyed a bumper crop" (Patterson et al., 2008, p. 147). Unfortunately, while he may have been a farmer, he was so different from the others that he wasn't seen as any more credible than Rogers, the academic.

Rogers' discovery, confirmed by looking at everything from how doctors start administering new drugs to how new technologies become popular, was that the people who are always first to adopt an innovation are not the people who will influence the majority. Rather, influencers are found among the 13.5 percent of the population who are the second group to try an innovation. These people are known as "early adopters" and "opinion leaders." What makes this group different from those first to adopt is that opinion leaders are respected and socially connected.

Opinion leaders also share the following characteristics:
- knowledgeable about the proposed change
- dedicated to using their knowledge to help rather than manipulate their colleagues.
- willing to spend the time in frequent face-to-face dialogue with their colleagues.

Who Has Influence?

Research
Spotlight on *Influencer*

If you are responsible for facilitating adult learning, it is vital that you work with opinion leaders. They are the people who will make or break any change effort. Talk with colleagues about successful and unsuccessful change efforts you have experienced, identifying the relative impacts of those who are first to adopt an innovation and the opinion leaders. Do you agree with Rogers' findings? Is it possible for a person to be both a first adopter and an opinion leader?

For an interesting perspective on the role of influence, see the website for my review of the book *Influencer: The Power to Change Anything* by Kerry Patterson and colleagues.

Of course, opinion leaders are helpful in a change effort only if there is a clear purpose that is motivating the group, and if specific behaviours have been identified. These behaviours must be *vital* ones—the high-leverage actions that spell out what people will actually do in order to achieve their desired purpose (see page 211). Your school's vision will help you determine which behaviours are vital.

Crafting a Vision

We can teach ourselves to see things the way they are. Only with vision can we begin to see things the way they can be.
—*Max DePree*

A vision is a narrative with clear indicators of success. As discussed on pages 106–107, we are drawn towards what we visualize. Just as race car drivers are instructed that when their car is out of control and headed for a wall, they should look at the recovery point and not the wall (Tice, 1999), we need to create and keep in mind a clear and compelling vision of what success looks like relative to the purpose we have established. We should *not* craft a vision statement based on what we think might be achievable under present conditions.

If your purpose, mission, and vision are related to engagement—and I'm assuming they are—you will want to consider including indicators of success for one or more of the different aspects of engagement discussed in this book. With thanks to Daniel Pink (2009), from whom I borrowed the idea, here is a Twitter summary of each of the first six sections of *Tuned Out*.

Section 1: Seeking
Whether you measure attendance, connection, or academics, too many students are disengaged. So are their teachers. We need a 21st c. plan.

Section 2: Competence
Engagement happens when our basic needs are satisfied and our competencies recognized. Having a growth mindset helps, too.

Section 3: Creativity
Creativity and innovation are essentials in our 21st c. world. Creative thinking makes a positive difference to engagement.

Section 4: Community
Adolescents are social beings who make varied use of social network sites. Both students and teachers need a sense of community.

Section 5: Context
Technology engages, but that counts only if it is in the service of learning. Many factors combine to create effective 21st c. rat parks.

Section 6: Challenge
Even the most reluctant learner wants challenge. The trick is to provide worthy challenges that meet the conditions of flow.

Triarchic Intelligences and Visioning

If you haven't already done so, consider completing the triarchic intelligences inventory on the website. Use it to determine your preference for one of the following three vision crafting activities.

Resources
Triarchic Intelligences Inventory

- √ Analytical—Review the sections of *Tuned Out* that relate to your purpose. Create checklists of indicators of success, checking each indicator against your mission statement. Make sure the indicators are written in enough detail that it will be easy to determine whether or not they are achieved.

√ Practical—Review student and school data to determine where there is the greatest potential for improvement relative to your purpose. Write a vision statement for that specific area, and make sure it includes the indicators of success teachers would see in a typical classroom day.

√ Creative—Respond to the prompts "What I'd really like to see…" and "It would be great if…" using any combination of text, images, and sounds to create a multimodal vision statement that paints a vivid picture of success indicators.

Your 140

Conversations
Tweet Us

Now that you are almost finished reading *Tuned Out*, how would you summarize this book in no more than 140 characters? Share your summary online through the website or, if you are a twitterer, please feel free to tweet it to the world.

Summary of Chapter Website Content		www.pearsoncanada.ca/tunedout
Conversations	**Resources**	**Research**
• Share Your Mission • Tweet Us	• Wordle • Triarchic Intelligences Inventory	• Twitter for Educators • Spotlight on *Influencer*

14 The Road Ahead

Two dozen years ago, I was browsing in a bookstore when I stumbled across a book that changed my teaching practice forever. I picked it up because I thought, then and now, that the title was the best description of teaching I'd ever read. The book is called *Sometimes a Shining Moment*, and it is the account of English teacher Eliot Wigginton's 20 years of teaching in a high school classroom.

Wigginton taught in Rabun Gap, a small community in the Appalachian Mountains of northeastern Georgia. The school was a combination of a boarding school with a religious orientation and a day school for students from the local community. Wigginton described the school in a letter to a friend:

> Just for starters, imagine creating a situation where a hundred adolescents are jerked out of a home situation that more often than not had been urban, fast-paced, and permissive, and plopped down in the middle of what to many of them seems a deathly quiet, maddeningly dull rural wasteland. Now complicate things further by making them adolescents who...are perceived as being primarily in need of that discipline which parents have been unable to provide. To meet this need, you create a school filled with rules and regulations governing every aspect of the students' lives....Now make it co-ed....And just to make things interesting, add 140 adolescents from the community and put them in daily classes with your captive population....Twist things a little further by making them country kids who deer hunt, squirrel hunt, dress funny, [and] talk funnier....
>
> (1985, p. 13)

To say that his students were highly disengaged would be a bit of an understatement. After many failed attempts, Wigginton decided to try engaging his students in authentic reasons for developing their communication skills: they would create a school magazine called *Foxfire*. To make connections to the experiences of students from the local community and to honour local knowledge and traditions, *Foxfire* contained not just poetry and school news, but also folklore, first-person accounts, and detailed instructions on how to do everything from cultivate ginseng to build a log cabin—all gathered by students who interviewed, watched, and worked alongside adults from the community.

Students published the first *Foxfire* magazine in 1966. The work was done on manual typewriters and duplicated on a mimeograph machine. Over the next 20 years, as interest in preserving the traditions of the people of the Appalachian Mountains increased, major publishers and foundations became involved. Ultimately, Wigginton and his students published 12 anthologies of articles from the magazine, as well as a series of special interest books such as *The Foxfire Book of Appalachian Toys and Games* and *The Foxfire Book of Appalachian Cookery*. The project also expanded to *Foxfire* collections of authentic Appalachian music and demonstration videos. It even inspired a major Broadway play called *Foxfire*.

I found *Sometimes a Shining Moment* as satisfying as its title because Wigginton gave an unvarnished account of the development of *Foxfire*, mistakes and all. He eloquently described the challenges he encountered as his program began to receive national attention, and as he fought to keep student learning and decision making at its centre. Wigginton's project-based approach to teaching impressed me, and the reflections he offered about his own learning inspired me.

When I'm inspired by something in education, I have a tendency to leap into the deep end of the pool. So perhaps it's not surprising that on the first school day in September 1993, I stood in front of the students in my combined Grade 7/8 class and told them that throughout our entire year together, all of our learning would happen within a project I called *Focus on Technology*.

Of course, in 1993 there wasn't anything like the technology we have today. (I do realize that young teachers will now expect me to say that I also walked to school uphill, in the snow, in my bare feet—I didn't!) When I referred to technology, I was talking about six different sets of "media tools": art, photography, video/film, sound, computers, and print. My thinking was that if we became literate in the uses and limitations of each of these media tools, we could study different perspectives on any topic through all six tools. We could also use these tools to create high quality responses and products.

I say "we" because the only media tool I was really familiar with was print. I'd never used a camcorder, never developed a photograph, and had used a computer only for word processing. My students were in a similar situation—when I asked who had used a computer during the previous week, only 37 percent of them had (and only to play games).

My students and I were truly going to be learning together, which was exactly what I wanted. I feel most alive when I am learning, and I needed to feel alive. The year before *Focus on Technology* had been my first year teaching in the intermediate division. I've written about that in the blog post, "Not Just in Training" (noted in Chapter 11). Additionally, though we were in the early days of computers in the classroom, the rhetoric about their usefulness in education was already at a fever pitch. Since there was little available in the way of educational software, I had plenty of opportunity to test my theory that if we gave adolescents access to the tools that (at the time) were being used only by adults, and if adults taught them how to use the tools effectively, students would be capable of so much more than we adults tended to believe.

I have a vivid memory of that first day when I announced that we were going to embark on this exciting adventure together. The students weren't engaged—at best they were skeptical; at worst, upset. Some of the rites of passage that these adolescents had come to expect from school were being disrupted. The Grade 7s had been looking forward to lockers (which they got) and to a timetable of separate subjects, each with a different teacher. My colleagues and I had decided to teach our own students as much as possible so that our work could be interdisciplinary and project-based.

The Grade 8s were upset because they were in a combined class. One student said, "Being in a 7/8 class last year, I saw all of the things the Grade 8s did, and I am watching to see if the program will stay the same or if it will change."

"I am watching." That statement summed up the attitude of my students, their parents, and my colleagues and administrators at the school. My enthusiasm was keeping the wolves at bay, but I knew I had to act fast in order to gain my students' trust and move them from their position as dispassionate and somewhat disgruntled observers to that of engaged participants. It wasn't going to be easy. *Focus on Technology* had minimal technology that first week.

I had spent the summer trying to scrounge equipment. I'd managed to beg a single computer and a dot matrix printer from my principal, and six basic cameras from a manufacturer. I was teaching in the art room so I had plenty of art supplies, and I knew I could borrow camcorders from the district's media centre. In early August I had finally convinced a major computer company to loan me six computers—they reneged on their commitment the day before school began. In the middle of September, relatives and friends of relatives took pity on me and loaned me their entry-level computers.

The first project was relatively technology-free. I had my students interview seniors in the local community. To prepare them for this work we did a walking tour of the community with a guide from the Local Architectural Conservation Authority, and we practised interview techniques as a whole class—first with each other, and then with a local artist. Armed with tape recorders, notepads, and reminders about being polite, students set off with partners to interview their "contacts." When they returned, we debriefed the experience, generating a list of "Top Ten Tips for Interviewing." (The #1 tip was "Make sure the equipment works.")

I knew that being trusted to walk to a house a few doors from the school and interview someone would engage students, but if the activity was to serve the goal of intellectual engagement with curriculum objectives, there needed to be a relevant purpose for the interviews.

To achieve this, I had prearranged with the publisher of the local newspaper to print a special four-page "Voices in the Village" insert featuring short articles written by my students. The publisher found advertisers who were happy to support the cost of the additional pages, so he gave me a deadline for the articles and reminded me that his reputation with his advertisers was riding on a bunch of teenagers coming through on time with quality work.

That proved to be a bit of a problem. Students finished their interviews a few days before the newspaper deadline and wrote their articles. The first drafts were terrible. I took them home that night, figured out what I hadn't taught that I should have, and went back the next day and taught it. That lesson—which was about focusing on a main idea, writing a strong lead, and quoting an interview subject fairly and accurately—had an impact on every student in my class. They were being trusted by adults to do real work, and that work was going to be published. They were determined not to disappoint the publisher, their interview contacts, me, their peers, or themselves.

All that day and into the early evening, the students worked together as I circulated from group to group. They voluntarily wrote and rewrote their articles until they were satisfied. Students who hadn't brought their lunches to school either called home and asked for them to be delivered or dashed home, ate quickly, and came back to school to keep working.

We celebrated the publication of "Voices in the Village" by inviting all of our interviewees, along with the students' parents, to an evening tea at the school. Students presented each interviewee with a carnation and a laminated copy of the newspaper insert, and gave a short speech of appreciation for the participation of the interviewee. In return, students were told by interviewees, parents, the newspaper publisher, and school administration that their work was impressive. Several people admitted that they hadn't thought the students had it in them, and they now realized they were wrong. My students glowed with pride.

Our learning community coalesced because of the "Voices in the Village" project. From that point on, my students saw themselves as people who could successfully meet any challenge. They trusted that if I asked them to do something really difficult—often something I didn't know how to do myself—we would work it out together.

We had some incredible opportunities that year. People were captivated by what we were trying to do, so doors opened for us. In the equipment line, we ultimately got a small darkroom so we could develop photos (digital cameras were not yet inexpensive and readily available), and the school paid for a colour printer, a small video editing suite, and a phone line into the classroom. We particularly needed the last item—the phone was a lifeline to an expert when something wasn't working or when a student wanted to try something new. It gave us access to the many professionals in the various forms of media who were more than willing to help students with their projects.

The equipment, however, was almost incidental to our success. What I learned from that year was that school could be an exhilarating experience when learning was the focus for both students and teacher, when our work was of real consequence, and when students had the opportunity to work alongside adults. I also learned that when intellectual engagement and emotional engagement were in place, school process engagement wasn't an issue. Parents had trouble convincing their children to stay home when they were ill and difficulty getting them to come home at night. I was delighted when students would call their parents on a Tuesday at 4:30 to ask permission to keep working, and parents would quip, "Okay, but I want you home by Friday!"

The *Focus on Technology* year was the most exhilarating of my career. I will always be grateful for that experience because I learned so many important lessons about both student and teacher engagement.

However, you will remember that I began this book by describing two roads through the woods of student and teacher disengagement, and urging that we look for a third—a road of moderation. There was no moderation during the *Focus on Technology* year. I don't remember sleeping. I lived on Diet Coke, fast food, and pure exhilaration. I gave that year everything I had, and when the next year's students arrived, I had nothing left to give. That was the year I talk about in "Michelle Made Me Crazy" (the blog post noted in Chapter 7), and I am as keen to forget being burned out as I am to remember being on fire.

Ultimately, what I have learned about student and teacher engagement is that it comes down to the teacher—to the integrity of being what you believe. Whether you are teaching students or adults, the only way to gain trust is to be real: to live your belief that the dignity and potential of the individual learner is paramount, and that your job is to help every learner be amazing.

What road through the woods will you choose? Whatever choice you make, be prepared for obstacles along the way. In stories and in life, nothing worthwhile has ever happened without the hero being tested—by all manner of alligators that appear along the way, or by a challenge that seems impossible, as in the following story based on a traditional tale.

After a long career in which he had achieved great success, a captain of industry was looking for someone wise enough to replace him when he retired. He asked his Human Resources Department to prepare a list of the best of the best, both from within his organization and beyond. Then he invited all of these people to gather at a grand palace he had rented for the occasion.

Standing in front of the palace door, he addressed the group: "I'm sure you are wondering why I have brought you here. The time has come for me to choose a successor, someone with the wisdom to preserve and build upon my achievements." At this, excited murmurs ran through the crowd, for this was a once-in-a-lifetime opportunity.

The captain of industry continued: "To select the person who will replace me, I have devised a challenge. The door you see behind me is the biggest, mightiest, heaviest door in all the land. Who among you has the wisdom to figure out how to open the door without any assistance?"

Some people immediately assumed that the door was locked and just shook their heads. Others estimated the door's dimensions in order to calculate its immense weight. A few tried to apply theories of effective problem solving, but to no avail. "It just can't be done," people began to whisper.

Soon every single person had given up—except one.

All eyes were on the one brave soul who walked up to the door, examined it closely with hands and eyes, took a deep breath, and gently pulled on the handle. Because the door had been left ever so slightly ajar, it swung open easily.

The captain of industry then turned his eyes away from the door and addressed the group. "Success in life and work depends on five ways of approaching the world," he said, "and my successor has just demonstrated them."

"Rely on your senses, not just your intellect, to understand the world around you.

Check your assumptions.

Have the courage to act with boldness and conviction.

Put your powers into action.

And do not be afraid to make mistakes."

The wonderful thing about being educators is that no matter how experienced we are, there is always room to grow—and there are always new challenges that require us to grow in our practice. Engaging today's students in a curriculum that will prepare them for a future we can't clearly see is just such a challenge, and one that, at times, might seem as impossible as opening the massive door in the story. It is my hope that this book, along with the website material, will help you find the road that is right for you and will embolden you to stride up to the door and open it—not only for yourself, but for those who rely on you to show them the way.

References

Alexander, B., Beyerstein, B., Hadaway, P., & Coambs, R. Effect of early and later colony housing on oral ingestion of morphine in rats. *Pharmacology, Biochemistry & Behavior, 13*, 571–576. Retrieved from http://sciencethatmatters.com/wp-content/uploads/2007/02/sdarticle.pdf

Anderson, N. J. (2002). *The role of metacognition in second language teaching and learning*. Washington, DC: ERIC Clearinghouse on Language and Linguistics. Retrieved from http://www.cal.org/resources/digest/0110anderson.html

Antonietti, A. (1999). Can students predict when imagery will allow them to discover the problem solution? *European Journal of Cognitive Psychology, 11*, 407–428.

Apple. (2008). *Apple Classrooms of Tomorrow—Today: Learning in the 21st century* [Background information]. Retrieved from http://ali.apple.com/acot2/global/files/ACOT2_Background.pdf

Applebee, A. N., Langer, J., Nystrand, M., & Gamoran, A. (2003). Discussion-based approaches to developing understanding: Classroom instruction and student performance in middle and high school English. *American Educational Research Journal*, Fall.

Ariely, D. (2008). *Predictably irrational: The hidden forces that shape our decisions*. New York, NY: HarperCollins.

Aronson, E. (2000). *Nobody left to hate: Teaching compassion after Columbine*. New York, NY: W.H. Freeman.

Assor, A., Kaplan, H., & Roth, G. (2002). Choice is good, but relevance is excellent: Autonomy-enhancing and suppressing teacher behaviours predicting students' engagement in schoolwork. *British Journal of Educational Psychology, 72*, 261–278.

Atkinson, R. K., Catrambone, R., & Merrill, M. M. (2003). Aiding transfer in statistics: Examining the use of conceptually oriented equations and elaborations during subgoal learning. *Journal of Educational Psychology, 95*, 762–763.

Ayers, W. (2001). *To teach: The journey of a teacher*. New York, NY: Teachers College Press.

Baird, A. A., Gruber, S. A., Fein, D. A., Maas, L. C., Steingard, R. J., Renshaw, P. F., & Yurgelun-Todd, D. A. (1999). Functional magnetic resonance imaging of facial affect recognition in children and adolescents. *Journal of the American Academy of Child and Adolescent Psychiatry, 38*(2), 195–199.

Baker, F. W. (2010). Media literacy: 21st century literacy skills. In H. H. Jacobs (Ed.), *Curriculum 21: Essential education for a changing world* (pp. 133–152). Alexandria, VA: ASCD.

Baltes, P., Lindenberger, U., & Staudinger, U. (2006). Life span theory in developmental psychology. In W. Damon & R. Lerner (Eds.), *Handbook of child psychology: Theoretical models of human development* (6th ed., Vol. 1, pp. 569–664). New York, NY: Wiley.

Bamford, A. (2003). *The visual literacy white paper*. Retrieved from http://www.adobe.com/uk/education/pdf/adobe_visual_literacy_paper.pdf

Barth, R. (1990). *Improving schools from within*. San Francisco, CA: Jossey-Bass.

Bauerlain, M. (2009). *The dumbest generation: How the digital age stupefies young Americans and jeopardizes our future*. Toronto: Penguin.

Baylor, A., & Ritchie, D. (2002). What factors facilitate teacher skill, teacher morale, and perceived student learning in technology-using classrooms? *Computers and Education, 39*(4), 395–414.

Begley, S. (2007). *Train your mind, change your brain*. New York, NY: Ballantine.

Bennis, W., & Biederman, P. (1998). *Organizing genius: The secrets of creative collaboration*. New York, NY: Basic Books.

Berns, G. (2005). *Satisfaction: Sensation seeking, novelty, and the science of finding true fulfillment*. New York, NY: Henry Holt and Company.

Bluestein, J. (2001). *Creating emotionally safe schools: A guide for educators and parents*. Deerfield Beach, FL: Health Communications.

Bosworth, K. (1995). Caring for others and being cared for: Students talk about caring in school. *Phi Delta Kappan, 76*(9), 686–693.

Bowen, C. W. (2000). A quantitative literature review of cooperative learning effects on high school and college chemistry achievement. *Journal of Chemical Education, 77*(1), 116–119.

Bricker, D., & Wright, J. (2009). *We know what you're thinking*. Toronto: HarperCollins.

Brooks-Young, S. (2007). *Digital-age literacy for teachers: Applying technology standards to everyday practice.* Washington, DC: International Society for Technology in Education.

Brown, J. S., Collins, A., & Duguid, P. (1989). Situated cognition and the culture of learning. *Educational Researcher, 18*(1), 32–42.

Brown, S., & Vaughn, C. (2009). *Play: How it shapes the brain, opens the imagination, and invigorates the soul.* Toronto: Penguin.

Buckley, J., Schneider, M., & Shang, Y. (2005). Fix it and they might stay: School facility quality and teacher retention in Washington, D.C. *Teachers College Record, 107*(5), 1107–1123.

Burke, J. (1995). *Connections.* Toronto: Little, Brown.

Buzan, T. (2005). *The ultimate book of mind maps.* London, England: Thorsons.

Chapman, E. (2003). Alternative approaches to assessing student engagement rates. *Practical Assessment, Research and Evaluation, 8*(13). Retrieved from http://PAREonline.net/getvn.asp?v=8&n=13

Chen, J. (2006). *Flow in games.* Retrieved from http://www.jenovachen.com/flowingames/Flow_in_games_final.pdf

Cherry, D., & Spiegel, J. (2006). *Leadership, myth, and metaphor: Finding common ground to guide effective school change.* Thousand Oaks, CA: Corwin.

Christensen, C. M., Horn, M. B., & Johnson, C. W. (2008). *Disrupting class: How disruptive innovation will change the way the world learns.* Toronto: McGraw Hill.

City, E. A., Elmore, R. F., Fiarman, S., & Teitel, L. (2009). *Instructional rounds in education: A network approach to improving teaching and learning.* Cambridge, MA: Harvard Education Press.

Coiro, J., & Dobler, E. (2007). Exploring the online reading comprehension strategies used by sixth-grade skilled readers to search for and locate information on the Internet. *Reading Research Quarterly, 42,* 214–257.

Colan, L. (2009). *Engaging the hearts and minds of all your employees.* Toronto: McGraw-Hill.

Collins, J. (2001). *Good to great: Why some companies make the leap...and others don't.* New York, NY: HarperCollins.

Cornett, C. E., & Smithrim, K. L. (2001). *The arts as meaning makers: Integrating literature and the arts throughout the curriculum* (Canadian ed.). Toronto: Pearson Canada.

Cotton, K. (1989). *Expectations and student outcomes* (School Improvement Research Series, Close-up #7). Retrieved from Northwest Regional Educational Laboratory website: http://www.nwrel.org/scpd/sirs/4/cu7.html

Csikszentmihalyi, M. (1990). *Flow: The psychology of optimal experience.* New York, NY: HarperCollins.

Csikszentmihalyi, M. (1996). *Creativity: Flow and the psychology of discovery and invention.* New York, NY: HarperCollins.

Csikszentmihalyi, M. (1997). *Finding flow: The psychology of engagement with everyday life.* New York, NY: Basic Books.

Csikszentmihalyi, M. (2003). *Good business: Leadership, flow, and the making of meaning.* Toronto: Penguin.

Csikszentmihalyi, M., & Larson, R. (1984). *Being adolescent: Conflict and growth in the teenage years.* New York, NY: Basic Books.

Curran, A. (2008). *The little book of big stuff about the brain: The true story of your amazing brain.* Bethel, CT: Crown House.

Daly, J. (2004). *Life on the screen: Visual literacy in education.* Retrieved from http://www.edutopia.org/life-screen

Danielson, C. (2009). *Talk about teaching! Leading professional conversations.* Thousand Oaks, CA: Corwin.

Dannetta, V. (2002). What factors influence a teacher's commitment to student learning? *Leadership and Policy in Schools, 1*(2), 144–171.

Day, C. (2004). *A passion for teaching.* London, England: RoutledgeFarmer.

Deal, T. E., & Peterson, K. D. (2009). *Shaping school culture: Pitfalls, paradoxes, & promises* (2nd ed.). San Francisco, CA: John Wiley & Sons.

Deci, E., Koestner, R., & Ryan, R. (2001). Extrinsic rewards and intrinsic motivation in education: Reconsidered once again. *Review of Educational Research, 71,* 1–27.

Dede, C. (2010). Learning, no matter where you are. *Journal of Staff Development, 31*(1), 10–17.

Dweck, C. (2006). *Mindset: The new psychology of success.* Toronto: Random House.

Erwin, J. C. (2004). *The classroom of choice: Giving students what they need and getting what you want.* Alexandria, VA: ASCD.

Feinstein, S. (2004). *Secrets of the teenage brain: Research-based strategies for reaching & teaching today's adolescents.* Thousand Oaks, CA: Corwin Press.

Ferguson, B., Tilleczek, K., Boydell, K., Rummens, K., Edney, D., & Michaud, J. (2005). *Early school leavers: Understanding the lived reality of student disengagement from secondary school.* Toronto: Ontario Ministry of Education and Training, Special Education Branch.

Ferguson, M. (1980). *The aquarian conspiracy.* Los Angeles, CA: J. P. Tarcher.

Ferriter, B. (2009). Taking the digital plunge. *Educational Leadership, 67*(1), 85–86.

Fisher, D., & Frey, N. (2008). *Better learning through structured teaching: A framework for the gradual release of responsibility.* Alexandria, VA: ASCD.

Fisher, D., & Frey, N. (2009). *Background knowledge: The missing piece of the comprehension puzzle*. Portsmouth, NH: Heinemann.

Flowers, N., Mertens, S., & Mulhall, P. (2000). What makes interdisciplinary teams effective? *Middle School Journal, 31*(6), 53–56.

Friedman, T. L. (2005). *The world is flat: A brief history of the twenty-first century*. New York: Farrar, Straus, & Giroux.

Fuster, J. M. (2003). *Cortex and mind: Unifying cognition*. New York, NY: Oxford University Press.

Gallup. (2008). *Employee engagement: What's your engagement ratio?* Retrieved from http://www.gallup.com/consulting/121535/Employee-Engagement-Overview-Brochure.aspx

Gallup. (2009). *Engagement research flyer*. Retrieved from http://www.gallupstudentpoll.com/122186/Engagement-Research-Flyer-August-2009.aspx

Gardner, H. (2006) *Changing minds: The art and science of changing our own and other people's minds*. Boston, MA: Harvard Business School Press.

Gardner, H. (2008). *5 Minds for the Future*. Boston, MA: Harvard Business Press.

Gee, J. P. (2007). *What video games have to teach us about learning and literacy*. New York: Palgrave Macmillan.

Geving, A. M. (2007). Identifying the types of student and teacher behaviours associated with teacher stress. *Teaching and Teacher Education, 23*, 624–640.

Gilbert, I. (2008). *The book of thunks*. Bethel, CT: Crown House.

Gillies, R. M. (2008). The effects of cooperative learning on junior high school students' behaviours, discourse, and learning during a science-based learning activity. *School Psychology International, 29*(3), 328–347.

Glasser, W. (1986). *Control theory in the classroom*. New York, NY: Harper and Row.

Goleman, D. (2006). *Emotional intelligence: Why it can matter more than IQ* (10th ed.). New York: Bantam.

Gollwitzer, P. (1999). Implementation intentions: Strong effects of simple plans. *American Psychologist, 54*, 493–503.

Goodlad, J. (2004). *A place called school* (20th anniversary ed.). Toronto: McGraw-Hill.

Gopnik, A., Meltzoff, A., & Kuhl, P. (1999). *The scientist in the crib: Minds, brains, and how children learn*. New York, NY: William Morrow.

Grandin, T. (2006). *Thinking in pictures: My life with autism* (Rev. ed.). Toronto: Random House.

Hallinan, J. T. (2009). *Why we make mistakes*. New York, NY: Broadway Books.

Hammond, C., Smink, J., & Drew, S. (2007). *Dropout risk factors and exemplary programs: A technical report*. Clemson, SC: National Dropout Prevention Center/Network. Retrieved from www.dropoutprevention.org/resource/major_reports/communities_in_schools.htm

Harvey, S., & Daniels, H. (2009). *Comprehension and collaboration: Inquiry circles in action*. Portsmouth, NH: Heinemann.

Haury, D. & Rillero, P. (1994). *Perspectives on hands-on science teaching*. Retrieved from http://www.ncrel.org/sdrs/areas/issues/content/cntareas/science/eric/eric-1.htm

Heath, C., & Heath, D. (2007). *Made to stick: Why some ideas survive and others die*. New York, NY: Random House.

Heath, C., & Heath, D. (2010). *Switch: How to change things when change is hard*. Toronto: Random House.

Hogan, K., Nastasi, B. K., & Pressley, M. (1999). Discourse patterns and collaborative scientific reasoning in peer and teacher-guided discussions. *Cognition & Instruction, 17*(4), 379–432.

Horst, H., Herr-Stephenson, B., & Robinson, L. (2010). Media ecologies. In M. Ito et al., *Hanging out, messing around, and geeking out: Kids living and learning with new media*. Cambridge, MA: Massachusetts Institute of Technology.

House, J. D. (2005). Classroom instruction and science achievement in Japan, Hong Kong, and Chinese Taipei: Results from the TIMSS 1999 assessment. *International Journal of Instructional Media, 32*(3), 295–311.

Huberman, M. (1993). *The lives of teachers*. New York, NY: Teachers College Press.

Human Resources and Skills Development Canada (HRSDC). Indicators of well-being in Canada. Retrieved from http://www4.hrsdc.gc.ca/.3ndic.1t.4r@-eng.jsp?iid=32

Hurley, S., & Charter, N. (Eds.). (2005). *Perspectives on imitation: From neuroscience to social science* (Vols. 1–2). Cambridge, MA: MIT Press.

Ito, M., Baumer, S., Bittanti, M., boyd, d., Cody, R., Herr-Stephenson, B., & Tripp, L. (2010). *Hanging out, messing around, and geeking out: Kids living and learning with new media*. Cambridge, MA: Massachusetts Institute of Technology.

Iyengar, S., & Lepper, M. (2000). When choice is demotivating: Can one desire too much of a good thing? *Journal of Personality and Social Psychology, 79*, 995–1006.

Jackson, A. W., & Davis, G. A. (2000). *Turning points 2000: Educating adolescents in the 21st century*. New York, NY: Teachers College Press.

Jacobs, H. H. (2010). New school versions: Reinventing and reuniting school program structures. In H. H. Jacobs (Ed.), *Curriculum 21: Essential education for a changing world* (pp. 60–79). Alexandria, VA: ASCD.

Jarvis, J. (2009). *What would Google do?* New York, NY: HarperCollins.

Jensen, E. (1998). *Teaching with the brain in mind*. Alexandria, VA: ASCD.

Jensen, E. (2001). *Arts with the brain in mind*. Alexandria, VA: ASCD.

Jeroski, S. (2007). *Research report: The wireless writing program 2004–2007*. Retrieved from http://www.prn.bc.ca/documents/WWP/WWP_finalreport2007.pdf

Johnson, L. F., Smith, R. S., Smythe, J. T., & Varon, R. K. (2009). *Challenge-based learning: An approach for our time*. Austin, TX: The New Media Consortium. Retrieved from www.nmc.org/publications/challenge-based-learning

Jukes, I. (2009). Did you know #1? Quick facts you might find interesting. Retrieved from http://committedsardine.com/blogpost.cfm?blogID=277&utm_source=Committed+Sardine+Blog+Update&utm_campaign=91287caefc-Blog_Update_Aug_28&utm_medium=email

Kahneman, D. (2000). Experienced utility and objective happiness: A moment-based approach. In D. Kahneman & A. Tversky (Eds.), *Choice, values and frames* (pp. 673–692). New York, NY: Cambridge University Press and the Russell Sage Foundation.

Kajder, S. B. (2003). *The tech-savvy English classroom*. Portland, ME: Stenhouse.

Kashdan, T. (2009). *Curious? Discover the missing ingredient to a fulfilling life*. New York, NY: HarperCollins.

Keene, E., & Zimmerman, S. (1997). *Mosaic of thought: Teaching comprehension in a reader's workshop*. Portsmouth, NH: Heinemann.

Kelly, K. (2006, May 14). Scan this book! *New York Times*. Retrieved from http://www.nytimes.com/2006/05/14/magazine/14publishing.html?_r=2&oref=slogin&pagewanted=all

Klem, A. M., & Connell, J. P. (2004). Relationships matter: Linking teacher support to student engagement and achievement. *Journal of School Health, 74*, 262–273.

Klusmann, U., Kunter, M., Trautwein, U., Ludtke, O., & Baumert, J. (2008). Engagement and emotional exhaustion in teachers: Does the school context make a difference? *Applied Psychology, 57*, 127–151.

Langer, E. (1989). Minding matters. In L. Berkowitz (Ed.), *Advances in experimental social psychology* (p. 22). New York, NY: Academic Press.

Lau, J., & Lazarus, W. (2002). *Pathways to our future: A multimedia training program for youth that works*. Santa Monica, CA: The Children's Partnership.

LeDoux, J. (2003). The emotional brain, fear, and the amygdala. *Cellular and Molecular Neurobiology, 23*(4–5), 727–738.

Leithwood, K., & Beatty, B. (2008). *Leading with teacher emotions in mind*. Thousand Oaks, CA: Corwin Press.

Lenhart, A., Kahne, J., Middaugh, E., Macgill, A., Evans, C., & Vitak, J. (2008). *Teens, video games and civics*. Retrieved from http://www.pewinternet.org/Reports/2008/Teens-Video-Games-and-Civics.aspx

Levin, B. (2008). *How to change 5000 schools: A practical and positive approach for leading change at every level*. Cambridge, MA: Harvard Education Press.

Lieras, C. (2008). Do skills and behaviours in high school matter? The contribution of non-cognitive factors in explaining differences in educational achievement and earnings. *Social Science Research, 37*(3), 888–902.

Lundy, K. G. (2004). *What do I do about the kid who…? 50 ways to turn teaching into learning*. Markham, ON: Pembroke.

Maich, S., & George, L. (2009). *The ego boom: Why the world really does revolve around you*. Toronto: Key Porter Books.

Marchese, T. (1998). The new conversations about learning: Insights from neuroscience and anthropology, cognitive science and workplace studies. Retrieved from http://www.newhorizons.org/lifelong/higher_ed/marchese.htm

Martin, R. (2007). *The opposable mind: How successful leaders win through integrative thinking*. Boston, MA: Harvard Business School Press.

Marzano, R., Pickering, D., & Pollock, J. (2001). *Classroom instruction that works*. Alexandria, VA: ASCD.

McAdams, D. (2001). Generativity in midlife. In M. Lachman (Ed.), *Handbook of midlife development* (pp. 395–443). New York, NY: John Wiley.

McCain, T. (2005). *Teaching for tomorrow: Teaching content and problem-solving skills*. Thousand Oaks, CA: Corwin Press.

McGivern, R. F., Andersen, J., Byrd, D., Mutter, K. L., & Reilly, J. (2002). Cognitive efficiency on a match to sample task decreases at the onset of puberty in children. *Brain and Cognition, 50*(1), 73–89.

McMillan, D. W., & Chavis, D. M. (1986). Sense of community: A definition and theory. *American Journal of Community Psychology, 14*(1), 6–23.

Medina, J. (2008). *Brain rules: 12 principles for surviving and thriving at work, home, and school*. Seattle, WA: Pear Press.

Mendelson, M. (2006). *Aboriginal peoples and post-secondary education in Canada*. Ottawa: Caledon Institute of Social Policy.

Mendler, A. N. (2000). *Motivating students who don't care: Successful techniques for educators*. Bloomington, IN: National Educational Service.

Michalko, M. (2001). *Cracking creativity: The secrets of creative genius*. Berkeley, CA: Ten Speed Press.

Michalko, M. (2006). *Thinkertoys: A handbook of creative-thinking techniques* (2nd ed.). Toronto: Ten Speed Press.

Milgram, S. (1963) Behavioral Study of Obedience. *Journal of Abnormal and Social Psychology, 67*, 371–378.

Milgram, S. (1974) *Obedience to authority: An experimental view.* New York, NY: Harper and Row.

Morgan, N., & Saxton, J. (2006). Asking better questions (2nd ed.). Markham, ON: Pembroke.

Myers, C. B., & Simpson, D. J. (1998). *Re-creating schools: Places where everyone learns and likes it.* Thousand Oaks, CA: Corwin.

Newmann, F., & Wehlage, G. (1993). Five standards for authentic instruction. *Educational Leadership, 50*(7), 8–12. Retrieved from http://pdonline.ascd.org/pd_online/diffinstr/el199304_newmann.html

Nunley, K. F. (2003). *A student's brain: The parent/teacher manual.* Kearney, NE: Morris.

Oettingen, G., & Gollwitzer, P. M. (2002). Self-regulation of goal pursuit: Turning hope thoughts into behaviour. *Psychological Inquiry, 13*, 304–307.

Owen, N. (2007). *More magic of metaphor: Stories for leaders, influencers and motivators.* Bethel, CT: Crown House.

Owen, N. (2008). *The magic of metaphor: 77 stories for teachers, trainers & thinkers.* Bethel, CT: Crown House.

Palincsar, A. S., & Brown, A. L. (1984). Reciprocal teaching of comprehension-fostering and comprehension-monitoring activities. *Cognition and Instruction, 1*, 117–175.

Palmer, P. (1998). *The courage to teach: Exploring the inner landscape of a teacher's life.* San Francisco, CA: Jossey-Bass.

Palmer, P. (2009). *A hidden wholeness: The journey toward an undivided life.* San Francisco, CA: Jossey-Bass.

Papert, S. (2002, August 24). How to make writing "hard fun." *Bangor Daily News*, p. A7. Retrieved from www.papert.org/articles/HardFun.html

Partnership for 21st Century Skills. (2004). *Framework for 21st century learning.* Retrieved from http://www.p21.org/index.php?option=com_content&task=view&id=254&Itemid=119

Patterson, K., Grenny, J., McMillan, R., & Switzler, A. (2002). *Crucial conversations: Tools for talking when stakes are high.* Toronto: McGraw-Hill.

Patterson, K., Grenny, J., Maxfield, D., McMillan, R., & Switzler, A. (2008). *Influencer: The power to change anything.* Toronto: McGraw-Hill.

Pearson, P. D., & Gallagher, G. (1983). The gradual release of responsibility model of instruction. *Contemporary Educational Psychology, 8*, 112–123.

Pichert, J. W., & Anderson, R. C. (1977). Taking different perspectives on a story. *Journal of Educational Psychology, 69*, 309–315.

Picoult, J. (2004). *My sister's keeper.* New York, NY: Atria.

Pink, D. (2006). *A whole new mind: Why right-brainers will rule the future.* New York, NY: Riverhead Books.

Pink, D. (2009). *Drive: The surprising truth about what motivates us.* Toronto: Penguin.

Polanyi, M. (1969). *Personal knowledge.* London, England: Routledge and Kegan Paul.

Poldrack, R., Clark, J., Pare-Blagoev, E., Shohamy, D., Myano, J., & Myers, C. (2001). Interactive memory systems in the human brain. *Nature, 414*, 546–550.

Postman, N., & Weingartner, C. (1969). *Teaching as a subversive activity.* New York, NY: Delacorte.

Prensky, M. (2001). Digital natives, digital immigrants. *On the Horizon, 9*(5). Retrieved from http://www.marcprensky.com/writing/Prensky%20-%20Digital%20Natives,%20Digital%20Immigrants%20-%20Part1.pdf

Raskind, M., Goldberg, R., Higgins, E., & Herman, L. (1999). Patterns of change and predictors of success in individuals with learning disabilities: Results from a twenty-year longitudinal study. *Learning Disabilities Research & Practice, 14*(1), 37–49.

Recht, D. R., & Leslie, L. (1988). Effect of prior knowledge on good and poor readers' memory of text. *Journal of Educational Psychology, 80*, 16–20.

Restak, R. (1995). *Brainscapes.* New York, NY: Hyperion.

Reyes, P., & Imber. M. (1992). Teachers' perceptions of the fairness of their workload and their commitment, job satisfaction, and morale: Implications for teacher evaluation. *Journal of Personnel Evaluation in Education, 5*(3), 291–302.

Reynolds, G. (2008). *Presentation Zen: Simple ideas on presentation design and delivery.* Berkeley, CA: New Riders.

Reynolds, G. (2010). *Presentation Zen Design: Simple design principles and techniques to enhance your presentations.* Berkeley, CA: New Riders.

Robertson, H., & Hord, S. (2004). Accessing student voices. In L. Brown Easton (Ed.), *Powerful designs for professional learning* (pp. 43–52). Oxford, OH: National Staff Development Council.

Robinson, K. (2001). *Out of our minds: Learning to be creative.* West Sussex, UK: Capstone.

Rogers, E. (1983). *Diffusion of innovations* (3rd ed.). New York, NY: Free Press.

Ross, J. A., Hogoboam-Gray, A., & Hannay, L. (2001). Effects of teacher efficacy on computer skills and computer cognitions of Canadian students in grades K–3. *The Elementary School Journal, 102*(2), 141–162.

Ross, J. A., McKeiver, S., & Hogoboam-Gray, A. (1997). Fluctuations in teacher efficacy during implementation of destreaming. *Canadian Journal of Education, 22*(3), 283–296.

Ruef, K. (2003). *The private eye: (5x) looking/thinking by analogy*. Seattle, WA: The Private Eye Project.

Ryan, M. J. (2009). *Adaptability: How to survive change you didn't ask for*. New York, NY: Broadway Books.

Sandholtz, J., Ringstaff, C., & Dwyer, D. (1994). *Student engagement: Views from technology-rich classrooms*. Apple Classrooms of Tomorrow (ACOT). Retrieved from http://www.apple.com/nl/images/pdf/acotlibrary/rpt21.pdf

Schaps, E. (1999). The child development project: In search of synergy. *Principal, 79*(1).

Schwartz, T., & Dunkin, B. (2000). Facilitating interdisciplinary hands-on learning using LabVIEW. *International Journal of Engineering Education, 16*(3), 218–227.

Senge, P. (1994). *The fifth discipline fieldbook*. New York, NY: Doubleday.

Sethi, A., & Mischel, W. (2000). The role of strategic attention deployment in development of self-regulation: Predicting preschoolers' delay of gratification from mother–toddler interactions. *Developmental Psychology, 36*(6), 767–777.

Shen, J. (1997). Teacher retention and attrition from public schools: Evidence from SASS91. *Journal of Educational Research, 91*(2), 33–39.

Shulman, L. S. (2004). *The wisdom of practice: Essays on teaching, learning, and learning to teach*. San Francisco, CA: Jossey-Bass.

Simmons, A. (2006). *The story factor: Inspiration, influence, and persuasion through the art of storytelling*. New York, NY: Basic Books.

Skinner, E. A., & Belmont, M. J. (1993). Motivation in the classroom: Reciprocal effects of teacher behaviour and student engagement across the school year. *Journal of Educational Psychology, 85*(4), 571–581.

Slavin, R. E. (1990). *Cooperative learning: Theory, research, and practice*. Needham Heights, MA: Allyn and Bacon.

Sternberg, R. (2001). *Teaching for successful intelligences*. Upper Saddle River, NJ: Pearson Education.

Sternberg, R. J., Grigorenko, E. L., Jarvin, L., Clinkenbeard, P., Ferrari, M., & Torff, B. (2000). The effectiveness of triarchic teaching and assessment. Retrieved from http://www.gifted.uconn.edu/nrcgt/newsletter/spring00/sprng002.html

Sullo, B. (2007). *Activating the desire to learn*. Alexandria, VA: ASCD.

Tapscott, D. (2009). *Grown up digital: How the net generation is changing your world*. Toronto: McGraw Hill.

Tice, L. (1999). *Imagine 21: Fast track to change*. Los Angeles, CA: The Pacific Institute.

Tichy, N. M., & Cohen, E. B. (1997). *The leadership engine: How winning companies build leaders at every level*. New York, NY: HarperBusiness.

Tschannen-Moran, M. (2004). *Trust matters: Leadership for successful schools*. San Francisco, CA: Jossey-Bass.

Van Overwalle, F., & De Metsenaere, M. (1990). The effects of attribution-based intervention and study strategy training on academic achievement in college freshmen. *British Journal of Educational Psychology, 60*, 299–311.

Video Game Culture: Leisure and Play Preferences of B.C. Teens. (1998, October). Simon Fraser University. Retrieved from http://www.media-awareness.ca/english/resources/research_documents/reports/violence/upload/Video-Game-Culture-Leisure-and-Play-Preferences-of-B-C-Teens-Report-pdf.pdf

von Oech, R. (2008). *A whack on the side of the head: How you can be more creative* (Rev. ed.). New York, NY: Hachette Book Group.

vos Savant, M. (1990). *Brain building: Exercising yourself smarter*. Toronto: Bantam.

Vygotsky, L. S. (1978). *Mind in society: The development of higher psychological processes* (M. Cole, V. John-Steiner, S. Scribner, & E. Souberman, Eds.). Cambridge, MA: Harvard University Press.

Vygotsky, L. S. (1986). *Thought and language*. Cambridge, MA: MIT Press.

Wald, P., & Castleberry, M. (Eds.). (2000). *Educators as learners: Creating a professional learning community in your school*. Alexandria, VA: ASCD.

Walling, D. R. (2005). *Visual knowing: Connecting art and ideas across the curriculum*. Thousand Oaks, CA: Corwin Press.

Warlick, D. F. (2009). *Redefining literacy 2.0* (2nd ed.). Columbus, OH: Linworth Books.

Weiss, E. (1999). Perceived workplace conditions and first-year teachers' morale, career choice commitment, and planned retention: A secondary analysis. *Teacher and Teacher Education, 15*(8), 861–879.

Wenglinsky, H. (1998). *Does it compute? The relationship between educational technology and student achievement in mathematics*. Princeton, NJ: ETS Policy Information Center.

West, T. G. (2009). *In the mind's eye: Creative visual thinkers, gifted dyslexics, and the rise of visual technologies* (2nd ed.). New York, NY: Prometheus Books.

Wheatley, M. (2002). *Turning to one another: Simple conversations to restore hope to the future*. San Francisco, CA: Berrett-Koehler.

Wiggins, G., & McTighe, J. (2005). *Understanding by design* (2nd ed.). Alexandria, VA: ASCD.

Wiggins, G., & McTighe, J. (2007). *Schooling by design: Mission, action, and achievement*. Alexandria, VA: ASCD.

Wigginton, E. (1985). *Sometimes a shining moment: The Foxfire experience*. Garden City, NY: Anchor Books.

Wilhelm, J. D. (2007). *Engaging readers and writers with inquiry: Promoting deep understandings in language arts and the content areas with guiding questions.* Toronto: Scholastic.

Willingham, D. T. (2009). *Why don't students like school? A cognitive scientist answers questions about how the mind works and what it means for the classroom.* San Francisco, CA: Jossey-Bass.

Willis, J. (2007). *Brain-friendly strategies for the inclusion classroom.* Alexandria, VA: ASCD.

Willms, J. D., Friesen, S., & Milton, P. (2009). *What did you do in school today? Transforming classrooms through social, academic, and intellectual engagement.* Toronto: Canadian Education Association.

Wilmarth, S. (2010). Five socio-technology trends that change everything in learning and teaching. In H. H. Jacobs (Ed.), *Curriculum 21: Essential education for a changing world.* Alexandria, VA: ASCD.

Winik, M. (2005). Gods and monsters. In F. Conlon & G. Hudson (Eds.), *I wanna be sedated: 30 writers on parenting teenagers* (pp. 217–223). Emeryville, CA: Seal Press.

Wiseman, F. (Producer/Director). (1994). *High school II* [Motion picture]. United States: Zipporah Films.

Wolfe, P. (2001). *Brain matters: Translating research into classroom practice.* Alexandria, VA: ASCD.

Wood, G. (2005). *Time to learn: How to create high schools that serve all students* (2nd ed.). Portsmouth, NH: Heinemann.

Wormeli, R. (2006). *Fair isn't always equal: Assessing and grading in the differentiated classroom.* Portland, ME: Stenhouse.

Wrzesniewski, A., McCauley, C. R., Rozin, P., & Schwartz, B. (1997). Jobs, careers, and callings: People's relations to their work. *Journal of Research in Personality, 31,* 21–33.

Yankelovich, D. (1999). *The magic of dialogue: Transforming conflict into cooperation.* New York, NY: Simon & Schuster.

Yazzie-Mintz, E. (2007). *Voices of students on engagement: A report on the 2006 high school survey of student engagement.* Bloomington, IN: Center for Evaluation and Education Policy, Indiana University. Retrieved from http://ceep.indiana.edu/hssse

Yero, J. (2002). *Teaching in mind: How teacher thinking shapes education.* Hamilton, MT: MindFlight Publishing.

Index

A

ability grouping, 141
Aboriginal learners, 114, 149, 179, 221
absenteeism. *see* student truancy
academic competence, 40
    requirements for, 46
academic engagement, 5, 196–198, 203–205
administrators. *see* leaders
adolescents
    relating to, 123–125
    role models, 124
    separation from adults, 123
    use of technology, 163–165
    and the workplace, 31
adopters
    early, 250
    first, 249
adults
    generative, 246
    use of technology, 123, 163–165
Aesop, 117
Alexander, Bruce, 158
alligators. *see* change, obstacles to
amygdala, 130
analogy
    definition, 91
    and kinesthetic learning, 91–93
    teaching with, 91
Apple, 20, 144, 174, 186–188, 236–237, 243
applied creativity, 78–80. *see also* creativity; practical creativity
apprenticeship programs, 109, 149
Ariely, Dan, 57

arts, interdisciplinary study, 112–116
ArtsSmarts, 113, 114, 194
Asimov, Isaac, 157
Asperger Syndrome, 72
at-risk students, 40, 178, 183
attendance, school. *see also* student truancy
    and disengagement, 9
attention deficit hyperactivity disorder, 56
autonomy, need for, 49, 70
avatars, 213
Ayers, William, 33, 44

B

backward design, 161
Barth, Roland, 125
basic competencies, 30
basic needs, 40
Bear, Judy, 114
beliefs, 76–77, 84–86, 98
    in conversation, 139–140
belonging, sense of
    in a community, 119
    and disengagement, 9
Bennis, Warren, 144
Berns, Gregory, 196–197
Biederman, Patricia Ward, 144
blogs, 153, 156
    in the classroom, 236–237
body language, 130–131
Bohr, Niels, 106
Bourke-White, Margaret, 103
brain, change-challenged, 207–208
brainstorming, 94

brainwriting, 94
Bricker, Darrell, 119, 163, 171
Brin, Sergey, 81
Britton, James, 36, 232
Brooks-Young, Susan, 163
burnout, professional, 12
Buzan, Tony, 88, 105

C

case learning, 220
case studies, 63, 65, 72, 73, 92, 103, 111–112, 113, 114, 115–116, 132, 147, 150, 151, 152, 153, 154, 155, 177, 179, 186–189, 193, 194, 221, 228, 229, 236–237
Castleberry, Michael, 242, 247
celebrations, 53
Central Park East SS, 232
challenge
    and disengagement, 10
    instructional, 160
    need for, 49, 196–198
    and video games, 199–201
challenge-based learning, 220
change
    and the brain, 207–208
    bringing about, 150
    collaboration in, 247
    images of, 247
    obstacles to, 240, 245
    planning for, 210–213
    support for, 246–247
checking in with students, 134–137
checklists, 210

Chen, Jenova, 200
choice in the classroom, 70–74
    personal interests, 72
choice theory, 40, 41
Christensen, Clayton, 23, 168, 169
classroom
    climate, 159, 234
    low-threat, 133
    physical arrangement, 234
    predictable, 176–177
Colan, Lee, 33, 37
collaboration, 241–242, 247
    characteristics of, 242
    power of, 248–249
collaborative IQ, 241–242
collective efficacy, 45
Collins, Jim, 19, 247
communications, 182–183
communities, professional learning, 127–128. *see also* networks, professional learning
community
    classroom as, 125–126
    definition, 118
    sense of, 118
community members, connecting with, 148–149
community scans, 110
competence, 30
competencies, 30–31. *see also* teacher competencies
compliance, experiment in, 248–249
computers. *see also* technology
    mass customization of, 43
Conceptual Age, 82, 162
concern, circle of, 241
confidence and disengagement, 10
connection, need for, 47–48
connections, learning through, 90–93
Connell, James, 6
Considine, David, 180
conversation, learning-focused, 232–234

conversation, professional
    clarifying thinking, 139–140
    establishing dialogue, 138–139
    honesty in, 140–141
    storytelling, 142–143
    value of, 127–128
cooperative education, 149
cooperative learning, 144–147
Cornett, Claudia, 115
creative, 75
creative industries, 82
creative process, rules of, 89
creative thinking, 82–83, 88–89, 94–95
creativity. *see also* applied creativity; practical creativity
    "capital c" creativity, 77
    definition, 77, 113
    on the job, 78–80
    myths about, 77–78
    "small c" creativity, 78
critical moves, 211
Csikszentmihalyi, Mihaly, 49, 77, 78, 197–198
curiosity, 226, 227
"curiosity gap theory," 7

D

Daniels, Harvey, 220
Danielson, Charlotte, 140
Day, Christopher, 13
Deal, Terrence, 148
debriefing with students, 137
Dede, Chris, 184–185
Dell computers, 43
design technology, 110–112
dialogue, establishing, 138–139
digital immigrants, 173–174
digitization, 172
disaffection, 6
discipline, classroom, 159
disengagement. *see* student disengagement; teacher disengagement

Disney, Walt, 89, 243
distance learning, 179
dopamine, 130, 196–197
Dorsey, Jack, 243
doublethink, 213
drawing and learning, 104
dropping out, 10, 178
drug addiction, 158–159
Dubach, Jean, 63
Dweck, Carol, 36, 47, 58
Dynamic Difficulty Adjustment (DDA), 199, 200

E

effort and success, 58–61
Einstein, Albert, 75, 77
e-learning, 179
electronic devices. *see* computers; technology
emotional engagement, 6
emotions, 130–133
employers, and worker competencies, 31–33
engagement. *see also* student engagement; teacher engagement
    in children, 34
    continuum of, 37–38
    defining, 5–6
    fluctuations in, 38
    measuring, 6–7
    obstacles to, 240
    and relevance, 62–65
    roots of, 37–41
    self-reporting, 7
    terms of, 2–14
    in the workplace, 31–33, 46–50
engagement needs
    of students, 46–50, 203–205
    of teachers, 46–50
environment, supportive, 234
Erikson, Erik, 246

Erwin, Jonathan, 64
expectations and performance, 205–207
expeditionary learning, 220
expertise, developing, 218–219
extracurricular events, 136

F

Facebook, 119–120
facial expressions, 130–131
failure, impact on students, 59, 205–206
fear, 131–133
Ferguson, Bruce, 10, 40
Ferriter, Bill, 185
Feynman, Richard, 235
figurative language, 90–93
Fisher, Douglas, 215
fixed mindset, 36, 66–67
flow, 197–198
flOw (video game), 200
Flowers, N., 192
focus groups, 136
Fort Battleford, SK, 114
Foxfire, 253–254
Frayer diagrams, 4–5, 216–217
Frey, Nancy, 215
Friesen, Sharon, 5, 6, 8, 9, 10, 11, 159–160, 200
Frost, Robert, 1
Fuster, Joaquin, 109
future of technology, 171–173

G

gallery walk, 94
Gallup, 8, 32
    Employee Engagement survey, 38, 47
Gardner, Howard, 67, 202–203
Gee, James, 199

geeking out, 122
geocaching, 147
George, Lianne, 41–42, 43
Glasser, William, 40, 41, 47
Glasser Quality School, 41
goal-directed behaviour, 54–55
goals
    helping students with, 56–57
    "just right," 55
    setting personal goals, 54–57
    shared, 55
    SMART goals, 57
Goleman, Daniel, 131
Gollwitzer, Peter, 211–212, 213
Goodlad, John, 224, 233
Google, 80, 164, 243
    productivity at, 81
gradual release of responsibility model, 214–217
Grandin, Temple, 106
graphic organizers, 105
group investigations, 220
groups, working in, 144–147
    geocaching, 147
growth mindset, 36, 66–67

H

habituation, 207
Haddon, Mark, 72
hands-on learning, 108–109
hanging out, 120–121
hard fun, 196
Harvey, William, 90
Heath, Chip and Dan, 19, 26, 206, 207, 211, 212
Hemingway, Ernest, 137
Heraclitus, 241
Hesiod, 44
hoax websites, 182
honesty in conversation, 140–141
hypothalamus, 70

I

ICT literacy, 180–183
    teaching suggestions, 181–183
ideas
    getting, 94–95
    power of, 232–238
ifspeak, 226
individuals, power to influence, 249–250
Industrial Age, schools in, 162
influence, circle of, 241
influencers, identifying, 249–250
Information Age, 82
Information and Communication Technology (ICT) literacy. *see* ICT literacy
innovation, 78–80
inquiry-based learning, 220–225
    characteristics of, 222
    at lesson level, 232–238
    reasons for not using, 224–225
    reasons to use, 222–224
instruction, differentiated, 205, 230–231.
    characteristics of, 230
instruction, engaging, 203–205
intellectual engagement, 6, 196–198, 203–205
intelligence, 66–69
    definition, 66
    types of, 67–69
interdisciplinary study, 110–116
    arts integration, 115–116
    ArtsSmarts, 113, 114, 194
    business simulation, 111–112
    First Nations culture, 114
Internet and mass customization, 43
interventions for at-risk students, 178
intrinsic motivation theory, 40
Iyengar, Sheena, 71

J

Jacobs, Heidi Hayes, 190, 191
Jensen, Eric, 53, 109, 131
Jobs, Steve, 144
Jukes, Ian, 164

K

Kahneman, Daniel, 246
Kajder, Sara, 181, 182
Kelly, Kevin, 172
kinesthetic learning, 108–109
    and analogy, 91–93
    and metaphor, 91–93
Klem, Adena, 6
knowledge, specialization of, 78–79
Koinonia, 138–143

L

leaders, 32
    activities for, 13, 18, 22, 24–25, 26–28, 33, 47–50, 53, 55, 61, 71, 86, 97, 99, 138–141, 143, 148, 171, 177, 183, 185, 186, 192, 207, 242, 244–245, 250
    scheduling, 190
learners
    developing, 51–74
    mindsets of, 36, 66–67
    short-term groups, 191
learning
    cooperative, 144–147
    distance, 179
    by doing, 108–109
    and emotions, 130–133
    environment for, 234
    inquiry-based, 220–225
    kinesthetic, 108–109
    and negative reinforcement, 248–249
    online, 179, 184–185
    place-based, 149
    professional, 127–128, 155, 184–185
    project-based, 221, 253–258
    role of technology, 167–171
    skills for real world, 202–203
    through service, 149
    through talk, 232–233
    time for, 159
    and video games, 199–201
Leavitt, Martine, 73
Leithwood, Ken, 45, 48
Lenhart, Amanda, 196
Lepper, Mark, 71
Levin, Ben, 27
literature circles, 220
Lucas, George, 182
Lundy, Kathy Gould, 103, 215

M

Maich, Steve, 41–42, 43
Mandelbrot, Benoit, 106
Maple Ridge–Pitt Meadows School District, 189
mapping, 105
Marchese, Theodore, 84
Marshmallow Test, 54–55
Martin, Roger, 202
Marzano, Robert, 55
Maslow, Abraham, 40
mass customization, 43
McCain, Ted, 202, 233
McTighe, Jay, 18, 19, 28, 161
Medina, John, 100, 101, 130, 132, 190
Meier, Deborah, 232
Mendler, Allen, 136
Merrill, Jean, 111
messing around, 121
metaphor
    definition, 90
    and kinesthetic learning, 91–93
    teaching with, 91

Michalko, Michael, 77, 89, 95, 98, 104, 139, 140
Milgram, Stanley, 248–249
Millar, Bart, 212
Milton, Penny, 5, 6, 8, 9, 10, 11, 159–160, 200
mind maps, 105
mindsets, 36, 66–67
minds-on learning, 108, 109
mirror neurons, 124
Mischel, Walter, 54
mission statements, 16–19, 227, 242–244
    for the 21st century, 20–23, 26–28
    helpful activities in writing, 245
    and vision statements, 24
Miyata, Cathy, 132
modelling behaviour, 124
Morgan, Norah, 227
motivation, 5
    and emotions, 130–133
    and engagement, 39–40
multiple intelligences, 67, 69
Mundy, Mary-Ruth C., 29

N

needs. *see also* engagement needs
    21st century, 41–44, 202–203
    basic, 40
Net Generation, expectations of, 80
networks, professional learning, 155, 184–185. *see also* communities, professional learning
Ning, 152
"No child left behind," 16
NorthWest Mounted Police, 114
novelty and learning, 176
Nowlan, Alden, 150
Nunley, Kathie, 70
"Nuremberg After Allied Bombing," 103

O

Obama, Barack, 244
Oliver, Mary, 214
online communities, 152–155. *see also* social networking sites
online learning, 179
opinion leaders, 250
opposites thinking, 35–37
Orwell, George, 213
Osborne, Alex, 95
Owen, Nick, 93, 142, 239
owl monkeys, 63

P

Page, Larry, 81
Palmer, Parker, 12, 22, 127, 128
Papert, Seymour, 196
parents, connecting with, 148
Partnership for 21st Century Skills, 126
Patterson, Kerry, 138, 140–141, 211, 249, 250
Peace River North School District, 186–189
Pecha Kucha, 101
performance competencies, 30
personalized computers, 43
Peterson, Kent, 148
Picoult, Jodi, 226
Pictorial Superiority Effect (PSE), 100
Pink, Daniel, 49, 82, 142, 162, 251
place-based learning, 149, 151
"Podcast Idol," 73
Polanyi, Michael, 79
Postman, Neil, 227
practical creativity, 87–116. *see also* applied creativity; creativity
    using figurative language, 90–93
predictability and learning, 176
Prensky, Marc, 173
presentations, 182–183
principals. *see* leaders

Problem-Based Learning (PBL), 220–225
problem solving, 95–99
project-based learning, 221, 253–258
project mood chart, 212
purpose, sense of, 48–49, 246
purposefulness, 246
purpose of school. *see* mission statements

Q

question generator, 226
questions and learning, 226–230
    open-ended questions, 226
Quest to Learn (Q2L), 201

R

rat parks, 158–159
real world
    and adolescent behaviours, 31
    skills needed for, 202–203
reclassifying, 94–95
Red Cross, 244
redoing work, 61
"relationship generation," 119
release, gradual, 214–217
relevance and engagement, 62–65
    genetics, 63
    personal connections, 65
    and student interests, 64
residential schools, 221
responsibility, gradual release of, 214–217
rewards
    alternatives to, 52–53
    unintended consequences of, 52
Reynolds, Garr, 183
Riel, Louis, 103
Robinson, Sir Ken, 77, 89, 110, 165
Rogers, Everett, 249–250
role models, 124
Ryan, M. J., 210, 213

S

Sagan, Carl, 91
Salen, Katie, 201
Saxton, Juliana, 227
SCAMPER, 95
schedules, school, 190
Schmidt, Eric, 172
school climate, 159–160, 177
school design, 190–194
    for the 21st century, 193–194
school dropouts, 10, 178
school process engagement, 5
schools
    physical space, 192–194
    residential, 221
    revolutionizing, 168–170
    size, 191
S.E.A.R.C.H., 181–182
self-awareness in teachers, 44–46
self-efficacy, 45
self-regard, focus on, 42
semantic web, 172
Senge, Peter, 138
service learning, 149
Shackleton, Sir Ernest, 195
Shulman, Lee, 50
simile, 90
Simmons, Annette, 143
simulations, 221
Sizer, Ted, 224
skipping school, 84–86
    solving, 96–99
Slavin, Robert, 144
SMART goals, 211
Smith, Larry, 137
Smithrim, Katharine, 115
social engagement, 6
social networking sites, 119–123, 243. *see also* online communities
    adult use of, 123
    teen use of, 120–123
social web, 171

Socrates, 138
Sternberg, Robert, 68, 69, 223
stimulus-response theory, 39
storytelling, 132, 142–143
stress, 132
student disengagement, 8–11. *see also* teacher disengagement
    at-risk students, 178
    and challenge, 10
    and confidence, 10
    and dropping out, 10
    factors requiring research, 11
    groups frequently affected, 8
    and opposites thinking, 35–37
    and school attendance, 9
    and sense of belonging, 9
student engagement, 5–6. *see also* engagement; teacher engagement
    promoting through questions, 227
    purpose of, 202–203
    requirements for, 46, 159–160, 203–205
    and technology, 161, 167–171
students
    at-risk, 178, 183
    setting personal goals, 54–57
    as teachers, 173–174
student truancy, 84–86
    solving, 96–99
success
    and effort, 58–61
    expectations for, 160
Sunchild E-Learning program, 179
surveys and questionnaires, 7

T

talk, learning-focused, 232–234
Tapscott, Don, 80, 119, 161
tasks, complex vs. difficult, 231
Taxonomy of Personal Engagement, 227
teacher competencies, 44–46
teacher disengagement, 12–14. *see also* student disengagement
    factors affecting, 12
    factors requiring research, 14
teacher engagement, 46–50. *see also* engagement; student engagement
teacher leaders. *see* leaders
teachers
    competent, 44–46
    creative, 82–83
    as digital immigrants, 173–174
    expectations of students, 205–207
    grouping, 192
    professional learning, 127–128, 155, 184–185
    professional relationships, 47–48
    relating to adolescents, 123–125, 159
team teaching, 191, 192
technology, 160–161. *see also* computers
    adaptive use, 170–171
    age-related use, 163–165
    and the arts, 115–116
    in the classroom, 165–166, 254–258
    as extension of mind, 170–171
    of the future, 171–173
    impact on education, 168–170
    infrastructure support for, 186–189
    and learning, 167–171
    learning through networks, 155
    managing use of, 177
    and thinking skills, 236–237
    as a tool, 169–171
    transformational use, 170–171
thinking
    clarifying, 139–140
    matrix, 236–237
    need to teach, 202
    teaching skills in, 235–237
threats, 131–133
    removing from classroom, 133
time, effective learning, 159
transfer of knowledge, 102–103, 203

triarchic intelligences, 68, 69, 251–252
tweets, 243
Twitter, 243–244

V

video games, 196
    and challenge, 199–201
vision statements, 24–25, 227
    for the 21st century, 26–28
    crafting, 250–252
    Twitter versions, 251
visualization, 106–107
visual literacy, 102
visuals in teaching, 100–103
    connecting to written text, 102–103
    images and artifacts, 103
    interpreting, 102
    presenting, 101
vital behaviours, 211
"Voices in the Village," 256–257
VoiceThread, 154
von Oech, Roger, 82, 92, 93, 94–95
vos Savant, Marilyn, 66
Vygotsky, Lev, 122, 197

W

Wald, Penelope, 242, 247
walk around reading, 215
Warlick, David, 180, 181–182
Web 1.0, 171
Web 2.0, 171, 184–185
Web 3.0, 172–173
webbing, 105
WebQuest, 221
Weingartner, Charles, 227
Wheatley, Margaret, 127, 128, 139
Wiggins, Grant, 18, 19, 28, 161
Wigginton, Eliot, 253–254
Wilhelm, Jeff, 203, 234

Willingham, Daniel, 142, 218
Willms, J. Douglas, 5, 6, 8, 9, 10, 11, 159–160, 200
Wilmarth, Stephen, 172
Wireless Writing Program, 186–189
Wiseman, Frederick, 232
Wood, George, 16, 18, 25, 28
word webs, 105
Wordle, 242

workplace
    21st century successes, 80, 82
    competencies in, 31–33
    expectations of workers, 79–80
    preparing students for, 162–163, 202–203
    relationships in, 47–48
Wormeli, Rick, 61
Wright, John, 119, 163, 171

Y

Yankelovich, D., 139
Yazzie-Mintz, Ethan, 8, 200
Yero, Judith, 84, 85
YouTube, 164

Z

zone. *see* flow
Zuckerberg, Mark, 119

About the Author

Karen Hume is a well-known Canadian teacher, administrator, author, speaker, and workshop leader. The winner of three "Teacher of the Year" awards, Karen has taught all but four grades in K–12 (she especially enjoyed Grades 7 and 8), and has also been a teacher-librarian. As an administrator, Karen worked in a high-needs K–8 school and then led her district's efforts in reculturing schools to meet the needs of at-risk and struggling learners in Grades 7–12.

Karen has her M.Ed. in curriculum and teacher development, has been a member of a university research group funded to investigate the role of talk and inquiry in the classroom, and is a member of the editorial board of an online action research journal.

Karen's writing, workshop facilitation, and keynote addresses revolve around differentiated instruction, which she sees as an organizing framework for everything that happens in teaching and learning at all levels of a school system. Her specific areas of interest within this framework include effective and responsive instruction and assessment; engaging both adolescent and adult learners; developing effective learning communities for students and adults; change processes for adult learners; literacy education; and evidence-informed decision making.

Also by Karen Hume

Differentiated Instruction

For Teachers

Start Where They Are: Differentiating for Success with the Young Adolescent

Karen Hume's first professional book for teachers includes theory, notes on classroom implications, and implementation suggestions. This text bridges theory and practice, targets the needs of the adolescent learner, and roots differentiated instruction within an effective classroom.

Includes CD with line masters
Also available in interactive eBook format
ISBN: 9780132069137 (Text and CD)
ISBN: 9780137133741 (eBook)

For School Leaders

Supporting and Sustaining Differentiated Instruction: An Administrator's Guide

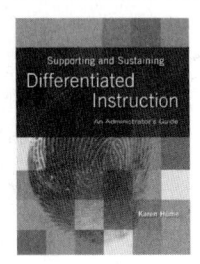

Specifically written to support school administrators as instructional leaders—because schools are places where students and teachers learn. These unique features support school leaders as they build professional learning communities:

- **Teaching Adults** provides lesson plans for administrators to use for staff professional learning opportunities
- **Process** offers steps for specific activities for a school-based process with teachers

Includes DVD with line masters and video
ISBN: 9780138127602

Assessment

For Teachers

Evidence to Action / 50 Tools and Techniques for Classroom Assessment

Evidence to Action: Engaging and Teaching Young Adolescents Through Assessment and *50 Tools and Techniques for Classroom Assessment* create a powerful new professional resource package for teachers. Together, the books and DVD unravel the sometimes complex topic of assessment and provide practical strategies and examples to help teachers embed assessment into everyday instruction.

Includes DVD with line masters and video
ISBN: 9780136083375

For School Leaders

The Evidence-Based School: An Administrator's Guide

A concise, timely resource that explores the topic of assessment with an administrator's needs and commitments in mind. This practical guide discusses how data can be used to inform classroom instruction and school-based professional learning and includes practical tips and strategies to engage staff in productive learning situations using student data.

Includes DVD with line masters and video
ISBN: 9780138140748

Visit www.pearsonschoolcanada.ca to learn more.